D0192623

COST ACCOUNTING
AND
COSTING METHODS

BY

HAROLD J. WHELDON, B.Com.(Lond.)

F.C.W.A.; A.C.I.S.; F.L.A.A.
Lecturer in Costing at the City of London College, etc.
Consultant on Costing Systems.

THE SCHOOL OF ACCOUNTANCY
SECRETARYSHIP, BANKING AND INSURANCE

Printed in Great Britain by
Richard Clay and Company, Ltd.,
Bungay, Suffolk.

PREFACE

THE chief purpose of this text-book is to provide a complete course in cost accounting and costing methods for students preparing for examinations in this subject, but, at the same time, it is hoped that it will be of value to manufacturers and accountants because of the many practical applications and the modern methods that are illustrated and described.

The book has been written in the light of many years' practical experience in factories, coupled with an intimate knowledge of the requirements of candidates for all the professional examinations, gained as a lecturer and teacher in the subject at a number of London and provincial colleges.

The importance of cost accounting is becoming more and more recognised every year as a vital factor in the administration of progressive manufacturing undertakings. This fact is appreciated by the various professional societies and other examining bodies, as is evidenced by the increasing extent to which searching questions on costing principles and methods are set in the examinations.

The author has made every endeavour to make this volume a comprehensive and complete survey of modern costing methods. Theory and practice are combined in the descriptions and explanations given.

The principles underlying all costing methods are enunciated and explained in considerable detail; but, in addition, many examples of the practical application of these principles have been included.

One of the great difficulties confronting those studying the subject is the diversity of industries to be considered, but this has been surmounted by dealing very fully with principles of general application, applying them to well-defined types of industry, and then giving demonstrations of systems and methods in actual use in particular undertakings.

The great majority of students have had no opportunity of becoming acquainted with the actual work and conditions

v

inside a factory, and even when they have acquired a good theoretical knowledge of costing, they are handicapped by being unable to see specimens of representative forms and cost accounts. This is a real difficulty, particularly for those studying for the advanced or final examinations, and it is for this reason that many forms and accounts actually in use in various modern factories have been reproduced as illustrations.

A number of examination questions, and entire examination papers set by various examining bodies, have been included by kind permission of the examining bodies concerned.

Many forms and specimen cost accounts which have been used to illustrate the text, and much detail of several of the methods described have been kindly supplied by prominent factory accountants and members of the Institute of Cost and Works Accountants, and to these the author expresses his warmest thanks. In this connection he desires specially to acknowledge the assistance afforded by the following :

C. Baron, F.C.W.A., of the City of Portsmouth Electricity Department, for details of electricity supply costs.

G. D. Belcher, F.C.W.A., A.I.S.A., of Fiat (England), Ltd., for specimen cost control accounts.

W. T. Boulton, F.C.W.A., for the detailed system of costing by " Hollerith " punched card tabulating machines.

R. A. Bransom, A.C.W.A., of the London County Council Mechanical Transport Department, for motor transport costing data forms.

The Chilton Class Journal Company of Philadelphia, U.S.A., for permission to include details of their standard cost system for motor transport, published in their *Commercial Car Journal.*

G. H. Clamp, F.C.W.A., Chief Accountant to the Royal Ordnance Factories, for the data on unit operation costs.

W. Desborough, O.B.E., for co-operating in the preparation of the chapter on Powers–Samas Tabulating Machines.

J. H. Duckworth, for several forms and information on standard costs and operation costs.

A. H. Gledhill, J.P., M.I.M.E., F.C.W.A., for permission to reproduce illustrations and data from his " Practical Costing."

International Time Recording Co., Ltd., for illustrations of their instruments and cards.

P. H. Lightbody, F.C.W.A., and Gledhill–Brook Time Recorders, Ltd., for supplying many illustrations of time cards.

Perry Keene, F.C.W.A., and the Austin Motor Co., Ltd., for co-operation and permission to include the chapter on Production Control Costing in the Motor-Car Industry.

W. Pickering, A.C.W.A., for the detailed information and forms for coal distillation costs.

H. N. Stutchbury, F.C.W.A., for specimen accounts and data of cordite process costs.

W. D. Turner, C.A., for preparing the account of Production Control Costing in the Motor-Car Industry.

A. Williamson, F.C.W.A., Costing Secretary of the British Federation of Master Printers, for the outline of the Federation's uniform system of printers' costs.

A. Wilson, F.I.S.A., and D. A. Palmer, for specimen cost sheets of a cutlery works.

W. R. Wintle, F.C.W.A., for the forms and details of iron foundry costing.

W. Crosskey, F.C.W.A., for Process Cost Sheets, concluding Chap. XVI.

H. J. Wheldon.

August 31, 1932.

PREFACE TO SECOND EDITION

I desire to express my thanks and appreciation to Sir Reginald Townsend, K.C.B., C.B.E., A.C.A., F.C.W.A., President of the Institute of Cost and Works Accountants 1932–1933, for reading through this book and giving many suggestions and ideas for its improvement, which have been incorporated in the present edition. Also to Donald L. Moran, F.C.W.A., President of the Institute of Cost and Works Accountants 1931–1932.

H. J. W.

May 1, 1934.

PREFACE TO THIRD EDITION

The present edition has provided the opportunity of extending the scope of the book to include Municipal Cost Accounting, and in addition to the acknowledgments in the text I desire to thank Mr. W. H. Boddington, B.Com., F.C.W.A., A.I.M.T.A. and Mr. A. W. Muse, F.C.W.A., F.L.A.A., for kindly reading through this additional matter and giving me their valued co-operation. The chapter on Electricity Supply Costs has been re-written and brought up to date. The remainder of the book has been revised and additional matter introduced.

H. J. W.

January 31, 1936.

PREFACE TO FOURTH EDITION

Notwithstanding that but little more than twelve months have elapsed since the publication of the third edition of this treatise, the need for a fourth edition has enabled me to revise the text completely, and to include additional matter where necessary. Numerous requests having reached me for a more elaborate treatment of the matter of Chap. XXIX dealing with the graphic presentation of facts, I may perhaps be permitted to direct readers to my book " Business Statistics and Statistical Method " issued by the publishers of this volume.

H. J. W.

PREFACE TO FIFTH EDITION

The continued approval of this book by Educational Authorities, Teachers and Students is a great encouragement to me to keep it abreast of the latest, established costing practice. In this edition, I have judged it necessary to make minor corrections only.

H. J. W.

September, 1938.

PREFACE TO SIXTH EDITION

The need for a further edition has given me an opportunity to enlarge the treatment of overhead expense, and to effect a number of minor additions and alterations in other chapters.

H. J. W.

August 15, 1940.

PREFACE TO SEVENTH EDITION

The demand for another edition has enabled me to introduce further alterations and additions, some arising from war-time conditions. New examples of Cost Sheets have been introduced. I thank Mr. J. E. Brett, A.S.A.A., and Mr. Wm. M. Johnston, A.C.W.A., for their co-operation in the revision of this edition.

H. J. W.

December, 1941.

PREFACE TO EIGHTH EDITION

In this edition, the third since the outbreak of war, a number of further additions and minor alterations have been made to amplify some of the descriptive matter in Chapters IV, VII and IX.

H. J. W.

January, 1944.

CONTENTS

FORMS AND ILLUSTRATIONS

INDUSTRIES AND PRODUCTS

THE COSTING OF WHICH IS DESCRIBED OR MENTIONED IN THIS BOOK

CHAPTER I

INTRODUCTION

THE development in industry in recent years, the ever-increasing application of more scientific methods in industrial processes, and the complex organisation which characterises the modern factory demand specialised technique for providing prompt and regular information regarding the cost of production for the guidance of the management.

When the prices of commodities are falling throughout the world, competition becomes more and more keen, and, to maintain its trade, a manufacturing business must reduce its costs of production to a minimum. When demand is brisk and profits are more easily earned, this necessity is apt to be overlooked. But, whatever the state of trade, the manufacturer should seek the fullest reward of his enterprise, and this can be secured only by vigilant control of all the expenses of production and marketing. Waste and concealed losses must be eliminated; efficiency in every direction must be developed. To achieve these ends, competent organisation, combined with an adequate system of control provided by efficient costing and cost accounts is imperative.

Costing Defined.—Costing is the proper allocation of expenditure, and involves the collection of costs for every order, job, process, service or unit, in order that suitably arranged data may be presented to a producer as a guide in the control of his business. It deals with the cost of production, selling and distribution.

Management aided by Costing.—There is a considerable lack of appreciation by many manufacturers of the value of costing. A usual comment is : " A cost system is no doubt useful to some, but my business is different." However " different " a business may be, there is expenditure on labour and materials, and expenses incurred in manufacturing, and also in disposing of the product. The Cost Accountant having an experience of factory organisation can devise a cost system, based on fundamental principles, for any industry. His function is obviously not to manufacture the goods, but to reveal in detail *where* the methods used produce a gain or a loss.

The costing scheme should not only find what various jobs

B

or operations have cost, but also what they should cost; it should indicate where losses and waste are occurring before the work is finished, in order that action may be taken to avoid loss and waste there and then.

The delegation of responsibility, and the division of labour and specialisation, are introduced into industry to secure efficient manufacturing, but every subdivision of effort tends to the possibility of waste, and an important function of management is to exercise such control as will minimise the waste. Adequate costing facilitates this.

Again, by the aid of cost reports and statistics prepared by the Cost Accountant, the management can decide whether the manufacture of certain products increases overhead expense disproportionately; whether to treat by-products, even if at a loss, to make possible a more important trade in another product; or whether the plant and machinery could be used more advantageously by concentrating on particular products to the exclusion of less profitable ones.

Costing essential to Industrial Control.—An efficient system of costing is an essential factor for industrial control under modern conditions of business, and as such may be regarded as an important part in the efforts of any management to secure business stability. The organisation of an undertaking has to be so controlled that the desired volume of production is secured at the least possible cost in relation to the scheduled quantity of the product. Cost Accounting provides the measurement of the degree to which this objective is attained, and thus has a definite place in the organisation of the business. All expense is localised, and thereby controlled in the light of the information provided by the cost records.

Costing in Periods of Trade Depression.—When business is not difficult to secure, many manufacturers are able to show a profit, notwithstanding the leakages which pass unchecked, but, in periods of trade depression, concealed inefficiencies have to be tracked down, and rigorous control must be exercised to ensure even modest margins of profit.

Failure to maintain normal output in times of acute trade depression results in overhead expenses not being recovered in full. The value of a costing system is even greater at such times, since by indicating where economies may be sought, waste eliminated, and efficiency increased, some of the loss occasioned by reduced turnover and falling prices may be avoided. Further, knowing real costs of production, a manufacturer can fix the lowest margin of profit on the reduced output when tendering; or, when embarking on a policy of cutting his prices, to increase turnover with the object of avoiding the loss of at least some of those irreducible fixed overheads inseparable from heavy investment in capital assets. Such a policy could not continue for an indefinite period, but may be justified during a trade depression until a revival of business occurs, in that, whilst loss may be suffered, the loss would otherwise be heavier. The policy is, however, a dangerous one, unless operated under the expert guidance of a cost accountant, and, in any case, may have harmful repercussions on the industry as a whole, unless judiciously managed. The Cost Accounts provide data for decisions as to how far such a policy may be carried.

Costing and Governmental Controls.—Limitation of supplies by Governmental action seriously affects the incidence of overhead expenses, particularly those of a " fixed " nature, and Government restrictions limiting increases in selling prices to actually incurred additional cost both demand careful costing, quite apart from the submission of costs necessitated when contracts subject to cost investigation are undertaken.

Cost Accounting and Price Fixing.—The preparation of accurate costs of production will guide a manufacturer when deciding upon his price-fixing policy, but, in very many instances, selling prices are governed only partly by the cost of production— the other influences being the economic law of supply and demand, the activities of competitors, trade associations, fixed price agreements, regulated supply, and the price policy of the management.

Estimates and Costs.—Estimates, it should be observed, are not costs, from which they differ in several ways. Usually, estimates are based on present or prospective market prices of materials and labour, and, while previous costs ascertained may be used as a guide in fixing prices, it is sometimes expedient to prepare estimates on a competitive basis, making quotations even below cost to avoid greater loss where there is a costly plant and the fixed overhead expenses are heavy.

Cost Accounts, however, record the actual costs of materials, wages, and expenses. It has been said very aptly that "an estimate is an opinion, price is a policy, and cost is a fact." The ascertained costs provide a measure for estimates, a guide to policy, and a control over current production.

Statistics and Costs.—The preparation of statistical returns and cost summaries must not be regarded as cost accounting, but rather as a method of presenting to the management results ascertained by the aid of the costing system. Statistical reports serve to interpret the Cost Accounts, and other information collected in the course of their compilation. Cost statistics not prepared in conjunction with Cost Accounts which interlock with the Financial Accounts are analogous to single-entry as compared with double-entry book-keeping. Such information fails for the want of proof. Uncertainty in costing is undesirable and dangerous.

Desirable Conditions for a Costing System.—The following general conditions should be observed as far as possible when installing a costing system :—

1. The arrangement of the system should be adapted to suit the general organisation of the particular business, subject to such alterations as may be unavoidable. Usually, any scheme to alter the plan of the business to adapt it to a costing system will be unsatisfactory, and, owing to resentment of officials, there is the probability that the fullest co-operation will not be given.

2. The technical aspects of the business should be carefully studied, and an effort made to secure the sympathetic assistance and support of the principal members of the works staff and of the workers generally.

3. The minimum amount of detail in which records are to be compiled should be arranged. Complete analyses are desirable, but over-elaboration must be avoided. The compilation of schedules and analyses with unnecessary details involving undue clerical work will make the system costly, and disproportionate to the benefits received. Still, the costing system should, without exception, cover the whole work of production and services.

4. The records to be made by foremen and workers should involve as little clerical work as possible. Printed forms should be provided, and all instructions written or printed. It is advantageous to provide written or printed instructions as to the origin, use, and disposition of each form.

5. To ensure reliable statistics, every original entry on factory forms should be supported by an examiner's signature, or counter-checks.

6. Promptitude, frequency, and regularity in the presentation of statistics and accounts must be arranged for.

7. The Cost Accounts and Financial Accounts should be either interlocked in one integral accounting scheme, or so arranged that the results shown by the two sets of accounts can be reconciled.

Summary of Purposes of Cost Accounts and Statistics.—The following summary may be useful to the student:

1. The figures recorded and summarised in the Financial Accounts are analysed and classified with reference to the cost of products and operations.

2. To arrive at the cost of production of every unit, job, operation, process, or department, and develop cost standards.

3. To indicate to the management any inefficiencies, and the extent of various forms of waste, whether of materials, time, expense, or in use of machinery, equipment, and tools.

4. To provide data for periodical Profit and Loss Accounts and Balance Sheets at such intervals as may be desired during the financial year.

5. To reveal sources of economies in production, having regard to methods, equipment, design, and output.

6. To provide actual figures of cost for comparison with estimates, and to serve as a guide for future estimates, or quotations, and to assist the management in their price-fixing policy.

7. Where Standard Costs are prepared, they show what the cost of production should be, with which the actual eventually recorded costs may be compared.

8. To present comparative cost data for different periods and various volumes of production output, and to provide guidance in the development of the business.

9. To indicate where articles or components can be bought more advantageously than made.

10. To record the relative production results of each unit of plant and machinery in use as a basis for examining its efficiency. A comparison with the performance of other types of machines may suggest the necessity for replacement.

11. To provide a perpetual inventory of stores and other materials.

12. To explain in detail the sources of profit or loss revealed in total in the Profit and Loss Account. The interlocking

of the Cost and Financial Accounts is a necessary corollary for this purpose, and the costing scheme must provide for this.

Standard Costs and Budgetary Control.—In well-developed industries, and in many individual factories which have been efficiently organised, systems of Standard Costs have been introduced in conjunction with pre-determined Expense Budgets. An Expense Budget is a schedule of all the elements of expense pre-determined in relation to an assumed output of production. Standard Costs are pre-determined costs in relation to an assumed volume of production which serve as a measure with which ascertained actual costs may be compared, to test the efficiency of production. The objective is to maintain actual costs as closely as possible to the Standard Costs. (See p. 317.)

The corollary to this procedure is the establishment of Budgetary Control, whereby every item of actual cost is so controlled by vigilant supervision as to make it conform, as nearly as possible, to the predetermined standard. This procedure has resulted in the elimination of waste and excess costs in every suitable instance where Budgetary Control has been properly instituted; in numerous cases the savings effected have been very considerable. A system of Standard Costs is most suitable for undertakings engaged in mass production or repetition work, process or unit operation manufacturing, or some form of continuous production as distinct from irregular job or order work. The subject of Standard Costing is dealt with more fully in later chapters.

Uniform Costing.—In a number of industries, uniform systems of costing have been introduced. In some cases, this has been the result of organisation by particular trade federations, in other cases, where a number of factories have become amalgamated under a central control, uniform systems have been put into operation. Such organisation provides a basis for comparing costs, and for discussion of common problems of production. As rationalisation proceeds, it would appear that there will be further developments of Uniform Costing systems.

Mechanised Cost Accounting.—Costs and statistics must be prepared with accuracy, speed, and regularity, and, in large works, this is only possible by the aid of sorting, tabulating, calculating, and other machines. Much valuable information is never secured because of the time and cost when using ordinary clerical methods.

In view of the rapid development in the use of machinery for preparing records, and particularly in the use of punched card tabulating machines, three chapters at the end of the book have been devoted to the subject.

Costing Terminology.—The science of costing has developed rapidly on both sides of the Atlantic, but the terminology used by writers reveals considerable lack of uniformity, as will be seen from the synonyms which are referred to in the following chapters. It is gratifying to know that the Institute of Cost and Works Accountants has set up a committee which has prepared a glossary of costing terms. This useful work by the Institute should lead to a much-needed standardisation, which it is to be hoped will be universally adopted. The terminology and definitions in this book conform with such standards.

EXAMINATION QUESTIONS

1. What are the essential features in the presentation of Costing results to the Management ?—*Institute of Cost and Works Accountants (Inter.).*

2. It has been stated that :
"Cost Accounts supply periodical Profit and Loss Statements independently of the financial accounts."
Comment on this statement and mention any precautions necessary in consequence of the fact referred to.—*London Chamber of Commerce.*

3. What are the main features in presentation of costing data ? Assuming it is your duty to write a monthly report on a factory where process costing is in use, what features would you expect to discuss ? Indicate briefly the form of your report.—*Institute of Cost and Works Accountants (Final).*

4. A small manufacturing business, until recently conducted by the proprietor has now been taken over by a Company of which the late proprietor is Managing Director. A considerable amount of new capital has been brought into the business to finance extensions. The late proprietor has conducted the business successfully for many years, he is an expert in the trade and felt no need of costing records.
Assume the products to be of any kind with the manufacture of which you are familiar, and write a report for the new Board, giving reasons for the introduction of a Costing system and outlining a suitable system.—*London Chamber of Commerce.*

5. What advantages would you expect to accrue from the institution of a uniform system of costing throughout an industry ?—*London Chamber of Commerce.*

6. What objects are to be obtained from the keeping of Cost Accounts that cannot be obtained from the usual Financial Accounts ?—*Royal Society of Arts (Advanced).*

7. What is meant by Standard Costs; in what circumstances may they safely be employed; what advantages do they offer ?—*Institute of Cost and Works Accountants (Inter.).*

8. Show that Cost Accounting is essential to industrial efficiency.—*Institute of Cost and Works Accountants (Inter.).*

9. What is meant by the expression "predetermined Costs" ? For what purposes are they used ?—*Institute of Cost and Works Accountants (Inter.).*

10. Give five examples of the manner in which Cost Accounting aids management.—*Institute of Cost and Works Accountants (Inter.)*.

11. Write a short essay on the uses of Costing in periods of industrial depression and explain how the information supplied by the Cost Accountant is best utilised.—*Institute of Cost and Works Accountants (Final)*.

12. What advantages would you claim for a scheme of Budgetary Control and what safeguards would you suggest in connection with its use ?—*Institute of Cost and Works Accountants (Final)*.

13. Do you consider there is any necessity for keeping Cost Accounts in a monopolistic industry ?   State your reason in full.—*Institute of Cost and Works Accountants (Final)*.

14. Distinguish between (a) estimates, (b) costs, (c) prices, and indicate how they are related to each other.—*Institute of Cost and Works Accountants (Final)*.

15. Write a short treatise of about 300–400 words on the modern trend of Cost Accounting.—*Institute of Cost and Works Accountants (Final)*.

16. What are the primary and secondary objects of scientific costing ? What other purposes can it be made to serve ?—*Institute of Cost and Works Accountants (Final)*.

17. What effect would a good system of Costing have on management ? —*Institute of Cost and Works Accountants (Final)*.

18. You are consulted by a manufacturing concern to advise them as to installing a system of Costing.   Write out a report to the board of directors detailing the general lines of your investigation, setting out the advantages to be gained by the adoption of such a system and indicating the directions in which its cost would be recovered.—*Institute of Cost and Works Accountants (Final)*.

19. Explain why Cost Accounts are said to be the key to economy in manufacture.—*Society of Incorporated Accountants and Auditors (Inter.)*.

20. It is contended that competition governs prices and that where production efficiency is good there is no need for a proper system of Costing.   What arguments would you advance to educate this opinion ? —*Institute of Cost and Works Accountants (Final)*.

21. Explain fully the advantages to a manufacturer or contractor of keeping Cost Accounts, and contrast the advantages with any possible disadvantages.—*Society of Incorporated Accountants and Auditors (Inter.)*.

22. A manufacturer has been recommended to have an efficient costing system installed, but is doubtful whether the results obtained will justify the expense incurred.   Indicate the benefits which will accrue if a proper system is installed, and state what additional information should be available to the manufacturer.—*Corporation of Accountants (Final)*.

23. A manufacturer has quoted for a certain contract at the price of £6,000, which is in accordance with estimate prepared by the Cost Accountant, as follows :

Labour	£2,000
Material	2,500
Overhead Charges	1,000
	£5,500
Profit	500
	£6,000

He has been offered the Contract at the price of £5,250.   Would you recommend the manufacturer to undertake the work at this price, bearing in mind that the trade is in a depressed condition and that orders are difficult to obtain ?   State your reasons for or against acceptance of the order.—*Corporation of Accountants (Final)*.

CHAPTER II

THE ELEMENTS OF COST

THE METHODS OF COSTING

The Analysis and Classification of Cost.—It is necessary to analyse and classify manufacturing costs, if management is to be provided with the data required for cost control.

A classification has to be made to arrive at the detailed costs of departments, processes, production orders, jobs, or other cost units. The total cost of production can be found without such analysis, and in most instances an average unit cost could be obtained, but none of the advantages of an analysed cost would be available.

Generally speaking, all expenditure may be divided into groups corresponding to the activities of a manufacturing concern, namely :

(a) Producing Departments or Shops. ⎫
(b) Service Departments.   ⎬ Expenditure of Manufacturing.
(c) Works Expenses.   ⎭
(d) Administration Expenses.
(e) Selling Expenses.
(f) Distribution Expenses.

Again, total cost can be separated under three broad headings, namely, Materials, Labour, and Expense, and these three groups of expenditure are known as the elements of cost.

THE ANALYSIS OF TOTAL COST

The total expenditure incidental to production, administration, selling, and distribution is analysed by the cost accountant according to the elements of cost. The elements of cost are :

(i) Direct Labour. ⎫
(ii) Direct Materials. ⎬ Prime Cost.
(iii) Direct Expenses. ⎭
(iv) Overhead Expenses—comprising (a) Departmental, (b) General, and (c) Services; and
(d) Administration, (e) Selling, (f) Distribution.

Works or Factory Cost. Total Cost.

9

The first three items constitute Prime Cost, so that the elements of cost may be said to comprise prime cost and overhead. Each item is defined and explained below.

Direct Labour.—This is all labour expended in altering the construction, composition, conformation, or condition of the product. The wages paid to skilled and unskilled workers for this labour can be allocated specifically to the particular cost accounts concerned—hence the term " Direct Wages," which may be defined as the measure of direct labour in terms of money. The term does not apply to services or processes where labour is analysed under other headings, such as specific operations or occupations.

Other descriptions sometimes used are : Process Labour; Productive Labour; Operating Labour.

Direct Material is all material that becomes a part of the product, the costs of which are directly charged as part of the Prime Cost. In other words, it is the material which can be measured and charged directly to the cost of the product.

The following groups of materials fall within the definition :

(i) All material specially purchased for a particular job, order, or process.

(ii) All materials requisitioned from the stores for particular production orders.

(iii) Components purchased or produced, and similarly requisitioned from the finished parts store.

(iv) Material passing from one operation or process to another, e.g. produced, converted, or part-manufactured material which is intended for further treatment or operations.

The following descriptions are used in the same sense as Direct Materials : Process Material; Prime Cost Material; Production Material; Stores Material; Constructional Material.

Raw Material.—Reference may be usefully made here to the term " Raw Material." In the majority of instances, the finished product of one industry is the raw material of another. Thus sheet steel may be the finished product of the steel rolling-mill, but the raw material of a metal-cutting works. The finished product of a wool-spinning mill becomes the raw material of the weaving mill. Pulp board is the finished product of mills which pulp timber, but this is part of the raw material of the paper-mill.

Circumstances arise when some direct materials are used in comparatively small quantities, and it would be a futile elaboration to make an analysis of them for the purpose of a direct charge. In the manufacture of hats or sewn boots it would be absurd to measure the value of the thread; or in making cardboard boxes, to determine the glue cost for fixing strips of linen used for binding the corners. Such direct material as this should be treated as a production expense item.

Direct Expenses.—This includes any expenditure other than direct material or direct labour directly incurred on a specific cost unit. Such special necessary expense is charged directly to the particular cost account concerned, as part of the prime cost. This item is sometimes termed " Chargeable Expenses."

The distinction between Direct Expense and Direct Departmental Expense should be observed :

When expenses can be allocated directly to a particular department, as, for instance, such items as power, light, and heat, indirect labour, rent, rates, water, gas, etc., they are described as Direct Departmental Expenses, but they are Indirect Expenses, so far as the allocation to particular cost units is concerned.

Overhead Expenses.—The three elements of cost just described constitute Prime Cost, and all expense over and above Prime Cost is Overhead, or, as it is frequently termed, " Oncost "—an unfortunate misnomer. Prime Cost plus all Works Overhead represents Works, or Factory Cost. Works Cost plus all other Overheads represents Total Cost.

"Overhead" may be defined as the cost of indirect material, indirect labour, and such other expenses including Services as cannot conveniently be charged direct to specific cost units.

There are four main groups into which Overhead may be sub-divided :

(a) Production or Factory Expense, including Services; often called Works Oncost.

(b) Administration Expense.

(c) Selling Expense.

(d) Distribution Expense.

All items of Overhead are dissected and collected under these four headings, and are subsequently distributed in some suitable manner which ensures their fair allocation to Departments or Centres for recovery upon each individual cost unit.

Overhead may also be classified as Fixed Overhead and Variable or Floating Overhead, and this aspect of expense analysis is discussed on pages 105 and 110.

This element of cost has a number of synonyms, such as Oncost, Establishment Charge, Burden, General Expense, Indirect Expense, and On-Charges.

Oncost is a term very frequently used for Overhead, but it is desirable that it should be discontinued, for the reason that Overhead is as much part of the cost as direct labour and prime cost materials, hence such expense is wrongly described as Oncost. In this book the term Overhead is used instead of Oncost.

THE SUB-DIVISIONS OF OVERHEAD EXPENSES

Production (or Factory) Expense is all indirect expenditure incurred by the undertaking from the receipt of the order until its completion ready for dispatch, either to the customer or to Finished Goods Store.

Other terms used are : Factory Overhead; Factory Oncost; Works Overhead; Works Oncost; Mill Oncost.

Examples of Production Expense, *i.e.* Works Overhead, are :

(a) Rent, rates, insurance, chargeable against the works, excluding any which can be apportioned to the general administration offices, selling departments, warehouse, and distribution.

(b) Indirect labour, *e.g.* supervision, such as salary of works managers, wages of foremen, etc.; shop clerical work; testing, gauging, and examining; indirect labour in connection with production shops (see page 13).

(c) Power (steam, gas, electric, hydraulic, compressed air) and other services in aid of production; process fuel; internal transport; Canteens, etc. (see page 137).

(d) Consumable stores, and all forms of indirect material, *i.e.* material which cannot be traced as part of the finished product, such as cotton waste, grease and oil, small tools, etc. (see below).

(e) Depreciation, maintenance, and repairs of buildings, plant, machinery, tools, etc.

Indirect Material.—In its strict sense, indirect material is material that cannot be traced as part of the product. Sometimes minor items of material which enter into production are treated as indirect material because of the futility of attempting minute analysis, as mentioned above in the last paragraph of the section dealing with direct materials (page 11).

Synonyms are : " Oncost Materials," " Expense Materials."

Indirect Labour.—This may be defined as labour expended that does not alter the construction, conformation, composition, or condition of the product. The term includes the labour of foremen, clerks, shop labourers, cleaners, and those engaged on maintenance and other general work not directly concerned with actual production. It also includes the technical and general management and supervision of the works. It is sometimes referred to as " non-productive " labour, but this is an undesirable description, and one which has fallen into disuse by cost accountants. Other synonyms are : " Oncost Labour," " Auxiliary Labour," " Ancillary Labour."

Indirect Wages.—The measure of indirect labour expressed in terms of money.

Administration Expense.—This consists of all expense incurred in the direction, control, and administration of an undertaking. It is sometimes called Office Oncost.

Examples are : The expenses in running the general offices, *e.g.* office rent, light, heat, salaries and wages of clerks, secretaries, accountants, general managers, directors, executives; legal and accounting machine services; investigations and experiments; financing expenses, and miscellaneous fixed charges.

Selling Expense.—This portion of the Overhead comprises the cost to producers or distributors of soliciting and securing orders for the articles or commodities dealt in, and of efforts to find and retain customers. It includes advertising; salaries and commission of the sales manager, travellers, agents; the cost of preparing tenders, and estimates for special selling projects; sales stock shortages; Rent of Sale Rooms and Offices; consumer service and service after sales, etc.

Distribution Expense.—This comprises all expenditure incurred from the time the product is completed in the works until it reaches its destination. Under this heading would be included Warehouse or Finished Stock Store charges, and the cost of transporting goods thereto, packing-cases, loading, carriage outwards, and of goods on sale or return, upkeep and running of delivery vehicles, despatch clerks and labourers, and other items of like nature.

Selling and Distribution Expenses are collected and analysed :—

(i) According to the nature of the expense, and also by function, *e.g.* advertising, salesmen, showrooms, storage, etc.

(ii) By location, *e.g.* representatives' territories, agents, markets, counties, countries, etc.; by departments, depots, etc.; or by type or grade of products. For the distribution of such costs various factors may be used, according to which is most suitable as regards incidence. Suggested factors are units of product, weights, values by selling turnover, time, distance, cubic capacity, invoices and so on. The object is to show the relationship of sales turnover to costs, and the relationship of sales turnover to the potential market. Hence the analysis of sales turnover and of these costs must be on the same basis. The effectiveness of these expenses towards profit earning can then be measured.

Factory Cost (or Works Cost).—This is that portion of total cost represented by the sum of the prime cost and expense incurred in producing an article up to the time it is completed at the factory. A proportion of general administration and accountancy expenses should be included to the extent that these services are directly connected with the factory. Selling and distribution expenses, however, do not form part of factory cost, but do form part of total cost.

Total Cost (All-In Cost).—Total Cost, or as it is often called, All-in Cost, is the entire expense incidental to production, administration, selling, and distribution.

Selling Price is made up of all the items included in total cost plus profit added, if any; or less loss, if sold below cost.

METHODS OF COSTING

General Observations.—*In the financial books* of an undertaking, the whole of the expenditure applicable to a given accounting period is posted in detail from the Cash Book, Journals, and other subsidiary books, to appropriate ledger accounts.

The capital and revenue expenditure, receipts, and credits are shown under suitable headings in the General or Impersonal Ledger, from which the Balance Sheet and Profit and Loss Account are prepared at suitable periods, usually half-yearly or yearly, but in some undertakings even monthly.

In the Cost Accounts the same revenue expenditure is analysed under the headings of the elements of cost, and is allocated to the separate cost accounts for particular orders, jobs, processes, services, or units in such a manner as will assist the management in the control of the business.

As the general financial accounts and the cost accounts are based on the same total expenditure, by allowing for certain exceptional items, *e.g.* bad debts, etc., it is possible to reconcile the final results shown by the two accounting systems as explained in Chapter XV.

The Methods of Cost Accounting.—The general principles are the same in every system of Cost Accounting, but the methods of collating and presenting the costs vary with the type of production to be costed.

Seven methods of costing may be identified :—

(a) *Unit Cost Accounting*, frequently referred to as " Output " or " Single " Costing. Represents the old " Departmental " costing based on an overall average cost.

(b) *Job Costing*, often called " Terminal " Costing. This term includes " Contract " Costing.

(c) *Batch Costing*, which is a form of Job Costing.

(d) *Process Costing*.

(e) *Multiple Costing*, also referred to as " Composite Costing."

(f) *Operation Costing*.

(g) *Operating or " Working " Cost Methods*.

Uniform Costing is a system of costing common to different factories or producers in the same industry and may include any of the above methods. It is described on page 260.

Standard Costs may be used in conjunction with all the above methods, but not with Job Costing when the orders are practically all dissimilar and non-repeating. (See page 315.)

Unit Costing (" Output " or " Single " Costing).—This may be defined as a method of costing by the unit of production where manufacture is continuous, and the units are identical, or may be made so by means of ratios. It may be employed in conjunction with batch, operation, or process costing, and is suitable for such undertakings as collieries, quarries, various kinds of mines, flour mills, steel works, brick and cement works, paper-mills, breweries, etc., in all of which there is a standard unit of production. It is also used in Municipal Costing. Examples of such units are detailed on pp. 248, 249, and 391.

Job Costing (includes " Terminal " and " Contract Costing ").—This method is used to cost jobs or contracts that are kept separate during manufacture or construction. It is applicable to job order work in factories and workshops, and work by builders, constructional engineers, shipbuilders, printers, municipal engineers, etc. The unit of cost is the job, order, or contract, and the accounts show the cost of each order.

Batch Costing.—The method of costing when orders or jobs are arranged in batches convenient for production, the batches being regarded as the units for costing purposes.

Process Costing.—The method of costing production by processes in which (a) the product of the process becomes the material of a subsequent process; or (b) where the different products and by-products (if any) are produced simultaneously at the same process; or (c) when the products, differing only in shape or form on completion, are not separately distinguishable from one another during one or more processes of manufacture. Typical industries which may use this method are : those concerned with chemicals, textiles, distilled products, foods, explosives, paints and varnish, etc. The cost of each process, and the costs per unit at each stage, are usually shown by the accounts.

Multiple Costing (or " Composite Costing ").—A method of costing by combining the costs of component parts of an assembled or aggregate product, separate costs being compiled for each of a variety of articles manufactured. This method is used in such factories as those manufacturing cycles, motor-cars, engines, wireless sets, machine tools, aeroplanes, and other complex products.

Operation Costing.—A method of costing by operations in connection with mass production, repetition work, and other forms of quantity production. It is used in factories where the production is in quantities of standardised lines with the object of working at a minimum cost. There is usually a constant and uninterrupted flow of production, making use of machine tools and equipment specially designed for each operation, and much division of labour in order to ensure a maximum output at each operation, *e.g.* components for products named under " Multiple Costing " above.

Operating Costing.—A method of costing the expenses incurred in the provision of services, such as those afforded by railways, tramways, motor coaches, carriers, gas, electricity, and water undertakings.

Each of these methods of costing is described in detail in later chapters.

"Time and Lime" Costing,* and "Cost Plus" Costing.— These refer to contracts placed with contractors on the basis of cost plus an agreed sum or percentage to cover overhead expenses and profit. The cost refers to direct labour, materials and admissible direct expenses, such as plant hire, transport of materials and plant, etc. Great care is required to see that only agreed and necessary items are admitted to cost. The method was much used before and during the Great War of 1914 to 1918, and is usually used only when there is need for rapid execution of contracts without waiting for the fixing of definite contract prices. The method is not regarded as satisfactory in normal circumstances owing to the possibility of abuse and the lack of incentive to minimise costs. When the method is used, the accounts are usually scrutinised by accountants appointed by the Authority which placed the contracts.

"Target" Costs.—These are used in connection with large constructional contracts, and refer to the method of carefully calculating the anticipated cost, usually by experienced surveyors in consultation with accountants. This anticipated cost is treated as the Target Cost, and on the cost so determined the contractor is paid either an agreed percentage or a fixed sum to cover his overheads and profit. The percentage may be determined by tenders, the lowest being usually accepted, or it may be one agreed directly with a contractor. In order to encourage economical work, it may be agreed to give the contractor a predetermined bonus, such as a percentage of any saving on the target cost.

Clauses may be included in the contract to provide conditions for unascertainable increases in such items as subsequent rises in wage rates, prices of materials, etc., and the cost of any

---

* Often erroneously referred to as " Time and Line," probably due to misquotation in early newspaper references.

C

required deviations in the work to be added to the target cost.

As in the case of cost plus profit contracts accountants independent of the contractor are usually employed to scrutinise the records and accounts. Contracts for supplies may be placed at target prices, on a cost basis with an agreed bonus if target price is reduced.

EXAMINATION QUESTIONS

1. What do you understand by—

(1) Direct Wages.   (3) Direct Material.
(2) Indirect Wages.   (4) Indirect Material.

Give an example in each case.

London Association of Accountants (Final).

2. State how you would allocate the following items under their headings of (a) Works Expenses; (b) Administration Expenses; (c) Selling Expenses; and (d) Distribution Expenses :

Depreciation of Offices.   Directors' Fees.
Salaries to Sales Managers.   Loss of weight in transit to cus-
Costing Department.   tomers.
Patent Fees.   Advertising.
Tran port.   Postages and Stationery.
Bill Discount.   Dividend on Investments received.
Rents.   Interest paid on Bank Overdraft.

Institute of Cost and Works Accountants (Inter.).

3. Define, and give examples of :—

Prime Cost.   Administrative Expenses.
Direct Expenses.   Standard Costs.
Works Oncost.   Selling Expenses.

London Chamber of Commerce.

4. Define :—

(a) Prime cost.
(b) Works cost.

Illustrate their relationships to the selling price of a manufactured commodity.—*Royal Society of Arts (Advanced).*

5. What components go to make up the selling price of a manufactured commodity ?—*Royal Society of Arts (Advanced).*

6. A holding company controls three factories, all of which make similar products. It is desired to introduce a system of uniform costing in the three factories. Describe briefly the principles on which you would base the system you would propose to install.—*Royal Society of Arts (Advanced).*

7. "Expenses should not lose their identity in the expense or on-cost statements." Give illustrations of what is meant by this and say how you would propose to ensure compliance with this principle.—*Royal Society of Arts (Advanced).*

8. What do you understand by the term "Oncost"? Upon what basis should it, in your opinion, be calculated? State your reasons.—*Chartered Institute of Secretaries (Inter.).*

9. "The principles underlying all systems of Costing are identical." Enumerate and define these principles.—*Society of Incorporated Account ants and Auditors (Inter.).*

10. What method of costing (Job, Operating, etc.) would apply to the following industries :

  (a) Coal Mining.
  (b) Shipbuilding.
  (c) Weaving.
  (d) Boot Manufacture.
  (e) Oil Refining.
  (f) Power Station.
  (g) Soap Manufacture.
  (h) Printing.
                Institute of Cost and Works Accountants (Inter.).

11. Explain the distinction between Process, Single, and Job Costing; state the industries to which each is suitable.—*London Chamber of Commerce.*

12. What would you take as the unit of cost in the following cases :

  (a) Iron Foundry.
  (b) Electricity Undertaking.
  (c) Machine Tool-makers.
  (d) Brewery.
  (e) Building Contractors.
  (f) Stevedore.
  (g) Railway Company.
                Royal Society of Arts (Advanced).

13. Describe briefly the different methods of costing known to you and the type of product to which they are respectively applicable.—*Royal Society of Arts (Advanced).*

14. Assume three methods of Costing. Job method, Process method and Unit method. What method would you apply in the following industries : Motor-car Manufacturing; Tanning; Electricity Supply; Coal Mining; Weaving; Iron Founding; Boot Manufacturing; Sugar Refinery; Shipbuilding.

State your reasons for the application.—*Institute of Cost and Works Accountants (Inter.).*

15. Discuss the preliminary steps you would take in installing a complete costing scheme in a factory hitherto without one. Name some of the first difficulties you would expect to arise, and how you would endeavour to overcome them.—*Institute of Cost and Works Accountants (Final).*

16. What are the main principles of Cost Accounting, and what faults would you expect to find in defective cost accounts ? Discuss the latter and show how these are prejudicial to effective management.—*Institute of Cost and Works Accountants (Final).*

17. What do you understand by the terms :
  (a) Process costs ; (b) Operating costs ?

In what types of industry do you consider these systems applicable ? —*Institute of Cost and Works Accountants (Inter.).*

18. Set out six items under each of the following classes of expense :
  (a) Production; (b) Administration; (c) Selling; (d) Distribution.

What effect on their respective proportions would you expect, when the turnover varies considerably in different periods ?—*Institute of Cost and Works Accountants (Inter.).*

19. Discuss the term " Scientific Management," and state how, in your opinion, the work of the Cost Accountant contributes to its successful operation.—*Institute of Cost and Works Accountants (Final).*

20. What methods of costing would you advocate in the case of the following manufactures ?   State reasons.
Ball bearings ; Beer ; Bicycles ; Biscuits ; Bricks.

Institute of Cost and Works Accountants (Final).

21. Which type of costing is most suitable for the following undertakings :
(*a*) Colliery ; (*b*) House Building ; (*c*) Furniture Manufacturing ; (*d*) Cold Storage Plant ; (*e*) Multiple Shop ; (*f*) Oil Refinery ?
Give reasons for your answer, explaining what result each system is designed to show.—*Society of Incorporated Accountants and Auditors (Final).*

22. State which method of Costing you would recommend for use in the following :
(1) Chemical Works ; (2) Colliery ; (3) Painter and Decorator ; (4) Hosiery Manufacturer ; (5) Constructional Engineer ; (6) Road Transport Company ; (7) Paper Mill.—*Corporation of Accountants (Final).*

23. What is costing and how would you define " cost " ?—*London Association of Certified Accountants (Final).*

24. What is the primary function of Cost Accounts, and what do you understand by the term " Cost Accounting " ?—*Incorporated Accountants (Inter.).*

25. Define the following and indicate in which industries or undertakings the different classes could be suitably applied :
(1) Single Costs ; (2) Terminal Costs ; (3) Operating Costs ; (4) Multiple Costs ; (5) Process Costs.—*Incorporated Accountants (Final).*

26. What items are always understood as being included when speaking of the following :
(1) Prime, First or Flat Cost ; (2) Total Cost, Gross Cost or Cost of Production ; (3) Selling Price ?—*Chartered Accountants (Inter.).*

27. What do you understand by the term " Unit of Cost " ?   Give the units that you consider most applicable to, or most used in, any four industries known to you.—*Incorporated Accountants (Inter.).*

CHAPTER III

FACTORY ORGANISATION IN CONJUNCTION WITH THE COSTING SYSTEM

Production Efficiency.—The organisation of a factory or workshop has for its aim efficient production—this efficiency being measured by the number of articles produced, the quality and price of the product, and the quickness of delivery. The requirements for successful competition are that production must be expeditious, correct, and at a minimum cost.

The attainment of these objectives demands careful organisation, good management, and the fullest use of plant and the other agents of production. The inclusion of a system of costing provides a reliable means of measuring the extent to which the management succeeds in achieving these objectives.

The Costing system can be so arranged that the management may be aware, not only what the cost of production should be, but also what it has actually been. It provides the only reliable means of collating data and analysing expenditure in relation to production for the guidance of the management. The financial accounts kept will reveal the amount of profit or loss realised, but the information provided by the Cost Accountant goes further than that by indicating where leakages, losses, and waste, occur, or where improvements are possible. The function of the Cost Accountant is to assist the Works Manager with information, and to measure for him in money value the results of production. The ascertained cost of all that is done also provides a guide for the future.

The Need for Co-operation.—It is essential that the works system and routine should include arrangements for providing the Cost Accountant with the figures and information necessary for preparing the cost data. A costing system, however good, cannot function properly if the works organisation is unsatisfactory, and, therefore, it is desirable that the system should be drawn up in collaboration with the Works Manager, and,

19

probably, departmental heads, so that full co-operation of all concerned may be secured. Every effort should be made to eliminate friction and departmental jealousy, and to adopt all suggestions which will tend to make the arrangements run smoothly with the least possible trouble in the workshops.

The Scheme of Administration and Management.—Particular and varying conditions in different industries and works make it impracticable to describe a standard system of works organisation which would be universally suitable, but the principles of works management and organisation can be outlined. For present purposes it will be sufficient to describe the functions of the various departments and officials in a representative works. Others are referred to in later chapters dealing with systems in specific industries. In large works, the duties and responsibilities are shared by more officials than in a small factory, hence, when studying the functions outlined below, it should be noted that in a smaller organisation one individual may combine several such functions within his sphere of responsibility. The main principle to observe is that each person should have his authority and responsibility well defined, so that overlapping of duties does not occur. Provision has to be made for fullest co-ordination and liaison.

The Main Divisions of Management

The administration of a manufacturing business is usually controlled by a Managing Director, or General Manager, and the main divisions of managerial responsibility can be identified, viz.:

(i) Secretarial and Financial.
(ii) Sales and Distribution of the products.
(iii) Production and Production Services.
(iv) Design and Research, in large concerns.

The Secretarial and Financial Management is usually the responsibility of the Secretary, or a director of a company, or, in many instances, of the Chief Accountant, or Chief Clerk. The functions usually include :

(a) Secretarial work, and control of the general office staff.
(b) The control of financing operations and the ordinary financial books of account.
(c) Collaboration with the Works Manager in regard to the financing aspect of equipment and production.

The Sales Manager is responsible for sales promotion in its various forms. He devises selling and advertising campaigns, controls the salesmen, submits estimates and tenders, and is responsible for all statistics relating to sales. He must collaborate with the Works Manager, or Planning Department, as to types and quantities of various goods likely to be required. For estimates and tenders he will consult the Cost Accountant, or, in some cases, the Rate-Fixer, who often functions as an estimator.

The third division—that of Production Management—is the most important from the point of view of this book, and will be considered in greater detail, using for purposes of illustration a large engineering works.

Production Management.—The organisation or production management is co-ordinated by the Works Manager, and the technical control is exercised by the Chief Engineer, or Chemist.

The Works Manager supervises all who are in the chain of control of production, the main sections of which are :

   (i) The Planning Department.
   (ii) The Production Departments, including Stores.
   (iii) The Service Departments.
   (iv) The Purchasing Department.

Much of his time is spent in smoothing out the difficulties of his subordinates, and giving decisions when special matters arise in respect of production. He must keep himself well informed of all that takes place in the works, and act as general controller in all matters relating to production.

In particular, the Works Manager usually controls the following sections :

(1) *Planning Department*, which may be responsible for—

(a) Arranging how and where the work is to be done and the issue of instructions.

(b) The Progress Department, which regulates the work in accordance with the time-table set by the Planning Department. Sometimes that department determines the sequence of operations, the Progress Department being responsible for the detailed arrangements.

(c) The Tool Drawing Office.

(d) The Rate-fixing and Time-study Department.

(e) The Tool-room, and, sometimes,

(*f*) The Tool Stores. The Tool-room and Store sometimes come under the control of the Production Department.

2. *The Production Department*, which controls

(*a*) Shop Superintendents, and through them the Foremen and Charge Hands.

(*b*) Stores Departments, *e.g.*:

    * (i) Main Stores of Materials.

    (ii) Part Finished Stores.

    (iii) Finished Stores.

    (iv) Tool Stores, if not supervised by the Planning Department.

    (v) Consumable Stores.

(*c*) Despatch Packing.

(*d*) Transport.

(*e*) Labour and Welfare.

3. *The Purchasing Department*, which is responsible for dealing with replenishment requisitions from the Stores; and for the securing of special direct material.

4. *The Inspection Department*, if not controlled by the Engineer (see below).

The Chief Engineer supervises the technical side of the works, and acts as technical consultant to almost every section of the works. He designs the articles to be made and any variations arising out of special specifications. It is his duty to study the latest technical information, and to propose improvements in design and materials, after proper research and experiment if necessary in conjunction with the Works Chemist.

The departments he is responsible for are :

(1) *The Drawing Office.*—Under the instructions of the Engineer, working drawings are prepared, and the necessary blue prints for use in the shops. A carefully indexed file of drawings and blue-prints is kept. The Tracers and Blue-print Room are supervised by the Chief Draughtsman.

Specifications of Material (sometimes called Bills of Material) suggested by the Engineer are prepared, and orders pass from the Engineer's Department to the Drawing Office and Planning Department for the issue of instructions.

(2) *Experiment and Research Department.*—New designs, improvements, and new methods are tried out in this depart-

* The stores are sometimes under the control of the Cost Accountant, or Financial Officer. The control is twofold: (*a*) financial, (*b*) physical.

ment. It is also responsible for testing materials, and examining them to ascertain whether they conform to specification. Various physical and chemical tests may be necessary, especially where metals and chemicals are used in the process of manufacture.

(3) *Inspection Department.*—The Chief Inspector must of necessity be a technical man who understands all manufacturing operations to enable him to trace reasons for defective work. Inspection duties can be divided into four sections :

(a) Inspection of purchased raw materials. Examination is made as to dimensions, tensile strength, chemical composition, finish, or other factors mentioned in the purchase specification. It should be noticed that the finished product of one industry, or department, may be the raw material of another.

(b) Inspection of goods purchased in a partly finished or machined condition. The examination is made to see that the articles agree with the specification. Where gauges have been supplied, copies will be used to test the articles, in addition to inspection of the general finish.

(c) Inspection of finished parts, or components, made in the factory. This may be conducted after every operation or process; but if this cannot be done without unduly large expense, the finished part is examined on completion. Each person examining will stamp or otherwise impress the articles with his own identification mark.

(d) Inspection of finished products for stock or despatch. Each part assembled is examined, *e.g.* the painting, polish, and general appearance, the fit if applicable, and the correct components or accessories. Quantities are also usually certified by the Inspection Department, showing the quantities rejected.

DEPARTMENTAL PROCEDURE

The Planning Department.—This department relieves the foremen of many responsibilities, and co-ordinates production by providing the plan of procedure and time-table for the whole works. Arrangements are made for the passing of each order through the shops. Not only the route, but also the machines to be used are specified, and the supply of requisite materials is ensured.

Attention has to be paid to machining and handling methods,

and to the volume of production which can be coped with by each department or shop. In matters of cost, the Cost Accountant has to be consulted, particularly in regard to alterations in procedure.

The Progress Department is responsible for the details of manufacture which have been arranged by the Planning Department. The latter will plan the sequence of operations, and the Progress Department details the particular machines to be used, regulates the work, and maintains its movement to time through every stage of manufacture. The Progress Department makes sure that materials required are in stock, or that specially purchased material is delivered to time. It obtains the specifications of materials and drawings from the Drawing Office, and sees that any necessary jigs or tools are available. Where special tools are required, drawings will be made and orders given for the making of the tools. Schedules are prepared for every movement of the work, so that the progress man knows what work is on each machine, and can be making preparations for the next job to follow. Graphic charts are often used, the Gantt Charts being particularly appropriate (see p. 378).

The Tool-Drawing Office is another part of the Planning Department, which is generally separate from the main Drawing Office.

The jigs, gauges, and tools required by the Planning Department are designed in the Tool-Drawing Office.

The Tool-Room is the department which produces the jigs, gauges, and tools required by the Production Department. It examines tools returned from the shops, and re-conditions them if this is necessary. The foreman in charge is usually a highly skilled man, and he is provided with machine tools, special furnaces for hardening, etc., and various instruments for measuring accurately. All tools made or returned from the shops are passed to the Tool Store, from which they are only issued on presentation of formal requisitions, see Ch. XIV.

The Rate-Fixer in some works may perform some of the functions of the Planning and Progress Departments. He may decide whether day- or piece-work is to be used, indicate the time allowed, and is responsible for fixing time or price rates for each piece or operation not produced or paid by ordinary time-work rates. A careful investigation is made in detail for every operation; timing is made with the aid of a stop-watch, and a reliable average time fixed, and, finally, the piece-work or premium-bonus rate. All factors which affect the work are considered, including the type of machine, its speed, and the kind of material to be worked upon. It is apparent that the Rate-Fixer must have a practical working knowledge of every machine, and thoroughly understand tool design. Careful enquiry into motion study methods, as advised by industrial psychologists, may lead to better results.

Production Department.—Immediately responsible to the Works Manager are the

Works or Shop Superintendents.—Each has one or more producing shops under his supervision and control.

Where there is a Labour Engagement Department, the Works Superintendent may be responsible for authorising the engagement of workers requisitioned by foremen. His chief duties are : representing the Works Manager, attending to matters delegated to him, and supervising the conduct of the shops for which he is responsible.

The Foreman is mainly concerned with supervision of the men and work in his shop. Through him all instructions and works orders pass to the workers, and his duty is to see these are duly and correctly carried out.

The foreman will see that proper shop records are kept of orders handed to the workers, and that time spent on each is correctly booked. The modern practice is to have this work done by a clerk assisting the foreman.

The work done in his shop will generally be inspected by him or his assistant, and he will see that machines are kept running, reporting defects to the Repair Department. In large shops, charge-hands may assist the foreman.

The Storekeeper is responsible for the care and custody of materials, and sometimes of finished stock. He must see that all materials are kept in an orderly manner, and that quantities are maintained in accordance with the maxima and minima which have been fixed by the management. Proper records of receipts and issues must be kept by him. He must see that nothing is issued, except on presentation of a duly authorised requisition. He is responsible for these requisitions being sent daily to the Cost Office.

If departmental stores are kept, in addition to the main

stores, an assistant storekeeper will be in charge of each. Stores procedure and organisation will be dealt with in a separate chapter.

Stores Audit.—It is usual to have a continuous check on the records and physical stock, a portion being done each day or week in a large works.

The Despatch Department is responsible for the packing and despatch of goods; for the checking of the quantity and weight of packages; and for the careful execution of delivery instructions given by customers.

Purchasing Department.—The buyer purchases materials for all purposes. Generally, materials have to be bought to specification. The requisitions upon which the buyer acts emanate from the storekeeper for replenishment of standard materials, and from the Engineer's Office or Drawing Office for special materials for a particular job or order.

The department must see that delivery is made within the time required for use. The most suitable markets must be known, quotations secured, and orders placed. Good indexes should be kept, and constantly revised, showing (a) the goods used by the factory, (b) suppliers, with their latest prices for such goods, time required for delivery, and other useful particulars. Purchasing procedure is detailed in the next chapter.

The Costing Department.—The Cost Accountant should be directly responsible to the General Manager, but must work in close collaboration with the engineer, and the Planning and Production Departments. The department is responsible for the preparation of the Cost Accounts, Returns for the guidance of the management, and particularly for indicating where loss, waste, inefficiency, and possibility of saving occur.

Particulars of expenditure of all kinds must be transmitted to it from the General Office, and, as both the Cost and Financial Accounts are based on the same original data, the scheme of accounts must be made to reconcile with those of the Financial Accountant's department. No attempt should be made to effect agreement in details, so long as the final results and main sectional totals are reconciled. Over-elaboration makes the department unnecessarily costly, and may even obscure rather than elucidate results. Whatever cost reports are prepared, they should be in a form readily understood by those managers for whom they are prepared.

The Cost Office is responsible for recording particulars of requisitions and prices for materials. These requisitions received from the Storekeeper must be checked against the shop requisition book counterfoils or duplicates to ensure none are missing. Prices and variations thereof are dealt with.

The Wages and Timekeeper's offices are usually under the control of the Cost Accountant, at least in so far as the calculation of times and amounts payable are concerned and the form in which records are entered up. The timekeeper is directly responsible for the recording of the times of workers, computing time and overtime, and the operation of attendance time recording devices. The Wages Office, from details supplied by the timekeeper, or from work tickets, makes up the pay-roll from which the Cashier pays. The detailed procedure of these departments is described in Chapters VI and VII.

Production Departments or Shops, and Production Services.— Production Department is the term used to connote the department in which the actual product for sale is manufactured or produced, in contradistinction to the service departments that are ancillary.

A Production Service is a facility available to a production department. Often it is applicable generally, and constantly available but only taken as required, *e.g.* power supply, steam supply, etc.

EXAMINATION QUESTIONS

1. By means of a suitable chart, describe the route through the works taken by an order from its reception, during all stages of manufacture, to its completion ready for dispatch.—*Institute of Cost and Works Accountants (Inter.).*

2. What scheme would you adopt whereby the Drawing Office, Planning Department, Jig and Tool Department, Estimating Department and Design Office can have advantageous service from the Cost Accounts ?—*Institute of Cost and Works Accountants (Final).*

3. What method would you employ to ensure that all requisitions finally reach the cost department ?—*Institute of Cost and Works Accountants (Inter.).*

4. What steps would you propose should be taken to avoid discrepancies between store-house records and the stores ledgers in respect of issues of materials and stores ?—*Institute of Cost and Works Accountants (Inter.).*

5. "No system of costing will prove successful if the organisation of the factory is bad." Comment on this statement. Who is the officer directly responsible for the organisation of a factory, and what is the extent of his control and responsibility ? Why are his methods of importance to the Professional Accountant ?—*Society of Incorporated Accountants and Auditors (Final).*

CHAPTER IV

PURCHASING AND STORES DEPARTMENTS PROCEDURE

Introductory.—In each industry, and in different works within an industry, the detailed organisation will vary according to particular conditions and ideas, but the general procedure and principles outlined in this chapter may be regarded as typical, although particularly suitable for an engineering or similar factory. The forms used as illustrations are based on some actually in use, but again will vary in ruling and wording to suit particular needs.

The storekeeper's duties are important, and the position is a responsible one. In his care are materials representing large sums, and he must see that these are safely stored, arranged in an orderly manner and accessible, all receipts and issues being properly recorded, and re-ordering promptly dealt with.

Quantities and kinds of materials will be decided upon by technical managers, the usual custom being to fix a maximum and minimum quantity of each material to be carried.

It is usual to keep separate stores for part-finished stocks, finished parts, finished stocks, raw materials, and consumable stores. In large works, it is sometimes the practice to have departmental stores for materials regularly required in the respective departments, supplies being drawn from the main stores. In such cases, an assistant storekeeper is in charge. Generally speaking, it is inadvisable to place departmental stores under the care of the foreman of the department.

The definitions of the kinds of stock are :

Raw Materials.—Materials purchased or produced, either in a natural or manufactured condition. Manufactured materials of one industry are often the raw materials of another.

Bulk Material is a term often used to describe material not in unit form directly suited to the work in hand, as, for instance, material not measurable except by weight or volume, sheets, bars, tubes, and bales.

Part-Finished Stock is work in progress that has not reached the stage of completion as a part or component.

Finished Parts are items, or sub-assemblies, put into store awaiting final assembly, or sale as spares. The term "components" refers to the separate pieces entering into a complete product.

Finished Stock is the completed product awaiting sale or despatch. Stock is so named after transfer from Work in Progress, physically and by entry in the accounts. Sometimes termed : Finished Stores, Completed Stock or Manufactured Stock.

Scrap Material.—Residue of materials, raw or manufactured, and spoilt materials arising in the course of manufacture, which are of no use for their original purpose.

Indirect Materials are those used which cannot be directly charged to, or traced as part of the product. They include :

Consumable Stores such as lubricants, waste, belt fasteners and dressings, and cleaning materials which are chargeable to expense accounts.

Classification Code for Materials.—The use of material specification code numbers is an advantage, not only to the Purchasing Department and Drawing Office, but also to the pricing clerk in the Works Office, in that ambiguity is eliminated. The code should consist of symbols and numbers, the symbol indicating a material or an item, and the number the size, pattern, etc. A simple example will make this clear. Screws, brass, and steel could be given the symbols B.S. and S.S. respectively, a number being added for each size, the first is sixteenths, the next two-lengths in eighths :—

B.S. 403 = Brass Screw $\frac{1}{4}'' \times \frac{3}{8}''$	S.S. 403			Steel screws
B.S. 704 = ,, ,, $\frac{7}{16}'' \times \frac{1}{2}''$	S.S. 704			of the same
B.S. 507 = ,, ,, $\frac{5}{16}'' \times \frac{5}{8}''$	S.S. 507	=		sizes as
B.S. 414 = ,, ,, $\frac{1}{4}'' \times 1\frac{3}{4}''$	S.S. 414			stated for
B.S. 418 = ,, ,, $\frac{1}{4}'' \times 2\frac{1}{4}''$	S.S. 418			brass.

The use of index letters for the purpose of identifying parts is illustrated in Fig. 62.

All standard articles will have identifying symbols and numbers, and, although the system may appear complicated, it will be found, in practice, that storemen, clerks, and draughtsmen find these codes easy to work with, since the code numbers of the more frequently used materials are readily memorised. In the Cost Office the pricing of issued material is facilitated and uncertainty as to size and kind of material is avoided.

In the Bills of Material prepared by the Drawing Office, stock materials are indicated by the appropriate code number, but full details have to be specified for special parts and materials which have to be manufactured or purchased outside.

The procedure for requisitioning, buying, and issuing materials will now be described.

Purchase Requisitions for Materials.—The Purchasing Department places all orders for materials and supplies in accordance with requisitions received from

(a) The storekeeper for all standard materials, the stocks of which require replenishment.

(b) The engineer, or Drawing Office, for special materials required for particular orders, but which are not ordinarily stocked.

Requisitions from the storekeeper are generally countersigned by the Works Manager, and those from the Drawing Office by the Chief Engineer, or the Works Manager.

The Drawing Office issues Specifications of Materials (often called Bills of Materials) for the guidance of the buying and other departments.

Purchase Requisitions—Form and Procedure.—The storekeeper, or other official, writes each purchase requisition in triplicate, the sheets being supplied in carbon manifold sets.

FIG. 1.

STOCK PURCHASE REQUISITION				
			No. 86. Date : 16 June, 19...	
Quantity.	Description.	Stock Code No.	Purchase Order No.	Supplier.
1 Cwt.	1½″ Copper Nails, Sq.	B. 36	M.S. 681	C. Hall & Co.
Signed Storekeeper : J. Stockwell.		Approved : T. S. Shaw.		

N.B.—Sometimes an additional column is included for the storekeeper to state the balance of material in stock, for the guidance of the manager and buyer. The last two columns are filled in by the buyer.

He signs this, and passes it to the Works Manager for approval. One copy is sent to the buyer, one to the Progress Department, and one is retained by the storekeeper. A suitable kind of requisition is shown in Fig. 1.

The storekeeper is guided, when requisitioning for stock, by the maximum and minimum quantity which he is authorised to work to in respect of each kind of material. The minimum stock for any article will be fixed by taking into consideration the rate of consumption, and the time necessary to obtain new deliveries.

FIG. 2.

A SPECIAL MATERIAL REQUISITION

SPECIAL PURCHASE REQUISITION

For Special Order No. : 2864.	Reqn. No. : 72.
Name of Customer : Jones & Co.	P.O. No. : 296.
Specification No. : 268.	Date of issue : 26 Feb., 19...
Drawing No. : 39.	Delivery by : 1 Mar., 19...

| Part No. | QUANTITY. | | Description. | ORDERED. | | | Delivery. |
	Per Set.	Total.		From	O/No.	Date.	
F.C. 7	1	1	Iron Cylinder, patt. 29 spec. List No. 38 (Parkinson)	Brown Bros.	273	27/2/19...	28/2
P.M. 81	3	12	Cp. Br. St. 243 (Thompson)	Simplex Co.	274	27/2/19 .	

The maximum stock is fixed by taking into account such *further* aspects as (a) keeping qualities, (b) storage space available, (c) extent to which price fluctuations may be important, (d) the amount of capital necessitated and available, (e) the risks of changing specifications or of obsolescence, (f) seasonal considerations as to both price and availability of supplies—e.g., market shortage or otherwise, (g) the incidence of insurance costs, which may be important for some materials, and (h) any restrictions imposed by local or national authority in regard to materials in which there are inherent risks, e.g., fire and explosion.

The usual ordering quantity may be stated on the Bin Cards, and for check control purposes, also on the Stock Record Sheets, and will indicate the usual market units, so as to avoid requisitions for irregular quantities. Sometimes an "ordering level" is stated. This is the point in the reduction of a stock

D

commodity when action to replenish should be taken. This point will depend upon the margin of time necessary to cover fluctuating consumption demands and possible abnormal delays by suppliers for replenishments.

Special Purchase Requisitions for direct materials for specific jobs are prepared by the Drawing Office; or, for standardised repetition work, the Planning Department may requisition on the basis of the original specification of material prepared by the Drawing Office. A Specification of Material (also known as a Bill of Material) is drawn up for special work by the Drawing Office (see Fig. 3). On this, stock material is indicated by code numbers, and the special material shown on it will be the subject of a special purchase requisition (see Fig. 2) which is sent to the Purchasing Department. Suitable brands or particular suppliers may be specified.

Specifications of Material (Bills of Material).—A Specification of Material is a complete schedule of parts and materials required for a particular order, prepared by the Drawing Office, and issued by it, together with the necessary blue prints of drawings. For standard products, printed copies of the Specification of Material may be kept in stock—there being blank spaces for any special details of modifications for a particular job.

The schedule details everything required, even to nuts, bolts, and screws, as well as weights and sizes.

A copy is retained in the Drawing Office, and one each is provided for the Purchasing Department, the Planning Department, and the foreman.

An example of a Specification of Material is shown in Fig. 3.

Organisation of the Purchasing Department.—The buyer in a manufacturing business has considerable responsibility, and, in a large concern, much money can be lost or saved by his department.

He requires a good technical knowledge of the industry, and a large measure of administrative and organising ability; he must keep in constant touch with market prices, reports and market tendencies, and have a working knowledge of contract law and procedure, and a practical understanding of the principles of economic laws.

In reference to the materials usually used, he should be provided with a schedule of technical specifications, each item

FIG. 3.

SPECIFICATION OF MATERIAL.

Number 268.

For Order No. PO. 296.   Electric Motor No. 7.   Assembly Drawing No. 39.   Date : 26 February, 19...

Symbol No. of Parts.	Description.	No. per set.	Total No.	Code No.	Description.	Quantity.	Remarks	Reqn. No.	Date.	Deliveries Specified.	Order No.
					MATERIALS.			FOR PURCHASE DEPARTMENT.			
E.M. 3 C.	Iron casing	2	2	M. 16	Standard	2	Stock	72	28/2	5/3	273
E.M. 3 B.	Core plates	10		P. 14	Slotted open type	20	Japanned wrought iron				
E.M. 3 F.	Frame	1		M. 15	Cast Iron	1	Stock				
	End rings	4		S. 27	Standard	4	Ref. 276				
F.C. 7	Iron cylinder, etc.	1			Parkinson	1	Stock				
	Ring bolts	4		B. 9	Standard	8	,,				
	Nuts ¼″	4		S.N. 4	,,	16	,,				
	Nuts ⅜″	2		S.N. 5	,,	2	St. 243				
	Brass cups	2		B.O. 2	Thompson	2					
P.M. 81	Brush holders, etc.	3	12	—		12		72	28/2	5/3	274

Drawing Office Copy.	Date Order : 24 Feb, 19... Delivery : 19 Mar. No. of Sheets : 4	Prepared by : J. H. Ross. Checked by : C. F. Davis.	Dated to stores : 26 Feb, 19... ,, from stores : 28 ,, 19... ,, to shops : 7 Mar, 19...

Note.—This schedule is often referred to as a " Bill of Material."

having a code number which will be quoted by those issuing purchase requisitions.

The department should keep files suitably indexed, both under the names of suppliers and materials. Records of prices and quotations for all materials should be kept in schedule form, arranged to show the seasonal and other movements of prices. (See Fig. 5.)

The systematic following up of deliveries by due date is important, and necessitates the prompt marking off of deliveries from the Goods Received Notes.

No purchases should be permitted, except upon receipt of duly authorised purchase requisitions, but, in the case of materials largely and regularly used, forward contracts may be made after consultation with the management. Where purchase contracts are placed, a record of orders issued against them and deliveries made should be kept. (Fig. 4.)

FIG. 4.

PURCHASE CONTRACT RECORD

File No. : 87.

Material : 1″ Copper Tubes.
Suppliers : Tube Mfg. Co.
Contract No. : 261/22 June, 19...
Completed : 25 Sept., 19...

Quantity : 20 Tons.
Price : £72 per Ton.
Free delivered.
Net monthly.
Total Cost : £1440.

ORDERED.			DELIVERED.				
Date.	Quantity. (Tons.)	Balance to Order. (Tons.)	Date.	Quantity. (Tons.)	Current Price. (Per Ton.) £	Value. £	Balance to Deliver. (Tons.)
19...			19...				
June 22	5	15	July 7	5	73	365	15
July 10	4	11	„ 12	2	73	146	13
Aug. 20	11	—	„ 30	2	74	148	11
			Aug. 14	5	73	365	6
			„ 21	2	75	150	4
			Sept. 8	4	74	296	—
	20			20		1470	

Procedure in the Purchasing Department.—On receipt of purchase requisitions the buyer will obtain quotations, or, for important requirements, may invite tenders for the supply of the materials required.

Consideration has to be given to more factors than price—namely, to specifications, conditions of delivery, various charges, times of delivery, terms of payment and discount. A good plan

Fig. 5. SCHEDULE OF QUOTATIONS

File No. : 32.

Material : 1″ Copper Tubes   Date : 20 June, 19...

	Rate. £	Amount. £ s. d.	Time for Delivery.	Terms.	Delivery.	Remarks.
Estimated cost or part price.	76	1520 0 0				
1. Hall & Co.	75	1500 0 0	7 days	Net monthly	Free	
2. Tube Mfg. Co.	72	1440 0 0	14 days	,,	,,	Accepted
3. Copper & Co., Ltd.	76	1520 0 0	4 weeks	,,	,,	
4. F. White & Co.	80	1600 0 0	10 days	,,	,,	
5.						

is to prepare a schedule of quotations to facilitate comparison (see Fig. 5), and to file this for reference on subsequent occasions.

A Purchase Order (see Fig. 6) is then written, preferably in triplicate, the original being sent to the supplier, the duplicate

Fig. 6.

PURCHASE ORDER.

ORDER.

No. 4721.

To Messrs. Smith, Jones & Co.,
Birmingham.

From A. Maker & Co., Ltd., Star Works, London, N.W.

Our ref. : Req. 284.   Date : 28/2/19...

Please supply, in accordance with the instructions herein, the following :

Particulars.	Price.	per	Delivery.
2 tons ⅞″ Mild Steel Bars, round.	£x	ton	At once

Delivery free at our Works.
Mark Order No. on invoice and advice note.
Terms : 5% Monthly Account.

For A. Maker & Co., Ltd.
C. Davis.

to the stores receiving clerk—the third copy being retained for reference purposes. The duplicate is useful for comparing with delivery notes, and for noting upon it the deliveries. Sometimes a duplicate is sent to the suppliers for confirmation purposes.

In some factories a Goods Ordered Book is kept, one page being allotted to each kind of material. It is ruled for recording the name of the supplier, the quantity ordered, description, price, order number, terms, and delivery date. (See Fig. 7.)

FIG. 7.

GOODS ORDERED BOOK

Material : Blue Wove.

Specification : Tub-sized, 18 lbs.

Page 76.

Code No. : H. 14.

Date of Order.	O/No.	Suppliers.	Quantity.	Price.	Terms.	Deliv. due.	DELIVERED.		Total.
							Date.	Quantity.	
19... Jan. 6	31	Sun Paper Makers, Ltd.	10 tons	6d. lb.	net monthly	Feb. 10 2 tons, bal. by Mar. 31	19... Feb. 10 ,, 26 ,, 28	2 tons 3 ,, 5 ,,	Tons. 10
Feb. 9	48	" X " Paper Mill, Ltd.	20 tons	5½d. lb.	do.	Apl. 20, bal. by May 2	Apl. 19	5 tons	5

The following up of deliveries on or before due date is important, and may be the duty of the storekeeper, or the Purchasing Department. If the receiving clerk's copies are filed according to the stated dates of delivery, he will know what materials to expect each day, and, when deliveries are made, the copy order can be marked with particulars of delivery, and returned to the buyer to mark off.

Procedure on Receipt of Materials.—Suppliers usually send a delivery note, or an advice of despatch, which is passed to the receiving clerk. Invoices received are passed direct to the office.

Full particulars of the goods should be entered in a Goods Received Book, or, preferably, on a Goods Received Note (see Fig. 8). The advantage of Goods Received Notes is that, after being filled in with particulars as to quantities and other information, they can be passed to the official responsible for approving the goods, who signs the notes, and sends them with the goods to the storekeeper. The receiving and approving of goods is sometimes the duty of the storekeeper himself, in which case he will prepare the G.R. Notes. It is not generally advisable,

Fig. 8.

GOODS RECEIVED NOTE							
From : Smith, Jones & Co., Birmingham.					G.R. No. 59. Date : 5 Mar., 19...		
Goods.	Quantity.	Packages.	Order No.	For Office Use. Rate.	£	s.	d.
			4721				
Carrier. L.M.S.	Received by. A. Jones	Goods Inspection Report. Correct. B. Hall					
Requisition No. 284	Noted on Progress Chart. 5/621	Bin No. 72	Stores Ledger. 212	Invoice No. 360	A/cs. Ref. P.J. 84		

however, for him to have the duty of passing invoices, the quantities on which can be checked against the G.R. Notes by the office. The bin number is inserted by the storekeeper on each G.R. Note, and the notes are sent to the progress clerk, who enters such particulars as may be required on the Progress Chart.

The Purchasing Department receives a copy of the G.R. Note together with the receiving clerk's copy of the Purchase Order, the order is marked off in the Order Book, and, in due course, the invoice is checked, and passed by the buyer.

If any material be rejected, details would be entered in the Goods Returned Book, and a debit note sent to the supplier. A duplicate of the note may be used for the Purchase Department and progress clerk.

Checking Inward Invoices.—When invoices are received, it is useful to impress each with a rubber stamp, as shown in Fig. 9. Invoices are numbered consecutively on entry into the Invoice Register. The Purchasing Department enters the Order Number, G.R. No. and signs for the correctness of the particulars, which he is able to check with his order, and the certified Goods Received Note. He should mark the Order-Book copy with the invoice number to preclude the passing of a duplicate invoice.

The calculations are checked in the Works Office, and the proper debits made to the appropriate material account in the Stores Ledger, except in the case of material purchased for a specific job, when the debit is made to the Cost Account for that job. In this office also the price and amount are entered on the Goods Received Note, the description and quantity previously entered by the receiving clerk being checked at the same time.

FIG. 9.

STAMP FOR INCOMING INVOICES

Regist. No.	Goods Correct.	Checked.	Noted Works Office.	Bought Jrl. Fo.	Passed for Payment.
360	A. Buyer	With order : A.B.	Charged to : Stores	84	C. Davis
Order No. 472	G.R. No. 59	Prices : A.B. Extens.: R.S.	Initials : L.C.	Charged to : Stores a/c	

The invoice is duly passed to the Accounts Office for entry in the Purchase Journal, from which the suppliers' Account is credited in the Bought Ledger. The respective totals of the columns in the Purchase Journal are debited in the Impersonal Ledger to the various accounts concerned. The detailed procedure for accounting and specimen entries are given in a later chapter.

Need for Reconciliation of Totals Debited.—In view of the ultimate need for reconciliation of the Cost and Financial Accounts which is discussed in Chapter XV, it should be noticed that so far as materials are concerned there must be a precise agreement between the total values entered in the Stores Ledger from the primary details entered on the Goods Received Notes, and the amounts incorporated in the financial accounts from the subsidiary books compiled from the suppliers' invoices. This is particularly necessary when the suppliers' invoices are not used in conjunction with the Goods Received Notes when the Stores Ledgers are entered up.

EXAMINATION QUESTIONS

1. State fully the duties and responsibilities of the storekeeper in any business with which you are familiar.—*London Chamber of Commerce.*

2. State briefly the main features of a suitable system for the Stock records of a factory, including the relations between these and the costing and general financial records.—*Institute of Chartered Accountants* (*Final*).

3. What do you understand by maximum and minimum stocks and ordering level ?—*Royal Society of Arts (Advanced)*.

4. Describe in detail a method of controlling the replenishment of stocks of manufactured component parts.—*Institute of Cost and Works Accountants (Inter.)*.

5. State briefly the main features of a system for the Stock records of a factory, including the relations between these and the costing and financial records.—*Institute of Chartered Accountants (Final)*

6. In many manufacturing businesses the materials used in the production of manufactured goods are obtained from general stores by requisition. The requisition notes are the means of securing information of direct materials chargeable to the cost of particular products. In some instances, purchases of materials are made for specific contracts and are relatively useless for general purposes. The materials thus purchased, however, pass through the Stores and are requisitioned as required. State what difference would be observed in the Stores Ledger records between such general stores and stores specially acquired for a specific contract. In the latter case, how would you propose to deal with the small surpluses of material which inevitably arise ? What objection would there be to including these surpluses in the annual stock-taking valuation ?—*London Association of Accountants (Final)*.

7. Do you consider that the storekeeper should see and pass invoices for material received ? What alternative method is suggested for checking the quantities and prices ?—*Institute of Cost and Works Accountants (Inter.)*.

8. In connection with a stock record the term " ordering level " is sometimes used. In what way does this differ from the terms " minimum " and " maximum " stocks ?—*Institute of Cost and Works Accountants (Inter.)*.

9. What are the factors which determine the maximum and minimum figures for stock control ? Illustrate your answer with examples. —*Institute of Cost and Works Accountants (Inter.)*.

10. Describe a system that would definitely link up the Purchasing Department, Goods Receiving Department, and Cost Department; giving all information for passing invoices, checking goods received and posting to Costs.—*Institute of Cost and Works Accountants (Inter.)*.

11. State what arrangements are necessary for installing a stores requisition system of material control in a factory where such a system has not been in use.—*Institute of Cost and Works Accountants (Final)*.

CHAPTER V

STORES ROUTINE

Receipt of Materials.—Purchased materials are passed into the custody of the storekeeper when they have been examined and approved. The storekeeper checks the quantities with the Goods Received Note, which he signs. When the storekeeper is directly responsible for receiving goods he will prepare the G.R. Notes.

Some articles or parts for stock are not purchased from outside suppliers, but made in the works. These will be inspected in the usual course, and are then passed into the stores. In order to keep the accounting uniform, it is desirable that a Goods Received Note be prepared for these articles. The necessary debits and credits, as between production and stores, will be dealt with by the Cost Office.

Issue of Materials.—Nothing should be issued by the storekeeper, except on presentation of a Stores Requisition. (Fig. 10.)

FIG. 10.

STORES REQUISITION								
Materials Required for : Job. E 513. _(Job or Process.)_ Department : Engines.					No. 76. Date : 20 July, 19...			
Quantity.	Description.	Code No.	Rate.	£	s.	d.	Notes.	
10 ft.	½″ Brass X.E.D.	B 102	12 lbs.	1/- lb.		12	0	

Foreman : F. Simpson. Workman : E. Barry.	Shop E. 3.	Storekeeper's initials : A. S.	Cost Office ref. : MA 364. Stores Ledger Fo. : 218.

Note.—The pricing out is done in the Cost Office.

39

A Stores Requisition is an authorisation to the storekeeper to issue raw material, finished parts, or other stores.

These forms are generally issued and signed by the shop foreman, but sometimes, in the case of special jobs, the particulars are determined by the Planning Department.

The Receipt and Issue of Special Materials (Materials Allocation).—Materials ordered for a specific job will be marked with the job number, and kept apart ready for issue. The foreman will be informed that the material is available. A good plan for this is for the Production Department to prepare a Stores Requisition, and send it to the foreman, who can sign it, and present it at the Stores when he is ready to use the material.

Stores Records.—Two records are usually kept of materials received, issued or transferred—namely, on the Bin Cards, or Stores Control Record, and in the Stores Ledger. The Bin Cards (or Stores Control Record) are written up in the Stores, but the Stores Ledger is sometimes kept by the Cost Department, or a stores office.

There is considerable advantage in this procedure, as it leaves the storekeeper with the minimum amount of clerical work, and the Stores Accounting Records are kept cleaner and more accurately by an experienced stores clerk.

A Stores Appropriation Record is often kept when it is not convenient to work to definite maxima and minima of certain types of material which may be required to meet orders. It may be used in connection with stores materials, or components, which are made in the works, and also ordered from outside, and is of great value to the Planning Department, in that it shows the quantity in stock and on order. The record may be combined in the ordinary Stores Control Record by providing a special column for the purpose, or a separate Stores Appropriation Ledger may be used. When the latter is adopted, the procedure is to debit each account with the quantities in stock and ordered. As a quantity is appropriated, it is credited, and the balance represents the quantity in stock and on order.

Finished Parts or Components Store.—These are items or sub-assemblies put into store awaiting final assembly or sale as spares. It is not unusual to keep these parts in a separate store, under the control of the Progress or Planning Department. It is usual to keep a Finished Parts Stock Record indicating the quantity and also in some cases the value of each class of finished part and its location in the stores. Stock orders for quantities of standard parts will be issued in batches convenient for economical manufacture. A Stores Appropriation Record is useful for the control. The cost, ascertained from the Works Order for the production of these stock orders, will ordinarily be the charging-out price, when components are issued on requisition for assembly on various Works Orders.

Transfers of Materials.—Transfers of materials from one departmental store to another should be recorded by means of a Stores Requisition signed by the storekeeper, and marked "Transfer." This memorandum can then be used in the office for the making of the necessary credit and debit.

Where transfers are numerous it is sometimes the practice to have special columns in the Stock Record Sheets or Bin Cards for recording the details of the transfers.

The transfer of material from one job to another in the works should be strictly prohibited, unless adequate procedure is arranged for a Material Transfer slip, showing all necessary data for crediting and debiting the cost accounts affected, as otherwise the records and cost accounts concerned would be incorrect. Such transfers occur where an urgent order has to be made and work started on a less urgent order may be appropriated. In such a case there must be provision for the re-issue of material to the job from which material already issued has been transferred. For excess material, the proper procedure is to return this to the Stores, when a Shop Credit Note can be made out.

Material Issued in Excess of Requirements.—Bulk material has to be issued at times in excess of the needs for a particular job. For instance, sheet iron or steel bars, which cannot be cut off in the Stores to the exact size required, or which can be more advantageously operated upon in the works when full size. The procedure is to charge out the full quantity issued, and, when the excess is returned to store, a Stores Debit Note is filled in, signed by the foreman, and handed to the storekeeper.

A Stores Debit Note is an authorisation to return to the storekeeper raw material, finished parts, or other stores no longer required by the factory. It is sometimes referred to as a Shop Credit Slip.

The various stock records and cost accounts are adjusted in due course from the details given on this form.

These debit notes may be drawn up in the same form as a Stores Requisition, but printed in red to distinguish them.

Bin Cards.—Materials are kept in appropriate bins, drawers, or other receptacles; some are stacked, others racked. For each kind of material or article, a separate record is kept on a Bin Card, showing in detail all receipts and issues. (See Fig. 11.)

FIG. 11.

BIN CARD

Description : ....   Bin No. : ......
....   Code No. : ......
Normal Quantity   Maximum : ......
to Order :   ....   Minimum : ......

RECEIPTS.			ISSUES.			BALANCE.	REMARKS.
Date.	G. R. No.	Quan-tity.	Date.	Req. No.	Quan-tity.	Quantity.	Goods on Order and Audit Notes.

Note.—The columns headed " quantity " may be ruled for tons, cwt., qrs., lbs.; cwt., qrs., lbs., oz.; gross, doz., units; or simply for units; yards, ft., ins.; gallons, qts., pts., oz. as may be necessary.

The Bin Cards are used, not only for detailing receipts and issues of material, but also to assist the storekeeper to control the stock. For each material, the maximum and minimum to be carried are stated on the card—these limits having been determined by the Production Department in the first instance. From time to time these maxima and minima may be altered to suit current requirements.

To facilitate ordering of further supplies, the normal quantity to order is sometimes stated at the head of the card. When materials are of a kind requiring advance ordering, an Ordering Level may be specified on the Bin Card.

Fig. 12.

STOREKEEPER'S MATERIAL CONTROL RECORD

Description : ....

Code No. : ....

Ordering Level : ....

LIMITS.

Maximum : ....

Minimum : ....

Quantity to Order : ....

Bin No. : ....

Unit : ....

RECEIPTS.			ISSUES.			BALANCE.	ON ORDER.					REMARKS AND STOCK COUNTS.
Date.	G.R. No.	Quantity.	Date.	Req. No.	Quantity.	Quantity.	Date.	Pur. Req. No.	Supplier.	Quantity.	Delivered.	Date.

The various receptacles in which materials are kept are numbered, the Bin Card for each being similarly numbered. Where identifying code-numbers are used for materials, it is advantageous to attach these to the bin, and to quote them on the Bin Card.

An alternative to Bin Cards kept with or near each kind of material is a Stores Material Control Record (Fig. 12) written up in the Stores in a loose-leaf book, or card file, in place of Bin Cards. On this record, as on the Bin Cards, quantities only are recorded, all money values being shown only in the Stores Ledger in the Office. An advantage of this record is that the storekeeper has all details close at hand, and can keep noted in it such information as quantities ordered, probable requirements for particular contracts, and other details. Where transfers between inter-departmental stores are numerous, an additional section may be included on the Stock Record Sheets for details of the transfers as distinct from issues to the shops.

Stores Ledger.—The Stores Ledger is kept in the Works Accounts Office, and is parallel with the Bin Cards, except that money values are shown. Correct stores accounting is as important as accounting for cash, hence the separation of this clerical work from the actual handling of the materials.

The ruling of the accounts may be as shown in Fig. 13, or follow the Bin Card ruling, with the addition of money columns as in Fig. 14.

In some factories it may be unnecessary to show money values in the Stores Ledger, but this is the exception, not the rule.

An account is opened in the Stores Ledger for every kind of material. A columnar account may be used for different sizes, etc., of one kind.

The debit side is prepared from the invoices and Stores Debit Notes—the credit side either directly from Stores Requisition Notes, or from an abstract summary compiled from them. The Stores Ledger folio should be marked against every item so posted. Tabulating machines are used in large works (see pp. 362–369).

Perpetual Inventory.—This may be defined as a method of recording Store balances after every receipt and issue, to facilitate regular checking and to obviate closing down for stock-taking. It is sometimes termed " Continuous Inventory."

FIG. 13.

STORES LEDGER

Material : ....   Code : ....   Maximum : ....   Folio :...
                                                        Minimum : ....

Dr.   RECEIVED.   ISSUED.

Date.	G.R. No.	Supplier or Remarks.	Quantity.	Rate.	£	s.	d.	Date.	Iss. Req. No.	Quantity.	Rate.	£	s.	d.	Notes.

FIG. 14.

STORES LEDGER (2nd type)

Article : ....   Code : ....   Maximum : ....   Folio :......
                                                        Minimum : ....

Date.	G.R. No.	Supplier.	Quantity. received.	Rate.	£	s.	d.	Date.	Req. No.	Quantity. issued.	Rate.	£	s.	d.	Balance Quantity.	Notes.

The Perpetual Inventory System.—The balance of any account in the Stores Ledger should agree with the balance shown on the Bin Card, or Stock Control Record, for the same item of material, and a frequent checking of these dual records should be made, as well as of the actual quantity in stock.

In large stores, a system of continuous checking is instituted, a number of items of material being counted daily, and compared with the Bin Cards and Stores Ledger by a Stores Audit Clerk. Discrepancies are inquired into; many may be clerical errors, which are corrected. When, however, the stock is incorrect, an investigation is made, after which any shortage, or surplus, is adjusted in the records to make them correspond with the physical count. This may be done conveniently by making out a Credit Note or Debit Note, as the case may be, for the difference, and, after obtaining authority to pass the adjustment through the Cost Journal, debiting (or crediting) a Stock Adjustment Account. The balance on that account is written off direct to Profit and Loss Account at appropriate times.

The usual causes of differences are : Incorrect entries, breakage, pilferage, evaporation, breaking bulk, short or over issues, absorption of moisture, price approximation or pricing method, and placing of stores in wrong bin.

The method of keeping Stores Accounts described above is known as the Perpetual or Continuous Inventory System. Its valuable advantages are :

(1) The long and costly work of a stocktaking count is avoided, and the stock of materials, as shown by the Stores Ledger (but not the Work in Progress), can be obtained quickly for the preparation of a Profit and Loss Account and Balance Sheet.

(2) A detailed, reliable check on the stores is obtained.

(3) Discrepancies are readily localised and discovered, giving an opportunity for preventing a recurrence in many cases.

(4) The moral effect on the staff tends to greater care, and serves as a deterrent to dishonesty.

(5) The audit extends to comparing the actual stock with the authorised maxima and minima, thus ensuring that adequate stocks are maintained within the prescribed limits.

(6) The storekeeper's duty of attending to replenishments is facilitated, as he is kept informed of the stock of every kind of material, thus ensuring uninterrupted and safe manufacturing stocks.

(7) The stock being kept within the limits decided upon by the management, the working capital sunk in stores materials cannot exceed the amount arranged for.

(8) The disadvantages of excessive stocks are avoided, as for instance :

(*a*) Loss of interest on capital locked up in stock. (*b*) Loss through deterioration. (*c*) Danger of depreciation in market values. (*d*) Risks of obsolescence.

The Pricing of Stores Material Issues.—The method of pricing materials issued largely depends upon the nature of the materials, the undertaking concerned, and the circumstances which require to be taken into consideration.

E

The purpose of Cost Accounts is to arrive at the actual cost of each job, or of each process or operation of manufacture, and, to this end, it is desirable to charge out stores material at cost.

Some accountants prefer that material issued should be charged to Cost Accounts at market prices ruling at the time the materials are used, because these are the prices which would have to be paid if the material were purchased at that time. This procedure introduces considerable confusion into the accounts, and at once involves departure from the principle of showing actual costs in the Cost Accounts.

There are a few kinds of business, however, where the particular nature of the transactions leads the management to desire that the Cost Accounts should represent the current position, and correspond with estimates, as well as that the efficiency of buying should be revealed, and this information is secured by charging stores at current market prices, regardless whether these are higher or lower than the actual figures paid.

The result of this procedure is that, in a period of falling prices, the costs of such manufacturers will show as lower than those of manufacturers who charge materials at actual prices paid at an earlier date. This does not mean that the first-named manufacturers are in a more competitive position, for the reason that when submitting estimates, or fixing prices, allowance must be made for the trend of market prices. Herein lies one of the chief points of difference between costs and estimates.

Mention must be made here also of materials which it is necessary to retain for purposes of maturing, of which perhaps the best example is timber. Logs are often sawn longitudinally, and left in this rough state for seasoning, as also is timber cut into suitable sizes. In such cases, the stock appreciates in value, and it is customary to increase the cost by at least the interest on the capital value the stock represents, and other special storage expense may also be added.

The method of valuing stores for the Annual Balance Sheet, it is important to observe, is quite independent of the system of pricing for costing purposes. The recognised method of pricing stores for the Balance Sheet compiled from the financial accounts, is at cost, or market value, whichever is the lower. The cost price referred to in this connection is the average cost price of the stores on hand, which, it may be assumed, will consist of the most recent purchases.

The use of the cost price method is a satisfactory one for the Cost Accounts as it avoids troublesome adjustments.

The Application of the Market Price Method for Stores Issues. —The materials are priced out at the market price ruling at the time of manufacture. It is usual to ignore small fluctuations, and to prepare a schedule of prices which is used by the Cost Office. As prices rise or fall, the price schedule is amended, thus ensuring revised charging in the Cost Accounts. The fluctuations create a difference on the Stores Account as a whole, and the book profit or loss due to this cause has to be written off through an adjustment account.

The value of Work in Progress at the date of the Balance Sheet will also require adjustment, as explained in a later paragraph. This method introduces difficult complications, and is not much used.

The Application of the Cost Price Method for Stores Issues.— The simplest case is where material has been purchased for a specific job, when a direct charge is made at cost to the account for that job. In costing, direct debits should be made whenever possible.

There are several ways of applying the cost price method for materials issued from the stores.

1. *The " First-in—First-out " Method.*—The stores are issued from the earliest lot delivered until exhausted, then from the next delivery—the charge in the accounts being the cost price of each lot. The Stores Ledger clerk can ascertain from the accounts when each consignment is completed. Where market fluctuations are frequent and considerable the method sometimes produces curious and unfair results as between one job and another. Further, if the transactions are numerous the method is unnecessarily involved. It is satisfactory in some cases.

2. *Fixed Prices Method.*—When market prices are fairly stable, with small variations, a fixed price may be adopted, but a price adjustment account is required. It is seldom that this method can be used, except in connection with Standard Costing described in a later chapter.

3. *Use of Average Purchase Prices.*—The average is not that of all of each material bought, but the average of the prices of quantities in stock at the time, and the prices of the quantities in each new delivery. The price to be charged may be fixed with each new delivery, or, say monthly, if particular conditions

permit. The following example will make the method clear :

200 items bought @ 1s.
150 charged out @ 1s.
___
50 balance @ 1s.
100 New delivery @ 1s. 6d.
___
150 balance now charged out at 1s. 4d. (the average of 50 @ 1s. and 100 @ 1s. 6d.).
It would be incorrect to charge @ 1s. 2d. (the average of 200 @ 1s. and 100 @ 1s. 6d.).

Whichever method is used, the cost of Stores used is recovered, and the Stores Ledger can be balanced, both as to quantities and money values, subject to minor adjustments for differences due to wastage, evaporation, and other losses.

Small Parts used in Large Quantities, when of little individual value, are not generally requisitioned and charged separately for each production order. The average quantity used will be predetermined and charged on that basis to each job. A quantity of each of such materials may be issued by the Stores to a Shop and a Shop Stores Account debited at an average cost price. This account will be credited, say weekly, with the estimated quantity for the number of orders dealt with, thereby eliminating much unnecessary detail.

Stores Expenses.—If of a general nature, these are included in Stores Overhead, but expenses particular to a specific order may be charged thereto in addition to the price of the material, as may be the cost of carriage inwards and handling.

The Value of Work in Progress at the date of the Balance Sheet will require adjustment, in the financial accounts, by way of depreciation, if market prices of material have fallen. This applies also to Finished Stock which has been valued at cost of manufacture.

In the event of market prices having risen, however, the stock (whether finished or in progress) should not be written up. An unrealised profit should not be anticipated in the accounts, but an expected loss should be reserved for.

This adjustment is necessary whether the materials are priced out at market price, or at average, or actual cost. The adjustments are more difficult when market prices are used.

Indirect Materials, sometimes called Consumable Stores, such as lubricants, engine waste, and cleaning materials, should be requisitioned in the same way as materials issued for manufacturing operations. The requisitions are summarised and charged to suitable expense accounts, as will be explained in a later chapter devoted to the subject (Chapter IX).

Turnover of Stores Material.—It is an advantage to compare the turnover of different grades and kinds of material as a means of detecting stock which does not move regularly, thus enabling the management to avoid keeping capital locked up in undesirable stocks. It is not an infrequent thing for a particular item of stock to be overlooked for considerable periods, unless means are taken to prevent such accumulations.

The rate of turnover should be taken for the stock as a whole, and of major kinds of material individually. The balance of stores, compared with the total withdrawals, indicates how many times a year the stock is renewed.

Tool Store procedure is described in Chapter XIV, p. 180.

EXAMINATION QUESTIONS

1. It is found that systematic thefts have taken place from the stores of a large company manufacturing small machine parts.

Beyond the entry of purchase invoices in the bought journal no records of stores have been kept.

You are desired to recommend an adequate system for the supervision of the stores in future, including the rulings of any books or forms you consider necessary. Prepare, therefore, whatever instructions or explanations you consider it advisable to issue to the persons who will keep the future stores records, and append your proposed rulings.— *London Chamber of Commerce.*

2. Describe a system of stock control which retains the advantages of a physical stock-taking without causing excessive work at the end of each accounting period.—*Institute of Cost and Works Accountants (Inter.).*

3. State the various methods of pricing Stores Requisitions with which you are familiar, and discuss their respective merits.—*Royal Society of Arts (Advanced).*

4. Select two of the following items and prepare a stock card, with varying prices, showing the rate you would use for each quantity into the shop, using your own figures :

    (1) Copper.
    (2) Bolts and Nuts.
    (3) Liquid Paint in tins.
    (4) Steel Bars.
    (5) Flour in sacks.
    (6) Raw Cotton.

Institute of Cost and Works Accountants (Inter.).

5. Draft a form of Bin or Locker Card with three specimen entries thereon, and explain the purpose and utility of such cards.—*Society of Incorporated Accountants and Auditors (Inter.).*

6. Twenty tons of material are purchased and taken into store, and

eventually used on six different contracts. State in chronological order the records in relation to this material, giving details of all forms which would be used and all entries in the cost books relating to same.

7. What are the various methods by which stores issues may be priced, and under what circumstances do you consider the practices can be varied with advantage ? State reasons.—*Institute of Cost and Works Accountants (Inter.)*

8. Timber Merchants often have very large stocks of timber in process of seasoning, this process takes several years.
State your views :
(a) With regard to the valuation of these stocks at each annual stock-taking.
(b) As to how the various expenses incurred during the process should be treated in costing the timber for sale.
London Chamber of Commerce.

9. Define the following and say on what basis each should be determined :
(a) Minimum stock.
(b) Maximum stock.
(c) Ordering level.
Royal Society of Arts (Advanced).

10. Draw up a specimen bin card for use, in a general store and give your reasoned advice as to whether it should be kept in the store office or alongside the goods to which it relates.—*Royal Society of Arts (Advanced).*

11. Copper is purchased at £60 a ton in January for general stock and is used in the following June when the market price has risen to £70 a ton. What figure would you use in your costs ? Give reasons for your answer.—*Royal Society of Arts (Advanced).*

12. In Costing, materials may be charged out to jobs at cost price, or at market price. Explain which method is in your view preferable, giving your reasons, and state how, under the respective methods, fluctuations in the Costing Accounts will arise, and under what headings they will appear.—*Institute of Chartered Accountants (Final).*

13. A manufacturing concern purchases from time to time large quantities of a commodity used in the manufacture of one of its products. The following are the details of purchases during the six months ended June 30th, 1930 :

1930.	Quantity.	Cost Price per 100.
		s. d.
February 2 . . .	10,000	10 0
March 15	25,000	10 6
April 20	20,000	9 6
May 3	15,000	9 0
June 1	12,000	9 0
June 20	3,000	8 6

There were 15,000 units in stock at January 1st, 1930, which were valued at 9s. 6d. per 100.
Quantities issued from store during the six months were as under :

1930.	
January 25	10,000
February 28	8,000
March 29	25,000
April 30	20,000
May 15	18,000
June 29	15,000

At what prices should the issues be charged and the closing stock valued ? Prepare a Stores Ledger Account illustrating your views.— *The Society of Incorporated Accountants and Auditors (Final).*

14. Distinguish between Stores and Stock. Under what circumstances, if any, would you as an Auditor feel justified in accepting a figure for Stores or Stock, knowing that an Inventory had not been made at the balancing date ?—*The Society of Incorporated Accountants and Auditors (Inter.).*

15. Departmental Stores situate in a works frequently interchange various materials. Describe an accounting system showing how these transactions should be recorded.—*Institute of Cost and Works Accountant (Inter.).*

16. What steps would you take to ascertain and to eliminate over-investment of capital in stocks ?—*Institute of Cost and Works Accountants (Inter.).*

17. Give specimen ruling of a stores requisition and describe fully its routine throughout the workshops and cost department.—*Institute of Cost and Works Accountants (Inter.).*

18. Assume all records of stock are kept in the Cost Office—devise a scheme for checking at irregular periods the actual stock in the storeroom.—*Institute of Cost and Works Accountants (Inter.).*

19. Discuss the respective merits and demerits of keeping store records of quantities :

 (a) Alongside the stocks to which they relate ;
 (b) In cabinets in an office conveniently placed in the storehouse;
 (c) In the cost office.

Institute of Cost and Works Accountants (Inter.).

20. Describe the arrangements you would make for stocktaking throughout a large works in order that completion may be reached as quickly as possible.—*Institute of Cost and Works Accountants (Inter.).*

21. Describe with sample card and a few specimen entries, the working of the maximum and minimum method of stock-keeping.—*Institute of Cost and Works Accountants (Inter.).*

22. In charging out materials to work orders, what alternative methods are available for dealing with the effect of market fluctuations on the values of materials in store ?—*Institute of Cost and Works Accountants (Inter.).*

23. Describe briefly how you would conduct the audit of a system of continuous stocktaking and what procedure you would adopt to deal with differences.—*Institute of Cost and Works Accountants (Inter.).*

24. Assume that it is the policy of a certain brass foundry to make monthly purchases of copper. The market rates have fallen :

	Per ton.
April 1929	£105
June 1929	20
May 1930	55
September 1930	45

How would you propose to price withdrawals from store for manufacture carried out during the period in question ? State on what basis you assume selling prices to be determined.—*Institute of Cost and Works Accountants (Inter.).*

25. For Balance Sheet purposes it is customary to value Stores at cost or market price, whichever is the lower. Would you adopt the same basis in charging out stores for costing purposes ? Give reasons for, and explain the effect of, the method you advocate.—*Society of Incorporated Accountants and Auditors (Inter.).*

26. You are instructed to organise a factory stores, and arrange for maximum and minimum quantities. Discuss the determining factors which would influence your decisions concerning these quantities.—*Institute of Cost and Works Accountants (Inter.).*

27. Describe what you consider to be an adequate system of checking the receipt of goods and payment for them.—*Institute of Cost and Works Accountants (Inter.).*

28. The moving of material from stores to, and in, departments involves both labour and overhead expenses. Do you consider these should all be recovered by a direct charge against material or as a departmental overhead? Briefly explain your reasons for the method you suggest.—*Institute of Cost and Works Accountants (Final).*

29. In a factory where "continuous stocktaking" is carried out periodically, discrepancies are discovered. Suggest possible causes of these discrepancies.—*Corporation of Accountants (Final).*

30. Briefly describe a system of recording the receipt and issue of goods from store to departments in any manufacturing business with which you are familiar.—*Chartered Secretaries (Inter.).*

31. In most factories many small parts, such as bolts, screws, nails, washers, etc., are used in large quantities in the process of manufacture. The parts in question are usually purchased by weight, and the price thereof may fluctuate considerably.

Outline a system by means of which the correct price at which such items should be charged in the factory costing records may be determined in order to prevent serious discrepancies between the total value of Stocks on Hand and the balance of stores purchased and issued. Include as part of your answer a specimen ruling for the Stores Ledger recommended to be used.—*Incorporated Accountants (Final).*

32. How would you record tools issued and returned? Who should authorise such issue?

What provision would you make in respect of such tools, where a workman is transferred to another department, and where tools are lost or broken? Draft a workmen's Tool Book.—*Incorporated Accountants (Final).*

33. A manufacturing company secures a contract necessitating the use of 20 tons of zinc sheets. Trace the procedure to be followed in the office and in the works in order that this material may be available, giving specimens of any two of the forms you would expect to be used. The price of the zinc sheets purchased would be about £24 per ton.—*Incorporated Accountants (Inter.).*

CHAPTER VI

LABOUR : TIME-KEEPING AND TIME-BOOKING

The Engagement of Labour.—When a worker is engaged, all desired information concerning him is entered on a Labour Engagement Record Sheet.

The practice, which is almost universal, is to allot to each worker a number, by which he is identified, and which is used for reference in the records and accounts. This number is variously known as his check number, ticket number, or, more usually now, in view of the prevalent use of time-recording clocks, as his clock number. Where there is a large number of employees, it is useful to reserve a block of numbers for each type of labour, or for each shop or department, *e.g.* 1 to 50 for the Foundry, 51 to 100 for the Machine Shop, and so on.

TIME-KEEPING METHODS

The methods of recording the gate, or factory, time of workers vary considerably, and, although, in most modern works time-recording clocks are used, very many still use older methods.

The Check or Disc Method.—Metal discs bearing the workers' numbers are placed on hooks on a board at the entrance to the works. The worker, on entering, removes his disc, and places it in a receptacle provided, or he may be required to hang it on another board, on a hook bearing his number. The box is removed at starting time, and a " late " box substituted.

The checks enable the timekeeper to enter up the Attendance Register, after which the checks may be handed back to the workers by a boy going round; or the discs may be replaced on a numbered board for checking out.

An easy method for entering up the time register is to mark off all but the discs left on the board at the time the box is closed; the time of the late-comers, if they are not locked out, is obtained by requiring them to present the discs at the time-keeper's window.

The Use of Time-Recording Clocks.—The substitution of mechanical for manual methods of time-keeping and time-booking has rendered records more exact; whilst the uses to which time-recording instruments may be put have revolutionised costing procedure.

The uses of time-recording clocks will be described under two sections : (1) Gate or attendance time records; (2) Job-time records.

1. ATTENDANCE TIME FOR PAY HOURS

The methods which may be used are :

   (a) Card Time Recorders, of which there are several varieties.
   (b) Key Recorders, using rolls of paper in a clock.
   (c) Dial Recorders, which record the numbers and times of the workers in various ways.

(a) **Card Time Recorders.**—These give a weekly printed and tabulated record of the arrival and departure of employees, on a single card for each. Some models give the times of incomings and outgoings in one colour printing only, others print automatically the time of all late arrivals, early departures, or over-time workers in red, so that irregular time is brought prominently to notice at a glance. This has an advantage in that short time and overtime can be easily dealt with by the time clerks when making up records for the pay roll, and, further, has a good moral effect on late-comers.

A rack or series of racks is placed near the clock, and a card bearing the worker's number is placed there for each worker. On entering, the card is taken by the worker, inserted in the clock, and, by depressing a lever, the time is printed on the card. In some models, the insertion of the card is sufficient to record the time without the use of a lever. The card is then placed by the worker in another rack on the other side of the clock, ready for the time of leaving the factory. Absentees can be noted by a glance at the racks.

The machines print the day of the week, hour and minute a.m. and p.m. Some models print the month and date in addition. When red printing is used to indicate late-comers and overtime, the clock automatically makes the necessary change over at the scheduled times.

Fig. 15.

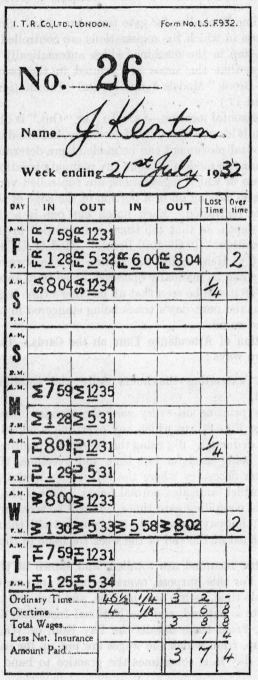

I. T. R. Co., Ltd., London.   Form No. L.S. F.932.

No. 26

Name _J. Kenton_

Week ending _21st July_ 19_32_

DAY	IN	OUT	IN	OUT	Lost Time	Over time
A.M. **F**	FR 7 59	FR 12 31				
P.M. **F**	FR 1 28	FR 5 32	FR 6 00	FR 8 04		2
A.M. **S**	SA 8 04	SA 12 34			1/4	
P.M. **S**						
A.M. **S**						
P.M. **S**						
A.M. **M**	7 59	12 35				
P.M. **M**	1 28	5 31				
A.M. **T**	8 01	12 31			1/4	
P.M. **T**	1 29	5 31				
A.M. **W**	8 00	12 33				
P.M. **W**	1 30	5 33	5 58	8 02		2
A.M. **T**	7 59	12 31				
P.M. **T**	1 25	5 34				

Ordinary Time	46 1/2	1/4		3	2	-
Overtime	4	1/8			6	8
Total Wages				3	8	8
Less Nat. Insurance					1	4
Amount Paid				3	7	4

Note.—P.M. registrations are indicated by a dash under the hour figure.

Card Time Recorders for gate times are of two kinds :

(1) Those in which the registrations are controlled vertically by a card step in the machine, which automatically rises each half day so that the times are printed in the proper space. ("Gledhill-Brook" Models A. and B., and "International." See Figs. 15 and 17.)

The horizontal location—*i.e.* "In" or "Out," is obtained by moving a shift lever, which may, if necessary, be locked in position. This horizontal movement can be made at pre-determined times on the automatic models without any manual operation.

(2) Those in which registrations are controlled vertically by the automatic cutting off of a portion of the edge of the card as the time is registered. Each notch cut out is a little more than type depth, so that the times are recorded in the correct vertical position. ("Gledhill-Brook" Models C. and F. C. See Fig. 16.) Here again the setting to the correct column horizontally can be manually operated, or be fully automatic.

In Fig. 16 it will be seen that all one day's time is grouped in one column, the next day's times being staggered in the second column, and so on.

Calculation of Attendance Time on the Cards.—This can be made in two ways :

1. By extending the hours daily and totalling at the week-end.

2. By printing on every card the standard weekly total hours (see Fig. 17), to which any overtime is added, and any lost time deducted. By using the two-colour printing mechanism, red being used for lost time and overtime, there is no calculation necessary where the full week's record is printed in blue, which indicates normal hours. This is the speediest method of compiling gate times. It will be seen on reference to Fig. 17, that pay stubs can be incorporated with the time card, and detached at the end of the week for issue to the workers.

The hours recorded are totalled, and shown at the foot of the card. For this purpose, overtime hours are counted as $1\frac{1}{4}$, $1\frac{1}{2}$, or double-time, as the case may be, and then the pay at the worker's rate is entered, and the National Insurance deductions are made. From these details the Pay Roll, or Wages Book, is entered up, from which the wages are put up for payment.

On pay day it is sometimes the practice to hand the com-

Fig. 16.

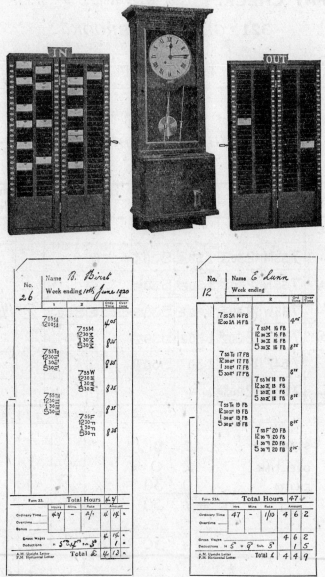

A "Clipper" Equipment for Time Recording or Job Costing.
Supplied by the Gledhill-Brook Time Recorders, Ltd.

FIG. 17.

PAY CHECK. *Week Ended 9 : 4 : 32*

321 *GLEDHILL BROOK.*

Received Pay...

Week Ended 9 : 4 : 32

321 *GLEDHILL BROOK.*

DAY	A.M.		P.M.		OVERTIME		O'TIME	
	IN	OUT	IN	OUT	IN	OUT	HRS.	EXTRA
Su.								
M.	7 55 M	12 30	1 30	5 30				
Tu.	7 55 Tu	12 30	1 30	5 30				
W.	7 55 W	12 30	1 30	5 30	6 00	8 00	2	½
Th.	7 55 Th	12 30	1 30	5 30				
F.	7 54 F	12 30	1 30	5 30				
Sa.	7 55 SA	12 00 SA						

		RATE	£	s.	d.
STANDARD	47 - 0				
OVERTIME	2 - 0				
EXTRA	0 - 30				
LOST	49 - 30				
	49 - 30	1/6	3	14	3
DEDUCT H. 9 U. 10 S.C. 2				1	9
NETT PAY			£ 3	12	6

Fig. 18.

I.T R.Co., Ltd   FORM NO. W. 1001

No. 14

NAME *a. Walker*

WEEK ENDING....*6th Feb*....................19*32*....

#	MON	TUE	WED	THU	FRI	SAT		
1	7 58		8 00	7 56	7 59	8 00		
2		8 01						
3								
4								
5	12 01		12 04		12 00			
6								
7	1 00	1 00	12 59	1 05	12 58	1 01		
8								
9		2 00		2 00				
10								
11								
12								
13	4 10		4 02		4 00			
14	4 31		4 32		4 30			
15		5 01		4 55				
16		5 29		5 16				
17			6 00		6 00			
18	6 16			6 29				
19		7 05						
20								
21								
22								
	8½	9¼	8½	8	8½	5		

ORDINARY TIME	46¾	1/3	2	18	5	TOTAL WAGES	3	0	3½
OVERTIME	1	1/10½		1	10½	LESS NAT. INS		1	4
						AMOUNT PAID	2	18	11½

Note.—Facsimile card (slightly reduced) used for overlapping or irregular times recorded on Model 1102 International Time Recorder.

pleted cards to the workers to check their wages; or, where a pay stub is provided as in Fig. 17, this portion is detached, and used in the same way. After checking the amount, the worker signs the card, and, on presenting it to the pay clerk, receives in exchange his pay envelope.

The International Time Recorders are used in the same way, and also can be adapted for irregular or overlapping comings

Fig. 19.

	7 58	18
	7 59	29
	7 59	24
	8 00	10
	8 00	27
*	1 00	27
*	1 00	10
*	1 00	14
*	1 01	24
*	1 01	18
*	1 01	29
	1 58	29
	1 58	18
	1 59	14
	1 59	24
	2 00	10
	2 00	27
*	6 00	27
*	6 00	24
*	6 00	18
*	6 00	12
*	6 01	10

Bundy Key and Time Record (slightly reduced).

* Signifies times of going out.

and goings of employees, as, for instance, in railway depots and large stores. The cards are printed in the form shown in Fig. 18.

The Self-Regulating International Electric Card Recorder is driven by a master clock, which controls any number of recorders, giving uniform time throughout the premises.

(b) **Key Recorders.**—Each employee is allotted a key bearing a number (Fig. 19), and when coming in or going out, he registers the time and his number by inserting his key in the recorder, giving it a quarter turn, and hanging it up on the proper board. As the keys are only taken from their proper hook when recording, and immediately replaced, they cannot be lost.

A printed impression of the hour, minute and distinctive number of the employee is made on a continuous roll of paper inside the recorder.   The advantage is that an unlimited number can register time at any hour of the day, and this saves the expense of several regulators.

This International Key Recorder—the original Bundy

Fig. 20.

Naylor, Jennings & Co. Ltd., Dyers, Finishers and Mercers, Yeadon, Yorks, use three International Dial Recorders, Model 112, in their well-equipped works.

Time Recorder—is satisfactory for ensuring true records of employees' times, but is not so suitable for accounting purposes.

(c) **Dial Recorders.**—These provide a daily or weekly record on sheets.   Hours worked may be transcribed direct to the Wages Book, or the sheets filed in a Guard Book, in the form of a Wages Book, with a separate wages summary. These International Dial Recorders (Dey Time Registers) require the worker to press the dial arm into a hole on the dial, each hole bearing a number corresponding to the number of the worker (Fig. 20).   The exact time is recorded

F

Fig. 21.

NAMES		FRIDAY	SAT
Ronald Wood	1	757 100 156 530	756 101
James B. Brook	2	801 100 159 531	757 101
Thos Cooke	3	757 101 158 530	800 101
Chas Leslie	4	759 101 200 531	759 101
Fredk Daley	5	800 100 159 530	800 101
Philip Brown	6	757 102 158 531	800 100
H. Horsfall	7	601 200	600 200
J. Atkinson	8	600 200	600 200
H. Simpson	9	758 101 159 532	757 101
Thos Terry	10	759 100 158 532	800 101
A. Duckett	11	800 102 159 530	759 10
Rbt. Godard	12	757 101 200 531 601 801	800 10
Fk. Knowles	13	800 101 157 530	756 100
M. Moore	14	757 100 200 531	800 10
P. Longbottom	15	758 102 200 531	759 100
Wm Radcliffe	16	800 102 200 531	759 10
Jack Sykes	17	759 100 157 531	800 10
N. Leyton	18	200 1000	200 1000
Geo. Martin	19	200 1000	200 1000
Robt. Clarke	20	757 101 200 531	759 10
David Gibson	21	758 102 200 531	800 100
Oliver Black	22	757 100 159 530 601 801	800 101
Len Butcher	23	757 101 200 530	759 101
John Hall	24	800 101 159 530	757 101
Harold Young	25	759 100 157 531	800 100
J. W. Wallace	26	800 101 200 531	800 101
Ivan Binks	27	759 101 159 531	800 12
Hot Womersley	28	800 101 159 530	759 100
Tim Dain	29	800 100 157 532	757 10
A. Stevenson	30	757 100 200 530	800 100

Employees' Names. Time Records. (Note irregular times of Nos. 7, 8, 18 and 19, representing Shift Workers.)

Note.—Facsimile sheet (slightly reduced) from International Dial Super-Automatic Time appear in red on the actual record

Week Ending 9th June 1932 THURSDAY	Ord Time	Over time	Pay On	Rate	£	s.	d.	Less Ins.	£	s.	D.	
158 530	47	—	47	1/04	3	2	8	1/4	3	1	4	1
159 531	48	—	48	1/4	3	4	.	1/4	3	2	8	2
158 530	48	—	48	1/6	3	12	.	1/4	3	10	8	3
202 531	48	—	48	1/4	3	4	.	1/4	3	2	8	4
158 530	48	—	48	1/4	3	4	.	1/4	3	2	8	5
158 531	48	—	48	1/6	3	12	.	1/4	3	10	8	6
	48	—	48	1/4	3	4	.	1/4	3	2	8	7
	48	—	48	1/2	2	16	.	1/3	2	14	9	8
200 531	48	—	48	1/4	3	4	.	1/4	3	2	8	9
159 532	48	—	48	1/4	3	4	.	1/4	3	2	8	10
200 530	47½	—	47½	1/8	3	19	2	1/4	3	17	10	11
159 530 559 801	48	6	55½	2/-	5	11	.	1/4	5	9	8	12
200 532	48	—	48	1/8	4	.	.	1/4	3	18	8	13
158 530	48	—	48	1/6	3	12	.	1/4	3	10	8	14
200 530	48	—	48	1/4	3	4	.	1/4	3	2	8	15
200 532	48	—	48	1/4	3	4	.	1/4	3	2	8	16
200 532	48	—	48	1/6	3	12	.	1/4	3	10	8	17
	48	—	48	1/8	4	.	.	1/4	3	18	8	18
	48	—	48	1/10	4	8	.	1/4	4	6	8	19
200 532	48	—	48	1/10	4	8	.	1/4	4	6	8	20
200 532	48	—	48	1/4	3	4	.	1/4	3	2	8	21
158 532 500 801	48	6	55½	1/4	3	14	.	1/4	3	12	8	22
159 530	48	—	48	1/6	3	12	.	1/4	3	10	8	23
200 500	47½	—	47½	1/4	3	3	4	1/4	3	2	.	24
159 530	48	—	48	1/4	3	4	.	1/4	3	2	8	25
200 530	47	—	47	1/2	2	14	10	1/3	2	13	7	26
200 531	47	—	47	1/4	3	2	8	1/4	3	1	4	27
158 530	48	—	48	1/4	3	4	.	1/4	3	2	8	28
159 531	48	—	48	1/2	2	16	.	1/3	2	14	9	29
	47½	—	47½	1/1	2	11	7½	1/4	2	10	3½	30

Actual Overtime worked.   Overtime is reckoned as time and a quarter.   Gross Wages.   Insurance deductions.   Net amount to pay.   Employees' Nos.

Recorder. (Weekly Model.) The records slightly thicker than the rest in the above illustration to indicate lost time and overtime.

against each employee's number on a sheet inside the machine. These machines are arranged for 50, 100 or 150 workers; and, to this extent, are not so elastic as the card recorders, with which extra workers can be provided for.

The numbering in these dial recorders can be arranged according to departments. Weekly sheets may be printed in any desired arrangement, allowing for " In " and " Out " records per day, and with wages analysis columns exactly as in existing Wages Books, providing for ordinary time, overtime, rate of pay, insurance deductions, net amount payable, and any further analysis columns desired. No transcribing is necessary if the sheets are filed in a permanent binder to form the wages book (see Fig. 21, which is reduced facsimile of a sheet actually printed by one of these recorders).

When making up wages from the clocked time sheets, it is only necessary to deduct lost time from the normal weekly hours, and add overtime. Lost time is shown by records *automatically* printed in red, and by blank spaces. Overtime records are also automatically printed in red.

The International Super-automatic Recorders automatically register the records in the correct place on the sheet whether a worker is coming in or going out. Although every employee does the same operation of pressing the lever, the machine places the record in the correct position without overstamping, or error, regardless of how irregular the times of entering or leaving may be, how times overlap, or how often the time schedule is altered.

EXAMINATION QUESTIONS

1. Set out the operations up and to and including the preparation of a wages sheet (or pay roll). Draw up specimen forms with typical entries. —*Royal Society of Arts* (*Advanced*).

2. State the relative advantages and disadvantages of recording time by :

    (*a*) Recorder clocks.
    (*b*) Depositing and picking up of tickets.
                     Royal Society of Arts (*Advanced*).

3. It is possible for a wages book to be so compiled and arranged that it will serve the purposes of both financial and costing books. Give a ruling for such a book, and add notes as to its use for the double purpose.—*The Institute of Incorporated Accountants and Auditors* (*Inter.*).

4. Draft a diagram illustrating the relationship of the Cost Accounts to the General Accounts of a business, as far as direct wages are concerned.—*The Society of Incorporated Accountants and Auditors (Final).*

5. Discuss the various types of mechanical time-recorders, stating which you prefer, and why.—*Institute of Cost and Works Accountants (Inter.).*

6. Describe the special features of the different types of time recorder clocks known to you.   In what position in the Works would you propose to locate them ?—*Institute of Cost and Works Accountants (Inter.).*

7. Compare the time-clock and disc methods of time recording for a factory employing a thousand workers.—*Institute of Cost and Works Accountants (Inter.).*

8. Draw up a skeleton wages list or pay-roll and enumerate, without describing, the operations leading up to its preparation on the assumption that clock cards are used for recording attendance and that the employees are paid on a time basis.—*Institute of Cost and Works Accountants (Inter.)*

CHAPTER VII

TIME-BOOKING METHODS

In addition to registering workers' time of arrival and departure it is necessary, in most instances, to record also particulars of work done, and the time spent on each order. There are several methods of obtaining this information, the principal being :

(a) Weekly Time-sheets.
(b) Daily Time-sheets or Reports.
(c) Job-tickets or Job-cards filled in by hand.
(d) Job Time-recording Instruments.

In some old-fashioned workshops job times are still taken by the crude method of chalking them on a board each day !

(a) **Weekly Time-sheets.**—The workers are required to fill in particulars of the time spent on each job every day. The method is not one giving precision, as the workers are inclined to enter only approximate times, and instead of entering the particulars as each job is done, or at the end of each day, they may even complete the time-sheet at the end of the week, if supervision is not strict.

A typical weekly time-sheet is shown in Fig. 22.

(b) **Daily Time-sheets.**—These have nearly the same shortcomings as the Weekly Time-sheets. It will be seen from the example (Fig. 23) that provision is made for recording the time spent on each job done during the day, but, although the form is signed by the foreman, there is a tendency for the times to be approximate only. If a strict foreman is in charge, greater accuracy may be obtained by having the job times entered on the forms in the foreman's office, but even with this arrangement idle or waste time is likely to be concealed. The method is convenient and suitable for some classes of work.

(c) **Job-tickets or Job-cards.**—The use of these for registering the time worked on each job or order is extensive. There is a

67

Fig. 22.

WEEKLY TIME-SHEET.

| Workman : .... | | | Joiner's Time-sheet | | | | | | |
| Clock No. : .... | | | Week ending 22 Feb., 193...... | | | | | | |

Name of Job.	No. of Job. or Rod*	Description of Work.	S.	M.	T.	W.	Th.	F.	Total.	
									Ordy.	O'time.

Workman's Signature :   Foreman's Signature :

Sheet to be made up *each day* and handed to Foreman on Friday.

N.B.—A separate coloured sheet is used for each trade, *e.g.* machinists, joiners, labourers, etc.

* " Rod " is a term for job used in joinery works.

Fig. 23.

DAILY TIME-SHEET.

Man's Name :			Date :		
Check No. :			Week No. :		
Machine No. :					

Works Order No.	Work done.	Time.		Hours.	Rate.			
		Start.	Finish.			£	s.	d.

Signed (worker) :	Certified (foreman) :	Office Ref. :

great variety of forms, as nearly every manufacturer draws up his job-tickets to suit his own particular needs.

The usual procedure is for the tickets to be issued to the workers from the foreman's office, to serve the dual purpose of providing instructions for the workers, and for entering upon the time spent on the work, and other information required by the Office. The time of starting and finishing the work is entered on the ticket (see Fig. 24) by the foreman, or by the

FIG. 24.

JOB-TICKET

Department :	Job No. : ....
Works Order No. :	Date : ....

Drawing No :	Time started : ....
Operation No. :	„ finished : ....
Machine No. :	Hours on Job : ....
Time allowance :	

Description of Job.	Hours.	Rate.	£	s.	d.

Worker's No. :	Certified	Office
Signature :	(foreman or	ref. :
	inspection) :	

workers, but this means that only one ticket can be issued at a time to each worker.   The time may be inserted by use of a special time-recording clock as described on another page.

When there are a number of operations in sequence, a job-card showing each operation may travel with the work through the various shops.

It is desirable that arrangements be made for recording, separately, idle or waste time, and for reconciling the gate times with the job times, unless the system used provides for a different check.

In some factories, where a large volume of detail has to be dealt with, mechanical sorting and tabulating machines, such as the Hollerith or Powers, are used, and it is convenient for the job-cards to be drawn up in a suitable form for the punching required for the purposes of the machine.   The specimens shown in Figs. 25 and 26 are typical of Gledhill-Brook clock cards for use with a Powers tabulator. They combine particulars of piece-work on one side, and on the other side the usual clock times.

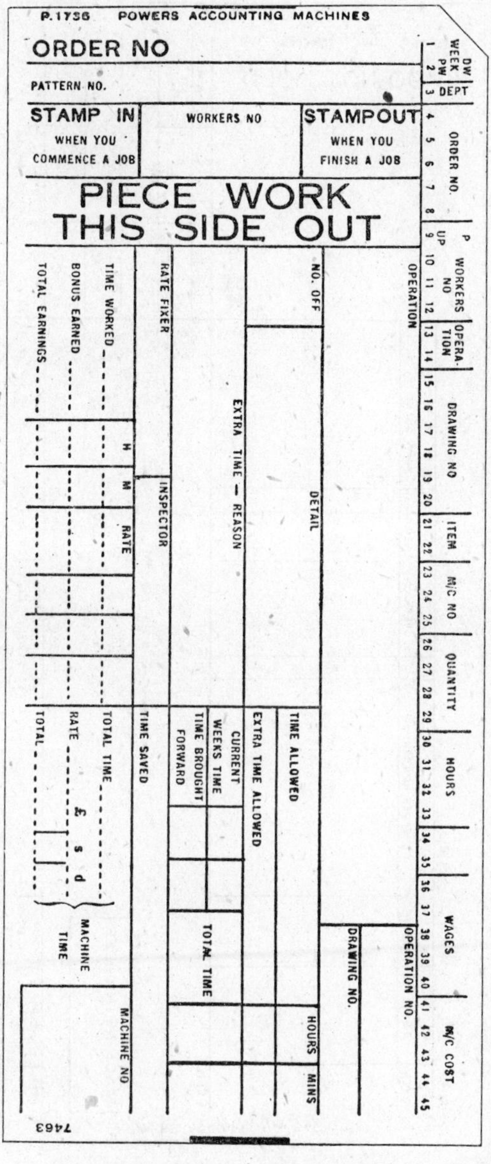

The use of tabulating and sorting machines is described in a later chapter.

(d) **Job Time-recording Instruments.** —In many factories time-recording clocks are used for ascertaining the time spent on each job or operation. There are several types of these recorders, which may be used by the workers themselves, or by the foreman or his clerk. The latter is the procedure when the workmen are not allowed by the rules of their trade union, as in the printing trade, to record such times mechanically.

A very adaptable instrument is the International Job Time-recorder, which prints on the job cards the time of starting and stopping on every job or operation, and with which any size, style, thickness, or shape of card or sheet may be used.

FIG. 25.

P.1756 POWERS ACCOUNTING MACHINES

ORDER NO

PATTERN NO.

STAMP IN — WHEN YOU COMMENCE A JOB

WORKERS NO

STAMP OUT — WHEN YOU FINISH A JOB

PIECE WORK THIS SIDE OUT

7463

Another type of recorder operates electrically, and when a number are in use in various shops they work without batteries direct from the electric mains, and are all automatically checked by the master clock every hour, and each clock sets itself to correct time. The worker simply inserts the job card when starting or finishing a job, and thus records accurate times.

The Gledhill-Brook Recording Clock, which clips off the edge of the clock cards, as previously described, is a very efficient instrument for recording job times. These machines are made to record in hours and minutes; hours and decimals of an hour; or in minutes only, whichever the system may require. There is an increasing use of the decimal hour time records.

The Procedure.— The procedure for recording job times with these various instruments will depend upon the nature and volume of the jobs; but the following may be mentioned:

Fig. 26.

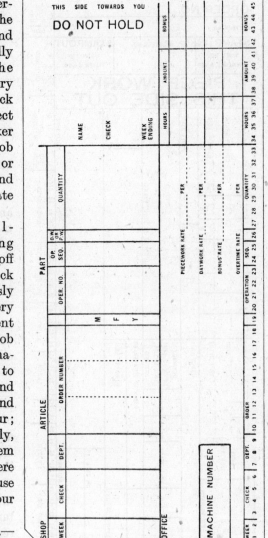

(1) *All Time on Jobs on a Weekly or Daily Card.*—If the jobs are not numerous each worker is provided with one card on which he clocks the time of starting and finishing each job or operation. The times are extended into appropriate columns by the Wages Section of the Cost Office, and transferred to a summary sheet. Fig. 29 illustrates a clock-card used in this manner.

(2) *A Separate Card per Job.*—If the jobs are too many to deal with as in (1) above a separate clock card for each may be used.

FIG. 27.—Job Time-recorder (International Model No. 1008).

FIG. 28.—Electric Job Time-recorder in Metal Case (International Model No. M.C. 1008).

The electric recorder is operated from a Master Clock (A.C. or D.C. current) or from electric light supply (A.C. controlled frequencies).

(3) *One Card for a Series of Operations.*—When there is a series of operations to be performed in sequence, a job clock-card may travel with the job from one shop to another until completion. At each operation the worker concerned clocks the time of starting and completing the operation for which he is responsible. Space is provided on the cards for stating the various operations, and for the Cost Office to insert the length of time worked on each, the rate of payment applicable and the extension of the value of the time worked. A job clock-card of this type is illustrated in Fig. 30.

Clocking Arrangements for Recording Job Times.—Time-recording instruments can be placed in convenient positions in the shops for use by the workers, or in the foreman's office,

FIG. 29.

I. T. R. Co. Ltd.			FORM No. L.S. F. 930.
DAILY COST CARD			
No. 21		DATE 31/5/32	
NAME James Knobson			

JOB No.	Time		Time Record
	OFF		⌒9 11
411	ON	' 11	⌒8 00
	OFF		⌒10 34
328	ON	1 19.	⌒9 15
	OFF		⌒12 01
1098.	ON	1. 25.	⌒10 36
	OFF		⌒3 21
756⁹	ON	2-23.	⌒12 58
	OFF		⌒3 53
438.	ON	. 25.	⌒3 28
	OFF		⌒5 31
521.	ON	1. 32.	⌒3 59
	OFF		
	ON		
	OFF		
	ON		
	OFF		
	ON		

International System

Daily Cost Card showing registrations printed by International
Time Recorder Model 1008.

where the forms or cards are marked with the time of issue or return.

In large factories, it is a growing practice to place the " In " and " Out " gate cards and clocks in the shops or departments, instead of at the main gate. This eliminates waste of time by the men on the way to the shops after clocking. In these circumstances, the same clock can then be used in suitable circumstances for timing job-cards as well. In the latter case, the clock and

Fig. 30.

| I.T.R. Co., Ltd. | JOB COST CARD | | | | | Form No. L.S.F. 931. |

ORDER No. _385_ **DRAWING No.** _72_ **PATTERN No.** _1568_

Special Instructions:- _____

Date	Started 1/6/32 Completed 2/6/32	OFFICE USE ONLY					
WORKMAN	OPERATION	COST	RATE		TIME TAKEN		RECORD
		s	d	s	d	Off / On	Hrs.	Mins.	
17	Dressing		11	1	-			54	854 800
4	Rough Turning	4	-	1	4		3	2	1158 856
9	Rough Planing	1	-	1	-		1	1	202 101
3	Turning	5	4	1	4		3	58	602 204
21	Planing		4	1	4			14	815 801
8	Grinding	2	-	1	4		1	29	946 817
7	Finishing	3	1	1	6		2	5	1157 952
11	Tempering		9	1	6			29	131 102
19	Cleaning Off		11	1	-			54	229 135
38	Finishing	1	7	1	6		1	5	339 234

I.T.R. Total Labour Cost — £ — : _19_ s. _11_ d

ENTER MATERIAL ISSUED ON REVERSE OF THIS CARD.

Job Cost Card showing time registrations against operations in sequence.
Records made on International Job Time Recorder Model 1008.

racks should be placed near the foreman's office or desk, which
is usually in a central position in the shop. A useful arrange-

ment, suggested by International Time Recording Co., Ltd., is shown in Fig. 31.

The two card-racks at the extreme right and left of the clock are for gate-time or wage-cards, and the rack between the clock and the " In " rack is for " Jobs in Operation." The one between the clock and the " Out " rack is for " Jobs Ahead." The foreman will also keep a file for job-cards made out ahead to be worked upon later, and from this he can fill the empty pockets in the " Jobs Ahead " rack, as they are emptied

Fig. 31.

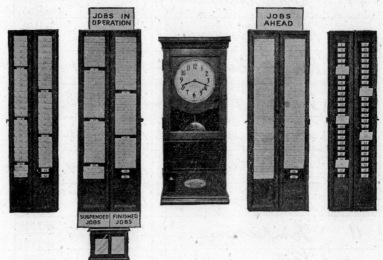

by the men. A box is kept near the clock for the cards relating to finished jobs and suspended jobs.

The worker arriving in the morning finds his gate-card and a job-card in his numbered pocket in the " Out " rack. He records his time on the gate-card, and places it in the " In " rack, where it remains until he leaves again. When he starts the job he " clocks on " the job-card. On completing it he " clocks off," places the card in the Finished Jobs Box, and takes the next job card from the " Jobs Ahead " rack, " clocks on " and places the card in the " Jobs in Operation " rack.

Should it be necessary to suspend work on a job, the worker " clocks off," and drops the card in the " Suspended Jobs Box." This card will be placed in the " Jobs Ahead " rack by the foreman later, for the same worker, or he may make another card out if a different worker has to finish the job.

The foreman files the finished job-cards by workers' numbers consecutively, and each morning the clerk from the Cost Department collects these.

The recorded job times can be checked in the Office against gate-times to ensure that the time paid for is all accounted for on the job-cards. Discrepancies must be regarded as lost time, and costed accordingly.

Different-coloured cards may often be used with advantage to denote the various departments, and different kinds of work, or to distinguish day-work from piece-work.

FIG. 32.

PIECE-WORK ORDER.			No. :			
Worker's Name :			Date :			
Clock No. :			Time Taken :			
Part :			Price :			
Operation :			Quantity :			
No. Made.	Passed.	Rejected.	Rate.	£	s.	d.
Signed Worker :		Signed Inspection :				
		Foreman :				

Piece-work Tickets.—Payment may be made according to the number of articles or quantity of output produced. In some factories, time is not recorded, in others it is as it should be (see p. 90). When a premium or bonus is paid for time saved, then both quantities and time must be recorded.

A form of piece-work ticket is shown in Fig. 32. Other examples made in the form of a clock-card for use with tabulating machines are shown in Figs. 25 and 26. The number or quantity produced is entered and signed for by the workers on the ticket or slip. When the work has been inspected, the ticket is countersigned by the person inspecting, or the foreman, and passed to the Office, where the prices are entered and extended. From these the pay-roll is entered, and the necessary details extracted for the Cost Accounts.

The Ticketograph Coupon System for Control of Piece-work.—The ticketograph is constructed for controlling costs and progress in a factory, whether the work is on a time or piece-work basis. The appliance is shown in use in Fig. 33. It imprints a ticket, composed of coupons, one coupon for each

FIG. 33.

International Ticketographs in use at WALLACE & WIER, LTD., Clothing Manufacturers, Glasgow, where also five International Time Recorders are installed.

The board behind the ticketograph holds the tickets of completed operations and serves as a progress record.

operation forming a part of any particular job. (See Figs. 34 and 35.) Each coupon carries the order and style number, quantity, cost of the operation it covers, or any other information desired, for the purpose of controlling cost. One to eighty-two coupons may be imprinted at a time.

The complete ticket, with the coupons, travels through the factory, attached to the article. As each worker completes his individual operation, he removes the coupon bearing his operation number. This is continued until the article is entirely finished.

Each productive worker is supplied with a coupon holder

book, and after he removes the coupon covering his operation, which is his *voucher for pay*, he places it in this book. At the end of the pay period he turns in his coupon-holder book

Fig. 34.

The Property of Priory Works, Alperton. Issue with this :— (1) Scale Card (2) Progress Card	Description of Garment	Colours :—	Size—
	Jumper	Parma	Womens
No. of P/T 3	This PRODUCTION CARD is to accompany the relative goods in each stage of progress through Factory—being returned to Office by Despatch Department. Special Instructions (if any)		

1	2	3	4	5	6	7	8	9	10
11	12	13	14	15	16	17	18	19	20

5537 Order No. — 6 Quantity (12 doz.) — 3008 Garment No. — 27-4 Required by (date)

Left-hand operations:

No.				Price per doz.	Operation	
20	5537	6	3008	Void	Extra H.E.	P.W.A.
18	5537	6	3008	Void	Extra M.R.	P.W.A.
16	5537	6	3008	6	Buttons (Machine)	P.W.A.
14	5537	6	3008	8	Button-Holes	P.W.A.
12	5537	6	3008	5	Machining : Hemming	P.W.A.
10	5537	6	3008	1/4	Machining : Hemming	P.W.A.
8	5537	6	3008	1/4	Quick-Seam	P.W.A.
6	5537	6	3008	1/6	Over-locking	P.W.A.
4	5537	6	3008	6	Cutting	P.W.A.
2	5537	6	3008	2/-	Knitting Trimmings	P.W.A.

Central panel:

Any other extra operation is to be noted on Coupon 21 below.

Extra Operation (No. 21)

Name & Price	O/N Qty No.	Worker's No.

All Workers please carefully note :—

Workers, before detaching Coupons, must place their Clock Number in the numbered square above corresponding to their operation. Remember the Coupon is your voucher for pay.

Coupons must not be detached until work has been passed as correct by your examiner.

Put your number on the back of your Coupon before putting it into your Coupon Book.

Your Wages will be made up from the Coupons—so take great care of them and the Coupon Book—remember they are the equivalent of Cash.

Knit on M/c No.

Form No. 8. 25/11/25

Right-hand operations:

No.				Price per doz.	Operation	
19	5537	6	3008	6	Pressing	P.W.A.
17	5537	6	3008	5/6	Head Finishing (throughout)	P.W.A.
15	5537	6	3008	2/2	Pockets (M.R.)	P.W.A.
13	5537	6	3008	8	Seam-Cover	P.W.A.
11	5537	6	3008	Void	Border Tacking	P.W.A.
9	5537	6	3008	Void	Binding	P.W.A.
7	5537	6	3008	1/-	Linking	P.W.A.
5	5537	6	3008	Void	Preparing (M.R.)	P.W.A.
3	5537	6	3008	12/-	Knitting Skirt	P.W.A.
1	5537	6	3008	16/-	Knitting Body, &c.	P.W.A.

International Ticketograph Production Card. (Reduced facsimile : actual size is about 9″ × 5½″.)

the coupons in which have been automatically counted. This will show what he actually earned, and also eliminates the checking afterwards, as the entire ticket is automatically checked when issued by the ticketograph.

G

FIG. 35.

	1 I	3 H	5 G	7 F	9 E	11 D	13 C	15 B	17 A	Despatch V	Warehouse or Cutting Room V
A	1 I	3 H	5 G	7 F	9 E	11 D	13 C	15 B	17 A	Despatch V	Warehouse or Cutting Room V
B	432	432	432	432	432	432	432	432	432	432	432
C	56	56	56	56	56	56	56	56	56	56	56
D	12	12	12	12	12	12	12	12	12	12	12
E	2/6	VOID	2/9	3½	2/6 *6½	1/11	6¾	4/-	3/3⅜		
F	V Cutting	Back-making	Piecing Up	Shaping	Sew Round	Closing	Neck-making	Felling	Brushing and Pressing		
G	1	3	5	7	9	11	13	15	17		
G		4	1	2	3	4					

PROGRESS

(The four coupons attached to this portion form progress reports and must be put in the collecting box immediately operation is finished.)

Workers, before detaching Coupons must place their Clock No. in the square corresponding to their operation. REMEMBER—the Coupon is your voucher for pay.

INTERNATIONAL TICKETOGRAPH SYSTEM—FORM NO. T 376

	2 F	4	6 G	8	10	12	14	16	18	Cost Office V	Making Department V
G	2	4	6	8	10	12	14	16	18		
A	2	4	6	8	10	12	14	16	18	Cost Office V	Making Department V
B	432	432	432	432	432	432	432	432	432	432	432
C	56	56	56	56	56	56	56	56	56	56	56
D	12	12	12	12	12	12	12	12	12	DB	
E	1/7	DB	7½	3/-	9¾	2/6	1/9	3/-	4/11		
F	V Fixing	Sleeve Making	Under Pressing	Linen to Edge	Baist Under	Baist Out	Stitching	Sleeving	Buttons and Button-holes		

N.B.—The figures in dark type are printed a line at a time by the Ticketograph by one pressure of a lever; for explanation see p. 80. The capital letters on the left are not part of the card, but are inserted for reference purposes in the explanation of the card. Average size about 10″ × 5½″, but the size depends on the number of operations.

* 6½d. on coupon No. 9 is an "extra" added by a "plussing" device.

The card of coupons and prices is printed for each particular job as needed. Those operations not required are cancelled, whilst the others are simultaneously priced, before the job goes into the factory.

For progress purposes the ticketograph also imprints on a portion of the coupon card progress coupons for each department which bear the job No., etc., and date by which the work must be finished. This ticket accompanies the article through the various departments and as the work is finished in a department the coupon belonging to that department is detached and immediately sent to the office, where it is placed with the counter-part stub or master-ticket, thereby enabling the production manager to see at a glance exactly where a job is and its state of progress.

A second specimen, showing the Progress portions, is shown in Fig. 35. The references on this example are :

A = operation No.
B = order No.
C = style No.
D = quantity to be made.
E = price per operation.
F = name of operation.
G = blank squares in which worker inserts his number on finishing operation.

The labour cost of the complete job is known by the symbol designating the price schedule (*e.g.*, D.B. on cost office coupon, Fig. 35).

This system not only keeps the office in close touch with the work in the factory, but also provides an incentive to each head of a department to get the work finished and the progress coupon delivered to the office, with the utmost dispatch.

This is a very efficient system, which is not so well known as it should be for piece-work involving many minor operations.

Preparation of the Pay-roll or Wages Sheets.—Whichever method of time-keeping, time-booking, premium bonus or piece-work recording is adopted, the wages due to the workers are entered up on the Pay-roll, Wages-sheets or Wages-book, as the case may be. A form of Wages Sheet is shown in Fig. 36.

In many modern factories the Pay-sheets are typed, extended, totalled, and analysed on specially constructed adding and calculating machines.

One type of International Dial Time-recording Clock prints the daily hours on a sheet which becomes the Pay-roll Sheet at

Fig. 36.

WAGES-SHEET OR PAY-ROLL

(N.B.—A separate sheet to each shop is desirable.)

Process :
Department or Shop : ....

Week ending : ....19...   Sheet No. : ......
Week No. : ......

Department Symbol No.	Check No.	Name.	Grade or Trade.	Hours.*	Rate.	Ordinary Wages.		Extra for Bonus.	Gross Wages.	Deductions. Fines.	Nat. Ins. Worker.		Net Wages. Paid.	Nat. Ins. Employer.	
						Time.	Piece-work.				H. & P.	Un.		H. & P.	Un.

(Separate columns for each item of deduction are provided.)

* Sometimes a column for each day of the week and total are included.

the end of the week (see Fig. 21). The pay rates and totals are entered and extended by hand or by machine.

Where Powers or Hollerith tabulating machines are used the Pay Roll may be printed from punched cards. All the columns are entered up and the necessary totals made and printed by the machine. The same cards can also be used for a labour cost analysis, and other punching may be made for special analyses.

A summary is made of the totals of the wages-sheets, together with an analysis of the amount of each denomination of money required by the cashier for making up the pay-envelopes, and a cheque for the total is drawn accordingly.

The pay-clerks make up the wages due to each worker, the respective amounts being placed in pay-envelopes or tins marked with the workers' numbers. If the number of employees is large, it is advisable to count out the money total for each sheet separately, so that when the pay-envelopes for the workers on a sheet are completed, any error in counting the individual amounts is localised. To make a recount of the whole to discover an error before the time fixed for paying out would be almost impossible, except in case of a small number of workers.

It is prudent to allot to different clerks, and change about, the duties of preparing the Pay-Roll, making up the wages envelopes, and paying out to the employees, to avoid the risks of fraud. Sometimes, a further safeguard is provided by requiring the foremen or a charge-hand to be present at the pay-box to identify the men, and to see that there is a recipient for every pay-envelope. After paying out, the pay-clerks and foremen should sign the Pay-Sheets, certifying that the wages have been paid as shown thereon.

Some large modern factories use automatic cash-counting machines, which rapidly count out the money due to each worker.

The Prevention of Fraud and Irregularities in the Pay-Roll.— Frauds in connection with the payment of wages occur every year owing to lack of proper precautions. The following is a summary of the safeguards which may be adopted to ensure that no fictitious names are entered, and that irregular payments are not made :

(1) A time-keeper should see that each worker clocks only one gate time-card; or places only one check in the time box where time-recording clocks are not used.

(2) When practicable, the time booked within the shops on jobs should be summarised and checked against time-cards, or time-sheets, for each worker.

(3) The time-keepers may be required to check the employees while at work in the shops from time to time.

(4) Time- and piece-work records should be counter-signed by the foreman.

(5) Piece-workers should check in and out in the same way as day-rate workers.

(6) Overtime should be sanctioned in advance, and an overtime slip should be made out or signed by the foreman, and given to the time-keeper.

(7) Workers leaving the factory during working hours should present pass-out slips, duly signed, stating the reason. The gate-man should hand these daily to the time-keeper, or Wages Office.

(8) The clerks who prepare the wages-sheets should not put up the pay envelopes.

(9) The actual paying-out to the workers should not be done by the clerks who prepare the wages-sheets, or pay-envelopes.

(10) The foreman, or charge-hand, should be present during the paying-out to see that all the pay-envelopes are distributed, and to identify the recipients.

EXAMINATION QUESTIONS

1. What objections do you have to—
    (a) A time-worker filling in his time sheet;
    (b) A piece-worker returning his production?
How would you recommend that these objections should be overcome?—*Institute of Cost and Works Accountants (Inter.)*.

2. Describe two methods of booking time to jobs and discuss the advantages or disadvantages of each.—*Royal Society of Arts (Advanced)*.

3. A factory is running on operation cards which travel with the work and all time is booked, when completed, on these cards. What means would you suggest to check these times against the employee's weekly time so as to ensure correct balancing?—*Institute of Cost and Works Accountants (Inter.)*.

4. A proposal is being considered to install clocks for stamping the times of commencement and finish of jobs or operations; and you, as Cost Accountant, are asked for your views. What advice would you give and, if favourable, what precautions would you suggest being taken to secure reasonable accuracy in the records?—*Royal Society of Arts (Advanced)*.

5. In a factory a group of millwrights are engaged in the installation and maintenance of plant in a series of independent shops. Sketch out

a specimen time sheet showing a number of entries covering work performed.—*Institute of Cost and Works Accountants (Inter.).*

6. What mechanical appliances can be used in preparing a pay-roll and in handling wages ?—*Institute of Cost and Works Accountants (Inter.).*

7. Discuss the various types of mechanical time recorders, stating which you prefer, and why. Include time in and out of the factory and the daily internal works time records.—*Institute of Cost and Works Accountants (Inter.).*

8. A factory producing parts in quantities uses job cards which follow the batches of work as they progress through shops, each operative booking his time on the cards. Some of the batches are in hand for several weeks. How would you ensure that each operative's time in any wage week is satisfactorily balanced ?—*Institute of Cost and Works Accountants (Inter.).*

9. Do you consider it to be essential that piece-workers should record the time taken for each article or batch of articles ? If you agree, to what purposes could the time record be put ?—*Institute of Cost and Works Accountants (Inter.).*

10. Describe the routine in the calculation and making up of pay-rolls and refer to any mechanical aids known to you. Describe the nature of the checking system to be employed for the verification of piecework and timework wages.—*Institute of Cost and Works Accountants (Inter.).*

11. Draw up a card to be used for recording piecework, showing the information that you consider to be essential. State what you assume to be the methods in use of (*a*) recording attendance, and (*b*) charging overheads to the products.—*Institute of Cost and Works Accountants (Inter.).*

12. How would you ensure that no " dummy " workmen are included in the pay-roll ? (part question).—*Society of Incorporated Accountants and Auditors (Final).*

13. Suggest a system of time recording and wages payment to minimise the risk of fraud.—*Corporation of Accountants (Final).*

14. You have been consulted by a furniture manufacturer regarding the methods which should be adopted in recording workers' time and charging same to Cost Accounts.

Write a memorandum giving your suggestions and stating the forms which should be used and also the entries which are required in the Cost Books and Financial Books. No Rulings of Forms are required. The business consists of manufacturing certain standard articles for stock and making up goods to customers' own specifications.—*Corporation of Accountants (Final).*

15. Is it necessary to keep time records for piece-workers ? Give reasons for your answer.—*Incorporated Accountants (Final).*

16. You are requested to draft with appropriate rulings a Time or Job Card suitable for a system where piece work is operated.—*Incorporated Accountants (Final).*

17. Draft a form of Wages Sheet and insert particulars of Wages payable to three workers in respect of Ordinary Time, Overtime and Premium Bonus. *Note.*—Oncost is allocated on the basis of Productive Labour Hours.—*Corporation of Accountants (Final).*

18. What checks would you advise in order to prevent fraud in connection with wages paid to workmen by a Road Contractor on a distant job where 50 per cent. of the labour is drawn from the local Labour Exchange and a certain number of such men are changed every week ?—*Incorporated Accountants (Inter.).*

CHAPTER VIII

METHODS OF REMUNERATION

General Considerations.—The cost of labour is a factor which requires most careful thought. It provides problems of major importance, and, on the solution of these, the success of any enterprise must largely depend.

Reduction in labour costs is one of the chief objectives of the Production Manager, and much guidance to this end can be secured from a suitably organised costing system. Low wages do not necessarily mean low costs—in fact, it is widely recognised now that efficiently organised factories may pay the highest wages, and yet have the lowest labour costs.

Many schemes for remunerating labour have been devised to secure more efficiency than is usually obtained from the common method of paying by the week, day, or hour, without regard to the amount of work or volume of production. Some systems have failed on account of their complexity, others have been introduced successfully in isolated undertakings only, but several have been used with advantage to both manufacturers and workers. Strikes and agitations have arisen where wages schemes are complex, and not understood by the workers, hence, in promoting a special method of payment, care must be taken to see that it is not only understood, but also appreciated as a reasonable one by the workers.

The nature of the industry and the particular circumstances in each factory must necessarily influence the choice of a system of payment, and the considerations which arise are mentioned below.

Factors to be Considered.—(1) *Efficiency in Production.* When volume of production is the important factor, labour control and remuneration may be devised to this end; but, when output is less important than great care and accuracy, wage payments based on production quantities are undesirable, unless competent inspection is arranged for.

(2) *Effect on the Workers.*—The attitude of the workers is of importance. Whatever system of payment is adopted, it should be readily understood by the workers, otherwise the fullest advantage will not be secured. For this reason, a simple scheme is usually the most satisfactory. Ordinary piece-work payments are easily understood, but two principles must be observed : first, that, when a rate has been fixed, it should not be altered (see p. 90 however) ; secondly, no limit to the amount of wages earned at the rate should be fixed.

The restriction as to lowering rates refers to those fixed by individual employers, but, when a national, or district, piece-rate is in operation within an industry, different considerations apply. Regard must be had, of course, to minimum rates fixed by Trade Boards in certain trades.

(3) *The Incidence of Overhead Expenses.*—A proportion of the general expenses of an undertaking, the " fixed " charges, do not fluctuate with the volume of output, consequently, any reduction in output results in an increased cost of production per unit of output. This is a factor of great importance, and is the basic feature of schemes for remunerating labour according to (*a*) volume of output, and (*b*) time saved in production. The ordinary time- or day-rate method of payment does not take this factor into account. As to the incidence of overtime see pp. 114 and 115.

(4) *Labour Turnover.*—Any changing of employees occasions loss to a manufacturer in several ways. In addition to the labour necessary for the engagement of a worker, there is the loss of his time and that of his instructor during the period of learning the routine of the works and the details of his duties. Statistics have shown that the loss due to labour turnover is of significance, and every effort is made to employ efficient workers, and to keep them satisfied, not only with the general working conditions, but by means of inducements linked up with the method of remuneration. When deciding upon the wages system, this aspect of the subject should be considered, in order to secure a contented staff.

METHODS OF REMUNERATION

The remuneration of the workers may be based on the time attended, the quantity of output produced, operation time, or a combination of these factors.

The methods used may be classified as follows :

1. Time (or Day-rate) Wages calculated on the basis of the time employed—extra payment being made for overtime.

2. Wages Paid on Results.

    (a) *Individual.*

        (1) Piece-work, of which there are four varieties :
            (i) Ordinary straight piece-work.
            (ii) The Balance System.
            (iii) The Balance and Debt System.
            (iv) Payment on " Points Values " of output.

        (2) Differential Piece-work, in which wages are calculated from piece-rates which vary with the quantity produced and the time taken.

        (3) Bonus Schemes.

            (i) Task Bonus or Efficiency Bonus payments based on time taken.
            (ii) Premium Bonus payments, based on a fixed proportion of time saved over time allowed.
            (iii) Differential Bonus System, based on a percentage determined by means of a sliding scale, in which the percentage is larger the more the time is saved.
            (iv) Fixed Bonus System. A stated sum per hour saved is paid.
            (v) Cost Premium Method, based on the saving effected in materials and time.

    (b) *Collective.*

        (1) Group piece-work contracts.
        (2) A bonus, in addition to time wages, which is dependent on the production output of the whole works, separate shops, or departments.

In addition to these methods of remuneration, there are schemes whereby the employees share in a portion of the profits, usually with the object of reducing labour turnover, and payments under such a scheme are conditional upon workers having been with the employer for specified minimum periods.

Time-work or Day-work Method.—The workers are paid by the hour, day, or week without regard to the output of work. It is customary in most industries to pay extra for overtime,

Sunday and holiday work, at rates of time and a quarter, time and a half, or double time, as the case may be.

A disadvantage of this method is that there is no special inducement to the workers to give more than average effort, or more than sufficient to ensure that their services will be retained. Although there may be, generally, a certain amount of interest in the work, there is, frequently, a tendency to take longer than need be in doing it. Efficient workers receive no more wages than those less capable or less diligent.

Circumstances exist in which time-work wages are particularly advantageous, as, for instance, in the tool-room and pattern-shop. The work there demands very skilled men; there is not much likelihood of jobs recurring, because nearly all are special. Care is more important than speedy work, and inducements for the men to work quickly might lead to greater loss than on time.

Time-work may also be satisfactory in small shops, where supervision can be close; and it is also generally accepted as suitable for general labourers, and other classes of indirect labour, even when schemes of payment by result are adopted for skilled workers.

Many large works operate successfully under this method of day-rate pay, but keen management is essential, and it may be that production costs could be lowered, even in these particular works, by introducing some method of payment offering greater inducements to the workers.

Apart from any loss of output owing to fullest efforts not being given when day-rate wages are paid, there is often much time lost by workers in such ways as : (1) deliberately (or otherwise) refraining from seeking the next job; (2) waiting until the foreman gives further instructions; (3) making a job last longer, to avoid starting another before meal-times, or before the time signals; or, (4) where supervision is not strict, making the work last a long time, if there is a shortage of jobs.

Time-work tends to higher production costs, because it does not offer monetary advantage for special effort, thereby failing to secure the maximum output. Supervision, however close, does not, as a rule, result in as high an output as is likely under schemes in which payment is made according to results.

The High-wage Plan.—There are some manufacturers who believe that day-rate wages can be as effective as bonus and piece-work schemes for securing a high state of efficiency, by paying a wage higher than usual for their locality or for their particular industry, and combining a policy of close management.

The plan may be summarised as follows :

(1) A high rate of wages is paid.

(2) Special effort and interest in the work is demanded from the workers.

(3) The high wages offered attract the most experienced and efficient workers, who, eager to retain such remunerative employment, use their best endeavours.

(4) Standards of efficiency and output are set, which the foremen are required to maintain.   Work is set for each man to do, and he must do it.

(5) The work set is not more than can be accomplished, without undue fatigue, in a day of eight hours.   This ensures a contented staff.   Overtime work is, generally, not permitted.

The most notable adherent to this plan is Mr. Henry Ford, who has published a statement that, throughout the Ford industries in America, the minimum wage paid for an eight-hour day is six dollars, except during a probationary period. He and many manufacturers have proved that high wages do not necessarily result in high costs, but that many costs are higher than they should be because of low wages which command only the less efficient workers.

PIECE-WORK METHODS OF PAYMENT

Ordinary Piece-work.—The worker is paid a stated fixed price for each unit completed, without recording the time taken on the work.   A modern introduction is the payment of piece work or bonus on " points " values of production operations. Differential rates, or a bonus, may be paid, having regard to time taken, and these are dealt with later.   The unit may be a single article, a series of articles, or an operation.

Piece-workers usually develop a high degree of speed through constant repetition of the same operations, with a result that a high level of output is maintained by industrious workers. The employer enjoys lower costs, as the output is increased, owing to the spread of the fixed overhead expenses over a greater number of units produced.   On the other hand, in their endeavours to increase the output, the workers may make the quality of the work a secondary consideration, so that a strict inspection of the work has to be provided, and this adds to the cost.

There is another aspect of the matter, which is not realised by piece-workers. They will, generally, strive to increase their output, but, at times, they may be satisfied to work slower, or absent themselves, believing that it is only they who lose thereby; they overlook the fact that overhead expenses form part of the cost, and that any reduction in output results in some increase in the cost per unit. For this reason piece-workers should, normally, be required to record their gate-time in the same way as day-rate workers, and also, normally, job-time as well can be required with advantage. In the case of out-workers who are paid piece-rates, loss of time is less important in this respect.

The determination of piece-rates calls for considerable care, because, when a rate has been fixed, and is found to be too high, there is much difficulty in reducing it, without creating dissatisfaction and friction. If, however, it is necessary to reduce a piece-rate, the distrust of the workers can usually be overcome by re-arranging the operations or units, and fixing new rates. The rate-fixer must consider and measure every movement that the worker has to make, and must time the operations with precision. If previous performances are used as a guide, the rate fixed must make sure that the workers have not been slowing down with the object of securing a higher piece-rate.

The basis for piece-rates is usually the recognised time-rate for the class of worker, and the estimated number of units which may be expected in a given time. Thus, with an hourly rate of 2s., with an estimated output of, say, 12 units per hour, the piece rate would be 2d. per unit; then, if in a day of 8 hours a worker produced 128 units, he would receive £1 1s. 4d., or 5s. 4d. more than if he received payment at the rate of 2s. an hour. But if only 80 units were completed in the 8 hours, the worker would receive only 13s. 4d., or 2s. 8d. less than if paid by the hour.

From the employer's point of view, the labour cost per unit is the same, but the total cost, in the second case, would be higher than in the first, because of the incidence of the over-head expenses. The difference in cost may be very considerable, seeing that overhead expenses may be as much as 100 per cent. or more, on labour wages.

The Balance System.—A worker is employed at a stated rate of wages per hour, and a piece-work price per job is fixed. If his earnings, at the piece-rate, are more than his time wages, he is paid this balance. Should the worker produce work which equals or is less than his time-wages, he is paid at his hourly rate for the time worked. As each job is calculated on its own basis, job-time has to be recorded.

The Balance and Debt System.—In this method, which is of doubtful validity and probably obsolete, the total earnings at piece-work prices are counted. If this total is more than the wages earned at the day-rates, the excess is paid as a balance. If the piece-work wages earned are less than the time-wages, the difference is carried forward against him as a " debt " to be deducted from any subsequent balance in his favour.

This method of payment has several disadvantages which may usefully be explained :

(a) A worker may draw a balance every week, giving the impression that he is competent. It may be, however, that the piece-rates are wrong. Some may be too high, and others too low, and whilst the worker may be incurring a debt on low-priced jobs, he may be gaining more than this on the high-priced ones, thus earning a balance, and the inaccuracies remain undiscovered. Thus, the individual job costs would be incorrect both as to the labour charge and the overhead allocation. If job times are recorded, the faults in pricing may be discovered.

(b) When a worker is in " debt," he frequently claims that the piece-work price is wrong, whereas the employer may contend that the worker is lacking in either competence or industry. It may be that some of the piece-rates are too low, and to discover which are wrong, job time-recording must be arranged for, otherwise discontent may develop.

(c) If two workers, with different day-rate pay, work on the same class of work at the same piece-price, the one with the higher day-rate shows a debt, or a small balance, whilst the other is rewarded with a larger balance.

(d) The carrying forward of a " debt " tends to a feeling of

discontent, a feature which is undesirable. These difficulties disappear in the bonus schemes described below.

Differential Piece-work Rates.

(1) *The Taylor System.*—A scheme to increase the output of
the workers was introduced in America by Dr. F. W. Taylor in
his treatise on Scientific Management, and is widely known as the
" Taylor System."

The Taylor system combines the time taken and the quantity
of work produced, so that graduated rates are paid. The rates
rise as the output in the allotted time increases beyond a stated
quantity per hour.

Rate-fixing for this scheme must be on a "scientific" basis,
after the manner first described by Dr. Taylor, otherwise unsatisfactory results develop to the loss of either the manufacturer or the workers, according to whether the rates are too
high, or too low, respectively. As rate-fixing on these lines
applies also to some of the bonus schemes referred to below, a
detailed description of it is included at the end of this chapter.

The features of the differential piece-rate system may be
summarised thus :

(1) Day wages are not guaranteed.

(2) A standard time for a job is computed by the rate-
fixer, and a piece-rate price is fixed.

(3) If the worker does the work in the standard time,
he is paid at this rate.

(4) If longer time is taken, payment may be made at
ordinary day-rates, or at a lower piece-rate price.

(5) If the job is done in less than the standard time, a
higher rate is paid, as, for instance, standard piece-rate, plus
$33\frac{1}{3}$ per cent.

(6) An important feature of the method is that inefficiency
is penalised, whilst efficient work is adequately rewarded.

Dr. Taylor's scheme has been improved upon, and, whilst
it tends to a much larger output, trials are reported to have
shown that, in their effort to earn the higher piece-rates, the
workmen spoilt a considerable amount of work.

(2) *The Merrick Differential or Multiple Piece-Rate Method*
resembles the Taylor system in that the piece-rate paid is
augmented in an increasing ratio as output rises above the

standard fixed; it differs by not imposing a penalty for taking longer than standard time.

(3) *Emerson's Efficiency System* is another American scheme, which combines ordinary fixed day wages with a differential piece-rate, as follows :

(1) Day-wages are guaranteed.

(2) A volume of output which is regarded as the standard is decided upon from previous output records and test observations. This standard represents 100 per cent.

(3) A bonus on wages is paid to a worker whose output exceeds two-thirds of the standard for any week.

(4) The bonus increases in a stated ratio to the increasing output up to and beyond the standard, *e.g.*

Fig. 37.

STANDARD OUTPUT = 1500 UNITS.

Workers' Output.		Earnings.
Quantity.	Efficiency.	
1. 750	50 per cent.	Below $\frac{2}{3}$ of standard, no bonus, day wage only.
2. 1350	90 per cent.	Time-wages plus Bonus 10 per cent.
3. 1500	100 per cent.	,, ,, ,, 20 ,, ,,
4. 1650	110 per cent.	,, ,, ,, 30 ,, ,,

Task Bonus Method of Payment.—The best-known example is the Gantt Task Bonus scheme, in which a job must be completed in not more than time-allowance set. The main features are :

(1) Day-wages are guaranteed.

(2) A definite task is set on which a bonus may be earned if completed within the time allowed.

(3) The time allowed is arrived at in a similar manner to that used by Taylor.

(4) The bonus is a fixed percentage on the time taken; there is no graduated scale as in the case of the premium systems described below.

(5) If more than time allowed for the job is taken, day-rate wages are paid without bonus.

(6) The time and bonus are fixed for each job, and when a job is completed the man goes on with the next. The pay earned thus consists of day-wages plus the sum of any bonuses for which the worker has qualified.

(7) The foreman receives a bonus if the workers reach the standard of efficiency qualifying for a bonus.

Example : Four men engaged on similar jobs, day-rate wages 1s. 9d. per hour; bonus 33⅓ per cent. on time taken, if job is done within 4 hours :

FIG. 38.

Man.	Time Taken.	Earned by Day-rate or Minimum. s. d.	Bonus. s. d.	Equal to Hourly Rate of s. d.
A	5 hrs.	8 9	none	1 9
B	4 hrs.	7 0	2 4	2 4
C	3½ hrs.	7 0	2 0½	2 7
D	3 hrs.	7 0	1 9	2 11

The system demands a careful calculation of the time necessary to do a job, so that the fixed overhead expenses can be taken into consideration to enable the bonus to be fixed so as to warrant paying this bonus, if standard time is improved upon.

Premium Bonus Methods of Payment.—The object of making wages dependent on the results achieved by the workers is chiefly to secure a greater output, and to lower the cost of production. The latter is secured when output is increased, because some of the overhead expenses are constant, and the amount chargeable to each unit of production becomes less as the volume of units made increases.

In piece-work systems, the labour charge in the costs remains constant.

The premium bonus schemes introduce a different principle. They are a combination of ordinary day-rate and piece-rate methods, but the bonus, or premium, is dealt with in terms of hours saved. The principle followed is that as the efficiency of organisation and equipment provided by the employer adds to the special efforts made by the workers, the benefit of any gain in output should be shared by the employer and the workers. The workers are offered an incentive to give their best efforts, and their interests are adequately protected; it is, likewise, advantageous to the employer to provide efficient plant, and a sound organisation, to ensure the maximum production.

The various premium bonus systems described differ chiefly in the method of calculating the bonus, and the proportions in which any saving is shared between worker and employer.

H

Like all methods of payment by results, the rate of pay, and, particularly, the rate of bonus, or premium, must be decided with extreme care by the management, bearing in mind that:

(1) If the terms are too liberal, there may be a loss rather than a gain to the business.

(2) If the terms are too low, the desired extra effort from the workers will not be secured, and the probability of friction and discontent arises.

For these reasons, the premiums should depend on times and rates scientifically fixed on the lines described at the end of this Chapter. It is highly probable that unreliable rate-fixing is responsible for the limited use which has been made of premium bonus schemes.

The attitude of the workers and their trade unions is more favourable to ordinary piece-work than to premium bonus schemes, probably on the assumption that the worker receives the full advantage of extra effort, and need only work to the extent to which he feels inclined. The scheme must be equitable to retain a contented efficient staff. An essential requirement under the premium bonus schemes is that jobs should be proceeded with in close succession throughout the hours the factory is open. Again, the more rapidly a job is completed the greater the average hourly rate earned by the workers, although the total amount paid per job decreases, thus the employer also secures reward for the efficiency of his organisation, which contributes, to an important extent, to the workers' ability to increase their output.

The Halsey Premium Bonus Scheme.—This American system originated by F. A. Halsey gives the worker a bonus of 50 per cent. of the time saved over the time allowed for a job. The procedure is the same as for the Halsey–Weir system described in the next paragraph.

The Halsey–Weir Premium Bonus Scheme.—This differs from the preceding one in that only 30 per cent. of the time saved is given as a premium to the worker.

The procedure for determining the premium bonus is briefly this:

(1) The job is carefully timed by making a time study of every movement and operation, supplemented by information provided by records of previous experience.

(2) To this estimated time is added a percentage which will give the worker a bonus of say, 33⅓ per cent., so that he can earn time and one-third if the job is completed in the estimated time. This means that 66⅔ per cent. has to be added to the estimated element time.

Example (Halsey Scheme) :

Estimated time	3 hours
add 66⅔ per cent.	2 ,,
Job time allowed	5 ,,

If the worker does the job in the 5 hours allowed, he receives no premium, being paid at his ordinary day-rate. If he takes 4 hours, thereby saving 1 hour, he gets a bonus of ½ hour, *i.e.*, 4½ hours' pay at his day-rate for 4 hours' work. If he does the job in the estimated time (3 hours) he receives 1 hour premium, *i.e.*, 4 hours' pay for 3 hours' work, thus securing the full bonus of 33⅓ per cent.

It should be noticed that :

(1) The worker has a guaranteed fixed hourly rate, even if he cannot do the work in less than the time allotted.

(2) The ratio of extra pay decreases when the allotted time is exceeded ; but increases steadily to the extent that time is saved. When half the allotted time is saved the bonus is 50 per cent. on time taken.

(3) Economy in time is directly encouraged by the fact that the worker can aim at a premium on every job.

(4) The calculation of the bonus is simple for the worker to understand ; bonus time is added to hours worked.

(5) The saving is divided equally between the employer and the worker, however large it may be.

The comparative table on p. 97 shows the operation of the system, as applied to five workmen engaged on the same task.

The Rowan Premium Bonus Scheme.—The system introduced by David Rowan, of Glasgow, in 1901, operates on somewhat similar lines as to time rating, but differs in two important respects :

(1) The premium, based on time saved, is added to the hourly pay-rate.

(2) The premium added to the pay-rate is the same percentage as the time saved represents of the time allowed.

Fig. 39.

THE HALSEY PREMIUM BONUS SCHEME

Workman.	Time Estimated.	Time Rate Allowed.	Time actually Taken.	Saving over Time Allowed.	Premium Time Given (Half Time Saved).	Representing Bonus per cent. on Time Taken.	Hours Paid in Lieu of Actual.	Wage paid at Day-rate of 1s. 6d. per Hr.			Equivalent to Rate per Hr. of :	
	Hrs.	Hrs.	Hrs.	Hrs.	Hrs.		Hrs.	£	s.	d.	s.	d.
A	9	15	15	nil	nil	—	15	1	2	6	1	6
B	9	15	9	6	3	$33\frac{1}{3}$	12		18	0	2	0
C	9	15	10	5	$2\frac{1}{2}$	25	$12\frac{1}{2}$		18	9	1	$10\frac{1}{4}$
D	9	15	8	7	$3\frac{1}{2}$	$43\frac{3}{4}$	$11\frac{1}{2}$		17	3	2	$1\frac{3}{4}$
E	9	15	$7\frac{1}{2}$	$7\frac{1}{2}$	$3\frac{3}{4}$	50	$11\frac{1}{4}$		16	$10\frac{1}{2}$	2	3

In other words, the bonus is fixed by adding to the ordinary day wages at hourly rates a percentage equal to the percentage by which the time allowed is reduced.

Example (Rowan Scheme) :

> Ordinary time rate 1s. 6d. per hour.
> Estimated time 3 hours for a job
> add $66\frac{2}{3}$ per cent. 2   „
>   ―
> Time allowed   5   „
> Job done in 3 hrs. 20 min.

Then the time saved is 1 hr. 40 min. and the premium is

$$\frac{5 - 3\ \text{hrs. } 20\ \text{min.}}{5\ \text{hrs.}} = \frac{100\ \text{min.}}{300\ \text{min.}} = \frac{1}{3}$$ or $33\frac{1}{3}$ per cent. and the

rate of pay will be 1s. 6d. plus $\frac{1}{3} = 2s.$ and the wages for the job, therefore, 6s. 8d.

The formula for the bonus percentage is :

$$\frac{\text{Time allowed} - \text{Time Taken}}{\text{Time Allowed}} \times 100$$

The actual total bonus value to be added to wages may be calculated at once also by the following formula :

$$\frac{\text{Time Saved} \times \text{Time Worked} \times \text{Time Rate}}{\text{Time Allowed}}$$

e.g. using the previous example :

$$\text{Total Bonus} = \frac{1\ \text{hr. } 40\ \text{min.} \times 3\ \text{hr. } 20\ \text{min.} \times 18d.}{5\ \text{hrs.}} = 20d.$$

Amount earned is $3\frac{1}{3}$ hrs. at 1s. 6d. $= 5s. + 1s.\ 8d.$
                                              $= 6s.\ 8d.$

The following comparative table, using the same figures as for the Halsey illustration (p. 96), shows how the Rowan method differs in results :

Fig. 40.

THE ROWAN PREMIUM BONUS SCHEME

Workman.	Time Estimated.	Time Rate Allowed.	Time Actually Taken.	Saving over Time Allowed.	Representing Percentage Bonus on Wages.	Ordinary Day-rate Wages at 1s. 6d. per Hour.			Total Wage + Bonus for Job.			Rate per Hour after Bonus Added.	
	Hrs.	Hrs.	Hrs.	Hrs.		£	s.	d.	£	s.	d.	s.	d.
A	9	15	15	nil	nil	1	2	6	1	2	6	1	6
B	9	15	9	6	40		13	6		18	11	2	1⅖
C	9	15	10	5	33⅓		15	0	1	0	0	2	0
D	9	15	8	7	46⅔		12	0		17	7	2	2⅜
E	9	15	7½	7½	50		11	3		16	10½	2	3

Notice that both systems give a bonus of 50 per cent. when the time allowed is halved, also that, although each of the men B to E receives a lower total wage per job, they do more jobs in a week than A, so that they earn considerably more total wages, as evidenced by the higher hourly rates.

From the employer's point of view, the method is safer than the Halsey–Weir scheme, in that the premium being proportionate to the time saved, the risks from mistakes in rate-fixing are less serious.   The worker finds it advantageous to save time up to 50 per cent., but, after this, his increase in wages is at a diminishing rate, whereas, under the Halsey–Weir system, it is progressive, and increases substantially.

A bonus of 100 per cent., or double wages, cannot be earned under the Rowan scheme.

The premium bonus schemes which have been devised have, usually, been the outcome of wage-incentive experiments in particular factories, hence, from time to time, different industrialists have published such schemes when they have been tested, and most of them are of American origin.

The Differential Bonus System is a variation of the premium bonus system. The bonus percentage is determined on a sliding-scale basis, and increases the more time is saved.   The result is that the quicker workers receive a larger bonus, showing also a greater percentage reward, and yet reduced costs are obtained.

The Fixed Bonus System.—A separate fixed bonus per hour is arranged for each section of the works, *e.g.* 4*d.* per hour in shop A, 6*d.* in shop B. The bonus, at the applicable rate, is paid on the number of hours saved on the standard time allowance. The time allowance is made for each job, and represents the time which would be taken by the average worker on day-rate wages.

Cost Premium Method of Payment by Results.—This is a method which may be used in connection with standard costs, but only to a limited extent, in view of the fact that materials as well as time are taken into account. The principle followed is to determine the standard cost of materials, labour, and expenses— a bonus being given if the actual cost is less than the standard. The assumption is that the workers can reduce costs by saving time, and by exercising care with materials, so that waste is eliminated as far as possible; a proportion of the saving so effected is distributed to the workers on some agreed basis.

Rate-fixing by Time Study Methods.—This is commonly called " scientific rate-fixing," following the lead given by Dr. F. W. Taylor. In the payment of work on " Points Values," the points are often based on this method.

The time taken to do a job on a machine tool is considered in three sections :

(1) The time taken in reading the drawing and instructions, and the handling of the tools to be used in the machine.

(2) The time setting the tools and handling the machine.

(3) The element time for the actual operations, when running.

The first two are timed in minutes, and this time is added to the running time necessary for the number of units, or pieces, which have to be made. The time for each operation when the machine is running is taken with a stop-watch, and is called the element time. To the total element time, an allowance for contingencies is added; this contingency allowance may be 20 per cent. or more, according to the type of machine.

The sum of these times represents the " estimated time " per article made. To this 66⅔ per cent. is added to allow of a bonus of 33⅓ per cent. This is the " time allowed " or " standard time."

If the time allowed is taken by the worker, he receives no bonus, but is paid at ordinary day-rate. If exactly the estimated time is taken, a bonus of one-third is earned.

The procedure for building up the rate and the application of it is shown in the following simple example :

	Element Time per Unit made in Minutes.	Time for Batch in Minutes.
Read instructions and drawing	—	3·5
Draw tools from store	—	7·0
Fix tool No. 1	—	2·0
Feed material	—	0·5
Turn	0·15	—
Fix tool-box in turret	—	0·5
Set tool	—	6·0
Turn	0·75	—
Set dies	—	5·5
Cut thread	0·20	—
Set parting of tool	—	4·5
Part off	0·50	—
Total times	1·60	29·5
Contingencies allowance 25 per cent.	0·40	
Total element (or running) Time	2·00	

Estimated Time for 144 units :—

$$29·5 + (2·00 \times 144) \text{ minutes} = 317·5 \text{ min.}$$

Standard Time allowed :—

$$317·5 + 66\tfrac{2}{3} \text{ per cent.} = \text{say, } 528 \text{ min.}$$

If 144 pieces are turned out in 528 minutes, ordinary time-rates are paid; but, if less time is taken, a bonus is paid according to the provisions of the system in operation.

Payment to Workers on a Collective Basis.—The methods of remuneration described so far concern the payment of individuals only; there are, however, apart from Joint Piece-Work, schemes which offer collective incentives to workers. They cannot, strictly, be regarded as wages, but collective extra payments which are made if stipulated conditions are fulfilled.

The Contract System.—A certain volume of work is placed with a foreman, leading hand, or other individual, which he undertakes to do at a fixed price, finding his own men to enable him to do the work. The men so engaged are paid by this individual, out of the price he receives, but the employers usually provide the materials, plant, and tools. The argument for this procedure is that the foreman must press the workmen to work quickly, and without waste of time, as his own pay, or profit, depends upon the surplus, after he has paid them.

This system is adopted in some instances by builders, shipbuilders, collieries, mines, iron and steel works, and steel rolling mills. It is also used for outworkers, as in ladies' clothing and tailoring trades.

Collective Bonus Schemes.—The encouragement of collective effort and interest is sometimes provided for by

(i) A bonus based on production results of the whole works or of a department.

(ii) Profit-sharing and co-partnership schemes.

These plans never provide results as profitable as direct bonuses to individuals.

The intention under these schemes is

(i) To create collective interest of all employees in the business.

(ii) To encourage the elimination of waste and loss of time.

(iii) To secure the co-operation of foremen and willing workers in watching that other members of the staff perform their duties reasonably.

(iv) Thereby to secure more economical production, and a high output.

The defects of these collective incentive schemes are :

(i) The amount received by individuals is usually too small when the bonus is shared by all employees.

(ii) The less industrious and slow workers share equally with the willing, efficient ones.

(iii) In the majority of schemes the intervals between bonus distributions is too long to retain sustained effort.

Examples of Collective Bonus and Profit-sharing Schemes.

(a) *Priestman's Production Bonus.*—A standard weekly production output is decided upon, and valued in points for each class of manufacture, and should the output in any week be above this standard, a bonus is awarded for distribution to the employees. The actual output each week is valued in points, on the same basis as the standard. The bonus paid is proportionate to any increase. For example, 500 workers in a 48-hours week are set a standard output valued at 60,000 points. One week this year there are 600 workers, from whom the production is valued at 72,000 points. No bonus would be payable—there being no increase because both the workers and the output were 20 per cent. more.   The next week 500 workers had an output worth 63,000 points—this being 5 per cent. above the standard set, each worker would receive 5 per cent. bonus on his wages.

(b) *Bonus based on Reduced Production Costs.*—This method depends on a standard cost of materials, day-wages, and such part of the overhead expense as it is possible for the employees to influence as to reduction. When actual cost falls below this standard, part of the saving is set aside as a bonus to the employees. The distribution may be on the basis of wages, and, usually, the rate of bonus is affected by the period of service. This is called the Collective Cost Premium bonus scheme.

(c) *Bonus based on Reduced Labour Costs.*—This is sometimes referred to as the Towne Gain-Sharing System, the method having been introduced by Mr. H. R. Towne. The bonus consists of half of any reduction in the cost of labour as ascertained for a suitable standard output, based on previous results.

The bonus is divided between the foremen and the operatives, as, for instance, 20 per cent. to the foreman, and 80 per cent. to the operatives.

As the bonus is usually paid half-yearly it loses much of its effect as an incentive to individual effort, although the share taken by foremen encourages their co-operation.

(d) *Profit-sharing and Co-partnership.*—There are many forms of these, but, despite efforts to increase their use, official records show that, of the many schemes that have been put into operation, many have been discontinued.

One of the principal purposes of these schemes is to reduce labour turnover.

The trade unions do not favour the principle.

Sometimes the bonus is distributed wholly, or in part, in shares carrying limited rights, and an elected employee may be asked to join the management; in other cases, a small percentage may be paid on wages and salaries, as though they were capital invested.

Criticisms which are sometimes advanced by labour officials are that bad management and lack of well-maintained plant reduce the profits, and, therefore, the bonus, whilst the share in the profits allotted to the workers is too small. In some cases there is a certain amount of distrust of the profits declared by the employers. For the purposes of this book it is not necessary to describe the details of any of these schemes.

EXAMINATION QUESTIONS

1. Discuss the relative advantages of a Piece-work System and a Premium Bonus System for the payment of wages.—*Institute of Cost and Works Accountants (Final).*

2. Describe the Premium Bonus system. What are its advantages and disadvantages respectively to employers and employees ?—*London Chamber of Commerce.*

3. When considering the advisability of carrying out a job by piece work or day work what relevant considerations would you urge for or against either method as affecting the ultimate cost ?—*Royal Society of Arts (Advanced).*

4. Would you adopt a Premium Bonus System, or alternatively, a straight Piece-work System in the case of :
   (a) The manufacture of small repetitive work ;
   (b) Fitting and erecting various classes of large machines ;
   (c) Spinning and weaving textile fabrics ?
   State reasons for your choice of system.—*Institute of Cost and Works Accountants (Inter.).*

5. What are the objections to straight piece-work as a method of remuneration and what remedies or alternatives would you recommend ?—*Institute of Cost and Works Accountants (Inter.).*

6. Describe briefly three methods of payment by results and indicate in each case the formula by which payment to the employee is computed. State what, in your opinion, are the respective advantages and disadvantages of each.—*Royal Society of Arts (Advanced).*

7. Your advice is asked as to the advantages and/or disadvantages of the following wages systems, which have been submitted to a manufacturer for the purpose of increasing the output and reducing the cost of production for the mutual benefit of both employer and employee :
   (a) Payment to the worker of a fixed premium of one-third of the saving for each hour saved on the standard time for the performance of a job.
   (b) Payment to the worker of a premium bearing the same percentage to the wages rate as the time saved bears to the standard time for the performance of a job.
   Illustrate your answer with a concrete example.—*Society of Incorporated Accountants and Auditors (Final).*

8. Under the Weir system of Premium bonus, the employer shares with the worker the time saved. Would you consider this an equitable arrangement ? State your reasons.—*Institute of Cost and Works Accountants (Inter.).*

9. State whether you would prefer the use of payment of wages by piece-work or on time in the following industries :
   (a) House Building ; (b) Coal Mining ; (c) Motor-car Manufacture. Give your reasons.—*Institute of Cost and Works Accountants (Inter.).*

10. What difficulties would you anticipate in connection with a proposal to clock times of starting and finishing operations on jobs, where payment is made normally by piece-work but with occasional breaks on time-work ? How would you propose to overcome these difficulties ?—*Institute of Cost and Works Accountants (Inter.).*

11. In what circumstances, if any, would you advise the payment of wages on the basis of hourly rate ? Give reasons.—*Institute of Cost and Works Accountants (Inter.).*

12. Describe briefly two plans of premium bonus. State which you prefer and your reasons.—*Institute of Cost and Works Accountants (Inter.).*

13. Sketch out a system of Payment by Results in any trade or industry in which you have experience.—*Institute of Cost and Works Accountants (Inter.).*

14. What are the general circumstances which render payment by results desirable or undesirable respectively ?—*Institute of Cost and Works Accountants (Inter.).*

15. What are the essential points to be considered in devising an efficient wage system ?—*Institute of Cost and Works Accountants (Inter.).*

16. Various methods of remunerating labour have been devised with the object of saving Indirect Charges. Give details of any two methods with which you are familiar and explain the systems necessary to ensure that the labour cost of the output is properly recorded and paid for.—*Society of Incorporated Accountants and Auditors (Inter.).*

17. In what circumstances would you differentiate in your costs, between the time taken in (*a*) making ready or setting up for a job preparatory to the running off on a machine, and (*b*) running off the job ? What objects would you aim at securing by such differentiation ? —*Institute of Cost and Works Accountants (Final).*

18. Detail the various methods of remunerating labour and consider each method from the point of view of costing and its probable influence on output.—*Society of Incorporated Accountants and Auditors (Inter.).*

19. It is proposed to institute a system of payment by results in a certain factory. State what safeguards must be provided for both the employers and the employees before the system can be successfully established.—*Corporation of Accountants (Final).*

20. A worker is remunerated under the Rowan Premium Bonus System with a guaranteed time-rate of 1*s*. 6*d*. per hour.

His time-cards for the week ended 5th December, 1934, show :

32 hours on Job No. 82; 6 hours on Job No. 83; 10 hours on Job. No. 84. The times allowed under Rowan Premium Bonus System are :

For Job No. 82, 36 hours; Job No. 83, 5 hours; Job No. 84, 12 hours. Calculate the wages cost of each job, and state the worker's gross wages for the week.—*Corporation of Accountants (Final).*

21. (*a*) State the advantages and disadvantages of the piece-work system of wages payment.

(*b*) Two piece-workers X and Y are paid at the rate of 4*s*. per article produced. In 36 hours X produced 18 articles and Y 24 articles. The material cost is 12*s*. per article and the oncost is 1*s*. per hour.

Prepare a statement showing which worker is more profitable to the employer.

22. An argument used by workers against the Rowan Premium Bonus System is that the same bonus can be obtained by a less efficient as by a highly efficient worker, *e.g.*, if hourly rate of wages is 2*s*. and standard time is 30 hours, a worker who performs the work in 21 hours is entitled to the same bonus as a worker who does so in 9 hours.

Prepare a statement to show whether this contention is correct or not, and give your opinion regarding same.—*Corporation of Accountants (Final).*

23. Name six different methods of computing the wages to be paid to workmen and describe fully two of these methods and state to which industry they are particularly appropriate.—*Institute of Cost and Works Accountants (Inter.).*

24. What are the advantages, or disadvantages, of the time basis of remunerating labour, and to what extent do you consider the interests of employer and employee are at variance under such a system ?—*Institute of Cost and Works Accountants (Inter.).*

25. A worker under the Halsey method of remuneration has a day rate of 54*s*. 11*d*. per week of 47 hours, plus a cost of living bonus of 12*s*. per week. He is given an 8 hours task to perform, which he accomplishes in 6 hours. He is allowed 30 per cent. of the time saved as premium bonus. What would be his total hourly rate of earnings ?—*Institute of Cost and Works Accountants (Inter.).*

CHAPTER IX

OVERHEAD

CLASSIFICATION

IT has been mentioned previously that Overhead may be analysed into four groups of expense, viz. Production, Administration, Selling, and Distribution. Manufacturing Overhead expense comprises the production expenses and all administration expenses other than the proportion allocated to selling and distribution. Manufacturing Overhead may be classified into three sections :

1. Indirect material.
2. Indirect labour.
3. Indirect expenses.

These three sections cover all the Overhead chargeable to production up to the time the finished products are placed in the Finished Stock Store, or are ready for despatch.

Fixed and Variable Charges.—In considering the method of accounting for Overhead, it is necessary to separate Fixed Charges and Variable Charges, sometimes referred to as Fixed and Floating Overhead (or Oncost) respectively.

Fixed Charges are expenses that do not vary substantially, or at all, with the volume of production, *e.g.* rent, rates, taxes (Schedule A), insurance, depreciation of plant, machinery, buildings and fixtures, and, if included in cost, interest on capital values used in the factory.

Variable Charges are expenses that fluctuate from period to period, not necessarily in direct proportion to the volume of production, but largely so, and in sympathy with it, *e.g.* indirect wages, power, repairs.

There is no hard and fast line between fixed and variable overhead, the distinction is often entirely dependent upon the *particular conditions* in any given undertaking.

Exceptional Expenses or Losses.—Generally these will be treated best by transferring them direct to Profit and Loss Account in order not to disturb the normal comparisons of cost. For example : Loss by damage through flood; removal of plant; abnormal wastage and spoilage of a large quantity of goods through an exceptional mistake; damage by fire not recovered by insurance; etc.

The Object of Classifying Overhead.—The sub-division of Overhead is made to enable the management to compare and to control the cost of each group with that for preceding periods, processes, jobs, or units, as well as with the budget, or predetermined estimated expense costs for the period under review.

The Use of Standing Order Numbers.—To make the classification effective for this purpose, it is necessary to provide a scheme for the collation and analysis of Overhead, and the headings under which the analysis is made should be clearly defined for everybody in the works who may be concerned.

The most usual method is to use a nomenclature of Standing Order Numbers, sometimes called Syllabus Order Numbers, because they are enumerated in a permanent list, or schedule, detailing the items to be included under each heading. Headings of expense are decided upon by the management, and each is given a distinguishing number, which is used to simplify charging, and to permit of easy reference in the accounting. The related types of expense may be numbered in groups, identified by a symbol, which is quoted with the number; or straight numbering may be used. For example :

Repairs—the numbers might be arranged under the group symbol R, then, say :

R. 11. Repairs to buildings.
R. 20.   ,,   ,, plant.

And, as it is necessary to further identify such expenses, sectionally, the scheme may be extended thus :

R. 11. Repairs to buildings (foundry).
R. 12.   ,,   ,, power-house.
R. 13.   ,,   ,, machine shop.
R. 14.   ,,   ,, office building,
            etc.
R. 21. Repairs to steam plant.
R. 22.   ,,   ,, transmission plant.
R. 23.   ,,   ,, electric power plant,
            etc.

Similarly, other symbols and numbers can be allotted to other items of expense. A separate series should be used for expenditure of a capital nature.

If straight numbering is used, the prefix S.O. (Standing Order) may be used for all expense numbers, to keep them distinct from Works Order, Production Order, or Job Order numbers, which are generally used to identify work other than that chargeable as an expense. Standing Works Order Numbers are sometimes used in connection with production in some factories, but more usually Standing Order Numbers are employed to designate expense accounts.

Whatever scheme of account numbering is adopted, items can be easily identified with departments by giving each department a number which can be used with the expense numbers, thus : S.O. 50/6 might mean, say, Repairs in shop No. 6.

A Scheme of Standing Order Numbers.—Every factory using expense numbers has its own particular scheme of nomenclature for standing order numbers, compiled to suit the needs of its cost accounting organisation.

Too minute an analysis should be avoided, as excessive detail may encumber supervision, and create clerical work which is more expensive than is commensurate with the advantages secured. As regards the scheme of numbering below, it should be observed that the analysis may be condensed, or expanded, according to the needs of the management.

Standing Order numbers may be used for capital additions and for overhead expenses. For convenience, both classes of expenditure are included in the scheme of suggested symbols and numbers given below. These, of course, are quite arbitrary.

Capital Additions (designated by *the symbol N*.).

N. 1 Series (capital expenditure on buildings) :

N. 11.   Power house.
N. 12.   Foundry building.
N. 13.   Automatics.
N. 14.   Assembling shop.
N. 15.   Office buildings, etc.

N. 2 Series (service plants) :

N. 21.   Steam plant.
N. 22.   Generators.
N. 23.   Heating buildings equipment, etc.

N. 3 Series (machinery) :

N. 31.   Milling machines.
N. 32.   Lathes, etc.

Note : The cost of fixing new plant is capitalised.

N. 4 Series (power transmission) :
- N. 41.   Shafting.
- N. 42.   Pulleys,

> etc.

N. 5 Series (internal transport) :
- N. 51.   Trolley tracks, overhead.
- N. 52.   Belt conveyors.
- N. 53.   Trucks,

> etc.

N. 6 Series (loose tools and gauges) :
- N. 61.   Gauges.
- N. 62.   Thermometers, pyrometers, etc.
- N. 63.   Small machine tools,

> etc.

N. 7 Series (fixtures and fittings) :
- N. 71.   In works offices.
- N. 72.   ,, administration offices.
- N. 73.   ,, stores.
- N. 74.   ,, warehouse,

> etc.

Factory Overhead.—*The symbol R.* designates repairs and maintenance.

R. 1 Series (repairs and maintenance of buildings) :
- R. 11.   Power-house.
- R. 12.   Foundry.
- R. 13.   Automatic shop.
- R. 18.   Offices,

> etc.

R. 2 Series (repairs and maintenance of Plant and machinery, including the cost of moving plant and refixing) :
- R. 21.   Steam boilers.
- R. 22.   Steam pipe-lines.
- R. 23.   Milling machines.
- R. 24.   Steam press,

> etc.

R. 3 Series (repairs to office machines, time-recorders, etc.) :
The symbol W. indicates idle time; lost time; overtime; material loss, waste, etc.

W. 1 Series (waiting and lost time) :
- W. 11. Machinery breakdown.
- W. 12. Waiting instructions.
- W. 13. Waiting for materials.
- W. 14. Expense of Idle Plant and Facilities disused owing to shortage of work. (See pp. 115, 151.)
- W. 15. Other waiting or idle time,
          etc.

W. 2 Series (material loss or waste) :
- W. 21. Faulty material.
- W. 22. Rejected articles.
- W. 23. Stores discrepancies,
          etc.

W. 3 Series (overtime, holidays, sickness) :
          and so on.

The Symbol S. for Shop Sundries :
- S. 11. Oiling and cleaning machinery, etc.
- S. 12. Shop cleaning, removal of scrap, etc.
- S. 13. Consumable shop stores.
- S. 14. Perishable tools,
          etc.

The Symbol T. for indirect labour, etc. :
- T. 1. Stocktaking and stores physical audit.
- T. 2. Inspection and testing.
- T. 3. Experimental and research.
- T. 4. Timekeeping and gate control.
- T. 5. Shop clerical work.
- T. 6. Drawing office expenses.

The Symbol A. for administration expenses :
- A. 1. Executive and management salaries.
- A. 2. Office rent, rates, etc.
- A. 3. Office upkeep.
- A. 4. Office supplies,
          etc.

The Symbol C. for selling expenses :
- C. 1. Sales office expenses.
- C. 2. Travellers' remuneration.
- C. 3. Catalogues, circulars, price-lists.
- C. 4. Estimating and tendering.

C. 5.   Press advertising.
C. 6.   Annual Exhibition expenses,
             etc.

The Symbol D. for distribution expenses :
D. 1.   Warehouse expenses.
D. 2.   Packing expense.
D. 3.   Loading expense.
D. 4.   Delivery by own vehicles.
D. 5.   Carriage and freight outwards,
             etc.

An Alternative Scheme.—Omit the group symbols, and number each item consecutively, the number having an identifying prefix, such as S.O. Each group could be distinguished by a series, *e.g.* S.O. 1 to 20 for capital additions; S.O. 50 to 100 for maintenance; S.O. 150 to 160 for waiting time, and so on.

If each department or shop is also numbered, by adding the shop number to the S.O. number, when possible, correct charging is secured. Thus, S.O. 58/12 might mean, say, repairs to plant in shop 12.

Items of Expense.—A list of specific items of expense which may have to be considered and accounted for is given below for the benefit of those who are unacquainted with the details of expense analysis. Special notice should be taken that in some cases certain classes of expense may be apportionable to more than one expense number, according to the incidence of the expense.

A. *Works Overhead (Fixed).*

1. Rent of buildings, land, storage space. When the manufacturer owns the property, an interest charge equivalent to rent may be made, or sometimes the Schedule A Valuation for Income Tax (Property Tax) is used.

2. Rates imposed by local authorities.

3. Insurance of factory property, machinery and the fixed annual charge (if any) for automatic fire alarms, sprinkler installation.

4. Depreciation of plant and machinery.

5. Depreciation of buildings.

6. Salaries of managers and principal officials are often included.

7. Interest on capital to the extent (if any) it is included as an item of cost.   (See Chapter XI.)

I

B. *Works Overhead* (*Variable or Floating*).

1. Maintenance and repairs (which includes materials and labour used by maintenance service departments plus the overhead apportioned to these departments).

(*a*) of Machinery.

(*b*) of Buildings, roads, etc.

(*c*) of Boilers.

(*d*) of Generators.

(*e*) of Hydraulic plant.

(*f*) of Electric motors and controllers, starters, switches, etc.

(*g*) of Lighting equipment, wiring, conduits, switchboards, etc.; and alarms.

(*h*) of Power plant, power-lines.

(*i*) of Transmission plant, shafts, pulleys, counter shafts, belting.

(*j*) of Material transport and handling plant, hoists, cranes, elevators, overhead trolley-lines, belt conveyor systems, trucks, etc.

(*k*) of Stores fixtures, bins, scales, etc.

(*l*) of Steam plant, compressed-air plant, etc., including pipe-lines.

(*m*) of Furnaces.

(*n*) of Dies, power-press, and foot-press.

(*o*) of Tools for turning, butting, milling, boring; power knives, saws, shears; chucks and tool holders.

(*p*) of Office equipment, office machines of all kinds, etc. (Works).

2. Oiling and cleaning machinery, shafting, motors, etc.

3. Miscellaneous operating supplies (consumable stores), *e.g.* cotton waste, cloths for wiping; belt dressing, fasteners, etc.; brushes for sweeping, dusting, scrubbing; oil, benzine, emery and sand paper, carborundum dust; cleaning compounds; lubricating oils, greases; cutting oils and compounds.

4. Perishable tools, small taps, dies, drills, files, emery wheels, polishing wheels, oil stones, saw blades, reamers, etc.

5. Waiting time (= idle time.)

(*a*) Machinery breakdown.

(*b*) Power supply cessation.

(*c*) Waiting for work instructions.

(d) Accident to workers.

(e) Waiting for material.

(f) Waiting for tools.

(g) Workers' time lost through air raid warnings, etc.

6. Holidays and sickness with pay.

7. Stocktaking and inventory physical check expenses.

8. Inspection and testing.

9. (a) Experimental and research work. (b) Designing for production. (c) Drawing office expense.

10. Timekeeping and gate control.

11. Supervision; foremen, assistants, superintendents; administration.

12. Shop clerical work, labour and supplies of works stationery.

13. Shop labouring, general indirect; shop cleaning, etc.

14. Stores expenses; carriage inwards (sometimes); storekeeper and assistants, and other charges, e.g. branding, measuring and cutting off materials for issue; but not expenses particular to a specific order.

15. Training and instructing trainees (wages and materials, less value of productive work).

16. Welfare; ambulance and first aid; dining facilities.

17. Waste—spoilt and lost materials, stock discrepancies, faulty work, etc.

18. Insurance, (a) national; (b) compensation; (c) employers' liability; (d) machinery breakdown; (e) war risks (stores, materials and work in progress).*

19. Overtime expenses. (See observations below.)

20. Power of all kinds; process fuel.

21. Steam service.

22. Lighting.

23. Heating.

24. Other services, e.g. fire protection, internal transport.

25. Transport of materials to the Works.

26. Air raid precaution expenses, including a proportion of capital expenditure for shelters, camouflage, etc., less Government grant.

* But not War Damage Act Contributions which are declared to be capital expenditure and are not admitted as a revenue expense. They should be debited direct to Profit and Loss Account, being in the nature of a capital levy.

C. *Administration Overhead* (*Fixed and Variable*).

    1. Salaries of executives, managers, etc.

    2. Clerical expenses.

    3. Office rent, rates, insurances. (Excluding those applicable to the Works.)

    4. Office lighting, heating, and cleaning.

    5. Office repairs and maintenance of buildings.

    6. Office repairs of equipment; machines.

    7. Stationery, postage, telephones.

    8. Legal charges.

    9. Financing charges.

   10. Investigations.

D. *Selling Overhead* (*Fixed and Variable*).

    1. Sales office expenses.

    2. Travellers' salaries, commission and expenses.

    3. Advertising; catalogues, price-lists; samples.

    4. Discounts allowed.

    5. Estimating; preparing drawings and designs for tenders.

E. *Distribution Overhead* (*Fixed and Variable*).

    1. Warehousing of finished goods; including War Risks and other insurance premiums.

    2. Packing and warehouse trucking.

    3. Loading; loading conveyors, charges for cranes, hoists, etc.

    4. Delivery—upkeep and running of vehicles; outward freight and carriage, except that charged to customers.

The Distribution of Overhead.—The object of classifying the overhead expenses is to facilitate their correct distribution to various departments, and thence to the cost units of production.

The procedure may be shown in the form of a general plan :

Fig. 41.

1. All overhead expenses are collected under the separate headings of expense (Standing Order Numbers).
2. All these separate totals of expense are apportioned to Production Departments (Shops) and Service Departments.
3. The total of each Service Department is apportioned on a suitable basis in accordance with the services rendered to the Production Departments that use, or are entitled to use, the services.
4. The total Overhead for each Production Department is divided equitably, so that every works order, or cost unit of production, is charged with its share of the expense of each department, or shop, through which it passes.

OBSERVATIONS ON CERTAIN KINDS OF EXPENSE

Works Expenses :

Estimating and Drawing Office Expenses may often be apportionable as between Works and Selling Overhead.

Royalties.—(*a*) Production. These can often be charged direct instead of in Works overhead expenses. (*b*) Selling (see p. 116).

Depreciation and Interest.—See next Chapter.

The Cost of Moving and Refixing Plant.—This is a works overhead expense and is so treated on the grounds that the new fixing outlay cannot have a longer life than the machine itself, and is sufficiently represented in capital by the balance of the original fixing charge. The cost of fixing new plant is usually capitalised and written down with the plant itself.

Rent Charge of Premises Owned.—As no rent is payable, it is usual to include some charge in the Overhead. This may be an amount equal to interest on the capital value, at a rate agreed by the management. Allowance for such an amount taken into cost must be made when reconciling with the Financial Accounts. When one factory is owned, and another is rented, the course suggested is desirable to secure comparable costs of products in each. This is the same principle as applies when comparing costs of products made by machines of different capital cost.

Inspection.—Whilst this is generally a works expense apportioned to the departments concerned, it is, sometimes, the practice, when convenient, to make this a direct charge to specific jobs. The matter largely depends on the type of product.

Tool-Setting.—If this expense is necessary for a specific order, it may be regarded as a direct charge. When a number of orders can be dealt with on a machine with one setting, the expense is included in the overhead rates.

Wages of Engineers and Millwrights of the Repair Service engaged in repairing machines must be apportioned to departments, or centres, and then to the machines. The cost can thus be included in the machine overhead. Caution is necessary when this staff is engaged on work of a capital nature; their time should then be charged to the appropriate Standing Order, or Account, Numbers for the Capital Accounts concerned.

Overtime and Special Night Work Wages.—When overtime or night work is necessary owing to the special desire of a customer to have the job completed or rushed through within the time specified, the extra payment for overtime is legitimately charged to the job as direct labour.

When, however, the overtime is regular, or intermittent but recurring, and is for the purpose of generally increasing the output of the factory, *e.g.*, to keep up with stock requirements or orders generally, the cost of the overtime is charged to Works Overhead Expense Account. A standing order number is provided for this.

Distinction should be made between special intermittent overtime and night-work and that which is regular and budgeted. The latter can be recovered in overhead rates; the former if not chargeable to a particular job, or if not suitable for inclusion in overhead will be written off to Profit and Loss Account.

Expense of Idle Machines and Facilities.—This, if due to shortage of work, as in a period of trade depression, should be recorded under a Standing Order Number and written off direct to Profit and Loss Account, otherwise idle time is included in overhead.* Hence Idle Time and Idle Facilities must not be confused. The position is discussed on pp. 150–151 and p. 154.

Carriage and Cartage Inwards (of Stores Materials).—This is usually treated as part of the Cost of the materials, and not as Overhead. (Distinguish transport of materials to the works, and internal transport facilities which are items of works overhead.)

Administration, Selling, and Distribution Expenses.—Separate totals of these three groups of expense must be made. Sometimes it is the particular conditions in a given business which decide the heading under which certain items are to be included.

An important aspect of the separate analysis of Factory and other overheads is that Work in Progress has to bear its proportionate charge for expenses applicable to manufacturing, *i.e.* all factory or works expense and a fair apportionment of general management expense, but with strict exclusion of any expense relating to selling and distribution. The latter expenses are applicable only to marketing, and are chargeable therefore against sales of finished products. The marketing and delivery expenses can usually only be apportioned on a basis determined by factors involved in marketing.

* Payments for time lost through air raids may be included in Works Overheads, preferably departmentally.

Examples of items appearing under the respective headings are as follows :

Administration.	Distribution.	Selling.
General Office Expenses.	Warehouse Rent.	*Advertising, Samples, Folders.
Managing Directors' Remuneration (if necessary apportioned).	Warehouse Labour and other Expenses.	Rent and other Expenses of Selling Office and Showrooms ; *Royalties.
Professional Fees.	Depot Expenses.	Travellers' Salary and Commission.
General Stationery.	*Finished Stock, Waste and Loss.	Market Research.
Bank Charges.	*Carriage.	Certain Trade Subscriptions.
Rents, etc., of Office.	*Packages and Containers for Dispatch Purposes.	Tendering and Estimating.
	Finished Stock Insurances.	*Bad Debts.

* See comments below.

The following observations on a few items must be noted :

Finished Stock Waste and Loss.   Distinguish between

(a) Unavoidable waste due to inherent qualities, *e.g.* shrinkage, evaporation, breaking bulk.

(b) Deterioration due to lapse of time, obsolescence, and abnormal damage or abnormal loss.

(c) Avoidable waste caused by faulty handling, storing, etc.

Losses like group (b) are probably best written off direct to Profit and Loss, but (a) and (c) included as part of the distribution overhead.

Carriage on Goods Dispatched.   When chargeable to customers this is a direct charge on individual orders and excluded from overhead ; otherwise it is a distribution expense, although by some it is included in Selling Overhead, being regarded as an inducement for buying.

Carriage on Returns of faulty goods due to bad manufacture is a Works Expense ; but if due to bad packing is a Distribution Expense.

Bad Debts.   When a fairly regular percentage of bad debts is incurred this item may be rightly included in Selling Overhead ; but when exceptional or abnormal at long irregular intervals is probably better excluded, and written off to Profit and Loss.

Royalties and other specific charges against particular lines, *e.g.* Sales Royalty on a patented article, are best shown separately so that they may be charged against the product concerned.

Packing, Wrapping, etc., essential for conveying an article in a way necessary for supply to the consumer is a Production Expense, but other forms of packing, casing, etc., are Distribution Expenses.

Advertising by Permanent Signs, Neon and Electric Signs, etc. Capital Outlay is generally apportioned over the estimated effective life of the sign. Special Shop Displays and similar expense will be charged in Overhead. The expense can be spread over a longer period than a year if the expense is still found to be effective.

General Administration Expense, sometimes called " Establishment Charges," is generally added as a percentage of total manufacturing cost, but sometimes as a charge per unit when unit output costing is applicable. It has no relation to such factors as are used for apportionment of factory expense.

Distribution Expense and Selling Expense.—Almost all industries have different problems affecting the allocation of these expenses. Consideration of sales planning and delivery differs in the case of (a) those businesses which rely on orders taken before production, *e.g.* heavy industries, such as steel works, makers of boilers, ships, locomotives, bridges, etc., who produce to customers' requirements. (b) Businesses selling from stock, *e.g.* tinned foods, medicines, soap, chocolate, hosiery, motors, etc.

As to the identification of selling and delivery expenses, it is usual to regard these as all expenses incurred on goods after they have been placed in the warehouse or finished stock store, or handed over to the Despatch Department.

Selling Expense is usually allocated on a flat rate basis as a percentage of sales value, or proportionate to effort, by lines.

Delivery Expense as an amount per unit, per unit of weight or of quantity.

For Control Purposes, however, an analysis of Selling Expenses is often made : (a) by classes, (b) by areas, districts or territories, and (c) by salesmen or agents.

. Where possible, allocation is made direct to particular products or groups, otherwise being apportioned according to sales turnover of each in value, numbers, or quantities, whichever is the more equitable. Modern sorting devices and tabulating machines greatly facilitate this work in the case of large users.

In some undertakings selling and delivery overhead is charged against each line of article, pack or group, or sometimes each area, and by sales analysis the net profit or loss is obtained by using a schedule as follows :

Articles or Area.	Works Cost.	Administration Overhead.	Selling Expenses.	Distribution Expenses.	Total.	Sales.	Net Profit or Loss.

In suitable cases separate analyses of Wholesale and Retail Sales may be undertaken.

Expenditure Excluded from Cost.

It is hardly necessary to observe that various expenditures on capital additions, capital losses and payments in the nature of disbursement of profits cannot be included properly in manufacturing or operational costs.   Examples are national taxation (income tax, national defence contribution, excess profits tax); expenses of raising capital, discount on loans or debentures; bonuses to directors and employees voted at annual meetings, which are appropriations of profits; and losses on investments.

It is regarded as undesirable to include financing expenses, and exceptional losses of a non-recurring nature, *e.g., abnormal* manufacturing loss or waste through misadventure.

Expenditures and Losses Inadmissible to Cost of Government Contracts have been specially mentioned in various official reports and publications both in Great Britain and the United States of America.   These include not only items mentioned in the preceding paragraph, but others, which, although normally included in general commercial costs, are not regarded as applicable or appropriate to the performance of specific government contracts. The following list comprises items named in various official publications issued in U.S.A. or this country.   For the guidance of students the items have been suitably grouped, and suggested reasons added :

1. *Interest on Capital,* borrowed or otherwise, however represented, including Bank Interest charges. Interest is regarded as an element of profit covered by the profit allowed on the contract.   In effect, the interest on borrowed capital constitutes the lender's share in the profit representing the

return on the money virtually invested, and the balance of the profit on that borrowed capital is the share due to the contractor for his management of the money and production. When looked at in this light interest is clearly not an item of cost.

2. *Capital Assets, Losses of*, arising from sale, exchange or uninsured destruction. Fees of assessors and advisers on such destruction losses (fire, bomb damage, etc.) come under this heading, being unrelated to operating cost.

3. Amortization or Writing Down of *unrealised appreciation* of assets values, *e.g.*, Plant and Buildings.

4. *Losses on other contracts.*

5. *Legal and Accounting Fees* specifically incurred in connection with re-organisations; security issues; issues of capital stock or shares; patent registrations and infringements; anti-trust litigation (U.S.A.); prosecution of claims of any kind, including taxation matters, against the government.

6. *Life Assurance Premiums* on the lives of officers (other than insurances against risks from explosions and other risks connected with manufacturing but not risks from enemy action).

7. *Stamp Duty, Taxes* (*U.S.A.*) *and Expenses* on issues and transfers of capital stock, shares and bonds, etc.

8. *Investments*, Losses on.

9. *Finance Charges*, discounts on bonds, debentures, etc.

10. Expenses, maintenance, repair, and depreciation of *unemployed assets* often referred to as excess facilities (plant, buildings, etc.), other than reasonable and necessary stand-by facilities.

12. *Strikes and Lock-Outs*, extraordinary expenses arising from.

13. *Fines* and penalties.

14. *Taxes*, in the nature of income-tax, national defence contribution, excess profits tax.

15. *Commissions*, bonuses and special premiums under whatever name, paid in connection with negotiations for, or procurement of a Government contract.

16. *Reserves for Contingencies.*

17. Contributions to Pension Funds other than annual ones to an approved contributory Pension Fund Scheme.

18. Pensions to ex-employees killed in action.

19. *Donations* other than subscriptions to regular trade associations. Contributions to *local* hospitals and certain charitable institutions are usually admitted to the extent that they constitute an ordinary and necessary business expense owing to the probable needs of employees arising from their work.

20. Entertainment expenses.

21. *Bad Debts* and reserves therefor; and expenses of collection.

22. *General Advertising and Selling Expenses.* Certain such expenses not in the nature of *general* advertising or selling may be admissible.

23. *Royalties* paid to officers, employees or directors (U.S.A.) and to others in certain circumstances, are usually inadmissible, and particularly when in the nature of appropriation of profit. (Some justifiable and reasonable royalties are stated to be admissible.)

24. *Directors' Remuneration* in excess of approved limits dependent on the size of the business and responsibilities. Disproportionate or unreasonable increases since the war, and bonuses paid as a percentage of profits are usually not admitted as being in the nature of appropriations of profit.

25. *War Damage Contributions*, which by statute are capital expenditure.

26. *Patents*, cost of new, and costs of renewing of any not applicable to the contract supply.

All the above items (except item 25) are specially mentioned in an official publication by the United States Government promulgated as Treasury Order No. 5000 under Section 2 (*b*) of an Act of June 28th, 1940, and other provisions (commonly called the Vinson–Trammell Act). Many were referred to in the official publication entitled " Report (No. 2) of the Treasury Standing Committee on Co-ordination of Departmental Action in regard to Contracts (Colwyn Committee)," published by H.M. Stationery Office, 31st October, 1918.

EXAMINATION QUESTIONS

[*Note :* in this book " Overhead " is used instead of the term " Oncost."]

1. Define " oncost." Give twelve examples of such expenses.—*Royal Society of Arts (Advanced).*

2. In valuing Work in Progress at stock-taking, is it right to include Oncost Expense in the valuation, or only Wages and Material Cost? Give reasons for your answer.—*London Association of Accountants (Final).*

3. A part of the products of a factory is of a seasonal nature, *e.g.,* Christmas puddings. How would you propose to apportion Oncosts to such products?—*Royal Society of Arts (Advanced).*

4. At a large factory it is decided to grant a week's paid holiday annually to every industrial worker, and it is being considered whether the works shall close down for a week or each employee be permitted to choose his own week for the holiday, subject to the general convenience of the works. You are asked to estimate the relative costs of the two schemes. Describe fully on what lines you would proceed to construct your estimates.—*Royal Society of Arts (Advanced).*

5. How would you treat the following expenses in your Cost Accounts :

(*a*) Advertising expenses; (*b*) Apprentices' premiums; (*c*) Fire insurance premium; (*d*) Workmen's Compensation Act Insurance premium; (*e*) Salesmen's Commission; (*f*) Carriage charges?—*Royal Society of Arts (Advanced).*

6. A manufacturer, working at high pressure, incurred considerable expenditure in over-time wages. Assume that the direct wages method of allocating Oncost is in use in this case, what effect do over-time wages have upon this method? Do you consider that the additional payment for overtime should be regarded as direct or productive wages, or should they be treated as Oncost? Give your reasons.—*London Association of Accountants (Final).*

7. State the various sources from which Oncost expenses arise and what means you would adopt for their collection, prior to allocating them to departments or absorbing them on the products.—*Royal Society of Arts (Advanced).*

8. In all large works, wages expenditure is incurred on engineers and millwrights engaged continuously on repairing machinery, running the power plant, and maintaining the general equipment of the works in good order. They are also frequently engaged on work, the cost of which is charged to Capital and not against Revenue. Their services extend to all the manufacturing departments. State very briefly how you would secure weekly information as to

(*a*) Capital expenditure.
(*b*) Wages expenditure incurred in connection with the power plant.
(*c*) Wages expenditure chargeable to each Manufacturing Department.

London Association of Accountants (Final).

9. The following figures give the experience of two manufacturers as regards the relation of Bad Debts to Sales during five separate years :

	1.	2.	3.	4.	5.
A.	£	£	£	£	£
Sales	127,500	113,460	140,989	150,604	151,728
Bad Debts	—	757	—	—	1,592
B.					
Sales	73,846	64,504	69,211	71,409	79,207
Bad Debts	494	407	652	729	648

Would you reckon Bad Debts as part of the Selling, Delivery, and General Administration expense in both cases ?—*London Association of Accountants* (*Final*).

10. The following is a summary of the expenditure of a business for 1929, viz. :

	£	£
Materials consumed . . . . : . .		24,927
Direct Wages—		
A Department	11,469	
B ,, ...	7,892	
C ,, ...	10,974	
		30,335
		£55,262
Oncost—		
A Department	16,280	
B ,, ...	3,426	
C ,, ...	9,842	
		29,548
Total Manufacturing Cost		84,810
Selling, Delivery and General Administration Charges		16,962
Carriage outward		4,728
Royalties on Golf Balls sold		746
Bad Debts		250
Discounts allowed to customers . . .		2,700
		£110,196

Can you suggest any reasons for the four last items being separately stated and not included in the Selling, Delivery, and General Administration Charges ?—*London Association of Accountants* (*Final*).

11. Do you consider Bad Debts to be part of the Oncost of a business ? Give reasons for your answer.—*London Association of Accountants* (*Final*).

12. The Selling and Distribution Expense of a manufacturing business is usually provided for in individual costs by a percentage applied to the total Works Cost of each article. Is there any special reason for so doing ? Why is it necessary to distinguish between the Oncost expenditure of manufacturing departments and the expenditure involved in marketing the products ?—*London Association of Accountants* (*Final*).

13. What do you understand by fixed oncost and floating oncost ? In a time of exceptional trading depression when selling prices are below the cost of production, what policy would you recommend a manufacturer to adopt in relation to Oncost rates when in keen competition with other suppliers ?—*London Association of Accountants* (*Final*).

14. How would you deal with the following matters in stores records, and what procedure would you adopt :

(*a*) Gain or loss in weight through climatic conditions.
(*b*) Breakages in stores.
(*c*) Scrap returned to store.
(*d*) Excess materials requisitioned returned to store without an advice ?—*Institute of Cost and Works Accountants* (*Inter.*).

15. Explain the term " Standing Works Order," and give a representative list of such orders.—*Institute of Cost and Works Accountants* (*Inter.*).

16. Detail the main headings of selling and distribution expenses in any industry with which you are familiar and say how you would propose to recover them.—*Institute of Cost and Works Accountants (Final)*.

17. At the present moment a considerable expense is incurred in preparing for tenders for contracts, many of which are not obtained. What charges are involved and how are these expenses dealt with in your cost accounts ?—*Institute of Cost and Works Accountants (Final)*.

18. Prepare a system of symbols whereby the direct and indirect expenses of production may readily be distributed to the proper location for recovery.—*Institute of Cost and Works Accountants (Final)*.

19. Overhead expenses fall into various groups; name these groups and give examples of the expenses of which they are comprised.—*Institute of Cost and Works Accountants (Final)*

20. Explain how overtime payment is made up in any industry with which you are familiar. Fully describe the method of payment as it concerns—daily overtime, intermittent late working and night work. Under what circumstances is overtime payment chargeable as direct wages or alternatively as overheads ?—*Institute of Cost and Works Accountants (Inter.)*.

21. Certain steel and other bar work is kept in the stores and a sawing machine is installed so that requisite lengths are cut, as required, before serving out to shops. Show how you would ensure the cost of handling and cutting being added to the issue price.—*Institute of Cost and Works Accountants (Inter.)*.

22. Along with materials stocked for customers' requirements certain materials belonging to customers are also stocked. Should both bear the same charges for storing and handling or how would you differentiate between them ? What expenses would be affected ?—*Institute of Cost and Works Accountants (Inter.)*.

23. A manufacturing concern whose selling expenses are greatly divergent for various products requires a suitable basis for allocation. What method would you recommend ?—*Institute of Cost and Works Accountants (Inter.)*.

24. A certain organisation finds it necessary to divide its expenses under three headings, viz.:

Factory Expense, Commercial Expense, and Erection Expense.
Under which heading would you place the following :
Shortages discovered on site; Transport; National Health Insurance; Advertising; Estimating; Design; Depreciation of Plant Machinery ?

Would any such expense fall under more than one of the headings specified ?—*Institute of Cost and Works Accountants (Inter.)*.

25. In what circumstances would you propose that the bonus paid for overtime or for night shift should be charged to :

(*a*) the particular jobs worked upon during the overtime or night shift periods;
(*b*) the shop overhead expenditure;
(*c*) general overhead expenditure ?

Institute of Cost and Works Accountants (Inter.).

26. Spoilt work is inevitable in most factories, but unless kept under control may tend to become excessive. What method of keeping this in check would you adopt ?—*Institute of Cost and Works Accountants (Inter.)*.

27. A serious fire occurs at a works and it is found impossible to recover more than half the value of the damage. What effect will this have upon the subsequent costs ?—*Institute of Cost and Works Accountants (Final)*.

28. Define—

    (a) Standing Works Order,
    (b) Fixed Oncost,
    (c) Unit of Production,
    (d) Budgetary Control,
    (e) Direct Labour,
    (f) Terminal Costs,
    (g) Multiple Costs,
    (h) Pre-determined Costs.
Corporation of Accountants (Final).

29. Define—

    Chargeable Expenses,
    Selling Expenses,
    Fixed Oncost,
    Fluctuating Oncost,
    Administration Expenses,

and give three examples of items which would be included under each heading.—*Corporation of Accountants (Final).*

30. A manufacturer groups his expenditure for costing purposes under the following main headings : (a) Cost of Manufacture ; (b) Manufacturing Expense ; (c) Administration and Selling Expenses. (i) Enumerate the items you would place under each heading, taking a *manufacturing* business of your own selection. (ii) Do you consider it necessary or advisable to elaborate the main headings as set out, and if so, to what extent ?—*Chartered Secretaries (Final).*

31. From the following particulars prepare a Profit and Loss Account in such form as you consider would be most useful for the Costing Department.

	£		£
Opening Stock :		Carriage on Purchases .	550
Raw Materials . .	24,500	,, on Sales . .	950
Finished Goods . .	5,450	Rent and Rates (a) . .	3,360
Closing Stock :		Fuel, Gas, etc. (a) . .	960
Raw Materials . .	21,450	Repairs to Plant . .	650
Finished Goods . .	3,900	Depreciation of Machinery	1,050
Wages :		Repairs to Premises (a) .	800
Productive . .	17,350	Office Expenses . .	1,970
Non-productive . .	3,250	Purchases of Material .	73,650
Salaries . . .	3,400	Sales	124,700

One-sixteenth of items marked (a) to be taken in respect of the Offices as distinct from the Works.—*Chartered Accountants (Final).*

32. Under what circumstances do you consider that Selling and Distributive Expenses should be brought into Cost Accounts ? What items of expenditure would come in that category ?—*Incorporated Accountants (Inter.).*

33. Define :—(a) Fixed Oncost; (b) Fluctuating Oncost.
State six items of expense which would be included under each heading. —*Corporation of Accountants (Final).*

34. Prepare a Schedule showing allocation of Oncost between three departments of a factory, viz. :—A, B, and C. The expenses for the year ended 31st March, 1934, extracted from the financial books are as follows :—

		£
Electric Light	. . . .	250
Electric Power	. . . .	640
Heating	. . . .	300
Workmen's Compensation Insurance	. . . .	140
Fire Insurance on Plant	. . . . .	64
Depreciation on Plant at 10 per cent. per annum	. .	300
Plant Repairs	. . . .	256
Material handling charges	. . . . .	500
Rent and Rates	. . . . . .	750

You also obtain the following information :—

	"A" Dept.	"B" Dept.	"C" Dept.
Direct Wages on Pro- duction . . .	£2,400	£1,600	£3,000
Floor Space . .	30 per cent.	20 per cent.	50 per cent.
Direct Wage Earners .	20 ,,	17 ,,	33 ,,
Materials Used . .	£2,000	£2,000	£4,000
Value of Plant . .	£1,000	£500	£1,500
	(20 machines)	(12 machines)	(32 machines)

Calculate the total oncost allocated to each department as a per-centage on the direct wages, and show the basis of your allocation for each item of expense.—*Corporation of Accountants (Final).*

35. On what bases would you analyse the following selling and dis-tribution expenses over a number of different types of commodities sold by a firm :—

Travellers' salaries and commissions; Expenses of warehouse; Storing finished goods; Advertising on a national scale; Expenses of own delivery vans; Sales manager's salary; Sales office expenses; Expenses of return-able packages; Expenses of provincial depots ?

—*Institute of Cost and Works Accountants (Final).*

CHAPTER X

OVERHEAD (*continued*)

DEPRECIATION AND INTEREST

Depreciation of Assets.—Depreciation is one of the items of fixed overhead, and adequate statistical data must be kept to ensure proper computation of the annual charge to be included in the accounts.

Depreciation represents the loss in value of the capital sunk in buildings, plant, machinery, and other equipment, due to normal and inevitable deterioration during the life of these assets. The term connotes a gradual though sure diminution in value through use. The cost of fixing new plant is capitalised and depreciated with the plant. The refixing of plant moved to another position is not capitalised but included in Overhead.

The definite determination of the exact amount of the loss due to depreciation is difficult, and various methods have been suggested and used.

It is necessary to distinguish between normal depreciation and other forms of loss in value of assets, thus :

Depreciation is the normal deterioration in value which takes place during the life of an asset. It is the loss in value due to use, abuse, wear and tear, the natural elements, or passage of time. ·

Obsolescence is the process by which an asset loses its value by falling into disuse, other than by wear and tear. The term is generally used to indicate loss of value of an asset, such as a machine or building, which is discarded before the expiration of its normal life, usually because of its inability to compete with one better adapted, or of more modern type. Thus the idea here is of sudden not gradual diminution in value. Again, if plant is scrapped before the costs of plant and fixing (when new) have all been written off, the balance of both capital value of the plant and the fixing of it are written off to Obsolescence Account.

Depletion is the exhaustion which takes place in natural resources by the removal of the valuable material inherent therein, *e.g.*, by the extraction of raw materials from mines, quarries, clay beds, gravel banks, forests and woodlands, oil, and other minerals from the ground, etc.

Inadequacy is a term that may be used to indicate the measure of inability of an asset, such as a machine, or building, to meet the demands of production made upon it.

The Fundamental Theory of Depreciation is parallel with the theory of investment, viz., that an investment should return interest whilst the principal is maintained undiminished until withdrawn. Applying this principle to buildings and machinery, it will be evident that, inasmuch as these assets will at some future time become valueless, despite the provision of maintenance and repairs, it is necessary, at regular intervals, to reserve from income an amount equal to the loss, so that at the time their useful life terminates there is a reserve on the books, which, with the residual value of the asset, will be equal to the original cost. Or, put in another way, there is sufficient reserve to replace the asset without diminishing the original capital. This reserve is represented by the depreciation which must be included as part of the cost of manufacturing. Before describing the methods for measuring depreciation, obsolescence may be considered with advantage.

Obsolescence, being of a different nature, is dealt with in another way. Obsolescence cannot, as a rule, be accurately anticipated, and its measurement is ascertained when it occurs.

In the case of a machine, an improved model, or a new invention, may render it necessary to make a change to enable the production costs to be kept low enough to be competitive.

Should loss occur through obsolescence, it is desirable that this be written off direct to Profit and Loss Account, in order that comparative costs may not be obscured by such an exceptional item. In some industries, however, obsolescence is anticipated and provided for to some extent by adding a suitable amount to the rate of depreciation. This latter method is approved by many accountants, and was expressly authorised by the British and American Governments in connection with contracts for war-time supplies requiring special plant, which, except for salvage, would have no substantial value to the manufacturer when the contracts were completed.

The Computation of Depreciation.—The determination of the exact life of an asset, and the actual rate of decrease in its value during that period is not possible, and reliance on estimates is necessary. There are several methods which are used :

(i) *The Straight-Line Method.*—This is a much used method, which is simple and effective. It requires little work for computing the amounts. The life of the machine, or other asset, is estimated, also the residual value. The cost, less the residual value (plus the cost of fixing, in the case of a new machine), divided by the estimated years of life determines the annual amount of depreciation to be charged. A separate calculation should be made for each machine. Allowance will be made for *regular* working of two or three shifts.

If, subsequently, capital additions are made to any asset, the rate for depreciation will be adjusted by dividing the sum of the addition and the then value of the asset by the anticipated remainder of years of life.

The use of a Plant and Machinery Register (Fig. 46) described on p. 125 facilitates the ascertainment of depreciation charges.

(ii) *The Reducing Balance Method.*—A constant percentage rate of depreciation is determined, which is written off the reducing balance of the capital value, the rate being so fixed that, at the end of the estimated life of the asset, only the residual scrap value remains. In favour of this method it is argued that a heavier depreciation charge is borne in the earlier years when repairs are lighter, and that the assumed increasing repair cost is counterbalanced, in later years, by the reduced annual charge of depreciation.

Figs. 42, 43 show the rates commonly applied when the reducing balance method is used. It not infrequently happens that, when these rates are used in the financial accounts, heavier rates are adopted in the Cost Accounts. When this occurs, the increase has to be written back for reconciliation purposes.

(iii) *The Sinking Fund Method* in which a fixed annual sum is charged against profits, and a similar amount is invested in gilt-edged securities, or, alternatively, in an endowment insurance policy. Interest on securities is re-invested, and thus added to the fund, so that the depreciation rate is somewhat lower than in the straight-line method.

(iv) *The Annuity Method* is generally used for leasehold buildings. A fixed annual sum is charged as depreciation, this

FIG. 42.

DEPRECIATION RATES

Asset.	Rate %.	Asset.	Rate %.
Buildings . . .	$2\frac{1}{2}$	Motor lorries . . .	15
Boilers	5	Steam ,, . . .	15
Electric cables . .	3	Motor omnibuses . .	20
,, motors . .	$7\frac{1}{2}$	,, vans . . .	20
,, dynamos . .	$7\frac{1}{2}$	Machines, general . .	$7\frac{1}{2}$–10
,, transformers .	$7\frac{1}{2}$	Shafting	5
Engines, Diesel . .	10	Tools	5
,, gas . . .	5	Type (printers) . .	10
,, steam . .	5	Rail wagons (own) .	$6\frac{1}{4}$
,, traction . .	20	Sulphuric acid plant .	15
Electric furnaces . .	$12\frac{1}{2}$	Farm machines (motor) .	15–$22\frac{1}{2}$
Patterns . . .	20–50	,, ,, (non-motor)	10

Note that foundations for machines are excluded.

FIG. 43.

TABLE SHOWING THE PERIOD REQUIRED TO REDUCE ORIGINAL COST TO 10 PER CENT. BY APPLYING DEPRECIATION RATES ON DIMINISHING BALANCE.

Rate.	Years (nearest).	Rate.	Years (nearest).	Rate.	Years (nearest).
Per cent.		Per cent.		Per cent.	
5	45	$12\frac{1}{2}$	17	30	7
6	37	15	14	$33\frac{1}{3}$	6
$7\frac{1}{2}$	30	20	10	40	5
10	22	25	8	—	—

being debited to Profit and Loss Account, and credited to the Lease Account. This sum is calculated at a rate which allows interest on the diminishing balance to be debited to the Lease Account each year. The leasehold is thus considered as an investment earning interest, which is credited to Profit and Loss Account.

(v) *The Production Method.*—This is not often used, because of the uncertainty of future output, and a varying rate and amount of depreciation has to be calculated and applied. The intention is to distribute more equally the depreciation charge over the cost of the output. During periods of normal production the rate of depreciation is lower, and the total sum charged is higher than when output is below normal. When output is low, the rate per unit is higher, but the total depreciation charge is lower.

Instead of using volume of production as the basis, productive hours may be used, but this may be unreliable, as provision is not made for the speed of operation, nor for the waiting, or idle, time.

(vi) *Revaluation Method.*—This method is sometimes used, particularly by builders and contractors. Plant is charged to a contract at book value, and, at the end of the contract, is revalued and credited, so that the contract bears the difference.

The method is applied to such items as Loose Tools, Horses, and, sometimes, Patterns. The procedure often adopted is to open a Loose Tools Account, etc., to which the cost is debited of all new tools (other than those purchased for a particular job which are debited direct to the job), and of repairs to tools. At the end of each accounting period, the amount of the revalued stock is credited, the difference on the account being the depreciation to be taken into expense accounts, thus :

FIG. 44.

LOOSE TOOLS STOCK ACCOUNT

Dr.   Cr.

19...			£	s.	d.	193...		c/d	£	s.	d.
Jan. 1	To Balance	b/f.	510	10	6	Dec. 31	By Stock on hand (per valuation) . .		641	14	0
Feb. 28	,, Purchases	12	51	0	9						
Mar. 31	,, Materials	17	32	1	3						
,,	,, Wages .	18	10	5	6	,,	,, Depreciation .	27	97	0	0
Nov. 30	,, Purchases	22	81	4	6						
Dec. 31	,, Materials	25	22	2	6						
,,	,, Wages .	26	31	9	0						
			£738	14	0				£738	14	0
19...											
Jan. 1	To Balance	b/d.	641	14	0						

The Use of a Plant and Machinery Register.

—In order that the total depreciation chargeable may be easily ascertained, it is a good plan to record particulars of each machine in a Plant Register, or Ledger, which may be in book or card form.

In Fig. 45 a form is provided for detailing particulars of machines of one class, a separate form being used for different groups. Each machine should be numbered to correspond with the entry in the register.

Another form of Plant Register is shown in Fig. 46. This makes provision for arriving at the value of plant in each shop, and the total amount of depreciation to be charged for each year. The amount of depreciation for each machine is also shown individually, which is useful when making separate machine rates. The total balance values are useful for Balance Sheet purposes.

Fig. 45.

MACHINERY REGISTER
Type of Machines. Turret Lathes.

Sheet No.: ....

Ref. No.	Description.	Date Purchased.	Cost.	Rate of Depreciation on Cost.	Amount per annum.	Remarks.
			£ s. d.		£ s. d.	
T.L. 1 T.L. 2 etc.	Herbert 7"	16 Jan. 19...	90 0 0	7½%	6 15 0	

Fig. 46.

PLANT REGISTER
Shop, or Department: .... Machine Shop No. 3.

Sheet No.: ....

Ref. No.	Description.	Date of Purchase.	Cost.	Rate of Depreciation.	1932.		1933.		etc.
					Depreciation.*	Balance Value.	Depreciation.*	Balance Value.	
			£		£ s. d.	£ s. d.	£ s. d.	£ s. d.	
MS 1	New Leader No. 3	16/1/19...	100	10%	10 — —	90 — —	9 — 9	81 19 3	
MS 2	10" Centre Capstan	21/2/19...	150	8%	12 — —	138 — —	11 — —	126 19 3	

* *Note.*—When using straight-line method the amount in these columns will remain constant.

· Interest on Capital

Interest on Capital as a Cost or Not.—Some accountants include interest as an element of cost, but many, probably the majority, do not. There are also instances where it would be difficult to argue against the inclusion of an interest charge, as, for example, when material has to be stored for lengthy periods, such as timber, which must be seasoned before use. If the timber is green when purchased, capital may be locked up for years; if timber, already seasoned, is bought, a supplier who has seasoned it must take the interest into account in his selling price, so that the purchaser then cannot avoid the interest charge.

The weight of opinion seems to be against the inclusion of interest in the cost accounts, and on the grounds of expediency alone it will usually be advisable to adopt that view in normal circumstances, so far as a general interest charge is concerned, but it is interesting to summarise the arguments which may be advanced both for and against including charges for interest on capital in the Cost Accounts :

In favour of including it.

(1) Interest is as much an item of cost as production wages. Wages are the reward of labour, interest the reward of capital. Human labour has often been displaced entirely by machinery, and the interest on the capital sunk in that machinery may be regarded as the " wages " of the machine. Interest is for the hire of capital.

(2) Real profit is not made until the " rent," or remuneration of capital, has been paid, as is the case when interest is included in cost.

(3) All production takes time, involving the retention of the fixed and floating assets which represent capital, and the inclusion of interest is a proper charge for that capital, whether borrowed or not. Stocks for maturing, such as timber, whisky, beer, etc., cost more for rent and interest through holding them than unmatured stocks, and it is reasoned that, though less obvious, the same factor affects all the assets.

(4) Comparative costs of various methods and processes cannot be true unless interest is taken into account, particularly where various grades of machinery, some very expensive, are used.

(5) Capital borrowed has to be paid a sum in interest. If this expense is incurred to make production possible, it is an expenditure which must be regarded as part of the cost. The manufacturer who uses his own capital should similarly be credited with a sum representing interest.

Against including it :

(1) Although interest on borrowed money is an expense, it is a matter for internal adjustment of profit. A manufacturer working with borrowed capital cannot charge more for his products than others using their own money. Interest must, therefore, be regarded as an appropriation of profit; and, if charged as part of the cost, the margin of profit is simply lower.

(2) The argument that interest is the reward of capital as much as wages are of labour is one of economics, not of costing.

(3) Even to include interest paid on borrowed capital only cannot be accepted, because it has no more connection with manufacturing cost than all the capital invested in the business. Interest in both cases is a matter of finance, not of manufacturing.

(4) Interest is merely an anticipation of profit.

(5) When manufactured stock is costed with interest included, the interest has to be written back for the purposes of the Balance Sheet, and Profit and Loss Account, which is an admission that interest is not a part of cost.

(6) The charging of interest in the Cost Accounts is an unnecessary complication, and may result in being misleading.

(7) The ascertainment of the capital employed during each costing period, and of the appropriate interest, is one of complexity and difficulty. The total capital in a business is continually changing in form in many ways; assets and liabilities fluctuate; reserves, undrawn profit and working capital will vary from time to time. Also, the rate of interest on money is repeatedly changing, so that any fixed rate used in the Cost Accounts would not always be true.

(8) No useful purpose is served by introducing the complexities which accompany the inclusion of interest, and for expediency alone it should be omitted.

(9) Where comparisons of different producing units and costs, taking into account interest, are required, these can be made in suitable statistical statements or reports.

(10) The charging of interest on the value of stocks held for maturing purposes is admitted as correct, but it simply represents appreciation in value of the material.

It may be noted that those who argue against interest as cost are usually prepared to admit the charge when special funds in the form of loans, have to be obtained for a specific contract. This is hardly logical.

In America the inclusion of interest is very widely accepted, and there are some accountants in Great Britain who include such a charge in costs. It is not admitted in the costs of costed Government contracts in this country or America as stated on page 118.

Interest Charge Necessary for Comparative Machine Costs.— The comparative cost of operating various machines, or plant, cannot be obtained correctly, unless there is a charge for the capital invested in each. The question whether loans or mortgages exist for financing is immaterial. A reasonable market rate of interest should be adopted, and, applying that rate to the capital cost of each machine, an amount to be included as an item of cost is found. The interest so debited in the machine rates should be credited to a Factory Interest Account.

Adjustments when Interest is Included.—The amount debited for assumed interest in the Cost Accounts cannot be taken into the financial books, and an adjustment must be made to bring the two sets of accounts into agreement. This is effected by summarising the total interest taken into account, and adding the total to the profit shown by the Cost Accounts.

Again, the value of work in progress and stock in hand, if taken from the Cost Accounts, will need to be reduced by the amount of interest included, otherwise a profit not realised would be shown.

Formulæ for Calculating Depreciation. (a) *Straight-Line Method.*

Let P = original cost of machine, including cost of fitting and accessories,

n = number of years of estimated useful life of machine,

R = residual scrap or second-hand value at end of n years,

D = annual sum to be charged as depreciation.

Then to produce £$(P - R)$ in n years

$$D = \frac{P - R}{n}.$$

(b) *Reducing Balance Method*. The annual percentage chargeable is constant; let this be k, and this applied to the reducing balance gives the annual sum to be charged, which may be called D_2.

At the end of—

The 1st year, the depreciation fund = £kP.
 ,, 2nd year, ,,   ,, = $kP + k(P - kP)$.
               = $P(2k - k^2)$.
               = $P[1 - (1 - 2k + k^2)]$.
               = $P[1 - (1 - k)^2]$.
 ,, 3rd year   ,,   ,, = $P[1 - (1 - k)^3]$.
 ,, nth year   ,,   ,, = $P[1 - (1 - k)^n]$.

i.e. $P - R = P[1 - (1 - k)^n]$.

$$\therefore \quad (1 - k)^n = \frac{R}{P}$$

and

$$k = 1 - \sqrt[n]{\frac{R}{P}}.$$

N.B.—The " n " root is obtained by the use of logarithms.

(c) *Sinking Fund Method*. The annual charge calculated is invested and earns interest.

Let r = interest on £1 per annum,
    D_3 = annual depreciation charge to the fund.

Then, at the end of

The 1st year, the depreciation fund = £D_3.
 ,, 2nd year   ,,   ,, = $D_3 + rD_3 + D_3$.
               = $2D_3 + rD_3$.
 ,, 3rd year   ,,   ,, = $3D_3 + 3rD_3 + r^2D_3$.
 ,, nth year   ,,   ,, = $\dfrac{D_3}{r}[(1 + r)^n - 1]$.

i.e. $P - R = \dfrac{D_3}{r}[(1 + r)^n - 1]$.

$$\therefore \quad D_3 = \frac{r(P - R)}{(1 + r)^n - 1}.$$

Comparison of the Effect of these Methods. The following comparative table shows the rate of accumulation of the depreciation fund for a machine where $P = £1000$, $R = £160$, $n = 21$ years and $r = 0·03$, *i.e.* interest at 3 per cent. per annum.

Years.	Accumulating Fund.		
	Straight-Line Method.	Fixed per cent. on Reducing Value.	Sinking-Fund Method.
	£	£	£
1	40	83·6	29·4
2	80	160	59·68
3	120	232	90·88
5	200	353·4	155·6
9	360	544	298
15	600	730	544
19	760	809·4	737
21	840	840	840

EXAMINATION QUESTIONS

1. Describe the methods known to you of charging depreciation on plant and machinery, and express your opinion on each. In the case of a firm that has adopted the method of charging a fixed percentage annually on the diminishing value of the assets and where Oncost is charged to the products by the machine-hour rate, how would you, in the build-up of these rates, treat two machines that were identical in type and capacity, one of which was new and the other ten years old ?—*Royal Society of Arts (Advanced)*.

2. Assume the depreciation of a machine has been recovered but the machine is still rendering useful service. Discuss the position which thus arises.—*Institute of Cost and Works Accountants (Inter.)*.

3. Discuss briefly the question of providing for Interest in Cost Accounts.—*Institute of Chartered Accountants (Final)*.

4. Distinguish between "Depreciation" and "Obsolescence," and state how each should be provided for in the calculation of cost.

A manufacturer installed a machine in January 1921 costing £1000, the estimated life of which was 20 years, and the residual value at the end of that time was £25. State the rate at which you consider depreciation should be provided.

In October 1929 the manufacturer purchased a new and improved model for £1100, and discarded the old one, which he sold for £200.

Write up the Plant Register to the end of 1929, so far as the machine purchased in 1921 is concerned, making the necessary annual entries on the basis you recommend and state how you would deal in the financial accounts with any balance standing after the sale has been completed in 1929. Further, how should this balance be treated, if at all, in the Cost Accounts of the business ?—*London Chamber of Commerce*.

5. Draft a suitable form for a Register of fixed plant, showing its original cost, annual depreciation provisions, additions and any other information you think useful. Enter thereon particulars of three machines for the last five years.—*London Chamber of Commerce*.

6. How would you classify the fixed assets of a factory for the purposes

131a COST ACCOUNTING AND COSTING METHODS

of depreciation? What rates of depreciation would you propose to apply to each on a fixed or diminishing value basis, whichever you may prefer?

Into what categories would you place the following:

(a) Foundations for machines; (b) Internal steam mains and radiators; (c) Wharves; (d) Surface drainage works?—*Royal Society of Arts (Advanced).*

7. How far and in what manner should the following be taken into account as elements of Cost:

Interest on Capital;
Depreciation (wear and tear);
Obsolescence?
Society of Incorporated Accountants and Auditors (Final).

8. For the purpose of comparing the costs of the same article produced by two different manufacturing organisations, A and B, how would you deal with:

(1) Bank Interest incurred by A and Mortgage Interest by B.
(2) Salary of Managing Director in A (A being a Limited Company), and the absence of any remuneration to the working proprietor of B (B not being a Limited Company).
(3) Rent paid by A. No rent paid by B (B owning its own premises).
(4) Depreciation charged in A's accounts only.
London Association of Accountants (Final).

9. State your views on the question of the inclusion of Interest as an element of cost.—*Society of Incorporated Accountants and Auditors (Final).*

10. The following charges are incurred by a manufacturing business:

(a) Repairs to Plant; (b) Repairs to Buildings; (c) Interest on Bank Overdraft; (d) Income Tax; (e) Carriage inwards and outwards.

State whether you would include all or any of them in costs of production, and of those which you consider should be included, indicate whether as direct or indirect charges.—*Society of Incorporated Accountants and Auditors (Inter.).*

11. What method would you adopt in apportioning depreciation on plant and machinery departmentally?—*Society of Incorporated Accountants and Auditors (Final).*

12. A machine written down to scrap value is continued in service. Would you or would you not continue to add depreciation to your costs? Discuss the situation which would arise.—*Institute of Cost and Works Accountants (Final).*

13. When considering the rate of depreciation of plant and machinery, what influence would expenditure on repairs have upon your recommendations? Give reasons for your answer.—*Institute of Cost and Works Accountants (Final).*

14. A firm of wine merchants store different vintages in their vaults for varying periods up to 50 years. What items of expense should they take into consideration in fixing prices for wines which have been stored for longer or shorter periods?—*Institute of Cost and Works Accountants (Final).*

15. Define:

(a) Depreciation; (b) Obsolescence; (c) Capital expenditure; (d) Hourly rate; (e) Machine rate; (f) Works cost.—*Institute of Cost and Works Accountants (Inter.).*

16. A machine, costing originally £1000, was reduced to £350 in the accounts by depreciation. An additional expenditure of £300 restored it to its original efficiency, and it was considered equal to new. How

would you deal with this in the factory records ?—*Institute of Cost and Works Accountants (Final).*

17. A firm has reserves invested in War Stock. State fully the objections, if any, to the interest being used to reduce expenses.—*Institute of Cost and Works Accountants (Final).*

18. Devise a form for plant recording purposes which would provide the Cost Accountant with the necessary information for the various types of machinery.—*Institute of Cost and Works Accountants (Final).*

19. Discuss the different methods of depreciation, place them in order of preference, and cite cases to which the differing methods might be satisfactorily applied.—*Institute of Cost and Works Accountants (Final).*

20. Assume that a bank overdraft has been incurred in order to purchase certain plant. Should the interest be charged to plant account or should it be merged in the general expenses ? Give reasons in either case.—*Institute of Cost and Works Accountants (Final).*

21. In some large works there is a tendency to accumulate obsolete stock or plant. What procedure would you recommend to ensure control of this problem ?—*Society of Incorporated Accountants and Auditors (Final).*

22. The following figures relate to the Capital and average turnover of three manufacturing businesses :

	A.	B.	C.
Capital employed	£157,500	£342,698	£96,427
Sales of Manufactures (av. of last three years)	£450,000	£300,000	£600,000

In preparing costs of individual products and making provision for profit what provision in your cost schedule would determine which of these businesses was the more profitable in relation to its capital ? Work out an approximate example with the aid of the above figures.—*London Association of Certified Accountants (Final).*

23. Briefly state the arguments for and against the inclusion of Interest on Capital as a charge against cost of production and discuss circumstances and cases in which the inclusion of such interest is (*a*) desirable, (*b*) not desirable. Give reasons for your answer.—*Incorporated Accountants (Final).*

24. Electricity is purchased on the basis of " x " shillings per K.V.A. of maximum demand plus " y " pence per B.T.U.

What investigations would you make in order to decide upon the departmental apportionment of the total charge for a period ? Assume that the load varies considerably from time to time in certain departments, and that meters are installed in all departments.—*Institute of Cost and Works Accountants (Final).*

CHAPTER XI

OVERHEAD (*continued*)

APPORTIONMENT TO DEPARTMENTS AND CENTRES

Departmentalisation of Expense.—The incidence of overhead expense in a factory, or other producing undertaking, is unequal as between the various sections of the organisation, and, consequently, if the management is to be able to control the cost of production, the sections, or departments, must be defined, and the expenses apportioned in some equitable manner. For the purposes of control, sectional or departmental activities are largely delegated to foremen or managers, and the results of their efforts are measured by the volume and quality of the output, and, particularly, by the costs of production.

The cost records have to provide for the ascertainment of departmental or sectional costs, and for the allocation of these costs to the products which pass through the operating departments. The underlying principle is that, in addition to the prime cost of material and direct labour, all the overhead expense incurred up to the time the finished product is placed in the Finished Goods Store, or is ready for dispatch to the customer, has to be regarded as part of the manufacturing cost, and be so distributed that each unit produced bears its correct proportion of the expense of each department through which it may pass. The management is then able to compare costs of the product within a department, or as between departments, and thus can measure efficiency, control the foremen better, and modify plans should this be necessary.

It is essential that, when there is more than one shop or department, a separate total of Overhead (or Oncost) must be ascertained and separate shop rates calculated as described in the next chapter, otherwise costs can rarely be correct.

Apportionment of Works Expense may, therefore, be defined as the process of determining the incidence of works expenses to departments and producing units or centres, and the division of those expenses proportionately. The apportionment may reflect the allocation of actual cost, or be the outcome of applying some formula appropriate to the respective classes of expenses.

Allocation of Works Expense is the term used in this book to designate the charging of apportioned departmental works expense to the cost units, or products.

The Methods of Apportioning Overhead to Departments.—As far as possible, any expense which is incurred for a specific order or cost unit is charged as direct expense to that order or unit, and such items are excluded from the Overhead. Overhead cannot be dealt with so simply, but is apportioned according to incidence, and, as incidence of different items of Overhead varies, several methods of apportionment have to be used :

(1) A direct charge to a particular department or section can be made for many items.

Examples.—Overtime of men engaged solely in the department; similarly, with general labour, National Insurance, and waiting time. Power, when separate meters or measurement is available, jobbing repairs.

(2) A charge for Overhead which is proportionate to departmental wages paid.

This method is unsatisfactory for general application, and, in fact, very few items vary strictly with the total wages paid in a department.

Example.—Premiums for Workmen's Compensation and Employers' Liability Insurances, which are fixed on the basis of wages paid.

(3) A percentage or proportion relative to departmental values of (*a*) buildings, (*b*) plant, or (*c*) buildings and plant combined.

Examples.—(*a*) *Based on Capital Value of Land and Buildings.* General Rates imposed by Local Authorities; depreciation and fire insurance of buildings, when each department has its own building ;

(*b*) *Based on Capital Value of Plant.*—Interest on capital, if included; insurance and depreciation of plant and machinery.

(*c*) *Based on Capital Value of Plant and Buildings.* Rates of Local Authorities when buildings contain rateable plant, *e.g.*, boiler-house. It should be observed that machinery for manufacturing is not included in the rating assessment, but other fixed plant, *e.g.*, main power transmission plant, is.* Also, when some buildings are old and

* Rating and Valuation Acts 1925 and 1928, Sec. 24, and Plant and Machinery (Valuation for Rating) Order, 1927 (S.R.O., 1927, No. 480), summarised at p. 141.

others new, replacement values may have to be used because of the change in money values.

(4) An apportionment proportional to either—

(a) Superficial or floor area of departmental buildings, or

(b) The cubic capacity of departmental buildings, whichever gives the truer result, having regard to the nature of the expense, the buildings and the type of industry.

Examples.—Lighting, heating, attendance, rent, fire precaution expenses, building service.

When the character of the buildings varies considerably, rent may be better allocated on capital value. Again, if the shops or rooms are of varying heights, cubic content may be a fairer basis than area in some businesses.

(5) An apportionment proportional to the departmental totals of production hours of (a) direct labour, or (b) in some circumstances, machines.

The direct labour-hour basis is usually the most equitable method of apportioning the majority of general overhead expense, where a more closely related basis is not available.

Examples.—Overtime and waiting time expense. Works management, administration and supervision. Works office expenses—stationery, sundries; Timekeeping and gate control; Experiment and research; Inter-departmental trucking.

In departments where both machine and bench work are done, it will usually be necessary to divide the Overhead of the factory into items which vary with the running time of machines, and the operating hours of direct labour, and then to apportion the two totals of expense in proportion to (a) machine running hours or (b) direct labour hours, using separate expense rates.

(6) Apportionment according to the *number* of employees in each shop is fairer for some expenses, *e.g.* canteen expense, timekeeping and wage department expenses, recreation ground and rest-room, etc.

(7) Apportionment by technical estimate, investigation, or measurement. Under this heading several useful methods are included, mostly of particular application, some of which are given by way of example :

Electric Light.—The number of lights or watts used in each department may be listed, and the departmental proportion of the total used charged to the departments. This is alternative to using floor area.

Electric Power.—Using a return of the operating time in connection with a schedule of h.p. of the machines in a department, a close estimate of the departmental charge is obtained. In some factories, departmental meters are used ; a consumption return gives the basis for apportionment.

Steam is apportioned on a consumption return. There are various methods of measuring steam used in departments. Sometimes, however, this charge is made, not on consumption, but on potential consumption, on the ground that the service is provided and available whenever required. One method is to base a minimum charge for standing expense and another for quantity consumed like a two-part tariff.

Water.—For process use will be metered and charged accordingly. When not metered, a technical estimate may be used. In small businesses, where the water charge is based on rateable value, and the use is fairly uniform, the same basis of allocation as for rates may be used.

Compressed Air.—See remarks under Steam.

Circumstances arise when some items of expense can only be estimated in consultation between the works engineer, the works chemist, or other official, and the cost accountant, but such a course is to be avoided, if possible.

Departments for Costing Purposes.—These are not necessarily only production departments or shops. Sometimes a production " centre " or unit is treated as a " department," instead of, or in addition to, the larger factory divisions. A " centre " may be an isolated work-bench, a machine, a group of machines of one type, or an activity. By this arrangement closer distribution of expense and more detailed control are aimed at. This method of minute departmentalisation of cost involves a considerable amount of analysis, and, in the majority of cases, the expense of the work would not be warranted. The value of the method lies in the more precise costs which are obtained, regardless of the variation in the product or the equipment. Unless great care is used in analysis, this elaboration may lead to erroneous results.

Service Departments are apportioned their fair share of the Overhead, in the same way as the operating departments. The total cost of each Service Department is afterwards distributed on a suitable basis to each of the operating departments concerned. The basis should be one which gives an

L

apportionment proportional to user, which local circumstances will usually decide.

THE ANALYSIS OF EXPENSE FOR DEPARTMENTAL APPORTIONMENT

Preparation of Expense Summary.—The inequalities of the calendar month make it advisable to adopt either thirteen periods of four weeks to the year, or fortnightly periods. The use of summaries using calendar months makes comparisons unsatis-

FIG. 47.

OVERHEAD EXPENSE SUMMARY

Four Weeks ended : ....

1. Production (or Factory) Expenses.

S.O. No.	Items.	Total.			Wages.			Pur-chases.			Stores Issues.			Petty Cash.			Trans-fers.		
		£	s.	d.	£	s.	d.	£	s.	d.	£	s.	d.	£	s.	d.	£	s.	d.
	(Each detailed separately)																		

2. Administration Expenses.

3. Selling and Distribution Expenses.

factory. Some mitigate the position by using in each quarter two four-weekly periods, and one of five weeks.

All Overhead may be usefully summarised in a statement drawn up to enable the management to compare the total expense under every heading, and to provide a check on the figures used in the accounts. (Fig. 47.)

The Departmental Analysis of Expense.—The dissection of all items of Production Overhead expense into the respective Production and Service Departments has to be considered next. The various bases of apportionment described in the preceding chapter, and in Fig. 52, are used. Wherever possible, expenses

Fig. 48.

APPORTIONMENT OF FACTORY EXPENSES
Four Weeks to 28 February, 19...

Items.	Total as per Summary.	General Factory Overhead.	Buildings.	SERVICES. Electricity Supply.	Steam Supply.	Motive Power.	Stores Expenses.	Heating Service.	Lighting Service.	PRODUCTION. Dept. A.	Dept. B.	Dept. C.
	£	£	£	£	£	£	£	£	£	£	£	£
Indirect Labour:												
Foremen	199		20	25	20	25	16	10	10	33	20	20
Storemen	40						40					
Shop clerks	32	32										
Labourers	256		20	10	40	10				50	76	50
Works salaries	797	797										
National Insurance	257	257										
Workmen's Compensation Insurance	269		2	1	1	1	2	1	1	92	84	84
Fire Insurance	32		1	1	1	1	1	1	1	9	8	8
Rent	30		20				4		3			
Rates	257		257		26							
Stationery, etc.	298	6	272									
Indirect Material	20			5	5		10					
Water	179	3			11	15		3	2	45	52	48
Electricity and Gas Pur.	14			7				14				
Coal	120					100			20			
Service Wages	582			240	220		20	122				
Repairs	250		130	40	26	47				9	7	5
Maintenance	536		85	50	80	32		25	8	61	134	75
Stores adjustment	70		70									
Dining-room	20	20										
Welfare	70	70										
Lighting Material	40							10	30			
Fire Protection	30		25						3			
Depreciation	8	8										
Transport (internal)	365			45	80	30				35	30	32
Sundry Expenses	100	40								36	24	40
Experimental	32	32										
	£4903	1265	902	424	519	269	93	186	78	370	435	362

Note.—General Factory Overhead and Services are further analysed in Fig. 49; Final Apportionment to Departments in Fig. 50. Examples of the bases upon which apportionments above are made, are suggested in Fig. 52 on p. 140.

are charged direct to departments, and it is only when this is not possible that the apportionment methods are applied.

The Procedure. All the items of production (or factory) expense are separately apportioned between (see Figs. 48–50) :

(1) General Overhead, affecting all departments, but which cannot be allocated direct to any.

(2) The Service Departments, as, for instance :

> (*a*) Land and buildings expense.
> (*b*) Electricity supply expense.
> (*c*) Steam supply expense.
> (*d*) Motive power.
> (*e*) Stores expense.
> (*f*) Heating.
> (*g*) Lighting.

All auxiliaries to the other Departments.

(3) Production Departments, *e.g.*, Dept. A; Dept. B; Dept. C.

It is then necessary to apportion the General Overhead (which has not been charged direct to any department) over all the Service and Production Departments affected.   (Fig. 49.)

Fig. 49.

INTER-SERVICE DEPARTMENTS TRANSFERS

Items.	Factory General Expenses.	SERVICE DEPARTMENTS.						
		Buildings Expense.	Electric Supply.	Steam Supply.	Motive Power.	Stores Expenses.	Heating Service.	Lighting Service.
	£	£	£	£	£	£	£	£
Totals as per analysis (Fig. 48) . .	1265	902	424	519	269	93	186	78
Transfers from General expenses . .	− 140	20	20	25	25	30	10	10
,, Buildings service .	—	− 340	50	100	80	60	30	20
,, Lighting service .	—	—	—	10	10	27	4	− 51
,, Heating service .	—	—	—	—	—	18	− 18	—
,, Steam service .	—	—	—	− 202	—	—	202	—
,, Electricity service .	—	—	− 494	—	304	—	—	190
Total for allocation to shops . . .	£1125	582	—	452	688	228	414	247

The total cost of each Service Department is then allocated proportionate to use, or in some cases potential use also, to the Production and other Service Departments. Note that some of these service departments serve other service departments for which an apportionment has to be made first. The final analysis is shown in Fig. 50.

FIG. 50.

APPORTIONMENT OF SERVICES AND EXPENSES

Expense Item.	Total as Analysis. (Fig. 49)	PRODUCTION DEPARTMENTS.		
		Dept. A.	Dept. B.	Dept. C.
	£	£	£	£
General factory expenses .	1125	320	398	407
Buildings Expenses . .	582	180	202	200
Steam Supply . . .	452	298	154	—
Motive Power . . .	688	168	194	326
Stores Expense . . .	228	182	24	22
Heating service . . .	414	131	129	154
Lighting service . .	247	80	82	85
Other expenses . . . as per Analysis (Fig. 48)	1167	370	435	362
	£4903	1729	1618	1556

Tool Department.—The Tool Department of an engineering works is responsible for the supply of

(1) Special tools for specific works orders.

(2) Other tools for general departmental use in the works.

(3) Tools occasionally for sale.

The cost of direct wages, material and the appropriate proportion of the Tool Department Overhead expended on the special tools is a specific charge to the jobs concerned.

The other tools are charged as tool expense to the various departments that use this service.

An account may be drawn up as shown below.

FIG. 51.   TOOL-ROOM ACCOUNT.

Dr.   Cr.

	Direct.	General.		To Works Orders.	General (To Shops).
	£	£		£	£
To Wages . .	65		By Production		
,, Materials .	123		Orders :		
,, Wages .		39	(detailed)	200	
,, Materials .		211	,, Charges to		
,, Expense Allocation Summary .	12	14	Standing Order Nos. :		
			Shop 1		76
			,, 2		69
			,, 3		84
			,, Balance forward		35
	£200	264		£200	264

The expenses are allocated proportionately to direct labour hours, or departmental machine hours, in some cases.

The Basis of Allocation.—In the preceding chapter the methods of apportioning overhead expense were discussed. In the following schedule the application of these methods is indicated :

Fig. 52.

Schedule showing Methods of Apportionment of Certain Items.

Expense.	Basis of Allocation.	Source or Production.			Adminis-tration.	Selling.
		No. 1.	No. 2.	No. 3.		
Depreciation	Capital value of asset; or for build-ings floor space					
Interest (if in-cluded)	ditto					
Electric power	H.P. hours in each shop					
Steam	Consumption re-turn—metered or calculated for use and potential use					
Compressed air						
Hydraulic power						
Gas	Metered					
Electric light	Number of lights or total depts. watts floor space or number of workers					
Building ser-vice	Area or capacity of buildings					
Welfare	Number of Workers					
National In-surance	Actual					
Workmen's Compensation	Total wages paid					
Rates	Department assess-ment values ; capi-tal values other-wise					
Heating	Area or capacity of departments					
Repairs	Direct in S.O. num-bers					
Dining-room expenses	Number of workers or labour hours					
Insurance	Capital values					
Overtime	Direct labour hours if not actual					
Stores expense	Number of requisi-tions or values or weight or direct wages, whichever suitable					

Example of *Apportionment* of rates and fire insurance in a foundry :

Fig. 53.

Department.	Rateable Value Buildings and Equipment.	Per Cent. per Dept.	Rates.			Fire Insurance.			Total.		
	£		£	s.	d.	£	s.	d.	£	s.	d.
Cupola Department . .	3,000	3·15	1	3	1		1	11	1	5	0
Moulding Shop	35,000	36·85	13	11	0	12	2	0	25	13	0
Core Shop .	10,000	10·52	3	17	11		6	6	4	4	5
Fettling Shop .	1,000	1·06		7	7			8		8	3
Smiths' Shop .	1,000	1·06		7	7			8		8	3
Machine Shop .	45,000	47·36	17	8	4	1	9	7	18	17	11
Totals .	£95,000	100·00	36	15	6	14	1	4	50	16	10
									per month		

Rateable Plant and Machinery.—The basis of apportionment has been referred to on page 133 (par 3 (*c*)). In order to establish the basis of division of the charge for Rates, regard must be had to the Plant and Machinery which is rateable. There are *five* classes of assets, in addition to Land and Buildings, which are rateable, under the provisions of Section 24 of the *Rating and Valuation Act*, 1925, and the *Machinery and Plant* (*Valuation for Rating*) *Order*, 1927. These provisions were made applicable to London by the *Rating and Valuation Act*, 1928.

The Rateable Classes, deemed to be part of the heriditament, are as follows :

Class 1*a*. Machinery and Plant used in connection with the generation, storage, primary transformation, or main transmission of power in the factory.

This includes :

(*a*) Steam Boilers (their settings, chimneys, furnaces, mechanical stokers, injectors, feed water pumps, economisers, etc.).
(*b*) Steam Engines, turbines, internal combustion engines, hot air engines.
(*c*) Engines and turbines (operated by steam, internal combustion, and hot air).
(*d*) Dynamos (couplings to engines and turbines, field exciter gear, etc.); Transformers, Cables and Conductors, Switchboards and other gear.
(*e*) Water Wheels, water turbines, sluice gates, etc.; Pumping Engines and other hydraulic plant; Windmills.
(*f*) Air Compressors, compressed air engines.
(*g*) Shafting couplings, clutches, pulleys, gears, etc.

Fig. 54.

EXPENSE ALLOCATION SUMMARY WITH BUDGET COMPARISON

Month ended.................

ITEMS.	TOTAL EXPENSES.		SERVICE DEPARTMENTS.*				MANUFACTURING SHOPS,							
			Steam.		Repairs.		Foundry.		Machining.		Automatics.		Assembly.	
	Budget.	Actual.	Budget.	Actual.	Budget.	Actual.	Budget.	Actual.	Budget.	Actual.	Budget.	Actual.	Budget.	Actual.
	£	£	£	£	£	£	£	£	£	£	£	£	£	£
Foremen . . .														
Management . .														
Inspection . .														
Rate-fixing . .														
Drawing Office .														
Office staff wages .														
Labour, indirect .														
General expenses .														
Indirect materials .														
Power-house (wages)														
Do. (materials)														
Depreciation . .														
Rents, rates, etc. .														
Repairs and maintenance :—														
Tools . .														
Buildings . .				£1,765		£1,245									
Service Departments :— Steam £1,765 Repairs £1,245			(These two totals are apportioned to the shops.)				£	£2,115	£	£4,305	£	£3,000	£	£645
Direct Wages .	£	£10,065	£		£		£	£2,097	£	£2,867	£	£2,997	£	£1,288
	£	£9,249						100%		150%		100%		50%
Percentage of expenses to direct wages†	...	...	...	...	...	...								

As many columns as there are services.

Or labour hour, or machine hour rate may be quoted.

(*h*) Steam and other Motors for driving any machinery or plant in this class.

(*i*) All accessories used with the above, *e.g.* cranes, truck tipplers, conveyors, gasholders, meters, gauges, storage, foundations, platforms, etc.

Main transmission of power means all transmission from the generating plant or point of supply up to and including (i) shafting or gearing driven by the prime mover, (ii) the main distribution boards in the case of electricity, (iii) the point where the main ceases in the case of hydraulic or pneumatic power (*i.e.* excludes branch service piping).

Class 1*b*. Machinery and Plant for heating, cooling, ventilating, lighting, draining or supplying water to the land or buildings of the factory, or for fire protection (*but not* if installed for the purposes of manufacturing or trade processes).

This includes:

(*a*) Heating: water heaters, calorifiers, valves, ducts, etc. Gas burners, heaters, radiators, pressure regulators, flues and chimneys, etc.; electric heaters, plugs, etc.

(*b*) Cooling: refrigerating machines, water screens and jets, fans and blowers.

(*c*) Ventilating: air intakes, air treatment plant; electric and gas heaters, etc., for making air movement.

(*d*) Lighting: gas burners, electric plugs, sockets, etc.

(*e*) Draining-pumps, tanks, sewage treatment plant, etc.

(*f*) Water supply pumps, tanks, sluice gates, etc.

(*g*) Fire hydrants, sprinklers, alarm systems, tanks and lightning conductors.

Class 2. Lifts and Elevators used for passengers.

Class 3. Railway and Tramway lines and tracks.

Class 4. Parts of Plant, or combination of plant and machinery, whenever and only to such extent as in the nature of a building or structure, in a long list named in the Schedule to the Act.

The following are examples from the list:

Blast furnaces.
Bins, bunkers.
Hoppers.
Kilns, ovens, stoves.
Chambers for processes.
Chimneys.
Coking ovens.
Condensers for acids, etc.
Crane gantries.

Cupolas.
Floating docks, pontoons and gangways.
Foundations, settings, gantries, stages, etc., for machinery.
Headgear (mines, etc.).
Racks.
Refuse destructors.
Retorts.
Ship slipways, etc.

Stills.
Superheaters.
Tanks.
Silos, stages, etc., for loading.
Towers for condensing chemical processes, etc., and water.
Turntables, weighbridges, wireless masts.

Comparison with Pre-determined Estimates.

—The control of expense is often secured by preparing a budget of every item of expense, a subject which is discussed in a later chapter, and, in these circumstances, the Allocation Summary may be appropriately ruled to permit of regular comparison. A condensed summary on these lines is shown in Fig. 54.

EXAMINATION QUESTIONS

1. It has been decided to omit from costs the expenses incurred in connection with idle facilities. What items would you debit to the account opened for this purpose and on what bases would you make your apportionments of common expenses ?—*Royal Society of Arts (Advanced)*.

2. State briefly why it is desirable, as a general rule, to make use of different Oncost rates for each Department of a manufacturing business ? In what circumstances would you consider this to be unnecessary ?—*London Association of Accountants (Final)*.

3. Under a system of piece-work there are certain indirect operations for which a day-rate is paid. In dealing with overhead expenses suggest how such day wages should be treated.—*Institute of Cost and Works Accountants (Final)*.

4. Describe fully a method of arriving at departmental hourly rates for Overhead.—*Institute of Cost and Works Accountants (Inter.)*.

5. State very briefly the chief benefits derived from a departmental division of Oncost expenditure :

    (1) From a Costing standpoint.
    (2) From the standpoint of financial control.

In what circumstances is departmentalisation unnecessary ?—*London Association of Accountants (Final)*.

6. State what procedure you would adopt to obtain a monthly schedule of departmental Overhead charges.—*Institute of Cost and Works Accountants (Inter.)*.

7. Describe the methods you would adopt to ascertain the cost of defective work. State the particular industry you refer to and say how you would propose to deal with the cost so ascertained.—*Royal Society of Arts (Advanced)*.

8. A factory generates steam from water pumped from its own wells by some of its own steam. In the cost accounts for these services a proportion of the total cost of each must be charged to the other, but until this has been done the total cost of each service cannot be ascertained. How should this difficulty be met ?—*Institute of Cost and Works Accountants (Inter.)*.

9. Write careful notes on treatment in Cost Accounts of any two of the following :

    (1) Material damaged in course of manufacture.
    (2) Idle time of expensive machinery irregularly used.
    (3) Expenditure in connection with a research department.
    (4) Established charges during a period in which the factory runs on very short time owing to trade depression.
    (5) Expenditure in connection with a Service Department maintained in connection with a manufacturing business.
London Chamber of Commerce.

10. Prepare a skeleton statement of the cost of production of electricity where the steam raised is used for the following purposes :

    (*a*) generation of electricity;
    (*b*) process work;
    (*c*) shop heating.
Institute of Cost and Works Accountants (Inter.).

11. A factory incurs a liability of roughly £10,000 per annum on account of rates levied by local authorities. Into what categories would you divide the fixed assets in order to departmentalise this charge; and how would you then proceed to apportion it?—*Institute of Cost and Works Accountants (Final).*

12. B. & Co. are invited to quote for 50,000 tons of a commodity. The firm find that the total cost of production is £55 per ton but are informed that the contract cannot be placed with them at a price higher than £52 per ton. B. & Co.'s overhead charges included in the total cost of production amount to £5 per ton, such overheads covering Management and Depreciation.

Under what circumstances would they be justified in reducing their quotation to £52 per ton?—*Society of Incorporated Accountants and Auditors (Final).*

13. State how you would deal with the following in the cost records of a manufacturer, viz. :

(*a*) Carriage Outwards.
(*b*) Carriage Inwards.
(*c*) Rent, Rates and Taxes.
(*d*) Repairs to Plant and Buildings.
(*e*) Fire Insurance Premiums.
(*f*) Expense of Welfare Department.
(*g*) Electric Power.
(*h*) Scrap Material.
(*i*) Foremen's Salaries.
(*j*) Manager's Salary.

The factory consists of four Productive Departments, with the usual Stores, Offices, etc., and the Costs of each Department are prepared separately. State any additional information you would require to enable you to arrive at the amount to be charged to each department.
Corporation of Accountants (Final).

14. State briefly the object of distinguishing between fixed and floating expense. The following is a schedule of the expenditure in three departments of a manufacturing business :

	Department.		
	A.	B.	C.
	£	£	£
Direct Wages	11,290	3,775	5,782
Indirect Wages	3,619	1,029	786
Toolmakers	542	629	311
Power consumed	1,047	273	196
Shop Sundries	184	100	126
Repairs to Plant	478	264	60
Depreciation of Plant	380	376	142
Rent and Rates	872	517	460
Stationery for Manufacturing Departments	28	37	15
Supervision Salaries	1,000	500	625
Storekeeper's Wages	175	142	130

Divide the oncost of each between fixed and floating oncost and show separately the fixed and floating oncost rates, measured in relation with the direct wages.—*London Association of Certified Accountants (Final).*

15. There are six heavy machines in a certain machine shop, the capital costs of which were as follows :
No. 1, £4620; No. 2, £2780; No. 3, £825; No. 4, £1278; No. 5, £6429; No. 6, £2500.

The oncost of this shop was charged to costs on the direct wages method, the shop rate being 400 per cent. Machines No. 1 and 5 were used intermittently but the others were almost continually in operation. What is the main objection to this method of allocating oncost, and what steps would you propose to remedy this objection ?—*London Association of Certified Accountants (Final).*

16. Explain briefly the principles that should govern the allocation of overhead expenses in a manufacturing business between : (*a*) manufacturing and selling departments respectively and (*b*) the respective manufacturing processes.—*Chartered Accountants (Final).*

17. " One of the advantages of a Cost System is its aid in the control of expenditure." Set out in summarised form the directions in which this control operates.—*Incorporated Accountants (Final).*

18. How would you arrive at the amount to be charged against a particular job for Depreciation of Plant and Machinery in a Factory where the rate of depreciation varied on the different items and machines ? —*Incorporated Accountants (Inter.).*

19. Explain the man-hour method of distributing overhead costs, and show in what instances the method is best applied in preference to other methods. Give an illustration of the manner in which the hourly rate is computed, and calculate the cost of an imaginary article showing the application of the above principle.—*Incorporated Accountants (Final).*

20. The Zenith Manufacturing Company consists of three Production Departments and two Service Departments. For the month of July, 1934, the direct departmental expenses were as follows :—

Production Departments, A, £1,200; B, £1,400; C, £1,700. Service Departments, P, £600; Q, £580.

The Cost of Service Department P is allocated to the other Departments on a percentage basis, viz. :—

Production Departments, A, 20 per cent.; B, 30 per cent.; C, 40 per cent. Service Department Q, 10 per cent.

The Cost of Service Department Q is allocated on the basis of total Wages, which were as follows :—

Production Departments, A, £3,000; B, £3,600; C, £2,400. Service Department P, £600.

Prepare a Statement showing distribution of the Service Department Oncost.—*Corporation of Accountants (Final).*

21. On what classes of fixed assets are local rates assessable ?—*Institute of Cost and Works Accountants (Inter.).*

22. The boiler plant in a factory supplies steam for electrical generating plant, heating, and for certain manufacturing processes, in addition to a number of pumping units in the Works. The Directors are considering the purchase of electrical power from outside. Indicate the principal costing factors which will influence their decision.—*Institute of Cost and Works Accountants (Final).*

23. The following are details of A's Selling, Delivery and General Administration Expense for 1934 :—

	£	£
Selling Expense :		
Provincial Travellers Salaries and Commission	9,279	
London Agents and London Office Salaries and Expenses	5,426	
Stationery and Advertising	7,246	
Cost of exhibiting at Home Fairs . . .	549	
		22,500
Delivery Expense :		
Carriage not recoverable from customers .	2,540	
Warehouse Salaries	3,429	
Packing Materials	1,531	
		7,500
General Administration :		
Head Office Salaries	8,420	
Printing and Stationery	1,175	
Accountants' Charges	315	
Incidentals	785	
Insurance	115	
Rent and Rates of Head Office . . .	1,250	
Depreciation of Office equipment . . .	40	
		12,100
Bank Interest	2,429	
Mortgage Interest	3,580	
Discounts allowed	11,891	
		17,900
		£60,000

The manufacturing costs of goods sold during 1934 were :—	
Through Provincial organisation	82,568
Through London Office	217,432
	£300,000

Calculate a Selling, Delivery and General Administration rate for :—

        (*a*) Provincial Sales
        (*b*) London Sales

based upon the selling price.—*London Association of Certified Accountants* (*Final*).

CHAPTER XII

DEPARTMENTAL OVERHEAD

ALLOCATION TO THE PRODUCT

Factors to be Considered.—The apportionment of Overhead to departments serves two main purposes :

(1) To provide comparisons, and facilitate control of total departmental expense.

(2) To provide a basis for determining the amount to be charged to each unit, or order, in respect of Overhead in each department taking part in the production.

A suitable basis for ascertaining the expense to be borne by each unit, or works order, must be decided upon. The expense so ascertained is charged to the appropriate Cost Account, and this procedure is usually referred to as the " recovery " of overhead expense.

The problem is complicated by the fact that many items of expense have to be estimated, because the expense will often not be incurred or recorded in the financial accounts until after the work in the factory is well advanced, or completed. As close an estimate of Overhead as possible must be made, having regard to expenses in the preceding period, *and also* to the trend of activity and cost in the immediate future. Allowance has to be made for any probable fall or increase in output. This is called budgetting the expense, and demands great care. Budgetting, and budgetary control, is dealt with in the chapter dealing with Standard Costs.

The Methods used for Charging Overhead to the Product.— There are a number of fundamental methods to be considered. There are also variations applicable in particular cases which need not be dealt with here. The methods to be described are :

(1) A prime cost percentage.
(2) A percentage on direct wages.

144

(3) A percentage on direct materials.

(4) A rate per unit produced.

(5) A rate per hour of direct labour.

(6) A rate per machine hour.

(7) A rate per production hour.

It will be demonstrated that, in the majority of cases, the first three methods are unsound. They are often used, however, for convenience.

Method 1. *A Percentage on Prime Cost.*—The total Overhead for the factory or each department is expressed as a percentage of the estimated total of direct material and direct labour, and the percentage rate so obtained is applied to each job, or works order.

Example : Factory Overhead £8,480 $\left.\begin{array}{l}\text{Total Direct Wages £4,000}\\ \text{Direct Materials £6,600}\end{array}\right\}$ If several departments these must be departmental totals.

Then the percentage to add to the prime cost of each job would be $\dfrac{£8,480}{10,600} \times 100 = 80\%.$

This method must be unreliable, and, in the majority of instances, inaccurate. The only thing in its favour is that it is simple, requires but little effort to calculate, and is quick and convenient. The only time it could be accurate would be when materials used are equal in price, the wages uniform, and the equipment used exactly similar on every job.

The criticism may be summarised thus :

(*a*) There is practically no relation between overhead and the cost of material and labour, except where these two elements are constant.

(*b*) Jobs and processes usually involve the use of different types and values of machinery, or labour equipment, and the charge for these cannot be proportionate to prime cost.

(*c*) The time taken is not considered, so that no allowance is made for the disparity between wages earned by different workers due to varying wage rates and speed of working.

Method 2. *A Percentage on Direct Wages.*—The simplicity of this method has led to its being rather widely used, despite the inaccuracies it produces. It involves but little work to arrive at the percentage used, and appears satisfactory to those who do not know the advantages of more accurate costs.

The percentage of Direct Wages to be added to prime cost is calculated thus :

Oncost £8,100; Direct Wages £9,000

then $\frac{8,100}{9,000} \times 100 = 90\%$.

A common practice is to use as a basis the Overhead and Direct Wages for the preceding year. In circumstances where the method can be applied, the totals used should be adjusted to meet any anticipated rise or fall in production in the period coming into review.

As with Method 1, the results obtained are usually unsatisfactory for the following reasons :

(a) No distinction is made when some of the workers are using expensive machines, and others are merely using hand tools, yet the first incur more expense than in the case of hand work.

(b) The wages of workers on the same kind of work and using similar equipment may, and usually do, vary, hence the charge for expenses must frequently be incorrect.

(c) There is no discrimination between slow and quick workers.

(d) The inaccurate application of Overhead may conceal a low rate of profit on some lines which it might be more profitable to discontinue.

(e) When used in connection with work done by piece-workers, the Overhead charged per piece remains constant, notwithstanding that : (i) some of the work may be done at a very rapid rate, and below the average time. (ii) Other work occupies more than average time, and yet still bears only the same amount of Overhead.

Compare the inequitable results shown in Fig. 55, which presumes similar work is done by both time- and piece-workers.

The piece-work which occupied the factory facilities for 15 hours is charged no more than that which took 10 hours.

FIG. 55.

COMPARISON OF EXPENSE RECOVERIES

	Time-Work at 2s. 6d. per hour.		Similar Work at 25s. per piece.	
	10 hrs.	15 hrs.	10 hrs.	15 hrs.
	£ s. d.	£ s. d.	£ s. d.	£ s. d.
Material	3 0 0	3 0 0	3 0 0	3 0 0
Direct wages . . .	1 5 0	1 17 6	1 5 0	1 5 0
Prime cost . . .	4 5 0	4 17 6	4 5 0	4 5 0
Works Overhead 150 per cent. on wages . .	1 17 6	2 16 3	1 17 6	1 17 6
Production cost . .	£6 2 6	£7 13 9	£6 2 6	£6 2 6

There are cases, but they are not common, where this method gives reasonably good results, namely, where similar articles are made by uniformly paid labour, using equipment not very dissimilar in value.

Method 3. *A Percentage on Direct Material.*—Practically the same type of objections apply to this method as to one first dealt with. The value of materials is generally too uncertain a basis to adopt for distributing overhead to the product. It is, however, sometimes used, because it is simple to operate, but it would be difficult to find an instance in which it would produce sound costs. It requires but a simple example to show the fallacy of using the method; both costs are probably incorrect, one being over-charged, and the other under-charged :

COST OF METAL CAPS

	In Brass.	In Steel.
	£ s. d.	£ s. d.
Materials	4 0 0	2 0 0
Labour	18 0	18 0
Prime cost	4 18 0	2 18 0
Works overhead 75 per cent. on materials .	3 0 0	1 10 0
Production cost	£7 18 0	£4 8 0

It cannot reasonably be contended that the same quantity of brass caps should be charged with double the amount of Overhead borne by the steel ones. Where materials are similar and values are regular this objection could not be raised.

M

Method 4.   *A Rate per Unit Produced.*—In works producing uniform units, as is often the case in process and single output manufacturing, this is a simple method which, under suitable conditions, gives an equitable distribution of Overhead.   Varying units of the same type can be converted on a ratio or points basis to a common unit equivalent.

The total Overhead expense is divided by the total number of articles, or units, expected to be produced, thus giving a rate per unit to be added to prime cost.

Method 5.   *A Rate per Direct-labour Hour.*—This method assumes that time is the dominant factor in relation to overhead expense, and the number of hours of direct labour worked is the basis adopted.

A rate is obtained by dividing the total Production Overhead of the centre or department by the total direct-labour hours, which totals have been estimated carefully, having regard to past records, and the budget figures for the immediate future.

When fixed departmentally, the results are surprisingly accurate in the majority of instances, particularly when manual labour only is used.   It is necessary, however, to use also a machine-hour rate, if costly machinery is used in addition to manual labour (see Method 6), otherwise the work turned out by hand labour will receive a proportionate share of the machine expense, which, of course, does not affect hand work.

There are one or two points which require care :

(*a*) A direct-labour hour rate should not be calculated for the works as a whole, because the product may not pass through all departments.

(*b*) When computing the total working hours, Bank Holidays and other holidays must be omitted.

(*c*) When both hand and machine work are done in one department, separate labour and machine rates may be calculated after careful allocation of expense.   It may even be necessary to have rates for individual machines in some instances.

The method necessitates additional records being kept, which causes some increase in clerical work, viz. :

(i) The number of direct-labour hours spent on each job or works order in each department.

(ii) The total number of direct-labour hours worked by all the workers in each department.

This extra work ensures more accurate costing, and provides information for better control of costs, so that actual total costs may be reduced.

Other advantages are :

(a) The defects of the methods previously described are overcome in that the Overhead charged to each order is unaffected by any fluctuations in labour rates or earnings, or in the price of materials.

(b) When used in conjunction with piece-work, satisfactory apportionment of Overhead is secured. If the piece-worker produces more units in a given time, he earns more, but the Overhead charge is less, being distributed over a larger number of units.

(c) The time statistics collected are useful for measuring production efficiency without the less stable wages factor.

(d) There can be separate direct-labour hour rates for sections within a shop or department, so that, if different types of equipment or machines are used in one department, the separate rates provide a reliable method for distributing Overhead. This procedure is more fully explained under the Machine-hour Rate method.

Method 6. *The Machine-hour Rate.*—The principle underlying this method is that Production Overhead expenses of a centre are distributable in proportion to the operating hours of the machines. In factories where production is largely by machinery, this method gives greater accuracy than any of those previously explained.

Considerable preliminary work is necessary to set up reliable rates, and the detailed records of time and expense call for additional clerical work and analysis, but the detailed costs secured will usually make the method well worth while.

A machine rate can be set up for each machine, but as, in a large factory, this method would probably create too many rates for convenient handling, and be too costly, it is often the practice to fix a rate for each group of machines estimated to have the same overhead expense. It should be noticed, however, that these group rates sometimes lead to some inaccuracy, but it is enough to make adjustments as necessary, and, in the long run, practice shows they are more reliable.

There are several ways of building up the Machine Rate, two of which may be considered here :

(a) By including only the expense directly concerning the machine, and arranging a separate direct-labour hour rate to cover other production overhead. This method is desirable when there is both manual and machine work in a shop.

(b) By considering each machine, or group of like machines, as a department for cost purposes, and setting up a comprehensive rate for each to cover the whole of the departmental overhead.

Method (7), *A Rate per Production-hour*, is a rate for a shop as in (b) above, and is useful for departmental process work, Steel Rolling Mills, etc.

The Principles for Computing the Machine-hour Rate.—All expenses applicable are summarised, and then analysed to each machine, or sectional group. The general principle is to charge in each machine rate every expense connected with the machine, its accommodation, upkeep, and running. In some instances, the direct labour of operating the machine is included, but such a course should generally be avoided. It may lead to erroneous results in all but exceptional circumstances.

When reviewing the cost of running a machine, it will be apparent that it falls into two divisions :

(a) The cost of the floor space occupied, including the proportion of general overhead expense apportionable to that floor space, and

(b) The expense of operating the machine, including interest on the capital outlay for the machine, depreciation, insurance, maintenance, repairs, and power. By dividing this total cost for a suitable period by the total estimated operating hours a cost per hour is established. (See Fig. 56.)

This machine-hour rate gives a fairly reliable basis for " recovering " the expenses, *i.e.* for calculating the amount of Overhead to be charged to a particular works order, whether that order represents a job, process, or operation.

A certain amount of discrepancy arises, however, owing to (i) the inevitable irregularity of operating time; (ii) the necessity for using an estimated number of running hours in advance. Again, the amount of idle or waiting-time and overtime, if exceptional, affects the accuracy of the machine rate. A decided trend of increase in non-operating machine times, owing to a variety of causes, would call for a revision of the rate, which would have to be increased, proportionately, if it were desired to recover all factory expense in the costs, but, where machines stand idle in times of trade depression, the loss on this account is best written off to avoid altering the rates seriously, which would render comparisons difficult or produce grotesque comparisons.

If the machine-hour rates are fixed with due regard to existing and anticipated circumstances, they provide a reasonably reliable means for allocating the Overhead.

Computing the Machine-hour Rate. Method I.—Where separate rates are used for machine-work and bench-work in a shop :

(i) All Factory Overhead, excluding all specifically relating to machines, having been duly apportioned over the respective shops or departments, the total for each shop may be further divided, on the basis of floor area, between the respective machines and work-benches. A proportion of the area of gangways, staircases, etc., will be included in the floor area for each division.

(ii) To the factory overhead so allocated to a particular machine, or group of machines, the expense of each machine is added, *e.g.* power, repairs, interest on capital outlay on the machine, depreciation, oil, etc.

(iii) The total general and machine expense so allotted to each machine is then divided by the estimated running hours for the year (or shorter period), and thus an inclusive machine-hour rate is arrived at. (See Fig. 56.)

Computing the Machine-hour Rate. Method II.—Only the cost of power, repairs, interest on capital value, depreciation, oil, and expenses specifically affecting each machine are included in the rate. All other Factory Overhead is included in a separate shop-rate per direct-labour hour, or such other rate, or percentage, as may be selected. Thus, one rate applies the machine expense to the product, and a second rate, or percentage, applies the general Factory Overhead.

The following is an example of a schedule for computing a machine-hour rate which includes shop expenses :

Fig. 56.

MACHINE EXPENSE SCHEDULE

Machine No. B. 23; Shop " A "

Description : ....   Date bought : ....
Maker :   ....   Cost : £600.
Power :   ....   Estimated life : 10 years.
Additions :   ....   Depreciation : 9% p.a.

Item.	Basis of Estimate.	Cost per Annum. £
Interest on capital outlay .	Cost £600. Interest 5%	30
Depreciation . . .	9% to reduce to £60 in 10 years	54
Insurance	Actual	2
Repairs and maintenance .	Estimated from records or otherwise	34
Indirect materials : oil, cotton, waste, etc.	Estimated on average issues	10
Rent of floor space allotted .	300 sq. ft. at 1s. 4d.	20
Superintendence and shop expenses	$\frac{300}{3000} \times £1,800$ (say)	180
Power	302 days of 8 hours less 20% idle time, estimated	190
Cost per annum		£520
Cost per operating hour (1,933 hrs.) . . . . Use, say, 5s. 5d. hr.		5·38s.

When a separate shop rate is used for general Factory Overhead these charges are omitted from the machine rate. Additional columns may be added for subsequent changes in the expense and rate.

Adjustment of Overhead Expense Account.—It will be apparent that whatever basis is used for allocating factory expense, there is little probability of an exact recovery of the total expense—there will be a balance under-recovered, or over-recovered.

This balance is due to the necessity of (1) estimating what the total expense will be; (2) estimating the output and working hours, and arises when :

(a) The total expense computed for a shop or department exceeds the estimate.

(b) The output or hours worked are less than assumed.

(c) The total expense is actually less than estimated.

(d) The output or hours worked exceed the estimate.

The result is revealed in the Shop Expense Control Accounts, the principle of the operation of which is shown in Fig. 57 :

FIG. 57.

No. 4. SHOP EXPENSE CONTROL ACCOUNT

Dr.		£			Cr.
193... Feb. 28	To Total expense apportioned to shop . .	720	193... Feb. 28 ,, ,,	By Expense "recovered" by machine rates as per summary . . ,, Do. by direct-labour hour rates on hand-work . . . ,, Balance under-recovered transferred to Overhead Adjustment Account . . .	598 103 19
		£720			£720

OVERHEAD ADJUSTMENT ACCOUNT

Dr.		£			Cr.
193... Feb. 28 ,,	To No. 1 Shop Expense Control Account . ,, No. 4 do. do. .	21 19	193... Feb. 28 ,, ,,	By No. 2 Shop Expense Control Account . ,, No. 3 do. do. . ,, Balance written off to Manufacturing Account . . .	5 4 31
		£40			£40

There are three methods of disposing of the balance under— or over—recovered :

(1) By transfer to General Expenses, and absorbing it in new shop rates to be fixed; this is undesirable, as it not only vitiates comparisons, but gives untrue results as between one period and another.

(2) By transfer to Manufacturing Account, or Profit and Loss Account, direct.

(3) By transfer to an Expense Adjustment Reserve Account. This is often used when there is a credit balance on the Expense Account.

When the balance represents unrecovered expense, it is usually best to transfer this to Manufacturing Account or Profit and Loss Account, thereby showing the loss through expenses being higher than estimated, or due to short or idle time. The arguments in favour of this are that the amount has been actually lost; that it is unfair to saddle the production of the period following with expense incurred at an earlier period; and that true comparisons are obtained, which is not the case if balances are absorbed in subsequent expense rates.

Idle Facilities and Idle Time Records.—Idle time of plant and machines represents a loss of a proportion of the expense which remains even when facilities are not in use. There is a small saving in power, and in a few other items. The cost of (*a*) intermittent idle or waiting time should be recorded separately from (*b*) the expense of idle plant, or facilities, in periods of short-time working, owing to depressed markets. To effect this, a weekly schedule of machine times worked and idle should be kept. The idle time (*a*) is charged up to Idle Time Expense Account at the appropriate rate for each machine ; (*b*) is debited to Idle Facilities Account for transfer to Profit and Loss Account.

When part of the plant is necessarily used for only a portion of the total working hours, or can be used only seasonally, the total expense for both working and resting time is included in the rate, which is calculated according to the estimated number of hours to be worked so that the cost of this lost time is absorbed.

Similarly, if a reserve machine is kept to ensure no stoppage in production, the expense in connection with both machines must be included in Overhead and included in the machine-hour rate of the machine normally used.

The principle is the same for both reserve machines and machines used only during a particular season of the year, *viz.* the total cost anticipated for the year must be recovered on the limited hours worked. This procedure applies to idle time that is of regular and unavoidable occurrence, resulting from methods of production which necessitate having machines that cannot be kept fully employed. But when idle time is attributable to shortage of work due to business conditions, as during acute trade depression, the expense of idle plant is not included in the machine rate, but taken direct to Profit and Loss Account. Idle Time due to delays between jobs, etc., or due to shop management faults, etc., is usually included in Overhead.

Allocation of Special Fixed Bonus, War Bonus, etc., usually paid as a lump sum, *e.g.* a War Bonus of 10*s*. a week of 47 hours. The allocation of this to jobs may be on the basis of time worked on each. Where piece-rate only is paid to workers, the jobs may be converted into the equivalent in hours, and the bonus apportioned accordingly on the basis of Direct Labour hours.

EXAMINATION QUESTIONS

1. What do you understand by the term Machine-Hour rate? Illustrate your answer by an example. What effect has restricted output upon a Machine-Hour rate?—*London Association of Accountants (Final)*.

2. Discuss the relative merits of charging out on-cost on the following bases:

(*a*) Time.
(*b*) Direct labour.
(*c*) Direct labour plus direct material.

Royal Society of Arts (Advanced).

3. In a Press Shop having several power presses are engaged three tool-setters.

(*a*) How would you account for their wages in the labour costs of the several products?
(*b*) If you were required to pay them upon results, what method would you adopt?

Institute of Cost and Works Accountants (Inter.).

4. The Overhead charges of a factory are allocated over the production on the " Productive Hour " basis. What do you understand this statement to mean?

A man and a boy complete similar jobs; materials cost £10 in each case. The man spends 12 hours on the work and is paid at the rate of 1*s*. 8*d*. per hour, whilst the boy takes 20 hours and is paid at the rate of 1*s*. per hour. Oncost is charged at the rate of 2*s*. 6*d*. per productive hour. Prepare a statement showing the cost in each case.

Do you approve of this method of allocating Oncost? If not, what do you suggest?—*London Chamber of Commerce*.

5. What do you understand by the term " Oncost "? Upon what basis should it, in your opinion, be calculated? State your reasons.—*Chartered Institute of Secretaries (Inter.)*.

6. For what productions would you advocate the following methods of charging Oncost respectively? Give reasons.

(*a*) Percentage on direct labour.
(*b*) Percentage on direct labour plus direct materials.
(*c*) Hourly labour rate.
(*d*) Machine-hour rate.

Royal Society of Arts (Advanced).

7. The Forward Manufacturing Co. prepare the following Cost Sheet for the month of March 1930:

Articles	A.	B.	C.	D.	E.	
Units	483	1096	809	401	730	Total.
	£	£	£	£	£	£
Direct Materials .	27	31	86	70	489	703
,, Wages .	91	16	114	191	-18	430
Prime Cost .	118	47	200	261	507	1133
Works Oncost 107						
Office ,, 176	29	12	50	65	127	283
Total Cost .	147	59	250	326	634	1416
Cost per Unit	6/1·04	1/0·9	6/3	16/3·1	17/4·4	

The material used was 218 tons, the proportion wasted on account of defects being 0·38 per cent. Wages averaged 1s. 10d. per hour. If you think the Cost Sheet contains errors of principle, restate it correctly, giving reasons.—*Institute of Chartered Accountants* (*Final*).

8. A manufacturing business is divided into three manufacturing departments, A, B, and C. The manufacturing expenditure is divided as follows :

	A. £	B. £	C. £	Total. £
Productive Wages	10,000	5,000	7,500	22,500
Oncost Expense	5,000	10,000	7,500	22,500
Material	—	—	—	45,000
				£90,000

The cost of producing an article is prepared as follows :

	£	s.	d.
Wages Cost, A. Department	0	7	6
,, ,, B. ,,	0	4	0
,, ,, C. ,,	0	10	0
	1	1	6
Oncost 100 per cent.	1	1	6
Material	2	0	0
	£4	3	0

What is the fundamental fallacy of this method, assuming the Productive Wages are an approximately accurate measure for the distribution of Oncost ? When would the method give reliable results ?

In your answers, ignore the fact that Selling, Delivery, and General Administration Expense is not covered in the cost.—*London Association of Accountants* (*Final*).

9. The output of a certain Casting by four different moulders in the same week was as follows :

A	.	.	.	.	81
B	.	.	.	.	49
C	.	.	.	.	73
D	.	.	.	.	90

Each was paid 9d. per piece. The cost department calculated by two methods the cost of output of each man as follows :

	A. £	A. s.	A. d.	B. £	B. s.	B. d.	C. £	C. s.	C. d.	D. £	D. s.	D. d.	Total. £	Total. s.	Total. d.
Wages	3	0	9	1	16	9	2	14	9	3	7	6	10	19	9
Oncost on man-hour method	2	4	0	2	4	0	2	4	0	2	4	0	8	16	0
	5	4	9	4	0	9	4	18	9	5	11	6	19	15	9
Wages	3	0	9	1	16	9	2	14	9	3	7	6	10	19	9
Oncost on Direct Wages method	2	8	8	1	9	6	2	3	10	2	14	0	8	16	0
	5	9	5	3	6	3	4	18	7	6	1	6	19	15	9

Which do you consider the most reliable method of calculating the cost of the Castings made by B and D? Why? In adopting the man-hour method for the purpose of estimates generally, do you see any weakness in the method?—*London Association of Accountants (Final)*.

10. Explain the machine-hour rate method of apportioning Indirect Charges, giving an illustration of the method by which the hourly rate is ascertained.—*Society of Incorporated Accountants and Auditors (Final)*.

11. When applied to the allocation of Oncost what do you understand by the terms (a) labour-hour rate, (b) machine-hour rate, and (c) production-hour rate? What would be the determining factor in each case?—*Society of Incorporated Accountants and Auditors (Inter.)*.

12. The charges attributable to a particular department having been ascertained, on what basis should they be apportioned over the work done in that department? Give reasons for your answer.—*Society of Incorporated Accountants and Auditors (Inter.)*.

13. In calculating " Oncost " what do you understand by the :

(a) Percentage method,
(b) Productive-Hour method,
(c) Machine-Hour method?

Society of Incorporated Accountants and Auditors (Final).

14. Where a commodity requires a similar quantity of materials and time occupied by labour in the manufacture of a given output, what variable factors would require consideration from time to time in fixing the selling price of that commodity?—*Society of Incorporated Accountants and Auditors (Final)*.

15. State the information required for arriving at a " Productive Labour Hourly Rate." What are the advantages and disadvantages as compared with :

1. Percentage method of allocation of overheads.
2. Machine-hour rate?

Institute of Cost and Works Accountants (Final).

16. A certain operation is equally well performed by hand as by machine, but the flow of work is intermittent. You are required to examine the problems which arise and make recommendations.—*Institute of Cost and Works Accountants (Final)*.

17. Prepare a machine-hour rate to recover the overhead expenses indicated below :

	Per hour.	Per annum.
	d.	£
Electric Power . . .	11½	
Steam	10	
Water	1½	
Repairs		53
Rent		27
Running Hours . . .		2000

Original Cost Price, £1250.
Book Value, £287.
Present Replacement Value, £1150.
Depreciation, 7½ per cent. per annum.
Institute of Cost and Works Accountants (Final).

18. A group of manufacturers received a request for each firm to apply " Overhead " by a fixed percentage upon direct labour. Do you consider this a sound suggestion? Discuss the request.—*Institute of Cost and Works Accountants (Final)*.

19. A certain factory pays its operators upon a straight piece-work

basis (no job clocking). The National awards (war bonus), however, are only based on time-rate. How would you deal with these awards in job costs ?—*Institute of Cost and Works Accountants (Inter.)*.

20. Three operatives are given a job on a piece-work basis and their weekly rates are, for 47 hours, A—65*s*., B—47*s*., C—38*s*. respectively, plus a War Bonus of 10*s*. per week. The piece-price of the job is £8 and their times are A—42 hours, B—52 hours and C—36 hours. Calculate the bonus to be allocated to each and show the actual labour cost of the job, including War Bonus.—*Institute of Cost and Works Accountants (Inter.)*.

21. Describe how you would measure the item of idle time and how you would deal with the same in your Cost Accounts.—*Institute of Cost and Works Accountants (Inter.)*.

22. In ascertaining a shop hourly rate, what would you use as the basis ? Give a list of the principal factors you would expect to include. —*Institute of Cost and Works Accountants (Inter.)*.

23. In setting up machine-hour rates of absorption of overheads, what provision would you make year by year for depreciation of the machines engaged in production ? How would you deal with expenses of plant of a general character ?—*Institute of Cost and Works Accountants (Final)*.

24. During a period of industrial depression, how would you deal with the expense relating to idle plant, assuming such expense to be considerable, and that the market conditions preclude its inclusion in estimate prices ? Detail the main items comprising such expense.— *Institute of Cost and Works Accountants (Final)*.

25. How would you proceed to determine machine-hour rates for absorption of overheads where the number of machines worked by one operator varies from time to time ?—*Institute of Cost and Works Accountants (Final)*.

26. During a period of acute trade depression, a manufacturer asks your advice as to continuing his costing system in view of the fact that the reductions in prices and turnover render the cost figures useless for the purposes of comparison and estimating. What advice would you give ?—*Society of Incorporated Accountants and Auditors (Inter.)*.

27. The Profit and Loss Account of a large Printing Works includes charges in respect of the following items :

Clerks' Salaries.	Travelling Expenses.
Stationery.	Carriage Outwards.
Interest on Loans.	Management Salaries.
Advertising.	Rent and Rates.
Discounts.	Auditor's Fees.

State carefully how you would proceed with regard to these items in preparing Cost Statements. In which cases should charges be made against individual printing jobs undertaken and how should the charge be ascertained ?—*London Chamber of Commerce*.

28. State the matters you would take into consideration in deciding which of the following systems of allocating Works Oncost you would recommend for adoption in a particular trade :

    (a) Prime Cost Method,
    (b) Productive Labour Hour Method,
    (c) Percentage on Direct Labour,
    (d) Machine Hour Rate.
                            Corporation of Accountants (Final).

29. What is the man-hour method of allocating Oncost ? In what circumstances would you recommend the adoption of this method ? Give an example showing the method of calculation.—*Corporation of Accountants (Final)*.

30. The following figures relate to one of the departments of a manufacturing business during the last five years :

	1929.	1930.	1931.	1932.	1933.
	£	£	£	£	£
Direct Wages . .	18,742	23,691	21,840	17,640	14,781
Oncost : Floating .	12,872	15,240	14,300	12,090	10,178
Fixed . .	7,400	7,829	7,891	7,642	7,789

The year 1933 was abnormally depressed, and it is considered that the average of the other four years would form a satisfactory standard of output. (1) Calculate an appropriate rate of standard oncost to the nearest 5 per cent. (2) Show what loss through unrecovered oncost was suffered in 1933. (3) State what provision (if any) the standard oncost made in 1933 towards the fixed oncost.—*London Association of Certified Accountants (Final).*

31. In comparing the relative costs of production in two manufacturing organisations, x and y, how would you deal with :

(1) Depreciation charged in the accounts of x at the rate of $7\frac{1}{2}$ per cent. per annum on the diminishing cost and in the accounts of y at 5 per cent. ?

(2) Debenture Interest paid by x and Bank Interest paid by y.

(3) Rent paid by x; no rent paid by y (owning its own premises).

(4) Discounts allowed by x; no discounts allowed by y.

London Association of Certified Accountants (Final).

32. The following is a schedule of the expenditure in three departments of a manufacturing business, viz. :

Cost of Supplying and Installing One No. 6 Hydraulic Pump.

	£	s.	d.
Wages of foundry workers, machinists, fitters and erectors	316	8	9
Materials	202	10	6
Wages and travelling expenses of outside erectors . .	38	2	10
Establishment Charges 150 per cent. . . .	835	13	1
	1,392	15	2
Profit 10 per cent.	139	5	6
	£1,532	0	8

State briefly what fundamental principles appear to be ignored in the calculation of this cost.—*London Association of Certified Accountants (Final).*

33. What is the object of a manufacturer keeping records showing how much it costs to keep each machine in running order ?—*Incorporated Accountants (Inter.).*

34. Discuss the various bases on which overhead expenses or oncosts may be distributed, and argue which of these bases you would recommend in the case of a cotton-spinning factory or other industry with which you are acquainted.—*Incorporated Accountants (Final).*

35. The expenses of running an engineering factory for last year were : Rent and Rates £2,680; Fuel £3261; Electric Lighting and Heating (gas) £478; Machinery Repairs £641; Insurance (Fire and Employers' Liability) £895; Interest on Capital £3,400; Wages, productive £32,000, non-productive £6,450; General Expenses £1,948; Depreciation of Machinery (10 per cent.) £3,865. There are three shops of equal size and capacity, but the machines employed differ considerably in cost and running hours. Which of the above items (if any) can, in your

opinion, be charged direct to the several shops, and which should be apportioned, and upon what basis ?—*Chartered Accountants (Final)*.

36. What is meant by a machine-hour rate, and how is it arrived at ? —*Incorporated Accountants (Inter.)*.

37. B. MacArthur, a jobbing printer, makes a practice of adding to the prime cost of his jobs a percentage of wages and materials to cover oncost, such percentage being calculated on figures in the accounts of the previous financial year. In spite of the fact that each job appears to show a fair margin of profit and the overhead expenses have not materially altered, MacArthur finds that the Profit and Loss Account shows a loss at the end of the year. How do you account for this ? If you do not approve of MacArthur's method of allocating oncost, how would you amend it ?—*Chartered Accountants (Final)*.

38. Give a pro-forma account illustrating the method of calculation of a Machine Hour Rate.—*Incorporated Accountants (Final)*.

39. What information would you require and to what points would you give special consideration if called upon to plan a Cost System for any manufacturing business with which you are familiar (to be named) ?— *Incorporated Accountants (Inter.)*.

40. Where departmental overhead charges are allocated on the basis of labour only, what considerations should determine whether to apportion according to wages paid or time spent ?—*Incorporated Accountants (Inter.)*.

41. The following figures relate to a printing works for a year :—

	£		£
Total Sales . . .	40,000	Lighting and Heating .	310
Materials used . .	6,900	Repairs to Machinery .	490
Labour . . .	15,000	Plant Depreciation at 7½	
Rent, Rates and Water .	650	per cent. per annum .	720
Power . . .	255	Other Overhead Charges .	10,000

Included in the Plant are four Linotype machines occupying one-sixth of the total floor area. They cost £2,000 two years ago, and it is estimated that their scrap value in twelve years time will not exceed £200.

You are asked to work out a machine-hour rate, assuming any further details you may consider necessary.—*Incorporated Accountants (Inter.)*.

42. Calculate Machine Hour Rate for Machine No. 7. which is one of seven machines in operation in a department of a factory. You are furnished with the following information :—

(1) Cost of Machine No. 7, £1,000.

(2) Estimated Scrap Value at finish of working life (10 years), £100.

(3) Normal running hours per annum, 1,800.

(4) Depreciation to be charged at 9 per cent. per annum.

(5) Machine No. 7 occupies one-fifth of floor space of department, the Rent, Rates, Lighting, etc., of which amount to £350 per annum.

(6) Charges for Electric Power supplied to Machine No. 7, £200 per annum.

(7) Charges for Oil, Waste, etc., supplied to Machine No. 7, £30 per annum.

(8) Repairs and Maintenance throughout working life of Machine estimated at £370.

(9) Cost of Supervision and other expenses applicable to Machine No. 7 estimated at £150 per annum.

Labour Cost of operating the machine to be ignored in making your calculations.—*Corporation of Accountants (Final)*.

CHAPTER XIII

JOB OR TERMINAL COSTING

Job Costing is the method of costing jobs or contracts that are kept separate during manufacture or construction. A separate Cost Account is kept for each individual job, or contract, until completion of the work, when the account is closed, showing the total cost and the profit or loss made. Owing to the nature of this class of Cost Accounts, the designation Terminal Costing is often used.

This method of costing is applied to :

(i) Contracts such as are undertaken by builders, general contractors, shipbuilders, constructional and mechanical engineers, etc.

(ii) Job orders in factories and workshops.

The principle is the same for both groups, but there are, generally, a few points of difference in procedure, owing to the different nature of the work on large building and constructional contracts, as against the more numerous job orders dealt with in factories.

The Procedure.—It is usual to give each contract, or order, a distinguishing number to facilitate reference in the books, and on the various forms which are used. This number identifies the Cost Account to which are charged the cost of labour, materials, and expenses.

The Cost of Materials

(a) *Stores Material.*—Materials from the Store are issued against a Stores Requisition (Fig. 10) which is the authority for the storekeeper to issue. Each requisition bears the number of the job for which it is required, and a weekly (or other period) summary is made, called a Materials Abstract, in which an analysis under job numbers is shown. (See Fig. 59.) The total value of the material under each job number is then debited to the appropriate Cost Account bearing the same number by posting from the Materials Abstract.

In some cases no Abstract is prepared, posting being direct from the priced requisitions (Slip posting method).

(b) *Direct Material.*—Sometimes material is purchased outside, or manufactured in the works, for a particular job or contract. The cost of this material will usually be debited direct to the Cost Account for the job concerned.

159

In the case of large constructional contracts, sub-contracts for specialised material, *e.g.* polished granite or heavy girders, are placed, the price for which is similarly a direct debit.

(c) *Materials Returned.*—It is sometimes necessary to issue certain kinds of material in excess of requirements, as, for instance, brass bars from which a number of parts may be made on a machine tool, and which can be worked upon better in full bars. The excess is later returned to the Store, accompanied by a Shop Credit Note, or what is the same thing, a Stores Debit Note, on which is stated the job to be credited.

(d) *Records of Material Issued.*—The Issue Requisitions show the quantity taken, and later, when they reach the Works Office, the quantities of each kind of material are priced, extended, and entered in the Stores Ledger, after which the Materials Abstract is entered up ready for posting to the Cost Ledger Accounts.

The necessary entries on the Stores Bin Cards are made at the time of issue by the storekeeper, and in the Stores Ledger by a clerk in the Cost Office. The totals of the analyses of the figures posted to the Stores Ledger are also posted to the Materials Control Accounts, thus providing for reconciliation with the Financial Accounts.

The Wages Abstract.—The wages paid to the workers will usually be calculated upon gate-times, piece-work tickets, or time-sheets, according to the arrangements in force. Full particulars of the amount paid to each, and the total, are recorded in the Wages Book, or Pay-Roll arranged departmentally.

An analysis is also made on a Wages Abstract, so that the number of hours and amount chargeable to each job or contract, or expense account, are ascertained. (Fig. 58.) In the case of builders and contractors, this analysis will be compiled from details provided on time-sheets, and the Abstract is usually in sections, according to trades, so that separate totals for each job for each class of work are obtained, *e.g.* bricklayers, plumbers, joiners, etc. The total against each job number is posted to the appropriate Cost Account. See also p. 406.

In factories using the job cost method, the hours and amounts chargeable to each job are recorded by one of the methods described in a previous chapter, as, for instance, job clock-cards, job-tickets, piece-work tickets, etc. From these the Wages

FIG. 58

WAGE ABSTRACT

Week ending February 7, 19...   No. 32.

JOB No. 90

Clock No.	Hrs.	Amount £ s. d.
12	4	8 0
13	8	16 0
18	2	5 8
21	1	2 3
	15	1 11 11

JOB No. 91

No.	Hrs.	Amount £ s. d.
22	5	7 6
23	4	8 0
	9	15 6

JOB No. 98

No.	Hrs.	Amount £ s. d.
23	4	8 0
17	40	4 0 0
	44	4 8 0

JOB No. 100

No.	Hrs.	Amount £ s. d.
12	4	8 0
18	2	5 6
21	2	4 0
	8	17 6

R. 13

No.	Hrs.	Amount £ s. d.
22	3	4 0 0
18	14	4 15 0
21	2	2 4 0
12	20	2 0 0
19	6	2 15 0
	45	4 19 0

N. 31

No.	Hrs.	Amount £ s. d.
14	8	16 0
17	8	16 0
21	3	3 0
22	40	3 0 0
	59	4 18 9

SUMMARY

Job No.	Hrs.	Amount £ s. d.	Cost Led. fol.
90	15	1 11 11	
91	9	15 6	
98	44	4 8 0	
100	8	17 6	
R. 13	45	4 19 0	
N. 31	59	4 18 9	
	180	17 10 8	

A portion of a wages abstract sheet. The total shown in the summary column must agree with the direct wages on the pay roll. Another form appears on p. 406.

FIG. 59.

STORES MATERIALS ABSTRACT

Week ending : February 7, 19...   No. 12.

JOB No. 90

I.R. No.	£ s. d.
91	4 9 0
95	3 0 0
	7 9 0

JOB No. 91

I.R. No.	£ s. d.
93	1 2 0
97	3 7 0
	4 9 0

JOB No. 98

I.R. No.	£ s. d.
92	7 15 0
	7 15 0

JOB No. 100

I.R. No.	£ s. d.
94	2 1 0
98	15 0
	2 16 0

R. 13

I.R. No.	£ s. d.
96	8 6 0
99	3 2 0
90	1 5 6
	12 13 6

N. 31

I.R. No.	£ s. d.
88	6 3 0
89	5 19 0
	12 2 0

SUMMARY

Job No.	£ s. d.	Cost Led. fol.
90	7 9 0	
91	4 9 0	
98	7 15 0	
100	2 16 0	
R. 13	12 13 6	
N. 31	12 2 0	
	47 4 6	

A portion of a stores material abstract sheet.

N

Abstract is prepared. A separate account of each kind of indirect labour is kept under Expense account numbers.

The total of the Wages Abstract must be agreed with the total of the pay-roll, thus ensuring that in total the charge for wages in the cost accounts will be in agreement with the financial accounts. The totals are posted to the Wages Control Account. (See Ch. XV.)

Posting the Cost Ledger.—The separate totals of materials and wages for each job are then posted to a Cost Ledger Account for the job (see form on pages 164 and 184). The Job or Contract Cost Ledger is often in card or loose-leaf form, a separate card or sheet being used for the cash account instead of the usual book form. The total of each class of indirect labour cannot be posted direct to the Job Accounts, but is posted to appropriate Expense Accounts. The indirect labour and indirect material expenses are recovered in the various Job Accounts by a rate on a suitable basis, *e.g.* a rate per direct-labour hour, a percentage on direct wages, etc., as explained in an earlier chapter. Reconciliation of Cost Ledger with the Financial Accounts is effected by means of Control Accounts as described in Ch. XV.

The procedure so far described is alike for both Contract Accounts and for Job Cost Accounts in a factory. The particular features of Contract Accounts will now be considered— the Accounts of a builder being used for illustration. Factory Job Costs will be described in the next Chapter.

Contract Cost Accounts

The Form of Cost Ledger Accounts (Contracts).—For builders and other contractors a suitable ruling for a Contract Account is shown in Fig. 60. For businesses with many small contracts the card form of Contract Cost Ledger is very convenient, as the accounts of completed jobs can be removed to a separate filing cabinet. Other forms appear on pages 184, 185 and 282.

An account is opened for each contract. The exact form of the account will depend upon individual requirements. For instance, the column headed " Wages " in Fig. 60 is often expanded into several columns, a separate one being used for labourers, bricklayers, joiners, plumbers, painters, etc. In the case of large building contracts it is not unusual to take two pages across the Prime Cost Book for each Contract Account, one page showing the Materials analysed under such headings as the management may require, and the other dealing similarly with wages analysed by trades. The totals are posted on completion of the contract, or, at intervals, to a summary Contract Cost Account, ruled similarly to the Contract Accounts themselves. (Fig. 60.)

The Wages portion of a Prime Cost Book is shown in Fig. 61.

(a) *Materials*.—In the Purchase Analysis Journal direct purchases for particular contracts will be extended into a separate column, and will be debited direct to the contract concerned. The stores materials are analysed in separate columns for joiners', masons', bricklayers', and plumbers' materials, as it is usual to keep separate Stores Accounts for these sections. The totals of these stores materials columns are posted to Stores Accounts in the Nominal Ledger. A separate Stores Ledger is kept on the lines described in a previous chapter.

The issues of materials are debited to the Contract Accounts from the Stores Materials Abstract (Fig. 59), and the grand total of the Abstract is posted to the credit of Stores Control Account in the Nominal Ledger.

(b) *Plant*. The value of plant sent to the site of a contract is debited to the Contract Account, the appropriate Plant Account being credited.*

When the contract is finished, such plant as may be returned to the yard is credited to the contract at its estimated value, usually much depreciated. Some special plant may not be suitable for any other work, as, for instance, wooden templates, and may be sold at scrap price. The price so obtained will be credited to the cost account for the contract. By this procedure each contract bears the depreciation cost of the use of the plant.

(c) *Sub-contracts* are dealt with in the same manner as special direct materials; they are debited to the Contract Account direct from the Purchases Analysis Journal.

(d) *Direct Expenses*.—Disbursements of this kind, *e.g.* Petty Cash, Plant hire, etc., are posted direct to the Contract Accounts concerned.

(e) *Indirect Expenses*.—These are debited to expense accounts from the Cash Book, Petty Cash Book and Purchases Analysis Journal. At the end of each month, the total of each expense

* Plant sent for use for short periods is not charged in this way, but instead an hourly-rate or daily-rate is used, the charge thus depending on the *time* used. Such a charge will be credited to Depreciation Account, except when a hire charge is debited for plant hired from other firms.

FIG. 60.

CONTRACT COST LEDGER ACCOUNT

The Southern Bank Ltd.,
New Premises, 296 High Street,
London.

Name.   Contract No.: ......

Week Ending	Ref.	DEBITS						CREDITS			Prime Cost.	Overhead Charges.	Total Cost to date.
		Stores Materials.	Direct Materials.	Plant, etc.	Wages.	Direct Expenses.	Total.	Stores returned.	Plant returned.	Total.			
		£ s. d.	£ s. d.	£ s. d.	£ s. d.	£ s. d.	£ s. d.	£ s. d.	£ s. d.	£ s. d.	£ s. d.	£ s. d.	£ s. d.

Note.—Compare with Job Cost Ledger Account on p. 184.

FIG. 61.

WAGES PORTION OF THE PRIME COST BOOK

Date of Contract: ....

Name (of Contract).   Contract No.: ......

Week Ended	Abst. No.	Labourers.	Bricklayers.	Joiners.	Painters.	Plumbers.	Machinists.	etc.	Total for Week.	Posted Contract A/c. Folio
		hrs. £ s. d.	hrs. £ s. d.	hrs. £ s. d.	hrs. £ s. d.	hrs. £ s. d.	hrs. £ s. d.		hrs. £ s. d.	

account is credited, being transferred to the debit of Expense Allocation Control Account.*

The total expense charged to the individual contract accounts is credited to that account. It is usual to apportion the total expenses first to the various shops, *e.g.* joiners, stonemasons, etc. The expense charge to each contract is then made as a rate per hour of direct labour, or, in the case of the Joiners' Shop, where power machines are used, partly as a machine-hour rate for each machine, and partly as a labour-hour rate for work not done by machine.

(f) *Closing Accounts of Finished Contracts.*—The value of the completed contract is credited to the Contract Account, and debited to the Customer's Account, thus making each contract a separate Trading Account. Any profit (or loss) is then transferred to the General Profit and Loss Account.

When big contracts are operated, payments on account are made against the architects' certificates for the work completed at given periods and deducted from work in progress at cost.

(g) *Uncompleted Contracts.*—The outlay on materials, labour, direct expenses and the current proportion of indirect expenses is treated as work in progress. When indirect expenses are not added until the completion of the contract, as is often the case, a Suspense Account is debited with the accrued charge for expenses.

It is an accepted principle that no profit should be taken credit for on uncompleted work, except in the case of very long contracts, when a conservative sum, say two-thirds of the profit accrued on the work certified by the architects, may be credited.

(h) *Jobbing Work.*—There is generally a considerable amount of jobbing work of a minor nature done whilst major contracts are in progress. It is, therefore, customary to open a Jobbing Account for each department, *e.g.*, joiners, plumbers, etc. The selling prices credited to these accounts are debited to the purchasers via the Sales Day Book, which may be in columnar form when separate departmental jobbing accounts are kept.

(i) *Haulage Expense.*—The lorries and carts used by a builder involve expense which can be treated separately. A Haulage Account is debited with the running expenses, *e.g.* fodder, petrol, oil, drivers' wages, repairs, depreciation, etc.

---

* Indirect Expenses not otherwise allocable may be allocated to the various contracts proportionately to the total expenditure on each, although the labour-hour method is usually equitable.

Each driver records on his time-sheet the time taken on each job and states for which contract. The haulage expense is then calculated at a rate per hour, and debited, accordingly, to the respective contracts. Any balance not definitely chargeable to contracts is included in General Operating Expense Account.

(j) *Specimen Contract Accounts.*—Under the procedure described above the Contract Ledger forms an integral part of the financial double-entry accounts. The control accounts and final accounts are exemplified below.

CONTRACT CONTROL ACCOUNTS

1. *Stores Materials Account*

Dr.				£	s.	d.				£	s.	d.
19...							19...				
Jan. 1	To Balance on hand . .	b/d.		860	0	0	Jan. 31	By Issues to Contracts . .	A6	410	0	0
,, 31	,, Purchases .	J6		710	0	0	Feb. 28	,, ,, . .	A8	270	0	0
Feb. 28	,, ,, .	J9		760	0	0		,, Jobbing A/c. .	A8	820	0	0
Mar. 31	,, ,, .	J11		970	0	0	Mar. 31	,, Issues to Contracts . .	A10	350	0	0
							,, Issues to Jobbing A/c. .	A10	760	0	0
							,, Stock on hand	c/d.	690	0	0
			£3300	0	0				£3300	0	0

2. *Wages Account*
(or a separate account for each department, Joiners, etc.)

Dr.				£	s.	d.				£	s.	d.
19...							19...				
Jan. 31	To Cash . .	81		1590	0	0	Mar. 31	By Sundry Contract A/cs. .	J12	2460	0	0
Feb. 28	,, ,, . .	90		1630	0	0	,,	,, Stonemasons Shop A/c. .		460	0	0
Mar. 31	,, ,, . .	98		1720	0	0	,,	,, Joiners Shop A/c. .		610	0	0
						,,	,, Jobbing (Joiners) Shop A/c. .		790	0	0
						,,	,, Expense Control A/c. (Indirect Labour)		620	0	0
			£4940	0	0				£4940	0	0

3. *Stonemasons' Shop Account*
(a similar account for Joiners, etc.)

Dr.				£	s.	d.				£	s.	d.
1 9...							19...				
Mar. 1	To Balance .	b/d.		120	0	0	Mar. 31	By Sundry Contracts A/cs. .	J12	600	0	0
,, 31	,, Wages .	98		460	0	0	,,	,, Jobbing A/c. .	J13	395	0	0
,,	,, Stores Materials .	1		290	0	0	,,	,, Balance, Work in Progress .	c/d.	195	0	0
,, Expenses Allocation .	5		320	0	0					
			£1190	0	0				£1190	0	0

4. *Jobbing Account (Joiners)*

Dr.   Cr.

19...			£	s.	d.	19...			£	s.	d.
Mar. 31	To Wages . .	98	790	0	0	Mar. 31	By Sales . .	J12	2735	0	0
,,	,, Stores Materials .	1	980	0	0						
,,	,, Expense Allocation	5	375	0	0						
,,	,, Profit to P. & L. A/c. .	J13	590	0	0						
			£2735	0	0				£2735	0	0

5. *Expenses Allocation Control*

Dr.   Cr.

19...			£	s.	d.	19...			£	s.	d.
Mar. 31	To Indirect Wages .	98	620	0	0	Mar. 31	By Sundry Contracts A/cs. .	J12	1729	0	0
,,	,, Rents and Rates	J9	900	0	0	,,	,, Shop Allocations:				
,,	,, Cartage .	,,	300	0	0		Stonemasons	3	320	0	0
,,	,, Office Expenses	,,	600	0	0		Joiners, etc. .	4	375	0	0
,,	,, Light, etc. .	,,	125	0	0		Jobbing		520	0	0
,,	,, Repairs .	,,	235	0	0		,, Adjustment to P. & L. A/c. (under allocated) .	J14	6	0	0
,,	,, Depreciation, etc. . .	,,	170	0	0						
			£2950	0	0				£2950	0	0

6. *Contracts Account*
for the three months ending March 31st, 19......

Dr.   Cr.

19...			£	s.	d.	19...			£	s.	d.
Mar. 31	To Loss on Contracts (from each a/c. detailed)	J12	69	0	0	Mar. 31	By Profits on Contracts (transferred in detail) . .	J12	2950	0	0
,,	,, Profit on Contracts to P. & L. A/c. .	J13	2881	0	0						
			£2950	0	0				£2950	0	0

Profit and Loss Account
for the three months ending March 31st, 19......

Dr.   Cr.

19...			£	s.	d.	19...			£	s.	d.
Mar. 31	To Expense A/c.	J15	6	0	0	Mar. 31	By Contracts A/c.	J13	2881	0	0
,,	,, Net Profit for the three months .		5230	0	0	,,	,, Jobbing Shops: Stonemasons	J14	615	0	0
							Joiners	,,	590	0	0
							etc. . .	,,	1150	0	0
			£5236	0	0				£5236	0	0

The following example of an individual Contract Account shows two methods of reserving for profits on an uncompleted contract, a prudent course to provide against possible losses before completion from any of various possible causes.

Contract No. 86.

	£
Labour on Site	40,500
Materials direct to Site less returns	42,000
do. from Store and Workshops	8,120
Plant sent to Site	6,200
Direct Expenses	2,300
General Overhead Expense apportioned to this contract	3,710
Materials on hand 30th June	630
Wages accrued at 30th June	780
Direct Expenses accrued	160
Valuation of Plant 30th June	4,990
Work not yet certified, at Cost	1,650
Amount certified by Architects	110,000
Cash received on account	90,000
Contract Price for Completed Contract . . .	125,000

Prepare the Contract Accounts to show the position at 30th June, retaining an adequate reserve against possible losses before completion of the contract.

The details of the expenditure would be posted to a Contract Ledger Account in the form shown on page 164, and the position of the Contract may be shown as follows :

Contract No. 86.

Dr.   Cr.

193.		£	193.		£
June 30	To Materials direct	42,000	June 30	By Material on hand c/d	630
,,	,, Other Materials .	8,120	,,	,, Plant Valuation c/d	4,990
,,	,, Wages . .	40,500	,,	,, Balance c/d . .	98,150
,,	,, Direct Expenses .	2,300			
,,	,, Plant . .	6,200			
,,	,, General Overhead .	3,710			
,,	,, Wages Accrued c/d	780			
,,	,, Direct Expenses Accrued c/d .	160			
		£103,770			£103,770
June 30	To Balance b/d . .	98,150	June 30	By Work Certified .	110,000
,,	,, ⅔ Profit to Profit & Loss Account *	9,000	,,	,, Work done not yet Certified c/d . .	1,650
,,	,, Balance of Profit c/d	4,500			
		£111,650			£111,650
July 1	To Materials on hand b/d	630	July 1	By Profit b/d . .	4,500
,,	,, Plant b/d . .	4,990	,,	,, Wages b/d . .	780
,,	,, Work not Certified b/d . . .	1,650	,,	,, Direct Expenses b/d	160

* Alternatively, instead of taking ⅔ of £13,500 profit, a more conservative sum could be calculated thus :

$\dfrac{\text{Cash Received £ } 90,000}{\text{Work Certified } 110,000} \times 9,000$, i.e. $\tfrac{9}{11} \times 9,000$, say £7,364,

which would increase the profit reserve carried down to £6,136.

Dr.			CONTRACTEE'S ACCOUNT		Cr
193. June 30	To Contract 86. Architects Certificates .	110,000	193. June 30 „	By Cash . . . „ Balance c/d . .	90,000 20,000
		£110,000			£110,000
July 1	To Balance b/d . .	20,000			

["Time and Lime" Contracts, and "Target" Contracts are described on page 17.]

In the next chapter is described the general procedure for job costs in factories. The reference therein to mechanical aids for costing where detail is considerable may be applicable to Contract Accounts in suitable cases.

EXAMINATION QUESTIONS

1. A small builder doing (a) Contract Work and (b) Jobbing Work has, hitherto, had only an annual Profit and Loss Account and Balance Sheet, showing the result of the whole of his operations.

His last annual account showed a loss when he had expected a profit. He desires to organise his business so that in future he can obtain a cost statement in respect of each contract or job separately. The additional work involved must be kept at a minimum.

Set out in detail your recommendations, showing clearly the connection, if any, between the new costing records and the existing financial books.

You may assume any figures, or further details you need in order to make your recommendations clear.—*London Chamber of Commerce.*

2. What is meant by Oncost? State briefly any two methods known to you of allocating Oncost to the cost of producing manufactured goods, indicating in both cases the principle underlying the method.— *London Association of Accountants (Final).*

3. Draw up a specimen cost ledger sheet for job costing.—*Royal Society of Arts (Advanced).*

4. A and B, contractors, obtained a contract to build houses, the contract price being £400,000.

Work commenced on January 1, 1929, and upon it the following expenditure was incurred during the year: Plant and Tools £20,000, Stores and Materials £72,000, Wages £65,000, Sundry Expenses £5,300 and Establishment Charges £11,700.

Certain of the materials costing £12,000 were unsuited to the contract and were sold for £14,500. A portion of the plant was scrapped and sold for £2,300.

The value of the plant and tools on site on December 31, 1929, was £6,200, and the value of stores and materials on hand £3,400. Cash received on account was £140,000, representing 80 per cent. of the work certified. The cost of work done but not certified was £21,900; this was certified later for £25,000.

A and B decided to estimate what further expenditure would be incurred in completing the contract, to compute from this estimate and the expenditure already incurred the total profit that would be made on the contract and to take to credit of Profit and Loss Account for the year 1929 that proportion of the total which corresponded to the work certified by December 31.

The estimate was as follows :

(a) That the contract would be completed by September 30, 1930.
(b) That the wages on the contract in 1930 would amount to £71,500

(c) That the cost of stores and materials required in addition to those in stock on December 31, 1929, would be £68,600 and that the further contract expenses would amount to £6,000.

(d) That a further £25,000 would have to be laid out on plant and tools and that the residual value of plant and tools on September 30, 1930, would be £3,000.

(e) That establishment charges would cost the same sum per month as in 1929.

(f) That 2½ per cent. of the total cost of the contract would be due to defects, temporary maintenance and contingencies.

Prepare Contract, Stores and Materials and Plant Accounts for the year ended December 31, 1929, and show your calculation of the amount credited to Profit and Loss Account for that year. Ignore shillings and pence.—*Institute of Chartered Accountants (Final)*.

5. From the following particulars relating to Electric Lighting Installation prepare a Cost Ledger account tabulated in order to show Materials, Wages, and Indirect Charges, in separate columns :

Contract No. 50 Cavendish Mansions,
(Estimate Book folio 5, Personal Ledger folio 109.)

1927.		£	s.	d.
Jan. 21	Requisition 1131, Cable (1 mile) . .	36	0	0
Feb. 10	,, D 40, Fuse Cases (six) .	27	0	0
Feb. 10	,, D 50, Dynamo . . .	71	5	0
Feb. 11	Tubing (1,300 feet)	7	6	0
Feb. 11	Bends (3 doz.)	1	10	0
Mar. 22	Cable (220 yds.)	11	0	0
April 26	Cr. Cable returned (110 yds.) . .	2	0	0
Mar. 28	Wages :—			
	Department A	30	0	0
	Department B	28	0	0
	Fitters	300	0	0

Indirect Charges :

(a) Department A—
30 per cent. on Wages.
(b) Department B—
25 per cent. on Wages.
(c) Fitters—
20 per cent. on Wages.

Distribution Charges :

10 per cent. on Shop cost.
Society of Incorporated Accountants and Auditors (Final).

6. Assuming a Contract Ledger to be ruled in the following columns :

Materials, Plant, Wages, Establishment Charges, Other Expenses,

enter under its appropriate heading the under-mentioned items of expenditure, and state how you would deal with returns of Materials and Plant :

Materials purchased for the Contract.
,,   returned from the Contract.
Plant purchased for the Contract.
,,   returned from the Contract.
Carriage and Freight.

Wages of General Foreman, Yard Wages and Storekeeper's Wages.
Fuel, Light and Water.
Rent and Rates of Works.
Income Tax.
Depreciation.
Office Salaries.
  ,,   Expenses.
  ,,   Rent, Rates and Taxes.
Travelling Expenses.

Society of Incorporated Accountants and Auditors (Final).

7. From the following information prepare the Job Account (with proper rulings) in the Cost Ledger :

JOB 165. (ROLLING MACHINE)
Direct Wages :

	Sept. 6.	Sept. 13.	Sept. 20.	Sept. 27.
Joiners . . .	£170	£140	£95	£130
Fitters . . .	105	90	110	120
Smiths . . .	75	45	50	60
Turners . . .	30	35	40	50

Direct Materials purchased for Job	£1500
Stores issued for Job	£550
Erection Expenses on site (Fitters and Assistants) . .	£115

Works Oncost to be charged at 60 per cent. on Direct Wages.
Office Oncost to be charged at 5 per cent. on Works Cost.
The Selling Price of the machine erected on site was £4,350.

State how the double entry in relation to these items is completed in the Cost Ledger.—*Society of Incorporated Accountants and Auditors (Inter.).*

8. Theoretically it may not be correct to bring into account any profit or loss on uncompleted contracts, but in practice strict adherence to this principle may have important consequences. Discuss the pros and cons of the question.—*Society of Incorporated Accountants and Auditors (Inter.).*

9. Submit a ruling for each of the following forms to be used by a Building Contractor, inserting specimen entries :

(a) Workman's Time Card.
(b) Weekly Wages Allocation Sheet.

Society of Incorporated Accountants and Auditors (Final).

10. The following particulars relate to the purchase and use of Cable (Class F in three sizes) :

1929.
Feb. 1.	Received from B. & J., 5 miles Size 3/11ths at £25 per mile.		
Feb. 1.	,,	,,	X. & Y., 3½ miles Size 2/9ths at £30 per mile
Feb. 25.	,,	,,	A. & C., 440 yards Size 1/9th at £16 per mile.
Feb. 10.	Issued for use on Contract No. 10, 2½ miles Size 3/11ths.		
Feb. 10.	,,	,,	on Contract No. 15, 3 miles Size 2/9ths.
Mar. 1.	,,	,,	on Contract No. 19, 220 yards Size 1/9th.
Apl. 24.	Returned to X. & Y., 440 yards Size 2/9ths.		
Apl. 24.	,,	,,	B. & J., 220 yards Size 3/11ths.

Prepare a Stores Ledger Account in relation to these Goods, adding such reference columns and other particulars as you think necessary and bringing down the balances as at April 30th. The market prices of the three sizes on that date were 3/11ths £26 per mile, 2/9ths £28 per mile, and 1/9th £15 10s. per mile.

11. Outline a Costing Scheme by the Card System suitable for a General Contractor's business, and indicate the advantages of the system for this particular trade.—*Society of Incorporated Accountants and Auditors* (*Final*).

12. The following are a week's transactions in respect of a building contract, No. 25 :

Wages paid	£560
Bricks ordered for the job and delivered direct . . .	200
Materials delivered from stock	75
Cash received on Architect's Certificate	600
Joinery delivered from Joinery Shop	370
Plant delivered from Yard	50
Cash payment on account to sub-contractor for plastering .	200
Plant returned to Yard	20

Show by Journal entries how these transactions will be recorded in the Cost Ledger, and prepare an interim Contract Account with the entries made.—*Society of Incorporated Accountants and Auditors* (*Final*).

13. Using the figures given in the previous question and assuming any others you may find necessary, draw up a statement showing how you would value the uncompleted contract at a balancing date. Add notes giving reasons for your workings.—*Society of Incorporated Accountants and Auditors* (*Final*).

14. A Building Contractor's financial year ends on 30th June, 1933. The following particulars relate to Contract No. 99, which is uncompleted at that date, viz. :—

Wages incurred to 30th June, 1933	£5,400
Materials purchased for contract	7,300
Plant „ „	2,000
Direct Expenses to 30th June, 1933	800
Materials in hand as at 30th June, 1933	1,000
Value of Plant „ „	1,700
Work certified by Architect	13,900
Cost of Work not yet certified	2,200
Agreed Contract Price	25,000
Cash received to account	12,500
Wages accrued due at 30th June, 1933	200
Direct Expenses „ „	100
Establishment Charges (proportion applicable to Contract No. 99 to 30th June, 1933)	1,200

Prepare Contract Account, crediting Profit and Loss Account with two-thirds of profit received, and carrying forward one-third as a reserve.—*Corporation of Accountants* (*Final*).

CHAPTER XIV

FACTORY JOB COSTING

The Works Order Number.—The costs are collected and recorded under the works order number, a separate cost account being set up for each number. By using a well-arranged numbering scheme, work of different categories, and work done in various departments, can be readily identified.

The method of numbering, and some of the procedure varies according to whether the order is for

(a) Repetition work.

(b) Work involving sectional operations, or the making of components for assembly.

(c) A simple straight job.

When an order is received, the Works Office allots a works order number to it. If necessary, the work will be divided into sections, and, in this case, a master order number would be given to the order as a whole, and sub-section order numbers to the parts composing it, e.g. sub-numbers for components.

In some works this is an elaborate process, often involving the setting up of many operations, for each of which the Rate-fixing Department decides the extent of each operation, and the time to be allowed for performing each.

For repetition work the Planning Department decides how the work is to be split up, draws up a schedule of jobs, and identifies each job, or operation, by a distinguishing number, or index letter. An index letter, or symbol combined with a number, is often used with great advantage. The example in Fig. 62 shows how a schedule of operations can be indexed; in this case, the operations for making a Clipper Card Sheath for a Gledhill-Brook time recorder.

The Works Order.—A Works Order, or ticket bearing the order number, is issued to each foreman who will be responsible for any of the work, e.g. machine-shop, fitters, assembly, inspec-

Fig. 62.   A Schedule of Operations

Clipper Card Sheath.

Illustration	Index Letter	Description
	R.C.A.	Milling Card Sheath Castings.
	R.C.B.	Drilling to Jig.
	R.C.C.	Mouthpieces, Drill & Oxidise
	R.C.D¹	Cutter Holder, Boring & Turning
	R.C.D²	Cutter Holder, Machining
	R.C.D³	" " Drilling to Jig & Tapping.
	R.C.E¹	Cutter Plates, Punching
	R.C.E²	" " Flatten Drill & Tap.
	R.C.F¹	Cutters, Machining.
	R.C.F²	" File to Jig
	R.C.F³	" Grinding after Hardening.
	R.C.G¹	Cutter Shanks, Cut off Straighten & Drill
	R.C.G²	" " Machining.
Casting.	R.C.H¹	Brass Top Plate Making
Casting.	R.C.H²	" Bottom Plate "
	R.C.I.	Aligning Stud, Make in Captan
	R.C.J.	Springs for Card Cutters.
	R.C.K.	Assembling Clipper Card Sheath Complete.

tion, etc. Sometimes a duplicate of the order is sent to the Stores, so that the necessary materials, small tools, and jigs required may be issued. This saves delay, which may occur if the writing of a Stores Requisition is left to the foreman; it also avoids the risk of ordering material in excess of requirements. This procedure ensures that the Cost Office has all the preliminary information before the work is commenced.

If it is planned that the order accompanies the work until complete, being then passed to the Cost Office when the finished articles are taken to the Finished Store, the Cost Office is sure that the order is completed, and can proceed to make up the cost.

The time of commencing may be written on the work-ticket, but in very many factories to-day special time-recording instruments are used, as already described in the chapter dealing with time booking methods.

Time Control of Operations.—When there are a number of operations, a useful plan is to issue an operation card, which details the number of the job, the time allowed for each operation (based on time " studies "), jigs, and drills required, and such other information as may be necessary. A specimen is shown in Fig. 63.

Recording Labour and Machine Time.—The time spent on each job must be taken both of direct labour and of machines. These are necessary for ensuring the correct charging of (a) direct labour against the job, and (b) the fair proportion of Overhead (or, as it is often misnamed, Oncost).

In nearly all efficient costing systems, the time spent on the job is the foundation upon which the costing is built. It is most important that these time records should be accurate, and, for this purpose, the time recorders already described are invaluable. As the procedure has been detailed already in Ch. VII, it is only necessary to mention the five methods which are commonly used, the circumstances in any particular factory determining which is the most suitable :

System 1. One clock card per man for weekly time, and one card per job for each man for costing purposes.

System 2. One card per man for weekly time and job time combined, together with total time for each job on the same card. Unfinished jobs are carried forward in spaces provided at the foot to the next week's time and job card.

FIG. 63.

CLIPPER CARD SHEATH.				
OPERATION CARD.	INDEX LETTER OF JOB	R.C.A		
QUANTITY	EACH.	30	60	120
TIME NOT TO EXCEED :—	½ hour.	15 Lrs.	30 Lrs.	60 Lrs.

JIGS REQUIRED.		DRILLS REQUIRED	
Jigs 461 ABCDEFGH		No 21 Drill $\frac{3}{16}$" Tap	Scheduled Time.
Operations	Castings to be dipped in acid before given out for machining.		Time each
1	Straighten & bed up to milling fixture 461.		10 mins.
2	Drill to Jig no 461A, 5 No 21 Holes. Burr.		4 "
3	Tap 5 No 21 Holes with ⁵⁄₁₆" Tap		1½ "
4	Clamp fixture 461 on hollow table No 1. Fasten card sheath casting with 5 screws supplied. Machine front of casting to sample & gauge 461 C. Recess for card - 085' deep. Wide slot must be in centre of casting		6 "
5	Fit gauge 461D, & CAM 461E, on hollow table No 1 Hold finished edge of casting against gauge 461 D. with CAM 461E, then clamp to table with clamps 461F & 461G. Now machine top end of casting, square with card slot. Only just clean up. File off all Burrs.		3 "
6	Hold in same way as last operation. Machine seating for cutter holder to be 312" ± 0a0 thick. Place packing 461 H under seating to prevent spring when cutting.		2½ "
7	Straighten after milling.		3 "
		Total	30 "

System 3. One card per man for weekly time and job time combined, and a master card, or cost sheet, for all men's time on each job.

System 4. One card for each job. Time " In " and " Out," and " On " and " Off," is clocked on the job card, and the total of each card is transferred to a summary card, no weekly card being used by the man.

System 5. For recording machine time in the case of automatic machines, one card per machine shows both productive and idle time, with a summary of job times at the foot. The man in charge of a group of machines uses a weekly clock card as well.

Standing Order Numbers.—In addition to production orders, there are many jobs in every factory which are done in connection with Service Departments, or are in the nature of an expense to the business. These must be scheduled and given a standing order number as described in Ch. IX. Items of cost are charged against these numbers in the same way as for works orders. There are several methods for collecting the labour time in Service Departments :

(1) The engineer's or foreman's starting ticket, or job ticket, detailing the job, is given to the workman, who, on starting, enters the time. Usually, the standing order number is already inserted; if not, this will be done by the foreman on passing the job. Material is requisitioned under the standing order number. On completion, the job ticket is passed to the Cost Office.

(2) Another procedure, using time-recorders, is as follows : The job ticket (Fig. 29), bearing the standing order number, is given to the workman, who " clocks " on a time card the time of starting. The standing order number is entered against the time on the clock card, which is then placed in the rack under the workman's number. The details on the cards so used by the men are then entered on a summary sheet, daily or weekly, a separate sheet (Fig. 64) being used for each standing order number.

(3) A separate clock card for each standing order number is kept in a rack. When a man does work on a particular order number, he " clocks " on the appropriate card, entering his number against the time. At the end of each week, the cards are ruled off, and the totals posted to the proper Expense Account. The cards can thus be used continuously until full, and may last several weeks.

o

Fig. 64.

UPKEEP OF SHOP TOOLS. K.30.

	Check No.	Men's Time						Boys and Girls' Time						Total Hours	Rate	Labour Cost £ s. d.			Machine Rate £ s. d.		
		Th.	F.	S.	M.	Tu.	W.	Th.	F.	S.	M.	Tu.	W.			£	s.	d.	£	s.	d.
Johnson	140	3			7		2							12	10D		10	·			
Smith	84	4	1			2								7	6D		3	6			
Tompkins	260		5				4							9	9		6	9			
Watkins	220	3		2	4									9	10		7	6			
Helliwell	160		1½		3		7							11½	1/-		11	6		11	6
James	310	4		5	1									10	1/-		10	·		5	·
Thompson	197		2		7		1½							10½	1/-		10	6		7	
Macpherson	360	1		7	6									14	9		10	6			
Bryce	18													4	8		2	8			
O'Grady	110	2		6	1		3							12	11		11	·			
Pearson	365								2	3	5-6			16	4		5	4		16	·
Williams	367							1		6	1			8	3		2	·			
Week's Total																4	11	3	1	19	6
																			6	10	9

Summary of Time for a Standing Order Number

Idle or Waste Time Standing Order No.—This is used for

(1) Time waiting for jobs, or materials.

(2) Time waiting for foreman.

(3) Waiting time, owing to breakdown of plant, Air Raids, etc.

These times should be recorded on the time-sheets, or may be "clocked" on appropriate clock cards. The cost of Idle Facilities must not be included here; it is best written off to Profit and Loss Account.

Time on Replacing Rejected Work.—When it is decided to make up the quantity of parts to the number originally ordered, of which some have been spoiled, or rejected, the time-card for the job will be re-stamped, thus getting a record of the extra time taken. A report of spoilt work forms the basis of a charge to the appropriate expense number.

Overtime Expense.—When the overtime is worked on a special job, say outside the works, or when it is due to the special desire of a customer to have the job completed or rushed through within the time specified, the extra payment for over-time is legitimately charged to the job as direct labour.

When, however, the overtime is for the purpose of generally increasing the output of the factory, e.g. to keep up with stock requirements or orders generally, the cost of the overtime is charged to Works Overhead Expense Account. A standing order number is provided for this.

The Pay-Roll and Wages Analysis.—The pay-roll is made up from the gate clock cards and piece-work tickets. If clock cards are not used, the entries are made from time-sheets. When a premium bonus, or other output or efficiency bonus, is paid, an extra column will be provided for inclusion of these amounts. (See Fig. 65.)

In the Cost Office the wages are dissected on Analysis Sheets, so that correct allocation of direct wages to jobs is made, and of indirect wages to the appropriate Expense and Service Departments Accounts. (See Fig. 66.) Statistical data regarding labour and departmental totals will also be prepared. (See Fig. 67.)

The Cost Office Analysis must agree in total with the total shown on the wages-sheet, thus ensuring that the Cost Accounts will be in complete agreement with the wages total in the Financial Accounts. This is a most important point. Reference to the totals in Figs. 65, 66 and 67 will demonstrate such agreement.

Fig. 65.

Factory Pay-Roll

Week Ending : ....

Clock No.	Employer's Insurance			Rate			Deductions									Hours	Gross Day Wage			Piece-work Bonus			Gross Day Wage P.W. Bonus			Nett Wages paid out.		
							Mutual Aid.			Sports Club.			Employees Insurance.															
	£	s.	d.	£	s.	d.	£	s.	d.	£	s.	d.	£	s.	d.		£	s.	d.	£	s.	d.	£	s.	d.	£	s.	d.
Totals	40	7	0				3	5	0	6	2	9	38	6	0	20,539.8	797	16	1	73	7	3	871	3	4	823	9	7

Fig. 66.

ANALYSIS OF INDIRECT WAGES AND DEPARTMENTS CHARGED   Week ended 5th May, 19......

Department No.	Name	Total Indirect Charged £ s. d.	Tool Making and Repairing £ s. d.	Repairs £ s. d.	Rejections £ s. d.	Clerical £ s. d.	Supervision (Charge Hands) £ s. d.	Labouring £ s. d.	Inspection £ s. d.	Added Time for Overtime £ s. d.	Idle Time £ s. d.	Service (separately analysed) £ s. d.
410	Foundry	10 12 0				1 1 6	2 4 4	1 1 5	8 10		5 2 11	
413	Plating	18 9	2 9	17 0	1 1 7	1 1 16	1 1 0	8 12	8 8 7	17 5		16 0
414	Enamelling	20 16 4	8 7	10 5	1 2 4	3 19 2	1 12 16	1 17 12	7 4	2 11 3		17 4
415	Polishing	114 8 7	55 4 4	8 2 3 1		1 15 1	9 0 4	2 17 2	11 8	1 1 1		
416	Machine (A)	9 2 5	5 9	1 19	5 15	1 2 15 11	8 5 17	1 17	16 8	1 10		18 19 6
421	Winding	35 5 10	5 2	1		2 4 11	5 17		16 12	10 5		11 5 11
433	Fitters	36 17 8							13 3			
434	Machine (M)										8 8	29 12 4
												32 8 2
	Total Manfg. Depts.	**£234 0 5**	**£63 15 8**	**£31 2 7**	**£7 4 3**	**£16 8 1**	**£33 8 9**	**£10 8 9**	**£61 1 10**	**£5 1 10**	**£5 8 8**	**£93 3 3**
401	Progress	51 13 3		27	27 6 11	23 9 5						
403	Heating Engineering	19 1 4				12 0 7				11		16 17
406	Drawing Office	16 11 7	8 11			12 2 1						
408	Inspection	8 10 6	4 4 8		1 3 11	1 9 0	4 2 16	3 6	4 11 6	10 6 1		19 6
409	Maintenance	33 18 6				15 11	3 16 12			1 10		11 5 11
412	Despatch	13 12 10										
418	Canteen	20 17 0				20 4 0						
419	General Office	46 17 11		3	8 4	3 7 11		13 13		10 5		12 8
420	Stores	42 16 8		2			4 7 0			3 10		
424	Experimental							4 17				
	Total Non-Manfg. Depts.	**£254 0 0**	**£4 8 11**	**£7 4 10**	**£32 15 11**	**£69 19 10**	**£15 6 10**	**£16 5 11**	**£4 11 6**	**£8 15 9**		**£93 19 3**
	Gross Totals	**£488 0 5**	**£68 4 7**	**£38 7 5**	**£40 0 2**	**£86 7 11**	**£49 6 10**	**£26 14 8**	**£65 13 4**	**£13 17 7**	**£5 8 8**	**£93 19 3**

Stores Materials.—The materials issued to jobs against requisitions, and materials purchased for specific jobs, are debited to the appropriate Cost Accounts, as described in the preceding chapter and Ch. V.

Tool Room and Tool Store Procedure.—The careful selection, and the making and maintenance, of tools for manufacturing purposes are of great importance. In connection with the organisation dealing with tools there are three divisions : (a) Manufacturing, (b) Maintenance and Inspection, (c) Storage and Issue.

Tool Manufacture.—The making of tools for production may be costed by the job costing method described in this chapter, the cost being charged to Standing Order Numbers.

Tool Storage and Issue.—The tool stock can be conveniently recorded by the use of bin card procedure already described. If written requisitions are used, they should be made out in triplicate; one copy is kept by the workman, one in a file at the bin in numerical order of the recipients, and one in a file on the tool-store clerk's desk arranged numerically according to tool nomenclature. When a tool is returned, the requisitions are withdrawn from the files and completed as to time and date of return for analysis purposes.

An alternative and common method is to issue brass checks to the workmen, numbered according to their clock numbers. A check is given in exchange for a tool, and is hung on a peg on the bin. Each tool bin has checks also, bearing the symbol and number of the tools. When the workman's check is placed by the bin, a tool check is removed to correspond, and is hung on a control board under the workman's number. Track of the tools is therefore easily kept.

Tools Returned.—These are examined and reconditioned before being replaced, and the cost (Fig. 64) is charged to Upkeep of Tools Expense Account.

The Allocation of Tool Expense.—All the expenses of running the Tool Room and Tool Store are collated and apportioned as overhead to machine departments, except for the value of tools capitalised. The basis of shop machine hours is useful for the purpose. Regard must be had to the fact that Tools are made for (1) Tool Room use, (2) other centres, (3) for sale.

Overhead Expenses—Manufacturing.—This group of expenses is very frequently termed Works Oncost, but Production (or Factory) Overhead is the correct description.

Fig. 67.

FACTORY LABOUR AND WAGES STATISTICS

Week ended 5th May, 19......

No.	Name	Working Male	Working Female	Hours Total	Per Person Male	Per Person Female	Gross Wages with Piecework £	s.	d.	Piecework Amount Paid £	s.	d.	% Efficiency	Direct £	s.	d.	Indirect £	s.	d.	Non-Manufacturing £	s.	d.	% Direct to Total	% Indirect to Total	% Non-Mfg. to Total
410	Foundry	21	9	1,381·3	46	45	51	17	11½	2	10	2½	98	36	6	10	10	11	10½	4	19	3	70	20	10
413	Plating	2	26	1,231·8	46	44	33	6	8	2	1	2	100	30	14	10	1	2	9	2	9	5	92	1	7
414	Enamelling	1	7	387·2	47	47	14	9	3	15	17	1	95	10	10	0	7	3	7	2	15	5	73	8	19
415	Polishing	15	10	1,175·2	44	47	58	15	9½	13	16	2	99	47	13	6	78	12	11½	3	9	4	81	13	6
416	Machine (A)	65	27	4,434·2	51	47	202	1	3	30	5	3	96	84	18	1		15	0	39	11	6	42	39	19
421	Winding	2	8	457·4	49	47	17	18	7	3	9	3	97	11	4	0	24	19	0	5	11	6	67	2	31
433	Fitters	49	3	2,432·5	46	45	136	19	3	3	5	4	99	99	4	1	24	19	10	12	15	15	73	18	9
434	Machine (M)	7	55	2,838·6	48	45	81	10	5½	3	5	6	86	56	0	11	13	3	3	12	6	8	69	16	15
	Total Manfg. Depts.	163	145	14,338·2	48	46	596	18	8½	70	4	10	—	376	9	3	136	17	9½	83	11	8	63	23	14
401	Progress	6	4	467·5	46	47	21	17	9											21	9	9			100
408	Inspection	12	12	1,179·7	46	46	51	3	3½											51	17	3½			100
409	Maintenance	14	2	869·3	53	49	44	3	6											44	3	6			100
412	Despatch	9	4	696·7	57	46	31	2	0											31	6	6			100
419	General Office	12	13	1,332·5	61	46	44	11	10					6	13	8	36	6	9½	44	33	10	14	75	11
420	Stores	11	8	874·	46	46	33	0	3½											33	0	3½			100
424	Experimental	12	—	781·9	64		48	5	1½	3	2	5	100							5	4	8			100
	Total Non-Manfg. Depts.	76	43	6,201·6	54	46	274	4	7½	3	2	4	100	6	13	8	36	6	6	231	4	2	3	13	84
	Gross Totals	239	188	20,539·8	50	46	871	3	4	73	7	3	98	383	2	11	173	4	7	314	15	10	44	20	36

FIG. 68.

ANALYSIS OF EXPENSE FOR DEPARTMENTAL RATES

MANUFACTURING EXPENSES.

FIGURES OBTAINED FROM	DESCRIPTION	Handling Materials	General Overhead	Machine Rates	Departmental Rates	Floor Space	Power	TOTAL
WAGES.	Unproductive Labour		✔					✔
	On Cost ,,		✔					✔
	Upkeep of Plant and Tools			✔	✔		✔	✔
	Foremen's Wages			✔	✔			✔
	Charge Hands ,,			✔	✔			✔
	Inspectors' ,,		✔					✔
	Experimental ,,		✔					✔
SALARIES.	Managers and Assistants' Salaries		✔					✔
	Draughtsmen's ,,		✔					✔
	Cost Office ,,		✔					✔
	Rate Fixing Office ,,		✔					✔
PURCHASES.	Miscellaneous Material used in manufacture and not chargeable direct to product		✔	✔	✔			✔
	Stationery and Material used by Works Staff		✔					✔
WAGES.	Wages for handling Stores and Material	✔						✔
	Storekeepers and Clerks' Wages	✔						✔
SPECIAL A/C.	Interest on Stocks held	✔						✔
	Losses due to leakage	✔						✔
TRADE EXPENSES.	Rent, Rates, Taxes, Repairs and Insurance					✔		✔
	Heating, Electricity, Gas, and Water					✔		✔
	Depreciation and Interest		✔	✔	✔	✔	✔	✔
SPECIAL A/C.	Extra Depreciation not provided for in amount allowed in Trading A/c.			✔	✔	✔		✔
	Interest on whole of Capital employed for manufacturing, less any amount already paid in Trade Expenses		✔	✔	✔	✔		✔
WAGES, SALARIES, PURCHASES, & TRADE EXPENSES.	Power and Transmission Charges					✔	✔	
	Wages and Material					✔		
	Total of A&B)					✔	✔	

	2nd DIVISION.					A	B	
A.	Floor Space Total as above divided to Departments according to area	✔	✔	✔	✔			
B.	Power Total as above allotted to machines according to power consumed	✔		✔	✔			
		✔	✔	✔	✔ =EQUALS=			✔

Note.—Bases for the analysis are suggested in Fig. 52, p. 140.

Factory Overhead, as manufacturing expenses are properly termed, should be apportioned to :

(*a*) Machine-hour rates.

(*b*) Direct Labour-hour rates (or other departmental rates).

(c) Expense of handling and storing materials.

(d) Balance not included in the above, to general factory
    Overhead.

The methods of calculating these various expense rates
have been described in Ch. XII.

The illustration in Fig. 68 gives a comprehensive view of
the analysis of Factory Overhead. The columns and divisions
of analysis will, of course, vary according to the specific requirements of each particular factory

Selling and Distribution Overhead.—The total factory cost
having been ascertained, there remains to be added the proper
proportion of selling and distribution expenses to each job.
These are sometimes distributed on a basis, such as a percentage on the cost of labour, or prime cost, or as a percentage
on the product sold. But see the observations on the apportionment of Selling Overhead made on p. 116. Whichever method is
used, it is useful to show what the percentage cost of selling is
in relation to both selling price and factory cost.

Posting the Cost Ledger (or Cost Sheet).—A Cost Account
(see Fig. 69) is opened for each job, and bears the same number
as the job. A Foundry Job Cost Account is shown in Fig. 126.
This account may take the form of a Summary Cost Sheet or
Card (see Fig. 70). The posting of wages, time and materials
is made from the Wages and Materials Abstracts. Selling and
distribution expense is added to the total so ascertained, using
the pre-determined percentage or other basis.

A useful form of summary or Job Cost Account is shown in
Fig. 70. The column for "hours" in each shop is needed for
calculating departmental overheads (Oncosts).

Control and Reconciliation Accounts.—No system is complete unless it is so linked up with the Financial Accounts that
the results shown by both Cost and Financial Accounts may
be reconciled. In other words, subject to appropriate adjustment of the balance on the Works Profit and Loss Account,
as compiled from the Cost Accounts, the net profit or loss should
be the same in both cases.

It has been shown that complete agreement is obtained
for wages and materials. It remains to demonstrate how far
the Overhead charged approximates to the total actual expense
incurred. In other words, it is necessary to test whether the
machine-hour rates and labour-hour rates (or other bases used)
do, in fact, " recover " the expenses incurred.

FIG. 69.

Order No. P.97.

JOB COST LEDGER ACCOUNT

Name of Customer : J. Smith.

Date 19/6/......
23/6/......
Completed 23/6/......

Particulars : 1 Gross Special Horn Scale Pocket Knives.

Dr.																Cr.		
Week Ending.	Ref.	Stores Materials			Special Materials.			Direct Expenses.			Hours.		Direct Wages.			Overhead (Works).			Total Works Cost.			Date.	Details.	Ref.	Amount.		
											Man.	Machine.				Rate.	£	s.	d.	£	s.	d.				£	s.	d.
		£	s.	d.	£	s.	d.	£	s.	d.	*Shop 1.*																	
											Shop 2.																	
											Shop 3.																	

Add : General Administration Overhead Account   £ ... ...
Distribution Overhead Account   ... ...
Selling Overhead Account   ... ...

Total Cost   £

Note.—The credit side of the account is sometimes omitted, the total cost of the completed job being then transferred to completed jobs summary. The above illustrates a special order, but frequently the orders will be for replenishment of stock, or even for a capital addition, etc. The Works Overhead is debited separately for each shop, as are the hours and wages.

Assume that the actual overhead expense incurred for the year was £13,000. On analysis, suppose £7,000 is allocated to Machine Shops, and £6,000 to non-machine work. Dividing

FIG. 70.

ALTERNATIVE FORM OF JOB COST LEDGER ACCOUNT

Name of Customer or No. 23/276.   Works Order No. 6327

Date of Order 30/12/1916.

Description: I.C.I. Spur wheel.

Date	Clock No.	OPERATION	Class	M.	T.	W.	Th.	F.	S.	Su.	Total Hours	Rate	WAGE £ s. d.	BONUS £ s. d.	Mach. No.	Hours	Rate	COST £ s. d.
1917																		
Jan 12	1	Bore & Turn		6	8	8	8				30	4d.	1 6 0½	6 6	82	30	9d	1 2 6
Jan 12	2	Cutting						8	5									
19				8	8	8	4				41	4d.	1 10 11½	5 8¾	115	36	7d.	1 16 -
19	3	Keyway?							2		2	3d.	1 5	4	42	2	6d	1 -
													2 18 4½	12 6¾				2 19 6

Date	Reqn. No.	MATERIALS DETAILS	T.	C.	Q.	lbs.	Quantity	Rate	£ s. d.	SUMMARY	£ s. d.
Jan 2	2764	Cast Iron	16	2	12		1	18/- cwt.	14 17 2	Wage ...	2 18 4½
										Bonus ...	12 6¾
										Machine Rate ...	2 19 6
										Other Rates ...	- - -
										Overhead ...	3 5 0
											9 15 5¼
										Material ...	14 17 2
										„ 10 % ...	1 9 8¾
											26 2 4
										Selling Expenses ...	4 - -
										Profit ...	3 - -
										Selling Price ...	33 2 4

by thirteen to find the actual charge for every four-weekly period, we have £540 against Machine Shops, and £460 against non-machine work.

On taking a summary of the hours, and "recoveries" of

Overhead, charged in all the various Job Accounts, we find
the total "recoveries" for the first four weeks are :

Recoveries by machine-hour rates . . £555
      ,,   ,, labour-hour rates . . 466

£1,021

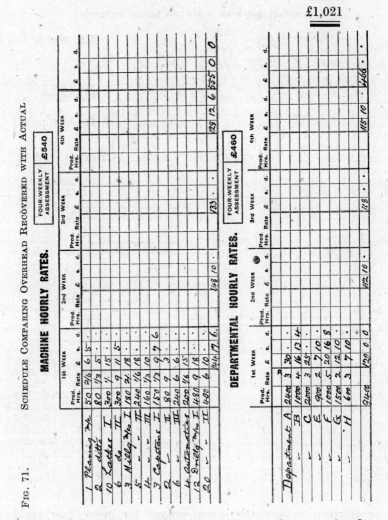

FIG. 71.

SCHEDULE COMPARING OVERHEAD RECOVERED WITH ACTUAL.

proving that the rates used are sufficient to cover the Overhead. The excess is not large, so no alteration in the rates
is necessary. The excess is transferred to Overhead Adjustment Account, and, at the end of the year, the balance on this

account is written off to Profit and Loss Account, thus bringing both sets of accounts into agreement.

A suitable form for summarising the Overhead recoveries for comparison with the actual expense is shown in Fig. 71. The figures shown therein are those used above.

To ensure accuracy in the Cost Accounts, and to prove that all the expenditure shown in the Financial and Cost Accounts is accounted for, and to secure the value of work in progress, suitable Control Accounts must be set up. These will form the subject-matter of a separate chapter.

JOB COSTS IN CONJUNCTION WITH THE FINANCIAL ACCOUNTS

The following set of abbreviated skeleton accounts (Figs. 72 to 80) illustrate how the Cost Totals Accounts may be arranged in conjunction with the Financial Accounts. The procedure of including in the latter the " Internal " Cost Accounts illustrated enables the accountant to show how total expenditure is accounted for in the Cost Accounts. When making up the usual Financial Accounts and Balance Sheet at the end of the year, these " Internal " Cost Accounts are ignored, thus enabling the ordinary accounts to be prepared in the usual way. The two sets of accounts are thus interlocked, without interfering with the customary double-entry financial system.

The skeleton accounts are annotated to make them self-explanatory. The accounts are referred to as Sheet 1, etc., as they are posted mechanically on loose leaf sheets.

FIG. 72.

ANALYSIS OF WAGES CHEQUE

Sheet No. 1.

Shops.	Productive Labour.	Non Productive Labour.	Supervision.	Total.
Shop 1	A	B	B	D
Shop 2				
Shop 3				
etc.				
Total				

Total D should agree with cheque and Pay-roll Total.
Post Total Productive Labour (A) to Debit of Internal Work in Progress Accounts.
Post Total Non-Productive Labour and Supervision (B) to Debit of Internal Overhead Accounts.

FIG. 73.

SUMMARY ISSUES OF MATERIALS

Sheet No. 2.

Requisitions.	Total.		Production.		Overhead Expense A/cs.		A/c.
Daily Totals . .	A		B		C		
Total . .							

Enter daily total of Requisitions in Column A.
Post Total of B to Credit of Internal Stock Account and Debit Internal Work in Progress Account.
Post Total of C to Debit of Expense Account and Credit Internal Stock Account, Sheet No. 6.

FIG. 74.

SUMMARY OF JOBS FINISHED

Sheet No. 3.

Job Nos.	Description.	Material.		Labour.		Overhead Expenses.	
		A		B		C	
	Totals . . .						

Make up as Jobs are completed.
Credit Total Internal Material (A) to Work in Progress Account and Debit Shop Account.
Credit Total Internal Labour (B) to Work in Progress Account and Debit Shop Account.
Credit Total Internal Overhead (C) to Work in Progress Account and Debit Shop Account.

FIG. 75.

INTERNAL SHOP ACCOUNTS

Sheet No. 4.

Dr.   Cr.

Sheet 3, col. A, B, C (Cost of Jobs Finished) .			Total Sales . . .		

The Balance on this account represents profit.

FIG. 76.

INTERNAL LABOUR—WORK IN PROGRESS ACCOUNT

Sheet No. 5 (a).

Dr.   Cr.

Sheet (1), col. A (from Wages Analysis) . .			Sheet (3), col. B (Finished Jobs) . . .		

FIG. 77.

INTERNAL MATERIAL—WORK IN PROGRESS ACCOUNT

Sheet No. 5 (b).

Sheet (2), col. B (Summary of Requisitions) .			Sheet (3), col. A (Finished Jobs) . .		

Balances of above accounts represents value of uncompleted jobs in hand in the shops.

Fig. 78.

Sheet No. 6.

INTERNAL STOCK ACCOUNT

Total purchases from Purchase Journal . .				Sheet (2), col. B (Total issues to Jobs) . . Sheet (2), col. C (Issues to Expense A/cs.) . .			

Balance represents approximate book value of stock on hand and is used for the periodical Profit and Loss Account.

Fig. 79.

Sheet No. 7.

INTERNAL OVERHEAD EXPENSE ACCOUNT

Dr.   Cr.

Total charged to respective shops from analysis of Expense A/cs. (plus outstandings and less paid in advance (Sheet (8), col. B)) . . Sheet (1), col. B . .				Sheet (3), col. C (Overhead charged to Finished Jobs) . . .			

Balance after allowing for Overheads on balance of Work in Progress Account will reveal whether all costs have been appropriated.

Fig. 80.

Sheet No. 8.

EXPENSE ANALYSIS

Expenses A/cs. (detailed).	Total.	Analysis to Shops.			
		Shop 1.	Shop 2.	Shop 3.	Etc.
	A	B	B	B	B

A. From individual Expense Accounts.
B. Debit each shop total to Internal Overheads, Sheet No. 7.

Batch Costing.—This is used when the production consists of limited repetition work where a definite number of articles are manufactured in one batch. Where a number of different parts enter into the article, sufficient for each batch are passed through the works for the quantity required. The cost of the operations on each batch is ascertained as described for job costing, the batches being treated as units for costing.

Operation Costing.—This is a method of costing by operations such as are necessary in mass-production work and repetition work. Often, in such cases, there is a need to manufacture to an economic price, and, consequently, the main purpose of the costing is to find the operation costs of Labour, Material, and

Overhead, to see that the manufacturing cost per unit at each operation is kept as closely as possible to the figure on which prices were fixed. Any tendency to increase, or decrease, is closely investigated, and comparative costs are kept.

In such work as this, it is a great advantage to set up standard costs, against which actual costs may be measured. Standard costs are dealt with in a later chapter, as also is a method of unit operation costing on pages 240–7.

Budgetary Control.—In order that close rates for applying Overhead to the product may be obtained, and also to control, generally, the productive costs, it is necessary to budget for sales, production, and expense. Such a budget is also necessary for installing standard costs. The subject is described on p. 317.

Uniform Job Cost System for Printers.—An outline of the principles of this system and some observations on Uniform Costing Systems in an industry are given in Ch. XX.

EXAMINATION QUESTIONS

1. Where job costs are used it is possible, after budgeting the expenses, to find the weekly cost of production and value the output. Draft a form which will provide the management with the approximate weekly turnover, including direct materials and the approximate profit.— *Institute of Cost and Works Accountants (Final).*

2. Draw up the following specimen forms for use in job costing at a works consisting of several departments :

    (a) Time and work sheet.
    (b) Cost ledger sheet.

Royal Society of Arts (Advanced).

3. What do you understand by work in progress ? Would you propose to keep separate accounts for each department or one account for the factory as a whole ? At what stage of manufacture would you cease to regard an article or component as work in progress ?—*Royal Society of Arts (Advanced).*

4. From the following information prepare the Job Account (with proper rulings) in the Cost Ledger :

Job 165.   (Rolling Machine)

Direct Wages :—

		Sept. 6.	Sept. 13.	Sept. 20.	Sept. 27.
		£	£	£	£
Joiners	. .	170	140	95	130
Fitters	. .	105	90	110	120
Smiths	. .	75	45	50	60
Turners	. .	30	35	40	50

Direct Materials purchased for Job : £1,500.
Stores issued for Job : £550.
Erection Expenses on site (Fitters and Assistants) : £115.
Works Oncost to be charged at 60 per cent. on Direct Wages.

Office Oncost to be charged at 5 per cent. on Works Cost.

The Selling Price of the machine erected on site was £4,350.

State how the double entry in relation to these items is completed in the Cost Ledger.—*Society of Incorporated Accountants and Auditors (Inter.).*

5. What is understood by the terms :

(a) Premium Bonus System of Wage Payment; (b) Job Tickets; (c) Bin Card; (d) Production Order; (e) Purchase Requisition; (f) Machine Rates?

Society of Incorporated Accountants and Auditors (Final).

6. Describe fully a costing system you would recommend for a motor garage with repair shop, petrol pumps, lock-up sheds for cars, and sales of motor accessories.—*Institute of Cost and Works Accountants (Final).*

7. In a job order business materials are used in all sorts of quantities. How would you ensure the individual job being duly debited with the cost and what method would you suggest to prove this ?—*Institute of Cost and Works Accountants (Inter.).*

8. An agent for a manufacturer utilises large stores and has a work-shop where parts are altered to suit customers' requirements. Sales are on a commission basis, out of which the agent has to meet his own warehouse expenses. Set out a suitable system to arrive at costs.—*Institute of Cost and Works Accountants (Final).*

9. Draw up a cost statement for a product with which you are familiar, showing, with suitable figures, labour, materials and charges on machine hour basis. What other expenses would you expect to add in order to complete the cost statement ?—*Institute of Cost and Works Accountants (Inter.).*

10. Select one of the following and set out a form of final cost, showing material, labour and overheads :

(1) Mechanical unit (steam, gas or electric);
(2) Complete building (say, small house);
(3) Box of " lead soldiers ";
(4) Bottle of fruit in syrup;
(5) Motor chassis, ready for body;
(6) Complete edition of a book, ready for delivery.

Institute of Cost and Works Accountants (Inter.).

11. Set out a complete form of cost for large non-repetition units of output showing as much detail as possible, with departmental establishment charges.—*Institute of Cost and Works Accountants (Final).*

12. Give ruling of a cost card suitable for any manufacturing business with which you are familiar, and detail the records from which it would be written up.—*Society of Incorporated Accountants and Auditors (Inter.).*

13. Explain the relationship existing between the Stores Ledger, Cost Ledger and Stock Ledger on the one hand, and the Impersonal Ledger and Cash Book on the other, in a factory where costing records are reconciled with the financial books.

Give the Journal entries illustrating the principles of double entry cost accounting in respect of :

(a) The payment of wages.
(b) The allocation of oncost.
(c) The issue of goods from stores to a production order.
(d) The transfer of finished goods to stock.

Society of Incorporated Accountants and Auditors (Final).

P

14. Discuss the relative advantages and disadvantages of : (a) Bound, (b) Loose-leaf, and (c) Card, Records for costing purposes.—*Incorporated Accountants (Final)*.

15. Calculate the cost of Job. No. 99, which is executed by three departments of a factory.

Productive Wages amounted to :—

Departments, X, £100 (900 hours); Y, £150 (1,500 hours); Z, £70 (600 hours).

Materials used amounted to :—

Departments, X, £150; Y, £140; Z, £50.

Works Oncost is calculated per productive labour hour, and Administration Oncost as a percentage of Works Cost.

The figures for the past year for the three departments are as follows :—

	Dept. X.	Dept. Y.	Dept. Z.
Productive Wages	£2,000	£1,600	£2,400
	(24,000 hrs.)	(18,000 hrs.)	(26,400 hrs.)
Materials	£1,900	£1,450	£2,000
Works Expenses	1,600	1,350	2,200
Administration Expenses	605	440	825

Corporation of Accountants (Final).

16. Gadgets, Ltd., manufacture various standard articles. The costs of Article No. 17 are as follows :—

	£	s.	d.
Materials used	9	0	0
Direct Wages	6	0	0
Direct Charges	1	0	0
Prime Cost	£16	0	0
Works Oncost (150 per cent. on Direct Wages)	9	0	0
Works Cost	£25	0	0
Office Oncost (10 per cent. on Works Cost)	2	10	0
Cost of Production	£27	10	0
Selling Oncost (rate per article)	5	10	0
Cost of Sales	33	0	0
Net Profit	5	0	0
Usual Selling Price	£38	0	0

The manufacturers are offered a Contract to supply 100 articles at the price of £25 each.

In what circumstances would it be advantageous to accept this contract ? Give reasons for your answer.

Works Expenses are 70 per cent. fixed and 30 per cent. fluctuating with production.

Office Expenses may be considered as constant irrespective of production.

Selling Expenses are 50 per cent. fixed and 50 per cent. fluctuating with Sales.—*Corporation of Accountants* (Final).

17. From the following information prepare the Contract Account in the Cost Ledger with a clear indication as to the completion of the double entry in relation to each item.

CONTRACT No. 135.

Week ending May

Wages—				1st.	8th.	15th.	22nd.	29th.
Riveters	.	.	.	£25	£45	£65	£75	£30
Fitters	.	,	.	95	85	80	220	110
Drillers	.	.	.	65	75	135	120	70
Labourers	.	.	.	32	60	45	20	15
Foremen	.	.	.	18	18	18	18	18

Materials used : From Store, £730; Direct Purchase, £4,500. Works Oncost, 50 per cent. on Wages. Office Oncost, 7½ per cent. on Works Cost. Contract Price quoted *ex* Works £8,000.—*Incorporated Accountants (Inter.)*

18. Where a business owns the Freehold of the premises, what would be a proper charge in lieu of rent, and what entries would be necessary in relation thereto in a double-entry costing system ?—*Incorporated Accountants (Inter.).*

19. Enumerate the books and documents which would be required for a complete costing system, adding explanatory notes where necessary. —*Incorporated Accountants (Inter.).*

20. A Manufacturing Company uses a certain raw material in production, and has in stock as at 31st December, 1933, 1,000 tons which cost £7 per ton. Purchases during the first four months of 1934 are made at varying rates. The quantities received into stock and used in manufacture are as follows :—

1934.		Purchased.		£	Used.
January	.	3,000 tons at £5 per ton .	.	15,000	2,000 tons
February	.	4,000 ,,	£5 10*s*. per ton .	22,000	3,000 ,,
March	.	6,000 ,,	£4 16*s*. 8*d*. per ton	29,000	7,000 ,,
April	.	4,000 ,,	£4 15*s*. per ton .	19,000	3,600 ,,

In the financial books the price at 31st December, 1933, was written down to £5 per ton.

Show in Cost Accounts :—

(*a*) The rate per ton to be charged to Manufacturing Costs for March in respect of material used.

(*b*) The price per ton for stocktaking purposes as at 30th April, 1934
Corporation of Accountants (Final).

CHAPTER XV

DOUBLE ENTRY COST ACCOUNTING

COST CONTROL ACCOUNTS

THE chief purposes of these accounts are :

(1) To provide a check for ensuring that all expenditure is accounted for in the Cost Accounts with double-entry proof.

(2) To provide a basis for reconciliation with the Financial Accounts.

(3) To provide a ready means of preparing monthly or periodical Balance Sheets and Profit and Loss Accounts.

In general, the Cost Control Accounts form the counterpart of the sectional items in the Financial Accounts and, if arranged in this way, they form an excellent basis for reconciliation.

Three Methods :

(1) Totals accounts are written up from the data supplied by the financial accountant, and summaries prepared by the cost accountant.

(2) Direct interlocking accounts between the cost and financial books are kept, using General and Cost Ledger Adjustment Accounts and an inter-system Journal.

(3) Direct interlocking by a Manufacturing or Work in Progress Account.

Control Totals Accounts Method.—A Main Cost Control Account is opened in the Cost Ledger, and a corresponding Manufacturing Account should be arranged in the Financial Books. It is desirable, in fact usually necessary, that the Financial Accounts should be arranged so that the main headings are representative of the principal divisions required for costing purposes. This facilitates the reconciliation of the two sets of accounts, and not infrequently provides better information for the management in the financial records.

192

The Main Cost Control Account starts with the balances brought forward from the previous month. The monthly totals under the various headings in the Financial Manufacturing Account are then posted from schedules supplied, as shown in Fig. 81. The sectional control accounts are debited with corresponding figures.

FIG. 81.

MAIN COST CONTROL ACCOUNT

Dr.   Cr.

19...Feb. 28			£	s.	d.	19...Feb. 1			£	s.	d.
To Sales (*less* Returns)	S2		3253	13	0		By Balance:				
,, Balance:	c/d.						Work in Progress .	b/d.	1832	15	0
Work in Progress .			1622	11	8		Stores on Hand	,,	781	0	0
Stores on Hand .	,,		664	6	4		Sales Stock on Hand . .	,,	820	2	6
Sales Stock on Hand .	,,		783	8	0	,, 28	,, Wages . .	S2	922	0	0
						,,	,, Materials . .	,,	620	0	0
						,,	,, Overhead:				
							Factory .	,,	360	0	0
							Administration	,,	160	0	0
							Selling .	,,	30	0	0
							Distribution .	,,	14	0	0
						,,	,, Profit and Loss A/c. (Profit) .	J3	784	1	6
			£6323	19	0				£6323	19	0
						19...Mar. 1	By Balance:				
							Work in Progress .	b/d.	1622	11	8
							Stores on Hand	,,	664	6	4
							Sales Stock on Hand . .	,,	783	8	0

The Cost Accounts must be reconciled to the above figure of profit. How this is done is shown in Fig. 86.

The sectional control accounts are as follows :

FIG. 82.

STORES MATERIALS CONTROL ACCOUNT

Dr.   Cr.

19...Feb. 1			£	s.	d.	19...Feb. 28			£	s.	d.
To Balance (opening stock brought down) .	b/d.		781	0	0		By Issues (*less* Returns) to work in Progress A/c.* .	A2	922	15	0
,, 28	,, Purchases (*less* Returns) .	S2	620	0	0	,,	,, Deficits in Stock † .	J4	24	2	0
,,	,, Components made . .	J4	210	3	4	,,	,, Balance : Stock in Hand	c/d.	664	6	4
			£1611	3	4				£1611	3	4
19...Mar. 1	To Balance .	b/d.	664	6	4						

* For each shop, but shown here in total.
† If a surplus, this adjusting entry would appear on the debit side.

Fig. 83.

WAGES CONTROL ACCOUNT

Dr.   Cr.

19...			£	s.	d.	19...			£	s.	d.
Feb. 7	To Direct Wages	S5	170	0	0	Feb. 28	By Work in Pro-gress* .	J5	545	0	0
„	„ Indirect „	„	71	0	0	„	„ Service Depts.*	„	163	0	0
Feb. 14	„ Direct „	S6	170	0	0	„	„ Factory Over-head . .	„	214	0	0
„	„ Indirect „	„	38	0	0						
Feb. 21	„ Direct „	S7	178	0	0						
„	„ Indirect „	„	52	0	0						
Feb. 28	„ Direct „	S8	190	0	0						
„	„ Indirect „	„	53	0	0						
			£922	0	0				£922	0	0

* Each shop separately detailed.

Fig. 84.

OVERHEAD EXPENSES CONTROL ACCOUNT

Dr.   Cr.

19...			£	s.	d.	19...			£	s.	d.
Feb. 28	To Actual Expen-diture :*					Feb. 28	By Shop A † . .	J6	282	15	0
	Factory Expense	S2	360	0	0	„	„ „ B . .	„	129	5	0
	Management .	„	160	0	0	„	„ „ C . .	„	169	0	0
	Selling Expense	„	30	0	0	„	„ Service Dept. A	„	121	18	0
	Distribution do.	„	14	0	0	„	„ Administration	„	31	2	0
„	„ Wages Control	J5	214	0	0	„	„ Sales Dept. Control .	„	30	0	0
						„	„ Despatch Dept. Control . .	„	14	0	0
			£778	0	0				£778	0	0

* As per schedule for period from financial department.
† These are from the cost office expense allocation analysis schedule.

Fig. 85.

SHOP " A " OVERHEAD CONTROL ACCOUNT

Dr.   Cr.

19...			£	s.	d.	19...			£	s.	d.
Feb. 28	To Overhead Con-trol A/c. .	J6	282	15	0	Feb. 28	By Recoveries per W. in P. A/c. as per sum-mary .	J8	319	13	0
„	„ Service Depts.	J7	46	0	0	„	„ Deficit to P. & L. A/c. (under-recovered) .	J8	9	2	0
			£328	15	0				£328	15	0

N.B.—The other Expense Control Accounts are omitted, as they operate on similar lines.

Other accounts for work in progress, finished stock and departments are similarly written up.

The general reconciliation with the profit shown in the Main Cost Control Account, which corresponds with that in the Financial Books, is provided by the Factory Profit and Loss Account (Fig. 86). Compare the method on p. 187.

Fig. 86.

FACTORY PROFIT AND LOSS ACCOUNT
for the month ending February 28th, 19......

Dr.   Cr.

19...Feb. 28			£	s.	d.	19...Feb. 28			£	s.	d.
To Cost of Sales A/c.	J8		2410	18	6	By Sales, less Returns	S2		3253	13	0
,, ,, Finished Stock A/c. (*deficit*)	J7		21	0	0	,, ,, Overhead (over-recovered Shop C)	J7		2	5	0
,, ,, Stores A/c. (*deficit*)			24	2	0						
,, ,, Overhead (*under-recovered*):											
Shop A	,,		9	2	0						
,, B, etc.	,,		6	14	0						
,, Balance, being Profit for month			784	1	6						
			£3255	18	0				£3255	18	0

Second Method of Control.—The procedure will be clear from the following journal entries, annotations and set of accounts. The accounts shown may be subdivided in practice. It is assumed the Financial Accounts are arranged to correspond. To make the Cost Ledger self-balancing, and to complete the double entry, a General Ledger Adjustment Account is introduced.

JOURNAL

	Dr.			Cr.		
	£	s.	d.	£	s.	d.
Stores Materials Control A/c.	2460	0	0			
To General Ledger Adjustment A/c.				2460	0	0
For goods purchased as per Purchases Book.						
Work in Progress A/c.	2670	0	0			
To Stores Materials Control A/c.				2670	0	0
For stores issues as per Abstract of Requisitions.						
Factory Overhead Control A/c.	7	1	0			
To Stores Material Control A/c.				7	1	0
Adjustment of stores shortage.						
Wages Control A/c.	3162	6	0			
To Gen. Led. Adjustment A/c.				3162	6	0
Total wages paid for four weeks.						
Work in Progress A/c.	2437	4	0			
Factory Overhead Control A/c.	725	2	0			
To Wages Control A/c.				3162	6	0
Division of total wages to Production and Expense A/cs. from Wages Analysis.						
Finished Stock Control A/c.	6808	8	6			
To Work in Progress A/c.						

	£	s.	d.			
Materials	2655	0	0			
Labour	2422	4	0			
Overhead	1731	4	6			
				6808	8	6

Completed goods passed to Finished Stock Store.

	Dr.			Cr.		
Overhead Adjustment A/c.	10	10	0			
To Factory Overhead Control A/c.				6	15	0
,, Administration ,, ,,				3	15	0
Adjustment of Expense under-recovered by the expense rates used.						

	Dr. £ s. d.	Cr. £ s. d.
Cost of Sales A/c. (or if not used, Trading A/c.) .	6652 8 6	
To Finished Stock Control A/c. . . .		6652 8 6
Goods issued from Finished Stock Store at cost against Sales Orders.		
Cost of Sales A/c.	285 7 6	
To Selling Overhead Expense Control A/c.* .		285 7 6
Transfer of selling expense recovered on finished stock.		
Overhead Expense Control A/c. . . .	1308 0 0	
To Gen. Led. Adjustment A/c. . . .		1308 0 0
Total actual apportioned expenses for the month.		
Factory Overhead Control A/c. . . .	685 10 0	
Administration Overhead ,, ...	337 2 6	
Selling * ,, ,, ...	285 7 6	
To Overhead Expense Control A/c. . .		1308 0 0
Analysis of total overhead transferred to appropriate sections.		
Work in Progress A/c.	1410 18 0	
To Factory Overhead . . .		1410 18 0
(Allocated)		
Work in Progress A/c.	333 7 6	
To Admin. Overhead		333 7 6
(Allocated)		
General Ledger Adjustment A/c. . . .	10,422 9 0	
To Profit and Loss A/c.		10,422 9 0
Sales as per Financial Books.		

Opening and Closing balances were :

	£ s. d.
Feb. 1. Stores Materials on hand	2700 0 0
Finished Stock ,, ,, ...	2550 0 0
,, Work in Progress :	
Materials	675 0 0
Labour	615 0 0
Overhead	210 0 0
,, General Ledger Adjustment A/c. . . .	6750 0 0
Feb. 28. Stores Materials	2482 19 0
,, Finished Stock	2706 0 0
,, Work in Progress :	
Materials	697 1 0
Labour	630 0 0
Overhead	216 0 0

FIG. 87.

THE CONTROL ACCOUNTS IN THE COST LEDGER
Stores Materials Control Accounts

Dr.		£	s.	d.		Cr.	£	s.	d.
19... Feb. 1	To Balance .	2700	0	0	19... Feb. 28	By Work in Progress A/c. (*issues*) .	2670	0	0
,, 28	,, Gen. Led. Adj. A/c. (*purchases*) .	2460	0	0	,,	,, Shortage adjustment transferred to Factory Overhead A/c. .	7	1	0
					,,	,, Stock on Hand	2482	19	0
		£5160	0	0			£5160	0	0
19... Mar. 1	To Balance .	2482	19	0					

* Not shown.

Wages Control Account

Dr.			£	s.	d.			£	s.	d.	Cr.
19... Feb. 7	To Gen. Led. Adj. A/c. (Wages paid) .		780	0	0	19... Feb. 28	By Work in Progress A/c. . . .	2437	4	0	
,, 14	Do. . .		796	10	0	,,	,, Factory Overhead A/c. (Indirect				
,, 21	Do. . .		786	18	0		Wages) .	725	2	0	
,, 28	Do. . .		798	18	0						
			£3162	6	0			£3162	6	0	

Overhead Expense Control Account

Dr.		£	s.	d.			£	s.	d.	Cr.
19... Feb. 28	To Gen. Led. Adj. A/c. (Total Expenses) .	1308	0	0	19... Feb. 28	By Factory Overhead A/c. . . .	685	10	0	
					,,	,, Administration Overhead A/c. .	337	2	6	
					,,	,, Selling Overhead A/c. . . .	285	7	6	
		£1308	0	0			£1308	0	0	

Factory Overhead Control Account

Dr.		£	s.	d.			£	s.	d.	Cr.
19... Feb. 28	To Overhead Control A/c. . . .	685	10	0	19... Feb. 28	Work in Progress : By Sundries (Allocations as per Abstract) .	1410	18	0	
,,	,, Wages Control A/c. (Indirect Wages) .	725	2	0		,, Adjustment A/c. Difference (under-recovered) .	6	15	0	
,,	,, Stores Adjustments	7	1	0						
		£1417	13	0			£1417	13	0	

Administration Overhead Control Account

Dr.		£	s.	d.			£	s.	d.	Cr.
19... Feb. 28	To Overhead Control A/c. . . .	337	2	6	19... Feb. 28	Work in Progress : By Sundries (as per Abstract) .	333	7	6	
						,, Adjustment A/c. Difference (under-recovered) .	3	15	0	
		£337	2	6			£337	2	6	

WORK IN PROGRESS ACCOUNT

Dr.			£	s.	d.				£	s.	d.	Cr.
19... Feb. 1	To Balance : £ Material . 675 Labour . 615 Overhead. 210	b/d.	1500	0	0	19... Feb. 28	By Finished Stock Control A/c. .	J60	6808	8	6	
Feb. 28	,, Materials A/c. .		2670	0	0	,,	,, Balance, Work in Progress : £ s. d. Material . 697 1 0					
,,	,, Wages A/c. .		2437	4	0		Labour . 630 0 0					
,,	,, Factory Over- head . .		1410	18	0		Overhead 216 0 0					
,,	,, Admin. Over- head .		333	7	6			c/d.	1543	1	0	
			£8351	9	6				£8351	9	6	

FINISHED STOCK CONTROL ACCOUNT

Dr.										Cr.		
			£	s.	d.				£	s.	d.
19... Feb. 1	To Balance	b/d.	2550	0	0	19... Feb. 28	By Cost of Sales A/c.	J62	6652	8	6
,, 28	,, Work in Progress A/c.	J60	6808	8	6	,,	,, Balance, Stock on hand	c/d.	2706	0	0
			£9358	8	6				£9358	8	6
19... Mar. 1	To Balance	b/d.	2706	0	0						

COST OF SALES ACCOUNT

Dr.										Cr.		
			£	s.	d.				£	s.	d.
19... Feb. 28	To Finished Stock A/c.	J62	6652	8	6	19... Feb. 28	By Profit and Loss A/c.	J63	6937	16	0
,,	,, Selling and Distribution Overhead	J63	285	7	6						
			£6937	16	0				£6937	16	0

OVERHEAD EXPENSES ADJUSTMENT ACCOUNT

Dr.										Cr.		
			£	s.	d.				£	s.	d.
19... Feb. 28	To Factory Overhead Control A/c. . 6 15 0					19... Feb. 28	By Profit and Loss A/c.	J64	10	10	0
,,	,, Admin. Overhead Control A/c. . 3 15 0	J64	10	10	0						
			£10	10	0				£10	10	0

PROFIT AND LOSS ACCOUNT

Dr.										Cr.		
			£	s.	d.				£	s.	d.
19... Feb. 28	To Cost of Sales A/c.	J63	6,937	16	0	19... Feb. 28	By Sales as per Gen. Led. Adjust. A/c.	J63	10,422	9	0
,,	,, Overhead Adjust. A/c.	J64	10	10	0						
,,	,, Net Profit to Gen. Led. Adjust. A/c.	J64	3,474	3	0						
			£10,422	9	0				£10,422	9	0

GENERAL LEDGER ADJUSTMENT ACCOUNT

Dr.			£	s.	d.				£	s.	d.	Cr.
19... Feb. 28	To Sales as per P. & L. A/c.		10,422	9	0	19... Feb. 1	By Balance .	b/d.	6,750	0	0	
,,	,, Stocks on hand:					Feb. 28	,, Stores Materials Control A/c. . .		2,460	0	0	
	Stores . .	c/d.	2,482	19	0	,,	,, Wages Control A/c. .		3,162	6	0	
	Stock . .	,,	2,706	0	0	,,	,, Overhead Control A/c.		1,308	0	0	
	Work in Progress . .	,,	1,543	1	0	,,	,, P. & L. A/c. balance .		3,474	3	0	
			£17,154	9	0				£17,154	9	0	
						19... Mar. 1	By Balance:					
							Stores . .	b/d.	2,482	19	0	
							Stock . .	,,	2,706	0	0	
							Work in Progress . .	,,	1,543	1	0	

Third Method of Control.—A Manufacturing Account (sometimes referred to as a Work in Progress Account, or a Cost Ledger Account) is opened in the Financial Books. An account of this nature may be opened for each department of the factory or for each type of goods manufactured.

A corresponding account, entered up on the reverse sides of the account in the Financial Books, may be kept in the Cost Ledger.

The following accounts in the Financial Books form the controls for the Cost Ledger. They are self-explanatory.

FIG. 88.

MANUFACTURING ACCOUNT

(or Cost Ledger Account)

for the 4 weeks ending February 28th, 19......

Dr.			£	s.	d.				£	s.	d.	Cr.
19... Feb. 1	To Balance, Stocks and Work in Progress b/d. . .		6,750	0	0	19... Feb. 28	By Finished Stock or Contracts .		6,052	8	6	
Feb. 28	,, Purchases (Stores)		2,360	0	0	,,	,, Work on Capital Additions to plant . .		600	0	0	
,,	,, Purchases (special for contracts) .		100	0	0	,,	,, Stocks on hand * .		5,189	19	0	
,,	,, Wages (total) .		3,162	6	0	,,	,, Work in Progress *		1,542	1	0	
,,	,, Overhead Expenses (excluding Selling and Distribution) . .		1,022	12	6	,,	,, Factory Overhead not recovered to P. & L. A/c. .		10	10	0	
			£13,394	18	6				£13,394	18	6	

* Carried down to next account.

FINISHED STOCK ACCOUNT

Dr.									Cr.		
19... Feb. 1 ,, 28	To Balance b/d. . ,, Manufacturing A/c. (Cost of Goods made) .	£ 2,550 6,052	s. 0 8	d. 0 6	19... Feb. 28 ,,	By Trading A/c. (Cost of Sales) . . ,, Stock on hand c/d	£ 5,896 2,706	s. 8 0	d. 6 0		
		£8,602	8	6			£8,602	8	6		

TRADING ACCOUNT

or the month ending February 28th, 19......

Dr.									Cr.		
19... Feb. 28 ,, ,,	To Cost of Sales . ,, Factory Overhead Adjustment . ,, Gross Profit c/d. .	£ 5,896 10 4,515	s. 8 10 10	d. 6 0 6	19... Feb. 28	By Sales (less returns and allowances).	£ 10,422	s. 9	d. 0		
		£10,422	9	0			£10,422	9	0		
,, ,,	To Selling and Distri- bution Overhead ,, Net Profit . .	285 4,230	7 3	6 0		By Gross Profit b/d. .	4,515	10	6		
		£4,515	10	6			£4,515	10	6		

Note.—Compare Contract Central Accounts on pp. 166–7.

Note on Reconciliation of Profit shown by Cost and Financial Books.—The net profit shown by the Financial Books usually differs from that shown by the Cost Ledger, and, generally, that of the Cost Accounts is less than the amount appearing in the financial Profit and Loss Account.

This may arise from several causes, and mention may be made, particularly, of depreciation and interest on Capital. Not infrequently, a higher rate of depreciation is used in the Cost Accounts, particularly if the Financial Accounts include only the rate allowed by the income tax authorities. Again, interest on capital does not appear in the financial accounts, but is frequently included in the Cost Accounts.

In addition to these items, the Overhead expense in the Financial Accounts is the actual expense incurred or chargeable for the period. In the Cost Accounts, the Overhead is applied by pre-determined rates as a rule, and, consequently, there is an under- or over-allocation of Overhead expense to be adjusted to bring the two results into line.

A Reconciliation Account may be prepared to bring the

result shown by the two accounting systems into agreement, thus :

FIG. 89.

PROFIT AND LOSS RECONCILIATION ACCOUNT
(Cost Ledger)

Dr.					Cr.			
19... Feb. 28	To Overhead under-recovered (Shop B).	£ 7	s. 5	d. 0	19... Feb. 28	By Net Profit as per Cost Ledger .	£ 2500	s. 0	d. 0
,,	,, Net Profit as per Financial A/cs. .	2740	5	0	,,	,, Depreciation charged in excess of that in Financial A/cs. .	150	0	0
					,,	,, Interest on Capital Assets not charged in Financial A/cs.	84	0	0
					,,	,, Overhead recovered in excess of actual (Shop A) .	13	10	0
		£2747	10	0			£2747	10	0

Tabular Control Account.—An account of this kind is particularly suitable for factories working on the job order system, where tabular Cost Ledger Accounts, or sheets, are kept for the various orders executed.

The total expenditure under each heading of cost is posted monthly from the Abstracts of Materials issued, Direct Expenses, Wages and Overhead. The items "Charged to Accounts" (Fig. 90) are from the Job Cost Summary, i.e., the summary of Costs of completed jobs.

The chief check provided is to prove that the totals, as per the schedules, agree with the total costs of orders, in case any items should have been mis-posted. An account of this type may be used for an individual large contract which extends over a long period.

FIG. 90.

TABULAR COST CONTROL ACCOUNT
(in the Cost Control Ledger)

Mnth.	Ref.	Abstracts : Totals.					Charged to Accounts : Totals of Completed Jobs.		
		Direct Purchases.	Stores.	Wages.	Overhead.	Total.	No.	Name.	
19... Jan.	b/d.	£ s. d. 15 0 0	£ s. d. 86 0 0	£ s. d. 53 0 0	£ s. d. 59 0 0	£ s. d. 81 0 0 213 0 0	92 83 97	J. Hows B. Pitts Jones & Co. In Progress	£ s. d. 132 0 0 41 0 0 23 0 0 98 0 0
						£294 0 0			£294 0 0
Feb.	b/d.					98 0 0			

1. The following represents the Trading and Profit and Loss Account (abridged) of a manufacturer of a patent fire extinguisher of a standard type.

TRADING AND PROFIT AND LOSS ACCOUNT FOR THE YEAR ENDED DEC. 31, 1929

	£	s.	d.		£	s.	d.
To Materials Used .	2915	0	0	By Sales . .	7500	0	0
„ Productive Wages	1861	0	0	„ Stock of Finished			
„ Factory Expenses	1405	10	0	Articles . .	181	5	0
„ Gross Profit (carried down) .	2052	15	0	„ Work in Progress :			
				£			
				Materials 280			
				Wages . 156			
				Factory			
				Expenses 117			
				——	553	0	0
	£8234	5	0		£8234	5	0
To Administration Expenses .	1365	0	0	By Gross Profit (brought down)	2052	15	0
„ Net Profit . .	687	15	0				
	£2052	15	0		£2052	15	0

1550 Extinguishers were manufactured during the year and 1500 were sold during the same period.

The cost records which had been kept showed that Factory Expenses worked out at 16s. 6d. and Administration Expenses at 18s. 1½d. per article produced, the Cost Accounts showing an estimated total profit of £703 2s. 6d. for the year.

From the foregoing information, you are required to prepare :

(a) Factory Expenses Oncost Account.

(b) Administration Expenses Oncost Account.

(c) An Account showing the reconciliation between the total figure of net profit as per the cost accounts and the figure of net profit shown in the financial books.

Institute of Cost and Works Accountants (Final).

2. Prepare in the Cost Ledger an expense account for the General Offices of a manufacturing business showing all the items which comprise the cost and indicate on the credit side how you would distribute the total cost.—*Institute of Cost and Works Accountants (Inter.).*

3. Explain the working of Stores Control Accounts. If at the time of stocktaking the quantity of counted stock should be found to differ considerably from the total shown in the Control Account, what conclusion would you draw, and why ?—*London Chamber of Commerce.*

4. What value do you attach to the reconciliation of Cost Accounts and Financial Accounts ? If you find at the end of an accounting period that there are serious differences, where would you expect to find these, and how would you deal with them in your Cost Accounts ?—*Institute of Cost and Works Accountants (Final).*

5. Describe briefly a Work in Progress Account and illustrate its relation to the Financial Accounts.—*Royal Society of Arts (Advanced).*

6. State shortly the means by which you would reconcile the Cost Accounts with the financial books of the business.—*Society of Incorporated Accountants and Auditors (Inter.).*

7 Prepare a manufacturing account, incorporating the following figures :

		£
Production Account (Factory output)	. . .	17,700
Work in progress, January 1	. . .	2,400
Work in progress, December 31	. . .	3,000

Materials, viz. :		£	
Stores (January 1)	. . .	1,500	
Purchases	. . .	5,400	
		6,900	
Less Stores (December 31)	. . .	1,740	
			5,160
Labour	. . . .		9,000
Rent, Rates and Taxes	. . .		1,000
Electric Power	. . . .		500
Electric Light	. . . .		140
Heating	. . . .		200
Superintendence and Clerical Assistance	. .		1,100
Small Tools	. . . .		400
Maintenance and Depreciation	. . .		500
Interest	. . . .		300

Society of Incorporated Accountants and Auditors (Final).

8. Under what general heads should the items appearing in a Trading and Profit and Loss Account be grouped for the purpose of comparing the financial and cost accounts of a business and to what element of cost will the expenditure under each head correspond ?

In spite of the close relationship between cost and financial accounts there are instances of important differences between the two sets of accounts. Indicate the nature of such differences.—*Society of Incorporated Accountants and Auditors (Inter.).*

9. What are the principal difficulties encountered in reconciliation of cost and financial accounts ? How are they overcome ?—*Institute of Cost and Works Accountants (Final).*

10. It is the practice in a certain factory to charge overheads to the products by means of pre-determined hourly rates. How would you propose to deal with the following under- or over-absorbed overhead at the end of an accounting period :

	Overhead incurred.	Overhead absorbed.	Balance.
Department A	. .	£2,000	£2,200	+£200
Department B	. .	£1,500	£1,300	—£200
Department C	. .	£1,100	£1,000	—£100

Institute of Cost and Works Accountants (Inter.).

11. Describe the method you would suggest for ensuring the agreement of works accounts with the financial accounts, showing the principal corresponding headings in each.—*Institute of Cost and Works Accountants (Final).*

12. Describe the means you would adopt in order to ascertain whether the total overheads as allocated to the Cost Accounts agree with the financial accounts at the end of a given period, and explain how you would deal with any differences.—*Institute of Cost and Works Accountants (Final).*

13. What provision should be made to ensure exact correspondence between the cost records and the financial accounts of a business ?—*Institute of Cost and Works Accountants (Final).*

14. Indicate the Cost Control accounts necessary for a manufactur-

ing business and define their functions.—*Institute of Cost and Works Accountants (Inter.).*

15. Where it is proved that the account of overheads applied to cost fall considerably short of the expense recovered in the financial accounts, what method would you adopt to ascertain and rectify the discrepancy ? —*Institute of Cost and Works Accountants (Final).*

16. Describe briefly how you would deal with under-recovered and over-recovered administrative and selling expenses. Should the following year's cost accounts be affected by either circumstance ?—*Institute of Cost and Works Accountants (Final).*

17. Describe how you would secure the interlocking of the cost accounts and the financial accounts for any business with which you are familiar.—*Institute of Cost and Works Accountants (Final).*

18. Describe with illustration a Work in Progress Account and state its uses. Mention the origin of the information contained in it, and explain its relation to the financial accounts.—*Institute of Cost and Works Accountants (Final).*

19. Explain the necessity for reconciling cost and financial accounts. State what disagreements you would expect to find and how you would deal with them.—*Institute of Cost and Works Accountants (Final).*

20. The products of a manufacturing concern are wide and various. At the end of the financial year the value of Stock and Work in Progress is urgently required. Describe a system that would give accurate and speedy returns.—*Institute of Cost and Works Accountants (Final).*

21. In connection with any system of Costing it is important to see that the Financial Accounts are kept in such a way as to afford a ready means of agreement of the total wages, materials, expenses and charges relating to each department. Explain precisely how this end can be achieved.—*Society of Incorporated Accountants and Auditors (Inter.).*

22. At a balancing date, the profit disclosed by the Manufacturing Account prepared from cost books is in excess of that shown by the Trading Account prepared from financial books. To what could such difference be attributable, and what steps would you take to obviate similar differences in future ?—*Society of Incorporated Accountants and Auditors (Inter.).*

23. A company owns the Freehold of its factory. Would you charge rent in the Cost Accounts, and, if so, how would you reconcile them with the Financial Accounts where there would normally be no charge for rent ?—*Society of Incorporated Accountants and Auditors (Inter.).*

24. A manufacturer seeks your assistance in connection with the organisation of his Stores records. You find that the keeping and balancing of a Stores Ledger would involve a large amount of detail and that the cost would be out of proportion to the benefits obtained. What procedure would you suggest for recording the movements of Stores that would also permit of the value of Stores on Hand being ascertained at any given date ?—*Society of Incorporated Accountants and Auditors (Final).*

25. The Cost Ledger of Morley Motors, Limited, showed the following balances as at 1st July, 1928 :

	£	£
Stores Ledger Account	5,250	—
Work in Progress Account	3,920	—
Finished Goods Account	2,790	—
Works Oncost Account	—	50
Administration Oncost Account	30	—
Cost Ledger Control Account	—	11,940
	£11,990	£11,990

Further balances resulting from the operations for the year ended 30th June, 1929, were :

Stores—Purchases	£18,000
Stores issued to Production Orders	19,650
Stores issued to Works and Repairs Orders	750
Wages	30,750
Productive Labour	29,500
Unproductive Labour	1,250
Carriage Inwards	300
Works Oncost allocated to Production Orders	8,950
Works Expenses	7,000
Administration Expenses	900
Administration Oncost allocated to Production Orders	920
Goods finished during the year	58,600
Finished Goods sold	60,000
Sales Expenses	670

Record the entries in the Cost Ledger Accounts for the year ended 30th June, 1929, and prepare a Schedule of Balances as at that date explaining what each balance represents.

26. The under-noted particulars are taken from the books of a manufacturing company which commenced business on 1st January, 1931. They relate to the six months ended 30th June, 1931. Show the following accounts as they would appear in the Cost Ledger, viz. :

(a) Completed Jobs Account.
(b) Work in Progress Account.
(c) Finished Stock Account.
(d) Works Oncost Account.
(e) Works Oncost Suspense Account.
(f) Office Oncost Account.
(g) Office Oncost Suspense Account.
(h) Manufacturing Account.

The Profit or Loss on Completed Contracts and Sales from Stock should also be shown.

Productive Wages on Completed Jobs	£400
Productive Wages on Work in Progress	100
Stores used on Completed Jobs	700
Stores used on Work in Progress	300
Direct Materials on Completed Jobs	100
Direct Materials on Work in Progress	20
Chargeable Expenses on Completed Jobs	20
Chargeable Expenses on Work in Progress	10
Transfers from Finished Stock to Completed Jobs	75

Works Oncost to be charged at 75 per cent. on Productive Wages.
Office Oncost to be charged at 10 per cent. on Works Cost.

Contract Price of Completed Contracts	£1,700
Sales from Finished Stock	350
Finished Stock on hand as at 30th June, 1931	250
Transfers from Completed Jobs to Finished Stock	475

The Ledger Accounts should be ruled off as at 30th June 1931, and balances, if any, brought down as at 1 July, 1931. No Journal Entries are required.—*Corporation of Accountants (Final).*

27. Detail the steps you would take to reconcile the Cost Accounts with the financial accounts, and state where you would expect to find discrepancies. Indicate the probable cause of the discrepancies and how you would deal with same in the cost books.—*Corporation of Accountants (Final).*

28. The following balances are shown in the Cost Ledger as at 1st January, 1933 :—

Q

	Dr.	Cr.
Work in Progress Account	£1,960	
Finished Stock Account	1,465	
Works Oncost Suspense Account . . .	100	
Office and Administration Oncost Suspense Account	50	
Stores Ledger Control Account . . .	2,625	
Cost Ledger Control Account		£6,200

Transactions for the year ended 31st December, 1933, were :—

Wages Paid			£16,000
Allocated :—Direct Labour . .	£15,300		
Indirect Labour .	700		
Works Oncost allocated to Production . .			4,675
Office and Administration Oncost allocated to Production			1,550
Stores issued to Production			9,825
Goods finished during year			30,000
Finished goods sold			33,000
Stores Purchased			9,000
Stores issued to Factory Repair Orders . .			375
Carriage Inwards on Stores used for Production			150
Works Expenses			3,500
Office and Administration Expenses . .			1,500

Write up Accounts in the Cost Ledger to record the above transactions, make ⁺he necessary transfers to Control Accounts, and carry down balances as at 31st December, 1933. Profit or Loss for the year is to be shown.—*Corporation of Accountants (Final).*

29. The following are the balances of a Cost Ledger at January 1st, 1932 :—

	Dr.	Cr.
Cost Ledger Control Account		£23,880
Stores Ledger Account	£10,500	
Work in Progress Account	7,840	
Finished Goods Account	5,580	
Works Oncost Account		100
Administration Oncost Account . . .	60	

The operations during the year 1932 were :—

Purchases			£36,000
Stores issued—			
Production Account . . .	£39,300		
Works and Repairs . . .	1,500		
			40,800
Wages (productive)			59,000
Wages (unproductive)			2,500
Carriage (inwards) . . . , . .			600
Works Oncost (Production Account) . .			17,900
Works Expenses			14,000
Administration Expenses			1,800
Administration Oncost (Production Account) .			1,840
Goods finished during the year . . .			117,200
Finished goods sold			120,000
Sales Expenses			1,340

(a) Record the entries in the Cost Ledger Accounts, and prepare a Trial Balance.

(b) Explain the relationship of the Balances in respect of the financial books of the undertaking.

Incorporated Accountants (Final).

30. The following are the Cost Ledger balances of A.B., Ltd., at 31st December, 1932 :—

	£	£
Stores Ledger Account	7,000	—
Work in Progress Account	4,000	—
Finished Goods Account	3,000	—
Works Oncost	—	70
Administration Oncost	40	—
Cost Ledger Control Account . . .	—	13,970
	£14,040	£14,040

At 31st December, 1933, the following further particulars resulted from operations for the year :—

Stores—Purchases	£20,000
Stores issued to Production Orders . . .	18,000
Stores issued to Factory Repairs Orders . . .	600
Wages	35,000
Productive Labour	33,600
Unproductive Labour	1,400
Carriage Inwards	400
Works Expenses	7,500
Works Oncost allocated to Production Orders . .	9,000
Administration Expenses	750
Administration Oncost allocated to Production Orders	900
Goods finished during the year	61,000
Finished Goods sold (Production Cost) . . .	63,000
Sales Expenses	700

Write up the Cost Ledger for the year to 31st December, 1933, and prepare a final Trial Balance. Make any comments that you think necessary on the resultant position.—*Incorporated Accountants (Final).*

31. In cases where there is a discrepancy between results disclosed by financial and cost accounts the latter sometimes give the more favourable apparent result. How would you account for this, and what would you advise to secure closer correspondence between the two sets of accounts ? —*Incorporated Accountants (Inter.).*

32. The costing records of the S.T. Manufacturing Co. reveal the following information in respect of the six months ended 30th June, 1933 :—

	£	£
Purchases	—	30,000
Stores on Hand	6,400	9,010
Stock of Finished Goods	9,740	10,250
Work in Progress	12,400	9,920
Carriage Inwards		450
Stores issued		27,600
Wages—Productive Labour		26,640
„ Unproductive Labour . . .		9,360
Works Expenses, including Rent, Power, etc. .		26,800
Repairs to Materials in Stores . . .		240
Cost of Completed Jobs		98,510
Cost of Finished Goods sold . . .		98,000
Selling Expenses		2,250
Office and Administration Expenses . .		5,300

The Journal shows that £36,530 and £5,260 were allocated to Work in Progress in respect of Works oncost and Office oncost respectively.

You are required to show how the above transactions would be recorded in the various Cost Ledger Accounts and to extract a Trial Balance as at 30th June, 1933.—*Incorporated Accountants (Final).*

CHAPTER XVI

PROCESS COSTING

Process Costing.—This is a method of Costing used to ascertain the cost of the product at each process, operation, or stage of manufacture, where processes are carried on having one or more of the following features :

(1) Where the product of one process becomes the material of another process or operation.

(2) Where there is simultaneous production, at one or more processes, of different products, with or without by-products.

(3) Where, during one or more processes or operations of a series, the products, or materials, are not distinguishable from one another, as, for instance, when the finished products differ finally only in shape or form.

The system provides for showing the Cost of the main products and of any by-products. The method is very different from Job Order Costing, where each job is separately costed. Orders may be combined for common process production to a certain stage, and then be costed for subsequent operations by Job Cost methods.

In most cases, Process Costing requires fewer forms, and less details, than are needed for Job Costs, but a closer analysis of operations. For example, there is not the need for the abstracting of labour to so many order numbers, and material is issued in bulk to departments, rather than to many specific jobs. In continuous processes, as in a coal distillation plant, the men are occupied continuously on each process.

The Application of the Method.—The industries in which Process Costs may be used are very many, in fact, except where Job, or Batch Costing, and Unit Operation Costing is necessary, a Process Costing system can usually be devised.

In particular, the following may be mentioned as a few examples :

Chemical works.   Textiles, weaving,
Soap-making.   spinning, etc.

206

Box-making.
Distillation processes.
Coking works.
Paper-mills.
Biscuit works.

Food products.
Canning factories.
Paint, ink, and varnish-
making, etc.

The General Features of Process Cost Systems.—An account is kept for each process or operation. Materials, labour, and expenses are debited, by-products and waste are credited, whilst the material, as modified at the first operation, is passed on to the next process. If by-products require further treatment, the same procedure is followed.

Put in another way, the " finished product " of the firs process becomes the "raw material " of the next one, and so on, until the final products are completed. Each Process Account, in fact, represents a subdivision of a Manufacturing Account, so that the works cost of each process is separately ascertained, and from which the unit cost at each operation may be calculated.

Single or Output Costing resembles Process Costing in which there is but one process where every unit is identical. Sometimes Unit Costing is combined with Process Costing, the method being to cost by the unit of production, where manufacture is continuous, and the units are identical, or can be made equivalent by means of ratios.

Departmental Costing differs in that separate products are, generally, dealt with in each department, whereas, in Process Costing, the same material passes from one operation or process to another in altered form. When two or more distinct varieties of goods are manufactured, separate departmental costs are desirable, so that the profit made by each department may be revealed.

Types of Process Work to be Considered.—The nature of the industry will determine the arrangement of the Process Accounts. Examples will be used to illustrate the types of manufacture which are frequently met with :

1. Where the raw material passes through a sequential series of processes before completion, there being no by-products, and no need for Stock Accounts at intermediate stages, e.g., glass bottle works, earthenware, paper-making, etc.

2. Where there are no by-products, but it is necessary to use a Stock Account for each process, or for some of the pro-

cesses, *e.g.*, engineering factories using mass production and repetition methods; cotton and wool textiles.

3. Where by-products arise, and have to be costed, *e.g.*, gas manufacture, coke-oven works, chemical works, distillation processes, refineries.

Standard Costs in Process Costing.—In industries where Process Costing is suitable, Standard Costs may be used with great advantage. Standard Costs provide a measure against which actual costs may be compared. Standard Costing, in connection with Process Accounts, gives the management an excellent measure of the efficiency of production, and it may be mentioned that accounting systems on these lines are being more widely used every year. This modern method is dealt with fully in another chapter.

The Use of Numerical Nomenclature.—In an earlier chapter the use of works order numbers and standing order numbers was described with examples. The identification of cost to processes by means of Process Order Numbers facilitates the collection of the necessary details, ensures a proper allocation of expenditure to each process, and simplifies expense analysis.

The adoption of departmental or process numbers is necessary when mechanical sorting and tabulatory machines are used, and these mechanical methods are being more widely adopted every year. In large factories these machines are indispensable, if prompt cost and production figures are required. Special chapters (Chs. XXVI–XXVIII) are devoted to costing by these remarkable machines.

A Theoretical Example of Process Costing.—In order that the practical illustrations of Process Costing may be more easily understood, the simple theoretical example below is given.

MAKING CHINA BOWLS

Process I. Grinding materials (white clay felspar and flints).
Process II. Pressing and casting in moulds and turning on lathe to remove excess material and inequalities of the exterior surface.
Process III. Articles placed in Saggars and baked.
Process IV. Glazing or decorating, and firing in glost oven.

N.B.—The grouping of processes as shown is merely arbitrary for illustration.

FIG. 91.

THE COST LEDGER ACCOUNTS

Dr.   1. *Grinding Account*   Cr.

19...		Fo.	£	s.	d.	19...		Fo.	Cwt.	Q.	lb.	£	s.	d.
	To Materials :					By Moulding								
	White clay .		20	0	0	A/c. .	2	33	0	0	98	2	0
	Felspar .		15	9	6								
	Flints .		5	7	6								
	,, Wages . .		21	0	0								
	,, Departmental expense as per allocation . .		36	5	0								
			£98	2	0			33	0	0	£98	2	0

Dr.   2. *Moulding and Turning Account*   Cr.

19...		Fo.	£	s.	d.	19...		Fo.	Qty.	£	s.	d.
	To Materials from Process I .	1	98	2	0	By Process III (Baking) .	3	3668	183	8	0
	,, Wages . .		60	0	0	(Unit cost 1s.)					
	,, Works expenses		25	6	0						
			£183	8	0			3668	£183	8	0

Dr.   3. *Baking Account*   Cr.

19...		Fo.	£	s.	d.	19...		Fo.	Qty.	£	s.	d.
	To Materials from Process II .	2	183	8	0	By Process IV (Glazing) .	4	3500	218	17	8
	,, Wages . .		15	0	8	,, Scrapped .		168	–	–	–
	,, Works expenses .		20	9	0						
			£218	17	8	(Unit cost 1s. 3d.)		3668	£218	17	8

Dr.   4. *Glazing Process*   Cr.

19...		Fo.	£	s.	d.	19...		Fo.	Qty.	£	s.	d.
	To Materials from Process III .	3	218	17	8	By Finished Stock A/c. .	5	3400	280	10	0
	,, Stores Materials . .		12	1	4	,, Scrapped and rejected .		100	–	–	–
	,, Wages . .		34	7	6						
	,, Works expenses .		15	3	6	(Unit cost 1s. 7·8d.)					
			£280	10	0			3500	£280	10	0

In the above *pro forma* accounts, which represent Process Accounts in their simplest form, it is assumed that the whole of the raw material is passed into manufacture, through each process in succession. At each process the unit cost is shown, and the unit cost of each process is represented by the difference between the cost per unit of one process and the preceding one. The " finished " product of Process I is the " raw material " of Process II, and so on, each transferred at cost.*

* Sometimes these transfers are made to show the transferring process a profit. The reason, and stock valuation problems arising, are dealt with on page 211.

Example of Process Accounts with Intermediate Stock Accounts

Process Stock Accounts.—In the preceding example no intermediate stocks of part-finished articles are held. It is necessary in some forms of manufacturing to accumulate stocks of articles at one or more of the operations, *e.g.*, when it is desired to complete subsequent operations or processes only when and in such quantities as may be required for specific orders.

This may occur, for instance, when standard articles are made by repetition work up to a certain stage, and completed to particular specifications of customers. In such cases there are usually well-defined stages of production.

When this procedure is adopted, it is convenient to introduce separate process Stock Accounts, which are debited at cost with the quantities made at each process. The quantities drawn from the Part-finished Goods Store are credited to this Stock Account, and debited at cost to the account of the next process. The procedure is illustrated in the following accounts:

Process I. Brass castings are made to a standard model suitable for machining to two styles.

Process II. Castings machined to the stock patterns.

Process III. The machined articles are polished and lacquered, or enamelled as may be required.

Fig. 92.

PROCESS I

Castings Account

Dr.		Fo.	£	s.	d.			Fo.	Unit cost s.	Unit cost d.	No. made	£	s.	d.	Cr.
19...	To Metal . .	6	60	9	0	19...	By Castings Stock A/c. .	2	2	0	1082	108	4	0	
	,, Wages . .	8	20	7	0										
	,, Patterns .	9	6	8	0										
	,, Foundry expenses .	J10	21	0	0										
			£108	4	0						1082	£108	4	0	

Castings Stock Account

Dr.		Fo.	No.	£	s.	d.			Fo.	Unit cost s.	Unit cost d.	No.	£	s.	d.	Cr.
19... Jan. 1	To Balance .	b/d.	802	88	1	0	19... Jan. 7	By Process II A/c. .	3	2	1	900	93	15	0	
,, 7	,, Castings A/c. (Process I) .	1	1082	108	4	0	,,	,, Stock .	c/d.	2	2	984	102	10	0	
			1884	£196	5	0						1884	£196	5	0	
Jan. 7	To Balance .	b/d.	984	102	10	0										

PROCESS II
Machining Account

Dr.			No.				19...		Fo.	Unit cost.		No.				Cr.
19...		Fo.		£	s.	d.	19...		Fo.	s.	d.		£	s.	d.	
Jan. 7	To Castings Stock A/c.	2	900	93	15	0	Jan. 14	By Process III A/c.	4	3	2	790	125	1	8	
Jan. 14	,, Labour	12	–	24	0	0	,,	,, Scrapped castings	–	–		10	–	–	–	
,,	,, Expenses as allocation	J13	–	21	0	0	,,	,, Work in Progress	c/d.	–		100	13	13	4	
			900	£138	15	0						900	£138	15	0	
Mar. 1	To Work in Progress.	b/d.	100	13	13	4										

PROCESS III
Finishing Account

Dr.			No.				19...		Fo.	Unit cost.		No.				Cr.
19...		Fo.		£	s.	d.	19...		Fo.	s.	d.		£	s.	d.	
Jan. 14	To Machining A/c.	3	790	125	1	8	Jan. 21	By Pieces rejected	–	–		15	–	–	–	
Jan. 21	,, Stores materials	15	–	8	0	0	,,	,, Finished Stock A/c.	J17	3	9·5	775	147	6	10	
,,	,, Wages	16	–	14	5	2										
			790	£147	6	10						790	£147	6	10	

Internal Process Profits.—Sometimes the output from one process is transferred to a subsequent process, not at cost as shown in the preceding examples, but at a price showing a profit to the transferor process. For instance, at a price corresponding to current wholesale market prices or at cost plus an agreed percentage. The object is (a) to show whether the cost of production competes with market prices, (b) to make each process stand on its own efficiency and economies, i.e. the transferee processes are not given the benefit, when comparing the cost at that stage with external prices, of economies effected in the earlier process.

It is an unnecessary complication in the accounts, as the desired comparisons could be prepared on separate cost reports for each process. The complexity brought into the accounts arises from the fact that these inter-process profits so introduced *remain included* in price of process stocks, finished stocks and work-in-progress, and, for Balance Sheet purposes, must be eliminated by the creation of proper reserves. Until actually sold, the profit on such stock, being unrealised, cannot be taken credit for, hence each process profit must be reduced by the profit in the value of the unsold stock.

The procedure may be illustrated from the following example :

PROCESS I.

	£		£
To Cost of Material, Labour and Expenses	225	By Transfer to Process II (Cost plus 33⅓% on Cost	300
„ Process Profit transferred . .	75		
	£300		£300

PROCESS II.

	£		£
To Process I Material . . .	300	By Completed Stock on hand at Cost	150
„ Other Material, Wages and Expenses	750	„ Transfer to Process III (Cost plus 33⅓% on Cost) . . .	1200
„ Process Profit transferred . .	300		
	£1350		£1350

In Process II the cost of the output transferred is £1050 less £150, *i.e.* £900. Of the £1,050 there is £300 from Process I, which includes 25% internal profit (N.B. 33⅓% on cost equals 25% on transfer price), hence the completed stock on hand, £150, contains some of that profit which should be reserved for thus :

$$25\% \text{ of } \frac{300}{1,050} \times 150 = £10\cdot7 \ ; \ \text{or } \frac{150}{1,050} \times 75 = £10\cdot7 \text{ Reserve.}$$

This is a reserve against the £300 profit shown for Process II.

At later processes similar calculations will have to be made in respect of any stock on hand at each process. Should the whole output be sold, then no reserve is required. The calculations become involved after the second process, because it is necessary to eliminate not only the proportion of profit in the preceding process, but also of that in *each* preceding process. This involves a chain of reserves being calculated, hence the objection to this method of pricing process materials transferred.

EXAMPLE OF ACCOUNTS OF PROCESSES WITH BY-PRODUCTS

Process Costs of By-products.—For the purpose of illustration assume that crude oil is distilled, producing (*a*) light oil, (*b*) medium oil, (*c*) heavy residue, which is used as fuel. The light and medium oils undergo further fractional distillation.

The processes may be summarised as follows :

1. Crude oil distilled, producing

   (*a*) Light oil; (*b*) Medium oil; (*c*) A residue which is used as fuel for the furnaces.

2. Light oil after passing through a treatment involving the use of sulphuric acid and caustic soda is fractionally distilled producing :

(*a*) Benzol; (*b*) Toluene; (*c*) Solvent naphtha, part of which is used in process No. III and some is sold.

3. Medium oil passes through a process requiring the use of sulphuric acid, caustic soda and solvent naphtha, and produces :

(*a*) Carbolic acid; (*b*) Chemical N; (*c*) Residue M, which is stored in drums for sale.

In the following accounts a column for Unit Cost as in Fig. 92 would usually be introduced, but is omitted here for simplicity.

Fig. 93.

THE PROCESS ACCOUNTS

1. *Crude Oil Distillation*

Dr.		Fo.	Qty. T.C.	£	s.	d.			Fo.	Qty. Gal.	£	s.	d.	Cr.
19... Feb. 28	To Materials (crude oil) .		2 0	200	9	6	19... Feb.28	By Light oil .		4000	160	0	0	
,,	,, Fuel .		–	22	10	0	,,	,, Medium oil .		3000	120	0	0	
,,	,, Wages .		–	42	11	6	,,	,, Residue to Fuel A/c. .		520	13	0	0	
,,	,, Expenses .		–	27	9	0								
				£293	0	0					£293	0	0	

Note.—After deducting an agreed or market value for fuel residue, this being debited to Fuel Account, the balance of the cost of the process is either allocated on the works chemist's formula based on average proportional quantities of each produced per ton of crude material as described in Ch. XVII, or, in some cases, the quantities of resulting products can be definitely measured in common units, and the cost be apportioned in proportion thereto.

2. *Light Oil Distillation Account*

Dr.		Fo.	Qty. Gals.	£	s.	d.			Fo.	Qty. Gals.	£	s.	d.	Cr.
19... Feb. 28	To Process I .	1	4000	160	0	0	19... Feb.28	By Benzol A/c. .		3800	245	10	0	
,,	,, Sulphuric Acid .	7	–	20	9	0	,,	,, Toluene A/c. .		50	15	2	6	
,,	,, Caustic Soda	8	–	15	0	6	,,	,, Solvent Naphtha A/c. .	S.2	100	12	0	6	
,,	,, Wages .	72	–	24	1	6	,,	Loss in Process .		50	–	–	–	
,,	,, Expenses .	18	–	53	2	0								
			4000	£272	13	0				4000	£272	13	0	

S.2 *Solvent Naphtha Account*

Dr.		Fo.	Qty. Gals.	£	s.	d.			Fo.	Qty. Gals.	£	s.	d.	Cr.
19... Feb. 1	To Balance (Stock) .	b/d.	209	24	0	0	19... Feb.28	By Process III (at Cost) .	3	90	11	12	6	
,, 28	,, Process II .	2	100	12	0	6	,,	,, Cost of Sales to Trading A/c. .	5	108	13	19	0	
,,	,, Storage expense .	18	–	3	10	0	,,	,, Balance (Stock) .	c/d.	111	13	19	0	
			309	£39	10	6				309	£39	10	6	
Mar. 1	To Balance (Stock) .	b/d.	111	13	19	0								

Note.—Similar accounts for benzol and toluene.

3. *Medium Oil Distillation Account*

Dr.   Cr.

19...		Fo.	Qty. Gals.	£	s.	d.	19...		Fo.	Qty. Gals.	£	s.	d.
Feb. 28	To Process I	1	3000	120	0	0	Feb.28	By Carbolic A/c.	5	2100	159	3	8
,,	,, Sulphuric Acid	7	–	15	7	0	,,	,, Chemical "N" A/c.	6	520	37	18	0
,,	,, Caustic Soda	8	–	10	18	0	,,	,, Residue "M" A/c.	S.4	360	30	6	4
,,	,, Solvent Naphtha A/c.	S.2	–	11	12	6	,,	,, Loss in Process	–	20	–	–	–
,,	,, Wages	72	–	23	2	6							
,,	,, Expenses	18	–	46	8	0							
			3000	£227	8	0				3000	£227	8	0

S.4 *Residue " M " Account*

Dr.   Cr.

19...		Fo.	Qty. Gals.	£	s.	d.	19...		Fo.	Qty. Gals.	£	s.	d.
Feb. 1	To Stock	b/d.	120	10	12	0	Feb.28	By Cost of Sales to Trading A/c.		319	31	18	0
Feb. 28	,, Process III	3	360	30	6	4	,,	,, Balance	c/d.	161	16	2	0
,,	,, Packing and storage	18	–	7	1	8							
			480	£48	0	0				480	£48	0	0

Note.—Similar accounts for carbolic acid and chemical " N."

TRADING AND PROFIT AND LOSS ACCOUNT
for the month ending February 28th, 19......

Dr.   Cr.

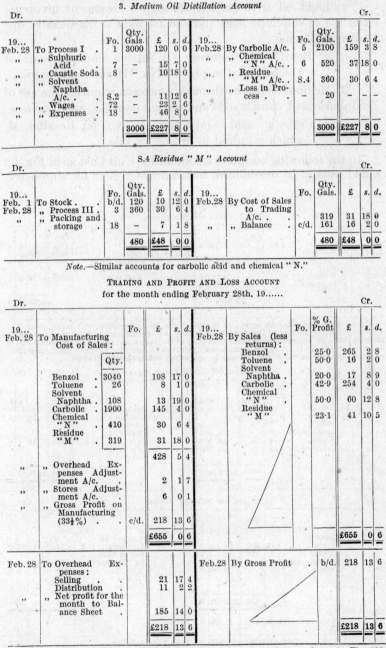

19...			Fo.	£	s.	d.	19...		Fo.	% G. Profit	£	s.	d.
Feb. 28	To Manufacturing Cost of Sales :						Feb.28	By Sales (less returns) :					
		Qty.						Benzol		25·0	265	2	8
	Benzol	3040		198	17	0		Toluene		50·0	16	2	0
	Toluene	26		8	1	0		Solvent Naphtha		20·0	17	8	9
	Solvent Naphtha	108		13	19	0		Carbolic		42·9	254	4	0
	Carbolic	1900		145	4	0		Chemical "N"		50·0	60	12	8
	Chemical "N"	410		30	6	4		Residue "M"		23·1	41	10	5
	Residue "M"	319		31	18	0							
				428	5	4							
,,	,, Overhead Expenses Adjustment A/c.			2	1	7							
,,	,, Stores Adjustment A/c.			6	0	1							
,,	,, Gross Profit on Manufacturing (33⅓%)		c/d.	218	13	6							
				£655	0	6					£655	0	6
Feb. 28	To Overhead Expenses :						Feb.28	By Gross Profit	b/d.		218	13	6
	Selling			21	17	4							
	Distribution			11	2	2							
,,	,, Net profit for the month to Balance Sheet			185	14	0							
				£218	13	6					£218	13	6

N.B.—Separate Trading Accounts may be used for each product as shown in **Fig. 106**, Ch. XVII.

Apportioning of Cost to By-products.—In the above accounts the apportionment of expenses to the products in each process is based on a proportion decided by a formula provided by the works chemist. Another method is to resolve the quantity of each product into its equivalent weight, in the terms of the original material, as is explained in Chapter XVII, dealing with Coal Distillation Accounts, and to apportion costs proportionately.

Intermediate Stock Accounts.—The use of separate Stock Accounts for each of the products and by-products facilitates the charging of any quantities which are used in other processes, as in Process I, where a by-product is used as furnace fuel, and in Process III, where solvent naphtha is used as a cleansing material, a quantity not so used being sold. In many cases the processes are so continuous that intermediate stocks do not arise.

Each process is carefully defined, and debited with materials used therein, and with its fair share of the works expenses. The correct charging of overhead expenses to processes is facilitated, and kept uniform, by using a schedule of expense-, or standing order numbers, and process and product cost numbers for the main accounts. When mechanical sorting and tabulating machines are used, this numerical system is necessary. The procedure for using these machines is described in Chapter XXVI.

Loss in Process.—In most processes there arises a loss of weight, or volume, in the course of manufacture, and this is particularly the case where there is water content, or where distillation, or disintegration, by heat or chemical action is necessitated, e.g., in foundry work; carbonisation of coal for coke and by-products; and distillation of crude oils. Careful cost control assists the manager to minimise these losses in some instances, but, in many cases, they are inherent and inevitable.

As all the material taken into process is duly debited to the appropriate process, normal loss has not to be separately debited; it is, however, entered on the credit side of the Process Account concerned, in the quantity column only. This results in the cost of the loss being thrown into the cost of the products recovered. Abnormal waste is excluded from cost by transferring the value direct to Works Profit and Loss Account.

Process Residuals and Process Scrap.—When residuals, or scrap, are recovered for use or for sale, usually the value is credited to the particular process, but sometimes direct to

Trading Account. To make residuals usable it may be necessary to pass them through a recovery, or renovating process, for which a separate account is required to ascertain the cost. Acids used in some chemical processes are frequently dealt with in this way.

The Application of Process Accounts to coal distillation works is dealt with in Ch. XVII.

EXAMPLE OF TABULAR PRESENTATION OF PROCESS COSTS
Manufacture of Cordite

Factory Organisation.—The system to be described has three distinct manufacturing departments. Each controls definite steps in the making of the product.

Service sections, in addition to the usual office and stores departments, comprise :

(*a*) Laboratory and research.
(*b*) Chemical plumbers.
(*c*) Maintenance of plant.
(*d*) Maintenance of buildings.

The Processes.—Cordite is made from a mixture, in certain proportions, of guncotton (nitro-cotton), and nitro-glycerine.

The three separate manufacturing departments are :

(1) Making guncotton.
(2) Making nitro-glycerine.
(3) Combining these ingredients and finishing the cordite as sticks of various lengths, or thickness ; or as long thread on reels.

The Procedure for Costing.—In the particular factory in which the procedure described is adopted, each process takes as a direct charge any expenses as they accrue, *e.g.* (*a*) trucking from one process to another is charged direct to the receiving process ; (*b*) maintenance of plant and buildings, for which purpose definite allocations are made possible. Only those expenses which cannot be broken down to a process charge directly are included in General Overhead.

The Process Operations.—Process I.—Dried cotton waste is nitrated in stoneware pans with a mixture of nitric and sulphuric acids of certain strengths. After a time, the acid is displaced by water. The used acid is led back to tanks for revivifying (By-process II). The nitrated cotton is trucked to Process II.

Fig. 94 shows the headings under which costs are collated.

Fig. 95 is an excerpt showing how these costs are set out to show a total cost, and a cost per lb. for each process for the use of the management.

It will be seen that this Cost Summary opens with the average cost for the preceding year. This provides a comparison for each of the thirteen four-weekly periods of the year. The

FIG. 94.

HEADINGS OF ACCOUNTS FOR NITRATION OF COTTON

Process.	Sectional Services.	General Overhead.

Materials :
Nitric acid.
  Sulphuric acid.
 	
Direct Labour.
 	
Water, Steam and Power :
  Steam.
  Electric power.
  M.W.B water.
  Hydraulic power.
  Fuel.
  Refrigeration.
  Compressed air.
  Pumping canal water.
 	
Foremen and Leading Hands.
 	
Indirect Labour
  Sweepers and cleaners.
  Attendance on motors.
  Oiling, cleaning and belt-
    men.
 	
Maintenance :
  Plant.
  Buildings.
 	
Miscellaneous :
  Depreciation.
  Consumable stores.
  Internal transport.
  Rates.
  Balance of process ex-
    penses.
	Water, Steam and Power :
	  Electric light.
	  Steam for heating.
	  Gas.
	
	Maintenance Services.
	
	Miscellaneous :
	  Care and custody of De-
	    partmental Stores.
	  Credit material returned
	    to Store.
	  Bookkeepers.
	  Sweepers and general
	    labour.
	  Allowance payments.
	  O.T. and N.S. Bonus.
	  Management (Chemists,
	    etc.).
	  Balance of Sectional ex-
	    expenses.
	
	Laboratory Testing.
		General Expenses :
		  Superintendence.
		  Registry, Pay and Order
		    Branches.
		  Worktakers, Wages and
		    Accounts.
		  General Stores.
		  Police, Fire Brigade and
		    Warders.
		  Maintenance of Grounds,
		    Mains, Canals, Perma-
		    nent Way, etc.
		  Non-effective charges.
		  Balance of general ex-
		    penses, includes water,
		    plant, buildings and
		    idle buildings.

average for the present year is inserted after the end of the year, and this is compared with the opening average for the preceding year. The value of this method is that the management can see at every period how the costs are moving. The Work in Progress for each period is recorded as shown in Fig. 96.

The By-processes for Acid are :

I. Manufacture of new nitric acid.

II. Concentration of weak used nitric acid.

For costing purposes, the bulks of the two acids are reduced

FIG. 95.

COST SHEET SHOWING CORDITE COSTS FOR EACH FOUR-WEEKS PERIOD
Production.

OUTPUT.	PERIOD. (4-weekly.)	MATERIALS.*				PROCESS STEAM AND OTHER SERVICES.			DIRECT LABOUR.			PROCESS STEAM AND OTHER SERVICES.		GENERAL OVERHEAD.	TOTAL PROCESS COST.	
		Qty. lbs.	Rate per lb. d.	Total. £ s. d.	Cost per Unit of lb. d.	Hours.	Total. £ s. d.	Rate per lb. d.	Qty.	Rate per lb. d.	£ s. d.	Rate.	£ s. d.	Cost per lb.	Total. £ s. d.
Average previous year.															
	1														
	2														
	3														
	4														
	5														
	6														
	7														
	8														
	9														
	10														
	11														
	12														
	13														
Total for Year															

* This section repeated for each of the three process materials.

FIG. 96.

PERIOD. (Four weekly.)	WORK IN PROGRESS. PROCESS I.						WORK IN PROGRESS. PROCESS II.					
	AT BEGINNING OF PERIOD.			AT END OF PERIOD.			AT BEGINNING OF PERIOD.			AT END OF PERIOD.		
	Quantity.	Rate.	Value.	Quantity.	Rate.	Value.	Quantity.	Rate.	Value.	Quantity.	Rate.	Value.
1												
2												
3												
4												
5												
6												
7												
8												
9												
10												
11												
12												
13												

By adding or deducting the quantities and values transferred from one process to another the actual output is ascertained.

R

to one nominal strength, referred to as 100 per cent. acid, *i.e.*, volume and analysis both taken into account.

The cost of these by-processes is built up by debiting material, labour and expense, and the value so ascertained is used for charging the acid to the Nitration Process above. Sulphuric acid is charged at purchased price for oleum. Sodium nitrate is heated with sulphuric acid, producing nitric acid.

The charge for acid to Process I is found by taking the stock of nitric and sulphuric acid at the beginning of each period, plus new acid made, or bought, less the quantity held at the end of the period. The balance represents acid lost in process, to be charged.

The cordite emerging in Process III has to be stoved. It is in different sizes, requiring varying times to dry. The expense is split up in direct proportion to the lbs. passing through, irrespective of size.

In this process, stocks not fully processed at the end of each four-weekly period have to be valued on a technical report as to the quantity in process, and the extent to which they have been subjected to the process. The stock is then valued proportionately.

Summary Costs.—The above procedure is used for finding the process costs per lb. to enable the management to test the works efficiency.

The summary costs are shown in two ways :

METHOD I

In Fig. 97 the cost is accumulated process by process, and is particularly valuable to the management, as it reveals which operation in the processes has caused variation in the cost of the finished product. The figures are from the process sheets (Fig. 95) and are entered in the order that they arise. (The figures shown are fictitious.)

METHOD II

In Fig. 98 the first portion of the table shows how the cost per lb. of material is arrived at. The second portion shows the additions for labour, process expenses, services overhead and general overhead, together with the output for the four-weekly period.

The Cost of Services.—As an example of how service departments are allocated to the respective operations, details of the water, steam, and power service are given in Fig. 99.

In the guncotton process, the rate per lb. in the first two items is found by dividing the value by the output.

FIG. 97.

ACCUMULATING COST PER LB. OF CORDITE.   Period No.: ....:...

Processes.	M.D. (Cost per lb. at each Stage).		
	This Period.	Last Period.	Average for Previous Year.
	d. per lb.		d. per lb.
Acid Nitric—Guncotton .	1·6334	1·5790	1·6874
„ —Nitro-glycerine.	1·7379	1·6800	1·7958
Prepared Cotton . .	6·5586	6·3400	6·7772
Nitrated Cotton . . .	6·8472	6·6190	7·0754
Boiled Nitrated Cotton .	7·2454	7·0039	7·4869
Finished ditto. . .	8·1397	7·8684	8·4110
Stoved Guncotton . .	8·5940	8·3075	8·8805
Nitro-Glycerine . .	7·8003	7·5403	8·0603
Mixed Paste . . .	8·4858	8·2029	8·7686
Incorporated Paste . .	13·0964	12·6598	13·5329

M.D.T. 5–2.   Table showing Cost of Cordite in different forms of finish.

Finishings.	This Period.	Last Period.	Average for Previous Year.	This Period.	Last Period.	This Period.	Last Period.
	d. per lb.		d. per lb.				
Incorporated Paste from above . .	13·0964	12·6598	13·5329				
Pressed Cordite	14·1635	13·6914	14·6356				
Stoved „	14·3826	13·9032	14·8619				
Reeled „	14·7178	14·2272	15·2086				
Drummed „	14·9229	14·4255	15·4203				
Packed „	15·0000	14·5000	15·5000				

In the next operation (nitration), the cost of nitration is £99; to this is added the whole of the cost of the prepared cotton of the previous operation (£18 15s.); and a proportion of the acid cost shown for the first operation, viz., $\frac{£6\ 15s.}{70,000} \times 100,000 = £9\ 12s.\ 10d.$ The total cost of this operation, £127 7s. 10d., divided by the output 140,000 lbs., gives a rate per lb. 0·2184d.

In the next operation (boiling), the output is less than the input; this is because some cotton was not fully boiled, and only the output shown was completed at the date.

Fig. 98.

Summary Cost of Cordite. Period : ....

Items of Cost.	Rate per ton.			Consumption of Raw Materials and cost per lb. of Cordite.			
				This Period.		Last Period.	
	£	s.	d.	lbs.	d.	lbs.	d.
Raw Materials :							
Cotton . . .	50	0	0	0·4795	2·7188	0·4653	2·6282
Nitrate of Soda .	5	0	0	0·9916	0·5824	0·9586	0·5630
Sulphuric Acid .	5	0	0	1·3952	0·7475	1·3487	0·7226
Glycerine . .	100	0	0	0·1278	1·3690	0·1235	1·3234
Acetone . .	100	0	0	0·4000	4·2857	0·3867	4·1428
Jelly . . .	10	0	0	0·0500	0·0536	0·3483	0·0518
Less Cr. Cotton & Fly					0·1502		0·1452
„ „ Nitre Cake .					0·0512		0·0495
Total (cost per lb. for period) . .					d. 9·5556		d. 9·2371

Items of Cost.	M.D.T. 5–2 Kind.					
	This Period.	Last Period.	This Period.	Last Period.	This Period.	Last Period.
	d.	d.				
Materials . . .	9·5556	9·2371				
Direct Labour . .	0·7400	0·7153				
Factory Expense :						
Process :						
Supervision .	0·1791	0·1731				
Indirect Labour .	0·0483	0·0467				
W.S.P. . .	0·7080	0·6844				
Maintenance .	0·7773	0·7514				
Miscellaneous .	0·2508	0·2424				
Sectional :						
W.S.P. . .	0·2081	0·2012				
Laboratory Testing	0·2218	0·2144				
Maintenance .	0·1131	0·1093				
Miscellaneous .	0·3758	0·3633				
General . .	1·8221	1·7614				
Total cost per lb.	15·0000	14·5000				
	lbs.	lbs.				
Output of Cordite .	150,000	150,000				

Proceeding in the same way, the final cost of water, steam and power per lb. (0·4768d.) is found, viz., this rate is the one applied (to the weight of guncotton prepared) to recover th

FIG. 99.

WATER, STEAM AND POWER SERVICE COSTS
Table showing Rate per lb. of Cordite to be Charged for these Services

Description.	Input of Product.	Output of Product.	£	s.	d.	Rate per lb.
Making Guncotton (Process I) :	lbs.	lbs.				d.
Nitric Acid		70,000	6	15	0	0·0231
Prepared Cotton		90,000	18	15	0	0·0500
Nitration of Cotton			99	0	0	
Prepared Cotton	90,000		18	15	0	
Nitric Acid	100,000		9	12	10	
£6 15s. × 100,000 ÷ 70,000 .		140,000	127	7	10	0·2184
Boiling Cotton			62	5	0	
Nitrated Cotton . . .	135,000		122	16	10	
£127 7s. 10d. × 135,000 ÷ 140,000		135,000	185	1	10	0·3290
Finishing Guncotton. . . .			59	0	0	
Boiled Cotton	138,000		189	4	1	
£185 1s. 10d. × 138,000 ÷ 135,000		135,000	248	4	1	0·4412
Stoving Guncotton . . .			20	0	0	
Finished Guncotton . . .	135,000		248	4	1	
135,000 lbs. for £248 4s. 1d.		135,000	268	4	1	0·4768*
Making Nitro-glycerine (Process II) :						
Nitric Acid		60,000	23	5	0	0·0930
Nitro-glycerine :						
Nitration			110	0	0	
Nitric Acid	45,000		17	8	9	
£23 5s. × 45,000 ÷ 60,000 .		60,000	127	8	9	0·5097*
Making Paste (Process III) :						
Mixing Paste			1	0	0	'
Nitro-glycerine . . .	46,000		97	14	0	
£127 8s. 9d. × 46,000 ÷ 60,000 .						
Guncotton (stoved) . .	98,500		195	13	10	
£268 4s. 1d. × 98,500 ÷ 135,000		144,500	294	7	10	0·4890
Incorporation of Paste . . .			60	10	0	
Paste	144,500		294	7	10	
144,500 lbs. for £294 7s. 10d.		150,000	354	17	10	0·5678*
Various Finishings (Process IV) :						
Pressed Cordite . . .			46	0	0	
Incorporated Paste . . .	150,000		354	17	10	
150,000 lbs. for £354 17s. 10d. . .		150,000	400	17	10	0·6414
Stoving Cordite	150,000	150,000	38	0	0	0·0608
Reeling Cordite	150,000	150,000	2	5	0	0·0036
Drumming Cordite . . .	150,000	150,000	1	7	0	0·0022
Packing Cordite	—	—	—	—	—	
Total. Water, Steam Power Charge						0·7080

* These are the rates applied at the respective processes to recover the cost of the Water, Steam, and Power Services chargeable to them.

cost of these services chargeable to guncotton. The same procedure is continued to find the charge per lb. against nitro-glycerine and subsequent operations.

Cost of Finishing Processes.—In Fig. 97 the cost up to, and including, the incorporated paste cost, is common to all sizes and finishes of completed product. From this point a break off is made, and the separate finishing costs for different sizes and styles are respectively added to the paste cost, the resultant costs per lb. being shown in the lower part of the table. This is because some of the final processes have a widely different labour charge; some based on labour hours, others on machine hours.

Efficiency Figures are prepared, as, for example :

(1) Cost per lb. of cordite of steam consumed.

(2) Cost of refrigeration per lb. of nitro-glycerine made.

The Tabular Presentation of Accounts illustrated has the advantage of showing all the details of cost of each process, and for all the four weekly periods of the year, in such a manner that the cost for successive periods is easily comparable with preceding periods, and with the average cost for the preceding year.

EXAMPLE OF PROCESS COST SHEETS.

Resin Manufacture

The specimen cost sheets given below are based on some in actual use, and the procedure for their compilation is as follows :

Daily time-sheets are filled in by the workers, a column being provided in which the Syllabus Order No. of the process concerned is entered by the office.

A weekly analysis of the wages sheets is then made to ascertain the time and cost chargeable against the respective processes. This analysis is transferred to a monthly summary (Form A).

FORM A.

DIRECT WAGES ANALYSIS SUMMARY FOR FOUR WEEKS ENDED 30TH SEPT., 193-.

Process or Service Dept.	S. Order No.	Sept. 9.			Sept. 16.			Sept. 23.			Sept. 30.			Total.		
		£	s.	d.	£	s.	d.	£	s.	d.	£	s.	d.	£	s.	d.
Batching Resin	1	6	0	0	7	0	0	10	0	0	7	0	0	30	0	0
Resin Making etc.	3	9	2	6	10	0	0	16	0	0	10	0	0	45	2	6

Expenses and Indirect Material Invoices are entered in an Analysis Purchase Journal; the monthly totals of the columns are posted to the Factory Expenses (Oncost) Schedule, a separate Schedule being compiled for each Process or Department.

DAILY REPORT OF ISSUE AND PRODUCING PLANT DETAILS

RESIN DEPARTMENT PRODUCTION RETURN

FORM B.

(Date)...........193-.

Batching						Resin Making						
Type of Resin.	No. of Batches.	Raw Materials Used (lbs.).			Total Weight.	Type of Resin.	No. of Batches.	Catalyst.	No. of Still Hours.	Weight of Resin (lbs.).		Remarks.
		Form-aldehyde.	Phenol.							To Powder.	To Despatch.	
X	2	541	541		1082	X	2		44	578		

(These Daily Reports summarised on Monthly Summary similarly ruled, one Monthly Summary for each Resin.)

Raw materials issued are listed daily, a monthly summary being compiled for each type of Resin. This summary also shows the production quantities for each type of Resin (Form B).

The Departmental Costs, apart from Raw Materials, are then gathered together on Forms C and D. The combined cost is then compiled on Form E from the information on Forms B, C and D.

FORM C.

PROCESS COST SHEET

From.. Date....................................

S.O. No. (of Process) 1.	Product: Batching Resin.		Quantity Produced. 255,732 lbs.			Period of Costing: 4 Weeks ending Sept. 30th, 193–.	
Items of Cost (other than Materials).	Quantity.	Price.	Value.			Unit.	
						Quantity.	Value.
			£	s.	d.	lbs.	d. per lb.
Wages (from Wages Analysis Summary) . . .			30	0	0		
Oncost:							
Indirect Wages . .			1	12	6		
Overtime Allowance .			1	15	0		
Plant Maintenance.							
Wages			3	10	0		
Materials . . .			5	0	0		
Trades Shop . . .			2	5	0		
Steam	126,593 lb.	62·500d.°/oo	32	19	4		
Electricity Lighting . .	224 kwH.	0·7500 d.		14	0		
Insurance, Direct . .				12	6		
Rent, ,, . .			1	13	0		
Rates, ,, . .				10	0		
Process Production Cost (excluding Materials)			£80	11	4		

Apportionment of Process Cost.

Product.	Wages.			Oncost.			Total.				
	£	s.	d.	£	s.	d.	£	s.	d.		
Resin X		3	0		5	1		8	1	1,082	0·090 *
,, Y		18	0	1	10	4	2	8	4	14,650	0·040
,, Z	28	19	0	48	15	11	77	14	11	240,000	0·078
As above	£30	0	0	£50	11	4	£80	11	4	£80 11 4	255,732

* Applied as a rate per lb. in Final Cost Sheet, see Form E (Operating Costs).

It will be noticed the costs on Forms C and D are all the operating costs (wages and expenses) only ; the materials are only brought to account in the Final Cost Sheet (Form E).

The manufacturing cost of wages and expenses is applied as a rate per lb. in Form E, under the heading " Operating Costs."

The stock of finished Resins is shown on the Final Schedule (Form E).

FORM D.

PROCESS COST SHEET

From........ .... Date.............................

S.O. No. (of Process) 3.	Product: Resin Making.	Quantity Produced 1232 Still Hours.	Period of Costing 4 Weeks ending September 30th, 193–.

Items of Cost (other than Materials).	Quantity.	Price.	Value.	Unit. Quantity.	Unit. Value.
			£ s. d.	lbs.	d. per lb.
Wages (direct from Wages Analysis Summary) . .			45 2 6		
Oncost:					
Supervision . . .			43 8 4		
Indirect Wages . . .			13 2 6		
Overtime Allowance . . .			3 7 8		
Plant Maintenance.					
Materials . . .			21 18 4		
Wages . . .			24 2 8		
Trades Shop . . .			16 4 8		
Special Maintenance . . .			20 0 0		
Steam . . .	402,000 lb.	62·5d. °/₀₀	104 13 9		
Electricity, Power . .	1,800 kwH.	·75d. kwH.	5 12 8		
,, Light . .	420 ,,	·75d. ,,	1 5 0		
Cooling Water . . .			34 2 0		
Insurance, Direct . . .			18 6		
Rent, ,, . . .			2 18 0		
Rates, ,, . . .			8 6		
Sundries . . .			18 11		
Gas . . .			6 3 2		
Make-up Water . . .			1 8 9		
Process Production Cost (excluding Materials)			£345 15 11		

Apportionment of Production Cost.

Still Hrs.	Product.	Wages.	*Oncost.	Total.	Still Hr. Cost of Oncost.	Value.	Unit. Quantity.	Unit. Value.
		£ s. d.	£ s. d.	£ s. d.	s.			
44	Resin X	11 2	10 14 9	11 5 11			578	4·690 †
120	,, Y	1 12 9	29 5 9	30 18 6			9,260	0·802
1068	,, Z	42 18 7	260 12 11	303 11 6			168,000	0·434
1232	As above	£45 2 6	£300 13 5	£345 15 11	4·881	£345 15 11	177,838	

  * Apportioned proportionately to still hours for each product.
  † Applied as a rate per lb. in Final Cost Sheet, Form E (see Operating Cost section).

FORM E.

COST SCHEDULE: RESINS (PACKED)

Four Weeks Ending .... 193..

Type.	Resin X.			Resin Y.			Resin Z.		
Details.	Usage. Per lb.	Price. *d.*	Cost *d.* per lb.	Usage. Per lb.	Price. *d.*	Cost. *d.* per lb.	Usage. Per lb.	Price. *d.*	Cost. *d.* per lb.
Raw Materials. Formaldehyde	0·936	4·000	3·744						
Phenol .	0·936	8·500	7·956						
Cresol . .									
Other Materials . .									
Operating Costs. S.O. No. 1 Batching .	1·872	0·090*	0·168						
S.O. No. 2 Batching .									
S.O. No. 3 Resin Making	1·000	4·690*	4·690						
Production and Cost .	578 lbs.		16·558						
	Quantity. lbs.	Rate. *d.* per lb.	Value. £ *s. d.*	Quantity. lbs.	Rate. *d.* per lb.	Value. £ *s. d.*	Quantity. lbs.	Rate. *d.* per lb.	Value. £ *s. d.*
Resin for Moulding Powder. Stock at 30th June, 193– .	620	17·200	44 8 8						
Production (as above) .	578	16·558	39 17 6						
	1198		84 6 2						
Stock at 30th Sept., 193–	480	16·558	33 2 4						
Used for Moulding Powder in this period .	718	17·111	51 3 10						
Resin for Sale. Stock at									
Production .									
Add Packing (S.O. No.)									
Stock at									
Despatched in period .									
Add to Unit Cost of Resin for Sale. †Works Overheads (at standard rate) . .			2·000						
Obsolescence (ditto) .			0·784						

* These two prices from Forms C and D (Unit Value column).
† All factory expenses other than applicable to departments, the standard being based on budget of total expenses and total estimated production.

EXAMINATION QUESTIONS

1. The following details are extracted from the costing records of an Oil Refinery for the week ended September 30 :

Purchase of 500 tons of Copra £20,000

	Crushing Plant. £	Refining Plant. £	Finishing. £
Cost of Labour	250	100	150
Electric Power	60	36	24
Sundry Materials . . .	10	200	—
Repairs to Machinery and Plant .	28	33	14
Steam	60	45	45
Factory Expenses	132	66	22
Cost of Casks			750

300 tons of Crude Oil were produced.
250 tons of Oil were produced by the refining process.
248 tons of Refined Oil were finished for delivery.

Copra Sacks sold	£40
175 tons of Copra Residue sold	£1,100
Loss in Weight in Crushing	25 tons
45 tons of By-products obtained from refining process .	£675

You are required to show the accounts in respect of each of the following stages of manufacture for the purpose of arriving at the cost per ton of each process, and the total cost per ton of the finished oil :

(a) Copra crushing process.
(b) Refining process.
(c) Finishing process, including casking.

Society of Incorporated Accountants and Auditors (*Final*).

2. What do you regard as the special features of process costs ? To what classes of manufacture are they generally applied ?—*Royal Society of Arts* (*Advanced*).

3. How would you deal with scrap material in process costs ? Give a concrete example.—*Institute of Cost and Works Accountants* (*Inter.*).

4. The manufacturing operations of a Limited Company involve three distinct processes in connection with the same unit. The practice has been to prepare a Cost Sheet for the processes as a whole, based upon the completed unit. The Cost Sheet for January 1929 appeared as follows :

			Total. £	Cost per unit (pence).
Direct Wages : Process A .	.	1,450		
,, B .	.	870		
,, C .	.	800	3,120	11·7
Raw Materials issued to				
Process A : 58,000 units			5,800	21·75
Machine Expenses : Process A	.	604		
,, B .		604		
,, C .		667	1,875	7·03
Factory Oncost . . .			725	2·72
Cost of . . .	64,000 units (C)		11,520	43·2
Deduct, Waste, etc	2,000 units (C)			1·4
Cost of Output of .	62,000 ,,		11,520	44·6

The Cost Sheets in the form given are obviously unsatisfactory; the variations in cost per process cannot be viewed and the expenses attributable to waste and faulty production in the individual processes are not accurately dealt with.

You are instructed to prepare Process Cost Sheets for January 1929 similar in form to the above, but based on the output of each individual process.

For this purpose, the following Statement of Stocks is furnished:

	Process:	A.	B.	C.
Jan. 1, 1929, Stock received on hand (units)		10,000	6,000	18,000
„ 31, „ Received		58,000	54,000	56,000
		68,000	60,000	74,000
„ „ „ *Delivered*		*54,000*	*56,000*	*62,000*
„ „ „ *Waste, etc.*		*1,000*	*2,000*	*2,000*
„ „ „ Stock on hand . . .		10,000	2,000	10,000

You are informed:

(1) That it is the practice to deliver to the next process all goods as and when completed and that no work has been done in any process upon units in stock at the end of the month.

(2) That Factory Oncost may be taken as 1*d*. per unit for each process on the total of units delivered.

(3) That Opening Stock of Process A and stock of raw material received into Process A may be taken at 2*s*. per unit.

(4) That Opening Stock of Process B and units received into that Process may be taken at the average cost of units delivered by Process A during the current month, and similarly as regards units received by Process C from Process B.

Prepare Process Cost Sheets accordingly. Calculations need not be carried beyond one decimal place.—*Institute of Chartered Accountants* (*Final*).

5. The Works Manager and the Sales Manager of a manufacturing firm are entitled to bonuses according to the results of the working of their respective departments.

The Works Manager's bonus is calculated as a percentage of the manufacturing profit each year, and for this purpose manufactured articles produced are to be credited to his department at an agreed price.

The Sales Manager's bonus is calculated as a percentage of the net profits each year, arrived at before charging the Works Manager's bonus.

The manufacture of the finished product comprises two processes: Process A in which the raw material purchased is treated, and Process B in which the material thus treated is worked up into the finished article.

During the year ended June 30, 1929, 3000 finished articles were produced, the agreed price at which they were to be credited to the Manufacturing department being £8 10*s*. per article, and the following figures represent extracts from the Firm's books for that period:

		£
Stocks at July 1, 1928 :— Raw Material	. . . .	800
Work in Progress (Process B)	. .	900
Finished Goods	. . . .	4,500
Stocks at June 30, 1929 :—Raw Material	. . . .	900
Work in Progress (Process B)	. .	500
Finished Goods	. . . .	5,000

Purchase of Raw Material	10,200
Sales of Raw Material	2,200
Purchases of Material used in Process B	3,600
Manufacturing Wages; Process A £5,000; Process B . .	3,000
Sales of Finished Goods	31,500
Establishment and Distribution Expenses (including Depreciation)	8,100

You are required :

(1) To raise accounts showing the amounts on which the bonuses of the respective Managers will be based for the above-named period.

(2) To state the cost per ton of Raw Material taken by Process B after treatment in Process A, the output of Process A being 500 tons.

Note.—Works Oncost is to be brought into account at the rate of 10 per cent. of the Manufacturing Wages in Process A and 20 per cent. of the Manufacturing Wages in Process B.—*Institute of Chartered Accountants (Final).*

6. The information given below is extracted from the Cost Accounts of a Factory producing a commodity in the manufacture of which three processes are involved. Prepare Process Cost Accounts showing the cost of the output and the cost per unit at each stage of manufacture :

(1) The operations in each separate process are completed daily.

(2) The value at which units are to be charged to Processes " B " and " C " is the cost per unit of Processes " A " and " A " plus " B " respectively.

	Process A.	B.	C.
Direct Wages . .	£640	£1,200	£2,925
Machine Expense . .	360	300	360
Factory Oncost . .	200	225	240
Raw Materials consumed .	2,400	—	—
	Units.	Units.	Units.
Production (gross) . . .	37,000	—	—
Wastage . . .	1,000	1,500	500
Stock, July 1, 1930 . .	—	4,000	16,500
Stock, July 31, 1930 . .	—	1,000	5,500

Society of Incorporated Accountants and Auditors (Final).

7. Prepare a Cost Sheet for any industry with which you are familiar, showing comparative figures at the end of four separate periods.—*Institute of Cost and Works Accountants (Final).*

8. How should by-products be dealt with in the cost records ? What varying circumstances should decide the exact method employed ?—*Institute of Cost and Works Accountants (Final).*

9. Where a product is put through several processes, the finished articles of one process become the raw material of the next. At what price should the transfer from process to process be made ? Illustrate your answer by a *pro forma* account assuming cost of Process 1 to be £700, Process 2 £880 (including cost No. 1), and Process 3 £1,200 (including cost of Processes 1 and 2).—*Society of Incorporated Accountants and Auditors (Final).*

10. A certain product passes through five distinct processes at a factory before it becomes a finished article ready for sale. Each process is dealt with in a separate department, but in the fourth process some of the raw material is purchased and not obtained from the prior processes. State and explain your views as to the price at which the trans-

fers from process to process should be made.—*Society of Incorporated Accountants and Auditors (Inter.)*.

11. Set out the headings for a cost statement for process manufacture, with a valuable by-product.—*Institute of Cost and Works Accountants (Final)*.

12. The sale of scrap brings in a substantial surplus over the cost of collection. Should this surplus be used to reduce the expense of handling and storing materials or treated as an ordinary sale? Give reasons for your view.—*Institute of Cost and Works Accountants (Final)*.

13. Product A yields by-products B and C.

The joint expenses of manufacture are :

Materials £500, Labour £400, Oncost £450, Total £1,350.

Subsequent expenses are as follows :

	A.	B.	C.
Materials	100	80	90
Labour	120	70	85
Oncost	130	50	75
	£350	£200	£250
The selling prices are . . .	£2,100	£1,000	£900
The estimated profits on sales are .	50%	50%	$33\frac{1}{3}$%

Show how you would apportion the joint expenses of manufacture.—*Society of Incorporated Accountants and Auditors (Final)*.

14. Draft a Cost Sheet for Mass Production Works with four operating departments designed to show the cost at each stage of manufacture, and the total cost of each unit of production. Utilise your knowledge of any such works with which you may be acquainted in answering the question.—*Society of Incorporated Accountants and Auditors (Final)*.

15. Where a product is put through several processes, the finished article of one process becomes the raw material of the next. At what price should the transfer from process to process be made? Illustrate your answer by a *pro forma* account, assuming cost of process 1 to be £700, process 2 £880 (including cost of No. 1), and process 3 £1,200 (including cost of processes 1 and 2).—*Society of Incorporated Accountants and Auditors (Final)*.

16. In certain factories the wastage of materials constitutes by-products. How would you deal with these in Cost Accounts where :—
(a) The by-product is of little value. (b) The by-product is of considerable value ?—
Society of Incorporated Accountants and Auditors (Inter.).

17. In the manufacture of a certain article breakages occur at various stages of manufacture.
(a) Discuss the treatment of such losses in the firm's cost accounts.
(b) Calculate the cost of breakage (if any) at the end of each process in the undermentioned case.

Assume that no expenditure has been incurred on the broken unit in the actual process where the breakage has taken place and the broken articles have no scrap value.

Process.	Total Additive Cost.	No. of Unbroken Units at End of Process.
	d.	
A	200	20
B	340	17
C	180	15

Society of Incorporated Accountants and Auditors (Final).

CHAPTER XVII

PROCESS COSTS (*continued*)

COAL CARBONISATION PLANT COSTS

Introduction.—Many useful products are obtained from the carbonisation of coal and the distillation of by-products. It may be mentioned that a ton of coal burned in a domestic fire-grate results in the destruction of nine gallons of tar, eight lbs. of fertilising substances, three gallons of benzole and nearly 12,000 cubic feet of gas.

The processes described in this chapter are for the commercial manufacture of coke and the recovery of the by-products in a modern plant, and the description is of a plant carbonising 500,000 tons of coal a year. Coal is a mineralised form of vegetable matter, and contains carbon, hydrogen, nitrogen, oxygen, a little sulphur and ash; *i.e.* it consists of carbon, ash and volatiles. It is from the last-named that by-products are obtained.

The Processes Described.—Small, clean coal is placed in air-tight silica ovens, and, with a modern battery, heated for approximately 17 hours at a temperature of about 1,110° C., which transforms the coal into coke, the volatile matter being collected through a connecting pipe fixed to each oven.

The hot gas is condensed by cooling, " scrubbed," and re-heated, whereby the by-products, tar, sulphate of ammonia and crude benzol, are obtained. The coal gas, approximately 12,000 cu. ft. per ton of coal, thus stripped of its by-products is used as fuel for heating the ovens, as power for driving gas engines, as fuel for boiler firing, and the surplus is used, or sold locally for town lighting purposes. The by-product processes will be referred to later.

The Cost of Materials. Calculating the Coal Equivalent per Product and Department.—Coal is the basic raw material for each product, and it is necessary to find the correct allocation, which is complicated by the fact that, after leaving the Coke

Department, the coal has to be measured in gaseous form, and reduced to a weight equivalent.

The constituents of coal vary according to the part of the country whence it is obtained. The by-products vary at different distillation temperatures, and according to the efficiency of the plant.

By measuring actual recoveries over a period of a year, a close approximation is obtained of the proportions in which products and by-products are produced per ton of coal carbonised, e.g. :

Per ton of Coal (2,240 *lbs.*)

70·0 per cent. coke.

9·5 gallons of tar.

8 lbs. of ammonia.

3·0 gals. of benzole.

11,850 cu. ft. of gas.

Knowing the gravity of the liquids, and the density of the gas, these quantities can be converted to a weight equivalent :

					lbs.
Approx. 192 gallons of tar	= 1 ton,	hence 9·5 gallons	=	111
,, 255 ,, benzole	= 1 ton,	,, 3·0 ,,	=	28
,, 1,000 cu. ft. of gas	= 37·5 lbs.	,, 11,850 cu. ft.	=	443
70 per cent. coke	=			1,572
Ammonia	=			8

Total weight recovered 2,162
Balance of ton (loss) 78

2,240 lbs.

There is always a loss in treating the coal of about 4 per cent., due to natural moisture. This moisture, driven off, is finally condensed, and the water absorbs the ammonia, forming ammonia liquor. When the ammonia is driven off and collected, the water (waste liquor) represents the 78 lbs. balance.

The water is used to quench the hot coke, and, therefore, this 78 lbs. is allocated to the Coke Department, thus giving the full total of 2,240 lbs. :

					lbs.	
Coke	.	.	.	.	1,650	
Tar	.	.	.	.	111	
Ammonia	.	.	.	.	8	per ton.
Benzole	.	.	.	.	28	
Coal gas	.	.	.	.	443	

2,240 lbs.

Allocation of Coal Gas.—As many of the expenses are apportioned to the various products on the equivalent coal value, it is necessary to apportion further the coal gas used by the works. The gas is measured by meters, or measuring instruments, to all the consumers, say, for example :

	Cu. ft.	Equal in lbs. to
Heating the ovens . . .	6,000	224
Used for Gas Engineer . .	225	8
„ boilers . . .	625	24
Sold outside	5,000	187
	11,850	443 as above.

A further allocation of the 6,000 cu. ft. (224 lbs.) used for heating ovens has to be made. The ovens are heated to the proper temperature for the reception of coal, and residue gas is used as supplementary heat during carbonisation.

This heat being essential for the production of coke, and other products, it is equitable to distribute the 224 lbs. coal charge over every department, pro-rata to the direct charge of coal against them, as follows :—

Fig. 100.

PROCESS ALLOCATION SCHEDULE

	Per Ton. lbs.	* Add used for Ovens. lbs.	Total Coal Allocation. lbs.	Per cent. per Ton.
Coke	1,650	183	1,833	82
Tar	111	12	123	6
Ammonia . . .	8	1	9	0·5
Benzole . . .	28	3	31	1
Gas Engines . .	8	1	9	0·5
Boilers . . .	24	3	27	1
Gas Sales . . .	187	21	208	9
Heating Ovens * . .	224	—	—	—
	2,240	224	2,240	100

The importance of the last two columns in the above table is that coal carbonised is used as the basis for allocation for a number of important items of overhead, as will be explained later.

Wages—Direct.—In the coking industry, the processes are for recovery of the products, rather than manufacture in the usual sense of the word. The labours of the workmen are

s

subordinate to the function of the chemical action in the various units of plant used in production. For this reason day-rates of wages are used instead of piece-rates. Direct wages relate to that class of labour employed in the direct process of recovery in every department. The plant is in constant operation day and night throughout the year, except in the extreme case where it has to close down because of industrial depression.

FIG. 101.

MAINTENANCE

Week Ending.	Coke.			Tar.			Ammonia.			Benzol.			Power.		
	£	s.	d.	£	s.	d.	£	s.	d.	£	s.	d.	£	s.	d.
Jan. 7	400	0	0	6	0	0	20	0	0	25	0	0	40	0	0
14	380	0	0	5	0	0	19	0	0	24	0	0	42	0	0
21	390	0	0	6	0	0	21	0	0	20	0	0	45	0	0
28	400	0	0	4	0	0	22	0	0	26	0	0	41	0	0
31	100	0	0	1	0	0	10	0	0	12	0	0	10	0	0
	1670	0	0	22	0	0	92	0	0	107	0	0	178	0	0

These figures are calculated from the Workmen's Time-Sheets, and the total

Each day is divided into three shifts, and the workmen record their time by time-recording clocks. The direct-labour time is a constant factor, because, should a man be off work for any reason, his place is at once filled by drawing from the maintenance staff another who is familiar with the duties. For instance, the Benzole Department has three direct workers, so that each week the department must be charged with twenty-one shifts, irrespective of which men work them.

The Wages-Book is drafted on departmental lines, thus providing a separate total of direct wages for each revenue and non-revenue department, in the same manner as shown for Maintenance Wages in Fig. 101.

Should the last day of the month conflict with the weekly pay-day all that is necessary is to calculate $\frac{2}{7}$ or $\frac{3}{7}$, as the case may be.

Indirect Wages consist of general labour and maintenance labour wages, *e.g.* fitters, joiners, blacksmiths, and electricians. As maintenance labour during a shift may be engaged on work affecting more than one department, Maintenance Time Sheets

are issued (Fig. 102) at the beginning of each week. The
workman states, briefly, the nature of the work done. The
foreman indicates the department to be charged. The cost
clerk completes the lower analysis, which provides the weekly
totals of time and wages. These totals are agreed with the
Wages Book, which is independently made up from the clock
cards.

Stores Materials.—The production cost accounts are only

WAGES ANALYSES

Gas.			Rectifica-tion.			Recovery.			Steam.			Main-tenance.			Total.		
£	s.	d.	£	s.	d.	£	s.	d.	£	s.	d.	£	s.	d.	£	s.	d.
2	0	0	2	0	0	12	0	0	10	0	0	100	0	0	617	0	0
1	10	0	2	10	0	6	0	0	4	0	0	98	0	0	582	0	0
1	10	0	2	0	0	4	0	0	6	10	0	100	0	0	596	0	0
2	10	0	2	10	0	8	0	0	12	0	0	120	0	0	638	0	0
	10	0		10	0	2	0	0	6	0	0	60	0	0	202	0	0
8	0	0	9	10	0	32	0	0	38	10	0	478	0	0	2635	0	0

2,635, must agree with the total maintenance in the Wages Books.

concerned with the amounts consumed (not purchased), and
the value of production (not sales). In the works under review
there are three Store Departments :

    (i) Manufacturing materials.
    (ii) Direct maintenance materials.
    (iii) General maintenance stores.

Manufacturing Materials.—These consist of sulphuric acid,
lime, bicarbonate of soda, creosote oil, soda ash and caustic
soda. They are used for extracting the ammonia and crude
benzole from the gas. Soda ash and caustic soda are used for
purifying the crude benzole.

The ratio of these materials to coal carbonised is known
from experience, so that contracts for supplies for three, six
or twelve months can be placed for automatic delivery of the
required quantity each week.

The cost clerk is advised of the weight of all materials received during each week (Fig. 103), and by adding the opening
stock and deducting the closing stock the amount consumed

Fig. 102.

MAINTENANCE WORK TIME-SHEET

WORKMAN'S TIME-SHEET	Dept. Ref.	ORDINARY HOURS	HOURS OVERTIME	TOTAL EQUIVALENT
For week ending 28 February, 19...				
Workman's No.: 39. Name : Tom Jones.				
Class : Electrician. Rate.				
W. (brief detail of work)	C T etc.	3 4	— 2	3 7
Th.				
F.				
S.				
Su.				
M.				
Tu.				

COST ACCOUNT ANALYSIS							A. Harris. FOREMAN		50
DEPT.	R	C	T	A	B	P			
WED.		3	7				10		
THUR.									
FRI.									
SAT.									
SUN.									CHECKED
MON.									
TUES.									
TOTAL							50		WAGES ABSTRACT
SHIFTS									
MONEY									

is arrived at. The materials are usually in storage tanks, so the closing stock can be measured. By applying the contract price the cost of materials consumed is found.

Fig. 103.

		THE COAL DISTILLATION CO.			
		GOODS RECEIVED			
No. 397.				*Week ending* 21 *February*, 19...	
Item No.	Quantity. No. or Weight.	Date Received.	Description.	From	Invoice No. and date.
1	1 ton	15/2/19...	B./C. Soda	Nat. Chem. Co., Ltd.	281 13/2/19...
2	5 tons	17/2/19...	Lime	X. Y. & Co.	285 15/2/19...
				Signed B. STOCKWELL.	

Direct Maintenance Materials.—These are for renewals, and replacements of plant, etc., and can be charged direct to a specific department.

The procedure for co-ordinating the purchasing, and the stores control, is as follows : A list of requisitions, signed by the Works Manager, is sent to the Purchase Department, together with a control card, showing ordering quantity, ordering level and minimum. After the placing of the purchase order, the control card is returned to the Stores Clerk showing :

1. Date ordered.
2. Order No.
3. Suppliers.
4. Delivery date.

On arrival of the goods, a stores received form is completed, sent to the Purchase Department for checking with the requisition and order, and with the invoice.

At the end of the month the invoices are entered in an analytical Purchase Journal (see Fig. 104) from which the direct maintenance materials charge is taken to the Control Account in the Cost Ledger.

General Stores.—These are kept on the perpetual inventory system described in an earlier chapter (p. 44).

FIG. 104.

PURCHASE ANALYSIS JOURNAL FOR DIRECT MAINTENANCE MATERIALS

1932.	Inv. No.	Name.	Total.	Coke.	Tar.	Amm.	Benzol.	Power.	Stores.	Etc.
			£ s. d.	£ s. d.	£ s. d.	£ s. d.	£ s. d.	£ s. d.	£ s. d.	
Jan. 1	1	John Brown Steel shaft	210 0 0	210 0 0						
12	2	W. Smith & Co. Nuts and bolts	40 0 0						40 0 0	
14	3	P. Brown & Co. Acid	1000 0 0						1000 0 0	
15	4	T. Jones & Co. Pipes	60 0 0		20 0 0	20 0 0	20 0 0			
			1310 0 0	210 0 0	20 0 0	20 0 0	20 0 0		1040 0 0	

Note.—The general maintenance materials are issued from stores, and abstracted in a form similar to that shown for wages.

Overhead Charges.

(a) *General :* The bases of allocation in the Coking Industry are indicated for various items below :

Workmen's Insurance, Compensation and Sick Fund.—Allocation proportionate to direct and indirect wages in each department.

National Insurance is a deduction from wages, definitely known.

Fire Insurance.—Proportionate to value insured in each department.

Electrical Breakdown Insurance.—As each item is usually specified, with values, on the policy, specific allocation is made.

Boiler Explosion Insurance.—Charged to steam service direct.

Rent, Laboratory Charges, Sundry Expenses affect the whole plant, and are allocated on the same basis as coal carbonised.

Administrative Salaries, Directors' Fees, Audit Fees and Staff Superannuation, are allocated on the basis of coal carbonised as calculated on p. 228.

Rates.—The usual method of floor space as a basis would be incorrect. The method used is to allocate on a capital basis for each section.

Depreciation is arrived at from the Plant Register, and charged in the usual way.

(b) *Service Departments :* The re-allocation of the cost of Service Departments to the Production Departments.

The Service Departments are :

  (1) Gas recovery apparatus.
  (2) Power supply.
  (3) Steam supply.
  (4) Maintenance and repairs (these have already been dealt with).

Recovery Expense.—The Recovery Department is of primary importance, as it embraces all the apparatus for withdrawing the gas from the ovens, and giving it sufficient pressure to overcome the resistance of the by-product plant. The pressure in the oven is insufficient to overcome the resistance set up by various units of apparatus through which the gas has to pass. An exhauster is provided, and this with other apparatus is called the Recovery Department.

This expense is allocated on the same basis as the coal charge (as shown in Fig. 100) to the departments, *e.g.* tar, ammonia, benzole, gas engine, steam, gas sold.

Power.—This is allocated on the basis of the H.P.-hours in each department.

General Maintenance Labour is allocated on the same basis as the coal carbonised.

Steam.—The allocation of the cost of the steam service is a complicated and difficult matter. There are to be considered such factors as whether live or exhaust steam is consumed and measured; whether it is converted into mechanical energy, or utilised for process work; what is the temperature and pressure of live steam as compared with exhaust steam; and what heat is lost in transit. It is, therefore, necessary to co-operate with the engineer. The following is an allocation made by the engineer taking the above factors into consideration :

Fig. 105.

STEAM ALLOCATION

One boiler evaporating 3,600 gallons or 36,000 lbs. of water per hour.

Department.	lbs.	%
Benzole	2,250	6
Benzole rectification	6,750	19
Power (steam engines)	9,000	25
Recovery (exhausters)	11,000	31
Ammonia (dryers)	4,000	11
Ovens (decarbonising oven tops) . .	3,000	8
	36,000	100%

FIG. 106.

		Expenditure.						Revenue.		
		£	s.	d.		T.	C.	£	s.	d.
COKE	Coal	7,380	0	0	COKE	11,700		7,020	0	0
	Direct Wages	200	10	0	BREEZE	1,200		840	0	0
	Materials	–	–	–	DUST	414		20	0	0
	Maintenance, Wages	400	0	0						
	,, Stores	520	10	0						
	Power	220	0	0						
	Overhead Charges	400	0	0						
	Depreciation	1,600	0	0						
		£10,721	0	0				£7,880	0	0
		£	s.	d.		T.	C.	Q.	£	s.	d.
TAR	Coal	540	0	0	TAR	800	0	0	2,000	0	0
	Direct Wages	–	–	–							
	Materials	40	0	0							
	Maintenance, Wages	100	0	0							
	,, Stores	60	0	0							
	Power	40	0	0							
	Overhead Charges	20	0	0							
	Depreciation	200	0	0							
		£1,000	0	0					£2,000	0	0
		£	s.	d.		T.	C.	Q.	£	s.	d.
AMMONIA	Coal	45	0	0	AMMONIA	220	0	0	1,100	0	0
	Direct Wages	40	0	0							
	Materials	700	0	0							
	Maintenance, Wages	60	0	0							
	,, Stores	40	0	0							
	Power	40	0	0							
	Overhead Charges	60	0	0							
	Depreciation	100	0	0							
		£1,085	0	0					£1,100	0	0
		£	s.	d.		Gallons.		£	s.	d.
CRUDE BENZOL	Coal	90	0	0	CRUDE BENZOL	70,000		2,041	13	4
	Direct Wages	10	0	0						
	Materials	200	0	0						
	Maintenance, Wages	40	0	0						
	,, Stores	60	0	0						
	Power	100	0	0						
	Overhead Charges	20	0	0						
	Depreciation	120	0	0						
		£640	0	0				£2,041	13	4

	Month.	Coal Carbonised.	Cost Price.	Department.	Profit / Loss.			Previous.
					January.			
		T. C.			£	s.	d.	
DRY		18,000 0	10/-	Coke .*	2,841	0	0	
				Tar	1,000	0	0	
				Ammonia	15	0	0	
				Benzol	1,401	13	4	
WET				Power	83	0	0	
				Gas	1,474	0	0	
				Benzol Rect.	1,288	6	8	
				* Loss.	£2,421	0	0	

The totals of the various items of Expenditure and Revenue

DISTILLATION CO.
COST AND REVENUE

January, 19...

		Expenditure.								Revenue.		
		£	s.	d.						£	s.	d.
POWER SUPPLY	Coal	45	0	0	POWER SUPPLIED	Units. 18,000 at 6d.				450	0	0
	Direct Wages	22	0	0								
	Materials	100	0	0								
	Maintenance, Wages	40	0	0								
	,, Stores	60	0	0								
	Power	–	–	–								
	Overhead Charges	60	0	0								
	Depreciation	40	0	0								
		£367	0	0						£450	0	0
		£	s.	d.						£	s.	d.
GAS	Coal	810	0	0	GAS SUPPLIED	Cubic Feet in 1000ths. 100,000 at 6d.				2,500	0	0
	Direct Wages	6	0	0								
	Materials	–	–	–								
	Maintenance, Wages	4	0	0								
	,, Stores	2	0	0								
	Power	100	0	0								
	Overhead Charges	4	0	0								
	Depreciation	100	0	0								
		£1,026	0	0						£2,500	0	0
		£	s.	d.		Re-cover.	Sales Price.	Gal-lonage.		£	s.	d.
BENZOL RECT.	Crude Benzol	2,041	13	4								
	Direct Wages	10	0	0								
	Materials	100	0	0	MOTOR SPIRIT	70%	1/3	49,000		3,062	10	0
	Maintenance, Wages	6	0	0	SOLVENT NAPHTHA	10%	1/-	7,000		350	0	0
	,, Stores	10	0	0	CREOSOTE	10%	3d.	7,000		87	10	0
	Power	–	–	–	*Loss*	10%						
	Overhead Charges	20	0	0								
	Depreciation	24	0	0								
		£2,211	13	4						£3,500	0	0

ACCOUNTS

		Cost Price.		Sales Price.		Recovery.	
To Date.		January.	Standard.	January.	Value.	Standard.	January.
		16/8		12/-			73·0%
		25/-		40/-			9·0 galls.
		98/8		100/-			27·5 lbs.
		2·7d.		7d.			3·9 galls.

should agree with the totals in the Financial Books.

The Accounts.—Each day the dispatch clerk prepares an advice showing particulars of all products dispatched during the day to the distributing depots, or to purchasers. Each class of product is listed on a different coloured form. (See Fig. 107.)

FIG. 107.

No. 903.

GOODS DISPATCHED NOTE

BY THE COAL DISTILLATION CO.

26 *Feb.*, 19...

Truck or Tank Number.	Description.	Gross Weight.				Tare.				Net Weight.				Depot or Consignee and Station.
		T.	C.	Q.	L.	T.	C.	Q.	L.	T.	C.	Q.	L.	
372	Crude Tar in drums													No. 4 Sales Depot
398	Ground neutral S./ Ammonia in bags													No. 2 Sales Depot.

Remarks: ....*Dispatch Clerk.*

From these an analytical Sales Book is entered up to show, at the end of each month, the total quantity and revenue of each particular by-product.

To check these totals, the cost clerk prepares a summary of all sales for the month, together with opening and closing stocks, and a cost sheet, which takes the form of a number of summarised manufacturing accounts, is prepared as in Fig. 106, to show the cost for the month for each process and the revenue credited. The profit (or loss) for the month is summarised by products at the foot of the sheet, together with the percentages of recovery.

Daily Check on Efficiency of Production.—The total production of each by-product is divided by the tonnage of coal carbonised. For this purpose, stock is taken at the end of each shift, this being done with the aid of a dip-rod, as the products are stored in tanks.

The Cost per Unit is obtained by dividing the expenditure incurred on each product by the number of units produced in each case. This should be compared with the cost of the previous month and of the previous year.

The Costs per Ton of Coal Carbonised.—In addition to the unit costs, it is advisable to follow the trend of each total class of expenditure, *i.e.* total wages, stores, or power produced, and to find the cost of each per ton of coal carbonised.

EXAMINATION QUESTIONS

1. Prepare a costing sheet for an industry with which you are familiar where process costing is carried out. Relate by diagram the cost accounts from which your information is collected, and illustrate briefly the relationship to the financial results.—*Institute of Cost and Works Accountants (Final).*

2. In the Chemical Industries, the same manufacturing processes frequently yield more than one marketable product, the selling prices of which are determined in the open market and are influenced greatly by the demand for such products day by day. For example, in producing Coal Gas, Coke and Tar are also produced as by-products. In such cases, can the cost of coal gas be ascertained ? If so, in what way ? If not, how is the selling price of coal gas to be fixed ?—*London Association of Accountants (Final).*

3. In a factory where process costing is in use, the unit of measurement varies in different processes for the same article (*e.g.*, in Process A the unit is weight, in Process B the unit is superficial area) and finally sold at a price per article. How would you deal with this problem in your costs ?—*Institute of Cost and Works Accountants (Inter.).*

4. The figures given below are taken from the Cost Accounts of various by-product departments of a Colliery Company. The Company is desirous of making a reasonable profit on the production of its by-products with a view to allowing the Coal Production Account a share in the profits on the coal used in obtaining the by-products. For this purpose a rate of profit of 10 per cent. on the total production of by-products is agreed upon. Show the profit or loss derived from each by-product, and what amount is transferable to the Coal Production Account :

	£
Coke Ovens :	
Cost of 75,000 tons of Coal	63,150
Coke Oven Expenses	14,790
Production of 46,500 tons of Coke	74,250
Benzol Plant :	
Cost of Creosote Oil	1,000
Benzol Plant Expenses	1,370
Benzol Production	6,120
Ammonia Plant :	
Cost of Sulphuric Acid	1,330
Plant Expenses	1,880
Ammonia Liquor Production	7,520
Sulphate of Ammonia Production	4,010
Tar Plant Production	3,100

Society of Incorporated Accountants and Auditors (Final).

5. A factory having its own gas-making plant utilises in its manufacturing processes the whole of the residual coke.

How would you determine the price at which to credit the gas factory for the coke so used ?—*Institute of Cost and Works Accountants (Inter.).*

CHAPTER XVIII

UNIT OPERATION COSTS

Application of the Method.—The details of Job or Terminal and Process Costing have been described in the preceding chapters, and the method dealt with in this chapter differs in that a series of operations are costed. This method is suitable where production is of a continuous nature, involving scrap, or waste, at various stages, and where, owing to the continuous flow of manufacture, and the difficulty of physically separating the scrap or waste arising from different batches, it is impracticable to cost the product by the batch, job, or process.

When the factory is operating on mass-production lines in this way, it happens that all operations are in process simultaneously, and the quantities passing through each operation, at one time, are in no direct relation to one another, which makes it almost impossible to arrange for manufacturing in batches.

Unit operation costs are an advantage also, where articles or components have to be stocked in a partly finished stage, to facilitate the execution of special orders, or for convenience of issue for later operations.

Effective Control of Unit Cost at each Operation.—This is secured inasmuch as, by this method, a detailed measure of efficiency is provided. Thus, at each operation, not only is the cost per article shown, but the cost per article of labour and material, and the total cost per finished article, which has passed through all the operations.

Again, the effect of the cost of defective work on the cost per article is shown, as well as the cumulative effect at each operation of waste in relation to subsequent operations. The principle underlying Unit Operation Costing is that each individual *operation* is costed, and from this operation cost the unit cost per article is ascertained. The method is particularly convenient when articles have to pass through one or more common opera-

tions, and, later, need subsequent operations in order to meet
the various special requirements of customers.

The Procedure : Example I. (Fig. 108).—In this example,
it is assumed, in order to simplify the description, that the whole
quantity required is put in hand, and that the exact numbers
passed as good at each operation are put through the next
operation. This procedure would be impracticable under actual
working conditions, but it will facilitate the explanation of the
necessary calculations.

A simple Unit Operation Cost Sheet, dealing only with one
element of cost, viz. direct labour, is shown in Fig. 108. It is a
simple sequential statement of quantities entering into five
operations of a process, drawn up to show the mathematical
procedure of the system. The columns are numbered for
reference in the following description :

FIG. 108.

UNIT OPERATION COSTS : EXAMPLE I (Labour only)

	Production Divisors.					Labour Costs.			
							Costs per 100.		
Opera-tion.	Gross.	Re-jects.	Net.	% of Rejects to net of each Opera-tion.	Ratio figure per 100 for cost of Final Net.	Value. £ s. d.	On Gross of each Opera-tion. s. d.	On Net of each Opera-tion. s. d.	On Final Net of each Opera-tion. s. d.
(1)	(2)	(3)	(4)	(5)	(6)	(7)	(8)	(9)	(10)
1st	100,000	25,000	75,000	33·33	200	50 0 0	1 0·00	1 4·00	2 0·00
2nd	75,000	5,000	70,000	7·14	150	18 15 0	6·00	6·43	9·00
3rd	70,000	5,000	65,000	7·69	140	87 10 0	2 6·00	2 8·31	3 6·00
4th	65,000	5,000	60,000	8·33	130	54 3 4	1 8·00	1 9·67	2 2·00
5th	60,000	10,000	50,000	20·00	120	25 0 0	10·00	1 0·00	1 0·00
					100	235 8 4	6 6·00	7 4·41	9 5·00

In columns 2, 3 and 4 of Fig. 108 the figures indicate that,
during the period under review, 100,000 articles, or components,
were put into process at the first operation, 25,000 were rejected
and 75,000 passed as good. Twenty-five thousand being 33·3
per cent. of 75,000, this percentage is recorded in column 5. The
total wages paid as direct labour for this operation was £50
(column 7). The number good at the first operation was worked
on at the second operation, with the result shown in line 2,
namely, that 5,000 were rejected and 70,000 passed as good—the
percentage of rejections to good being 7·14, and the wages paid
£18 15s.

The Use of Ratio Numbers.—In column 6, which is described as the ratio figure per 100 for calculating the cost of the final net, the intention is to indicate the number required to be put in hand at each operation in order to provide the quantity necessary to complete the order, which for this purpose is taken as 100. In the example given, it is evident that 100,000 articles have to be put into process at the first operation, in order to give 50,000 good productions at operation (5). The relationship of these two numbers is obviously 2 to 1, hence the figure in line 1, column (6), is shown as 200. Similarly, for the second, third, fourth, and fifth operations the respective relationships between

FIG. 109.

UNIT OPERATION COSTS : EXAMPLE II (Labour only)

Production Divisors.				% of Rejects to net of each Operation.	Ratio figure per 100 for cost of Final Net.	Labour Costs.			
							Costs per 100.		
Operation.	Gross.	Rejects.	Net.			Value.	On Gross of each Operation.	On Net of each Operation.	On Final Net of each Operation.
						£ s. d.	s. d.	s. d.	s. d.
(1)	(2)	(3)	(4)	(5)	(6)	(7)	(8)	(9)	(10)
1st	120,000	30,000	90,000	33·33	200	60 0 0	1 0·00	1 4·00	2 0·00
2nd	112,500	7,500	105,000	7·14	150	28 2 6	6·00	6·43	9·00
3rd	105,000	7,500	97,500	7·69	140	131 5 0	2 6·00	2 8·31	3 6·00
4th	130,000	10,000	120,000	8·33	130	108 6 8	1 8·00	1 9·67	2 2·00
5th	96,000	16,000	80,000	20·00	120	40 0 0	10·00	1 0·00	1 0·00
					100	367 14 2	6 6·00	7 4·41	9 5·00

the numbers put into process and the number finally completed (50,000) are :—150, 140, 130 and 120.

The Procedure : Example II showing Labour Cost when Quantities at each Operation are Unrelated.—As already mentioned, such a simple case as is outlined in Example I is never met with in practice, and the problem with which the cost accountant is faced is one where all the operations are being carried on simultaneously, and where the quantities being dealt with, at the different operations, bear no regular relation to one another. Such circumstances are illustrated in the Cost Sheet shown in Fig. 109, but, so that the method of calculating the various figures may be more easily followed, the figures in columns (5) and (8) are given as being the same in both Figs. 108 and 109. It is obvious that the figures in columns (9) and (10), being based on the figures in columns (5) and (8), will also be the same in both cost sheets.

In Cost Sheet 2 (Fig. 109) the relationship between the numbers put into process (120,000), and the numbers finally completed (80,000), and the ratio figures, is not as obvious as in Cost Sheet 1 (Fig. 108), and, therefore, it is necessary to indicate how the ratio figures are in practice determined. The procedure is as follows : The percentages in column 5 are first worked out for all the operations. Then it is necessary to work backwards. The percentage at the last operation is added to the base of 100 to give the figures in column (6), viz. : 120. The percentage in column (5) at the previous operation is now applied to the figure in column (6), 120, and, by addition thereto, gives the figure for this operation in column (6), namely, 130, 8·33 per cent. of 120, added to 120. In a similar way, the other ratio figures in column 6 are determined, and the result is this chain percentage, or set of ratio figures. In column 7 are stated the sums paid as wages for direct labour at each operation; by dividing these sums of money by the gross numbers in column (2), and multiplying by a hundred, the labour cost per hundred articles or components on gross numbers (column 8) is obtained. By dividing the same Wages Values by the net numbers good at each operation (column 4), and multiplying by 100, the labour cost per hundred on the net number (column 9) is found. By multiplying the gross cost per hundred articles in column 8 by the ratio in column 6 the labour cost per hundred on the numbers finally passed as good, column 10 is obtained. In other words, if it costs one shilling per hundred articles dealt with in the first operation, and, as indicated in column 6, it is necessary to put into process two, at this stage, for every one that is finally passed as good, it will be obvious that the gross cost of one shilling must be raised in this proportion. and that the full labour cost is twice a shilling or two shillings per hundred at this stage, which is the figure shown as the final net cost in column 10.

Information Deduced from Cost Sheet 2.—From the practical figures in the second cost sheet (Fig. 109) the following deductions can be made :

1. The direct-labour cost per hundred final articles, or components, is 9s. 5d. (column 10).

2. It is necessary to put into operation, at the first stage, two articles for every one completed (column 6).

3. That, at each operation, the cumulative effect on direct labour of the waste or defective components arising at subsequent operations is the difference between the labour on the net of each operation (column 9), and the labour on the final net (column 10).

4. The direct labour cost of waste is 2s. 11d. (column 10 minus column 8). (This is a partial measure of the permissible expenditure that may be incurred to lessen defective work.)

5. A basis for the valuation of direct labour in work in progress.

FIG. 110.

UNIT OPERATION COSTS (Work in Progress)

Work in Progress

At end of 1st Operation $= \dfrac{\text{Nos. in Progress}}{100} \times 1 \overset{s.}{} 4\overset{d.}{\cdot}00.$

At end of 2nd Operation $= \dfrac{\text{Nos. in Progress}}{100} \times (1 \overset{s.}{} 4\overset{d.}{\cdot}00 + 6\overset{d.}{\cdot}43 + 7\cdot14\% \text{ of } 1 \overset{s.}{} 4\overset{d.}{\cdot}00).$

$= \dfrac{\text{Nos. in Progress}}{100} \times 1 \overset{s.}{} 11\overset{d.}{\cdot}57.$

At end of 3rd Operation $= \dfrac{\text{Nos. in Progress}}{100} \times (1 \overset{s.}{} 11\overset{d.}{\cdot}57 + 2 \overset{s.}{} 8\overset{d.}{\cdot}31 + 7\cdot69\% \text{ of } 1 \overset{s.}{} 11\overset{d.}{\cdot}57).$

$= \dfrac{\text{Nos. in Progress}}{100} \times 4 \overset{s.}{} 9\overset{d.}{\cdot}70.$

At end of 4th Operation $= \dfrac{\text{Nos. in Progress}}{100} \times (4 \overset{s.}{} 9\overset{d.}{\cdot}70 + 1 \overset{s.}{} 9\overset{d.}{\cdot}67 + 8\cdot33\% \text{ of } 4 \overset{s.}{} 9\overset{d.}{\cdot}70).$

$= \dfrac{\text{Nos. in Progress}}{100} \times 7 \overset{s.}{} 0\overset{d.}{\cdot}17.$

At end of 5th Operation $= \dfrac{\text{Nos. in Progress}}{100} \times (7 \overset{s.}{} 0\overset{d.}{\cdot}17 + 1 \overset{s.}{} 0\overset{d.}{\cdot}00 + 20\% \text{ of } 7 \overset{s.}{} 0\overset{d.}{\cdot}17).$

$= \dfrac{\text{Nos. in Progress}}{100} \times 9 \overset{s.}{} 5$ which agrees with the total of Col. 10 in Fig. 109.

Valuation of Work in Progress.—The valuation of direct labour included in work in progress is based on the figures shown in columns 5 and 9, and is calculated as detailed in Fig. 110.

To arrive at the valuation of labour of work in progress at the end of the first operation, the numbers of articles in progress must be multiplied by the net labour cost at this operation. For those articles in process at the end of the second operation, it is obvious that the direct labour expended in respect of each hundred is the net cost at each operation through which the articles have passed, viz. 1s. 4·00d. plus 6·43d., and that inasmuch as these articles have passed through the second operation, the net cost, at the first operation, must be increased by the defective percentage at the second operation (7·14 per cent.). This gives the cost as 1s. 11·57d., as detailed in Fig. 110. Similarly for the third, fourth, and fifth operations, and it will be seen that the articles in process at the fifth operation are valued at 9s. 5d. per hundred, which agrees, as, of course, it must, with the total in column 10.

Once the above principles and procedure have been mastered, the Cost Accountant should have no great difficulty in applying them to meet the requirements of his particular problem.

Essential Requirements for the Method.—There are certain essential requirements which must be observed in order to put this method of costing into successful operation :

1. A list of standard operations numbered in sequence. In this connection one small difficulty that is constantly arising, namely, casual or repeat operations, has to be considered, as, for example, re-examination or extra cleaning. In view of the fact that this is not part of the regular sequence of work, the calculation of a defective figure for this operation, and its inclusion in the chain percentage, would vitiate the result. The proper treatment in such case is to link up the expenditure at this casual, or repeat operation, to the expenditure on the prior standard operation, and apply the defective percentage, after allowing for waste at both the standard and the casual operations, to the total labour expense so obtained.

2. Frequent and regular clearance of all waste. The frequency of the clearances will depend upon circumstances, and should preferably be, at least, daily.

3. Frequent and regular reports by standard operation numbers of :

(a) Rejections or preventable waste (this in order to determine figures for columns 3 and 5).

(b) Scrap other than rejections, that is, legitimate scrap. The reason for this is that the ratio figure is not affected by this consideration, when the calculations are being made on the basis of numbers, and not on the basis of weight.

4. It is frequently impracticable to count numbers at the various operations, and the output is weighed, or measured, and then converted into numbers for purpose of payment.

T

It follows, therefore, as there will be slight variations in the thickness of the material, or, in other dimensions, or in its specific gravity, provision must be made for :

(a) Frequent check weighings of the articles, or components, in order to confirm or correct the conversion factor of weight to numbers, and, in addition, as a check upon the scrap returns, where legitimate scrap arises.

(b) Frequent check weighings and counts of quantities removed from machines with the lubricant adhering to them. The object here is to prevent fraud, as it is not unknown for a bucket of lubricant to be thrown into the component in order to depress the scales.

Overhead.—So far one element of cost only—" Direct Labour "—has been dealt with, and it is necessary to make a few observations as to treatment of Overhead.

In order not to complicate the problem unduly, it is assumed that overhead is charged to the product on a time basis, by means of the machine-hour rate. This being so, the absorption at each operation on the gross numbers is known, and it can be dealt with on precisely similar lines to direct labour—that is, by the application of the ratio figure at each operation. There is one point that requires special mention in this connection, and that is in the case of examination operations. Assuming that the cost of examination is treated as an overhead expense, it will still be necessary to show examination as an operation, and to show the numbers examined, rejected, and accepted, respectively, at this operation, because the percentage of rejections here has a vital effect upon the ratio figure, as rejections are, generally, heaviest at examination operations. In this case, there will be no money entry in the account, as the expense being dealt with as overhead has already been provided for.

Material.—The treatment of the material element is simple in the case illustrated in Cost Sheet 2 (Fig. 109), as it will only be necessary to apply the ratio figure at the first operation to the value of the unit of material at that operation. In practice, however, the problem is rarely so simple, and the determination of the unit cost of material calls for some consideration, especially where there is legitimate scrap such as webbing, turnings, etc., as well as defective or rejected components, or articles. In such a case it is necessary to calculate a new ratio figure, introducing the legitimate scrap at each operation where it occurs, as such legitimate scrap does not enter into the ratio figure for direct labour.

The system described was introduced by Sir Reginald Townsend and developed by Mr. G. H. Clamp, F.C.W.A., who has contributed this chapter.

EXAMINATION QUESTIONS

1. The manufacture of an article is carried out on mass production lines, and consists of five operations.

The following are details for a period, the operation numbers indicating their sequence :

Operation number.	Gross numbers of articles worked upon.	Numbers defective at each operation.	Total wages paid for each operation.		
			£	s.	d.
1	5000	300	19	11	8
2	4500	500	33	6	8
3	6000	300	35	12	6
4	3500	400	32	5	10
5	5000	500	18	15	0

You are required to determine from these figures the labour cost per 100 articles for the period, having regard to the effect at each operation of the cumulative percentage of defectives at the subsequent operations. Accuracy to the nearest penny will suffice.—*Royal Society of Arts (Advanced)*.

2. By what method would you cost an article, the manufacture of which went on uninterruptedly, and where wastage occurred at various stages of manufacture and assembly ?—*Royal Society of Arts (Advanced)*.

3. In the preparation of periodical cost figures for repetition work, how would you indicate clearly the causes of fluctuations ? Illustrate your answer with two examples.—*Institute of Cost and Works Accountants (Final)*.

4. A number of articles varying in size and style can only be completed after an interval between each process. The articles may be batched for certain processes, but the time involved varies for each article, and in some cases is of short duration. How would you ascertain the cost of each article when complete ?—*Institute of Cost and Works Accountants (Final)*.

5. Machine parts requiring ten operations to complete are required in large quantities, and in every operation defective work is inevitable. How should they be put in hand in the shop in order to ensure accurate costing and replacement of scrapped parts ?—*Institute of Cost and Works Accountants (Intermediate)*.

6. A product involving the assembly of a number of small components is manufactured under the batch method, the numbers put in hand at the first operation of each component being sufficient to provide for the anticipated defectives and to allow for the final assembly of the numbers required in the batch. The excess numbers at the first operation vary for the different components and are based on past experience. How would you propose to ascertain the cost of the defective parts ?— *Institute of Cost and Works Accountants (Final)*.

CHAPTER XIX

UNIT OR SINGLE (OUTPUT) COSTING

SINGLE (Output) Costing, or Unit Costing, is a method of costing by the unit of production, where manufacture is continuous, and the units are identical, or can be made so by means of ratios. It may be applied to particular processes in conjunction with Process Accounts, or to Operation and Batch Costing.

The method is used in undertakings where there is a uniform product, of which there is a natural unit of cost. The work in such undertakings does not lend itself to Job Costing.

In most cases, the general accounts can be arranged in such a way that the Manufacturing, or Working Account, furnishes the total cost, and the detailed unit costs, when the expenditure is brought into relation with the output.

The accounts are designed to show :

(a) The total cost of the output for any required period.

(b) The unit cost in detail under the respective expense headings.

Examples of industries in which the method may be used, together with a suggested unit of cost, are :

Industry.	Unit Cost.
Steel works	per ton of steel.
Quarries	per ton of stone.
Collieries	per ton of coal raised.
Milling	per sack of flour.
Breweries	per barrel of beer racked.
Gold mines	per ounce of gold recovered or per ton of ore crushed.
Copper mines	per ton of copper.

Industry.	Unit Cost.
Paper-mill . .	per ton (or per lb.) of paper.
Textile factory .	per yard of material.
Envelope-making	per thousand envelopes.
Brick-making .	per thousand bricks.
Spinning mill .	per lb. of yarn.
Electro-plating .	per sq. inch plated (or per article if uniform).

The unit selected may be weight, measurement, or the filled container (box, barrel, sack, bag, etc.).

Departmental Application.—Although used for undertakings having a single unit of output, the method may be applied in factories where separate articles are made in different departments. Also where distinct operations, or processes, are separated departmentally, but, in these instances, departmental or process costs can be adopted in conjunction with departmental output. See for example Foundry Costs, page 267.

The Procedure.—In addition to arranging the required divisions in the Financial Accounts, it is usual to make up cost-sheets for short periods, such as a week, fortnight or month.

From the nature of the work, a Raw Material Account or Accounts can be operated conveniently in conjunction with the Manufacturing (or Working) Account. (See Fig. 111.)

The summary accounts are ruled with additional columns to show the detailed cost per unit. A column for percentage cost is often included.

Abstracts of the materials used, quantity, and value are prepared. The material is priced at cost on the " first in, first out " principle, or on the average cost. The average is made on the sum of the balance in stock, and the next delivery.

As in Process Costing, there occurs, sometimes, a loss of weight, or volume, in process. Such a loss in quantity (as distinct from value) should be shown in the account in total and as a cost per unit.

Wages are debited from the analysis summary.

Expenses are prepared in schedule form from the Impersonal Ledger. Only the proportion applicable for the period should be included, and, in the case of indirect or expense materials, only the actual quantity consumed.

Example of Manufacturing Accounts.—The following accounts show the use of Raw Material, Manufacturing and Trading Accounts for a factory making envelopes by machinery.

Comparative Costs.—By preparing summaries monthly, or for successive weeks for a year, the unit costs can be compared

FIG. 111.

ENVELOPE-MAKING FACTORY ACCOUNT

Raw Material

Flat Paper—Superfine, Angle, Grade 9

Dr.													Cr.
19... Feb. 1 „ 28	To Stock . „ Purchases	Rms. 40 930	Fo. b/d. J7	£ 13 309	s. 17 18	d. 0 0	Feb.28 19.... „	By Issues to Machinists as abstract „ Stock .	Rms. 900 70	Fo. J8 c/d.	£ 300 23	s. 0 15	d. 0 0
		970		£323	15	0			970		323	15	0
19... Mar. 1	To Stock .	70	b/d.	23	15	0							

Note.—Similar stock accounts for other grades of materials.

Manufacturing Account

for the month ending February 28th, 19......

Dr.											Cr.
			Cost per M. d.	£	s.	d.			Fo. c/d.	£ 1400	s. 0	d. 0

Output 16,000 thousands.

			Cost per M. d.	£	s.	d.			Fo. c/d.	£	s.	d.
19... Feb. 28	To Materials : Rms. M.						19... Feb.28	By Trading A/c. „ Loss in	c/d.	1400	0	0
	G.9 900 7,200		10	300	0	6	„	Punching (... lb.) = 1% . .		–	–	–
	G.12 700 5,600		12	280	5	0		„ Spoils in				
	G.16 400 3,200		24	320	10	0		Making (80				
	16,000	13·5		900	15	6		m.) = ½% .		–	–	–
„	„ To Direct Wages : Punchers . .		1·0	65	18	0	„	„ Sales of Cut- tings and				
	Machinists . .		4·0	264	2	0		Waste (...... cwt.). .			15	6
			5·0	1230	15	6						
„	„ Overhead (Fac- tory) : *Fixed*— Depreciation £35 Rent, etc. . 61											
	—		1·4	96	0	0						
	Variable— Labour . 38 Power . 12 Ind. Mat. . 7 Other. . 17											
	—		1·1	74	0	0						
			7·5	£1400	15	6				£1400	15	6
	Av. works cost .		21·0									

Trading and Profit and Loss Account

February 19......

Dr. | | | | | | | | | Cr.

| 19...
Feb. 1

Feb. 28

"

"

" | To Envelope Stock
b/d. . .
" Manufactured
per Mfg. A/c.
b/d. . .

Less Stock on
hand . .
Cost of Sales
" Gross Profit
c/d. . . | M.
20,000

16,000
36,000
13,330
22,670 | £
2650

1400
4050
1500
2550
850
£3400 | s.
7

0
7
0
7
2
10 | d.
6

0
6
0
6
6
0 | 19...
Feb.28 | By Sales . | M.
22,670 | £
3400

£3400 | s.
10

10 | d.
0

0 |

		% on Sales.	£	s.	d.	19... Feb.28	By Gross Pro- fit b/d. .	% on Sales	£	s.	d.
	To Administrative Expense . " Selling Ex- pense . " Distribution Expense . " Net Profit for month	8·5 7·0 3·0 6·5	289 238 102 221 £850	0 1 0 0 2	0 8 4 6 6			25	850 £850	2 2	6 6

Fig. 112.

SCHEDULE OF COMPARATIVE COSTS

Items.*	Month of			Same Month last Year.			Total to date since Stocktaking.			Total same Period last Year.		
	£ s. d.		Cost per Unit.	£ s. d.		Cost per Unit.	£ s. d.		Cost per Unit.	£ s. d.		Cost per Unit.
Raw Materials : 1............ 2............ etc. Manufacturing A/c. : (detailed Works Ex- penses) Trading A/c. : (detailed expenses of (*a*) Administration (*b*) Selling (*c*) Distribution) Net Profit . .												
Output in Units .												

* These are the details as shown in the Manufacturing and Trading Account in the Cost Ledger.

and used by the management for following the trend of cost for control purposes. The percentages in the Manufacturing and Trading Accounts are particularly helpful. In the latter account, it is the percentage to sales that is shown. Suggested forms for comparison of costs are shown in Figs. 112 and 113, and alternative forms are given in Figs. 117 and 140.

Specimen Accounts and Cost Sheets for several types of undertaking are given in this chapter. Their form is optional,

Fig. 113.

SERVICE DEPARTMENTS

Comparative Costs

A/c. Ref. No.	Services.	Week Ending : .... 19... Production....................Tons		Average cost per		Columns Repeat for each week.
		Hrs.	£	Hr.	Ton.	
20	Electric Power .					
21	Boiler House .					
22	Compressed Air .					
23	Water . .					
24	Transport . .					
25	Buildings . .					
26	Coal . . .					
27	Stores . .					
28	Testing and Laboratory .					
29	Acid Recovering .					
	Totals .					

and usually depends on the ideas of the cost accountant in control.

Cost Sheets.—These are prepared for the use of the management, and, consequently, they must include all the essential details which will assist the manager in checking the efficiency of production. In addition to the simplified forms given in this chapter, reference may be made with advantage to those shown for Process Accounts (Figs. 95, 106). Explanatory comments necessary are given with each Cost Sheet illustrated, viz. Paper-mill (Fig. 114); Colliery (Fig. 115); Steel Rolling-mill (Fig. 116); Expenses (Steel Mill) (Fig. 117); Machine Envelope-making (Fig. 111). See also Foundry Costs, Fig. 124.

FIG. 114.

PAPER MILL COST SHEET

Mill No. : ......   Date, 4 July. 19...
Production Order No. 962 for Parchment Writing Paper.
No. of Engines : 48 in 4 Chests.   Quantity 4½ tons.

Formula for Materials for the Order: (see note at foot).

Chests No.	Engines of Raw Materials.					
	No. 1 Rag.	No. 2 Rag.	Special Rag.	Wood.	Broken Paper.	Etc.
1	5	2	2	1	2	
2	5	2	2	1	2	
3	5	2	2	1	2	
4	5	2	2	1	2	
Total Engines	20	8	8	4	8	

	Cwt.	Qr.	lb.	s.	d.	£	s.	d.	£	s.	d.
Materials :											
Engine-Material.											
20 No. 1 Rag . .	40	0	0	27	6	55	0	0			
8 No. 2 „ . .	16	0	0	17	0	13	12	0			
8 Spec. „ . .	16	0	0	19	0	15	4	0			
	72	0	0			83	16	0			
8 Papers . .	16	0	0	15	0	12	0	0			
4 Wood . .	8	0	0	18	6	7	8	0			
48 Total .	96	0	0								
Add for loss on boil of rags .	10	3	5			12	11	5			
Less Waste in machine salle	4	0	24			3	3	1			
									112	12	4
Rag Sorters' Wages . .									14	2	8
Other Materials :											
Caustic 635 gal. . .	4	0	15	14	3	2	18	11			
Antichlor 120 „ . .		1	24	14	0		6	6			
Bleach 120 „ . .	1	1	6	6	9		9	6			
Alum 12 pail . .		1	12	5	6		2	0			
									3	16	11
Starch 100 lb. . .		3	16	25	6	1	2	10			
Resin Size 40 qts. . .							16	8			
Soap		2	24	50	6	1	16	0			
									3	15	6
Gelatine . . .	84	3	2	40	0				8	9	7
									142	17	0
Wages as per abstract .									152	4	5
Fuel Coal . . .									8	0	0
Mill expenses as per schedule .									72	0	0

Output : Actual weight 84 cwt. = 88·3%.   Making cost   **£375 | 1 | 5**
  of engine-material.   Cost per lb. 9½d.

Note.—(1) Engines and chests are containers of raw materials twelve engines to one chest. (2) The total cost, divided by the weight of output, gives the cost per lb. of paper made.

Fig. 115.

COLLIERY COST SHEET

Name of Pit : ....   Week Ending : ....

Days occupied : ......   Coal raised : ...... tons.   Last week : ...... tons.

	This week.		Last week.	
	Totals.	Cost per Ton.	Totals.	Cost per Ton.
Underground— **Wages—** Getting Transport Deputies and Checkers Roads and Faults	£	£	£	£
Expenses— Pit Props Stables Stores Sundries				
Cost per ton	£	£	£	£
Surface— **Wages—** Labour Joiners and Fitters Pumping, Winding, etc. Weigh-house **Expenses—** Stores Repairs Transport Sundries				
Cost per ton	£	£	£	£
Establishment and Other Expenses— Royalties Rent and Rates General Expenses— (In detail) Insurance Capital Sinking Fund				
Cost per ton	£	£	£	£
Total Cost per ton	£	£	£	£
Average Price realised per ton	£	£	£	£

Note.—The output stated on the form is the gross tonnage raised. Some of this is used in the colliery and some is supplied free to employees, the cost of which is included in the colliery expenses.

FIG. 116.

STEEL ROLLING-MILL

Summary of Production and Costs

Week ending : .... 19...

Department.	Production.		Total Expense. W.E. :			(Columns Repeat.)
				Average per		
	Tons.	Hours Worked.	£	Hr.	Ton.	
Hot Mill 1 . .						
„ 2 . .						
Total Hot Mills .			£			
Cold Mill 1 . .						
„ 3 . .						
„ 4 . .						
Total Cold Mills.			£			
Pickling Shop 1 . .						
„ „ 2 .						
Total Pickling .			£			
Annealing 1 . .						
„ 2 . .						
„ 6 . .						
Total Annealing.			£			
Paring and splitting .						
Cutting to length .						
Shearing . . .						
Hardening and Tempering .						
Polishing . . .						
Grinding . . .						
Warehouse . .						
Delivery Charges .						
Total Miscellaneous Processes .			£			
Steel Service . .						
Scrap „ . .						
Total Steel Service						
Grand Total .			£			

Note.—This is a total cost statement. A similar cost sheet is prepared with a column for each heading of expense, *e.g.* Indirect Wages, Coal Used, Stoves. Repairs, Services, etc., a special sheet for each week.

Fig. 117.

STEEL MILL

Expenses Cost Summary, 19...

A./c. Ref. No.	Details.	4 Weeks Average Year :			Week Ending :			Repeat each Week.
		£	Average per		£	Average per		
			Hr.	Ton.		Hr.	Ton.	
S.O. No.								
12	Indirect Wages . .							
15	Coal used . . .							
16	Acid used . . .							
30	Stores used . .							
210	Repairs . .							
211	Rolls or Pots . .							
212	Furnace . .							
213	Machinery . .							
	Service Depts. . .							
	Administration . .							
	Fixed Charges . .							
	Total . .							
	Direct Wages . .							
	Total Expense .	£						
	Distributed Expenses (recovered) :							
	Production Orders .							
	Foundry ,, .							
	Specific repairs on job Nos. . . .							
	Dept. repairs . .							
	Service Allocation to Depts. . . .							
	Miscellaneous . .							
	Total recovered	£						
	Balance of Expenses (under-recovered) to Profit and Loss A/c. . . .	£						
	Production ...... cwts.							
	Hrs. worked ...... hrs.							
	Coal used ...... cwts.							
	Pickelette used ... lbs.							
	Electricity ,, ... units							

Note.—The upper portion are actual expenditures; the middle portion the amounts allocated by pre-determined rates. The balance is written off to Profit and Loss Account.

Fig. 117a.

CANNED FOODS

Form of Cost Summary for 48,000 1 lb. tins of "Quick" Meals

	Nominal Weight.	Weight Used.	Price per Unit.	Details.	Total Cost.	Cost per Dozen Tins.
Ingredients.	Lbs.	Lbs.		£	£	s. d.
Meat						
Potatoes						
Carrots						
Peas						
Gravy						
	49,000	Weight or Quantity.				
less Residuals.						
Meat—Bones, Fat, Gristle, Kidneys, Suet, Sweepings, Muslin Bags, Blood and "Turn of Scale." ...% on usage						
Potatoes—Peelings and "Turn of Scale." ...% on usage						
Carrots—Peelings and "Turn of Scale." ...% on usage						
Peas—Rejects, Sweepings and "Turn of Scale." ...% on usage						
Total Tins filled .	49,000					
less Sale of imperfect tins	1,000					
Total usable tins . .	48,000					
Labour.						
Handling Ingredients .						
Preparing Ingredients .						
Filling Tins . . .						
Exhausting Tins . .						
Retorting Tins . .						
Lacquering Tins . .						
Labelling Tins . .						
Packing into Cases .						
Wiring and Nailing Cases						
Stacking Cases . .						
Supplies.						
Tins		49,500				
less damaged (...%) and sold for scrap .		500				
		49,000				
Lacquer and Thinnings.						
Labels		50,000				
less wastage (...%)		2,000				
		48,000				
Cases		1,008				
less damaged (...%) and sold for firewood .		8				
		1,000				
Packing Sundries : Nails, Wires, Stencils, etc.						
Departmental Overheads at ... pence per dozen						
General Works Overheads at ... pence per dozen						
Administrative Overheads . .						

Notes.—1. In practice, full details of Residuals, Packing Sundries, etc., would be shown, item by item.

    2. The "Turn of Scale" is the fractional amount which is put into the tin over and above the theoretical quantity.

    3. Subsidiary schedules could be attached showing details of recipe, preparation of gravy stock, etc.

    4. Further columns could be added for comparisons with previous periods, etc.

    5. A "Remarks" column could record such information as causes of excessive wastage, etc.

Fig. 117b.

COTTON WOOL

Form of Cost Summary for the production of 100,000 lbs. of Bleached Cotton Wool

	Price.	Unit.	Details.	Total Cost.	Cost per 100 lbs.
				£	
101,770·0 lbs. *Grey Cotton* . . .					
Bleaching					
11,194·7 *less* 11% Loss in Bleaching					
90,575·3					
20,535·8 lbs. *Bleached Cotton* . . .					
111,111·1					
11,111·1 *less* 10% Loss in Carding .					
..., waste sold for .					
100,000·0 lbs.					
Labour. Scutching					
Carding					
Packing					
Baling					
Maintenance					
Supplies. Interleaving Paper . Quantity.					
Packeting Paper .					
Labels . . .					
Hessian . . .					
Twine . . .					
Mill Overheads at ... pence per lb.					
Administrative Overheads					

Notes.—1. Further columns could be added for comparisons with previous periods, cost per lb., etc.

    2. A " Remarks " column could record such information as causes of excessive process losses, etc.

    3. Overheads based on throughput. In general it will be advisable to shew a separate rate for " fixed " expenses and variable," as by doing so the costs are more correctly presented.

EXAMINATION QUESTIONS

1. The following balances have been abstracted from the books of the Merton Colliery Company, Limited, in respect of the month ended on December 31, 1930 :

	£
Stock of Coal at December 1, 1930	750
Wages paid : Colliers	3500
Underground	1600
Surface	1000
Timber	460
Stores	120
Royalties	650
Depreciation (for the month)	650
Repairs	240
Stable Expenses	110
Rent and Rates	200
Pithead Office : Salaries	100
Postages, Telephones, etc.	30
Insurances	200
Heating and Lighting	50
Selling Expenses : Agency Charges	300
Advertising	50
Office Sundries	40
Bank Charges	50
Discounts, Dr.	250
Bad Debts	150
Rents of Cottages, Cr.	100
Coal Sales	11,000

The value of the stock of coal at December 31, 1930, is £900.
Coal Stock at the beginning was 1000 tons (£750).
Coal Stock at the end was   1200 tons.
Sales for the period were 8800 tons.

Calculate pithead cost and total cost, per ton of production; and prepare a statement for the information of the Board at their next monthly meeting exhibiting the result of the working.—*London Chamber of Commerce, Senior.*

2. Draw up a summary cost statement for any product you select and give such information therein as you think necessary for the management.—*Royal Society of Arts (Advanced).*

3. From the following information prepare a monthly Cost Sheet of the Sand-Lime Brickworks, showing cost and profit per M bricks. *Note*—M = 1000.)

Materials used : Lime :   895 tons at 50s. per ton.
                 Coal :   820 tons at 30s. per ton.
                 Sand :   1s. per M bricks made.
                 Stores : £632 10s.

Labour : Sand Digging and Running, £500.
         Brick-making, £2000.
Factory Oncost : 25 per cent. of direct charges.
Office Oncost : 10 per cent. of Factory Cost.
Bricks sold : 3500 M at 55s. per M.
Stock of bricks at beginning of month : 100 M.
Stock of bricks at end of month : 600 M.

Society of Incorporated Accountants and Auditors (Inter.)

4. The following particulars relate to the working of a colliery for one month :

	£	s.	d.
Wages	5,166	13	4
Stores	250	0	0
Timber	291	13	4
Repairs and Renewals	150	0	0
Depreciation	260	8	4
Tramways	141	13	4

Total Coal raised, 10,000 tons.

The colliery company own the freehold, and the annual value of the property is taken at £2,400. The *total* administration expenses for the month were £2,000, which included Selling and Distributing Charges.

You are required to make any necessary allocations (stating the bases used) and to prepare the Colliery Cost Sheet for the month showing the cost per ton of coal raised.—*Society of Incorporated Accountants and Auditors* (*Inter.*).

5. The Excelsior Manufacturing Co., Limited, deal in a Speciality selling at £40 per unit. The Trading and Profit and Loss Accounts of the Company for the year ended 31st December, 1928, are as follows :

TRADING ACCOUNT.

1928.				1928.		
Jan. 1.	To Stock	.	£4,000	Dec. 31.	By Sales .	. £30,000
Dec. 31.	,, Materials	.	7,750		,, Stock	. 2,000
	,, Wages	.	12,000			
	,, Gross Profit	.	8,250			
			£32,000			£32,000

PROFIT AND LOSS ACCOUNT.

1928.				1928.		
Dec. 31.	To Office Expenses	.	£3,000	Dec. 31.	By Gross Profit	£8,250
	,, Depreciation	.	1,500			
	,, Directors' Fees	.	750			
	,, Net Profit	.	3,000			
			£8,250			£8,250

Prepare, in detail, a Cost Sheet showing the cost of production and distribution per unit.—*Society of Incorporated Accountants and Auditors* (*Final*).

6. Select an industry and set out, as fully as possible, a form of final cost and include therein sufficient information to permit of a selling price being obtained.—*Institute of Cost and Works Accountants* (*Inter.*).

7. Prepare a statement showing the assembly of the cost sheet suitable for one of the following :

(*a*) A one-pound fancy cardboard box of assorted chocolates.

(*b*) A two-pound jar of marmalade.

(*c*) A seven-pound bar of soap.

Institute of Cost and Works Accountants (*Final*).

8. A factory requiring timber, purchases in bulk and stores for seasoning. Separate stores are used for boards, after sawing and planing

to thickness, from which they are drawn into shops for manufacture of repetition parts. Cutting, sawing, planing and spindling machines are in use. Describe the method of costing you would advocate.—*Institute of Cost and Works Accountants (Final).*

9. Draft a monthly report to the Directors, showing all information which you consider should be given by the Cost Accountant. Give your answer as fully as possible.—*Institute of Cost and Works Accountants (Final).*

10. In assembling costs the margin between works cost and selling price is available for :

(*a*) Selling and Distribution Costs.
(*b*) Administration Costs.
(*c*) Profit or Loss.

These items are sometimes expressed as a percentage on selling prices. What objections may be raised to this method and what alternatives are available ?—*Institute of Cost and Works Accountants (Final).*

11. In the process of electro-deposition a number of jobs are treated simultaneously in the deposition baths. It is not practicable to charge the labour involved direct to the jobs. How would you propose to cost the work done ?—*Institute of Cost and Works Accountants (Final).*

12. The following extract of costing information relates to Commodity A for the six months ended June 30, 1928 :

Purchases—Raw Materials	£30,000
Direct Wages	25,000
Rent, Rates, Insurance and Works Oncost	10,000
Carriage Inwards	360
Stock—January 1, 1928 :	
Raw Materials	5,000
Finished Product—1,000 tons	4,000
Stock—June 30, 1928 :	
Raw Materials	5,560
Finished Product—2,000 tons	8,000
Work in Progress, January 1, 1928	1,200
Work in Progress, June 30, 1928	4,000
Cost of Factory Supervision	2,000
Sales—Finished Product	75,000

Advertising, Discounts Allowed and Selling Costs—5*s*. per ton sold. 16,000 tons of the commodity were produced during the period. You are required to ascertain :

(*a*) The value of the raw materials used
(*b*) The cost of the output for the period.
(*c*) The cost of the turnover for the period.
(*d*) The net profit for the period.
(*e*) The net profit per ton of the commodity.
     Society of Incorporated Accountants and Auditors (Final).

13. Prepare a Cost Sheet of any manufacturing business with which you may be familiar, insert *pro forma* entries and show how the total cost of an article (or group of articles) is arrived at. Explain carefully the source of each entry you make and the method you have adopted of allocating indirect charges.—*Chartered Secretaries (Final).*

14. Select an article in common use, describe the materials, labour and expenses entering into its cost of production, and frame a Cost Sheet calculated to present to the manufacturer details of the cost of production.—*Incorporated Accountants (Final).*

U

15. From the undermentioned particulars, prepare a cost sheet of the Northern Brickworks, Limited, indicating cost and profit per 1,000 bricks.

> Wages (Clay getting, Machines, Drying, Setting, Burning, Drawing, Sorting, Loading), £7,500.
> Coal: 5,000 tons at 15s. per ton.
> Royalties at 1s. 6d. per 1,000 bricks made.
> Depreciation of Plant and Machinery, 10 per cent. (Capital outlay of £15,000).
> Removal of Overburden at 1s. per 1,000 bricks.
> Works Oncost, 10 per cent. of Wages and Coal.
> Office Oncost, 2½ per cent. of Wages and Coal.
> Bricks made, 10,152,284 (allow for waste 1½ per cent. of output).
> Bricks sold, 8,000,000 at 40s. per 1,000.
> Stock of Bricks January 1st, 2,000,000 at 30s. per 1,000.
> Stock of Bricks December 31st, 4,000,000 at 30s. per 1,000.
>
> *Incorporated Accountants (Final).*

16. Below is enumerated expenditure in the manufacture of X :—

	Three months ended	
	30/9/33.	31/12/33.
Raw Materials	2,550	2,800
Fuel	670	690
Electric Power	130	134
Process and General Wages . . .	6,030	6,350
Repairs	208	240
Haulage	92	106
Light and Water	40	40
Rent	200	200
Rates and Insurance	30	30
Salaries and General Expenses . . .	700	700
Administration	500	500
Depreciation	250	250
	£11,400	£12,040
Make (tons)	15,200	17,200

Prepare a cost sheet showing the comparative (itemised and total) cost per ton for each of the two periods.—*Incorporated Accountants (Final).*

17. B. Jones manufactures Vacuum Cleaners. He makes three types, namely, the "Midget," the "Standard" and the "De Luxe." His accounts to December 31st, 1934, his first year of production, were as under :—

	£			£
To Materials Consumed .	6,500	By Sales . .		16,380
,, Direct Labour . .	3,150	,, Stock of Finished		
,, Factory Expenses .	2,700	Machines . .		385
,, Gross Profit, carried		,, Work in Progress :—		
down . . .	5,180	Materials .	465	
		Labour .	150	
		Factory Oncost	150	
				765
	£17,530			£17,530

	£		£
To Office Expenses . .	1,400	By Gross Profit, brought	
„ Selling Expenses .	700	down . . .	5,180
„ Net Profit . .	3,080		
	£5,180		£5,180

He has kept rough Cost Accounts charging out Materials and Labour at actual cost, "Factory Oncost" at 100 per cent. on Labour, and "Office and Selling Oncost" at 15 per cent. on Factory Cost. Finished Machines and Work in progress are valued at Factory Cost.

The following figures are taken from his Cost Accounts :—

	Midget.			Standard.			De Luxe.		
	£	s.	d.	£	s.	d.	£	s.	d.
Average Cost of Materials per finished Cleaner	1	5	0	2	5	0	3	10	0
Average Cost of Labour per finished Cleaner		15	0	1	0	0	1	5	0
Number of finished Cleaners manufactured	1,550			1,230			320		
Vacuum Cleaners sold . . .	1,500			1,200			300		
Sale Price per Cleaner . . .	4	4	0	6	6	0	8	8	0

Prepare :—

(a) Statement showing, on the basis of Jones's Cost Accounts, (1) the total profit, and (2) the profit per Vacuum Cleaner sold.

(b) Reconciliation of the Profit shown by these Cost Accounts with the Profit and Loss Account balance of £3,080.—*Incorporated Accountants (Final).*

CHAPTER XX

UNIFORM COSTING AND THE BRITISH MASTER PRINTERS' COSTING SYSTEM

1. UNIFORM COSTING SYSTEMS

The Development of Uniform Costing.—Amalgamations and close working arrangements between groups of manufacturers in particular industries, and organisation for rationalisation, have necessitated, to a certain extent, the establishment of some degree of uniform costing by industries. In the case of particular manufacturers who control a number of factories situated in different districts, co-ordinated uniform costing has been introduced in order that the costs at each factory may be properly comparable. Uniformity of application of principles; of allocation and recovery of overhead expenses; and of determining cost and selling prices are found to be advantageous for comparing efficiencies and as a means of controlling unit costs.

Again, in the case of electricity supply undertakings, owing to the rules laid down in the Second Schedule of the *Electricity (Supply) Act*, 1926, for ascertaining the cost of production of electricity, at which cost the Board of Electricity Commissioners purchase the current produced, most undertakings operating under the scheme have arranged their costing on similar lines. (See Ch. XXIII.)

In a different class may be considered those uniform systems which have been devised and introduced into particular industries by various federations or associations of manufacturers, as, for example, in such industries as paper-bag making, printing, etc. One of the purposes of these particular schemes is to render competition less destructive, by ensuring that all the members know what is included in cost, and how to arrive at it. Other purposes of this type of uniform costing are connected with a standardised method of collecting figures in order to fix selling prices on a basis acceptable to those engaged in the industry. Of the systems organised by trade associations that of the British Master Printers' Federation was the first serious attempt at devising a uniform system of costing, and is probably the most complete. An official outline of the system is given in this chapter.

Requirements for Uniform Costing.—Apart from any decision whether single, process, or job costing is desirable, the following details require to be determined :

(1) The bases for the apportionment and allocation of overhead.

(2) The departments, sections or production centres to be used for analysis and comparison of costs.

(3) What items shall be regarded as factory as distinct from administration expense.

(4) How expenses of administration, distribution and selling shall be applied to prime cost, *i.e.* the basis of recovery rates.

(5) How expenses in connection with the buying, storing, handling and issuing of stores materials shall be treated.

(6) What rates of depreciation shall be applied to plant and machines.

(7) Whether interest on capital is to be included, and, if so, how, and on what basis.

(8) What rent charge is to be made for buildings if freehold or leasehold.

(9) How service departmental costs shall be arrived at.

(10) The demarcation between direct and indirect wages.

(11) In the case of time- and piece-work, whether the time or wage basis, or both, shall be used for determining expense rates.

(12) What organisation can be set up to prepare comparative statistics for the use of those adopting the uniform system. Privacy of individual data and confidence in the co-ordinating office are essential factors.

The Purposes and Value of Uniform Costing.—In a group of amalgamated manufacturers, or in the case of a firm controlling a number of factories, actual detailed costs can be compared, standard costs may be set up, and controls by comparisons secured. The most economical and suitable distribution of orders received can be made. Actual relative and efficiencies of production can be compared. By suitable organisation costs may be reduced.

Where manufacturers are only associated, or where the system is organised by a manufacturers' federation, less precise cost comparisons may be available, but useful general comparisons may be provided, as for instance :

(a) The cost value of production on some common basis, e.g. per £ of direct wages or other factor.

(b) The cost of rent, light, heat, etc., on the basis of say per 1000 sq. feet.

(c) The ratio of indirect labour to direct labour, say by units, by operations, or by processes.

(d) The output per hour for similar operations.

(e) The ratio of each kind of expense to prime cost, or to direct wages.

By these means comparison (a) of efficiencies, (b) of costs by selected units, (c) of periodical averages of costs of different firms, etc., can be made.

It will be obvious that greater advantage is obtained by those actually controlling a group of factories than by individual manufacturers operating a common system organised for their particular industry.

2. The British Master Printers' Costing System

Outline of the System.—In 1911 the Federation of Master Printers set up a special committee charged with the responsibility of compiling a system of Costing that could be uniformly applied to printing businesses of all sizes. How well the Committee succeeded in their efforts is proved by the fact that to-day (1940) the cost of probably more than 80 per cent. of the work produced by printers in this country is found by means of this system.

Budget of Expenses.—Operational costs are established by means of a budget, based on the expenses incurred for either a year, or, where deemed necessary, a shorter period. Direct allocation of expenses to departments, and, later, to operations (both hand and machine), is one of the main principles of the system.

Use of Hourly Cost Rates.—Inclusive hourly cost rates are set up for all operations. These rates comprise wages, direct expenses as departmentalised, and overhead expenses that are not possible of departmentalisation.

Expenses of Stores, etc.—The cost of buying, receiving, storing, issuing, and delivering direct material is ascertained and recovered as " handling charges," by adding to the cost of material a fixed percentage of the invoice price.

Interest on capital employed in the business is taken in as an item of cost, due, partly, to the fact that hand and machine operations are essential to the production of every order, and, sometimes, a choice of these operations may be deemed desirable; machines vary enormously in price, and one type of machine may serve equally as well for certain classes of work as another type of a higher value. Depreciation is taken in on the basis of diminishing value.

Testing the Rates used.—In order to prove the correctness, or otherwise, of the set-up hourly rates, and, also, to ascertain whether the full costs are being recovered on the volume of the work produced, two *weekly* statements are prepared :

On a form, Federation Form No. 4, called the " Value of Production," is tabulated the whole of the hours of " chargeable " (*i.e.*, productive) time for all operations, gathered from daily time-dockets. This time is shown against the name of each hand-worker and each machine. In addition, the non-chargeable time is collated. Thus, not only is the total time of each worker shown, but the ratio of chargeable to non-chargeable time of each individual is apparent. Columns are provided for progressive totals of both sets of figures, and it is thus possible to make comparisons over chosen periods.

On another form (Federation Form No. 3) are tabulated weekly the departmental wages and expenses, the latter being fixed on a basis of a fiftieth part of the annual budget figures. To the sum of these two items is added the ascertained percentage to recover the overhead expenses, and the total represents the cost of production for the department concerned.

Effect of the Overhead Rates used.—The application of overhead expenses by a percentage of the departmental cost has the effect of increasing the cost of production when pressure of work increases the departmental wages, and, correspondingly, decreases the cost of production when lack of work reduces the departmental wages bill. This applies to the normal fluctuations, and not to abnormal conditions, which would necessitate a recasting of the budget.

The departmental totals of value of production from Form 4 can be compared with the cost of production, and the difference shown as a surplus, or a deficit, as the case may be.

These two forms provide the management with information of great value as to whether the capacity of the factory to produce is being maintained.

The Federation publish a text-book containing full details of the system, and illustrations of a great variety of forms for use in connection with the system, but these are too numerous to reproduce in this book.

The Departments into which costs are divided are dependent upon the size and nature of the business. For a large firm they would be as follows : composing, foundry, machining, ruling, binding, lithography, materials. The composing may be further divided into hand composing, monotype and linotype.

The Basis of Allocation Used.

Rent, Rates, Heat, Light, and Water are in most cases apportioned to departments on the basis of square feet of area.

Fire Insurance.—That on buildings by area; on plant and contents according to value in each department; on standing formes and work on litho stones and plates, separate accounts with a view to recovery by a definite charge.

Insurance for consequential loss (profits and standing charges) is treated as general overhead.

Workmen's Compensation and employers' liability payments, on the basis of wages paid in each department.

Interest on Capital.—A charge of at least 5 per cent. is debited to each department on the value of the plant and stock therein. Interest on the balance of the capital in the business is included in general overhead.

Depreciation.—Usually, type 10 per cent., plant $7\frac{1}{2}$ per cent. off the diminishing value. Replacement values of pre-war plant should be used.

Loss in melt of metal used by monotype and linotype plant depends on the frequency of melting ; 2 per cent. per melt (of which there are two) is usually taken, and by multiplying 4 per cent. by the total value of metal melted, the depreciation per annum is arrived at.

Holiday Payments.—The cost of fixed holidays, and annual

holidays given to employees is included in the annual expense budget for each department, thus the cost is evenly distributed over the year.

General Expenses on Materials.—Handling charges, *e.g.*

Fig. 118.

PRINTER'S COST SHEET

Customer's Name and Address : F. Smith & Co., High Street, London.   Work Ticket No. 391.

Details : 20,000 Annual Reports as per Work Ticket, La. Post 4to fly, printed black and red.

Composing Room.*						Materials.					
19...	State Hand or Mono.	Hrs.	£	*s.*	*d.*	19... Aug. 2			£	*s.*	*d.*
July30	W. Jones, Hand Comp. . .	3½					10,080 Sheets Cr. Ld. L. Post .		9	10	0
,, 31	W. Jones, Hand Comp. . .	6½					Ink No. 8 . .			5	0
Aug. 3	W. Jones, Author's corrections .	2					,, No. 4 . .			2	6
							20 m. Envelopes .	11/-	11	0	0
							Add handling charges .	20%	4	3	6
	At 5*s.* 6*d.* .	12	£3	6	0				£25	1	0

Machine Room.							Outwork.					
19... Aug. 2	Man. 15	Machine. E 3	Time. 8	Rate	£	*s.*	*d.*	19... Aug. 7			£	*s.*	*d.*
,, 3	,,	,,	8					Addressing Envelopes .		2	0	0
,, 4	,,	,,	8					Add charges .	12½%	1	12	6
,, 5	,,	,,	6									
			30	4/6	£6	15	0			£3	12	6

Binding Room.							Summary.				
19... Aug. 5		Hrs 10	At. 2/-	£ 1	*s.* 0	*d.* 0				£	*s.*	*d.*
	Folding . .						Composing		3	6	0
	Cutting . .	—			4	6	Machining		6	15	0
	Piecework .	—			16	0	Binding		3	14	6
	% on 16*s* .		1	14	0		Materials		25	1	0
							Sundries		3	12	6
			£3	14	6				£42	9	0

* Where mono- or linotype composing is used a separate section may be introduced, as this will be charged at a different hourly rate from hand composing.

The form is kept in the office and entered up daily from the daily dockets, and on completion is filed with the Work Ticket.

The hourly rates are used only for the purpose of an example.

buying, receiving, storing, issuing, delivering, are added to the cost of materials; also a proportion for management and office expenses.

The remaining general expenses, *i.e.* travellers' salaries, commission, expenses, spoilage and the sundry expenses, are also applied as a percentage on materials. In the case of customers' own paper, an addition is made for handling and storage cost.

Cost Sheets.—A convenient form of cost sheet is shown in Fig. 118.

EXAMINATION QUESTIONS

1. Outline a system of Costing suited to the Printing Trade. How would you recommend the following expenses should be allocated? Power, Depreciation, Fire Insurance, Workmen's Compensation, Repairs and Renewals of Machinery and Plant, General Expenses. —*London Chamber of Commerce.*

2. Printing machines are made to print appropriate sizes of paper and usually cost more as the sizes increase. To meet the requirements of customers it frequently happens that a small sheet must be printed on a large machine. What procedure should be adopted when assembling the costs of the job ?—*Institute of Cost and Works Accountants (Final).*

3. What information from a uniform Cost System would you suggest as *particularly* useful to manufacturers in the same line of business ?— *Institute of Cost and Works Accountants (Final).*

4. What steps would you take to establish a system of uniform costing for fixing price standards in an industry controlled by a Combine ?—*Institute of Cost and Works Accountants (Final).*

5. What items of general expense would you expect to show most change per centum as a result of a combine? Indicate the direction of, and reasons for, these changes.—*Institute of Cost and Works Accountants (Inter.).*

6. Your firm propose making an amalgamation with another, and wish you, as Cost Accountant, to investigate and report. What especial features would you take into consideration for that report ?—*Institute of Cost and Works Accountants (Final).*

7. The studio and design department of a printing business prepares ideas which are sometimes accepted by clients, but a large proportion of the work so produced is abandoned as unsuitable. How do you consider the cost of such a service should be recovered? Give your reasons.—*Institute of Cost and Works Accountants (Inter.).*

8. A proposal is being considered to amalgamate two factories at an estimated cost of £50,000. The savings expected to result therefrom are estimated at £20,000 per annum. State broadly the details of the savings, aggregating £20,000, that you would assume to follow on the amalgamation, and how you, as Cost Accountant, could contribute to the discussion of the proposal.—*Institute of Cost and Works Accountants (Final).*

9. How would you propose to deal with the following items in your costs : (*a*) Warehousing expenses incurred in a printing business ? (Part of Question.)—*Royal Society of Arts (Advanced).*

10. State concisely your opinion as to the possibility of standardising costing systems in particular industries. Give reasons showing whether it is or is not desirable to attempt this task.—*Society of Incorporated Accountants and Auditors (Final).*

11. From the following data prepare six prices per thousand for printing an art wrapper, viz. :—

(*a*) First orders of 50,000; 100,000 and 250,000. (*b*) Repeat orders for 50,000; 100,000 and 250,000. Cost of sketch and lithographic work, £40. Making machines ready for printing, £20. All other work (per thousand), £2. Add for general overhead and profit, 25 per cent.— *Institute of Cost and Works Accountants (Final).*

CHAPTER XXI

IRON FOUNDRY COSTS

The Costs in an Iron Foundry are required as follows :

The Cost of the Pattern Shop.
The Melting Department or Cupola Cost.
The Moulding Shop Cost.
The Fettling and Cleaning Department Costs.
The Smiths' Shop Costs in the Foundry.

The procedure described in this chapter is that for a General Foundry, making all sorts of iron castings, and not a highly specialised one.

Where the work is constant and uniform in a foundry, that is, where a more or less single product is made, a method worked out on similar lines to the machine rate is often employed for job-costing and estimating. Each man and boy is regarded as a centre of production. The whole of the expenses is then carefully analysed, and charged on varying bases, to the centre of production, the total to each centre being divided by the normal hours worked. This gives a working expense rate to each operator in the foundry, and is an alternative to the percentage method here advocated.

Statistical Records Required.—(1) A daily charge sheet for the cupola (Fig. 119) should be prepared giving details of :

(*a*) The various grades of iron used in pig.
(*b*) Coke, limestone, etc.
(*c*) The number of charges.
(*d*) The quantity of new scrap put in, as against own scrap produced previously.

(2) The previous day's weight of scrap produced by runners, risers, heads, spare metal, tackle, etc.

This has a bearing on the coke consumption per ton of iron melted.

(3) The loss in melting. This is difficult to obtain, especially in large foundries, and in such cases should be pre-determined.

Tests can be taken over a short period of a week, or more, to ascertain the loss by :

(a) Keeping a record of all iron going into the cupola.
(b) After ladles are lined, weighing them.
(c) Filling the ladles from the cupola, skimming them and re-weighing.

Fig. 119.

DAILY CUPOLA RECORD

Date : ....

Metal charged :	Tons.	Cwt.
Pig Iron		
Bought Scrap		
Own Scrap		
Total . . .		
Coke consumed		
Limestone consumed		
Castings Produced		
Loss in Melting		
Coke Consumed per Ton of Metal Melted		

The difference between each day's weighing into and out of the cupola will represent, under normal conditions, a fair index to the loss in melting (see Fig. 120). Much depends on the quality of pig and scrap used, but, taking tests in different periods in the year, a percentage is found, which can be used with reasonably accurate results.

The Use of these Records :

(1) The total input less the loss in melting gives the total output.

(2) Total output minus the weight of saleable castings, wasters and sundry tackle represents the runners, risers, heads and metal over-melted.

(3) The amount of loss in melting is a guide to the quality of the scrap and pig purchased.

(4) The coke consumption per ton of metal melted reflects the quality of the coke purchased.

FIG. 120.

CUPOLA PRODUCTION RECORD

Input. | Output.

	Scrap Metal.		Cupola Coke.		Lime-stone.	Pig Iron, all qualities.		Total Iron Input.	Date 1932.	Saleable Castings made and felled.	Wasters.	Runners, Risers, Tackle, Core Irons, etc.	Total Iron Output.	% of Cupola Waste.
Date 1932.	Bought.	Returned to Cupola.	Bed.	Melt-ing.		Other kinds.	Foun-dry.							
	T. C.	T. C.	T. C.	T. C.	T. C.	T. C. Haematite	T. C.	T. C. Q. L.		T. C. Q. L.	T. C. Q. L.	T. C. Q. L.	T. C. Q. L.	
Feb. 1	4 0	3 10	15	2 0	13	2 0	12 6	21 16 0 0	Feb. 1	11 13 0 3	1 1 3 12	7 15 3 1	20 10 2 16	5·85
2									2					
3									3					
4									4					
5									5					
6	Not Blowing								6					
7									7					
8									8					
9									9					
10									10					
11									11					
12									12					
13									13					
14	Blowing for special cast								14					
15									15					
16									16					
17									17					
18									18					
19									19					
20									20					
21									21					
22									22					
23									23					
24									24					
25									25					
26									26					
27									27					
28									28					
29									29					
Totals								£						Average % for month.

(a) The input side should be checked approximately by the stocktaking figures on the 1st of each month. See Stock Book Record.
(b) The Stock Book figure should be the one to use in costing, as there may possibly be some fault with the Cupola Record. Its chief value lies in the percentage of waste figure, and the effect of buying good or poor scrap, coke, etc.
(c) The last column shows the waste due to moisture, gas, etc.

Alternative Method to find Metal Melted.—Ignore the total output of the cupola, take the total weight of the saleable good castings, the wasters, and the tackle, and apply the percentage loss in melting, say, 6 per cent.

Then for an output of 100 tons the formula would be $\frac{100 \times 100}{94} = 106$ tons 8 cwt., approximately, of metal melted on the assumption that all other metal melted represented by runners, risers, etc., has been duly returned to the cupola and used over again.   This is not so accurate as the first method.

Production Record.—This is made for each day's cast, showing :

(a) Weight of every casting (after fettling).
(b) Number of castings made.
(c) Waste castings in a separate column, and cause of waste.
(d) The Job Number and Works Order Number.

An example of a cupola production record actually used is shown in Fig. 120.   For the use of this record in Foundry Job Costs see p. 279 (re Cupola Cost).

Materials—Issues.—The issue of materials used in moulding is best made from a Stores, and charged out on a " used " basis.   This facilitates weekly costing, and serves as a check against goods inwards and stock-taking inventories.

Other materials, such as sand, coal, coke, etc., must be estimated for any period less than a month, when the stock books will give the necessary information.   (See Fig. 121.)

Stores Issue Requisitions are used for such indirect materials as :

Oils.	Small tools.	Brushes.	Riddles, etc.
Grease.	Buckets.	Shovels.	
Waste.	Bellows.	Belting.	

Materials—The Stock Book.—A form of Stock Book is shown in Fig. 121, and indicates the quantity " used " each month.   The stock on hand at the beginning of the month is brought forward and entered up under each class of material, such as hæmatite pig, hæmatite scrap, ordinary scrap, sand, coal and other items shown at foot of Fig. 121.

The amounts purchased as per the accounts are added, and

Fig. 121.

Stock Record Ledger

Stock of Materials at 28 February, 19...

	White Iron.	Foundry Quality. No. 2.	Haematite.					Goldendale Pig.
Stock (opening)			20	10	75/-	76 17 6		
Invoiced—(items detailed)			50	–	76/-	190 0 0		
			carr. paid					
Carriage & Wag. Hire Haulage			50	–	3d.	12 6		
Transferred			70	10	75/10	267 10 0		
Used			60	10	76/-	230 0 0		
Stock (closing)			10	0	75/-	37 10 0		
Stock Invoiced—(items detailed)								
(Words and rulings are repeated as above)	Limestone.	Stove Coke.	Cupola Coke.					Steel Scrap.

Sections are repeated for each material. Other headings are Silky, Foundry 1, Low Silicon, Haematite Scrap, C. I. Scrap, Sand, Ganister, Coal, Coal-dust, Core Oil, Core Gum Manure, Blacking, Straw Ropes, Plumbago, Wood Wool.

from the totals the stocks on hand at the end of the month are deducted, leaving the balance "used." This balance should approximately tally, in respect of iron, with the aggregate total of daily recorded issues.

This record provides average prices, and if the market is not fairly constant it may be necessary to adopt a market valuation for charging out.

Materials—Stocktaking of Materials on the "Used" Basis.— Stocktaking, *physically*, is of prime importance in the case of materials used in bulk. All materials on hand on the first of each month, whether under cover or in the open yard, must be recorded, by actual weight if possible, or by actual count.

The method of keeping a stock record of receipts and issues known as the "Book Stock" is not usually satisfactory.

The materials used in each department are :

Melting Department.—Coke, ganister, limestone, bricks, fireclay, oxygen, feeding irons, etc.

Moulding Shop.—Sand, cowhair, manure, blacking, plumbago, chaplets, sprigs, coal dust, small tools.

Core Shop.—Sand, coke, coal, straw ropes, wood wool, core gum, resin, core oil, wax wire, iron wire, small tools, core irons.

Fettling Shop.—All tools for chipping; materials for cleaning, such as brushes, file card, sand-blast material, goggles, filling compounds, etc.

WAGES ANALYSIS

1. Direct Wages are analysed under departmental headings as follows :

Melting Department—Cupola.—Cupola tenters, labourers handling iron and fuel, stocking and weighing-in.

Moulding Shop.—Wages of moulders and helpers in dry sand, green sand, and loam moulding; machine moulding; bench or stump moulding.

Core Shop.—Wages of core-makers and helpers, including core-turning machine workers.

Fettling and Cleaning Department.—Wages of fettlers and blasters, chippers, tumbling and inspection.

Smiths' Shop in Foundry.—Smiths and strikers.

Machine Shop.—In foundries dealing with small castings there may be a machining shop, but as the costing in this department follows the usual procedure in an engineering works, which has already been dealt with in other chapters, and is not essential to the understanding of foundry costing, it is thought unnecessary to deal with it here.

2. **Indirect Wages** are analysed separately to the various shops as far as possible, and, where miscellaneous, affecting several departments, the total is apportioned, say, on the basis of Direct Wages or Direct Labour Hours, in each department. (Fig. 122.)

FIG. 122.

APPORTIONMENT OF INDIRECT LABOUR
[Foremen, yard labour, etc., not allocated to shops.]

Month.	Total.	Foundry Departments.												
		Cupola.			Moulding Shop.			Core Shop.			Fettling Shop.			Smiths' Shop.
Direct Labour Proportion .	£ 2000 100%	£ 100 5%			£ 1600 80%			£ 200 10%			£ 50 2½%			£ 50 2½%
	£	£	s.	d.	£	s.	d.	£	s.	d.	£	s.	d.	£	s.	d.
Jan. . . Feb. . . etc.	248	11	18	0	200	8	0	23	16	0	5	19	0	5	19	0

Indirect Labour.

The Indirect Labour in the shops is as follows :

Cupola.—Allocation from schedule (Fig. 122).

Moulding Shop.*—Labour in and about the shop, sand milling, sand mixing, breaking runners and risers, delivering castings to fettlers, lining ladles, pattern carrying; proportion from above schedule.

Core Shop.*—Sand mixers, sand wheelers, oven men, men about shop, delivering cores to foundry, cleaning up; proportion from schedule.

Fettling Shop.—Labourers, cleaning up, proportion of foreman's wages, yard labour weighman, casting store clerk.

* It is usual to analyse further, finding separate totals for green sand, dry sand and loam moulding.

x

The respective departmental direct and indirect wages are shown in the Monthly Cost Summary. (See Fig. 124.)

Works Overhead " Running " Expenses.—An analysis of these is made to the departments, on suitable bases, but direct wherever they can be, such as Electric Power, etc.

Repairs and Maintenance.—The labour is charged up against Standing Order Numbers, suitably coded, for such expenses as :

Buildings.	Core-turning machines.
Cranes.	Cupola stoves.
Loam mills.	Electrical equipment.
Compressors.	Blowers, etc.
Moulding machines.	

The materials issued from stores will be similarly charged out against requisitions on which standing Order Numbers are shown. In addition, there are purchases generally requisitioned for immediate use, e.g.

Wheels for crane tracks.	Timber.
Ropes for cranes.	Bricks.
Iron for tools.	Cement,
Electrical equipment parts.	etc.

These latter will be analysed in the Purchases Book, suitably ruled with columns in addition to those for various stock materials, and other purchases.

A form of schedule for monthly repairs is shown in Fig. 123.

Overhauls, Renewals and Heavy Repairs to Plant.—A provision, based on previous experience, is made to ensure a fairly level cost per ton, which will cover any such expense. A Suspense Account may be opened, and to this are credited the amounts charged to each department monthly. When overhauls of a heavy nature occur, the cost is debited to this Suspense Account.

Depreciation.—A rate to cover depreciation in each department should be applied to each part of the equipment, and a monthly charge made against current costs.

Moulding Equipment (Loose).—This expense consists of such items as flasks, boxes, iron patterns, etc., which are in general use. Watch has to be kept on this expenditure, as this equipment is often broken and thrown into the cupola, and, unless

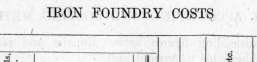

Fig. 123.

MONTHLY SCHEDULE—FOUNDRY REPAIRS

Source of Expense.	Total.	Cupolas and Equipment.	Moulding Shop.							Fettling Shop.				
			Overhead and Jib Cranes.	Loco-Crane.	Buildings and Crane Track.	Tools and Chains.	Loam Mills.	Electric Equipment.	Moulding Machines.	etc.	All Buildings.	Cranes.	Sand Blast Plant.	Tumblers.	Tools, etc.
	£													
Foundry:														
Fitters														
Machine shop														
Smiths' "														
Pattern "														
Labourers "														
Carpenters "														
Purchased items														
General Expenses (detailed)														

(SCHEDULE continued)

	Core Shop.			Smiths' Shop.				Machine and Fitting Shop.					
	Stoves and Ovens.	Other Drying Apparatus.	Sand Mixers.	All Buildings.	All Buildings.	Hearths and Anvils.	etc.	Buildings.	Lathes.	Drills.	Milling.	Grinding.	etc.
As above, etc.													

checked, misleading figures arise. Repairs and renewals of these are chargeable to current cost.

New boxes, etc., which have to be made, should be charged as a rate per ton of castings made. The rate is revised periodically, to ensure recovering the cost of this equipment, less the residual, or scrap value, as may be decided.

A Loose Plant Account is used to control the making of box parts, core bars, and special tackle. It is debited with the total making cost of these items, and credited with the amounts which have been debited to the summary foundry cost, at a rate per ton of castings made, as described in the preceding paragraph. It is thus equivalent to a depreciation account.

Overhead Charges Account.—This shows the collection and distribution of overheads. A proportion of each item of expense is apportioned on an appropriate basis to each shop for power, lighting, insurance, rates, depreciation, laboratory, compensation, medical supplies, water, sundry stores, etc. Where possible, the charge is direct to the shop concerned. The total overhead for each shop is allocated to the various orders dealt with, usually *pro rata* to weight or hours.

General Administration Expense is shown separately on the monthly summary. It is applied to individual jobs on the basis of the *total* direct labour by the percentage shown in the monthly summary. A Control Account is used, which shows the total debited to the Foundry, and the amount recovered on jobs.

Pattern Shop.—It is usual to keep a separate trading account for the Pattern Shop.

Practically the whole of the cost of patterns and repairs of old patterns is a " direct " charge against the Foundry, except for patterns for sale or for contracts worked for other firms, when pattern costs for these are charged to the castings orders, or pattern orders. The cost consists of wages, materials, and shop overhead, apportioned to this department, plus the proper proportion of management charges.

Monthly Foundry Summary Cost.—A form actually used is shown in Fig. 124. At the head of the form is entered the weight of the various classes of output, and this is followed by the total cost and cost per ton for each department. It forms the basis for costing jobs.

The item " Suspense Account " is the charge to cover

FIG. 124.

FOUNDRY SUMMARY COST

Month of ....

				Tons.	Cwts.	Qrs.	Lbs.	Percentage.
		Saleable Castings . .		315	10	—	22	57
		Box Parts . .		11	1	1	18	2
		Iron Patterns . .		—	—	—	—	—
Tons.	Cwts.	Total Saleable . .		326	11	2	12	59
Saleable Tons 326 Divisor.	12	Waster Castings . .		38	14	3	20	7
		Tackle and Plant .		99	12	2	21	18
		Runners, Risers, Heads, etc., etc. . .		55	7	—	6	10
		Total Cast . .		520	6	1	3	94%

					Amount.			Total.			Cost per Ton.		Total Cost per Ton.	
	Tons.	Cwts.	Rate.		£	s.	d.	£	s.	d.	s.	d.	s.	d.
1. Metal.														
Foundry Pig Iron .	381	16	58/-		1107	4	5							
Hematite Pig Iron .	23	10	75/-		88	2	6							
„ Scrap .	34	7½	67/-		115	2	3							
Cold Blast Iron .	—	—			—	—	—							
Steel Scrap . .	2	10	45/-		5	12	6							
Cast Scrap (new) ⎫ „ (own) ⎭	111	7½	42/6		236	12	11							
Total = 100% .	553	10½	56/1·24		1552	14	7							
Credit for Wasters, Runners, Risers, and Tackle .	193	14·2·19	40/-		387	9	4	1165	5	3			71	4·29
2. Cupola Cost (Cost per Ton of Iron Melted).			s.	d.										
Wages . . .			2	9·96		78	6	8				4	9·56		
Ganister, 13 tons at 22s. 6d.				6·34		14	12	6					10·75		
Limestone, 16 tons at 7s. 2d. .				2·49		5	14	8					4·21		
Coke (cwts. per ton melted iron, 2 C. 10 lb.), 58 tons, 2 cwt. at 32s. . . .			3	4·31		92	19	2				5	8·31		
Sundry Stores, etc. . .				3·79		8	15	0					6·43		
Laboratory . . .				1·52		3	10	0					2·57		
Repairs, etc., as per Schedule .				8·42		19	8	4				1	2·27		
Suspense Account . .				5·26		12	0	0					8·82		
Depreciation . . .			1	5·16		39	11	9				2	5·09		
Proportion of Power, Light, Rates, etc. . . .			9	11·19					274	18	1			16	10·01
3. Moulding Shop.														
Wages : Moulding in Dry Sand . .						150	2	10				9	2·33		
„ „ in Green Sand . .						310	1	4				18	11·85		
„ „ in Loam Sand . .						580	14	5				35	6·74		
„ „ by Machines . .						38	4	5				2	4·09		
Indirect Labour, as per Schedule .						401	1	3				24	6·72		
Repairs, etc., as per Schedule .						249	4	4				15	3·14		
Suspense Account ⎫ Depreciation ⎭ . . .						129	0	0				7	10·79		
Proportion of Power, Light, Rates, etc. . .						145	1	11				8	10·62		
Materials used :														
Sand						40	10	0				2	5·76		
Manure						12	2	10					8·92		
Blacking						13	8	0					9·85		
Coal						6	17	6					5·05		
Plumbago . . .						9	0	4					6·63		
Sprigs, Studs, and Chaplets .						7	11	7					5·57		
Coal Dust						15	0	0					11·02		
Cow Hair						—	—	—					—		
Sundry Stores, etc. . .						19	8	9				1	2·28		
Pattern Shop Direct Charges .						321	6	10				19	8·14		
Percentage of Overhead Expense to Direct Wages .	48·49%													
Total Percentage . .	73·86%								2448	16	4			149	11·50

Carried Forward . . .

277

	Amount.			Total.			Cost per Ton.		Total Cost per Ton.	
	£	s.	d.	£	s.	d.	s.	d.	s.	d.
Brought Forward . .										
4. Core-Making Shop.										
Wages in Moulding Shop ⎱	218	0	2				13	4·20		
„ Core Shop ⎰										
Indirect Labour as per Schedule .	84	0	0				5	1·73		
Repairs, etc., as per Schedule . .	29	13	5				1	9·81		
Suspense Account ⎱ . . .	16	0	0					11·76		
Depreciation ⎰										
Proportion of Power, Light, Rates, etc. .	41	16	2				2	6·72		
Materials Used :										
Sand	38	8	8				2	4·24		
Coal	30	12	0				1	10·49		
Coke	20	5	3				1	2·90		
Straw Ropes . . .	25	5	6				1	6·57		
Wood Wool . . .		11	2					0·41		
Core Gum . . .	3	1	3					2·25		
Core Oil . . .		14	0					0·51		
Rosin	—	—	—							
Wax Wire . . .	1	15	6					1·30		
Sundry Stores, etc. . .	7	0	0					5·14		
Percentage of Overhead Expense to Direct Wages . 40·12%				517	3	1			31	8·03
Total Percentage . . 65·49%										
5. Fettling and Cleaning Shop.										
Wages	114	2	11				6	11·88		
Indirect Labour, as per Schedule . .	22	1	9				1	4·23		
Repairs, etc., as per Schedule . .	8	3	3					6·00		
Suspense Account ⎱ . . .	3	0	0					2·20		
Depreciation ⎰										
Proportion of Power, Light, Rates, etc. .	9	12	8					7·08		
Sundry Materials and Stores . .	2	18	6					2·15		
Percentage of Overhead Expense to Direct Wages . 20·78%				159	19	1			9	9·54
Total Percentage . . 46·15%										
6. Smiths' Shop.										
Direct Wages	19	19	9				1	2·69		
Coke	4	10	0					3·31		
Sundry Stores	1	0	0					0·73		
Iron and Steel (Direct Materials) .	5	2	9					3·78		
Repairs, etc., as per Schedule .	1	12	6					1·19		
Suspense Account ⎱ . . .	1	0	0					0·73		
Depreciation ⎰										
Proportion of Power, Light, Rates, etc. .	6	10	0					4·78		
Percentage of Overhead Expense to Direct Wages . 73·16%				39	15	0			2	5·21
Total Percentage . . 98·53%										
7. General Expense and Establishment Charges.										
Salaries of Manager, Clerks, and Officials	203	14	9				12	5·71		
Salaries of Salesmen and Expenses .	59	7	7				3	7·63		
General Charges (i.e. Directors, Auditors, Law Charges, etc.) .	76	0	0				4	7·85		
Telegrams, Telephones, Stationery, etc. .	24	0	0				1	5·64		
Percentage of General Expense to whole of Direct Wages for Foundry . . . . 25·37%				363	2	4			22	2·83
8. Total Foundry Cost for Unmachined Castings . . . . .£										
Machine Shop.										
Wages : Machining Direct to Customer's Orders										
„ Fitting Direct to Customer's Orders										
„ On Repair Work for Foundry (to Repairs Schedule) . .										
Direct Materials to Customer's Orders .										
Establishment Charges and Overhead Expense to Customer's Orders .										
Establishment Charges and Overhead Expense to Repair Work (to Repairs Schedule)										
Total Foundry Cost . . .£				£4968	19	2			304	3·41

Stock and Production Statement.	Tons.	Cwts.	Qrs.	Lbs.	Rate.	£	s.	d.
Stock of Castings at beginning of Month .	84	2	1	7	300/0·00	1261	14	8
Cost of Good Castings in current Month .	326	11	2	12	304/3·41	4968	19	2
Total	410	13	3	19	303/5·05	6230	13	10
Less Castings in Stock at end of Month	68	9	1	4	300/0·00	1026	19	0
Cost of Castings delivered during Month .	342	4	2	15	304/1·28	£5203	14	10

average cost of overhauls and heavy repairs. The percentages show the relation between the direct and indirect cost of each shop.

The Cost of Jobs.—The data collated and shown in the Summary Cost are the basis for costing any particular job, class-cost, or tonnage cost, that may be required.

A Cost Account for each job is opened in the Cost Ledger (see Fig. 126), and debited with all actual expenditure in wages and material, together with the proper allocation of works over-head, and administration overhead, as indicated by the various percentages and rates ascertained in the Summary Cost Sheet.

Wages.—The job times and wages are recorded and abstracted in the usual manner.

Materials.—Purchases specially made for specific jobs are debited direct, and stores materials from the abstract compiled from requisition issue slips.

The correct charge for iron used requires careful records of mixtures to avoid an average cost per ton. The procedure is as follows : the Foundry Office supplies a return giving the mixture for all special work, for example :

Cylinder, O/No. 2932.
20 per cent. hæmatite iron.
3 per cent. steel.
77 per cent. ordinary foundry iron.

When the iron cost for all the special work has been worked out, then the remainder is common to all other castings made.

An Iron Account for distribution to orders, showing the weight, total cost and cost per ton for each, is illustrated in Fig. 125.

Overhead.—The following bases for distribution to jobs are used :

Cupola Cost.—The total cost of the melting department, as per summary cost, is divided by the total weight of metal

FIG. 125.

Name of Customer or O/No.	Description		Weight Cast.	Weight with Cupola Waste Added.	Hematite Pig. Weight.	Rate	£ s. d.	No. 4 Weight.
	Couplings, Frames	100% Hematite	4 13 1 7½					
			4 13 1 7½	4 18 2 10	4 18 2 10		17 16 4	
	Couplings	33 % Hematite	3 2 3					
	Pistons	57 % Foundry	4 0 16					
	Spur Wheels, etc.	10% Steel	2 6 1 10½					
	Surge Wheels, Flywheels	,,	6 17 3 19					
	Surge Wheels, Rope Pulley	,,	1 17 3 8½					
	Blocks	,,	4 0 7					
	Pulley	,,	1 13					
	Crushers	,,	2 14 2 8					
	Haulages	,,	4 18 0 18					
	Sliding Collar	,,	5 0 0					
	Beds	,,	7 10 2 0					
	Cylinder Covers	,,	3 1					
			27 3 0 20	28 13 3 10	9 11 1 3		34 11 4	
	Firebars	{ 20% Steel / 80% Foundry }	5 14 2 3½					
			5 14 2 3½	6 1 0 0				
	Liners	{ 40% Hematite / 20% Steel / 40% Foundry }	2 14 0 20½					
			2 14 0 20½	2 17 1 0	1 2 3 17		4 2 9	
	Hammer Block	{ 40% Hematite / 25% Steel / 35% Foundry }	1 4 0 0	1 5 1 9	10 0 14		1 16 7	
	Cylinders and Ram	{ 26% Forge 4 / 10% Steel / 64% Foundry }	11 19 1 0	12 12 3 4				3 6 0 21
	Tackle for Loam Moulding	{ 25% Hematite / 75% Foundry }	46 9 0 0	49 1 2 0	2 8 3 1		8 16 2	
	Cradles	{ 25% Hematite / 25% Steel / 50% Forge }	3 4 0 0	3 7 2 14	16 3 17		3 1 1	1 13 3 7
	Pipes	{ 100% All Foundry }	278 17 0 16¼	294 12 1 23				
			341 13 1 16¼					
	Cylinders and Rams	{ 10% Steel / 10% Hematite / 25% Forge / 55% Foundry }	24 18 1 7					
			24 18 1 7	26 6 2 0	2 12 0 0		9 12 0	6 11 2 14
	Weighbridge Plates	{ 20% Hematite / 80% Foundry }	1 8 0 21					
			1 8 0 21	1 9 3 2	6 0 0		1 1 9	
	Crushers	20% Hematite	12 18 3 10					
	Sleeves	5% Steel	6 1 0					
	Haulages	75% Foundry	11 16 0 2					
			25 11 0 12	27 0 0 0	5 8 0 0		19 3 0	
			433 16 0 23½	458 6 2 16	27 14 2 6		100 1 0	11 11 2 14

DISTRIBUTION TO ORDERS

Forge.			Steel Scrap.				Foundry Quality Pig Iron and Scrap Metal.								Total Amount.			Rate per Ton.	
Rate.	£ s. d.		Weight.	Rate.	£ s. d.		Weight.	Rate.	£ s. d.						£ s. d.			s. d.	
															17 16 4				
															17 16 4			76	4·42
															10 8				
															12 6				
															7 0 4				
															20 17 6				
															5 14 7				
															12 4				
															1 1				
															8 5 2				
															14 17 2				
															15 1				
															22 15 6				
															2 4				
			2 17 1 16		6 2 0		16 5 0 19		41 10 11						82 4 3			60	5·63
															14 18 11				
			1 4 0 0		2 11 1		4 17 0 0		12 7 10						14 18 11			52	2·33
															8 5 7				
			11 1 22		1 4 4		1 2 3 17		2 18 6						8 5 7			61	1·48
			6 1 7		13 6		8 3 16		1 2 9						3 12 10			60	8·57
	8 14 10		1 5 1 4		2 13 10		8 1 1 7		20 12 2						32 0 10			53	6·83
			16 3 17		1 16 0		45 15 3 10		117 0 1						127 12 3			54	11·35
	4 9 4						16 3 18		2 3 2						9 13 7			60	5·94
			7 0 5		15 0		294 5 1 18		710 3 9						710 18 9			50	11·87
															883 18 3			51	8·89
															65 13 1				
	17 7 9		2 12 2 15		4 19 6		14 10 0 27		33 13 10						65 13 1			52	8·40
															3 16 11				
							1 3 3 2		2 15 2						3 16 11			54	7·07
															36 19 7				
															17 2				
															32 9 4				
			1 7 0 0		2 11 10		20 5 0 0		48 11 3						70 6 1			55	0·26
	30 11 11		11 8 0 2		23 7 1	407 12 1 22		992 19 5							£1146 19 5			52	10·55

FIG. 126.

FOUNDRY JOB COST ACCOUNT.

Order No. 396. One C. I. Bedplate. Messrs. H. & Y. Jones, London.

Date.	Direct Wages.					Indirect.	Description.	Date Cast.	Materials.					Establishment Charges	Cupola Cost.	Total Cost.
	Moulding.	Core Making.	Fettling.	Moulding Tackle Core Irons.	Direct Labour Assisting Moulders.	Wages Foundry Labour.			Saleable Weight.	Wasters.	Tackle, etc.	Iron Cost.	Moulding and Core-making Materials Cost.			

Notes.—(*a*) Credit is given at the prevailing market price for scrap for wasters and tackle returned to the cupola.
(*b*) Every completed Job cost is posted to a Job Cost Summary and the total of the latter should balance with the Foundry Summary Cost (Fig. 124).

282

poured (Fig. 120).   Each job is debited on the basis of saleable
weight and wasters with its proportion.

Moulding Shop Cost.—Each job is debited with the actual
cost of moulding, and the overhead, at a percentage on direct

FIG. 127.

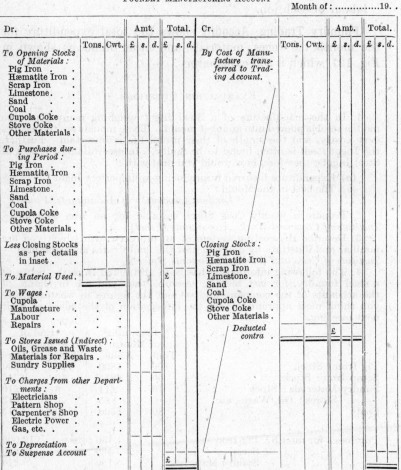

COST LEDGER
FOUNDRY MANUFACTURING ACCOUNT

Month of : ....19. .

Dr.	Tons.	Cwt.	Amt. £	s.	d.	Total. £	s.	d.	Cr.	Tons.	Cwt.	Amt. £	s.	d.	Total. £	s.	d.
To Opening Stocks of Materials :									By Cost of Manufacture transferred to Trading Account.								
Pig Iron .																	
Hæmatite Iron .																	
Scrap Iron .																	
Limestone. .																	
Sand . .																	
Coal . .																	
Cupola Coke .																	
Stove Coke .																	
Other Materials .																	
To Purchases during Period :																	
Pig Iron .																	
Hæmatite Iron .																	
Scrap Iron .																	
Limestone. .																	
Sand . .																	
Coal . .																	
Cupola Coke .																	
Stove Coke .																	
Other Materials .																	
Less Closing Stocks as per details in inset . .									*Closing Stocks :*								
									Pig Iron .								
To Material Used.				£					Hæmatite Iron .								
									Scrap Iron .								
To Wages :									Limestone. .								
Cupola									Sand . .								
Manufacture . . .									Coal . .								
Labour . . .									Cupola Coke .								
Repairs . . .									Stove Coke .								
									Other Materials .								
To Stores Issued (Indirect) :									*Deducted contra* .				£				
Oils, Grease and Waste .																	
Materials for Repairs . .																	
Sundry Supplies . .																	
To Charges from other Departments :																	
Electricians . . .																	
Pattern Shop . .																	
Carpenter's Shop . .																	
Electric Power . . .																	
Gas, etc. . . .																	
To Depreciation . .																	
To Suspense Account .				£													

labour in moulding, as per the Summary Cost.   In the case
of cored castings, the core-making cost is similarly arrived at.

Pattern Shop Charge is distributed on an actual cost basis
to every job where pattern-making is involved.

Fettling and Cleaning expense is applied on a tonnage

basis, excepting in the few cases where a direct charge can be made.

Smiths' Forgings.—The overhead is applied as a percentage on direct labour, as shown in the Summary Cost.

Administration.—Expense is charged by the percentage rate, as per the Summary Cost, on the *whole* of the direct labour of each job.

Foundry Trading Account shows the total expenditure for the month on wages, materials, and other items as shown in Fig. 127, which is self-explanatory.

EXAMINATION QUESTIONS

1. In the manufacture of a Steel Ingot weighing many tons, the molten steel is poured into an ingot mould. These moulds are themselves very costly, and the length of their useful life is uncertain. Further, the Ingot itself is often found to be faulty. In ascertaining the cost of Steel Ingots, therefore, how would you deal with :

    (a) Expenditure incurred in producing an imperfect Ingot;
    (b) The cost of the Mould ?

               London Association of Accountants (Final).

2. Prepare a weekly Cost Sheet suitable for an iron foundry.—*Institute of Costs and Works Accountants (Final).*

3. Describe the costing system of an industry with which you are familiar and illustrate by diagram how the final figures are assembled.—*Institute of Costs and Works Accountants (Inter.).*

4. The following information has been abstracted from the books of a steel foundry, for last month. Assume that you are in charge of the accounts of the company and set out the figures in whatever way you think most appropriate, for the information of the board at their next meeting.

	Beginning of Month.		End of Month.	
	Tons.	Value.	Tons.	Value.
Pig Iron : Stock	100	£800	120	£1,000
Scrap Iron : Stock . . .	50	£275	40	£245
Sundry Materials : Stock . .	10	£11	8	£10
,, Stores : Oil, Waste, etc. .	—	£5	—	£12
Coal	80	£300	40	£115

		£
Purchases for month : Pig Iron . . .	1,450 tons	12,000
,, ,, ,, Scrap ,, . . .	490 ,, .	2,940
,, ,, ,, Sundry Materials . .	150 ,, .	210
,, ,, ,, ,, Stores	.	100
Wages : Works	.	7,840
,, Office	.	120
Travellers : Salary and Expenses	.	210
Coal Purchases : Works	630 tons	1,890
,, used in Offices	.	20
Power and Light : Works	.	650
Office Lighting	.	25

		£
Repairs : Works		487
Depreciation : Works		840
Additions to Buildings		45
„ „ Machinery and Plant		530
Gas, Water, etc. : Works		76
Rent and Rates : Works		725
„ „ „ Offices		25
Sales : Scrap and Sundries	100 tons .	500
„ Castings	1,850 „ .	29,600

London Chamber of Commerce.

5. How would you deal with the case of Patterns in your cost accounts ?—*Institute of Cost and Works Accountants (Inter.).*

6. In an Iron Foundry producing medium weight Castings, the piece-work rates of Wages paid for each operation are adopted as the measure of the Oncost in each department. The piece-work rates applicable to a certain Casting are :

	s.	d.
Moulding	15	0
Core-making	3	0
Dressing	2	0

and the Oncost rates are :

Moulding	80%
Core-making	50%
Dressing	33⅓%

The weight of this Casting when moulded is 1 cwt., but in the dressing operation it loses 4 lbs. of its weight. Its selling price is invoiced " per cwt." and the cost of Selling, Delivery and General Administration is 2s. 4d. per cwt., calculated on the weight sold. Calculate the selling price of this Casting per cwt., after providing for :

7s. per cwt. for melted metal cost.
Loss in weight above mentioned.
10 per cent. profit on total cost.

Ignore scrap value of metal produced by the dressing operation.—*London Association of Accountants (Final).*

7. Enumerate the items which would go to make up Oncost in a Foundry, and explain two methods of allocating these charges.—*Society of Incorporated Accountants and Auditors (Inter.).*

8. Prepare a detailed Cost Sheet, with figures, in relation to any manufactured article with which you are familiar, and explain the basis on which you have arrived at the proportion of Oncost expenses.—*Society of Incorporated Accountants and Auditors (Inter.).*

9. How would you propose to cost the products of a brass foundry where castings are made that vary considerably as regards weight, intricacy and mixture of virgin and scrap metals ?—*Institute of Cost and Works Accountants (Inter.).*

10. Assume that it is the policy of a certain brass foundry to make monthly purchases of copper. The market rates have fallen :

	Per ton.
April, 1929	£105
June, 1929	20
May, 1930	55
September, 1930	45

How would you propose to price withdrawals from store for manufacture carried out during the period in question ?   State on what basis you assume selling prices to be determined.—*Institute of Cost and Works Accountants (Inter.).*

11. Set out a form of final cost for a product with the manufacture of which you are familiar, and give as much detail as possible.—*Institute of Cost and Works Accountants (Inter.).*

12. How would you charge out the expenditure incurred in the Pattern Shop ?—*Institute of Cost and Works Accountants (Final).*

13. A certain works contains a Foundry, Power House, Pattern Shop, Tool Room and three distinct Machining and Erection Shops.   You are requested to advise the management upon the distribution of expense. How will you proceed ?—*Institute of Cost and Works Accountants (Final).*

12. The following are some of the main items of overhead expenditure of a foundry :

> General labour for firing, carrying, etc. ;
> Examiners ;
> Supervision ;
> Coke for melting metal and drying moulds ;
> Crucibles for melting metal ;
> Sand for making moulds.

From the nature of the work it is impracticable to record times of the various operations other than those of moulding, core making and trimming.

In these circumstances on what bases would you propose to recover the overheads in the cost of the castings made ?—*Institute of Cost and Works Accountants (Inter.).*

13. How would you distribute overheads in the case of a foundry producing a variety of large and small castings ?—*Institute of Cost and Works Accountants (Inter.).*

14. An iron foundry makes heavy castings in loam, castings from patterns and machine-made castings.   Describe a system of costing suitable for such work.—*Institute of Cost and Works Accountants (Final).*

15. Give a list of General Expenses for one of the following industries, showing in columns, without figures, which of them relate to (a) Works Overhead, (b) Distribution and Selling, (c) General Administration :—Iron Foundry ; Motor Works ; Food Factory ; Soap Works ; Printing Works. —*Institute of Cost and Works Accountants (Final).*

16. In many industries the making of costly patterns or, in other cases, dies, is necessary before production of an article can take place. The effect of this initial expense upon the cost of producing the article depends upon the quantity of articles likely to be required.   How would you deal with this factor of cost—

> (a) In preparing estimates of the cost of any particular article ?
> (b) In determining the Oncost expense of the Department making use of the pattern or dies ?

Patterns frequently require to be repaired or altered after use.   How would you deal with this expense in preparing the required information under (a) and (b) ?—*London Association of Certified Accountants (Final).*

CHAPTER XXII

OPERATING COSTS

Unit Cost of Services.—Undertakings engaged in rendering services may be divided into two groups :

(a) Various forms of transport of goods and/or passengers.

(b) Public utility concerns, supplying a service, such as water, electricity or gas.

This method of costing is different from that used in connection with production manufacturing, but may apply to some forms of factory services. The difference lies chiefly in the manner of assembling the cost data, and in its allocation to cost units. A brief description of the costing for various kinds of undertakings falling within the above groups will suffice to demonstrate the procedure.

(1) MOTOR TRANSPORT COSTS

The Purpose.—The records are desired to show the total cost of operating each vehicle, and then to apply this cost to particular units. For example, it may be desired to know the cost per mile, per ton, per passenger, or the cost per ton-mile, per passenger-mile, per parcel-mile, etc.

The costs so ascertained are useful for :

(a) Comparison between the cost of using motor vehicles owned, and that of using other types of transport, either owned, or hired.

(b) Determining what should be charged against departments, or others, using the service.

(c) Determining at what price the use of a vehicle can be charged, profitably, to anyone hiring a vehicle.

(d) Comparing the cost of maintaining and running one vehicle with that of another of the same type and capacity.

The Collection of Data.—The following procedure is that followed by a large business, employing a fleet of **twenty motor vehicles.**

A daily Report Card is supplied for each car, stating in the space provided at the head of the card (see Fig. 128) the Vehicle No., driver's name, date, route, and time of departure.

At the foot are recorded details of :

(a) Petrol, oil, and other supplies provided by the garage.

(b) Time spent on the car for washing, cleaning, and attending to minor adjustments by the mechanics.

(c) The times of signing on and off by the driver and his assistant.

FIG. 128.

DAILY RECORD CARD

Vehicle No. :				Date : ....19...			
Driver :				Time left Garage :			
Route No. :				Time returned :			
			Trip Record.				
Trip No.	From	To	Tons or Packages.		Miles.	Time.	
			Out.	Collected en route.		Out.	In.
1 2 3 4 5 6 etc.							
		Totals					

Supplies.	Workers' Time.	Exceptional Delays.
Petrol :	Driver :	Loading delays : ......
Oil :	Assistant :	Traffic delays : ....
Grease :	Cleaners :	Accidents : ....
etc.	Mechanics :	

Space is provided for the driver, or dispatch clerk, to enter details as to the trips made and the number of packages taken, or the weight. From the speedometer readings, the number of miles run on each trip is recorded, and the time out and in for each trip is entered.

Repairs and adjustments required may be noted by the driver on the back of the card. The particulars of the repairs, etc., are recorded by the garage mechanics on repair tickets, or on the back of the card, and the office costs the work.

The cards are exchanged daily, the completed ones being sent to the Cost Office, where the data are tabulated on analysis sheets; a separate sheet is kept for each car. At the end of the month, the totals of the analysis sheets are transferred to a Monthly Cost Summary for each car.

The Cost Summary.—The Cost Summary for each car will contain the following analysis of expense (Fig. 129), and the cost and performance statement (Fig. 130).

Fig. 129.

MONTHLY CHARGES

Car No. 19.   Month ended February, 19...

A. Operating Charges.				B. Maintenance Charges.			
	£	s.	d.		£	s.	d.
Petrol				Tyres . . .			
Oil				Repairs . . .			
Grease . . .				Overhaul . . .			
etc. . .				Spare Car . . .			
Driver . . .				Garage Charge . .			
Assistant . . .				etc. . . .			
Mechanics . .							
Total . .	52	12	5	Total . .	6	15	3

C. Fixed Charges.				Proportion for Month.		
				£	s.	d.
Insurance at £...... per year						
Interest at .... % ,, ...						
Depreciation at .... % ,, ...						
Tax, licence at £...... ,, ...						
Other items at £...... ,, ...						
Total				8	12	4

Notes on Transport Costs.—The costs are divided, as shown in Fig. 130, into three sections, namely, Operating Charges, Maintenance Charges, and Fixed Charges.

Operating and Running Costs.—These vary from day to day, and are incurred by the actual operation of the vehicle; expenses which would not be incurred if the vehicle were placed in storage come under the general head of operating expenses, *e.g.* petrol, oil, wages, etc.

Maintenance Charges.—These include wear on tyres, repairs, and overhauls, painting, hire of spare vehicles when cars are under repair, garage rental, etc.

Y

Fixed Charges.—These are incurred whether a car is operating or not. They include insurance, depreciation, interest and tax.

The Ton-Mile.—Two understandings of the unit ton-mile are in use at the present time. These are known as the " abso-

Fig. 130.

MOTOR TRANSPORT COSTS.

Monthly Cost Sheet.

No. of Car : 19.   Month of February, 19...

Capacity in lbs. : ....   Chassis No. : ....

1. Total Capital cost, complete	£1123·95
Performance Record.	
2. Days operated	26
3. Days idle	4
4. Days maintained (Item 2 + Item 3) . . .	30
5. Total hours operated	232
6. Total miles covered	803
7. Total trips made	28
8. Total tons or packages or stops or passengers . .	2792
Performance Averages.	
9. Average miles per day maintained (Item 6 ÷ Item 4) .	26·76
10. Average miles per day operated (Item 6 ÷ Item 2) .	30·88
11. Average miles per trip (Item 6 ÷ Item 7) . .	28·67
12. Average tons, stops or packages per trip (Item 8 ÷ Item 7)	99·7
13. Average commercial ton miles, package miles or stop-miles per trip $\dfrac{(\text{Item } 11 \times \text{Item } 12)}{2}$	1429·20
Costs for the Month.	
14. Total expenses for month (Sum of Items A, B, and C in fig. 129)	£68
15. Cost per day operated (Item 14 ÷ Item 2) . .	£2·61
16. Cost per day maintained (Item 14 ÷ Item 4) . .	£2·27
17. Cost per mile operated (Item 14 ÷ Item 6) . .	1s. 8·3d.
18. Total commercial ton-miles, package-miles or stop-miles (Item 7 × Item 13)	40,017·6
19. Cost per commercial ton-mile, package-mile or stop-mile (Item 14 ÷ Item 18)	0·46d.

Note.—For passenger vehicles substitute " passengers " for " tons," etc.

lute " ton-mile and the " commercial " ton-mile. The absolute ton-mile may be defined as the carrying of a mass of 1 ton over a distance of 1 mile. The absolute ton-mile takes into consideration the number of tons hauled, and the distances over which all, or portions of the load, were carried. For instance, if a vehicle started from some certain point with a load of 5 tons and travelled 2 miles, it would have accomplished 5 × 2=10 absolute ton-miles of work. If, at the 2-mile point, the vehicle had

delivered 1 ton, leaving 4 tons of load, which it delivered 3 miles
farther along on the route, the absolute ton-mileage would have
been $3 \times 4 = 12$. If it then returned empty over the 5 miles to
the starting point, the absolute ton-mileage of this portion
of the trip would have been $5 \times 0 = 0$. The total ton-mileage
of the entire trip is the summation of the number of work units
accomplished on each portion, or $10 + 12 + 0 = 22$ absolute
ton-miles.

The Commercial Ton-Mile.—The calculation of the absolute
ton-miles is too inconvenient to make when a car takes a load
which is delivered in portions at different points upon the route;
and even more so if goods are also picked up en route. Therefore, a more simple system has been devised, known as the
Commercial Ton-Mile. This commercial ton-mile is obtained
by multiplying the tonnage carried on any trip by the mileage
of that trip divided by 2. This is a very simple operation
containing only one multiplication.

Example.—A car leaves with a load of 5 tons, travels 15
miles, delivers the load, and returns empty.

Absolute Ton-Miles $= (5 \times 15) + (0 \times 15) = 75$.
Commercial Ton-Miles $= (5 \times 30) \div 2 = 75$.

The ton-mileage must recognise the trip. This requires that
we define the meaning of the word "trip." A trip in most
cases means the operation of a car starting from any given point
until it again returns to that point for another load. In some
cases, a trip may consume a full day, or in overland haulage
work, 2 or 3 days. Perhaps the bearing of the trip upon the
ton-mileage performed by any car during any given trip may best
be expressed by an example, in order to prove that commercial
ton-mileage cannot be obtained by simply multiplying the tonnage hauled in a day by the mileage covered in a day. Suppose
a car makes two trips, as in the above example. The total
commercial ton-miles would be: $75 \times 2 = 150$. If, on the
other hand, an attempt were made to multiply the tonnage
carried per order to obtain the ton-mileage, the error of this
method is evident because the false ton-mileage would be (5 plus
5 equals 10) $\times$ (30 plus 30 equals 60), with a total of 600 ton-
miles, or 4 times the proper commercial ton-mileage.

The commercial ton-mile gives no error when loads are delivered in one lot, and only a comparatively small ratio of error

where cars are used for delivering and collecting at points during a trip.

Recovery of Transport Department Costs may be made by charging to departments or orders on such bases as (a) a calculated rate per hour per vehicle, (b) a rate per vehicle mile, (c) use of standard load rates. The standard load is the maximum load for articles of each department having regard to bulk and weight. Thus Dept. X goods, 1 load = 2 tons; Dept. Y 1 load = 3 tons, *i.e.* ratio 2 : 3. If total weights carried for X and Y are 1500 tons and 500 tons, *i.e.* ratio 3 : 1, then charges to the Departments would be $\left\{\begin{matrix} 2:3 \\ 3:1 \end{matrix}\right\}$ multiplied = 6 : 3, *i.e.* 2 : 1 or $\frac{2}{3}$ the total transport cost is charged to X and $\frac{1}{3}$ to Y.

Motor Transport Cost Ledger Accounts.—The abbreviated specimen cost accounts and summaries, Figs. 131 to 137, illustrate the procedure for recording the detailed costs. Fig. 138 is a specimen Job Repair Cost Sheet. These accounts and summaries are self-explanatory.

Fig. 136.

QUARTERLY COST SURVEY

(N.B.—Quarterly totals for group posted to Group Cost Survey.)

Class B.

Vehicle.	Repairs.			Running Charges.			Standing.			Total.			Mileage.
	£	s.	d.	£	s.	d.	£	s.	d.	£	s.	d.	
B26	138	4	6	146	4	7	51	4	6	335	13	7	6167
B27	34	4	11	253	2	9	51	4	6	338	12	2	7943
B28	100	18	9	137	3	1	51	4	6	289	6	4	4841
	£1315	9	0	£2250	6	0	£1100	0	9	£4665	15	9	90,419

TRADING ACCOUNT							
	£	s.	d.		£	s.	d.
To Charges for Quarter .	4665	15	9	By Balance brought forward	165	0	0
,, Balance carried forward .	20	3	3	,, 40,419 miles at 1s. .	4520	19	0
	£4685	19	0		£4685	19	0

(2) COSTS OF RAILWAYS AND TRAMWAYS

The expenses are analysed under such headings as :

Power Supply ; locomotives, fuel, oil, repairs.
Maintenance :
(a) Permanent way, its upkeep and renewals ;
(b) Buildings, *e.g.* offices, sheds, stations, repairs shop expense, stores, etc. ;
(c) Rolling Stock, repairs to carriages or cars, axles and wheels, motors and controllers, lighting equipment.   (*Contd. p.* 296.)

Fig. 131.

RUNNING COST LEDGER ACCOUNT.

Vehicle No. 93.
Class A.

Date.	Refs.	Miles.	Gallons.	M.p.g.	Petrol. £ s. d.	Tyres and Tubes. £ s. d.	Lubricants. £ s. d.	Driver's Wages. £ s. d.	Service Overheads.	Miscellaneous.	Total. £ s. d.
19...											
April 2	1276	140	14	10·0	14 0						14 0
	D 1							2 10 0			2 10 0
6	41164					4 14 6					4 14 6
9	1277	160	16	10·0	16 0						16 0
9	D 2							3 0 0			3 0 0
12	31847						2 6				2 6
16	D 3							2 15 1			2 15 1
etc.	1278	150	15	10·0	15 0						15 0

Fig. 132.

STANDING CHARGES COST LEDGER ACCOUNT.

Vehicle No. 93.
Class A.

Date.	Ref.	Capital Value. £ s. d.	Depreciation = 5% per Qr. £ s. d.	Interest 1¼% per Qr. £ s. d.	Licence. £ s. d.	Insurance. £ s. d.	Garage. £ s. d.	Miscellaneous. £ s. d.	Total. £ s. d.
19...									
Jan. 16	L.11				20 0 0				20 0 0
Jan. 17	J.16					14 0 0			14 0 0
Mar. 31	D.1	500 0 0	25 0 0	6 15 0					31 10 0

Note.—Accounts as above are kept for each vehicle.

FIG. 133.

REPAIR COST LEDGER ACCOUNT

Vehicle 224
Class D.

Depot.	Date.	Works Order.	Hours. Power.	Hours. Total.	Days at Works.	Wages. £ s. d.	Overheads. £ s. d.	Materials. £ s. d.	Depot Mechanic's Wages. £ s. d.	Break-down Service. £ s. d.	Sub-Total. £ s. d.	Credit Re-covered. £ s. d.	A/c. No.	Total. £ s. d.
Fulham	19.. April 2 June 19 July 27	1,167	70	740	68	65 10 10	65 10 10	74 4 8	4 1 3 2 1 6	4 .. 10	209 16 4 4 1 3 2 1 6	4 4 0 .. 10 0	143 187	
	30.6.32		70	740	68	65 10 10	65 10 10	74 4 8	6 2 9	4 .. 10	215 19 1	4 10 0		£211 9 1

FIG. 134.

VEHICLE COST SUMMARY.

Vehicle A116.

Quarter.	Repairs. £ s. d.	Running. £ s. d.	Standing Charges. £ s. d.	Total. £ s. d.	Mileage.	Rate per Mile. s. d.	Amount Recovered. £ s. d.	Profit. £ s. d.	Loss. £ s. d.
19.. March	138 14 6	146 4 7	51 4 6	338 3 7	6234	1 0	311 14 0		26 9 7
June	34 4 4	256 18 4	50 8 3	341 11 4	8246	1 0	412 6 0	70 14 8	

Note.—Accounts as the two above are kept for each vehicle.

FIG. 135.

GROUP COST SUMMARY.

Group C.

Quarter.	Mileage.	Repairs. £ s. d.	Cost per Mile.	Running Costs. £ s. d.	Cost per Mile.	Standing Charges. £ s. d.	Cost per Mile.	Total. £ s. d.	Cost per Mile.
19.. March	549,672	8,264 19 2	3·61	14,846 18 8	6·48	6,847 1 11	2·99	29,958 19 9	13·08
June	617,849	7,969 1 7	3·09	16,163 12 6	6·28	7,794 18 8	2·64	30,927 12 9	12·01

A group cost of several cars which are alike.

Fig. 137.

LEDGER ACCOUNTS
Quarter ended March 31st, 19......
Paint Account

19... Mar. 31	To Paint Materials, Painters' Tools, etc.	£ 147	s. 7	d. 9	19... Jan. 1	By Balance brought forward	£ 21	s. 6	d. 6
"	" Balance carried forward		19	0	Mar. 31	" Charges recovered: 3387 hrs. at 9d.	127	0	3
		£148	6	9			£148	6	9

Breakdown Service Account

19... Mar. 31	To Sundry Charges	£ 46	s. 16	d. 7	19... Jan. 1	By Balance brought forward	£ 6	s. 1	d. 7
"	" Balance carried forward	9	6	8	Mar. 31	" Charges recovered: Vehicle A/c.: £ s. d. A119 . 4 10 0 B76 . 3 0 0 Etc.	50	1	8
		£56	3	3			£56	3	3

Labour Charges Account

19... Mar. 31	To Holidays	£ 400	s. 0	d. 0	19... Jan. 1	By Balance brought forward	£ 106	s. 18	d. 4
"	" Sickness	560	16	7	Mar. 31	" Charges recovered: 147,164 hrs. at 3d.	1839	11	0
"	" Supervision	260	14	4					
"	" Pensions	308	8	1					
"	" Insurance	320	16	6					
"	" Balance carried forward	95	13	10					
		£1946	9	4			£1946	9	4

FIG. 138.

MOTOR REPAIR JOB COST SHEET

WAGES.						Vehicle : A119.		Date : 2.4.32.	
Trade.	Hrs.	At.	£	s.	d.	Date Received. 2.4.32.	Date into Service. 8.6.32.	Days at Works. 68	

Trade	Hrs.	At. (s. d.)	£	s.	d.
Mechanical Section :					
Charge Hand	20	2 3	2	5	0
Mechanic	180	2 0	18	0	0
Fitter	220	1 8	18	6	8
Labourer	100	1 4	6	13	4
Coach Section :					
Coachbuilder	80	2 0½	8	3	4
Trimmer	30	2 1	3	2	6
Labourer	40	1 3¾	2	12	6
Paint Section :					
Painter	40	2 0	4	0	0
Brush Hand	30	1 7	2	7	6
	740		£65	10	10

WORKS ORDER 1167.
Top Overhaul and Repaint. Est. 762.

	£	s.	d.
Labour	65	10	10
Overhead (100%)	65	10	10
Materials: £ s. d.			
Repairs Stores 71 12 2			
70 Hours Paint at 9d. . 2 12 6	74	4	8
Breakdown Gang : 4½ hours at £1 per hour	4	10	0
	£209	16	4

T. GREEN, *Engr. Supt.*

If a scheduled classification is drawn up, suitable Standing Order Nos. may be used. The Wages Analysis Sheets can be ruled to correspond with those for other expenses.

The statistics which are prepared show the following data for the current period, and a comparison with the same particulars in other periods corresponding :

Car-Miles.	*Passengers.*	*Goods.*
Number run.	Expenditure per person carried.	Cost per ton-mile.
Number per hour.		Number of tons carried.
Expenditure per car-mile.	Receipts per person carried.	Weight per mile.
Receipts per car-mile.	Number carried at each fare (1*d.*, 2*d.*, 3*d.*, etc.).	Etc.
	Cost per 100-seat mile.	

Comparative Cost Statements.—The method of summarising total costs for a period is shown in Fig. 139, which relates to Electric Tramway Costs, Fig. 140, Boiler House Costs, and on pages 394 and 395, Municipal Services.

(3) BOILER-HOUSE COSTS

The necessary statistics for arriving at the cost of steam produced and used are based on accounts prepared by the Cost Office and technical data provided by the Engineering Department as to steam pressures, evaporations, meter readings, and distribution to processes, factory heating, turbines, losses, etc.

Boiler-House Expenses.—The expenses may be considered under the following headings :

Supervision.—Wages of foreman, and a proportion of the Works engineer's salary.

Labour.—Coal handling, stokers, and ash removers.

Maintenance.—Repair labour wages and materials. Furnace repairs, replacement of fire irons, grate bars, etc.

Indirect Materials.—Boiler-house service materials and small tools.

Fuel.—Cost of coal, including cartage, handling from waggons or barges, stacking and storage. The Engineering Department calculates the amount of coal needed for the operating hours for a given period, and issues purchase requisitions and specification. The purchase cost is notified to the Cost Office, and, from daily returns of coal consumed, the debit for each costing period is ascertained.

Fig. 139.

ELECTRIC TRAMWAY COSTS

For the month ended : ....19...

Items.	Amount.			Per Car Mile, or 100-Seat Mile.*					
				This Year.			Last Year.		
	£	s.	d.	£	s.	d.	£	s.	d.
Power-Generation :—									
Wages and Salaries									
Fuel									
Stores Materials									
Maintenance and Repairs—									
Buildings									
Steam Plant									
Dynamos, etc.									
Accumulators									
Sundry Expenses									
Total									
Power-Purchased (if any)									
Total									
Power-Distribution :—									
Wages and Salaries									
Stores									
Maintenance and Repairs									
Plant									
Cables									
Other items									
Total									
Operating Expenses :—									
Salaries									
Wages—Inspectors									
Clerks, etc.									
Drivers, etc.									
Track, etc.									
Stores									
General Expenses									
Total									
Buildings :—									
Wages									
Stores									
Total									
Permanent Way :—									
Wages and Salaries									
Maintenance									
Renewals									
Total									
Cars and Equipment :—									
Wages									
Repairs									
Stores									
Total									
Grand Total for month									

* N.B.—Additional unit cost columns, such as " Per Passenger," or " Per Passenger Mile " may be added.

Water.—Cost of supply softening plant and purification. Any chemical purifiers may be included in this cost.

Fixed Overhead.—Rent, rates, depreciation, insurance, and interest, if included. It should be noted here that the capital value of the boiler-house plant is included in the rating

FIG. 140.

BOILER-HOUSE COST SHEET

For the month of June 19...

S.O. Nos.	Expense items.	Total Cost.		Cost per 1000 lbs. of Steam.				Incr. or decr. %.
		This Year.	Last Year.	This Year.		Last Year.		
		£	£	s.	d.	s.	d.	
	Fuel							
	„ Handling							
	Ash Removal and Disposal							
	Electric Power							
	Stokers and Coal Wheelers							
	Water Purchased							
	„ Softening							
	Boiler Cleansing							
	Sundry Indirect Materials							
	Gas and Electric Light							
	Maintenance Services :							
	Fixed Plant							
	Meters							
	Boilers							
	Economisers							
	Softening Plant							
	Mechanical Stokers							
	Steam Service Pipes							
	Barrows							
	Weighing Machine, Tools, etc.							
	Coal Bunkers							
	Furnace							
	Miscellaneous Expenses :							
	Supervision							
	Sweepers, Cleaners and General Labour							
	Rent, Rates, etc.							
	Depreciation Plant							
	„ Buildings							
	Renewals							
	Steam Mains							
	Allocation of General Charges							
	Total							

Steam Produced in 1000's lbs. : ......   Less Boiler House Use : ......   Less Mains Losses : ......   Total Consumption : ......

Remarks :

assessment, whereas that in manufacturing machinery is not. This must be borne in mind when apportioning rates as between shops, and departments, and boiler house.

Statistical Reports by Engineer.—Daily returns as to boiler operations are required, such as the hours in use for each boiler, temperature readings, pressures, coal consumption in lbs., steam produced in lbs., evaporation per lb. of coal fired, average flow of steam in lbs. per hour, the head of steam in B.T.U., water consumption, departmental consumption as per gauges, meters, or estimates, etc.

Cost Sheets.—A Monthly Cost Sheet, showing boiler-house costs in total, and per 1000 lbs. of steam, is prepared. (Fig. 140.)

A Coal Stock Card or Record for the month showing the weight and cost of deliveries to the works, withdrawals for use, and showing balance on hand, is required.

The Cost of Coal and Ash Handling may form the matter for a separate Cost Return as shown in Fig. 141.

Fig. 141.

COAL AND ASH COST STATEMENT

1. Coal.	Tons.	Price.	Amount.		
			£	s.	d.
Coal at Works					
Unloading Charges					
Storing ,, ...					
Crushing ,, ...					
Conveying ,, ...					
Cost at Boilers					
2. Ash.					
Conveying from Furnaces . . .					
Disposal					
Cost					

Allocation of Steam Cost.—This is usually based on technical data of consumption supplied by the engineer. Separate consumption returns for factory heating and process work per department should be provided. Important processes may use many thousands of lbs. of steam per hour, others but a few thousands per day. Meters may be used, but they are expensive and complicated to use and are used only when there is large consumption.

A simple system is to ascertain by technical calculation the *rate of steam consumption* in lbs. per hour in normal use for each consuming appliance connected with mains and service pipes. A record is kept of the times during which each unit is consuming steam. From this, by applying the consumption rate per hour a reasonably reliable record for steam allocation is obtained. A basis of charging for potential use, as well as consumption, is sometimes adopted, *e.g.* one method is to base a minimum charge for standing expense and another for quantity consumed, applying the charges as for a two-part tariff. See also pp. 135, 235, and Fig. 105.

EXAMINATION QUESTIONS

1. A large Store maintains a fleet of motor lorries for delivery purposes. Prepare a statement showing the costs of working in the manner in which, as Accountant to the Company, you would present these to the Board. You may supply for the purpose any figures or other information you think necessary.—*London Chamber of Commerce.*

2. A Department Store maintains a fleet of ten motor vans for its delivery service. On investigation you find the facts to be as follows :

> The average cost of the vans was £1000 each.
> Wages on vans amount to £4 10s. per week per van.
> Total Garage Rent, Rates, Heating, etc., are £390 per annum.
> Total Garage Wages are £200 per annum.
> Repairs to vans cost £1250 per annum.
> Depreciation 20 per cent. per annum.
> Tyres are dealt with by contractors at a cost of £50 per annum per van.
> Petrol costs £1100 per annum for the fleet.
> Oil and Stores cost £600 per annum.
> Insurance, all risks, for the fleet £200 per annum.
> Licences £550 per annum.

The average run of each van is 350 miles per week. For the purpose of this question it may be assumed that total costs can be allocated equally over the ten vans.

State your views as to the periodical returns of working which should be submitted to the Management, and, from the information given, draft the first of such returns.—*London Chamber of Commerce.*

3. A company owns ten motor omnibuses running on five different routes in the same city. The Management wish to have a weekly statement of working, and, in particular, wish to consider whether or not it would pay them to withdraw the buses from certain routes.

Prepare, supplying yourself any figures necessary, the statement for last week, and indicate the sources from which, in practice, you would obtain the figures.

Would you make any, and if so what, use of a chart or charts in this case ?—*London Chamber of Commerce.*

4. What system of Costing is usually adopted, and for what reasons, in the following :

> Railway Companies;
> Gas and Power Undertakings;
> Hospitals ?
> > *Society of Incorporated Accountants and Auditors* (*Final*).

5. In Railways, etc., it is usual to work out:

(*a*) The cost per mile run. Draft an abstract, using imaginary figures, giving the average cost per mile.

(*b*) To what use are the figures put for standardisation purposes?—*Society of Incorporated Accountants and Auditors (Final)*.

6. Show, with as much information as possible, a cost sheet of a motor transport company handling passenger and goods traffic, using petrol or steam vehicles, or both.—*Institute of Cost and Works Accountants (Final)*.

7. A transport company owning and operating passenger and goods vehicles runs services as follows:

(*a*) Steam lorries for goods only—long distance.
(*b*) Petrol charabancs for passengers—long distance.
(*c*) Petrol buses for combined goods and passengers—short distance.

In what form would you present cost sheets for the above?—*Institute of Cost and Works Accountants (Final)*.

8. Show a *pro forma* cost sheet for a power plant in an industrial works and suggest, in the absence of meters, how the cost of power should be allocated departmentally.—*Institute of Cost and Works Accountants (Final)*.

9. State the advantages and disadvantages of using the following units for comparing the operating costs of road transport:

Per ton.
Per mile.
Per ton-mile.

Institute of Cost and Works Accountants (Inter.).

10. Describe briefly how you would allocate the overhead expenses in the cost of a large road transport company.—*Institute of Cost and Works Accountants (Inter.)*.

11. On what basis would you prepare the costs of a road transport business using different types of vehicles, carrying different kinds of loads to a variety of destinations, sometimes returning empty and sometimes bringing back return loads; assuming the management must be furnished with means of comparing the relative cost and efficiency of the different types of vehicle?—*Institute of Cost and Works Accountants (Final)*.

12. The Excelsior Delivery Company operates a fleet of motor vehicles. Prepare a Statement showing the cost per mile for the month of April, 1933, from the following particulars, viz.:—

	£	s.	d.
Wages for month	100	0	0
Petrol used for month	70	0	0
Oil, etc., used for month	8	11	8
Original cost of vehicles on April 1st, 1931 . .	2000	0	0
Depreciation at 25 per cent. per annum on diminishing value to be written off.			
Miles run during month, 20,000			
Repairs during year ended March 31st, 1933 . .	312	0	0
Tyres, Tubes, etc., during year ended March 31st, 1933	240	0	0
Licences, Insurance, etc., during year ended March 31st, 1933	252	0	0
Garage Rent and Rates during year ended March 31st, 1933	156	0	0
General Expenses during year ended March 31st, 1933	480	0	0

Corporation of Accountants (Final).

13. A Motor Haulage Contractor submits the following information for the month of September, 1933, regarding one of his Motor Lorries, and desires to know—

(1) The average miles per day operated; (2) The average miles per trip; (3) The average tons per trip; (4) The average commercial-ton miles per trip, and (5) The total commercial ton-miles for the month.

Days maintained, 30; days operated, 25; days idle, 5; total miles covered, 1250; total trips made, 35; total hours operated, 130; total tons conveyed, 198.—*Corporation of Accountants (Final).*

CHAPTER XXIII

OPERATING COSTS (*continued*)

(4) ELECTRICITY SUPPLY COSTING

THE cost of operating an Electricity Supply Undertaking can be considered under two main heads :

1. The generation or production of the electrical energy.
2. The distribution of this from the power station to the consumer.

It will be convenient to deal with each portion separately.

Uniform Costing for Generation.—The passing of the Electricity (Supply) Act, 1926, and the subsequent setting up of the Central Electricity Board, have resulted in the Electricity Supply Industry adopting, so far as the production side is concerned, a uniform method of costing. The Board can be regarded as an administrative organisation, charged with the duty of supplying to authorised undertakers at cost price, in accordance with the provisions of a scheme prepared by the Electricity Commissioners. The owners of a generating station, if selected for the purpose, are to operate the station as, and when, the Board may direct, and to conduct such operations with due regard to economy and efficiency. They must sell to the Board all electricity generated at the station, the price paid by the Board being the cost of production.

Official Cost of Production Rules.—The Second Schedule of the Act enumerates the rules for determining the cost of production as follows :

(*a*) The sums expended for fuel, oil, water, and stores consumed, for salaries and wages, and any contributions for pensions, superannuation and insurance of officers and servants, for repairs and maintenance of buildings and plant, and for renewals not chargeable to capital account;

(*b*) Sums paid as rents, rates and taxes (other than taxes on profits), and for insurance in respect of the station;

301

(c) The proper proportion of management and general establishment charges of the station;

(d) Any other expenses on revenue account attributable to the station;

(e) Interest (exclusive of interest payable out of capital) on money properly expended for capital purposes of the Generating Station and the plant suitable to, and used for, the purpose of generating electricity there, and interest on working capital;

(f) An allowance for depreciation.

The need for a uniform method of production costing throughout the industry was obvious from the time the 1926 Act became law, and undertakings have remodelled their cost accounts to meet the requirements of the Board.

Ascertaining the Costs

Cost of Production.—The details of cost of production are as follows:—

(a) Works Costs :

(1) *Fuel.*—Usually, this item is the cost of the fuel fed to the boiler hoppers, or furnaces, during the calendar month according to the Coal Stock Books. The price is the average price delivered to the generating station, opening stocks being valued at cost, and purchases, since stocktaking, being brought in at cost delivered to the generating station site. Coal is the largest single item of Works Cost, and operating data with regard to coal should be available to the Station Superintendent daily, so that the efficiency of the steam plant can be verified constantly. The information required would be :

Total coal burnt.
Total units generated.
Lbs. of coal per unit generated.
Cost of coal delivered to boiler hoppers.
Cost in pence per unit generated.
Average calorific value in British Thermal Units.
Thermal efficiency.

A useful method of checking coal consumption is by using coal meters, which can be erected on the boilers. These meters measure the cubic content of the coal passing to the furnaces, and are calibrated to register in pounds. They are usually "set" to deal with dry coal, however, and, consequently, cannot take into consideration any variations of moisture content in the coal, and an estimate to adjust is necessary.

Included in the cost of fuel are also :

(a) Fuel handling charges. These are the expenses incurred in handling fuel after delivery to site, including conveyance to boiler hoppers, and repairs and maintenance of fuel handling and storage equipment, which includes :—

Barges.	Railway Sidings and Track.
Capstans.	Ships.
Coal Chutes.	Tipplers.
Fuel Bunkers.	Transporters.
Fuel Conveyors, Cranes and Telphers.	Trimming Plant.
Horses.	Unloading Apparatus.
Jetties.	Vehicles.
Locomotives.	Weighing Plant.

(b) Fuel preparation charges. Where pulverised fuel is in use, repairs and maintenance of the equipment, and the operation expenses incurred in treating the fuel between delivery to pulverising equipment and delivery to furnaces, are included under this heading.

(c) Ash handling charges. These are the costs incurred in handling and disposing of the ash, including repairs and maintenance of ash handling plant.

The value of the sale of ashes is brought in as a credit to fuel costs.

(2) *Steam Purchased.*—If any steam is purchased from, say, a refuse destructor, the cost is included under this head.

(3) *Oil, Waste, and Stores Consumed.*—This is the value of general engine-room stores issued from stock for such purposes as cleaning, etc. Material issued for repairs and maintenance is charged direct to the appropriate repairs and maintenance heading.

(4) *Water.*—This is the value of the water used during the month in the generating station. The supply is usually metered.

(5) *Salaries of Generating Staff.*—This includes the salaries of officials wholly engaged on the generating side of the undertaking. The salaries of officials who are partly engaged on generation but not wholly employed at the generating station are charged to the total management account.

z

Fig. 142.

MAINTENANCE ACCOUNTS.

Sub-heading.	Further Sub-divisions.	
Boilers.	Boilers. Air Ducts. Boiler Brickwork. Boiler Framework. Boiler Fittings. Boiler Meters. Chimneys (Steel). Economisers. Fans (Mechanical portions of). Flues.	Preheaters. Pulverised Fuel Burners. Reheaters (separately fired). Soot Blowers. Stokers. Superheaters. Tubes. Walls. Water Screens.
Engines.	Main and House Turbines and Condensers.	
Other Mechanical Plant.	Air Compressors. Air Extraction Plant. Cranes (other than Fuel and Ash Handling Cranes). Evaporators. Extraction Pumps. Feed Pumps. Feed Ranges and Valves. Feed Water Heaters. Feed Water Treatment Plant. Fire Fighting Equipment.	Hotwells. Oil Filtering Plant. Pumps (General Service). Repair Shop Equipment. Steam Accumulators. Steam Ranges and Valves. Steam Receivers. Tanks. Testing Equipment. Transformer Oil Pumps and Coolers.
Generators.	Generators. Air Coolers. Air Filters. Alternator Air Ducts. Alternator Fans. Alternator Main Transformers.	Exciters. Exciter Sets. House Service-Alternators. Main Alternators.
Other Electrical Plant.	Auxiliary Driving Motors. Cables (Main and Control). Charging Sets. Converting Plant and Batteries used for Generation. Internal Telephone Equipment.	Meters. Reactors (where allocated to Generation). Relays. Switchgear. Wiring and Electrical Heating and Lighting Equipment. Works Transformers.
Buildings.	Buildings. Bins, Racks, etc. in Stores. Chimneys (Brick and Concrete). Domestic Water Supply and Sanitary Arrangements.	Furniture. Water or Steam Heating Installations. Wells used exclusively for feed water.

MAINTENANCE ACCOUNTS (continued).

Circulating Water Plant.	Auxiliary Pumping Plant. Circulating Water Screens. Circulating Water Treatment Plant. Intake and Outlet Culverts.	Pipe Lines. Reservoirs. Sprayers. Towers. Wells (other than those used exclusively for feed water).

(6) *Wages (Operation only).*—These are the wages of workmen employed in attending to the operation of the station only, such as stokers, drivers, switchboard attendants, etc. Wages of workmen engaged on the repairs and maintenance of plant and buildings are charged direct to such heads.

(7) *Repairs and Maintenance.*—This includes costs of material, labour, and contract work allocated under the sub-headings set out in Fig. 142.

(8) *Renewals not chargeable to Capital Account.*—These costs are sub-divided in the same way as Repairs and Maintenance, and include such items as replacements of worn-out parts, etc.

Note.—Employers' contributions under the Insurance Acts, Workmen's Compensation Acts, and for superannuation are allocated to the appropriate salaries and wages, and included under the above items.

(b) **Overhead Charges.**—All overhead charges for production are the subject of an estimate at the commencement of the Board's financial year. One-twelfth of the estimate is charged each calendar month and the adjustment with actual cost incurred is made at the close of the twelfth month. The items which make up total overhead costs are:

(1) *Management and General.*—The procedure is to charge in detail all management expenses to a total management account which is inclusive of both generation and distribution. Items which make up management are: salaries of staff not wholly employed on generation or distribution, printing and stationery, law and valuation expenses, etc. The portion of the management costs chargeable to production is based on the capacity of the generating station. The prescribed amount is 2s. per kilowatt of installed capacity, plus £500 per annum, or 2s. 3d. per kilowatt per annum, the choice being left to the discretion of the Generating Authority.

That is to say, a station that could meet a demand of, say, 50,000 kilowatts at any one time, could charge to production either £5500 or £5625 per annum. The latter would probably be charged, as it is of course recoverable from the Central Electricity Board. The remainder of the total of management expenses is chargeable to distribution.

(2) *Rents.*—These include such rentals as the ground rent of the generating station site, rentals of land used for ash disposal, siding rents, etc.

(3) *Rates.*—Most Electricity Supply Authorities are assessed for rates on the profits of the undertaking as a whole. The method of apportionment most favoured is the division of the rateable value in proportion to capital value of generation works and other works.

(4) *Insurance.*—The premiums charged to production are for policies such as fire insurance, boiler insurance, etc., which belong to generation solely.

(5) *Interest.*—This covers interest on all expenditure attributable to the generating station and plant. In general, plant on the generator side of the station bus-bars is included, but distribution plant housed in the station for convenience (*e.g.* convertors, transformers and switchgear used for controlling supplies taken from the station) is excluded. Interest on working capital is included under this head, and is based on the monthly cost of production totals.

(6) *Depreciation Allowance.*—In the case of a local authority, the depreciation allowance is an amount equal to the sinking-fund charges properly attributable to the generating station and plant. Where the owners of the station are a company, an amount determined in accordance with a scale fixed by special order is charged.

The Unit of Cost.—The above represents " cost of production." The unit of cost for presenting production cost data is the Board of Trade kilowatt-hour or unit of electricity generated. That is to say, the values shown under the cost headings enumerated above are divided by the number of units generated during the period, and presented as cost in pence per unit.

The following is an example of a monthly cost statement (with dummy figures) for presentation to the Central Electricity Board.

A.—Works Costs					Details.	£	Per Unit.
Fuel Consumed—						£ 6,909	Pence.
(a) Coal 9,754 tons at 14/2 per ton							
(b) Coke ....tons at.................per ton							
(c) Oil ....tons at.................per ton							
(d) Gas...........thou. cu. ft. at..............per 1,000 cu. ft.							
(e) Refuse, etc.							
Total						6,909	0·1495
(f) Fuel Handling and Storage Charges					174		
(g) Fuel Preparation Charges							
(h) Ash Handling Charges					122		
(i) Flue Gas Treatment Charges					20		
(j) N.H.I., etc.					13		
Total						329	0·0071
Total						7,238	0·1566
Less (k) Proceeds of Sale of Ashes, etc.					205		
(l) Proceeds from Sale of Steam							
Total						205	0·0044
Total Fuel						7,033	0·1522
Steam Purchased							
Lubricating Oil, Water and Stores Consumed—							
(a) Oil and Stores					10		
(b) Water :—							
(i) Charged by Meter 810 thousand gals.					35		
(ii) Other Variable Charges							
Total Oil, Water and Stores						45	0·0010
Salaries and Wages of Generating Station Staff (Operation only)						792	0·0171

	Salaries and Wages.	Materials.	Contract Work.	Total.			
Repairs and Maintenance—	£	£	£	£			
(a) Boilers	310	66	32	408			
(b) Engines	19	158		177			
(c) Other Mechanical Plant	69	19		88			
(d) Generators	6	15		21			
(e) Other Electrical Plant	72	40	35	147			
(f) Buildings	98	46		144			
(g) Circulating Water Plant	6	22		28			
(h) Salaries							
(i) N.H.I., etc.	32			32			
Total Repairs and Maintenance	612	366	67	1045		1,045	0·0226
Total Works Costs						£8,915	0·1929

B.—Overhead Charges (Generation only)		
Agreed Monthly Estimate	4,356	0·0942
Non-Recurring Revenue Expenses—		
(a) Charges *re* Loans	13	0·0003
(b)		
(c)		
Total Overhead Charges	£4,369	0·0945
Total Costs	£13,284	0·2874

It may be as well to explain that the " unit " of electricity
is 1000 watts (1 kilowatt) of current for 1 hour—hence the
alternative term of " kilowatt-hour." The quantity of watts
is the result of multiplying amperes × volts, the amperes being

the amount of current and the volts being the pressure of the current.

Two Part Costs.—The total cost of producing electricity is made up of two distinct parts, owing, largely, to the fact that electricity cannot be manufactured uniformly, and placed into stock, until a customer is found. The rate of output is dependent upon the immediate demand, and is produced accordingly. Consequently, the rate of demand, and the time it occurs, influence considerably the cost at which the current can be produced, and, of course, at which it can be sold. The two parts are :

(1) The fixed or standing charges which are dependent upon the maximum rate of demand (maximum load in kilowatts) and independent of duration of demand or hours of use.

(2) The running charges which are proportional to the number of kilowatt-hours, or Board of Trade units.

(a) *The Fixed Charges.*—The cost of providing the capital that has been expended on generating plant, buildings, etc., which comprises such charges as interest, loan repayment, depreciation, etc. The fixed charges also embrace the cost of coal required to keep up the temperature of boilers, salaries and wages of that part of the staff necessary for keeping steam up in boilers, and machinery in readiness to supply. All these charges are fixed, no matter how much, or how little, the plant is in use, but they do bear a relationship to the maximum load in kilowatts on the generating station, and hence this cost can be properly expressed in terms of a fixed charge per month (or other period), in pounds or shillings per kilowatt of maximum demand.

(b) *The Running Charges* include coal for steam other than that required for stand-by losses, wages over and above the stand-by wages previously referred to, a large proportion of repairs and maintenance of plant, etc., and oil, water, and sundry stores. Each unit produced involves an amount of cost in coal, wages, stores, etc. (*i.e.* running charges), which can be definitely expressed as a cost per unit.

The Load Factor.—The division of the costs between standing and running charges is based on the load factor of the generating station which is :

$$\frac{\text{Units generated} \times 100}{\text{Maximum Demand in kilowatt} \times \text{hours of supply period.}}$$

Example :—

$$\frac{3,800,000 \times 100}{18,400 \times 720} = 28 \cdot 68 \text{ per cent.}$$

In other words, the load factor is the ratio of actual output in units generated to the possible output, if the maximum load demanded were continually in use throughout the period of supply.

Division of Cost based on Load Factor.—The load factor is applied by agreed formulæ to the different classes of cost, and the division is made accordingly.

Let us take an actual example.   (Fig. 143.)

Fig. 143.

Class.	Total cost for month.	Per cent. charged to Standing Costs say.	Standing Costs.	Running Costs.
	£		£	£
Fuel	3200	10	320	2880
Oil, Waste, Water, etc. . .	25	20	5	20
Salaries and Wages . . .	600	90	540	60
Repairs and Maintenance . .	450	70	315	135
Management Proportion . .	400	100	400	—
Rents, Rates and Insurance .	480	100	480	—
Interest and Depreciation . .	2500	100	2500	—
Totals . . .	£7655		£4560	£3095

Assume a generating station with an output in units for the month of 3,800,000 has a maximum demand on station of 18,400 K.W.

By dividing the standing costs by the maximum demand, $\frac{£4,560}{18,400}$, and the running costs by the units generated, $\frac{£3,095}{3,800,000}$, we get : 4s. 11d. per kilowatt of maximum demand, plus 0·1,955d. per unit, as our cost of production during the month.

The example quoted above is in a simplified form, but should be sufficient to explain the general principle. It is of interest to note that the price at which a " selected " station Authority may purchase supplies from the Board is based on this principle.

The Costs of Distribution.—The operation of the Central Electricity Board does not affect the working, or the costing methods, in connection with the distribution systems of Authorised Undertakers. Undertakers distribute and sell supplies to their own consumers, even though they themselves are required to purchase those supplies, in bulk, from the Board. A Committee has recently been set up by the Government, however, to review the existing organisation of distribution with the following terms of reference :

" To bring under review the organisation of the distribution of electricity in Great Britain, including the control of statutory electricity companies by other companies.

" To advise on methods by which improvements can be effected with a view to ensuring the standardisation of systems, pressures and methods of charge, further extending facilities (including supplies in rural areas) and reducing costs ; and to make recommendations."

It was on the recommendations of the Weir Committee that the Electricity (Supply) Act of 1926 was passed, with the resultant centralised control of generation and the adoption of uniformity of costing methods for this side of the industry.

New legislation affecting Distribution, probably along similar lines, will undoubtedly ensue from the recommendations of the new Committee.

The costs of distribution, although perhaps of less interest than those of generation, nevertheless form a considerable part of the whole costs of the undertaking. In most cases, it will be found that capital expenditure on distribution works covers approximately 60 per cent. of the whole.

The costs are built up in an orthodox way, by allocating wages, values of stores issued, transport charges, etc., to specific service headings. Stores are usually housed, for convenience, at different points of the supply area, and, as the Stores Ledgers and records are kept at the main Stores near the Generating Station, a system of transfer records is necessary. Costs are assembled under the following service heads (Fig. 144) :

Fig. 144.

SERVICE ACCOUNTS

Service Head.	Further Sub-division of Cost.
Salaries of Technical Staff . .	Distribution Engineer District Engineers, etc.
Repairs and Maintenance of cable network.	Main cables Service cables
Repairs and Maintenance of Apparatus on consumer's premises.	Transformers Meters Switches Fuses Domestic apparatus on hire, etc.
Repairs and Maintenance at Distributing Stations.	Buildings Switchgear Transformers, etc.
Public Lamps	Repairs and Maintenance Renewals
Rents	Wayleave rentals Stores rents, etc.
Rates	Proportion of rates attributable to distribution. Rates outside the Borough Boundaries assembled under rating authorities.
Insurances	Sub-divided under classes of insurance.
Proportion of Management Costs. Loan Charges.	Distribution Stations Main Cables Service cables, etc.

Employer's contributions under the Insurance Acts, Workmen's Compensation Acts, and for superannuation, are allocated to the appropriate headings as for Generation.

Separate costs are kept for each vehicle of transport owned by the undertaking, and the totals divided, weekly or monthly, amongst the services in proportion to mileage, or hours of use.

As regards the overhead costs, such as rents, rates, management, etc., estimates for the financial year are made in advance, and apportionments for the period allotted, the adjustment taking place at the end of the year.

Distribution statistics are presented to the responsible official periodically, the data being in the form of cost in pence per unit of electricity sold. The units sold figure is obtained from the totals of consumers' meters, as per the sales records.

The Cost of Capital Works.—Special attention is given to the costing of capital works, and the form of assembly and presentation is based on the requirements of the Electricity Commissioners. Application for sanction to borrow for capital works is, first of all, made to the Commissioners, and expenditure has to be accounted for in a specified form. The examples for mains (Figs. 145 and 146) will convey to the reader some idea of what is necessary.

Tariffs.—The tariff of charge to the consumer for electricity supplied to him must bear some relation to the cost to the Electricity Undertaking. From the preceding remarks in this chapter under "Two-part costs," it will be evident that every consumer or class of consumer involves the supply undertaking in two expenses :

(1) Each consumer's installation requires that a definite amount of plant shall be in readiness in the supply station to meet the requirements of that particular consumer. The cost of this may be met by charging the consumer a fixed charge per annum based on his maximum demand.

(2) A running charge, varying with the actual amount of energy consumed, which may be met by an additional charge to the consumer of so much per kilowatt hour or Board of Trade unit.

Note.—The division of generation costs into two parts are set out, under broad headings, in Fig. 143.

The demand from the different classes of consumers varies considerably, and hence the widely different rates for supply that make up an Electricity Supply Authority's scale of charges. The two-part tariff which is now so popular with the industry, and which charges a fixed amount per quarter, plus a charge per unit consumed, is the nearest attempt to base the charge to the consumer on the principles of cost. This method is, of course, rather more complicated to the consumer than the simple flat-rate method, and it might be argued that it is seldom satisfactory to sell on a cost basis, as the value of the commodity

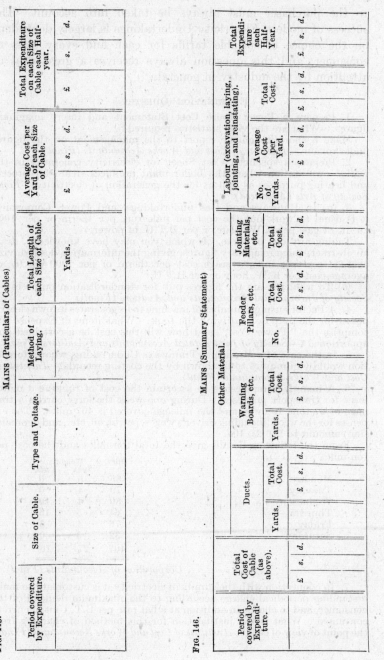

FIG. 145.

MAINS (Particulars of Cables)

Period covered by Expenditure.	Size of Cable.	Type and Voltage.	Method of Laying.	Total Length of each Size of Cable. Yards.	Average Cost per Yard of each Size of Cable. £ s. d.	Total Expenditure on each Size of Cable each Half-year. £ s. d.

FIG. 146.

MAINS (Summary Statement)

Period covered by Expenditure.	Total Cost of Cable (as above). £ s. d.	Other Material								Labour (excavation, laying, jointing, and reinstating).			Total Expenditure each Half-Year. £ s. d.
		Ducts.		Warning Boards, etc.		Feeder Pillars, etc.		Jointing Materials, etc.		No. of Yards.	Average Cost per Yard.	Total Cost.	
		Yards.	Total Cost. £ s. d.	Yards.	Total Cost. £ s. d.	No.	Total Cost. £ s. d.	Total Cost. £ s. d.			£ s. d.	£ s. d.	

to the purchaser must always be taken into account. The success of modern Electricity Undertakings is largely dependent on the choice of suitable tariffs for each and every class of consumer, and this question always receives a great deal of attention by the industry in general.

Examination Questions

1. Prepare a Power-House Cost Statement and insert imaginary figures. What are the vital statistics required?

Make a short imaginary report to the management on the figures under review.—*Institute of Cost and Works Accountants (Final).*

2. Prepare a specimen Cost Sheet for electricity generated in the works' own station where the boiler plant produces steam for process and heating purposes as well as for the generation of electricity.—*Royal Society of Arts (Advanced).*

3. (a) In Railways and Gas undertakings, and Power Companies, it is usual to work out the cost per mile run, per therm or per 1000 cu. ft. of gas, per K.W. hour or per B.T.U. of power.

Taking any one of these, of which you may have knowledge, draft an abstract, using imaginary figures, giving the information desired, viz., average cost per mile, average cost per therm or per 1000 cu. ft., or average cost per K.W. hour or per B.T.U.

(b) To what use are the figures put for standardisation purposes?—*Society of Incorporated Accountants and Auditors (Final).*

4. A Factory using a number of machine tools generates its own electric power for the purpose of driving the tools. What items of Expense will comprise the " Power Cost," and how will this cost be ascertained and apportioned?—*Society of Incorporated Accountants and Auditors (Final).*

5. In the case of a Municipal Tramways Undertaking, what information would you require to be shown by the costing records?—*Institute of Cost and Works Accountants (Final).*

6. A manufacturer desires to ascertain the cost of running a motor lorry for transport purposes. During one week the lorry carries a tonnage of 27 tons 10 cwts. and the mileage covered is 407 miles. The expenses for the week (including driver's wages, petrol, oil, etc., and depreciation) amount to £16 2s. 10d.

From the following details give the total ton-miles and the cost per ton-mile.

	Miles.	Weight.	
		Tons.	Cwts.
Monday	85	6	0
Tuesday	70	4	0
Wednesday	80	4	10
Thursday	64	5	15
Friday	76	4	5
Saturday	32	3	0
	407	27	10

Corporation of Accountants (Final).

7. In connection with the supply of electricity it is customary to make a standing periodical charge according to the maximum demand of the consumer, and to charge in addition at a flat rate per B.T. Unit of current consumed. What is the justification for this method of charging from the point of view of cost?—*Institute of Cost and Works Accountants (Final).*

CHAPTER XXIV

STANDARD COSTS

Standard Costs are pre-determined, or budgetted, estimates of cost to manufacture a single unit, or a number of units of product, during a specified immediate future period. They are used as a measure with which the Actual Cost, as ascertained, may be compared. In some systems all the costing is figured at standard rates, the cost resulting being afterwards converted to Actual by means of ratios.

Standard Costs are usually the planned costs of the product under current and anticipated conditions, but, sometimes, they are the costs under normal or ideal conditions of efficiency, based upon an assumed given output, and having regard to current conditions. They are revised to conform to supernormal or subnormal conditions, but more particularly to allow for persisting alterations in the prices of material and labour.

Standard Costing is a method of detailing the costs whereby statistics are prepared detailing : (a) the Standard Cost; (b) the Actual Cost; and (c) the ratio between these costs, for every product.

It will be obvious that, if the Standard Cost is one based on normal or ideal working, the system is an excellent one for revealing the degree of efficiency obtained in actual production, and often provides an incentive for improving performance and operating conditions.

It is usual to regard Normal Output as the output which the factory is capable of dealing with, based on recorded experience and present conditions. The work done under conditions of normal output is calculated to involve a definite corresponding amount of expenses, from which Standard Costs are fixed, thus forming the measure against which actual performance is comparable. Any change in machines or facilities has to be taken into consideration.

The standards cannot be fixed by total production, if adequate

315

control is to be made possible, but by arriving at separate departmental or process costs; in fact, it may be necessary to subdivide still further, *e.g.*, to the cost of operating each individual machine.

It will be obvious that when first deciding upon standards, much careful analysis and consideration of costs are demanded, but afterwards the work is not more, and often is less, than in many of the less modern cost systems in use to-day.

The Presentation of Facts.—There are several methods of showing or using the Standard Costs in the Statistics and Accounts, but the most usual one is to record the Standard and Actual Costs for each item in adjacent columns. This permits of ready and detailed comparison, both item by item, and in totals.

The Utility of Standard Costs has been widely recognised in recent years, particularly in the United States, and, to a considerable extent, in Great Britain. In the principal factories in this country producing on a large scale, as, for instance, in the textile industry, electrical and other engineering, biscuit-making, and chemical industries, Standard Costs are in use, and there is every indication that Standard Costing will be used to a very large extent in future.

Much depends upon the arrangement of the records as to whether a Standard Costing system entails additional clerical work. In some instances it has resulted in less work. In a certain American factory making a standard product, cost variances only are recorded. It may be said that, even if the procedure does involve additional clerical work, the close control effected enables considerable saving to be made in production costs.

Standard Costing can be introduced most advantageously in process, unit operation, and mass-production costing, or whenever there is repetition production, but not in those factories where dissimilar non-recurring jobs are undertaken.

The Chief Advantages secured may be summarised as follows :

(*a*) Actual performance is readily comparable with the pre-determined standards, showing separately profits or losses thereon on different classes or units of manufacture.

(*b*) Variations from standard can be detected in detail, enabling the management to investigate the cause. Inefficiencies of labour, of the use of materials, and of the operation of machines, are discovered.

(c) Gains or losses due to market fluctuations in prices of raw materials, as distinct from variations due to manufacturing conversion, are revealed.

(d) The effects on costs of variations in the price and use of materials, the rates of labour wages, the volume of production, and altered overhead expense, are demonstrated at short intervals.

This information enables the management to see whether shops or processes are being worked economically, and are producing a satisfactory output. It further serves as a guide whether prices can be adjusted to meet competition. In periods of trade depression, the records show at what price work may be undertaken to secure trade sufficient to cover overheads.

Budgetary Control Needed.—The budgetary control of sales, production, and finance is almost a necessity for the most advantageous and successful use of a Standard Costing system. For budgetary control all factors affecting production and cost are pre-determined as closely as possible. Sales quotas are determined in consultation with the Sales Manager and the selling staff. The cost of financing is carefully considered. The volume of production and its planning are fixed. From the budget, so prepared, the standard cost of each product is calculated.

In the setting up of these standards, consideration is given to statistics of production costs in the preceding periods, but total reliance on these is inadvisable, it being more satisfactory to have regard to the tendency of prices of materials and labour, and to the prospects of the immediate future. It will be apparent that marketing conditions, financing methods, selling methods, purchasing power, mechanical equipment, production possibilities, and labour conditions all have an influence on standards, and for determining Standard Costs they must be taken into consideration.

The determination of standards is a long and difficult task, and, consequently, it is not usual to vary the standards unduly. By the use of cost ratios, or efficiency percentages, such a course is rendered unnecessary. It is convenient, however, to alter the standards if labour or prices of materials are definitely changed for the future.

The Use of Ratios.—Ratios may be used with great advantage for showing the costs and efficiency of production more clearly than cost totals. The ratios between standard and actual costs are very convenient for the purpose.

Take, for example, the following figures :

    Standard Cost (labour) £6000
    Actual Cost recorded £8000

then the measure of efficiency of labour is only 75 per cent., assuming rates have not changed, viz. :

$$\frac{6000}{8000} \times 100 = 75 \text{ per cent.}$$

and the labour cost ratio is therefore 133·3, as follows :

$$\frac{8000}{6000} \times 100 = 133\tfrac{1}{3}.$$

The Standard Cost of material, labour, and overhead being known, by applying the current efficiency percentage to each the actual costs are ascertained. This is an advantage for current estimating.

The formula is as follows :

$$\text{Current Actual Cost} = \frac{\text{Standard Cost}}{\text{Efficiency percentage}}$$

The Procedure for Determining Standards.—For each product a Standard Cost is fixed for each element of cost :

(a) *Materials.*—Using the specification of material as to quantities and qualities, and allowing for average scrap, or waste, a standard price is settled, having regard to the current rates, and those of the immediate future. A price book showing standard prices is compiled for use.

(b) *Labour.*—The detailed operations both for machine and hand labour are settled, and a labour cost is fixed for each operation. This may be based on piece-work rates, bonus rates, or on standard times and rates, settled by test or experience. A schedule of standard rates is drawn up for use of the cost clerk.

(c) *Overhead.*—The budgetted expenses in connection with the budgetted production for respective departments, for shops, or even for particular machines, enables a standard rate, or percentage, to be calculated. This rate may be based on machine-hours, or direct-labour hours, or may be a percentage on wages, materials, or prime cost.

The Methods of Recording the Costs.—There are alternative schemes for recording costs in Standard Costing.

One method is to enter Standard and Actual values in adjacent columns. Another is to enter the Standard values in conjunction with ratios. The differences between Standard and Actual Costs are transferred to Cost Variation Accounts.

A simple illustration of the first method is as follows (Fig. 148) :

FIG. 148.

STORES MATERIAL ACCOUNT

Dr.   Cr.

			Standard.			Actual.						Standard.			Actual.		
			£	s.	d.	£	s.	d.				£	s.	d.	£	s.	d.
19... Jan. 1	To Balance .	b/d	166	13	4	177	3	4	19... Jan. 31	By Issues to Shops .	18	57	6	8	63	6	8
31	,, Receipts .	17	61	6	8	65	10	0	,,	,, Stock on Hand .	c/d	170	13	4	179	6	8
			228	0	0	242	13	4				228	0	0	242	13	4
19... Feb. 1	To Balance .	b/d	170	13	4	179	6	8									

The operation of the Work in Progress Account for each type of product is as follows :

Debit.	*Credit.*
Materials issued for the month at Standard rates (converted to actual by use of ratios as per Stores Material Account). Wages at Standard and Actual. Overhead at Standard.	Monthly production at Standard and Actual values (and debit at same figures to Finished Goods, Account).

The cost ratio must be ascertained to enable the final accounts to be completed.

Application of Cost Ratios.

Example : Details for Work in Progress Account (Materials only) :

100 Articles using exact standard quantity of material at 5s. each standard value would cost £25 (no waste).

The actual cost works out at 6s. each, *i.e.*, £30, owing to materials being dearer.

Through spoilage, etc., only ninety articles pass inspection,

A A

which, at standard value, are credited at 5s., i.e., £22 10s., and at actual value £30, because only ninety good articles have been produced out of 100 pieces of material costing 6s. each.

The Work in Progress Account would then be entered up as follows (materials only):

FIG. 149.

WORK IN PROGRESS ACCOUNT

Dr.   Cr.

	Standard.			Actual.			Ratio.		Standard.			Actual.			Ratio.
	£	s.	d.	£	s.	d.			£	s.	d.	£	s.	d.	
Materials . .	25	0	0	30	0	0	120	Finished Stock Account .	22	10	0	30	0	0	133·3

These ratios convey useful information :

The ratio 120 represents the relation to standard of the actual value of the material used due to price variation. The ratio 133·3 represents the relation of the Actual Cost of the actual production to the budgetted Standard Cost of that production. The £22 10s. credited (standard), as against £25 debited (also standard), shows an efficiency of 90 per cent. in the *use* of materials, apart from labour and other costs.

When finished goods are issued against sale orders, they cannot be debited at Standard Cost, but must be at Actual. The issues at Standard Cost price are, therefore, converted to actual, thus :

$$\text{Actual Cost} = \frac{\text{Standard}}{\text{Efficiency per cent.}} = \frac{£22 \ 10s.}{75} \times 100$$

$$= £30$$

$$\text{or} = 22 \cdot 10s. \times 133 \cdot 3 = £30$$

The Standard value, therefore, of each lot issued is converted for the charge to Trading Account (or Cost of Sales Account) by multiplying by the ratio as shown.

The **Causes for Variation from Standard** may be any or all of the following :

(1) Variation in price of material.

(2) Variation due to waste of material.

(3) Variation due to change of wage rate.

(4) Variation due to Workers' inefficiency, or idle time.

(5) Variation due to fixed overhead expense, if volume of production is above or below estimated quantity.

(6) Variation due to variable overhead caused by idle time, defective work, changed expense.

Checking the Efficiency of Labour.—A weekly, or monthly, schedule may be prepared. Fig. 150 shows a suitable form, which is self-explanatory.

FIG. 150.

PERCENTAGE EFFICIENCY OF OPERATORS

Jobs Closed Weekend : .... Paid Weekend : ....

Clock No.	Shop Order.	Code.	Operation Number.	Quantity Made.	Actual Hours.	Standard Cost Per 1000.	Standard Labour Cost.			Actual Labour Cost.			% Efficiency.
						£	£	s.	d.	£	s.	d.	

Examples of Standard Cost Accounts are given in the next chapter.

EXAMINATION QUESTIONS

1. Illustrate, with necessary forms, how you would present the following information to the management :

(a) The actual yield of a product with which you are familiar, illustrating the effect on cost of variation from standard yield.
(b) Maintenance cost in the factory.
(c) Productive and non-productive labour, showing relationship of piece-work and time-work.
Institute of Cost and Works Accountants (Final).

2. Define : Prime Cost;
Direct Expenses;
Works Oncost;

and explain the utility of " Standard Costs " and the mode of their calculation.—*London Chamber of Commerce.*

3. What do you know of Budgetary Control ? Under what circumstances do you consider it would be most successfully used ?—*Institute of Cost and Works Accountants (Final).*

4. What do you understand by Standard Costs ? To what industries or classes of production do you consider them applicable ? How are they compiled and how are they used to reflect efficiency in manufacture ?—*Royal Society of Arts (Advanced).*

5. Describe the method adopted for setting up a Standard Cost. Give an example of an industry to which such a system might be applied and state the advantages which, in your opinion, might be expected to accrue therefrom.—*London Chamber of Commerce*

6. What do you understand by Standard Costs ? Wherein do they differ from Actual Costs ?—*Royal Society of Arts (Advanced).*

7. Describe fully the contribution that the Cost Accountant could make towards the preparation of a budget of income and expenditure for any period.—*Institute of Cost and Works Accountants (Final).*

8. Under any scheme of budgetary control, how would you provide for fluctuations in proportions of overheads ? Explain your answer fully.—*Institute of Cost and Works Accountants (Final).*

9. What system do you recommend in order to secure the accuracy of the pre-determined figures upon which selling prices are fixed ?—*Society of Incorporated Accountants and Auditors (Final).*

10. A manufacturer prepared Standard Costs and ascertains that these vary considerably from the figures in the actual costs. Suggest reasons for the variations.—*Corporation of Accountants (Final).*

11. Prepare a statement showing comparisons over periods of actual cost with the standard, emphasising differences and the reasons for them. Use hypothetical figures covering three periods.—*Institute of Cost and Works Accountants (Final).*

CHAPTER XXV

STANDARD COSTS (*continued*)

EXAMPLE I

Factory and Costing Procedure.—It is desirable to trace the procedure in the factory for accumulating the data required for the accounts.

(*a*) **Materials.**—The issue of materials follows the putting in hand of the production order. The production orders are based on the sales orders received, or the pre-determined production programme. The material requisitions, in duplicate,

FIG. 151.

MATERIAL REQUISITION
(Standard Costing)

Department: *Automatic, No. 37.*   Req. No. *492.*
Order No.: *L. 2749.*   Expense No.: ....
Part No.: *34.*   Credit A/c.: *P.S. 23.*
Date: *3 June, 19......*

Qty.	Unit.	Material.	Qty. Delivered.	Bal.* on Hand.	Price.				Value.				
					Stand.		Act.		Stand.			Act.	
					s.	*d.*	*s.*	*d.*	£	*s.*	*d.*	£	*s.*	*d.*
448	lb.	2-in. rd. cold rolled steel	448	2000	22	0	22	6	4	8	0	4	10	0

Signed: J. HOPKINS,   Issued by: T. DANIELS,
        Storekeeper.   *Foreman.*

* A useful figure to include as a check on the Bin Card and on the Stores Ledger Account.

are issued along with the production order in many factories; in others, their issue is the responsibility of the foreman. The duplicate is retained by the storekeeper for entering up the bin card; the duplicate is sent to the stores ledger clerk, who prices and extends it at both Standard and Actual prices (see Fig. 151).

323

The Material Account is credited at Actual, thus keeping that account at the actual cost throughout.

Cost Office Procedure.—Requisitions are summarised, one summary being at Actual, the other at Standard. The Actual Cost Summary total is credited to Material Control Account, and debited to Material Variation Account. The Standard Cost Summary total is credited to Material Variation Account, and debited to work in Progress Control Account.

The requisitions are analysed under works order numbers, and posted to the debit of the Cost Accounts therefor.

FIG. 152.

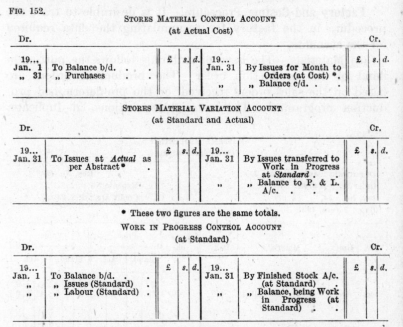

STORES MATERIAL CONTROL ACCOUNT
(at Actual Cost)

Dr.										Cr.		
19... Jan. 1 „ 31	To Balance b/d. . . „ Purchases . .		£	s.	d.	19... Jan. 31 „	By Issues for Month to Orders (at Cost) *. „ Balance c/d. . .			£	s.	d.

STORES MATERIAL VARIATION ACCOUNT
(at Standard and Actual)

Dr.										Cr.		
19... Jan. 31	To Issues at *Actual* as per Abstract * .		£	s.	d.	19... Jan. 31 „	By Issues transferred to Work in Progress at *Standard* . . „ Balance to P. & L. A/c. . . .			£	s.	d.

* These two figures are the same totals.

WORK IN PROGRESS CONTROL ACCOUNT
(at Standard)

Dr.										Cr.		
19... Jan. 1 „ „	To Balance b/d. . . „ Issues (Standard) . „ Labour (Standard) .		£	s.	d.	19... Jan. 31 „	By Finished Stock A/c. (at Standard) . „ Balance, being Work in Progress (at Standard) . .			£	s.	d.

This procedure keeps the Work in Progress Account at Standard Cost, and the Stores Material Account at Actual.

(b) **Labour.**—In Standard Costing procedure direct labour is usually paid at piece-rates or bonus rates; indirect at day-rates.

The procedure for recording gate time and job times has already been described. The total of the pay-roll, and that of the labour abstract, should be agreed.

Cost Office Procedure.—Two accounts are opened in the Cost Ledger : (1) Standard Labour Account; (2) Labour Variation Account.

The Labour Wages Abstract, based on job tickets priced at Standard, is totalled, and debited to Standard Labour Account.

There will only be labour wage variations if a change has been made in premium bonus or piece-rates, or if a job has been done at day-rate wages, although, normally, done at premium bonus or piece-work rates.

Any variation which does occur will be debited, or credited, to the Labour Variation Account, according to whether the difference is over or under standard.

The debit to Work in Progress is at Standard.

The general procedure is on the same lines as for materials.

(c) **Overhead** (= Oncost).—The many items of fixed and Variable Overhead make it difficult to get an exact distribution of it to the shops and the products; even though a time basis, machine-hour, or direct wages basis, may be used. The use of Standard rates, based on past record, but modified by the trend of the immediate future, is a usual method of procedure, which will need no alteration. The chief point to observe is that separate rates are fixed for each shop, and, usually, for each machine, or production centre.

Fixed charges, such as rent, depreciation, interest on capital, etc., continue whatever the output. Variable Overhead varies substantially, but not exactly, in proportion to output. For these reasons, it is often the practice to apply fixed and variable overhead by separate rates.

Overhead Control Account is debited with Actual expenses, and credited with Standard expenses recovered on the works orders, etc. The Work in Progress Account is also debited with the Standard recoveries in total.

There is, usually, a difference on the Overhead Control Account, due to over or under recovery of expense. This balance is transferred to Overhead Adjustment Account, thus clearing the account.

The Adjustment Account is closed by transferring the balance of it to the Profit and Loss Account at the end of each accounting period. It may be noted that this account is, sometimes, called " Over- or Under-Applied Expense Account."

(d) **Standard Cost Record Sheet.**—This is used for compiling the Standard Cost. When there are a number of components made or purchased, and these are eventually assembled into one complete unit, a separate cost sheet must be written up for each part, and one for the assembled product.

FIG. 153.

STANDARD COST RECORD SHEET

(for Component Parts)

Pattern No. : (*of a casting*).
Name of Part : *Steel frame.*
Material Specification : *2-in. cold rolled steel.*
Date completed : *24/6/19......*
Qty. per set : *50 lbs.*

Sheet No. : *2941.*
Part No. or Assembled ⎱ *C.P. 391*
Unit No.   ⎰ *for A.U.73*
Destination : *Assembly A.U.73.*

Shop No.	Operations.		Direct Labour.		Overhead.		Materials.
	No.	Details.	Machine time.	Cost.	Rate on Wages.	Amount.	
				s. *d.*		*s.* *d.*	*s.* *d.*
O7	1	*Press*	2 hrs.	5 0	75%	3 9	20/5/19...... 8 3
O8	2	*Drill*	1 ,,	3 9	100%	3 9	
Etc.	3	*Burr*					
	4						

Entered by :	Direct Labour, Hours per Unit.	Machine, Hours per Unit.	Rejects, % to add to Materials.	STANDARD COST PER UNIT.		Factory Cost.		
						£	s.	d.
F. Smith	2	1·25	2%	Material . . .		2	5	0
				Labour . . .		1	17	0
				Overhead . . .		1	19	0
				Total . .		£6	1	0

FIG. 154.

STANDARD COST RECORD SHEET

(for Assembly Units)

Shop No. : *09.*
Order No. : *347.*

Description :
Switchboard Exchange.

Sheet No. : *394.*
Assembled Unit No. :
A.U.73.

Component Cost Ref.	Part No.	No. Used.	Material.			Labour.			Overhead.			Total.		
			£	s.	d.	£	s.	d.	£	s.	d.	£	s.	d.
2941 Etc.	*C.P.391*	1	2	5	0	1	17	0	1	19	0	6	1	0
Total Assembled Cost .														

The specimen given in Fig. 153 is completed for the costs of each component. Each component Cost Sheet shows the standard cost per unit. The component costs are used for the assembling cost, for which Fig. 154 is a suggested form. In other words, the component Standard Cost Record Sheets provide the standard cost figure per unit for each component made; from these the assembled unit cost is built up, as shown in the example.

(e) **A Set of Standard Cost Control Accounts.**—These show the operation of the method described, and are sufficiently annotated to be self-explanatory.

STANDARD COST CONTROL ACCOUNTS

(1) *Stores Material Control Account*

Dr.					Cr.
		£			£
To Stock on Hand . .	b/d.	6800	By Issues as per Abstract, at Actual (Direct) . .	To 2	4000
„ Purchases for Month at Actual . . .		3000	„ Do. (Indirect) to Factory Overhead . . .	To 5	2000
			„ Balance, Stock on Hand	c/d.	3800
		£9800	(*All at Actual*) . . .		£9800

(2) *Stores Material Variation Account*

Dr.					Cr.
		£			£
To Issues to Jobs at Actual .	a/c.1	4000	By Issues to Jobs at Standard as per Work in Progress A/c. . .	To 6	3800
			„ Balance, being difference between Actual and Standard transferred to Profit and Loss A/c.	J	200
		£4000			£4000

(3) *Labour Wages Control Account*

Dr.					Cr.
		£			£
To Wages paid for Month (Actual) . . .		5000	By Direct Labour, total as per Abstract, to Variation A/c. . . .	To 4	3000
			„ Indirect Labour to Factory Overhead . .	To 5	1800
			„ Balance accrued . .	c/d.	200
		£5000	(*All at Actual*) . . .		£5000

(4) *Labour Wages Variation Account*

Dr.		£			£	Cr.
To Direct Wages debited to Jobs at Actual .	Fr. 3	3000	By Direct Wages at Standard to Work in Progress . .	To 6	3100	
„ Balance, being difference between Actual and Standard transferred to Profit and Loss A/c. .	J	100				
		£3100			£3100	

(5) *Factory Overhead Control Account*

Dr.		£			£	Cr.
To Indirect Material at Actual . .	Fr. 1	2000	By Overhead recovered by Rates at Standard (Total debited to Work in Progress A/c.) .	To 6	7800	
„ „ Labour at Actual	Fr. 3	1800				
„ „ Other Expenses (Actual) . .	J	1200				
„ „ Fixed Overhead (Actual) . .	J	3000	„ By Profit and Loss A/c., difference between Actual and Standard, under-recovered . .	J	200	
		£8000			£8000	

(6) *Work in Progress Control Account*

Dr.		£			£	Cr.
To Balance in Progress	b/f.	6,000	By Completed Work to Finished Stock A/c. at Standard . .	To 7	16,700	
„ Direct Material Issues at Standard . .	Fr. 1	3,800				
„ Direct Labour at Standard	Fr. 4	3,100	„ Balance, Work in Progress, at Standard .	c/d.	4,000	
„ Factory Overhead charged to Jobs at Standard Rates . .	Fr. 5	7,800				
		£20,700			£20,700	

(7) *Finished Stock Control Account*

Dr.		£			£	Cr.
To Balance, Stock on Hand, at Standard . .	b/f.	9,200	By Issues against Sales Orders, to Cost of Sales A/c. at Standard .	J	17,800	
„ Completed Work from Work in Progress A/c. .	Fr. 6	16,700	„ Balance on Hand at Standard . . .	c/d.	8,100	
		£25,900			£25,900	

EXAMPLE II

Accounting in Standard Values.—In this method all entries in the accounts are at Standard prices or rates, the conversion to Actual being effected by adjustment of totals, and the transfer of the amount of variations to Cost Variance Accounts.

Procedure for Standard Costing. (a) *The Purchase Journal.*—
The usual columnar journal is used, but a column for standard
cost values is added. (Fig. 155.)

As Invoices are passed against the Goods Received Notes,

FIG. 155.

PURCHASE JOURNAL

Inv. No.	Suppliers'.	Fo.	Amount of each Invoice. (Actual.)	Sub-Totals. (Actual.)	Sub-Totals. (Standard value.)	Stores Materials. (Standard price.)	Repairs Materials. (Actual.)	Other Expenses. (Actual.)
			£ s. d.	£ s. d.	£ s. d.	£ s. d.	£ s. d.	£ s. d.

the Standard price is entered under the Actual, ready for the
journal clerk.

The Actual values are entered in the first and second columns
in the usual manner, the Standard values in the third column.
The extension into the analysis columns is at standard for
Stores Materials, but at Actual for all the columns provided

FIG. 156.

STORES MATERIAL ACCOUNT
(Standard Values)

Dr.							Cr.	
19... Jan. 1	To Balance	b/d.	£ 9,366 s. 0 d. 0	19... Jan. 31	By Issues as per Abstracts	J4	£ 4,917 s. 0 d. 0
„ 31	„ Purchases	J3	3,556 10 0	„	„ „ Balance	c/d.	8,005 10 0
			£12,922 10 0				£12,922 10 0
19... Feb. 1	To Balance	b/d.	8,005 10 0				

for expense items. These totals are debited in the Cost Control
Accounts, *e.g.*, Fig. 156.

At the end of each week or month the difference between
totals of materials purchased is found, and posted to a Material
Cost Variance Account. (Fig. 157.)

If required, a separate account may be kept for each class
of material.

Materials Issued from Store.—These are made in the usual way against requisitions. When pricing out these issues in the Cost Office, the Actual and Standard prices are entered.

The various materials accounts in the Stores Ledger are credited at both values, the individual Cost Accounts being debited, and the totals are also credited to Stores Material Account, as shown above (Fig. 156), and debited to Work in Progress Account, at Standard value. The variance between Actual and Standard is posted to the Materials Cost Variance Account (debit or credit according to which is greater, Actual or Standard). (Fig. 157.)

Labour Wages.—These are dealt with on the same lines.

Factory Overhead.—Allocations to shops and to jobs or

FIG. 157.

MATERIALS COST VARIANCE ACCOUNT

Dr.				£	s.	d.				£	s.	d.
19... Jan. 1	To Balance (Variance on Stock in Hand)	b/d.		279	5	6	19... Jan. 31	By Variance* on Issues as per Abstracts .	J4	57	0	0
,, 31	,, Variance on Purchases .	J3		159	4	6	,,	,, Balance .		381	10	0
				£438	10	0				£438	10	0
19... Feb. 1	To Balance .	b/d.		381	10	0						

* Transferred to Cost Variance Control Account.

processes are at Standard pre-determined rates, as budgeted. The under-, or over-allocated overhead as revealed by the Overhead Control Account is transferred to Cost Variance Account.

Completed Work is credited to Work in Progress at Standard Cost. These totals are debited to Finished Stock Account.

Cost of Sales Account.—On issuing finished stock the Standard price is converted, by means of the ascertained ratio of Standard and Actual, to Actual values.

The Cost Variance Account (Fig. 158).—The balance of this account shows the net cost variance on production, plus the variance on Cost of Sales.

The balance on the Materials Cost Variance Account added to (or deducted) from the balance of Materials Account gives the Actual value of stock on hand. Similarly, with Finished Stock Account.

The Variance on Overhead Expense Control Account represents the difference between budgeted and Actual expense incurred. The Control Cost Variance Account (Fig. 158) is closed at the end of the month by crediting the variance trans-

FIG. 158.

CONTROL COST VARIANCE ACCOUNT

Dr.				£	s.	d.				£	s.	d.
19... Jan. 1	To Balance	b/d.		485	10	0	19... Jan.31	By Variance on Fin- ished Stock, to Cost of Sales				
Jan. 31	,, Variance on Stock	J4		177	10	0		A/c.	J4	104	2	0
,,	,, Variance on Ma- terials Issued .	J4		57	0	0	,,	,, Overhead Over- recovered to Profit and Loss				
								A/c.	J5	70	0	0
							,,	,, Balance	c/d.	545	18	0
				£720	0	0				£720	0	0
19... Feb. 1	To Balance	b/d.										

FIG. 159.

ACTUAL COST SUMMARY

Route : Order No. :
Date : Code :
Description : Qty. :

	Actual Cost of Order.			Actual Cost per 1000.	Standard Cost per 1000.
	£	s.	d.	Dec. of £	Dec. of £
Manufactured Material					
Purchased Material					
Labour					
Overhead					
Total Cost					

Standard Cost Variation Efficiency.	Standard Cost of Order.			Standard over Act. Cr.			Actual over Std. Dr.		
	£	s.	d.	£	s.	d.	£	s.	d.

ferred to the Cost of Sales Account. If over- or under-allocation of Overhead is included in this account, the amount is transferred to Manufacturing or Profit and Loss Account.

The balance remaining on the account represents the variance on materials and stock on hand, and is carried down as a balance.

The final accounts (Manufacturing and Profit and Loss Accounts) are then completed in the usual manner.

A Specimen Cost Summary.—The form shown in Fig. 159 is an Actual Cost Summary for a Works Order completed. It shows to what extent the Actual cost has varied from the Standard.

Checking Stores Records.—It should be noticed that the use of Standard pricing of stores materials enables balancing to be effected either in money values or quantities, because, by dividing the money value balance of any particular class of material by the price, the quantities can be checked. This is not possible when varying actual prices are used.

EXAMPLE III

ACCOUNTING IN STANDARD AND ACTUAL VALUES WITH RATIOS

In this method the records are entered at Actual and Standard values in adjacent columns, together with the ratio.

Materials.—A total Control Account for stores materials is kept. In the Stores Ledger the account for each class of material is ruled to show Standard and Actual cost and the cost ratio. The balances of the accounts in the Stores Ledger should agree in total with the balance of the Materials Control Account.

Costing Issues of Materials.—Standard prices are entered on the requisitions in the Cost Office, together with the current ratio between Standards and Actual.

The totals, from the Materials Abstracts, are credited to Materials Control Account (see Fig. 156), and debited to Work in Progress Account, at both values.

The issues to various works order numbers are debited thereto, and credited to the respective Materials Accounts in the Stores Ledger, at both Standard and Actual prices.

Materials issued for Standing Orders are charged at Actual prices.

A Stores Ledger Account on these lines is shown in Fig. 160.

Charging Labour and Overhead.—For job order work a job-card is issued to the worker for each operation. The time occupied in doing the work is recorded, together with the number

Fig. 160.

STORES LEDGER ACCOUNT (STANDARD COSTING)
½-in Steel Tubes. Code S. 102

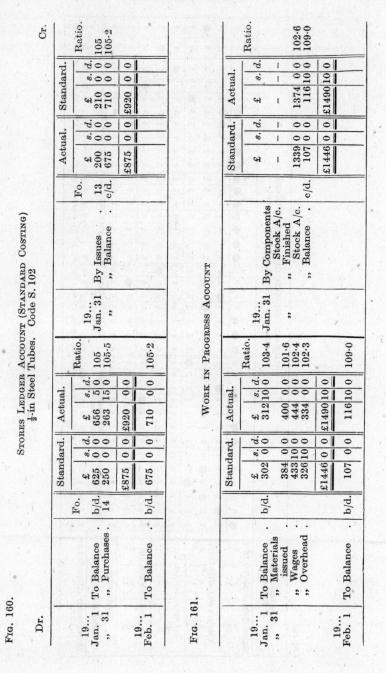

Dr.

19...		Fo.	Standard £ s. d.	Actual £ s. d.	Ratio.
Jan. 1	To Balance	b/d.	625 0 0	656 5 0	105
" 31	" Purchases	14	250 0 0	263 15 0	105·5
			£875 0 0	£920 0 0	105·2
19...					
Feb. 1	To Balance	b/d.	675 0 0	710 0 0	105·2

Cr.

19...		Fo.	Actual £ s. d.	Standard £ s. d.	Ratio.
Jan. 31	By Issues	13	200 0 0	210 0 0	105
" "	" Balance	c/d.	675 0 0	710 0 0	105·2
			£875 0 0	£920 0 0	

Fig. 161.

WORK IN PROGRESS ACCOUNT

Dr.

19...		Fo.	Standard £ s. d.	Actual £ s. d.	Ratio.
Jan. 1	To Balance	b/d.	302 0 0	312 10 0	103·4
" 31	" Materials issued		384 0 0	400 0 0	101·6
	" Wages		433 10 0	444 0 0	102·4
	" Overhead		326 10 0	334 0 0	102·3
			£1446 0 0	£1490 10 0	109·0
19...					
Feb. 1	To Balance	b/d.	107 0 0	116 10 0	109·0

Cr.

19...		Fo.	Standard £ s. d.	Actual £ s. d.	Ratio.
Jan. 31	By Components Stock A/c.		1339 0 0	1374 0 0	102·6
"	" Finished Stock A/c.		107 0 0	116 10 0	109·0
	" Balance	c/d.			
			£1446 0 0	£1490 10 0	

FIG. 162.

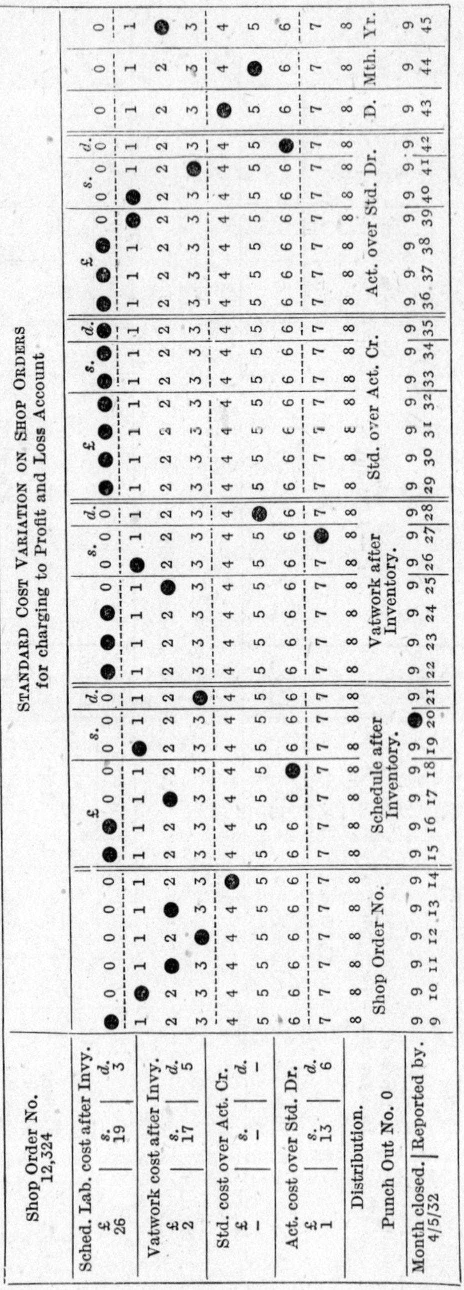
Shop Order No. 12,324
Sched. Lab. cost after Invy. £ 26 s. 19 d. 3
Vatwork cost after Invy. £ 2 s. 17 d. 5
Std. cost over Act. Cr. £ – s. – d. –
Act. cost over Std. Dr. £ 1 s. 13 d. 6
Distribution.
Punch Out No. 0
Month closed. 4/5/32
Reported by.
STANDARD COST VARIATION ON SHOP ORDERS for charging to Profit and Loss Account
Shop Order No.
Schedule after Inventory.
Vatwork after Inventory.
Std. over Act. Cr.
Act. over Std. Dr.
D.
Mth.
Yr.

of articles passing inspection. The day-rate, bonus rate or piece-work price is entered by the Cost Office, and a summary of these cards for each worker forms the basis for the pay-roll. A special column is provided for Standard Cost based on a labour-hour or piece rate at Standard price.

Overhead is added on the card. The total so added to all jobs is credited to Overhead Control Account.

The total of labour wages paid is debited to Work in Progress. (Fig. 161.)

Completed Orders.—These are summarised monthly and credited at Standard and Actual to Work in Progress (see Fig. 161); corresponding debits are made to Components Stock Account, and Finished Stock Account.

Cost of Sales.—The Standard Cost of goods issued against sales orders is entered on the duplicate of the invoice, or other record is kept.

By grouping like kinds of goods it is sometimes possible to apply the converting cost ratio to the totals. If not, this has to be done for the total of each type of stock sold. The Standard Cost is multiplied by the cost ratio to convert the total to Actual value for the Trading Account.

Standard Costing and Mechanical Tabulating.—The use of tabulating and sorting machines, such as the Powers or Hollerith, considerably facilitates prompt and accurate accounts and statistics. Material requisitions made on cards for punching speed up the summarising and sorting by materials at Actual and Standard, and by product classes. Labour efficiencies are readily ascertained, and also the cost variations on shop orders, a procedure which is slow when done by hand.

The example in Fig. 162 is a card actually used for arriving at cost variations from standards by a company making plated electrical components.

Standard Prices and Rates List.—For the purpose of pricing materials, components, etc., a schedule of standard prices and rates is compiled for use by the Standard Cost Clerk.

EXAMINATION QUESTIONS

1. How can cost data be utilised to aid the management in detecting losses, and aid them in effecting economies ? Illustrate by forms and concrete examples.—*Institute of Cost and Works Accountants (Inter.).*

2. Give instances where efficiencies are indicated in costing information.—*Royal Society of Arts (Advanced).*

B B

3. State, shortly, the advantage of Standard Costs, indicating the industries to which they are particularly applicable.—*Society of Incorporated Accountants and Auditors (Final).*

4. Explain the principles and objects of Standard Costs.—*Society of Incorporated Accountants and Auditors (Inter.).*

5. Define "Standard Costs," and state what you consider to be their value.—*Society of Incorporated Accountants and Auditors (Inter.).*

6. Explain the significance of Standard Costs as compared with Actual Costs and show how they are applied and what information is obtained from their application.—*Society of Incorporated Accountants and Auditors (Final).*

7. How would you treat the following as to their effect on Standard Costs :

(a) Exceptional expenditure, *e.g.*, abnormally large and expensive repairs due to explosion or flood and not covered by insurance.

(b) Prolonged periods of overtime.—*Institute of Cost and Works Accountants (Final).*

8. Having completed the necessary arrangements for budgetary control, what steps would you take to ensure its proper influence upon the future period of working, to which it relates? Give your answer fully.—*Institute of Cost and Works Accountants (Final).*

9. What is meant by Standard Costs; in what circumstances may they be safely employed; what advantages do they offer?—*Institute of Cost and Works Accountants (Inter.).*

10. What is meant by the expression "pre-determined costs"? For what purposes are they used and how are they prepared?—*Institute of Cost and Works Accountants (Inter.).*

11. Describe fully the basis upon which Standard Costs are obtained and state their uses to the management. Illustrate your answer with an example.—*Institute of Cost and Works Accountants (Inter.).*

12. Define the following terms :

(a) Standard Costs as applied to a product.
(b) Uniform Costs as applied to an industry.
(c) Process Costs.
(d) Test Costs.

Institute of Cost and Works Accountants (Final).

13. In drawing up a scheme of Budgetary Control, what considerations should be taken into account, and how should they be provided for?—*Institute of Cost and Works Accountants (Final).*

14. Three Feeder Departments supply the manufacturing departments at pre-determined cost prices. At the end of the financial year two have made a book profit of £3,000 and £8,000 respectively, and the other has made a loss of £2,700. How would you deal with this situation?—*Institute of Cost and Works Accountants (Final).*

15. In valuing inventories should Standard Cost be used instead of actual cost, or market price, if the standard cost be lower than either of these? State your reasons.—*Institute of Cost and Works Accountants (Final).*

CHAPTER XXVI

MECHANISED COST ACCOUNTING

The Punched-Card Systems using Sorting and Tabulating Machines.—The equipment consists of the Card, the Key Punch, the Verifying Key Punch, the Electrical Sorting Machine and the Electrical Tabulating Machine. The Hollerith Sorting and Tabulating Machines are hired at a monthly rental which covers all costs of maintenance and service. The Punches are sold outright and have a life of about ten years. The Powers–Samas equipment can be hired or purchased.

Coding.—It is necessary that all essential data required for analytical and accounting purposes which appear on original documents be expressed in such a way as will enable it to be dealt with mechanically. This is accomplished by transferring the original data, previously translated into numerals, to special cards by means of punched holes. The punching is done on a simple punching machine, which can be operated by a girl after very few lessons.

The first essential is the compilation of a numerical index or code by which, for example, each Workman, Operation, Job, Account, Commodity, Stores Item and so forth, can be identified.

The principle upon which the code is designed depends very largely upon the organisation of the individual business, and on the information which the accountant requires for the proper presentation of the accounts and statistical records. For example, a code which has been found most useful for stores is a six-figure one, divided into two sections, the first three figures representing the group, and the second three figures the item in the group. If a code of this description is used, stores can be divided into 999 groups, each with a capacity of 999 items.

An interesting feature of both these systems is the provision for printing alphabetical descriptions, or names from punched holes. This feature reduces the necessity for coding all information, and makes it possible to produce complete legible statements, without the supplementary operation of typewriting or handwriting the descriptions, at the rate of 6,000 cards per hour listing and adding.

The Punched Card.—Hollerith cards are of uniform size, $7\frac{3}{8}$ in. by $3\frac{1}{4}$ in., each having printed on it 38, 60, or 80 vertical columns of numerals from 0 to 9 (Fig. 163). Within the limits of these columns the card may be arranged to provide for the information required for any particular business.

The Powers–Samas card can be designed to carry any number of columns from 45 to 130 (Fig. 171), and each individual column can record digits up to 39. Similarly, three columns can

FIG. 163.

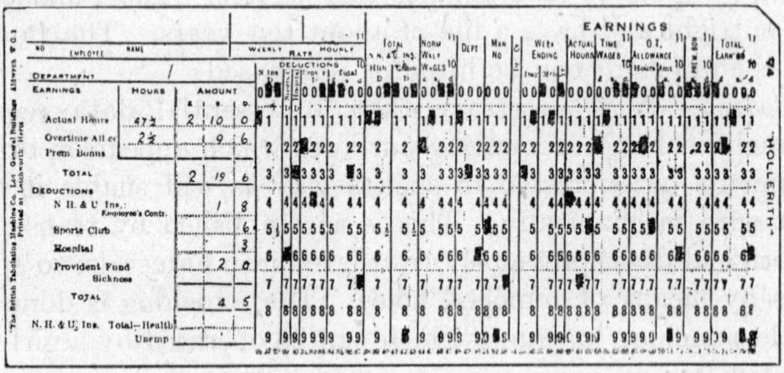

The 80 Column Hollerith Card (reduced).

be used to record digits up to 9,999, thus greatly extending the capacity of both the Hollerith and Powers–Samas cards.

The columns of figures enclosed by the vertical lines on the card are known as " fields." A " field " may occupy one or as many more columns as are necessary to record the information required. The heading of the " field " denotes the nature of the information therein, such as Month, Department, Quantity, Value, Job Number, etc.

When perforated or punched, the card is in all essentials a translation in numerical form of all the details recorded on the original document, whether it be a Stores Issue Requisition, a Job Card, a Time Distribution Sheet, or other record. Many analyses can be obtained from the one card, without the necessity of again referring to the original document.

"Dual" Cards.—A " dual " card is one used as an original

document as well as for a punched record. For example, a dual card, to be used as a Requisition and Issue Voucher, would be drawn up in the usual Requisition form. It would follow the usual course of procedure for a Requisition—details would be filled in by the person requiring the goods, the goods would be issued, and the necessary extensions and allocations made and coded. The original document, in this case a card, is then passed to the punch operators for punching, and then becomes also a record card. This dual form of card not only effects a considerable saving in stationery, but as there is from first to last only one document to handle, the liability of error is minimised.

The Key Punch.—The perforations in the cards are made by means of a Key Punch, operated electrically, or by hand. It is somewhat similar to a typewriting machine, and juniors can punch from 200 to 400 cards an hour.

There is an electrical duplicating punch which duplicates automatically on several cards, one at a time, the information common to all of them. Cards are fed in from the magazine, and when punched are ejected automatically. A " Master " card giving the information to be duplicated is placed in position at the top part of the machine. The whole, or part only, of a card can be duplicated as desired. When part only is duplicated, the remaining figures are punched in the usual way by depression of the keys.

Reproducing and Multiplying Punches.

(1) The Hollerith Reproducing Punch. This machine performs three functions :—

(a) The reproduction of information in one set of cards into another set, not necessarily in the same relative position.

(b) Gang punching of common information from a master card.

(c) The comparing of one group of cards with another and the automatic detection of any variation in punching.

(2) The Hollerith Multiplying Punch. This machine is unique. Hollerith cards are punched containing a Multiplier and a multiplicand, and are then fed into this punch,

which makes the necessary calculation and punches the product into any selected position of the same card. Further, any number of cards can be multiplied by a common Multiplier. The machine can be supplied to work entirely in decimals, or the rate may be expressed in pence and decimal parts of a penny or, alternatively, in shillings and decimal parts of a shilling, when a sterling answer can be given and punched.

The speed varies with the number of digits in the Multiplier from 700/1,400 calculations per hour.

Verification Punch.—As the value of the information produced by the Tabulating Machine depends on the accuracy of the holes punched in the card, a machine is provided, known

Fig. 164.

Powers–Samas Automatic Key Punch and Verifier.

as the Verification Key Punch, to verify mechanically the original punching. In operation, it is exactly similar to a Key Punch, but should an error have been made in the original operation, the card remains stationary in the machine, thus compelling the operator's attention to the mistake.

Once a card is punched it becomes a basic document, a permanent unchangeable record, which can be mechanically sorted, and from which the information punched therein can be printed, added or subtracted automatically as desired. As the punched holes cannot change position, the card must always reproduce accurately the figures represented by the punchings.

The Sorting Machine.—This is used for the purpose of arranging the punched cards in any desired order or classification, such as Man Number, Job Number, Article Number, Nominal Account, Traveller, Department, etc. A pointer may be set against the column on which it is desired the sorting process

FIG. 165.

Powers–Samas Alphabetical Printing Tabulator.

shall take place. After pressing the starting button, the sorting of the cards by Hollerith or Powers machines will proceed automatically at the rate of 24,000 per hour. The machine is so designed that once the cards have been placed in the Stacker it may be left unattended until all the cards have been sorted.

Tabulating.—After the cards have been sorted, the final phase

WEEK	GROUP	SHOP	OPN.	HOURS	WORKER	TIME	P.W.B.	TOTAL	ORDER NO.	M
T		20 40 60		20	20 40 60 80	20 11	20 CR 11	20 11		

T.S.F. 1208 9013   POWERS-SAMAS ACCOUNTING MACHINES   TRADE MARK   ACTAB   PAT. NO. 398223   REG   NO. 771461   LABOUR COSTING

FIG. 166.—Powers-Four Printing Tabulator, and Card Designed for Job Costing. (Actual size.)

of tabulating takes place. With the Hollerith machine the cards are placed in a hopper and the machine feeds them one by one past a series of brushes, which sense electrically the position of the various holes in the card, and so actuate, first, the adding, and, secondly, the printing mechanism. There is a roller to take the paper or forms on which the results are to be printed. This is similar to a typewriting carriage, and may be set for single,

Fig. 167.

Hollerith 38-Column Electric Tabulator, and (below) Key-Punch.

double or treble line spacing; may be moved from left to right; and will produce carbon copies, etc. The machine is constructed to add quantities of varying currencies, weights or units; to count the cards as they pass through the machine; to accumulate both sub- and grand-totals; and to list and add all the information on every card, item by item, as they pass through the machine. It is entirely automatic, and will pass 9000 cards an hour. A system using these machines is described in Ch. XXVII.

A recent feature added is a new method of Total Rolling or transferring from one counter to another, thus providing cross adding, and cross subtraction. This permits debits to be collected in one counter, and credits in another, when the machine will automatically produce the balance, either debit or credit.

The Powers–Samas machine reproduces information in a somewhat similar manner, but the system senses punched holes by positive mechanical means, and only the drive of the machines is electrical. For these machines, therefore, either Alternating or Direct Current may be used. Fig. 166 is an example of a Powers Card.

SMALL CARD TABULATORS.

(i) *The " Powers-Four " Machine.*—An economical machine placed on the market by the Powers–Samas Company, and known as the " Powers-Four," meets the needs of those numerous concerns which do not require the large capacity provided by the Standard Machines. The " Powers-Four " Machines operate from a much smaller card ($2'' \times 4\frac{11}{16}''$) carrying 36 columns instead of the 45 to 130 available on the Standard card. (Fig. 166.)

The Sorter and Tabulator of the " Powers-Four " Machines are of course smaller than those of the Standard set, but have ample capacity for all normal requirements. The Sorter has a speed of 24,000 cards per hour, and the Tabulator runs at 4,800 cards per hour.

(ii) *Hollerith 38-Column Tabulator.*—A small 38-column card is used, and the machine may have two, three or four counters, according to requirements. It embodies the Rolling Total feature already referred to, and provides for the smaller user all the advantages of the Hollerith System at a very much lower cost.

Needle-Sorting by Hand is explained on p. 417.

1. What method of recording work would you recommend for a factory employing over 1000 workers, and how would you propose to deal with the information so recorded, up to the stage of posting the Cost Ledgers? Give an idea of the numbers of transactions at each stage justifying your proposed treatment.—*Royal Society of Arts* (*Advanced*).

CHAPTER XXVII

MECHANISED COST ACCOUNTING (*cont.*)—COSTING IN ROLLED STEEL FACTORY

COMPLETE SYSTEM USING "HOLLERITH" TABULATING MACHINES

Introduction.—This chapter describes the application of the "Hollerith" Punched-Card System and Tabulating Machines to the accounting and costing records of Messrs. J. J. Habershon & Sons, Ltd., the well-known manufacturers of hot- and cold-rolled steel strips and sheets, whose kind co-operation has made the publication of such a detailed record possible.

The costing system installed in these modern and efficient mills, which are situated in Rotherham, is based on standard hourly rates, both for machines and for labour, but the Hollerith System can be equally well adapted to all other methods, such as the percentage and premium bonus schemes, which may be in force in other trades.

The primary advantage of the punched-card tabulating method of accounting is to ascertain and balance the cost of production quickly and efficiently, and, from these figures, to prepare a weekly Manufacturing Account and Balance Sheet.

The forms and accounts described are given in folded sheets at the end of the book.

Brief Description of the Product.—In this case, the raw material consists of billets and slabs of steel purchased from steel-makers, and, occasionally, strip and sheets already hot-rolled down to a pre-determined size. Material is not manufactured for stock, but only to customers' requirements, which may vary as follows :

(1) *Quality* : No limits arise, as any quality specified may be rolled.

(2) *Width* : Steel from $\frac{1}{4}$ in. to 36 ins. in width may be rolled.

(3) *Thickness* : Strip may be rolled down to a thickness of 0·0015 in.

(4) *Length* : Strip can be supplied in long random lengths, or specified lengths coiled up, or in specified lengths flat.

(5) *Finish* : It can be supplied soft, hard, black, bright, hardened and tempered, polished, or with round, sheared or ground edges.

List of Production Centres :

(1)	Hot-Rolling.	(9)	Hardening.
(2)	Annealing.	(10)	Tempering.
(3)	Cleaning.	(11)	Polishing.
(4)	Cold-Rolling.	(12)	Edge-dressing.
(5)	Shearing.	(13)	Grinding.
(6)	Paring.	(14)	Cutting to Length.
(7)	Slitting.	(15)	Flattening.
(8)	Straightening.	(16)	Circle Cutting.

These have not been given in the order of manufacture, as this varies according to quality, size, and finish. All processes are not necessarily applied to every order.

The Numerical Codes.—All statistical information has to be expressed in a numerical code suitable for the purpose of the tabulating machine. Although alphabetical description can be used, coding of such information is necessary in order to reduce the machine time for sorting purposes, and thus increase the capacity of the Hollerith machines in practical use. A carefully planned and comprehensive numerical code has therefore to be decided upon as the first step towards the installation of the equipment. Nominal and Control Account headings are given numbers ranging between 0 and 99, in accordance with the following list, and where sub-divisions of main accounts are necessary, the sub-account code must be given, together with a description.

01. *Petty Cash.*

02. *Bank.*

03. *Investments.*—Each investment is numbered, commencing at 1, those being the sub-account code numbers.

04. *Bills Receivable.*

05. *Accounts Receivable.*—Sub-divisions of this account are the Customers' Ledger Accounts. These must be kept in loose-leaf ledgers on the straightforward alphabetical vowel division system. Each vowel of each letter is allotted a number within the range of 0 to 99. This number therefore indicates the letter. Each of these numbers is followed by three more numbers indicating the customer's account. It is possible for 999 accounts to be opened for each letter of the alphabet.

11. *Raw Material Store.*—Raw Material is received from steel-makers in lots identified by a letter and a number, both being painted upon it. The letter indicates the quality of the steel and the number is the actual cast number. A separate stock card, as per **Form A,** * is opened for each cast of steel received, and the makers' numbers are used to identify them. These numbers are, therefore, the sub-accounts of this main account.

12. *Coal and Coke.*—Each class of fuel is given a number commencing at 1, and these are the sub-account numbers.

13. *Stores (Consumable).*—This heading covers consumable materials, small loose tools, utensils, implements and articles of all kinds for the maintenance, repair, and renewals of buildings, plant, and machinery. All these materials are first of all grouped under ten headings, each heading covering articles of a like nature, or articles used for similar purposes. Then, within each group, commodities having a definite similarity or relationship are arranged in sub-groups, and, within each sub-group, each commodity is numbered. A five-figure code is used. The first figure—reading left to right—indicates the main group. The next figure indicates the sub-group, and then there is provision for 999 commodities to be separately numbered within each sub-group. Each commodity number, of course, consists of the full five figures, so that groups and sub-groups are always indicated, and these numbers form the further sub-division of Account No. 13.

14. *Work in Progress.*—The sub-accounts are, of course, the records of each works order, and its number is the sub-account code. The products must be classified under main headings, and each group is allotted a block of numbers within the range of 1 to 99999.

15. *Partly Manufactured Stock.*—In addition to raw material being stocked in billet and slab form, controlled by Account No. 11, it may also be stocked in the form of hot- and cold-rolled strip and sheets. Each size is given a separate number, which forms the sub-account code.

21. *Land, Buildings, Plant, and Machinery.*—These are first

---

* All the forms referred to in this chapter are to be found in the two large illustrations, Appendices I and II, at the end of this book.

classified under ten main headings, and within each group, each building, machine, etc., is given a number within the range of 1 to 999.

22. *Loose Plant.*—The remarks made in 21 apply here.

32. *Accounts Payable.*—The sub-account code is made up of the suppliers' account numbers.

33. *Wages.*

34. *Salaries.*

35. *Repairs and Renewals or Special Expenditure.*—This account only controls, in total, expenditure on expense Job Numbers. A Job Number must be given to all work involving large expenditure, either on repairs, renewals, improvements, or capital. Regularly occurring repairs and maintenance are charged direct to the department concerned, and are not controlled by this account.

37. *Current Charges.*—This account controls all items of an expense nature which occur either irregularly, or vary each week. Examples of these, together with their sub-account numbers, are as follows :

    11. Electricity.
    14. Carriage and Cartage.
    30. National Insurance.
    41. Legal and Audit Charges.
    46. General Expenses.

38. *Fixed Charges.*—As the heading implies, only items of a fixed amount, or near enough to be called fixed, are controlled by this account. Examples of these are :

    10. Insurance.
    20. Rents Payable.
    30. Rates.

42. *Surplus.*

51. *Profit and Loss Account.*

52. *Trading Account.*—The numbers allotted to production orders will make up the sub-account code.

53. *Foundry Trading Account.*—The repairs and renewals necessitate the use of large quantities of iron and brass castings of all kinds and sizes. In this case the factory possesses its own foundry, and the output is grouped under main headings, according to similarity, and

method of casting or moulding. Within each group the castings or batches of castings made to each Stores Requisition are given a separate number. These Foundry Order Numbers make up the sub-account code to this account.

61. *Sales.*—The remarks made in 14 account apply here also.
62. *Miscellaneous Income.*
99. *Overhead.*—This account controls in total all debits and credits made in detail to departments, production centres, processes, or services. The sub-account code is made up of the numbers allotted to these, and a three-figure code is sufficient to identify them. Examples of these are as follows :

110. No. 1 Hot Mill.
120. No. 2 Hot Mill.
211. No. 1 Cold Mill Strong Rolls.
241. No. 4 Cold Mill Strong Rolls.
242. No. 4 Cold Mill Small Rolls.
301. No. 1 Pickling Department.
302. No. 2 Pickling Department.
311. No. 1 Annealing Department.
312. No. 2 Annealing Department.
394. Warehouse.
431. Sentinel Lorry.
500. Electric Power Service.
563. Stores Service.
600. Roll Turning.
610. Machine Shop.
620. Fitters.
900. General Works Expenses.

In each case the hundreds column identifies the group of departments, etc. For instance :

100 signifies Hot-Rolling Departments.
200   ,,   Cold-Rolling   ,,
300   ,,   Auxiliary processes or production centres.
400   ,,   Transport.
500   ,,   Services.
600   ,,   Maintenance Departments.
900   ,,   General Overhead Accounts.

Further indication is provided by the tens column. For instance, in the Hot- and Cold-Rolling Mills this column identifies the department, and in the 300 group it identifies the production centre, or process. The same remarks apply to the other groups. It will now be obvious that in the units column there is provision for nine sub-divisions of the tens, where necessary. Examples of these will be noticed in the 300 group.

In order to provide an analysis of charges to each department, etc., a further two-figure code is used, which allows for ninety-nine possible analysis headings. These are allocated in the following way:

00—19. Wages and Salaries Analysis.
20. Fuel.
21—29. Stores under classification.
21—29. Stores under classification heads.
30—39. Repairs and Renewals classified under predetermined plant headings.
55. Miscellaneous Expenses.
58. Current Charges.
59. Annual and Fixed Charges.
70—82. Redistribution of Services.
85—89. Various Administration Expenses.
90. Miscellaneous Credits.
91—99. Overhead Earned.

A sample printed Code Sheet is shown in Form B. One of these is headed for each department, production centre, service, and Overhead Account, and the printed code descriptions are fixed and unalterable throughout. All blank lines are filled in to suit each main account requirements. It follows, therefore, that any departmental account code necessitates seven figures, and they appear in the following form:

9,911,019 = No. 1 Hot Mill supervision.
9,916,020 = No. 6 Hot Mill Fuel.
9,921,121 = No. 1 Cold Mill Strong Rolls—Oils and Greases for Rolling.
9,931,137 = No. 1 Annealing Department—Repairs to Furnaces.

Documents and Original Entries.—Every transaction of an

c c

accounting nature appearing on any document must, therefore, be coded, either during the initial stages of preparation, or during the first use which is made of it, and it is generally necessary to decimalise weight when not so expressed at first. For reference purposes, a code number is given to each class of transaction. They are as follows :

0. *Miscellaneous.*—This class includes those which cannot be classified with the others. They are, however, referenced on the punched cards by means of a sub-code in columns 14 and 15. They include :—

01. Private Cash Book.
02. General Cash Book.
03. Petty Cash Book.
04. Financial Transfer Journal.
60. Cost Transfer Journal.
61. Salaries Distribution Sheet.
62. Fixed Charges Distribution Sheet.
63. Current Charges Distribution Sheet.
64. Coal Distribution Sheet.

1. *Sales Invoices and Credit Notes.*
2. *Purchase Invoices and Credit Notes.*
3. *Issues of Consumable Stores.*—This heading only covers issues and returns, but not purchases, of consumable supplies, and maintenance and repair items. In this case a dual card is used. The actual card punched is the original requisition filled in by the person requisitioning, and detached from a pad. A sample of this card is shown in Form C.
4. *Raw Material Issues.*—All details are obtained from Hot Mill Work Reports, which give Mill Outputs, Stoppages and Material consumed. A sample of this form is shown in Form D.
5. *Partly Manufactured Stock.*—Issues are entered upon dual cards.
6. *Wages.*—This heading refers to the distribution of wages, and does not include the making up of the pay-roll. Every man's time is accounted for on a work-sheet; an operator working alone fills in his own report; an assistant or one of a gang on the same job has his time filled in by the charge-hand on the latter's own report.

Every time-report is certified correct by a foreman. The design of the form is varied to suit the class of operator, and standard analysis headings and code numbers are printed in. Some of these are as per Forms E, F, G, H, and J. This reduces to a minimum the workman's time filling in and clerical time coding. Completed time sheets are handed in to the Time Office at the close of each shift, and are checked off, as regards total time, with the actual clock-cards. Analysis code numbers are inserted against those items which are not already entered against a printed code.

7. *Overhead.*—This is the term used to cover transactions affecting Control Account No. 99. These items appear upon Time-Sheets, Mill Reports, Process Returns, etc.

Annual and Fixed Charges are analysed to a weekly basis and punched upon cards, which can be used over and over again each week until they are either too worn, or the basis is altered.

Description and Use of Punched-Card Records.—Hollerith Cards are of standard size, but the capacity may be varied by altering the number of the columns. Where great detail is required, an 80-column card may be used, but in the actual case under review, a 45-column card is of sufficient capacity. The card in question is divided into what are known as " fields," of which there are fifteen. Each card punched represents one transaction, and may be compared to an entry in a journal, because it actually records the account to be debited, and the account to be credited. A similar card form is shown in Form K.

Column No. 1 records the class of transaction previously described.

Column No. 2 records the day.

Column No. 3 records the month.

Columns 4–15 are used to record references, such as Invoice and Requisition numbers; also sizes, units of issue, and qualities, and mill and shift numbers and grade of worker, where applicable.

Columns 16–22 state the account to be debited.

Columns 23–29 state the account to be credited.

Column 30 whenever Time appears, signifies whether such time is ordinary or overtime, " 1 " being punched for the former, and " 2 " for the latter.

Columns 31, 32 and 33 show the time spent upon orders—33 being for decimals of an hour—and in the case of Raw Material issues, the number of billets or slabs is punched in these columns.

Columns 34–39 give weight expressed in hundredweights and decimals to two places.

Columns 40–45 give money values correct to three decimal places of a pound.

Accounting Routine : (a) *Data transferred to Punched Cards.*— Thus, after all documents for a week have been cleared, every transaction recorded on them will have been transferred in code form to a punched card.   In effect, these transactions have been journalised mechanically.   Therefore, if the cards are sorted to the order of Credit Account and tabulated, and then re-sorted to the order of Debit Account and tabulated, it will be found that the totals of each tabulation will agree.   This is actually done, as will be explained further on, and it enables a weekly Profit and Loss Account and Balance Sheet to be produced.

A Card for every Works Order.—The ultimate aim of the system is, of course, the ascertaining of cost of production. This cannot be done by means of departmental and process costs, because of the wide variation in time taken on different orders, according to the size, quality, and finish.   Each order is therefore dealt with separately.   A cost card, as per Form L, is opened for every Works Order Number.   These are termed "Progress and Cost Cards," and they are folded over and filed in Visible Index Pockets, such as Kardex, so as to leave the bottom strip, containing the vital references, visible.

Progress and Cost Analysis.—The progress records, *i.e.* all facts, except money values, are entered up direct from work and time-sheets after every shift is finished.   Money values are posted up from a tabulation of Account No. 14 cards.   It is called "Progress and Cost Analysis," and a sample of this tabulation is shown in Form M.   Every batch of material issued is given a Production Order Number.   The size, quality, and finish govern the classification, and a block of numbers is allocated to each class.   Charges are made to orders in the following manner :

1. *Material.*—The actual material used is charged at cost price.

2. *Direct Labour.*—The actual cost is charged, but for the sake of convenience this is included in the Overhead Rate.

3. *Overhead.*—Standard Hourly Rates are in operation for each department, process, and production centre covering all indirect expenses.

Analysis of Overhead.—In connection with Overhead, actual expenses are analysed and accumulated to each department, production centre, process and service, each period of four or five weeks. The year is divided into eight periods of four weeks each and four periods of five weeks each—two fours being followed by a five in each quarter.

Distribution of Overhead.—At the end of each period, services, balances on Maintenance Departments, and general Overhead Accounts are distributed over the producing departments and processes, in a predetermined manner, and these distributions are punched up on cards. By including these cards in the last week of a period, it follows that all charges are concentrated upon producing departments, etc. The figures now arrived at, therefore, are the total costs of operating such departments for the period.

Adjustment of Under- or Over-applied Overhead.—By making a tabulation of departmental sub-accounts 91 to 99, it is possible to find the amounts charged to orders by Standard rates. The differences between Actual and Standard are transferred direct to Profit and Loss Account under the heading "Balance of Manufacturing Expenses." These differences may be caused by overtime, or plant idleness.

Sales and Cost of Sales.—Actual sales of completed orders are credited on the Cost Cards from a sales tabulation each week. All punched cards recording charges to orders (Debits and Credits to 14 Account) are filed to order numbers in a separate drawer. At the end of each week, those orders which have been completed are listed, and these cards are sorted out of the filing drawer. They are then tabulated to order number and also summarised to classification. The Sales Cards are dealt with similarly, and the results give profits and losses to orders and to classes. The Weekly Profit and Loss Account is shown as in Form N.

Special Expenditure (Heavy Repairs and New Plant).—It will be seen that very few figures are required to provide the net operating results for the week. Special Expenditure requires further explanation. Control Account No. 35 records all expenditure on extra heavy repairs, renewals and on new plant. A number is given to each job and all charges are left on Account No. 35 until a job is completed. These charges, therefore, are shown as deductions on the Weekly Statements, but immediately a job is completed its allocation is decided and a credit entry (red ink) will appear against this heading for the amount involved. All debit entries are made in black ink and all credits in red ink throughout the system.

Proving Totals at Every Stage.—At every stage in the preparation of cards, totals are agreed with some known figure. For instance, when a bundle of invoices has passed through the punching and verifying section, the cards are run through the Tabulator for a total of Weight or Money, or both. The tabulated total is agreed with the Invoice Register Total, in which the invoices have already been entered. Each class of card, distinguished by the punching in Column 1, is filed together, and when all documents for a week are passed out completed, the cards are tabulated, each class separately, to obtain totals of Quantity and Money for comparison with the same totals after all weekly figures have been obtained from the cards. This procedure is a safeguard against missing cards.

Statistics for Works Manager.—In the meantime, however, various tabulations have been made of information for Works Manager's use from the same cards which are going to be used for financial and Works Accounting purposes. The following are three examples :

(1) Weekly Order Analysis of Raw Material Issued.—This shows the quantity (weight and number of pieces) of each size of each cast (Quality) issued to every order separately, showing in respect of each issue the Hot Mill in which it was rolled and the date and shift.

(2) Wages Analysis.—This shows the total time and wages paid to each grade of operator, indicating in each case the Control Account which has been debited— usually 14, 35, 53 or 99. Overtime and ordinary time are tabulated separately.

(3) Overtime Analysis.—Overtime worked by each man, showing the periods on Saturday afternoon and on Sunday separately from those worked during the week.

Tabulating for Control Accounts.—When the necessary subsidiary tabulations are completed each week, all cards of every class are taken together and sorted into the order of Credit Account (Columns 23 to 29). The cards are then tabulated, and by the Hollerith system of automatic control, the tabulated figures give, in respect of each account credited, the details making up the total credit, showing also all the accounts which have been debited. The cards are then re-sorted to the order of Debit Account (Columns 16 to 22), and the same procedure is repeated on the Tabulator, but, of course, the results of the accounts are reversed. These two tabulations are then posted into a Control Ledger, quite a simple record, showing in respect of each account the total debits and credits, and in detail every other account affected, but all in code, no descriptions being necessary.

Profit and Loss Account and Balance Sheet Weekly.—At the end of each period the balances on Control Accounts are extracted, by the use of Comptometers, and a more detailed Profit and Loss Account is completed, together with a summary Balance Sheet. Of course, each week the transfers necessitated by the completion of a Weekly Profit and Loss Account have already been dealt with. Form O shows how the Profit and Loss Account for a complete period may be compiled. The left-hand Weight and Money columns contain the Period results. The right-hand columns contain the totals of all weeks to date, from the beginning of the financial year. On the reverse side of the same sheet is provision for the Sales Analysis for the same two periods of time. The information is copied from tabulations actually printed on the tabulator by using the Sales and Work in Progress Cards, and controlling the Order Classification. Below the Sales Analysis is provision for a very brief Balance Sheet.

Tabulation of Detailed Overhead.—To revert once again to the Weekly Tabulations, Account No. 99 is taken out in absolute detail. On the Debit Side, by controlling on Columns 18 to 22, we obtain in respect of each department, production centre, process and service, totals of each sub-account, descriptions of which have already been given. And by also controlling on Columns 23 and 24, we are told which of the Credit Control Accounts are affected by every Debit Item, or, in other words, these two columns indicate whether those items are Wages, Materials or Overhead, etc. The Credit Account items are obtained in the reverse way by controlling on Columns 25 to 29, and 16 and 17. These sub-account totals of both Debit and Credit items are required in respect of each period in the year. As each weekly tabulation of Account No. 99 is the condensation of a large number of cards, it follows that the total cards for each four- or five-weekly period would occupy a long time on the Tabulator. This difficulty is overcome by punching a card for each tabulated item every week, and using these summary cards for the purpose. In the same way, each period tabulation is punched up on cards in order to provide totals for the year.

Comparative Cost Summaries and Averages.—The Period Tabulations provide the figures for the Summary of Production Costs and Averages, samples of which forms are attached.

Form P shows all departments, etc., for each period analysed under the main headings shown, and provision is made for the actual costs per hour and per ton to be inserted.

Form Q is opened for each department, and allows for period figures to be compared with each other and with the average of four weeks of the previous year.

The Annual Tabulation of Account No. 99 furnishes the information for the Analysis of Production Costs and Averages, as in Form R. This gives absolute detail and provides for a comparison of five years. These various forms give dissections of costs for comparison with the standard hourly rates in operation.

Pay-Roll and Labour Statistics.—The Pay-roll is produced on the Hollerith Tabulator in pounds, shillings, and pence, through the medium of a Hollerith dual purpose card. Every man clocks on, using a similar clock card to that shown in Form S. After the Time Office staff have finished with all operators' cards, they are sent forward to the Comptometer Section for time earnings to be calculated and bonus earnings to be entered upon the card itself. They are then punched up and a tabulated Pay-roll is produced, as per Form T. Columns 24 and 25 contain codes of deduction, and enable an analysis of total deductions to be made. After the completion of the Pay-roll and the stamping of the Health and Unemployment Insurance Cards, the above-mentioned Hollerith dual clock cards are filed away in Man Number order. At the end of each Income Tax half-year, these cards are used to produce on the Tabulator a total of each man's earnings, for entry upon the form supplied by the Revenue

Authorities. The weekly earnings of each man are shown, thus providing quick reference whenever periodical earnings of men are required for compensation and other purposes.

FIG. 167 A.

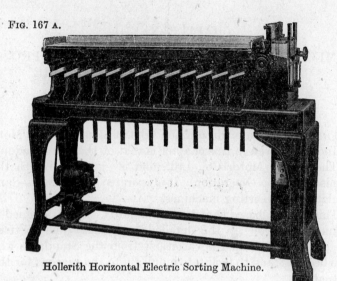

Hollerith Horizontal Electric Sorting Machine.

EXAMINATION QUESTIONS

1. State the method of costing applicable to an undertaking with which you are familiar, and set out briefly the advantages of such method.— *Society of Incorporated Accountants and Auditors (Inter.).*

2. Set out what you consider to be the advantages and disadvantages of using, as primary documents, cards that are to be used on punching and tabulating machinery. What precautions would you take to obviate any of the disadvantages anticipated?—*Institute of Cost and Works Accountants (Inter.).*

CHAPTER XXVIII

MECHANISED COST ACCOUNTING (*cont.*)—PRO-DUCTION CONTROL COSTING IN THE MOTOR-CAR INDUSTRY

System using Powers–Samas Machines

The description of Production Control Costing in the Motor-car Industry given in this chapter is that of the system adopted by The Austin Motor Co., Ltd., and is given here with their permission and co-operation. It is operated with Powers–Samas tabulating and sorting machines.

This system, based as it is on Standard Costs, is designed not so much to throw up the detailed cost of any one particular job, but to throw up the variations from the Standards which have been set, and to facilitate inquiry into the reasons for these fluctuations.

It is of interest to note that this company do not work on an hourly basis. The whole of the time recording is designed round the minute. The operations on each part number are timed as occupying so many minutes. Special time clocks for recording these minutes have been installed.

Another interesting feature is that material is controlled in terms of chassis numbers. It is known for instance at any time to what chassis number there is material available to build.

Wages.—Fig. 168 shows the Standard Labour Card on which are recorded all of the details relative to each operation on each part by each employee. Columns 35–37 and 38–40 show respectively the time allowed on the job and the time taken, from which are calculated the bonus points earned by the employee. A tabulation of these cards to show the totals by part and operation is given in Fig. 169.

At present the employees are grouped into five distinct grades, and it is an essential of the piece-work scheme that they earn more than a certain pre-determined bonus constantly. In fact, all the men who do not earn this fixed bonus are removed from the pay-roll. High bonus means high output, and there-

358

fore all of the tabulations are carefully scrutinised with a view
to eliminating all second-rate labour. These remarks of course
only hold good in so far as the basic piece-work rates are
correct; the checking of these rates, however, is continuous,
but it is a firmly fixed rule that no piece-work price once made
is ever cut. It is the recognition of this fact by the employees

FIG. 168.

WAGES CARD

Cols.		
1– 2.	Week.	
3– 6.	Check number.	
7.	Class.	
8–12.	Part number.	
13–14.	Operation number.	
15.	Type and S.O. number.	
16–20.	Works control number.	
21.	Account number.	
22–24.	Rate.	
25–28.	Quantity.	
29–31.	Time allowed each.	
32–34.	Machine number.	
35–37.	Time allowed total.	
38–40.	Time taken total.	
41–44.	Amount.	
45.	Sort.	

This card is of particular interest as it makes full use of the supplementary
punching positions. For instance, " Class " occupies one column, but by allocating nine supplementary positions shown printed at the top of the card (*i.e.*
the top three rows of figures) it is possible to punch " Classes " up to 99,
instead of classes only 1–9, which is the normal limitation of punched cards.

that largely accounts for their high standard of application and
output.

Pay-Roll.—The minutes worked, saved or lost each day
are booked on the reverse of each worker's time card daily,
and are certified by the inspectors. At the end of the pay
week the cards are evaluated and passed to the Powers-Punch
operators, who punch a card of the design of Fig. 171 for each
worker.

The cards are tabulated in department order and check
number. This operation gives a totalled and completed pay-roll.

FIG. 169.

WAGES.

THE AUSTIN MOTOR CO. LTD.   FORM NO. 799

CHECK NO	WEEK	CLASS	PART NO.	OPERATION NO.	TYPE	S.O. NO.	CONTROL NO.	ACCOUNT NO.	RATE	QUANTITY	TIME ALLOWED EACH	TIME ALLOWED TOTAL (MINUTES)	TIME TAKEN TOTAL (MINUTES)	AMOUNT UNITS	SORT
10613	44	1	3G 91	1	2164	166	240		2128	1005	45	452	255		86
10910	44	1	3G 91	2	2161	166	240		2128	1005	45	452	255		88
		1							1021	1000	22	220	195		22
10941	44	1	3G 91	3	2164	166	240		1021	1008	22	220	195		22
									1957	1000	34	340	225		62
10505	44	1	3G 91	4	2129	166	240		1957	1000	34	340	1325		62
11417	44	1	3G 91	4	2129	166	240		21708	1500	2000	30000	1275		5785
29127	43	1	3G 91	4	2129	164	240		21128	1508	2000	29960	1755		5765 / 591
									2170	1148	2200				
29102	41	1	3G 91	5	2129	164	240		6468	448	20000	30005	4305		1734
29102	43	1	3G 91	5	2129	164	240		1872	52	1500	75	75		129
29125		1	3G 91	5	2129	164	240		1872	215	150		42		13

FIG. 170.

SCRAP ACCOUNT

THE AUSTIN MOTOR CO. LTD.   FORM NO. 795

DATE MONTH	DATE DAY	CLASS (1. MATERIAL SCRAP, 2. OPERATORS SCRAP, 3. FOR RECTIFICATION)	PART NO.	OPERATION NO.	CONTROL NO.	INSPECTION DEPT. SHEET NO.	QUANTITY	MATERIAL TOTAL VALUE PENCE	LABOUR TOTAL VALUE PENCE
9	6	1	1A 71278	4	16155	2755	20001	365	104
9	6	1	1A 71168	4	16155	2755	34	35033	91
9	6	1	1A 70388	3	16155	2755	2126	57399	52473
9	6	1	1E 70050	1.13	16155	2755		395	363
9	6	1	1F 70050	3	16155	2755		2321	968
9	6	2	1A 70044	13	16155	2758	20	2018	245
9	6	2	1A 70044	1	16155	2755	22	33559	441
9	6	2	1A 70049	23	16155	2755	21	33333	13
9	6	2	1A 70051	6	16155	2755			15

The totals also give at the end of each department the required number of £1 notes, 10s. notes, half-crowns, florins, shillings, sixpences and threepenny pieces to make up the cash. This arrangement is found exceedingly useful, and considerably expedites the work of the Brandt Automatic Cashier when making up the pay packets.

Upon the completion of the pay-roll, the cards are segregated

Fig. 171.

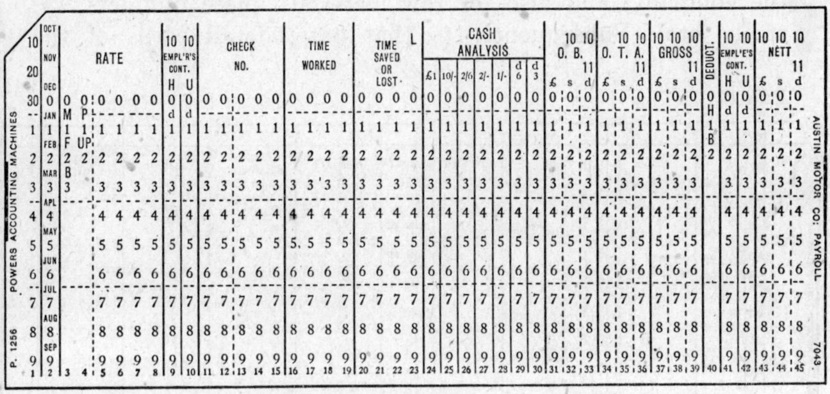

PAY-ROLL CARD

Cols. 1–2.   Date.
3.   Male, female or boy.
4.   Productive or unproductive.
5–8.   Employee's wage rate.
9–10.   Employer's contributions, National Health and Unemployment Insurance.
11–15.   Check number (cols. 11–12 also designate department).
16–19.   Total minutes worked during the week.
20–23.   Total minutes saved or lost during week.
24–30.   Cash make-up in nett wages.
31–33.   Output bonus.
34–36.   Overtime allowance.
37–39.   Gross wages.
40.   Hospital and benevolent deductions.
41–42.   Employee's contribution.
43–45.   Nett wages.

by class of labour and department, to obtain figures relating to efficiency :

Time worked, time saved, time lost by Department.
„   „   „   „   „   by Class of Labour.
Output Bonus earned by Service Departments.
„   „   „   by Producing Departments.
Overtime allowance by Department for Overhead Allocation purposes, etc.

Material Control.—As already stated, material is controlled in terms of chassis numbers. This of course only applies once the material has been definitely ordered. Fig. 172 shows the form of card from which are produced all the data relating to the buying of components and raw material. The quantities of this card are recorded in units, and not in terms of chassis numbers. At a given date a Master Card is punched giving the buying position on each piece that is not manufactured by the company, and also for raw materials, piece numbers, *i.e.* steels, etc. Subsequently to that date, detail cards of the

FIG. 172.

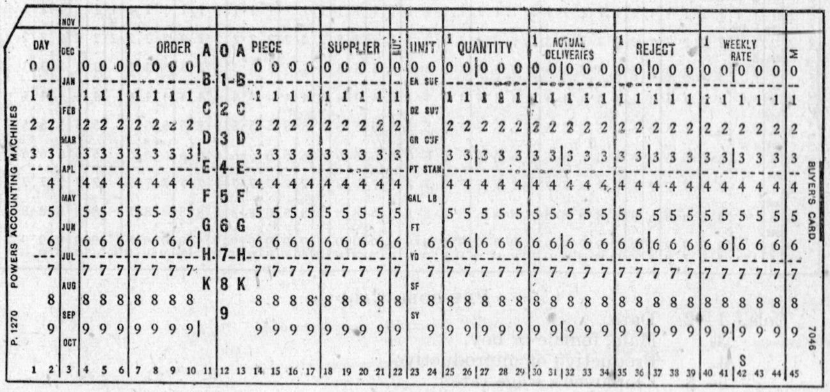

BUYER'S CARD

Cols. 1– 3.	Date.	Cols. 23–24.	Unit.
4– 6.	Spare.	25–29.	Quantity ordered.
7–11.	Order.	30–34.	Actual deliveries made.
12–17.	Piece number.	35–39.	Pieces rejected.
18–21.	Supplier.	40–44.	Weekly rate of delivery.
22.	Buyer's number.	45.	Master of detail cards.

same design and wording are punched for each order, quoting quantity ordered, and weekly rate of delivery required. Cards are also punched from the receiving departments' records, giving the actual deliveries made, and rejects, as, and when they arise. Periodically (weekly) both the Master and the Detail Cards are sorted by piece number, and tabulations are taken which show at that date, the total quantity ordered, the total deliveries made, and the total rejects for each piece number. Thus, when an order is complete, the actual deliveries less the rejects must equal the quantity ordered.

Fig. 173.

THE AUSTIN MOTOR CO. LTD.

STORES ISSUES.

FORM NO. 796

DATE		PART NO.	FROM CONTROL NO.	TO CONTROL NO.	PREFIX OR SUFFIX	SHOP ORDER NO.	QUANTITY		UNIT	VALUE PER UNIT		TOTAL VALUE		PARAGON NO.	
							UNITS	DECIMALS		£	DECIMALS	£	DECIMALS		
21	6	2 K 761	0085	202500		2119	300							78756	
21	6	2 K 761	0085	202500		2119	300					*		78756	
21	6	2 K 843	0085	165400			240							76717	1
21	6	2 K 843	0085	165400			240					*		76717	
17	6	2 K 900	0085	162500		2148	1000							76469	
17	6	2 K 900	0085	162500		2148	1000					*		76469	
15	6	2 K 1162	0085	162400			840							74682	1
17	6	2 K 1162	0085	195400			120							74675	1
16	6	2 K 1162	0085	208600			240							74782	1
15	6	2 K 1162	0085	162400			1200					*		234139	
22	6	2 K 1163	0085	201500		2148	2000							79361	
21	6	2 K 1163	0085	162500		2148	18000							79020	
17	6	2 K 1163	0085	165500		2156	4000							76420	
15	6	2 K 1163	0085	702400			180							74768	1
21	6	2 K 1163	0085	165500		2148	6000							78680	
21	6	2 K 1163	0085	165400			240							76718	1
22	6	2 K 1163	0085	201500		8600	30420					*		454967	
21	6	2 K 1164	0085	162500		2148	3000							79021	
20	6	2 K 1164	0085	165500		2148	3000							77563	
15	6	2 K 1164	0085	162400			600							74679	1
16	6	2 K 1164	0085	203500			420							74726	1
17	6	2 K 1164	0085	165500		2148	12000							76504	
20	6	2 K 1164	0085	40600			1440							76652	1
21	6	2 K 1164	0085	208600			240							76720	1
21	6	2 K 1164	0085	162500		6444	30700					*		535865	
17	6	2 K 1165	0085	165500		2056	3000							77228	
21	6	2 K 1165	0085	165500		2148	1500							78511	
17	6	2 K 1165	0085	165500		4204	4500					*		155739	
21	6	2 K 1172	0085	162500		2148	1500							79022	
20	6	2 K 1172	0085	165500		2148	3000							77564	
21	6	2 K 1172	0085	162500		4296	4500					*		156586	
17	6	2 K 1178	0085	165500		2156	2000							75926	
17	6	2 K 1178	0085	165500		2156	2000					*		75926	
21	6	2 K 1201	0085	130500		2119	2000							78727	
17	6	2 K 1201	0085	165500		2156	8000							76421	
17	6	2 K 1201	0085	165500		2156	3200							75973	
17	6	2 K 1201	0085	165500		2156	1350							75948	
17	6	2 K 120		165500		2148	15							76505	

Various other reports are also made from the cards, such as :

(1) Quantity outstanding on order by piece number.
(2) Total Rejects from each supplier.
(3) Commitments by Type of Car, *e.g.* 7 H.P., 12 H.P., etc.
(4) Commitments by Buyer.
(5) Quantity ordered by each piece number.

Tabulations from these cards are finally forwarded to the Purchase Ledger Section to facilitate the passing of accounts for payments.

Stores Issues.—For each issue from stores of materials for production, a card is punched and a weekly tabulation is made as shown in Fig. 173, which shows the issues of parts from control No. 85 (a sub-store or inspection point).

Scrap Control.—Parts are inspected at regular points in the shops. Cards are punched from Inspection Sheets and tabulated to show the scrap at each inspection point and the reasons for rejection. Fig. 170 illustrates a tabulation of rejections during one day at control No. 1615 by scheduled reasons 1 and 2.

Production Control.—The most valuable part of the system is that devoted to the Control of Production. The form of card used on this work is given in Fig. 174. These cards are punched on printing punches, the information punched being recorded automatically at the same time along the top edge of the card.

The Master Card.—At the commencement of every financial year, a Master Card is punched for each piece number, showing the production position on each piece at that date. This information is procured from the stock-taking, and Work-in-Progress Records already described.

When a Master Card is fully punched, it is interesting to note the information recorded thereon. Thus, from the Master Card, shown in Fig. 174, we infer the following facts :

(1) There are sufficient quantities of Piece 1A1456 on order to build up to Chassis 23,500.
(2) Quantities to build up to Chassis 23,450 have been received.
(3) Sufficient quantities have been passed by the receiving deck to stores to build Chassis 23,230.

(4) Sufficient quantities to build up to Chassis 23,200 have been issued from stores.

(5) Sufficient quantities (fully machined) are available in the finished stores to build up to Chassis 23,000.

FIG. 174.

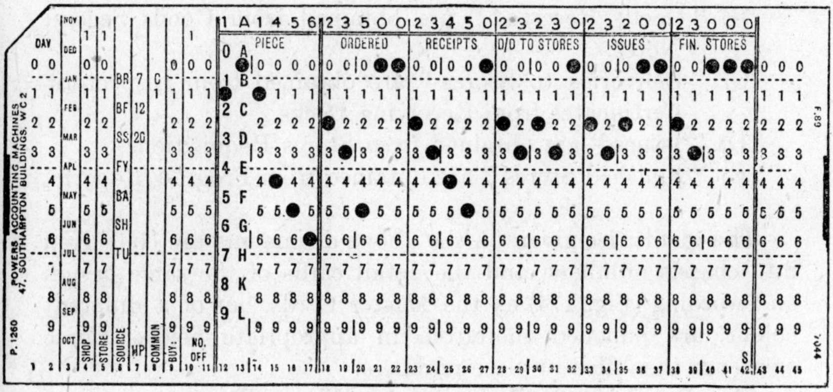

MASTER PRODUCTION CONTROL CARD

Cols. 1– 3. Date.
      4. Shop number.
      5. Store number.
      6. Source (bought out rough, bought out finished, stamp, foundry, bar, sheet and turn).
      7. Common (to designate if piece is common to 7 H.P., 12 H.P. and 20 H.P. chassis).
  10–11. Number required on each chassis (e.g., 1 if propeller shafts, 4 if piston, etc.).
  12–17. Piece.
  18–22. Quantity (in terms of chassis number) ordered.
  23–27. Receipts (in terms of chassis number) on receiving deck.
  28–32. Deliveries to Stores (in chassis number).
  33–37. Issues to production (in chassis number).
  38–42. Return from production to finished store (in chassis number).

Cards of the same design and wording, but of different colour, are used for detail additions and deductions referred to on p. 366.

Further :

(6) The difference between fields 1 and 2 gives Pieces ordered but not received.

(7) The difference between fields 2 and 3 gives Pieces received but held up for inspection.

(8) The difference between fields 3 and 4 gives Pieces in stock.

(9) The difference between fields 4 and 5 gives Pieces in Work-in-Progress.

D D

The Detail Card (Additions).—Data are received from various sources regarding the movement of pieces and materials; the main ones are given :

(A) " Goods Ordered " are obtained from Buyers' Tabulations.

(B) " Goods Received " are obtained from Goods Second Notes.

(C) " Deliveries to Stores " are obtained from Inspectors' Certificates from Receiving Decks.

(D) " Issues " are obtained from Stores Requisitions.

(E) " Finished Stores " are obtained from Progress Reports.

The quantities given on the above documents are converted into chassis numbers, and the detail cards of the same design and wording (Fig. 174) as the Master Cards, but of a different colour, are punched therefrom in appropriate fields. These cards are then filed in piece numbers.

The Detail Card (Deductions).—Where Pieces are found to be incorrect either on the Receiving Deck or in course of machining, cards are punched for these scrap quantities. The cards (Fig. 174) are deduction cards, as obviously the Pieces concerned cannot be regarded as being available for production. After punching the cards are filed in piece number.

Tabulations.—Twice weekly all the Master and Detail Cards are together run through the Sorter on piece number. The Cards are now tabulated on to Kalamazoo Sheets. The tabulator takes the Master Card for each Piece, adds to it all the " addition " cards, and deducts " deduction " cards, and then prints only the final results for each piece number.

The Tabulation appears thus :

FIG. 175.   CHASSIS NUMBER.............

Piece No.	Ordered (1).*	Receipts. (2).	D/D to Stores. (3).	Issues. (4).	Finished Stores. (5).
1 A 1	23,904	23,607	23,600	23,580	23,490
1 A 2	23,700	23,650	23,600	23,556	23,500
1 A 3	23,490	23,400	23,400	23,360	23,300

* These numbers refer to the "fields" on the cards.

The progress of each piece number is seen at a glance. Thus from the above we see that of Piece 1 A 1 there are sufficient ready to build up to Chassis 23,490. There are also :

90	Pieces of 1 A 1 in Production			*i.e.*	Field 4	less	Field 5
20	,,	,,	,,	Rough Stores	,,	,,	3	,,	,,	4
7	,,	,,	,,	Held up on Receiving Deck	,,	,,	2	,,	,,	3
297	,,	,,	,,	Outstanding on order	,,	,,	1	,,	,,	2

From the office copy of the above tabulation, new Master Cards are punched in preparation for the building up of the next Production Control schedules.

All Production Estimates receive special attention. Thus upon an Output being determined, it is known, by reference to certain charts, what chassis numbers should be in progress during any given week. At short intervals, therefore, the current Master Production Cards are sorted in Fields 1, 2, 3, 4, 5. This arranges the piece numbers in chassis order, and it is a simple matter to extract all cards below the given chassis numbers.

The Cards are then re-sorted back into piece number and a tabulation gives :

(1) The piece number behind Order.
(2) ,, ,, ,, ,, Delivery.
(3) ,, ,, ,, ,, Delivery to Stores.
(4) ,, ,, ,, ,, Issues to Production.
(5) ,, ,, ,, ,, Deliveries to Finished Stores.

It should be noted particularly that the company use to the full the benefits which can be obtained from mechanical accounting. They very rightly insist on up-to-date figures. Figures which are twenty-four hours old are valueless to the company.

To get out the results on time, the machines are worked both day and night. Throughout the night, a special shift is employed on producing the statistics relative to the previous day's work, and at nine o'clock the following morning each executive has on his desk all the essential statistics covering his own department for the preceding day. The value of such a system is too obvious to require stressing.

Stocktaking.—A Card as in Fig. 176 is punched from the counting slips filled in by the stocktakers, and is used for all pieces in progress through the shops. As a Piece may be in

various stages of manufacture at the time of stocktaking, the
punched card, when sorted and tabulated under piece number,
collects all Pieces together in the three totals. The work of
pricing is therefore simplified, one pricing being made for all
Pieces of a like nature in the Rough and Finished groups, while
the number of extensions for that Piece, if in progress, depends
upon the different number of operations involved. Stock sheets
are produced, therefore, giving the total number of Pieces,
Rough, In Operation, and Finished.

FIG. 176.

STOCKTAKING CARD FOR WORK IN PROGRESS AND FINISHED PARTS IN
SHOPS

Cols. 1– 3.   Spare.
      4.   Common (to designate those parts common to 7 H.P., 12 H.P.,
             and 20 H.P. chassis).
   5–11.   Location of stock.
  12–17.   Piece number.
  18–21.   Total quantity counted.
  22–24.   Unit.
  25–26.   Operation number completed (for use with cols. 31–34).
  27–30.   Pieces rough.
  31–34.   Pieces in operation or process.
  35–38.   Pieces finished.

The top copy is sent to the Cost Department, who price the
items, and therefrom punch a card as in Fig. 177.

Cards as in Fig. 177 are distributed to all stores for all stock
not located as Work-in-Progress. The above cards deal with
Raw Material, Service, Stationery, and Non-Productive Material
Stores.

The cards are appropriately filled in by the stocktakers and
returned to the Cost Department for coding (in case of Raw
Material, etc.), and pricing. The cards are then punched.

Note that in no case have extensions been made. The accuracy of the punching receives special attention from the auditors of the company, but not more than usual scrutiny is given the cards by the Powers Department, and yet it was found by the auditors (who carried out a check of every card) that, though over 50,000 cards were involved, errors had only occurred in four places.

Rapid Stock Valuation.—After completion of checking, the

FIG. 177.

LOCATION	PS OP	CR OP	TYPE A/C	CODE OR PIECE NO	MATERIAL RATE d dec.	LABOUR RATE d dec.	QUANTITY	OPER.	
0 0 0 0	0 0	0 0	0 0 0	0 0 0 0 0 0 0	0 0 0 0 0 0 0 0	0 0 0 0 0 0	0 0 0 0 0	0 0 0	CODE OR PIECE
1 1 1 1	1 1	1 1	1 1 1	1 1 1 1 1 1 L	1 1 1 1 1 1 1 1	1 1 1 1 1 1	1 1 1 1 1	1 1 1	MATERIAL RATE d dec. EA.
2 2 2 2	2 2	2 2	2 2 2	2 2 2 2 2 2 2	2 2 2 2 2 2 2 2	2 2 2 2 2 2	2 2 2 2 2	2 2 2	
3 3 3 3	3 3	3 3	3 3 3	3 3 3 3 3 3 3	3 3 3 3 3 3 3 3	3 3 3 3 3 3	3 3 3 3 3	3 3 3	LABOUR RATE d dec. EA.
4 4 4 4	4 4	4 4	4 4 4	4 4 4 4 4 4 4	4 4 4 4 4 4 4 4	4 4 4 4 4 4	4 4 4 4 4	4 4 4	
5 5 5 5	5 5	5 5	5 5 5	5 5 5 5 5 5 5	5 5 5 5 5 5 5 5	5 5 5 5 5 5	5 5 5 5 5	5 5 5	QUANTITY EA.
6 6 6 6	6 6	6 6	6 6 6	6 6 6 6 6 6 6	6 6 6 6 6 6 6 6	6 6 6 6 6 6	6 6 6 6 6	6 6 6	

POWERS ACCOUNTING MACHINES

DESCRIPTION.

LAST OPERATION

RATED BY...........

P. 1278   7049

1 2 3 4 5 6 7 8 9 10 11 12 13 14 15 16 17 18 19 20 21 22 23 24 25 26 27 28 29 30 31 32 33 34 35 36 37 38 39 40 41 42 43 44 45

STOCK VALUATION CARD
Priced in Cost Office

Cols. 1– 4. Location (not such a detailed location as on Fig. 176).
     5. Punching operator.
   6– 7. Checking operator.
  8–10. Nominal Account (Analysis Account).
 11–18. Code or price number.
 19–24. Material rate.
 25–30. Labour rate.
 31–35. Quantity.
 36–38. Operation number.

cards are "Digited." That is, sortings are made on the quantity field, and tabulations made adding the unit prices. The final result of five sortings and five tabulations is the total value of stock. 120,000 extensions are reduced to forty-five extensions with a consequent very large saving of time. This is the quickest method of stock valuation known. The details of the procedure are as follows :

The usual method of bulk extension by punched cards is to sort the cards by *Rate* and add quantity. In the following method the cards are sorted by *Quantity* and totalled on rate, and it makes no difference to the accuracy if tons are added to feet or lbs. to pints.   Thus :

SPECIMEN ITEMS TO BE EXTENDED

Quantity.	Labour Price.		Material Price.		Labour Value.			Material Value.		
	s.	d.	s.	d.	£	s.	d.	£	s.	d.
11		4		3		3	8		2	9
21		1		2		1	9		3	6
21	2	6		6	2	12	6		10	6
2	2	0	1	0		4	0		2	0
12	1	6	1	3		18	0		15	0
12		3		9		3	0		9	0
22		4		2		7	4		3	8
Total Value					£4	10	3	£2	6	5

Operation 1.

Sort on Unit Column (*) Tabulate adding Price. Thus :

Operation 2.

Sort and Tabulate on tens column (*) of Quantity. Thus :

	Labour Price.		Material Price.			Labour Price.		Material Price.	
	s.	d.	s.	d.		s.	d.	s.	d.
11*		4		3	*11		4		3
21*		1		2	*12		3		9
21*	2	6		6	*12	1	6	1	3
	2	11		11		2	1	2	3
2*	2	0	1	0					
12*		3		9	*21		1		2
12*	1	6	1	3	*21	2	6	6	
22*		4		2	*22		4		2
	4	1	3	2		2	11		10

Operation 3.

Multiply Cash Totals by designation digits : add the results and the answer is the Total Value of Stock.   Thus :

	Labour Price.			Material Price.			Labour Value.			Material Value.		
		s.	d.		s.	d.	£	s.	d.	£	s.	d.
Op. 1.	1 × 2	11		1 ×		11		2	11			11
„	2 × 4	1		2 × 3	2			8	2		6	4
Op. 2.	10 × 2	1		10 × 2	3		1	0	10	1	2	6
„	20 × 2	11		20 ×		10	2	18	4		16	8
Total Value of Stock							£4	10	3	£2	6	5

From the above it will be seen that with stock items whose quantities can be accommodated in a four-column field (*i.e.* 9999) only thirty-six multiplication sums are necessary, even if there are a million items to be dealt with. In a test, " Digiting " work which took five hours by calculating machines took forty minutes on Powers.

EXAMINATION QUESTIONS

1. A Production Order is issued for the manufacture of 1000 Type " A " Motor-cars, for which will be required, among other items, 4000 Components " B." Trace by means of a diagram the process of such Components through the cost and financial books from the time of purchase to their subsequent use in fulfilling the Production Order, assuming that upon inspection 50 of the Components are rejected as being not up to standard.—*Society of Incorporated Accountants and Auditors (Final).*

2. Draw up a ruling for a Stores Received and Stores Issued record. —*Institute of Costs and Works Accountants (Inter.).*

3. Prepare a specimen stores requisition or withdrawal note and trace its progress through the organisation up to its final filing. How would you ensure that all requisitions reach the cost department ?

4. State the price per ton to be charged to Manufacturing Costs for material used during the month of *September*, 1931, and the price per ton for stocktaking purposes as at 31*st October*, 1931, from the following particulars taken from the account of a certain Raw Material, viz :

<blockquote>
Stock as at 30th June, 1931, 500 tons at £3 per ton.
Purchases—July, 600 tons at £3 per ton.
Aug., 500 tons at £3 12s. per ton.
Sept., 600 tons at £3 3s. per ton.
Oct., 700 tons at £3 8s. per ton
Material used—July, 400 tons.
Aug., 600 tons.
Sept., 500 tons.
Oct., 600 tons.
</blockquote>

Corporation of Accountants (Final).

5. The 1932 Accounts of a company manufacturing Motor-cars disclosed the following facts :

Materials Consumed £178,000, Direct Wages £194,000, Factory Overhead Expenses £29,100, Establishment and General Expenses £28,077. You are asked to prepare a statement showing the price at which the company should sell its cars during 1933, assuming :

(1) That it is estimated that each car will require materials to the value of £312, and wages £120; (2) that during 1933 the factory overhead expenses will bear the same ratio to direct wages as in 1932; (3) that the percentage of establishment and general expenses on factory cost will be the same in 1933 as in 1932; (4) that the selling price will show a profit of 25 per cent. on the total cost.—*Chartered Secretaries (Final).*

CHAPTER XXIX

GRAPHIC PRESENTATION OF FACTS, STATISTICS AND BUDGETS

I. GRAPHS AND CHARTS

The Utility of Charts.—Figures presented in columns, tables, or series are difficult to visualise. Points of importance, especially as to the relationships of sets of figures, are easily overlooked. If the same facts are presented graphically, a clearer mental picture of the figures is secured at once. The relative importance of varying magnitudes is revealed without mental effort.

To the cost accountant and factory manager the graphic chart represents useful facts at a glance, such as production costs, movement of expenses, units of output, the position and movement of stocks, facts about labour, wages, and volume of production. Sometimes the charts do more, in that the trend or tendency of facts and events is often indicated, assuming that conditions continue as ascertained and represented on the charts.

The Functions of Graphic Charts,* from the points of view of the management of industrial undertakings, are :

(1) To facilitate comparisons of magnitude of items of cost and production, usually by means of line or bar charts on squared paper.

(2) To compare relative increases, or decreases, in various sets of figures. If variation percentages are charted, the line chart is best shown on " ratio " or " logarithmic " ruled paper, or the figures plotted should be logarithms of the numbers.

Other comparisons, as of the proportion that several parts represent of the whole, *e.g.*, the proportion that each of the three elements of cost represents of total cost, may be made by bar, or block diagrams, circular " pie " charts, or trilinear charts.

Line Charts.—These are commonly prepared on paper ruled

---

* The construction and use of charts, diagrams and tables is more fully described in the author's " Business Statistics and Statistical Method " issued by the publishers of this work.

into squares by intersecting horizontal and vertical lines, usually in multiples of ten.

If two lines OY and OX are drawn, as shown in Fig. 178, on squared paper, the point of intersection O is called the *origin* ; the base line OX, the *abscissa* ; and the line OY, the *ordinate*.

If the daily output of articles for the first four days of the month were (1) 100; (2) 300; (3) 600; (4) 500, these facts can be plotted on squared paper, as in Fig. 178. By using each square on the abscissa as a day, and each one on the ordinate as 100 units, a vertical line drawn from each point on the base line will intersect a horizontal line drawn from each point on the ordinate.

FIG. 178.

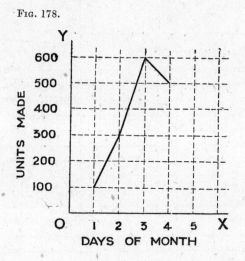

If now a line is drawn connecting each point of intersection, this portrays how the units made have varied in number each day. The connecting line is called a plotted graph, or curve. The graph shows, at once, whether the quantity made is increasing, decreasing, or stationary. This is the most usual method of presenting data in graph form.

Using the Line Chart.—As the squares on the chart are all equal in size, all similar increases, or decreases, in figures plotted are represented by the same vertical distance on it. If, therefore, two or more comparable sets of figures are plotted on squared paper, the vertical rise and fall of the curve indicates the magnitude of each series plotted in terms of actual quantities.

Example : The following figures are shown in the form of a line chart, in Fig. 179.

Date.		Units Produced.	Total Cost.	Prime Cost.
			£	£
January	. .	300	160	60
February	. .	250	130	50
March	. . .	300	170	60
April	. . .	275	160	55
May	. .	340	180	70
June	. .	200	140	40
July	. .	150	110	30
August	. . .	150	100	30
September	. .	175	110	35
October	. .	250	130	50
November	. .	325	170	70
December	. .	310	160	60

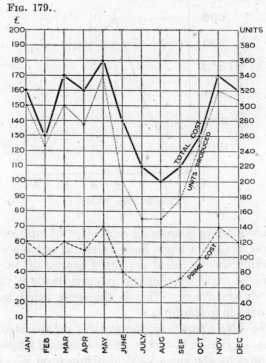

FIG. 179.

It is suggested that line graphs may usefully be used to show :

(1) Actual cost, compared with standard cost.

(2) Number of employees and total wages paid.

(3) Labour-hours worked and total wages paid.

(4) Departmental allocation of overhead and recoveries made on jobs.

(5) Comparison between cost of direct labour, materials used, and standing charges.

(6) Output of two or more similar shops or machines.

(7) Production output for two comparable periods.

(8) Actual overhead expense and budgeted expense.

(9) Production or cost for present period compared with moving average.

When several curves are used on the same chart to show data of the same nature, but for diverse periods, lines of distinctive colours, or types, may be used. Too many lines on one chart interfere with legibility, and should be avoided. The base line should always be zero, otherwise a false view may be given. The method described above is the *natural scale method*.

The Disadvantage of the Natural Scale Method.—A rise, or fall, of equal magnitude is represented by the same vertical distance on the chart, *e.g.*, Units produced : 2000 last month, and 3000 this month—increase 1000 units; but assume that the output figures were 50,000 and 51,000—also an increase of 1000 units. Then, in both cases, the graph would show exactly the same rise in the curve, yet, in the first, the increase was 50 per cent., and, in the second, only 2 per cent. Such curves are likely to be deceptive when attempting to consider the *ratio* of rise or fall. The difficulty is overcome by using a special ratio ruling, or by plotting the figures on a logarithmic scale. Such charts are sometimes called Logarithmic Historigrams.

Ratio Ruling or Logarithmic Scale Graphs.—To show percentage variations, it is necessary either

(*a*) To use ratio ruling, or,

(*b*) To use logarithms of the actual numbers on semi-logarithmic charts.

For the latter method, the logarithms of the numbers are plotted on the chart, and this has the effect of plotting *ratios* of rise and fall; *not* the rises and falls themselves. If the latter are desired, they may be shown by figures inserted on the right-hand side of the squared paper, but these are not plotted on the chart.

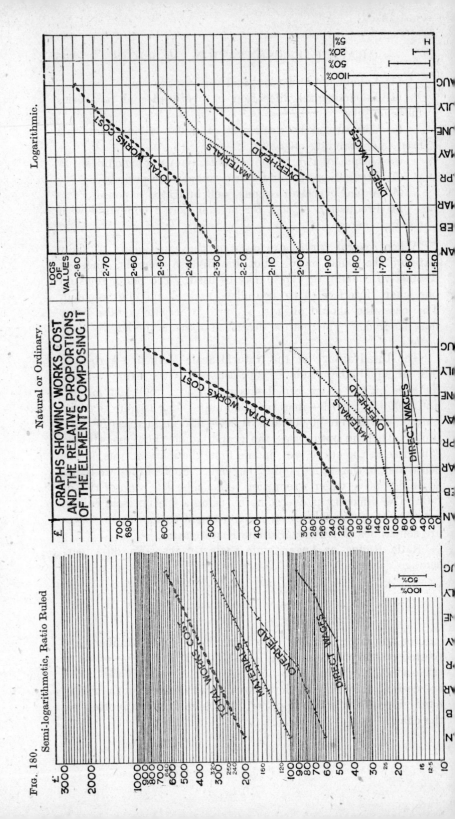

FIG. 180.

GRAPHS SHOWING WORKS COST
AND THE RELATIVE PROPORTIONS
OF THE ELEMENTS COMPOSING IT

Natural or Ordinary.

Logarithmic.

Semi-logarithmic, Ratio Ruled

In Fig. 180, the centre graph shows curves plotted on ordinary squared paper, representing actual figures. The right-hand graph shows the same curves plotted on squared paper using a logarithmic scale, *i.e.* using logs of the numbers, thus representing ratios. The left-hand graph shows the same curve plotted on ratio ruled, or semilogarithmic paper. In the left- and right-hand graphs, the same vertical distance between any two points represents an equal percentage difference on *any* part of the graphs.

It is not necessary or even desirable for the base line to be zero in using the Logarithmic Scale, but it is essential for the Natural Scale previously described. The same ratio exists at any portion of the scale on the graph. This advantage is not secured when the Natural Scale is used.

Ratio Ruling.—The horizontal lines are ruled in a manner which represents multiplication, instead of addition, as in the natural scale ruling. Thus, the same distance between lines is used to represent a rise from 2 to 3, as from 4 to 6, 6 to 9, 60 to 90. In other words, a graph curve shows a *proportionate* increase, or decrease, in the figures plotted, instead of the actual differences.

Two parallel lines plotted in a ratio chart indicate that the two series of figures plotted are increasing, or decreasing, in the same ratio. It is important to remember that where absolute figures and variations, as distinct from relative variations, are to be charted, the natural scale rectilinear chart is required.

Progress Charts.—There are two useful methods of graphically showing progress of work, etc. :

(*a*) Prepare a natural scale graph of the scheduled quantities in a stated time, and then plot the actual quantities, as the work proceeds.

(*b*) By using horizontal " bars." The scheduled work is represented by a horizontal line, with quantities budgeted for at each point of time. As the work proceeds, another bar, drawn thicker or in another colour, is run parallel to the scheduled bar. If quantities produced are less than those scheduled, the line will fall short of the line representing scheduled quantities. When the weekly (or daily) schedule is exceeded, the excess is drawn above, as in the third week in Fig. 181.

Example : A Progress Chart of the following facts is shown in Fig. 181.

	Scheduled.	Completed.
1st week . . .	80 Units	70 Units
2nd ,, . . .	70 ,,	80 ,,
3rd ,, . . .	100 ,,	130 ,,
4th ,, . . .	90 ,,	80 ,,
Total . . .	340 Units	360 Units

FIG. 181.

The fine lines and the numbers to the left of them represent scheduled work. The numbers on the right are the progressive totals. The thick lines show the actual work done each week. The fine, continuous line represents the scheduled work for four weeks (340 units). The thick line below this is the actual work done in the four weeks (360), *i.e.* twenty units more than scheduled.

This type of chart is one which has been very extensively developed by H. L. Gantt, and it is usually called the Gantt Chart.

A number of different facts may be represented on one chart, by using different thicknesses of line, or by different coloured inks. The former method is necessary, if blue prints are to be made of the chart for circulation in the factory.

The Uses of Progress Charts.—The following remarks have particular reference to the Gantt type, which is useful for :

(1) All comparisons of scheduled work and time with actual, and to show progress, and to serve as an incentive to maintain lay-out of production ; and for showing,

(2) Running times of machines possible as compared with actual. Any space at the end of the thick line, representing actual, can be explained by letters and footnotes, thus :

FIG. 182.

B. Machine breakdown.   M. Waiting for materials.

(3) Labour hours can be similarly treated, giving reasons for short time, etc. A separate chart for each man can be drawn for the use of the foreman; or, for each shop, for the manager to check the foreman's results. Lettering can be used to indicate absence, slow workers, sickness, accidents, tool or machine breakage, faulty material, waiting for orders, etc.

(4) The load, or number of orders, or quantity of work, assigned to shops, machines or men, can be indicated to ensure even distribution.

Other Methods of Graphic Presentation

Circular or " Pie " Charts.—Different elements which go to make up a total, e.g. the value of materials, labour, and over-

Fig. 183.

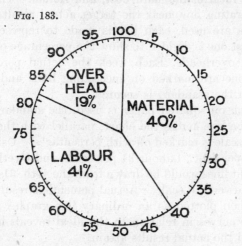

head, can be represented by sectors drawn on a circle, of which the circumference has been marked off into 100 parts. The percentage cost of each sector can thus be measured as in Fig. 183. The sectors may be coloured.

Vertical Bar Charts.

(a) These may be used on ordinary squared paper to compare series, much in the same way as line graphs, but, instead of connecting the plotted points with lines, a "bar" is dropped from each point to the base line.

(*b*) Bars of equal length may be used, each being divided into 100 parts, as in the circular chart; percentages are then shown by different shadings, or colourings.

Organisation Charts may be used to show the relationship of :

(*a*) Different officials in relation to each other, and to the manager. (Fig. 184.)

(*b*) The sequence of operation on work.

FIG. 184.

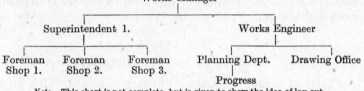

Works Manager

Superintendent 1.

Works Engineer

Foreman Shop 1.   Foreman Shop 2.   Foreman Shop 3.   Planning Dept.   Drawing Office

Progress

Note.—This chart is not complete, but is given to show the idea of lay-out.

Charting Ideal or Standard Cost, and Actual.—This is useful for demonstrating how near the target actual results come. If vertical bars are used, each bar is made to represent 100 per cent., the first one is divided to show the percentage of materials, labour, and overhead. Each week the actual percentages of the work done are marked on succeeding bars, and thus comparison with the standard is secured.

If a graph on squared paper is used, the standard, or ideal, is shown by a line across the chart, parallel with the base line; the vertical scale is marked off with percentages. Using figures : Material 40 per cent., Labour 31 per cent., and Overhead 29 per cent., straight lines would be drawn from the 40th, 31st, and 29th points on the vertical scale. Actual percentage results, week by week, are then plotted as an ordinary line graph. The movement of the curves in relation to the ideal reveals how near to the standard the actual results attain.

The Trilinear Chart.—The triangular chart is used to show the relative percentage values of three components, the sum of which is always equal to 100 per cent. However the individual values of the three items may vary, so long as the sum of them is 100 per cent., a single point on the trilinear chart will demonstrate these values.

For example, the percentage of total cost represented by the three elements of cost, material, labour and overhead may be shown graphically on a trilinear chart in the following manner : Draw an equilateral triangle (it is not essential to use an

equal-sided triangle but the procedure is simplified by doing so).
Mark the base line as, say, material cost, and the other sides of
the triangle direct labour and overhead respectively.

The altitude of the triangle, *i.e.* a line from the apex to the
centre of the base line, represents 100 per cent. and the sum of the
perpendiculars from any point within the triangle to the sides
will also be equal to 100 per cent.

Example:

Assume that the total cost (100 per cent.) is made up thus :
Material 50 per cent., labour 30 per cent., and overhead 20 per
cent.   Then on the chart (Fig. 185) where the 50 line parallel to
the base is intersected by the 30 line and the 20 line parallel respectively to the labour and overhead sides, a point S is found.

FIG. 185.

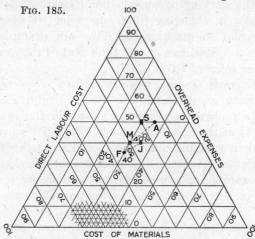

This point is perpendicularly placed 50 per cent. from the
material base, 30 per cent. from the labour side, and 20 per cent.
from the expenses side.   The sum of the perpendiculars is 100
per cent.   If S is regarded as the ideal or standard proportion of
the elements of cost, this point is then the objective.   Now take
the actual percentages recorded for four months as follows :

		Standard.	Jan.	Feb.	March.	April.
Material	. .	50	40	35	40	50
Labour	. .	30	35	30	30	35
Overhead	. .	20	25	35	30	15
Total Cost	.	100	100	100	100	100

On plotting these figures, the points ascertained show the degree
to which production costs have approached the standard.   The

E E

triangles used are ruled as section paper is ruled, with the difference that the intersecting lines are parallel to the sides instead of square. A portion of Fig. 185 has been ruled to illustrate this.

II. STATISTICAL DATA TO AID MANAGERIAL CONTROL

The detailed information necessarily collected for the purposes of the compilation of costs permits of the preparation of other statistics of considerable value for managerial control and the formulation of policy.

Labour and Wages Statistics provide much information of value for staffing control and the supervision of efficiency of utilisation in the various shops and services. Fig. 67 on p. 181 is an example. Losses through labour turnover, *i.e.* changes in the working personnel, time losses from late coming, shop time lost in changing from one order to the next, idle time in relation to machine use, etc., are examples of controllable losses. Statistics of overtime worked require analyses. Examples are referred to on p. 361.

Raw Materials Issued and Production Reports play an important part in managerial control. Useful examples of mechanically prepared reports are shown in the inset Appendices I and II at the end of this book. Material control (issues, purchases, deliveries and quantities, scrap and rejections) necessitates tabulation reports. Examples are described in pp. 362–367. An example of a production record is given on p. 269 In process costing statistics of production efficiencies may be presented.

Sales Statistics for classes of product, areas, salesmen, etc. form a guide for production, pricing and selling policy.

III. BUDGETS AND BUDGETARY CONTROL

The practical importance of Budgetary Control and its wide adoption by many manufacturers have been shown by the prominence given to the subject at various International Congresses for Scientific Management, particularly those of Geneva 1930 and London 1935. In relation to the benefits obtained, the cost of preparing budgets and maintaining a system of Budgetary Control has been found to be negligible.

Budgets are prepared for (*a*) Sales, (*b*) Production, (*c*) Overheads, (*d*) Stock purposes, (*e*) Financing arrangements, (*f*) Trading Account.

Sales Budget.—(i) *Period Covered.* This is usually the key to the other budgets prepared. The usual period covered by the budget is (*a*) one year in the case of trading from stock, *e.g.* in light industries and miscellaneous suppliers to wholesalers, retailers and the public; (*b*) three months where production occurs after sales orders have been taken, *e.g.* basic producers in the heavy industries which produce mostly for other industries.

Other notes on the subject appear on pp. 6 and 317.

The statistics for comparison are often prepared for each four-weekly period, and in many cases daily and weekly as well.

The budget may be (1) by classes of product or lines, (2) by quantities and items, (3) by geographical sales areas or travellers' grounds.

(ii) *Basis.* Sales Budgets may be based on past records, current reports on present conditions in various markets, and sometimes on an economic volume of production, in which case a selling policy and organisation is adopted to stimulate sales to absorb that output.

In distributive industries the total sales are not very difficult to assess, but in some cases the results of new lines and advertising campaigns affect estimates as to existing productions. In the basic industries regard has to be had to the trend of trade in the industries supplied, hence the shorter period for such budgets.

The Production Budget is usually based on the Sales Budget.

The advantages are that production can be planned to make the most economical use of machine and plant capacity and labour. The scheduling of departmental expense rates for recovery of overhead (or oncost) as well as piece rates and bonus rates is facilitated, peak loads can often be minimised, overtime expense may be curtailed and better opportunity for controlling production costs is available. The introduction of Standard Costing methods is possible and costing routine generally is facilitated.

The Purchasing and Stock Budget enables advantage to be taken of a long view purchasing programme, advantageous contracts can often be entered into, and better regulation of stocks is obtained.

Trading Account Budgets based on the other budgets are facilitated by the adoption of standard production costs. Sometimes standards of expenses for varying volumes of factory output are adopted. General policy of production and sales can be reviewed and the probable trend of financial results provided may be of great assistance from an administrative and financial point of view, particularly for determining forward policy.

In general an important value of Budgetary Control is that the interdependence and need for co-ordination of all sectional activities of the undertaking are emphasised, thus tending to both economy and efficiency.

EXAMINATION QUESTIONS

1. State the principal uses of Charts and Graphs in Costing; suggest any necessary cautions in their use. Give examples of three matters in regard to which you consider this method of illustration would be useful, and describe the kind of chart you would suggest in each case.—*London Chamber of Commerce.*

2. Give an example of the use of graphical representation and explain its uses.—*Royal Society of Arts (Advanced).*

3. Express graphically on the squared paper provided the following information. What deductions would you expect the works manager to make from it and what further information would he probably call for in this connection ?

Period.	No. Produced.	Total Cost.			Cost per Unit.		
		£	s.	d.	£	s.	d.
Jan. to March	400	4200	0	0	10	10	0
April	200	1900	0	0	9	10	0
May	250	2062	10	0	8	5	0
June	250	2000	0	0	8	0	0
July	200	1700	0	0	8	10	0
August	200	1700	0	0	8	10	0
September	300	2400	0	0	8	0	0
Oct. to Dec.	500	5000	0	0	10	0	0

Royal Society of Arts (Advanced).

3A. By means of a suitable chart describe the route through the works taken by an order from its reception, during all stages of manufacture, to its completion ready for despatch.—*Institute of Cost and Works Accountants (Inter).*

4. Prepare a Trilinear Chart indicating the relative percentages of Material, Labour and Overhead Costs based on the following monthly totals and showing the average percentages for the six months :

	Material.	Labour.	Overheads.
	£	£	£
January	87,002	65,028	53,282
February	90,104	64,193	52,177
March	95,671	64,311	51,808
April	98,880	64,012	50,722
May	100,101	63,628	49,724
June	105,762	63,117	49,281

Institute of Cost and Works Accountants (Final).

5. Prepare a Circular Percentage Chart for each of the following months showing the totals given :

	June. £	July. £	August. £	September. £
Materials	58,069	61,937	68,722	66,418
Labour	34,086	34,712	35,988	35,511
Overheads	25,721	25,982	25,814	24,981
Selling	11,241	11,388	12,721	13,814
Profit	14,892	15,982	16,718	16,219

Institute of Cost and Works Accountants (Final).

6. From the following information, set out a suitable form of chart :

	July.	Aug.	Sept.	Oct.	Nov.	Dec.
Number produced	1,500	1,860	1,230	1,580	2,130	600

Wages earned :

	£	£	£	£	£	£
Foundry	890	985	855	875	1,180	290
Automatic Machines	1,620	1,880	1,480	1,610	1,980	950
Milling section	1,555	1,740	1,390	1,420	1,980	810
Assembly	890	965	920	900	1,010	380
Total	£4,955	£5,570	£4,645	£4,805	£6,150	£2,430

Institute of Cost and Works Accountants (Inter.)

7. A Foundry's output for six months shows the following :

	Tons.	Wages. £	Value. £
January	378	151	1,240
February	429	142	1,728
March	527	178	1,823
April	264	115	1,026
May	591	157	1,948
June	438	163	1,717

Graph this table, also show value per ton, and criticise the results.—*Institute of Cost and Works Accountants (Inter.).*

8.

	Direct Wages. £	Materials. £	Works Overhead. £
January	1,590	1,660	985
February	2,065	2,245	1,100
March	2,025	2,320	1,005
April	1,870	1,990	965
May	1,680	1,820	1,040
June	2,140	2,495	1,365

Plot a chart setting out the above on a percentage basis, using the method you consider the most suitable for the purpose.—*Institute of Cost and Works Accountants (Inter.).*

9. Bearing in mind that all wages are *not* directly chargeable, design a graph which would enable the management to see whether wages were keeping step with other expenses.—*Institute of Cost and Works Accountants (Inter.).*

10. Prepare a set of charts and briefly describe how they may be used to enable the management effectively to control the factory and direct sales organisation.—*Institute of Cost and Works Accountants (Final)*.

11. State the chief advantages of a semi-logarithmic chart.—*Society of Incorporated Accountants and Auditors (Final)*.

12. Define a logarithmic historigram. For what purpose is it used and what are its weaknesses ?—*Society of Incorporated Accountants and Auditors (Final)*.

13. What do you understand by the following extract from a paper by a well-known writer on the subject ?—

"The problem of cost accounts is fundamentally a question, not of technique, but of policy—not how to get certain figures, but what figures to try to get and how to combine them."—*Society of Incorporated Accountants (Inter.)*.

14. The Directors of the Manufacturing Co., Ltd., hand you the undermentioned particulars, with the request that you will report to them generally as to whether the margin between cost of production (which includes overhead charges) and realised prices is sufficient to warrant the Board in assuming that for the year 1934 they will be able to anticipate maintaining a dividend of 7 per cent. on Preference Shares amounting to £2,000,000 and a dividend of not less than 5 per cent. on Ordinary Shares of £2,000,000.

From the total sales given for January, 1934, and the corresponding month of the previous year, you will require to make an intelligent fore-cast of the probable sales for the whole of the year 1934. If, in course of your consideration of the figures, you reach the conclusion that sale prices should be further shaded, or increased, in the case of any of the commodities, A to M, your opinion would be valued. Draft your report.

Commodity.	Total Sales, January		Average Price realised per ton, January, 1934.	Total Cost of Production per ton, January, 1934.		
	1934.	1933.				
	Tons.	Tons.	£	£	s.	d.
A	7,573	4,761	6	5	5	0
B	5,247	1,725	20	18	5	0
C	1,970	1,903	12	11	10	0
D	322	812	3	1	10	0
E	50	59	41	38	0	0
F	35	7	31	29	0	0
G	6,880	4,700	5	4	10	0
H	1,008	347	9	7	0	0
I	649	673	7	5	15	0
J	3	135	4	4	0	0
K	681	338	20	17	0	0
L	6,840	9,232	4	3	10	0
M	3,449	2,163	2	1	5	0
	34,707	26,855				

The same ratio of increase in sales for January, 1934, over January, 1933, was maintained throughout the first quarter of 1934.

Any fall in prices will no doubt be compensated for by a corresponding fall in the cost of production.—*Society of Incorporated Accountants (Final)*.

CHAPTER XXX
MUNICIPAL COSTING

Introduction.—In recent years the question of costing by Local Authorities has been prominent, and in view of the importance of Municipal Cost Accounting, the Institute of Cost and Works Accountants adopted certain measures to stimulate wider interest in the subject, including the introduction of a Municipal Session at their National Cost Conferences and of a Municipal Cost Accounting section in their official journal *The Cost Accountant*. Later, in 1932, the Report of the Committee on Public Expenditure (England and Wales), presided over by Sir William Ray, was published, and, to quote Mr. R. G. Nicholson, Borough Treasurer of Rotherham, " the keynote of which might be said to be Costing." The following year a Departmental Committee was appointed by the Minister of Health to consider Highways Costing, there being represented on this Committee the Institute of Municipal Treasurers and Accountants. The Research Committee of that Institute further undertook the task of investigation for the preparation of a standardised Abstract of Accounts. The adoption of a standardised form of abstract would be a big step towards uniformity in Costing.

There is, however, no generally accepted uniform system for Municipal Costing, but the subject-matter of this chapter is based on actual systems in use, and is written from information supplied or published by the following Municipal Officers to whom the author extends his thanks and appreciation :

W. H. Boddington, B.Com., F.C.W.A., A.I.M.T.A., Deputy Borough Treasurer, Leyton Corporation; J. Rowland Boffey, A.I.M.T.A., Deputy Borough Accountant, Reigate Corporation; C. H. Durman, A.C.W.A., Cost Accountant, Portsmouth Corporation; A. W. Muse. F.C.W.A., F.L.A.A., of Birmingham Corporation, Public Works Department; R. G. Nicholson, A.C.A., F.I.M.T.A., Borough Treasurer, Rotherham Corporation.

General Observations.—One of the methods of financial control employed by local authorities is the operation of a system of modern costing. Costing is beneficially employed in connection with trading undertakings of local authorities as well as in rate fund services, and facilitates the submission of accurate claims for Government grants. Mr. W. H. Boddington points out that municipal cost accounts, as operated to-day, are merely an extension of the classification of financial transactions of local authorities, and are the result of the development of the recommendations appearing in the Report of the Departmental Committee on the Accounts of Local Authorities, 1907.

In many municipal offices mechanical devices are used for classifying and tabulating records, account posting, etc., expeditiously. These are particularly useful for Stores accounting and control, the analysis and distribution of wages and overhead expenses, and the preparation of comparative cost statements.

Centralised or Decentralised Costing System.—A controversy exists as to whether Municipal Costing should be centralised and operated by a properly qualified cost accountant under the responsibility of the Chief Financial Officer ; or whether separate costing should be performed by the departments by which works are carried out, the costing being controlled by the technical officer in each.

In general, municipal cost control is usually carried out departmentally by separate executives, e.g. Birmingham and Manchester, but in a number of Local Authorities complete centralisation has been adopted successfully, e.g. Rotherham and Dundee, and there is a slowly growing movement towards such centralisation.

It is generally contended by Borough Engineers and other executives, that the Engineer is the appropriate official to have control of the Cost Accounting ; and by Municipal Financial Officers that the costing should be centralised and under their control. Mr. R. G. Nicholson expresses the view that the matter depends upon the general financial organisation. " In the case of the great majority of Local Authorities, the Financial Accounts are centralised, and where such conditions prevail a Centralised Costing Scheme is undoubtedly the most efficient and economic proposal." On the other hand, the financial organisation in the large cities is usually a decentralised one, each trading department and the more important rating departments having its own separate Cost Accountant and staff. In some cases there is a supervising Cost Accountant for co-ordination of the departmental costing, this official being subject to the general supervision of the Chief Financial Officer. It would appear a matter for local consideration, but the following arguments for and against must be considered, bearing in mind the fundamental need for closest co-operation between departmental officials and the Costing Department.

Arguments for a Centralised Municipal Costing System.—

(1) Cost control under an accountant experienced in accountancy and costing is desirable, because scientific costing involves technical operations in modern accountancy necessitating the professional skill of a technical qualified Cost Accountant.

(2) A departmental executive, such as the Engineer, should not be responsible for costing his own work, as this violates an important principle in efficient organisation and control.

(3) A municipal costing system should form an integral part of the financial accounting system, or be so linked with it as to provide proper reconciliation between the two sets of accounts. Centralised costing simplifies recon-ciliation with the financial accounts.

(4) The Financial Department has details of all expenditure and charges, many of which are not immediately available to other departments, and is therefore more capable of compiling complete costs and the full and proper proportion of overhead expense. The interest of other departments is to report the lowest working costs, and may result in the exclusion of certain allocations, say of overheads.

(5) Economy may be effected in that mechanical account-ing devices can be used to full advantage, and less staff may be needed for centralised work. Some mechanical units can only be employed profitably when there is a large volume of transactions, a condition which decentralisation prevents.

(6) Other economies may be possible in connection with wages department, stores accounting, etc., but whilst a central stores, central wages office and central transport department might be conveniently arranged, these are not

essential for centralised accounting purposes, if practical considerations otherwise demand.

(7) The contention that the executive departments cannot obtain the cost information as and when required has been disproved in practice. Costs can be supplied as quickly and promptly, and more complete by a well-organised central cost office. Time-tables for reports can be worked to, and special daily costs can be arranged for when necessary.

(8) Statistics can be compiled concurrently with cost records, and all statistical data are available in one place.

(9) Centralised control under the Financial Officer gives to the Council and the Public more confidence in reported results.

The Contentions against Centralised Costing are :

(1) Owing to the widely different types of technical services spread over a wide area, most Financial Officers have not a trained cost staff available for adequate cost control, although they invariably have excellent financial control.

(2) A technical executive does not appreciate cost reports prepared independently on work performed, when he is not fully cognisant of how they are compiled.

(3) Urgent cost information is frequently required while work is proceeding, and this is more easily obtained with departmental costing.

(4) Items of cost are better understood by the technical executive concerned, and easier reference for decisions is possible when costing is in his department. The Cost Accountant should be responsible to that head, and not to the Financial Officer, who is not competent to decide matters involving technical considerations.

(5) Co-operation with the Chief Financial Officer is better than centralisation under his control.

(6) Planning must be done departmentally, hence a central cost department could not obtain all necessary information, except through detailed reports which create unnecessary expense and trouble.

(7) It is impracticable when there are trading and non-trading departments each with separate financial control.

(8) There is no advantage, some claim, in having the costing centralised, with cost accounts forming an integral part of the general accounting system.

Uniform Costing in Local Authorities has not been adopted, although much discussion on the subject has taken place. The difficulty arises, chiefly because of varying local conditions. Speaking at a National Cost Conference, Mr. G. A. Bryant, Cost Accountant to the Norwich City Council, pointed out that to achieve uniform costing throughout, all Local Authorities must have uniformity in estimating, in the financial accounts and in the methods of costing. Certain of the public works and services lend themselves to the adoption of uniform standard units for comparative purposes, but for others definite units could not be prescribed. Mr. A. W. Muse suggests that uniform costs could be set up for comparison as between different classes of authority for (*inter alia*) :—

Road and Street Works, Sewer Works, Public Lighting, Refuse Collection and Disposal, Sewage Disposal, Passenger Transport and Housing Maintenance.

In general, it may be stated that the comparison which would be available under uniform costing methods would be useful for testing efficiencies and effecting economies, but no basis for instituting such uniformity has been found. For Municipal Costing there is, it is claimed, no fixity or static condition to permit of useful uniform costing, but alternatively it is advanced that the adoption of standard costs would provide a basis for comparative purposes more effectively.

Municipal Administration, so far as works and services are concerned, operating under the Council and Committees, is generally under the control of the Engineer and Surveyor; Engineering Assistants and District Surveyors superintend Road, Bridge and Sewer Works; Architectural Assistants deal with Building and Housing Works; the Lighting Superintendent is responsible for Street Lighting; the Cleansing and Transport Superintendent deals with Street Cleansing, Refuse Collection and Disposal, and Transport. Revenue Producing Departments and Social Services each have their superintendents or managers, and expenditure of all departments is controlled by the Chief Financial Officer.

The important feature is that the activities of Local Authorities are controlled by Committees of the Council, and revenue expenditure is usually limited by allocation.

Unit and Job Costing.—Services and works upon which

municipal expenditure is incurred may be dealt with by : (1) The Unit Costing Method or (2) The Job Costing Method.

Unit Costing for municipal purposes is the costing of a Public Service to a convenient unit of cost. It provides a method of comparison of cost of similar service undertaken by the Local Authority in different districts and at different times. It is conceded generally that to secure the maximum benefit from such Unit Costing unit costs ascertained by all Local Authorities should be properly comparable, as by this means efficiency of services of one Local Authority in comparison with others could be tested ; the difficulties in the way of this have already been mentioned.

Units of Cost for Local Authorities.—The schedule below shows suitable units of cost which may be adopted. It is compiled from particulars supplied by municipal accountants (chiefly Mr. W. H. Boddington of the Leyton Corporation and Mr. A. W. Muse of the Birmingham Corporation) and articles published in *The Cost Accountant*, the official journal of the *Institute of Cost and Works Accountants*. The variety of services operated by Local Authorities necessitates many cost units, but in addition it is advantageous for purposes of comparison and control to define many sub-units, *e.g.* : compare the unit for " Highways " and those for " Road and Street Works " in the schedule of Units on p. 392. The application of unit costing to various municipal services and works has received considerable attention in recent years.

Observations on Cost Units.—

(1) *Coding.*—Before work is commenced on capital works, plans, bills of quantities, and estimates are prepared. The Bill of Quantities is used by the cost clerk as a basis for preparing code numbers against which costs are to be charged. Similarly, a scheme of code numbers can be set up for desired units in connection with service works ; see, for example, those given on pp. 399 and 400.

The important matter is to define precisely the cost units so coded. Consultation with the Borough Engineer will usually be desirable when deciding the units to be adopted. The staff soon becomes familiar with the code numbers, and all invoices, debit notes, etc., are boldly marked with the appropriate code number.

(2) *Defined Units.*—Many units in the schedule on p. 392

are natural ones in common use by Municipal Cost Accountants. Some may be of particular value only to one district or type of work. Thus, clearly defined units and instructions as to their meaning are set out in the annual return on Refuse Collection and Disposal required by the Ministry of Health, from which comparative cost figures are compiled and published.

(3) *Varying Factors* sometimes prevent uniformity in units as between municipalities, but unit costs may be ascertained for internal comparisons. Thus *Sewer Works* may vary owing to depth of excavation, sizes of pipes, brickwork, and sometimes tunnelling ; *Street Lighting* units will depend upon whether gas or electricity is the illuminant, and whether different types and numbers of burners are in use ; *Street Cleansing*, the recognised unit of " per 10,000 super yards " should properly be based on types of streets, but this has not been adopted ; *Sewage Disposal* units have been fixed, and uniformity as between Local Authorities is aimed at. It has been suggested by Mr. J. W. Drury, F.C.W.A. and Mr. J. Finch, A.M.Inst.S.P., of Rotherham, that a unit based on the following formula would be better than the " Million gallons per dry weather flow " Unit :—

$$\begin{array}{l} \text{Volume of sewage in} \\ \text{millions of gallons} \end{array} \times \begin{array}{l} \text{Strength of} \\ \text{tank effluent} \end{array} \times \begin{array}{l} \text{Percentage of} \\ \text{purification} \end{array} = \begin{array}{l} \text{Number of D.F.}\dagger \\ \text{Sewage Units.} \end{array}$$

Schedule of Units of Cost for Municipalities.

RATE FUND SERVICES :—

Education—per scholar in average attendance, per 1000 of population.
Public Assistance—per 1000 of population.
Hospitals—per occupied bed.
  (a) Wards : per patient-day.
  (b) Dispensary : per prescription.
  (c) Nurses' Homes : per nurse.

Road and Street Works (Non-Capital Expense) :—
  1. Street Cleansing—per 10,000 super yards for each type of surface. (Watering, Gritting, Snow removal, and Sweeping.)
  2. Surface Repairs—per super yard (for each type of material).
  3. Tar Spraying—per super yard (for each type of material : bitumen, cold spray, high-viscosity tar, etc.).
  4. Traffic Lines—per 100 yards of white line (i.e. length × times painted).
  5. Grass Verges Maintenance—per 1000 super yards.
  6. Tram Track Maintenance—per yard of track.

Road Works (Capital Expenditure) :—
  1. Carriageway—per cubic yard excavated.
    per cubic yard of filling.
    per super yard of foundation (thickness and type).
    per super yard of surface (each type).

* See comments above.

  2. Footway—per super yard of foundation.
    per super yard of paving (each type).
  3. Kerb and Channel—per lineal yard of concrete bed.
    per lineal yard of kerb (each type).
    per lineal yard of channel (each type).
  4. Drainage—per cubic yard excavated.
    per super yard foundation.
    per lineal yard piping (each type).
    per manhole complete.
    per gully fixed.
    per pumping hour (when applicable).
  5. Other Work—per lineal yard fencing.
    per super yard grass verge laid.
    per refuge erected.
    per traffic signal erected, etc.

Highways—per 10,000 super yards per mile, per 1000 of population.
Sewers, Construction *—per mile or per yard laid.
Sewage Disposal *—per million gallons dry weather flow and per head of population.
Street Lighting—per lamp.
    per mile.
    per 1000 of population.
N.B.—Sub-units according to type of lamp and illuminant may be used for comparative cost purposes, e.g.—
Electric—per 100-watt lamp.
Gas—per high-pressure lamp.
    per low-pressure lamp having regard to number of burners.

† i.e. Drury-Finch Units.

ROAD FUND SERVICES (*cont.*) :—

Refuse Collection—per ton or per cubic yard.
   per 1000 population.
Refuse Disposal—per ton or per cubic yard.
   per 1000 of population.
Parks—per acre.
   per 1000 of population.
Tennis Courts, etc.—per player.
Libraries—per 1000 of population.
Baths—per bather.
Wash Houses—per washer.
Fire-Brigade—per fireman.
   per call.
   per 1000 of population.
Police—per constable.
   per mile of highway patrolled.
   per case.
   per 1000 of population.

TRADING OR REVENUE PRODUCING DEPART-
   MENTS :—

Gas—per 1000 cu. ft. made.
   per 1000 cu. ft. sold.
   per ton of coal carbonised.
Electricity—per 1000 units generated.
   per 1000 units sold, etc.
Passenger Transport *—per car-mile (some
   use the 100-seat-mile.
   per passenger or passenger-mile.
Water—per 1000 galls. consumed (*d.*).
   per million galls. consumed (£'s).
   per 1000 of population.
Housing—per house (of each type, *e.g.*,
   3-bedroom non-parlour, 2-bedroom parlour, etc.).
Markets—per 1000 animals for sale.
   per stand or pitch.
Slaughterhouses—per 1000 animals slaugh-
   tered.

* See comments on p. 391.

The Compilation of Standards for Comparative Purposes.—

The operations of a year may be selected for standard comparisons for future expenditure, care being taken to ensure that
the figures represent normal outlay or costs.

The standards may be set up for departments and also for
convenient types of expenditure, the following being a useful
form :—

EXPENDITURE STANDARDS.

Services.	Headings of Expenditure.						Departmental Standards.
	01.	02.	03.	04.	05.	etc.	
A. *Rate Fund.*							£ £
.... 1.							
.... 2.							
Street Cleansing. . 3.							
Baths Establishments 4.							
(see p. 400) etc.							
B. *Trading Depts.*							
Tramways . . 21.							
Electricity . . 31.							
etc.							

Departmental executives can be notified of the actual
controllable expenditure, compared with the standard, at convenient periods of a month, etc., on a form shown on p. 393.

Non-controllable expenditure like interest payments, sinking
fund contributions, rates, taxes, etc., may be omitted to give
emphasis to the items controllable departmentally.

Standards are amended periodically to allow for extended
or reduced activities.   The standards set up are not necessarily
the ideal or perfect position, but simply a basis for comparisons.

In addition to departmental expenditure standards, standards
may be set up for various units of cost in each of the authority's
services.

BATHS ESTABLISHMENTS.

Expense Code No.	Standard.	Estimate Year Ended ...... 193..			Actual ...... months to ...... 193..			Percentage of Actual to	
								Standard.	Estimate.
41.01 41.02 etc.	£	£	s.	d.	£	s.	d.	%	%

Municipal Overheads fall into two main categories :—

(1) Administration Expenses of Central Departments, *i.e.* legal and financial departments, salaries and expenses, and the Municipal Buildings, Council Chamber and Committee Rooms.

(2) Overheads of the Departmental Works, Services and Trading Departments, viz.: (*a*) Departmental office expenses (including accounting staff and proportion of Central Expenses); (*b*) Supervisory Charges (including salaries of the executive officer and technical staff and wages of foremen); (*c*) Depot Expenses (or Stores Expenses) including wages of superintendent and men handling materials.

Items in Group (1) are usually allocated at the close of the financial year, and the amount is that actually incurred; those in Group (2) are distributed during the year, since rechargeable accounts, bearing their proportion of overheads, are normally rendered monthly. For Costing purposes *all* overheads should be distributed over services and works.

Allocation of Overheads. Many methods are used and no uniform plan has been adopted.

Group 1. Some apportion Central Expenses from officials' diaries, but this laborious analysis can be avoided by establishing Duty Schedules for the various officials, thus permitting allocation on an approximate time basis, which should be sufficiently accurate.

All other expenses not allocable on one of the customary bases (floor space, etc.) should follow the remuneration proportions. Needlessly meticulous analysis should be avoided.

Group 2. A useful method is to allocate wages and salaries

weekly (or monthly) to (a) Departments' own works, (b) Works for Corporation Departments, (c) Works for Private Parties. Remaining expenses can then be apportioned proportionately to these totals, excepting where any can be allocated by usual methods to each of these divisions.

Summary Cost Sheets showing operating costs may be prepared in the form presented on pp. 394 and 395, which are from a lecture by Mr. W. H. Boddington to the Institute of Municipal Treasurers and Accountants Students Societies.

Motor Buses.	Expenditure.		Per 100 Seat Mile.	Per Bus Mile.	Per Passenger.
	£	%.	d.	d.	d.
Traffic Expenses	38,879	40·29	11·46	4·47	0·68
Repairs and Maintenance	12,732	13·19	3·76	1·46	0·22
Power	23,686	24·54	6·98	2·72	0·41
	75,297	78·02	22·20	8·65	1·31
Other Expenses	9,946	10·31	2·93	1·14	0·17
Working Expenses	85,243	88·33	25·13	9·79	1·48
Loan Charges	9,096	9·43	2·68	1·05	0·16
General Charges	2,164	2·24	0·64	0·25	0·04
	96,503	100·00	28·45	11·09	1·68

Income.

		Per 100 Seat Mile.	Per Bus Mile.	Per Passenger.
		d.	d.	d.
Income	92,673	27·33	10·66	1·61
Deficiency	3,830			

Bus Mileage	2,086,918
Passengers	13,791,497
Average number of buses in commission	51
Average seating capacity	39

A Central Costs Bureau or National Cost Dept. is considered by many Municipal Officers to be desirable, and Mr. W. H. Boddington has suggested that it might serve the following purposes :—(a) to evolve a comprehensive scheme of unit

Water Supply.					Cost per 1000 Gallons Consumed.	Cost per Million Gallons Consumed.	Cost per 1000 of Population Supplied.
	£	£	£	%	d.	£	£
Expenditure :							
Catchment Area and Storage .		5,360			5·19	0·35	1·44	26·28
Distribution .		8,842			8·57	0·57	2·38	43·34
Working Expenses		14,202			13·76	0·92	3·82	69·62
Rates and Taxes	20,659			20·02	1·33	5·56	101·27
Loan Charges .	57,163			55·40	3·69	15·38	280·21
General Charges	11,161			10·82	0·72	3·00	54·71
		88,983					
			103,185	100·00	6·66	27·76	505·81
Income :							
Grants . .		1,995					
Other Receipts .		101,581					
			103,576		Thousand of gallons consumed . . . 3,716,284		
Surplus . .			£391		Population Supplied . 204,000		

costing, (b) to prepare standardised tabulations of costs prepared throughout the country, (c) to undertake research for setting up of cost units and standard costs, e.g. different standards for the corresponding service in different groups of authorities, varied according to population, topography and other factors, and

Mental Hospital.	Average No. of Occupied Beds, 581. Patient Days, 211,289. Expenditure.			Cost.	
				Per Occupied. Bed.	Per Patient Day.
	£	£	%	£	s.
Salaries . . .	14,421		39·87	24·82	1·37
Provisions . . .	5,646		15·61	9·72	0·53
Heating, Lighting and Cleaning . .	1,801		4·98	3·10	0·17
Medicines and Appliances	183		0·51	0·32	0·02
Furnishings . . .	739		2·04	1·27	0·07
Miscellaneous . .	7,175		19·84	12·35	0·68
		29,965	82·85	51·58	2·84
Loan Charges . .		5,755	15·91	9·91	0·54
General Charges .		450	1·24	0·77	0·04
		36,170	100·00	62·26	3·42
Income . . .		6,719			
NET COST . . .		£29,451		50·69	2·79

possibly the standards divided into " constants " and "variants," (d) to compile and publish cost returns, (e) to foster healthy competition, and (f) to facilitate investigations and indicate where costs are excessive and how economies may be possible.

Costing Scheme for Borough Engineer's Department.—The scheme is a centralised system employed by Mr. R. G. Nicholson, A.C.A., F.I.M.T.A., Borough Treasurer of Rotherham, by whose courtesy it is here described. In general, it is applicable to all Public Services, including Trading Departments. As 20,000 accounts entailing 200,000 postings a year are operated in the Rotherham scheme, the work is facilitated by the use of a Burroughs Stores and Cost Posting Machine and a Burroughs Listing Machine ; an operator can post 100 items an hour to the ledger cards.

Stores Accounting.—All materials are coded under a five-figure code ; the first two numbers indicate the class, and the others the article. Thus, 02001, (02) represent cement, lime, etc., class and (001) a grade of cement.

Goods bought in bulk are recorded in the smallest units likely to be used. Thus cement is entered in units of quarters, *e.g.*, 10 tons = 10 × 80 qrs. ; an issue of 7 tons 16 cwt. 3 qrs. would be recorded as 627 units.

The Price for charging out stores issued is the average price

---

STORES LEDGER.　　　　　　　　　Catalogue No. 02001.

Description : Portland Cement-Pelican.

Supplier : 1. Dukes, Ltd. ....　Ordering Level.　　Bin No.: Y.6.
　　　　　2. ....　Maximum Stk.
　　　　　3. ....　　　　　　　　　Unit: 1 Qr.
　　　　　4. ....　Minimum.

Issues.			Receipts.				Price.	Supplier No.	Date.	Balance.			
Qty.	Value.			Qty.	Value.			£			Qty.	Value.		
	£	s.	d.		£	s.	d.					£	s.	d.
643	15	13	9	3,200	78	0	0	0·02437	1	Apl. 2	3,200	78	0	0
				10	4	10				„	2,557	62	0	0
										„	2,567	62	11	1

per unit of the stock on hand after posting all goods received to date. The calculation is done mechanically, and decimals of £1 are used. A new average is made after each new delivery inwards.

Goods Inwards Tickets are prepared in triplicate from delivery notes, one copy for Cost Office, one for Borough Engineer, one for Stores Dept.

In Borough Engineer's Dept. the tickets are sorted in suppliers' name order. When invoice is received it is checked to G. R. Ticket, and when passed, the G. R. Ticket is filed in a separate file for priced tickets. Outstanding invoices are thus easily ascertained.

GOODS INWARD TICKET 10,729.		
Supplier : G. T. Duke, Ltd.	Storekeeper's Initials.	Date : 12.3.36
		Order No.: 9815
Description : Cement-pelican		Invoice passed : Highways Apl. 1936
Quantity : 10 tons	If direct charge.	Vehicle No. ....
		Estimate No. ....
		Job. No. ....
Quantity in Units.	Rate.	Amounts.	
800		£ 19 s. 10 d. 0	Stores Catalogue No.: 02001

Stores Issues Requisitions are used in the usual manner (see p. 39). In the Rotherham scheme these are made in duplicate, as one copy is used for Stores Ledger posting, and one as a posting medium for the Cost Ledger as described later. The goods are unitised and priced from the Stores Ledger Cards, both copies being priced together to avoid error. *Returns to Stores* are made on Stores Returns Notes and similarly dealt with.

A separate ticket is prepared for each item on a requisition, these tickets being used for easier posting by machine.

STORES REQUISITION No. 1944.		
Date		
Please supply to............................		
Charge to Job : Wickersley Rd. (No. 2753).		
Qty.	Description.	Storekeeper's Catalogue No.
7 16 3 3 tons 3½ ,,	Cement Pebbles Sand	02001 05002 08016
Foreman : J. W. B.		Storekeeper : W. S.
Carter's signature : J. Hill		

STORES ISSUES POSTING TICKET.

STORES ISSUE TICKET.		
Where Used : Wickersley Rd.		Date : 30.3.
Description : Cement		Reqn. No. 1944
Quantity : 7 tons 16 cwt. 3 grs.		Estimate No. 22/6
		Job. No. 2753
Units. Rate, £. Amount. 627 0·02437 £15 6 0		Stores Catal. No. 02001

Stores Returns Notes similarly printed in red as credits. Tickets for each department printed on paper of distinctive colour to facilitate sorting.

Posting to the Stores Ledger is done weekly in one total for each material. The quantities and amounts are listed first to find the posting total. (This operation is equivalent to summarising issues on to a Materials Abstract, see p. 161, as is done when posting tickets are not prepared.)

A Stores Control Account is used. Weekly totals of Stores Inwards and Returns to Stores are posted from the Tally Roll lists to the credit ; and of Stores Issues to the debit of this account. The balance of this account thus shows the value of Book Stock at any date. Regular routine physical check and adjustments keep this balance reconciled with the Actual Stock after the manner detailed on p. 45.

The Cost Accounting.—*A Cost Code* carefully devised and flexible is recommended.

A code number is given to each heading of expenditure, in each of the sections of the Engineer's Department such as :

Classified Roads.   Refuse Collection and
Non-Classified Roads.   Disposal.
Street Cleansing.   Sewage Disposal, etc.

Sub-code numbers are given to sub-headings of expenditure. If, within a heading of expenditure, particular costs are required, Job Orders are issued, each having a separate Job Order number.

The following are four examples of a code classification, the first two being those used at Rotherham :

Cost Code.

Classified Roads*—First Class.

Code No.		Sub-Code (used in conjunction with each Code No. as required).	
18	A.618 * Moorgate and Corporation Street.	1.	Carriageway Maintenance.
		2.	do. Foundations.
19	A.630 Sheffield Road, . . . and Doncaster Road.	3.	do. Hot Surface Treatment.
		4.	do. Cold Treatment.
20	A.632 Wortley Road, . . .	5.	do. Re-surfacing in Similar
22	A.6021 Broom Road and . . .		Material.
25	Traffic Signals (Maintenance)	6.	do. do. Improved Material.
26	do. (Installation)	7.	Footpaths, Maintenance.
		8.	do. Surface Dressing.
		9.	do. do. Improved Materials.
		10.	do. New.
		11.	Verges and Fences.
		12.	Surface Water Drainage.
		13.	Kerbing and Channelling.
		14.	Traffic Signals Maintenance.
		15.	do. New.
		16.	Signs and White Lines, etc.
		17.	Bridges.
		18.	Sundries.
		19.	Capital Works defrayed out of Revenue.
		20.	Loan Charges.

Sewerage Works.

(The code list is arranged to facilitate the preparation of the Annual Cost Returns of the Ministry of Health for Sewage Disposal Works.)

Code for Heads of Expenditure.	Sub-Code for Costing Kinds of Sewage Treatment.
125. Salaries.	1. Screening and Tank Treatment.
126. Wages and National Insurance.	2. Filtration and Humus Tank Treatment.
127. Materials (excluding Repairs and Chemicals).	3. Activated Sludge Treatment.
128. Chemicals.	4. Sludge Treatment, including Humus Sludge.
129. Haulage.	5. Pumping.
130. Ejectors Power.	6. Unallocated Expenditure.
131. Electricity at Works.	7. Capital.
132. Repairs to Buildings, etc.	8. Ejectors and Pumps.
133. Ejectors and Pump Maintenance.	9. Stable Expenses.
134. Rates, Rent, Insurance.	10. Holidays.
135. Loan Charges.	11. Pensions.
136. Sundries.	

Housing Construction.—A Code No. allotted to each building estate, *e.g.* erection of 100 houses in red brick and rough cast at Town Estate (30 parlour, 50 non-parlour).

* This refers to the Ministry of Transport's Classification of Roads.

Sub-Code Nos.		Operation Sub-Code Nos. Common to All Types.
01	Parlour, 3-bedroom houses.	1. Clearing and Excavating.
02	Non-parlour, 3-bedroom houses.	2. Foundations.
03	do. 2-bedroom houses.	3. Brickwork.
04	2 Blocks of 6 each in red brick.	4. Tiling.
05	3 do. 4 each in rough cast.	5. Slating.
etc.		6. Plastering (internal).
		7. do. (external).
		8. Carpentery.
		9. Joinery.
		10. Glazing.
		11. Plumbing.
		12. Drains.
		13. Fences, etc.
		14. Painting and Decorating.
		15. Hearths, etc.
		16. Making good after Tradesmen.

Public Baths Expenditure.—In the code below, the first number in the code designates the Baths Department; the second, a particular Baths Establishment; the last two the heading of expenditure :—

BATHS ESTABLISHMENTS

	No. 1. High St.	No. 2. Hill St.	No. 3. City Rd.
Wages	41.01	42.01	43.01
National Insurance . . .	41.02	42.02	43.02
Coal and Cartage . . .	41·03	42.03	43.03
Towels and Soap . . .	41.04	42.04	43.04
Water	41.05	42.05	43.05
Electricity	41.06	42·06	43.06
Telephones	41.07	42.07	43.07
Printing, Advertising . .	41.08	42.08	43.08
Rent, Rates, Taxes . . .	41.09	42.09	43.09
Insurance	41.10	42.10	43.10
Repairs	41.11	42.11	43.11
Sundries	41.12	42.12	43.12
Capital items	41.20	42.20	43.20

Example of the Use of the Code.—Surface-Dressing Classified Road A.6021 (Broom Road) Code reference for costing is 22/8. Traffic signal maintenance on Sheffield Rd. (A.630), 19/14. For Wages expended on Activated Sludge Treatment the Cost Code is 126/3. If there is a Job Order to be separately costed then the Code numbers are quoted with the addition of the Job Number.

Job Order Work.—Orders are issued in quadruplicate, two

go to the Foreman, one to the Cost Office, one is retained in the Borough Engineer's Office. Separate Cost Accounts are opened for these orders. When completed and approved by the Engineer, any re-chargeable jobs are then passed to the Rental Section of the Borough Treasurer's Department for collection.

Collection and Analysis of Expenditure Data.—This is dealt with under the usual headings, as : Wages, Stores, Materials, Direct Charges, Services (Motors, Rollers, Plant Hire, etc.).

Wages.—The Time Record of gangs of labourers is prepared by a timekeeper. Skilled men fill in individual Time Sheets.

| Borough Engineer's Dept. Section : Highways No. 1. | | | | | | | | | | Time Record. Week-ending 2nd April, 19... | | | | |

Classification No.	Check No.	Name.	1st day.	2nd day.	3rd day.	4th day.	5th day.	6th day.	7th day.	Total. Ord.	O.T.	Extras.	Rate.
420	420	Rusling, F.	Job Hrs. 4490 8½	2753 8½	2753 8½	2753 8½	2753 4½		2753 8½	47	—	—	1/1
422	422	Sandown, T.	Job Hrs. 4490 8½	4490·4 2753 4½	2753 8½	2753 8½	2753 8½		2753 8½	47	—	—	1/1
		etc.											

The Borough Engineer's Department prepares Wages Sheets from the Time Sheets, both of which are passed to the Cost Office.

From this information it is usual for the Cost Office to prepare a Wages Abstract (see p. 161), but at Rotherham Wages Tickets are prepared (one for each job upon which each man has worked) for posting purposes by machine to the Cost Ledger Cards :—

Borough Engineer's Dept.				WAGES TICKET.	
Week ending : 24th Apl., 193... Section : Highways No. 1.				Check No.	420
				Classification No.	
Hours.			Rate.	Amount.	Vehicle No.	
Ord.	O.T.	Total. 38¼	1/1	£ s. d.	Estimate No.	22/6
				2 1 8	Job No.	2753

The aggregate for each man is agreed with his wage on the Wages Sheet; the total aggregate of wages posted to the Cost Accounts is agreed with total wages paid.

Materials from Stores.—The total of requisitions of each material for each job or account number is posted from the Materials Abstract to the Cost Ledger Accounts. At Rotherham this is done by sorting the Materials Cost Tickets into code and job number order ready for the machine operator to post direct to the Cost Ledger Cards.

Materials Delivered Direct to Jobs.—The procedure as to ordering and recording is the same as for Stores Materials, except: (1) the foreman signs the Delivery Note and sends to the Storekeeper, (2) instead of the Stores Code Number the proper job or estimate number is quoted on the Goods Received Note.

Direct Expenses are dealt with by debits as for Stores Issues. Direct charges such as Insurance, Road Charges, Rates, etc., are debited under proper allocation to code and job numbers.

COST LEDGER ACCOUNT.

Class 1. Roads. A.6021. Code No. 22/6
Wickersley Road. Job No. 2753
Job. *Repairs to Carriageway from Stag Lane to Middle Lane.*

Date.	Wages.			Stores.			Other Items.				Total to Date.	Remarks.
	£	s.	d.	£	s.	d.	Ref. No.	£	s.	d.		

[*Abbreviated.*] *As the card is used for machine posting, money columns are not printed.*

Subsidiary Services.—Motor Transport, Rollers, Plant Hire, Stores, Private Works, Establishment, etc., are each costed as such by allocating expenditure so appropriated.

Stores expenses include stores wages, repairs, heating, lighting, rates, insurance, loan charges, etc., at the stores and the cost of transport handling of materials into stores.

Any main service utilising a subsidiary service is debited on a predetermined basis defined below. All such debits are posted in the column headed "Other Items" shown on the specimen Cost Ledger Account above. Amounts so debited are credited to the appropriate Subsidiary Service Cost

Account, or may be dealt with through a Service Expense Control Account.

The Basis for Charging Use of Subsidiary Services.

(a) *Motor Transport.*—Time Sheets are used as prime records for miles run, petrol, oil and time on each job. The Time Sheets as required by the Road Traffic Acts should be used. A flat rate per hour is computed for each vehicle based on records so kept, together with maintenance expense and usual annual charges for depreciation, licences, insurance, etc. The charges to jobs, etc., are listed to find what each vehicle has earned, and then the posting tickets are resorted and listed under Jobs and Code Numbers, these totals being posted to the appropriate Cost Accounts.

SPECIMEN TIME SHEETS.

Borough Engineer's Dept.   PLANT OR TIMBER ON HIRE.

Estimate or Job No.	Quantity.	Description.	Date Issued.	Date Returned.	Time to be Charged.	Rate.

CARTER'S (HORSE TRANSPORT) TIME SHEET.

Carter...

Week ending .... 19...

Date.	From.	To.	Destination.	No. of Loads.	Hours Worked.

MOTOR TRANSPORT AND ROLLERS TIME SHEET   Date...................

Mileage Recorder. Start............ Finish............ Total..............

Driver .... Mate .... Vehicle No............

Tues.

Wed.

A/c No.	Destination.	Arrive.	Depart.	Time.	Details of Load.	Weight.	Recd. by.

Issues: Petrol............... Oil	Driver's Remarks :	Job No.	Hrs.	Road.
Verified by .... M.T. Supt.	Allocated by			

(b) *Horse Transport.*—Each carter prepares a time sheet showing jobs upon which engaged, and particulars of loads carried. The accounting is the same as for motors.

(c) *Rollers* are dealt with as for Motor Transport.

(d) *Plant*, namely Air Compressors, Concrete Mixers, Watch Boxes, Woodworking Machinery, Cranes, etc. A separate Cost Account is kept for each unit.

A Plant Register provides details of depreciation, etc.

A Plant Day Book is used at the Depot to record the jobs on which plant is used each week. The Cost Office extracts the data for charging up. In the scheme under review posting tickets are prepared for use with the Burrough's Posting Machine.

(e) *Tools* such as picks, shovels, etc., are charged as a percentage on prime cost to each job. The rate is based on the annual maintenance cost and is revised annually.

(f) *Timber*, scaffolds, etc., are charged on a hire basis as for plant.

(g) *Stores Expenses.*—A percentage calculated to cover handling, etc., is added to the value of Stores Issued. (*Note.*—Special rates are used in the case of Stores charged to Classified Roads and Ministry of Transport Grant Jobs calculated on a unit basis, *e.g.* handling charges per cwt. bag of cement, per man-hole cover and frame, per gully grate, etc.). All the stores materials for a particular cost account are listed and totalled, on which the percentage is added in one operation and one machine posting.

Establishment Charges, including the Town Clerk's, Borough Treasurer's and Borough Engineer's Departments, should be apportioned over all the Services of the Corporation. Owing to many complications as to a suitable basis, no general apportionment is made at Rotherham, but some apportionment is made in respect of re-chargeable work, and is charged as a fixed percentage. (See, however, p. 393.)

Cost Control Accounts.—The main heads of the Cost Code are identical with the heads of expenditure in the annual estimates, and therefore of the Financial Books.

In the scheme described the Tally Roll List Totals are the totals posted to the Cost Accounts. By posting corresponding totals to the respective Control Accounts (say quarterly) the latter provide a complete analysis of expenditure under Estimate Headings, and these figures may be used for posting the expenditure side of the Financial Accounts.

Returns of Cost Supplied to Departments.—Weekly Returns

are supplied to the Borough Engineer showing the cost of each Classified and non-Classified Road (with amounts under each sub-code head); detailed cost of Collection and Disposal of Refuse; cost of each vehicle under sub-codes and its earnings; costs of all other services; cost of special jobs week by week and on completion. Also a monthly return of his expenditure under appropriate Estimate headings.

Returns are made within seven days of the end of a week.

Other departments receive similarly detailed returns.

Departmental Returns include a charge for annual expenses such as Rates, Insurance, Loan Charges, etc., monthly. These apportionments are debited to the appropriate Cost Code No. and credited to Suspense Account. When invoices for these are passed for payment by the Committee the Suspense Account is debited, thus clearing the Account.

Operation of the Scheme.—Mr. Nicholson is satisfied that the preparation of the large number of posting tickets involves less work and time than the making of analyses and abstracts. Sorting is quicker, as is machine posting as compared with hand posting. Further economy and efficiency has been achieved by the adoption of a Centralised Costing Scheme.

Alternative Municipal Costing Scheme.—This system is similar in many respects to the one just described, but is departmental and suitable for manual posting. The details and forms have been kindly supplied by Mr. J. Rowland Boffey, Deputy Borough Accountant, Reigate.

The Code System is as already described, and when possible should correspond with the Chief Financial Officer's Rate Estimates, amplified with any desired sub-coding.

The following remarks refer to the Borough Surveyor's Section, and the costing is not centralised.

Manual Labour.—Daily time sheets are prepared, and summarised weekly. These documents are used for preparation of the Pay Sheets.

The Pay Sheets are analysed on the Wages Analysis Abstract under Job or Code Numbers. The total for each number is posted to the appropriate Cost Sheet or Cost Account.

Materials.—A daily return of Materials Issued is sent to the Costing Section by the Storekeeper. Values are there inserted and the total of the sheet is transferred to a summary, viz., The

Materials Issued Abstract. This abstract is merely a summary of the daily totals for a quarter.

WAGES ABSTRACT.

SUMMARY OF DAILY TIME SHEETS.

Reigate Corporation.   Highways Dept.

Week ended ....   Total Job Costs to Wages
                                            Analysis Abstract fo. 28/9 £.........

Check No.	Wages. £ s. d.	206/2. £ s. d.	208/3. £ s. d.		240/6. £ s. d.	etc.	etc.	Total (Cross casts). £ s. d.
				[Sheet (16 columns) broken for convenience of printing.]				
		306/1 £ s. d.	307/3 £ s. d.		etc.			
		401/2 £ s. d.	402/1 £ s. d.		etc.			
£								Total

The amount for each job is transferred weekly to the Wages Analysis Abstract, on which weekly time sheets are also analysed. An abbreviated form of Abstract is shown on p. 161.

Each issue on the Daily Return is posted (a) to the credit of the Stores Ledger, the folio of the ledger being inserted on the Return, (b) to the debit of the appropriate Cost Account. For the latter the posting reference is the Stores Ledger Folio.

Returns to Stores are similarly dealt with on separate sheets.

The postings to the Job Cost Ledger are in red ink in the Materials column, as a separate credit column is not used.

Direct Costs.—As Centralised Costing is not in operation, the posting from analysed committee schedules or expenditure analysis book cannot be done. The procedure (using invoices of the Roads and Bridges Committee only) is as follows : Invoices are analysed in the Finance Dept., so that the amount charged to each Rate Estimate head is available each month. Also, assuming the two systems are operating on the same Estimate Code, the expenditure is available under Cost Code numbers (jobs, etc.). Such totals can thus be posted direct to the Cost Accounts, using the Expenditure Journal or Committee Schedule as reference, but a Cost Journal is more convenient for dealing with headings sub-coded—one section for Direct Costs Analysis, another for Annual Charges. Annual charges are allocated over the four quarters of the year.

The Annual Charges section of the Journal has six Cash Columns ; one, estimate for the year ; two to five, for the quarterly allocations ; six, for the actual payment. The quarterly allocations are provisional until payment is made, when any difference is apportioned over the remaining quarters. The quarterly allocations are predetermined at the beginning of the year.

The total of Direct Costs is posted to the Direct Costs Control Account, which has three columns, one for each month of the quarter. (See Materials Control Account on p. 414.)

Transport.—Returns are provided as specimen on p. 408. The daily total charges are summarised in a Vehicle Quarterly Abstract, but the Daily Return is used for posting to the respective Job Cost Accounts. Charges are on an hourly-rate basis.

Tools and Plant.—A percentage (usually about 1½ per cent.) is added to prime cost of each job using plant to cover this item.

Recoverable Job Costs.—Instruction sheets are issued to foremen, who insert date of completion and pass to the Cost Office.

Job Cost Sheets are ruled off quarterly for balancing purposes.

CONTROL ACCOUNTS.

Balancing the System.—At the end of each quarter it is essential to extract the analysis of Wages, Materials, Transport, etc., in order to provide the information for posting to the

HIGHWAYS AND WORKS DEPT.   REIGATE CORPORATION   DATE : 16 Sept, 19.....

LORRY NO. 3   DRIVER : R. Jones   Mate ....

Journey No.	Place of Loading.	Place of Delivery.	Material Hauled.	Actual Weight Carried.		Miles Covered.		Ton Mileage.	Time for each Journey.		Hrs.	Job. Cost No.	Rate : 3/- hr.		
				Tons.	Cwts.	Loaded.	Empty.		Departed.	Arrived.			£	s.	d.
1	Reigate Depot	Castlefield Rd.	Tarmac	2	0	2 1/16		4·2	7.30	7.45	1	200/1		3	0
2	Castlefield Rd.	Tip. Brighton Rd.	Old Tarmac	1	10	3		4·5	8.45	9.0	1	do.		3	0
3															
4															
etc.															
TOTALS															

Details of Standing Time to be entered above on the line under the preceding Journey.

Mileometer Readings :
Finish . . 18,733
Start . . 18,700

TOTAL MILES RUN   33

Examined by ....

For Office use	At Work. Hours.	Under Repairs. Hours.	Idle Time. Hours.	No. of Journeys (loaded).
	Mileage (loaded).	Mileage (empty).	Tonnage (carr'd).	Ton Mileage.

I hereby certify the above particulars to be correct.

(Signed) .... Driver.

Examined and Certified Correct .... Superintendent.

REIGATE CORPORATION

RECOVERABLE JOB COSTS ABSTRACT

BOROUGH ENGINEER AND SURVEYOR'S DEPARTMENT

FOR THE QUARTER ENDED December, 19...

Job No.	Works in Progress—Brought Forward			Expenditure for Quarter			Total Costs to end of Quarter			Works in Progress—Carried Forward			Direct Costs Completed Jobs			Add—Profits as per Cost Sheets (losses in red)			Total Recoverable			Account No.	Housing Repairs Accounts			School Repairs			Miscellaneous Jobs		
	£	s.	d.	£	s.	d.	£	s.	d.	£	s.	d.	£	s.	d.	£	s.	d.	£	s.	d.		£	s.	d.	£	s.	d.	£	s.	d.
Forward	190	0	0	1850	5	0	2040	5	0	184	11	9	1855	19	3	92	16	0	1948	15	3		233	16	5	40	10	0	1674	8	10
521	9	5	0	3	9	1	12	9	1	12	9	10																			
522	1	5	0	15	10	0	15	6	11	6	15	11																			
523				10	10	3	10	10	3	10	2	3	15	10	0	15	15	6	16	5	6	3243	16	5	6				17	7	3
524				16	10	9	16	10	9				16	10	9	16	16	6	17	7	3	3244									
£	200	10	0	1901	9	0	2101	19	0	214	5	0	1888	0	0	94	8	0	1982	8	0		250	1	11	40	10	0	1691	16	1

[Note.—More columns may be utilised for further analysis.]

REIGATE CORPORATION   BOROUGH ENGINEER AND SURVEYOR'S DEPARTMENT

RECOVERABLE JOB COSTS CONTROL ACCOUNT
December Quarter 19...

Dr.   Folio 9   Cr.

Abstract from Summary.

	£	s.	d.
To Works in Progress brought forward	200	12	0
„ Expenditure for Quarter	1901	13	0
„ Administration (as per contra)	94	8	0
	£2196	13	0

Analysis of expenditure for Quarter as per quarterly abstract to Borough Accountant—

	£	s.	d.	D.P.S.
Labour	900	9	0	9
Materials	700	11	0	7
Haulage and Rolling	250	11	9	12
	1851	11	9	
	50	1	3	
Direct expenditure	£1901	13	0	

Abstract from Summary.

	£	s.	d.
By Direct Costs—completed jobs	1888	0	0
„ Administration—profits less losses	94	8	0
Recoverable	1982	8	0
„ Works in Progress carried forward	214	5	0
	£2196	13	0

REIGATE CORPORATION—BOROUGH ENGINEER AND SURVEYOR'S DEPARTMENT

JOB COSTS

Remarks: Resurfacing, Castlefield Road.
Commenced: 12 Sept., 19.... Completed:

Code No.: 200/1
Estimate: £350 15s. 0d.

Week ended.	Manual Labour.		Materials (Credits deducted).		Lorries.		Team Labour.		Steam Roller.		Petrol Roller.		Gully Emptier.		Direct.		Weekly Total.		Progressive Total Cost.	
	Fo. ML.	£ s. d.	Fo. M.	£ s. d.	Fo. L.	£ s. d.	Fo. TL.	£ s. d.	Fo. SR.	£ s. d.	Fo. PR.	£ s. d.	Fo. G.	£ s. d.	Fo. D.	£ s. d.	Fo.	£ s. d.		£ s. d.
18th Sept.	29	29 10 2	153	29 18 0	3	1 6 0			10	1 6 0					7	10 0		41 10 2		41 10 2
																		95 0 6		136 10 2
																		100 5 0		236 15 8
																		89 10 0		326 5 8
Totals.																		£326 5 8		

G G

General Rate Fund Ledger, and balancing the costing accounts. The form of Job Cost ruling in this system renders this information readily available (pp. 409 to 411).

Where sub-coding has been introduced, it will be necessary to summarise several Job Cost Sheets on to one sheet to provide totals for the " rate estimate " items of expenditure, and when this has been done, the total of the columns of the Job Costs Sheets, and sectional controls introduced, should be transferred to a Job Costs Extract Book.

This extract book will contain separate pages for Wages, Materials, Tools and Plant, and Transport, and additional columns for sub-totalling as required for Ledger purposes, together with folio columns. The Transport page should contain analysis columns corresponding with the columns on the Job Cost Sheets.

Transport Control Account.—A Control Account is opened for each vehicle (see specimen on p. 413), the debit side showing the cost of running the vehicle for the quarter as transferred from the Job Cost Sheets already completed. The Credit side entry being the total of the daily returns obtained from the Vehicle Abstract or Quarterly Summary.

When more than one vehicle of the same class is in use, a control account for the whole of the vehicles of that class should be kept on the columnar form. This shows deficits brought forward, costs for quarter, and surpluses carried forward, against surpluses brought forward, allocations for quarter and deficits carried forward, and can be utilised for fixing the hourly charge for the next quarter. (See specimen on p. 414.)

The hours the vehicles have been used can be ascertained by dividing the current hourly rate into the total of the column termed " allocation charges for the quarter." The deficit or surplus divided by this number of hours, will show the increase or decrease which should be made in the hourly charge for the next quarter. If thought essential this deficit or surplus can be allocated proportionately to the headings of expenditure concerned as shown in the Jobs Extract Book. In any case the charge for the next quarter must be provisional, and the costs of the previous quarter or quarters must act as a basis.

Wages Control Account is debited with the actual wages paid and credited with the total in the Job Extracts Book, which is regularly agreed with the wages paid.

REIGATE CORPORATION

DR.

FOLIO ☐

SPECIMEN TRANSPORT CENTRAL ACCOUNT

BOROUGH ENGINEER AND SURVEYOR'S DEPARTMENT

No........3 Ford Lorry.......CONTROL ACCOUNT

......September.......QUARTER, 19...

CR.

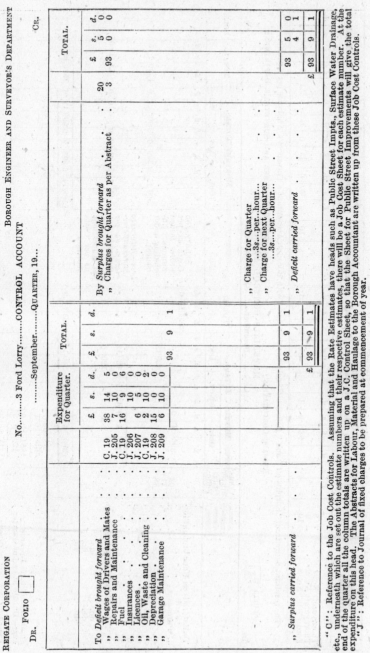

		Expenditure for Quarter			Total		
		£	s.	d.	£	s.	d.
To *Deficit brought forward*							
,, Wages of Drivers and Mates	C. 19	38	14	5			
,, Repairs and Maintenance	J. 205	7	10	0			
,, Fuel	C. 19	16	9	6			
,, Insurances	J. 206	6	10	0			
,, Licences	J. 207	2	5	0			
,, Oil, Waste and Cleaning	C. 19	15	0	2			
,, Depreciation	J. 208	6	10	0			
,, Garage Maintenance	J. 209				93	9	1
,, *Surplus carried forward*							
					£93	9	1

		Total		
		£	s.	d.
By *Surplus brought forward*	20	93	5	0
,, Charges for Quarter as per Abstract	3			
		0	1	
,, Charge for Quarter ...3s...per..hour...				
,, Charge for next Quarter ...3s...per..hour...		93	4	9
,, *Deficit carried forward*				
		£93	9	1

"C": Reference to the Job Cost Controls. Assuming that the Rate Estimates have heads such as Public Street Impts., Surface Water Drainage, etc., underneath which are set out the estimate numbers and their respective estimates, there will be a Job Cost Sheet for each estimate number. At the end of the quarter all the column totals are written up on a J.C. Control Sheet, so that the Sheet for Public Street Improvements will give the total expenditure on this head. The Abstracts for Labour, Material and Haulage to the Borough Accountant are written up from these Job Cost Controls.
"J": Reference to Journal of fixed charges to be prepared at commencement of year.

REIGATE CORPORATION

BOROUGH ENGINEER AND SURVEYOR'S DEPARTMENT

LORRIES COST CONTROL ACCOUNT

......September.......QUARTER 193...

Dr. Folio 20

Cr.

Vehicle Particulars.	Job Cost Control No.	Deficit Brought Forward.			Costs for Quarter.			Surplus Carried Forward.			Totals.			Analysis Abstract No.	Fol.	Surplus Brought Forward.			Allocations for Quarter.			Deficit Carried Forward.			Totals.		
		£	s.	d.	£	s.	d.	£	s.	d.	£	s.	d.			£	s.	d.	£	s.	d.	£	s.	d.	£	s.	d.
Thornycroft No. 1 ..	8																										
Thornycroft No. 2 ..	9																										
Ford No. 3 ..	10				93	9	1				93	9	1		10	5	0		93	0	0	4	1	93	9	1	

The resultant figure from "Surplus c/f" and "Deficit c/f" columns shall agree with Borough Accountant's Transport a/c balance periodically.

REIGATE CORPORATION

BOROUGH ENGINEER AND SURVEYOR'S DEPARTMENT

MATERIALS CONTROL ACCOUNT

......December.......QUARTER 193...

Dr. Folio 3

Cr.

	Committee Order Folio.	Oct.		Nov.		Dec.		TOTAL.		
		£ s. d.		£ s. d.		£ s. d.		£ s. d.		
To Materials on Hand brought forward . . .										
,, Purchases	63	390 4 0		900 15 6		420 12 0		2031 10 6		
do.	71									
do.	88									
do.										
do. (Unpaid at Quarter end)						120 0 3		120 0 3		
do.										
do.										
do.		390 4 0		900 15 6		540 12 3		1881 11 9		
do.		£390 4 0		£900 15 6		£540 12 3		3863 2 3		

Reconciliation

1831 11 9
120 0 3
£1711 11 6

Summary of Stores Inwards .
Less—Unpaid at end of Quarter .
Passed for Payment in Quarter .

	Oct.		Nov.		Dec.		TOTAL.		Fols.
	£ s. d.		£ s. d.		£ s. d.		£ s. d.		
By Sundry Job Costs as per Stores Issued Summary (including under issues) .	599 15 9		399 10 9		600 1 6		1599 7 6		
Less—Returns to Stores and over-issues as per Summary	11 1 3		1 0 6		10 0		12 11 9		
Net Allocations as per Costs Abstract	588 14 6		398 9		599 11 6		1586 15 9		
	£588 14 6		398 9		599 11 6		1586 15 9		
By Materials on hand as per Inventory .							2276 6 6		
							£3863 2 3		

Materials Control Account.—Monthly payments for purchases are debited, and at the end of each quarter outstanding unpaid invoices allowed for bringing the total into agreement with the Stores Inwards Abstract. The total of the Stores Issued Abstract is credited, Returns to Store being shown as a deduction. The net total should agree with the Job Extracts Book. The opening and closing balances agree with the balance on the Stores Ledger and with the Stocktaking List (when such is prepared).

The Totals are posted monthly as shown in the specimen account on p. 414.

Tools and Plant Control Account and Plant Book.—The opening balance will be transferred from the previous quarter's account; to this will be added the quarter's outlay on new tools, repairs and maintenance transferred from the appropriate Job Costs Sheets. The total charges for the quarter will be credited from the Jobs Extract Book and the closing balance inserted from the Tools and Plant Book.

The Tools and Plant Book should contain a separate page for each group of Tools and Plant, each group being " written down " annually in accordance with the known lives of the various classes of tools. Any deficit or surplus should be carried forward each quarter, and the final surplus or balance at the end of the year should be transferred to the Job Costs Sheet sectional control for " Other Roads and Bridges."

Recoverable Job Costs are dealt with as already described.

Organisation Time Table.—The following schedule provides a useful survey of the system described :—

TIME TABLE AND ORGANISATION OF COSTING SYSTEM

Daily Duties—Outside Staff.

Time Sheets.
Drivers' Returns.
Materials :—
1. Received Sheet.
2. Issued Sheet.
3. Returns to Stores Sheet.
4. Stores Book Entries.
5. Emergency Requisitions—materials for Stock.

Daily Duties—Costing Staff.

Vehicles—Daily Returns :—
1. Extensions of charges to jobs for user.
2. Posting of charges to Job Costs.
3. Daily totals to appropriate abstract for each vehicle.

Materials Received Sheet :—
1. Insertion of cost of materials from invoices.
2. Posting to Stores Ledger.
3. Daily total to abstract.

Materials Issued :—
1. Insertion of value of materials used.
2. Posting to Stores Ledger.
3. Daily total to abstract.
4. Posting issues to Job Costs.

Returns to Stores :—

1. Insertion of value of materials returned.
2. Posting to Stores Ledger.
3. Daily total to abstract.
4. Crediting to Job Costs (in red—materials column).

Recoverable Jobs :—

1. Issuing Instruction Sheets—new jobs.
2. Recording dates of jobs completed on Job Costs.

Weekly Duties—Outside Staff.

Time Sheets.

Weekly Duties—Costing Staff.

Craftsmen's Analysis Sheets—Thursday morning.
Preparation of Pay Sheets—Wednesday to Thursday noon.
Wages Analysis Abstract—Monday.
Wages Posting to Job Costs—Tuesday.

Monthly Duties—Costing Staff.

Materials—Storekeeper's Requirements :—

1. Insertion of estimated prices.
2. Preparation for Chairman's signature.
3. Issuing Orders to Tradesmen.

Materials—Invoices :—

1. Checking with Daily Materials Received Sheet.
2. Insertion of Order number and invoice amount in Requisition Binder.
3. Summarising materials invoices for Committee schedules.

Direct Expenditure—Invoices :—

1. Checking with Requisition Books.*
2. Summarising and allocations for schedules for Committee.*
3. Insertion of estimate numbers.*

Direct Costs :—

1. Apportionment of annual charges—first week of year.
2. Analysis of copies of Committee schedules.
3. Totals to Journal.
4. Posting to Job Costs.

Quarterly Duties—First 10 Days.

Working Day.	Duty.
1st.	Reconciliation of Stocktaking Sheets
	Preparation of Over-Issues Sheet (copy to Storekeeper)
	Preparation of Under-Issues Sheet (copy to Storekeeper)
	Total quarterly abstracts for vehicles
	Total vehicle columns on job cost sheets
	Total materials — received abstract
	Total materials—issued abstract
	Total materials—returns abstract
2nd.	Post Over and Under-Issues Sheets to Stores Ledger
	Post total over-issues to Abstract (Returns)
	Post total under-issues to Issues Abstract
	Prepare quarterly Reconciliation of Stores Ledger Accounts
	Post Over and Under-Issues to Job Costs
	Total materials columns on Job Cost Sheets
	Total direct expenditure on Job Cost Sheets
3rd.	Balance and rule off all Stores Ledger Accounts
	Quarterly Reconciliation and Materials Control Account
	Agree total of materials columns on Job Cost Sheets
	Total Wages columns on Job Cost Sheets
4th.	Job Costs Sectional Controls (green sheets)
	Prepare Control Account for each vehicle
	Determine charges for vehicles for quarter from Transport Control Accounts (sections)

* Three days before Committee.

Quarterly Duties—First 10 Days (cont.)—

Working Day.	Duty.
4th.	Recoverable Job Costs ruled off and Quarterly Summary of expenditure
	Wages for quarter—lists agreed
	Chief Financial Officer's Jobs Extract Book—Wages Analysis
5th.	Recoverable Job Costs Abstract and verify jobs stated as incomplete.

Working Day.	Duty.
5th.	Reconcile amounts due with Income Ledger.
	Journal quarterly total to Control Account.
	Chief Financial Officer's Job Extract Book :—
	1. Vehicles Section.
	2. Materials Section.
	3. Direct Expenditure Section.
6th.	Close all control accounts.
7th to 10th.	All daily and weekly duties for the first 10 days of the quarter to be brought up-to-date.

All posting to Job Costs on some approved method of Carbon Posting.

Note.—Certain of the daily duties, such as analysing the vehicles returns, may be suspended during the first 10 days of the quarter to facilitate the quarterly balancing. But the extension of such period should only be sanctioned in exceptional circumstances, and the work should, in any circumstances, be right up-to-date by the end of the first month of the quarter.

Concluding Notes on the System.—Despite the fact that the job costs are posted weekly, it is simple to provide daily costs of any work in progress when required by the technical section.

One of the most important advantages of the system is that each of the units, viz. of Labour, Materials and Haulage, is balanced in the Costs section, and the returns provided to the Borough Accountant for incorporation in his ledgers are proved by the control accounts.

By subcoding the Borough Accountant's Rate estimate numbers, which constitute the main code, any job is kept separate in whole or in part for unit costing.

Mechanical Accounting.—In municipalities where the volume of work is sufficiently great the punched-card system for sorting and tabulating on such machines as the Powers and Hollerith can be employed. Mr. G. A. Bryant, F.C.W.A., of Norwich Corporation, has devised and operated such a scheme, and Birmingham Corporation has employed Hollerith machines since 1916.

Needle-Sorting by Hand, of which the Paramount System is an example, can be used for smaller installations.

Cards of any convenient size or shape are supplied ready punched with a series of holes along one or more edges, the number and position of the holes being determined by the headings on the card. Each hole stands for a number or value, in relation to the headings. Codes are used to reduce the number of holes to a convenient limit.

The details written on the card are represented on the edge of the card by snipping out the holes representing each item. This is done with a pair of nippers or by a key punch for large numbers.

When a stack of cards has been so slotted, say for materials and labour charged against jobs, all the cards for labour on a particular job can be separated easily, by passing a long needle through the appropriate hole and lifting the cards edgeways. Those cards with the holes cut away drop, leaving the others on the needle. Cards of a particular slotting when placed in a stack show a channel, and should a wrong card be in the bundle its presence is at once noticeable, thus giving a visible check in accuracy. Summaries can be then made on listing and adding machines.

The Use of Machines.—Many operations in connection with costing can only be done mechanically in the largest Local Authorities offices. It is the adoption of mechanical devices which gives full and regularly prompt returns so necessary to adequate control by executive officers.

Cost Control Accounts for Municipalities.—The following is a simple example of a set of control accounts described by Mr. C. H. Durman, of Portsmouth Corporation, in *The Cost Accountant*.

Different municipalities have different methods of keeping the financial records, and whilst the system to be described may be adapted to any set of circumstances, it will simplify matters if certain assumptions are made regarding the method of keeping the accounts, and then the operation of the system is described within those set conditions. The first assumption is that the Abstract of Accounts is compiled from a General Ledger, to which postings are made from three possible sources, viz :—

(a) *The Transfer Journal*—which records charges made by one committee on another and in which is analysed the charges for rates, telephones, insurance, etc. ;

(b) *The Invoice Journal*—a term which is self-explanatory ; and

(c) *The General Payments Journal*—which records such

other expenses as purchase of property and sundry periodical payments, such as road rentals, car and cycle allowances, etc.

To simplify the description it has been assumed that the records deal only with the expenditure of one committee.

The essence of the scheme is to place the entire responsibility for the analysis of the expenditure into the hands of the Cost Office and for that office to pass the results of the analysis on to the Financial Office. In this latter office an Adjustment Account is kept to record the expenditure of the committee in total, and at the end of each quarter, or other appropriate period, the Cost Office compiles a series of Transfers which the Financial Office uses to clear the Adjustment Account and to debit the appropriate heads of expenditure in the General Ledger. A similar Adjustment Account is kept by the Cost Office, but in reverse order, thus making the two accounts complementary. That is, although both accounts are posted from the same source, the debits in the one appear as credits in the other, and *vice versa*. A series of Control Accounts kept by the Cost Office serves to complete the double entry.

Adjustment Accounts.—These accounts are concerned only with financial transactions and deal simply with wages, materials, disbursements and hired haulage, each of which will be discussed in turn. In the books of the Cost Office the account is termed " General Ledger Adjustment Account," whilst in the financial books it bears the name " Cost Office Adjustment Account." At the beginning of the financial year there is a balance to the account representing the value of stores in hand. During the year the items just mentioned and the totals of the Cost Office Transfers will be posted to the account and the balance at the end of the year will again represent the value of stocks.

Control Accounts.—These deal with the totals of the elements of cost, there being one account for each element. At the end of the financial year the balance of each of these accounts should be nil, with the exception of the Stores Control Account, which has a balance representing the value of stores in hand.

Wages Paid.—Wages are analysed by the Cost Office and agreed in total with the pay roll. This total is then journalised as follows :—

	Journal Entry No. 1.		
		£	£
Costing Books—			
Wages Control A/c. . . . . . *Dr.*	2	1200	
To General Ledger Adjustment A/c. .	1		1200
Being wages paid.			
Financial Books—			
Cost Office Adjustment A/c. . . . *Dr.*	1	1200	
To Cash			1200
Being wages paid.			

Disbursements.—This term has been used in a comprehensive fashion to include invoices for direct charges to jobs, and transactions passing through the Transfer Journal and General Payments Journal. As far as the invoices are concerned, these are posted by the Cost Office into an analysed Invoice Journal, from whence they are debited to the various cost accounts. At the end of each month the invoices are passed to the Financial Office with the total attached. They are then entered, in total, into a single column Invoice Journal, and from there posted to the Cost Office Adjustment Account. The General Payments Journal is kept by the Financial Office, and it is quite convenient for the Cost Office to use it as a posting medium. The Transfer Journal, also kept by the Financial Office, deals with many transactions that are not necessarily costing items. In order to separate the relevant items from the irrelevant it is convenient to have two columns in the Journal headed " Cost Office Adjustment Account " and " Cost Office Adjustment Account— Contra Expenditure." This will be found greatly to facilitate the work of the Cost Office and will ensure that they post only those items applicable to their accounts. The journal entries necessary for disbursement are :—

	Journal Entry No. 2.		
		£	£
Costing Books—			
Disbursements Control A/c. . . . *Dr.*	4	600	
To General Ledger Adjustment A/c. .	1		600
Being sundry disbursements.			
Financial Books—			
Cost Office Adjustment A/c. . . . *Dr.*	1	600	
To sundry persons			600
Being sundry disbursements.			

Materials Purchased.—These are really nothing but disbursements in the eyes of the Financial Office, but as a separate Control Account is necessary for them in the Costing Books, they have been dealt with separately. The invoices will be entered into the stores ledgers *via* a Goods Inwards Journal and then passed on to the Financial Office with the total attached as in the case of ordinary invoices. The following journal entries will be applicable :—

		Journal Entry No. 3.	
		£	£
Costing Books—			
Stores Control A/c. . . . Dr.	3	1500	
To General Ledger Adjustment A/c. .	1		1500
Being materials purchased.			
Financial Books—			
Cost Office Adjustment A/c. . . . Dr.	1	1500	
To sundry tradesmen			1500
Being materials purchased.			

Hired Haulage.—This is another sub-section of disbursements as far as the Financial Office is concerned, but the Cost Office opens a separate control account for the item :—

		Journal Entry No. 4.	
		£	£
Costing Books—			
Hired Haulage Control A/c. . . . Dr.	5	400	
To General Ledger Adjustment A/c. .	1		400
Being invoices received in respect of Hired Haulage.			
Financial Books—			
Cost Office Adjustment A/c. . . . Dr.	1	400	
To sundry contractors			400
Being invoices received in respect of Hired Haulage.			

Treatment of Costing Transactions.—Each week postings are made to the various cost accounts in respect of wages, materials, disbursements, hired haulage, Corporation haulage, plant charges and oncost. The total of each of these elements of cost is ascertained and utilised to make the following journal entry :—

	Journal Entry No. 5.		
Costing Books—		£	£
Work in Progress A/c. . . . . *Dr.*	9	4300	
To Sundries :			
Wages Control A/c.	2		1200
Stores Control A/c.	3		1300
Disbursements Control A/c. . .	4		600
Hired Haulage Control A/c. . .	5		400
Corporation Haulage Control A/c. .	6		300
Plant Charges Control A/c. . .	7		50
Oncost Control A/c.	8		450
Being work in progress for week ended......			

These transactions are recorded by the Cost Office only ; they are purely items of cost and necessitate no corresponding entry in the financial books. Similar postings are made week by week until the quarterly transfers are prepared for the Financial Office. These are journalised in the following manner :—

	Journal Entry No. 6.		
Costing Books—		£	£
Sundries : *Dr.*			
To Work in Progress A/c. . . .	9		4300
General Ledger Adjustment A/c. . .	1	3500	
Corporation Haulage Control A/c. .	6	300	
Plant Charges Control A/c. . . .	7	50	
Oncost Control A/c.	8	450	
Being transfers for quarter ended			
Financial Books—			
Sundry Jobs . . . . . . *Dr.*		4300	
To Sundries :			
Cost Office Adjustment A/c. . .	1		3500
Income : Use of Corporation Haulage	2		300
Use of Plant	2		50
Supervision and Establishment Charges	2		450
Being costing transfers for quarter ended...			

With regard to rechargeable works, such as road reinstatements for the Gas, Water and Electricity Companies, private contractors, etc., the Cost Office enters the amount of the charge into the Day Book when the account is sent, and the Financial Office posts the Sundry Debtors Ledger in the usual way. At the end of the financial year an analysis of the Day Book under the headings of Adjustment Account, Corporation Haulage, etc., is prepared in order that the necessary entries may be made in the appropriate accounts. For the purpose of this description it has been assumed that this analysis is incorporated in Journal Entry No. 6, above.

To complete the illustration, assume that the value of stores in hand at the commencement of the year was £2,400. This would have stood as a debit balance in the Cost Office Adjustment Account and the Stores Control Account, and as a credit balance in the General Ledger Adjustment Account. The ledger accounts incorporating the above transactions would then appear as shown hereunder.

It will be found convenient to have a separate Adjustment Account and a separate set of Control Accounts for each committee. This will necessitate transfers between the various accounts when, for instance, one committee's lorries are used by another committee's works staff.

The system ensures complete and direct interlocking of the accounts, and the following advantages are to be gained from its adoption :—

(1) Automatic reconciliation is ensured.

(2) The elimination of analysed Invoice Journals in the Financial Office results in the work of that office being relieved during the busy billing period.

(3) The work of analysis is left entirely in the hands of the costing staff, who are more conversant with the work concerned.

(4) The costing books are controlled on a double entry basis.

Costing Books.

DR.   CR.

GENERAL LEDGER ADJUSTMENT ACCOUNT.   Account No. 1.

		£				£
To Work in Progress A/c. .	. 6	3500	By Balance brought forward .			2400
„ Balance carried forward .	.	2600	„ Wages A/c. .	.	1	1200
			„ Disbursements A/c. .	.	2	600
			„ Stores A/c. .	.	3	1500
			„ Hired Haulage A/c. .	.	4	400
		6100				6100
			„ Balance brought forward .			2600

WAGES CONTROL ACCOUNT.   Account No. 2.

		£			£
To General Ledger Adjustment A/c.	1	1200	By Work in Progress A/c.	. 5	1200

Dr.   Cr.

STORES CONTROL ACCOUNT.   Account No. 3.

	£		£
To Balance brought forward .	2400	By Work in Progress A/c. . 5	1300
,, General Ledger Adjustment A/c. 3	1500	,, Balance carried forward .	2600
	3900		3900
,, Balance brought forward .	£2600		

DISBURSEMENTS CONTROL ACCOUNT.   Account No. 4.

	£		£
To General Ledger Adjustment A/c. 2	600	By Work in Progress A/c. . 5	600

HIRED HAULAGE CONTROL ACCOUNT.   Account No. 5.

	£		£
To General Ledger Adjustment A/c. 4	400	By Work in Progress A/c. . 5	400

CORPORATION HAULAGE CONTROL ACCOUNT.   Account No. 6.

	£		£
To Work in Progress A/c. . . 6	300	By Work in Progress A/c. . 5	300

PLANT CHARGES CONTROL ACCOUNT.   Account No. 7.

	£		£
To Work in Progress A/c. . . 6	50	By Work in Progress A/c. . 5	50

ONCOST CONTROL ACCOUNT.   Account No. 8.

	£		£
To Work in Progress A/c. . . 6	450	By Work in Progress A/c. . 5	450

WORK IN PROGRESS ACCOUNT.   Account No. 9.

	£		£
To Sundries 5	4300	By Sundries 6	4300

Financial Books.

COST OFFICE ADJUSTMENT ACCOUNT.   Account No. 1.

	£		£
To Balance brought forward .	2400	By Sundries 6	3500
,, Wages paid 1	1200	,, Balance carried forward .	2600
,, Disbursements . . . 2	600		
,, ,, . . . 3	1500		
,, ,, . . . 4	400		
	6100		6100
,, Balance brought forward .	£2600		

GENERAL LEDGER—INCOME.   Account No. 2.

Fo.	Use of Corporation Vehicles.	Fo.	Use of Plant.	Fo.	Supervision and Establishment Charges.
6	£300	6	£50	6	£450

Note.—General Ledger Expenditure Accounts, Sundry Debtors, Sundry Creditors and Cash Account have been omitted from the above.

Examination Questions

1. Set out the principal headings under which you would expect municipal expenditure to be allocated, and state how capital additions are dealt with.—*Institute of Cost and Works Accountants (Final).*

2. Discuss the merits and demerits of centralised costing for Municipal Trading undertakings.—*Institute of Cost and Works Accountants (Final).*

3. State, with reasons, on what bases you would allocate overheads in any three of the following :—

Builder and contractor;
Non-ferrous foundry;
Farmer;
Milk products;
Printers;
Municipal department for dust removal.
Institute of Cost and Works Accountants (Inter.).

4. Draw up a skeleton periodical cost summary of the running of public baths and washhouses, with such statistical statements as you would consider necessary.—*Institute of Cost and Works Accountants (Final).*

5. Set out a final form of cost, complete with imaginary entries, for one of the following :—

(1) Motor Car or Lorry;
(2) Any form of Metal Toy;
(3) Furniture or Joinery work;
(4) Finished Building;
(5) Chemical process with by-products;
(6) Municipal Trading Undertaking.
Institute of Cost and Works Accountants (Final).

6. Statistics of a public transport undertaking are based on :

(a) car mile; (b) passenger mile; (c) route mile; (d) vehicle hour.

Discuss the respective merits of each in their application to costs.—*Institute of Cost and Works Accountants (Final).*

7. Describe and comment on the official Costing returns issued in connection with any four services administered by local authorities.—*Institute of Municipal Treasurers and Accountants (Inter.).*

8. A local authority administering an area with a population of 100,000 and providing the usual municipal and sanitary services, possesses an electricity and transport undertaking. A discussion has arisen on the question of centralisation of the costing sections of the various departments.

Prepare a report on the advantages of, and objections to such a proposal.—*Institute of Municipal Treasurers and Accountants (Final).*

9. What do you understand by " Oncost " ?

Give the principal items of oncost you would expect to find in a cleansing Department.—*Institute of Municipal Treasurers and Accountants (Final).*

10. Indicate some factors to be taken into account in comparing the maintenance unit costs of a hospital with those of similar institutions of other local authorities.—*Institute of Municipal Treasurers and Accountants (Final).*

11. What kind of information should be deducible from an efficient costing system ?—*Institute of Municipal Treasurers and Accountants (Inter.).*

12. State the factors which may cause differences in Unit costs.—*Institute of Municipal Treasurers and Accountants (Inter.).*

13. A Costing system is being installed in connection with a Highways Department. Draft instructions to (a) the Storekeeper, (b) General Foreman, (c) the Ganger or Charge-hand, on the way to deal with stores required on a job, and surplus stores returned from a job.—*Institute of Municipal Treasurers and Accountants (Final).*

14. Using hypothetical figures, draft a monthly cost-sheet for a commercial motor transport vehicle. The sheet should be made up of three sections, viz. :—(a) Performance record; (b) Performance averages; (c) Costs for month.—*Institute of Municipal Treasurers and Accountants (Final).*

15. What do you understand by Unit costing?
How could this system be applied to the following services :—(a) Police ; (b) Roads ; (c) Hospitals ; (d) Sewers ; (e) Street Lighting ?—*Institute of Municipal Treasurers and Accountants (Final).*

16. Outline a general scheme of Stock-keeping for a Municipal Body having a number of depot stores within the area, much of the material being necessarily interchangeable. What system of control would you recommend, assuming the area to be a large one ?—*Institute of Cost and Works Accountants (Inter.).*

INSTITUTE OF CHARTERED ACCOUNTANTS

ADVANCED BOOK-KEEPING AND ACCOUNTANCY

Second Paper

Time allowance—3 hours

IMPORTANT NOTICE.—Special value will be given to the answers to the first four questions. Of the remaining six questions, Candidates must NOT attempt more than four.

1. The manufacturing operations of a Limited Company involve three distinct processes in connection with the same unit. The practice has been to prepare a Cost Sheet for the processes as a whole, based upon the completed unit. The Cost Sheet for January, 1929, appeared as follows :

			Total. £	Cost per unit (pence).
Direct Wages : Process A	.	. 1,450		
,, B	.	. 870		
,, C	.	. 800	3,120	11·7
Raw Materials issued to				
Process A : 58,000 units	.	.	5,800	21·75
Machine Expenses : Process A	.	604		
,, B	.	604		
,, C	.	667	1,875	7·03
Factory Oncost	. . .	.	725	2·72
Cost of . . .	64,000 units (C)		11,520	43·2
Deduct, Waste, etc.	2,000 units (C)			1·4
Cost of Output of .	62,000 ,,		11,520	44·6

The Cost Sheets in the form given are obviously unsatisfactory ; the variations in cost per process cannot be viewed and the expenses attributable to waste and faulty production in the individual processes are not accurately dealt with.

You are instructed to prepare Process Cost Sheets for January 1929 similar in form to the above, but based on the output of each individual process.

427

HH

For this purpose, the following Statement of Stocks is furnished :

Process :	A.	B.	C.
Jan. 1, 1929, Stock on hand (units) .	10,000	6,000	18,000
„ 31, „ Received . . .	58,000	54,000	56,000
	68,000	60,000	74,000
„ „ „ *Delivered* . . .	54,000	56,000	62,000
„ „ „ *Waste, etc* . . .	4,000	2,000	2,000
„ „ „ Stock on hand . .	10,000	2,000	10,000

You are informed :

(1) That it is the practice to deliver to the next process all goods as and when completed, and that no work has been done in any process upon units in stock at the end of the month.

(2) That Factory Oncost may be taken as 1*d.* per unit for each process on the total of units delivered.

(3) That Opening Stock of Process A and stock of raw material received into Process A may be taken at 2*s.* per unit.

(4) That Opening Stock of Process B and units received into that Process may be taken at the average cost of units delivered by Process A during the current month, and similarly as regards units received by Process C from Process B.

Prepare Process Cost Sheets accordingly. Calculations need not be carried beyond one decimal place.

[*N.B.—The remaining questions in this paper which do not refer to costing are omitted.*]

NOVEMBER, 1931

4. ZYX Co., Ltd., manufacture lemon squash.

Prepare from the following balances and records Manufacturing, Trading and Profit and Loss Accounts, showing in them such percentages and figures per case as will furnish costing information and facilitate periodical comparisons.

	£		£
Stocks at cost, on Jan. 1st, 1931 :		Factory Rent . . .	594
		Carriage Inwards . .	382
Bottled Lemon Squash.	2,112	Distributing Charges .	522
Ingredients . .	4,784	Office Salaries and Expenses	2,080
Bottles, etc. . .	1,226	Selling Expenses . .	904
Purchases :		Stocks at cost, on June 30th, 1931 :	
Ingredients . .	10,432	Ingredients . . .	3,775
Bottles, etc. . .	3,128	Bottles, etc. . .	1,007
Factory Wages . .	5,120	Sales	26,294
Factory Expenses . .	628		

The stock of bottled lemon squash on June 30, 1931, was 12,500 cases ; 7,000 cases produced during the period had been invoiced out at £1,824 and treated as sales, but were still held by customers on sale or return on June 30, 1931.

Messina lemons purchased at 24*s.* a case during the year 1930 have been found unsuitable for manufacture ; the Sales include 1,260 cases of these lemons sold during the period at 18*s.* a case and 180 cases were still in stock on June 30, 1931, when the market value was 16*s.* a case.

100,000 cases of bottled lemon squash were produced during the six months.

7. M, Ltd., have for many years had an average of six motor lorries and have kept a separate Operation and Maintenance Account for each. They ask you to advise them at what average age it is economical to renew.

How will you proceed in order to determine your advice ?

MAY, 1932

4. A Company owning its own premises and engaged in the printing trade has, in addition to offices and stock rooms, the following departments : Mechanical Composition, Hand Composition, Letterpress, Binders. The motive power is steam, and exhaust steam is used for heating.

Supplying your own data, give the form of the statement which would be prepared to show the cost of the Power and Heating Department and the allocation thereof to the other departments. Indicate the basis of distribution.

5. A Limited Company purchased a special machine for £2,500, the cost of erection being £80. It was expected that the machine would last ten years, and a Depreciation Fund, invested outside the business, was created to replace the machine at the end of that time. At the expiration of nine years, however, the directors decided that, as the machine could not be worked profitably, it should be scrapped and a more modern one purchased. At that date the balance of the Depreciation Fund Account was £2,375, and this was represented by an investment in 5 per cent. War Stock, which was subsequently sold for £2,305. The cost of dismantling the machine was £30, and, with the exception of parts, estimated to be worth £20, retained to be used on the new machine, the old one was sold as scrap for £40.

Give the ledger accounts concerned and show how these matters would be dealt with in the books of the Company.

THE SOCIETY OF INCORPORATED ACCOUNTANTS AND AUDITORS

INTERMEDIATE EXAMINATION. MAY, 1932

Time allowed—1 hour

COST ACCOUNTS

1. Costing systems are classified according to the requirements they are designed to meet. Enumerate them, and give one example of a business to which each is applicable.

2. Outline a system of costing you would recommend for a factory producing wireless parts and sets, bearing in mind the fact that large numbers of parts are produced, most of them of small value. What principle would govern your recommendations ?

3. The following is a summarised record of all transactions relating to Contract G 72 :

		£
Materials purchased direct	. . . . .	635
Materials supplied from Stores	. . . .	260
Wages	. . . .	1,072
Expenses directly chargeable	. . . . .	147
Materials returned to Stores	. . . . .	120
Contract Price	. . . . . .	2,500
Works on-cost	. . . .	25 per cent. of direct wages
Office on-cost	. . . .	10 per cent. of prime cost

Open the necessary Accounts in the Cost Ledger and record the transactions therein in order to show the double entry in each case.

4. At the close of a balancing period it is found that the credit for office on-cost in the Cost Ledger is considerably less than the total expenses shown in the financial books. The percentage of on-cost was based on the accounts of the previous period. What conclusions would you draw, and what would you recommend to prevent a recurrence of the discrepancy ?

5. " Reduction of cost is the natural result of *mass production*." Discuss this statement, giving your opinion how far, if at all, it is justified.

THE SOCIETY OF INCORPORATED ACCOUNTANTS AND AUDITORS

FINAL EXAMINATION. MAY, 1932

Time allowed—1½ hour

COST ACCOUNTS

1. The M.M. Colliery Co., Ltd., which, in addition to its usual colliery business, also builds its own Wagons and keeps them in repair, desires to improve its storekeeping system.

You are asked to devise a system which will, in your view, prove effective, and which will also be helpful for stocktaking purposes.

Draft your report, giving rulings of such necessary bin or locker cards as you may deem desirable.

2. Into what class of costing would you place the following :

(a) The manufacture of cycles, boots, furniture or hosiery ?
(b) The building of a bridge or a ship ?
(c) The manufacture per barrel or per ton of a commodity ?
(d) The manufacture of chemicals where one commodity when made is utilised in the making of other commodities ?
(e) Railway, Tramway or Electric Power undertakings.

3. Should interest on Capital or Loans be taken into account in arriving at costing results ?

Give reasons for your answer.

4. (a) Define the Bonus or Premium system for the remuneration of Labour.

(b) A worker is given ten hours to do a piece of work, his rate being 2s. per hour, plus a bonus of one-tenth of the wages earned for each hour saved. How would this affect the worker and the manufacturer in a case where one hour was saved and in another where five hours were saved in doing of work ?

What, if any, defect can you detect in the system ?

5. In what way would you provide for wages of boilermen, time-keepers, storekeepers and the like, in cases where such wages cannot be related directly to a particular job ?

6. Upon what basis would you value work in progress ? Would you carry the full estimated profits on such work to the Profit and Loss Account ?

7. Draw up a system of cost accounts for a house builder, indicating the manner in which the cost accounts would be co-ordinated with the financial books of the business.

8. Show the following figures graphically by diagram :

Year.	Sales.	Labour and Materials.	Selling and General Expenses.	Profit.
	£	£	£	£
1928	20,000	16,000	2,000	2,000
1929	25,000	20,300	2,300	2,400
1930	24,000	19,500	2,200	2,300
1931	22,000	18,000	2,100	1,900

THE INSTITUTE OF COST AND WORKS ACCOUNTANTS
(LIMITED BY GUARANTEE)

INTERMEDIATE EXAMINATION. DECEMBER, 1931

COSTING. Part I.—Labour   *Time allowed—2 hours*

N.B.—The Candidate's examination number and trade must be stated at the top of every sheet used : his name must NOT appear anywhere on his paper.

Questions numbered 1, 2, 3 and 4 are compulsory. Candidates should attempt two only out of the remaining questions numbered 5, 6 and 7.

1. A decision is taken that a certain class of labour expense that has formerly been charged direct shall in future be charged to overheads. What is gained or lost thereby ?

2. Describe the special features of the different types of time recorder clocks known to you. In what position in the Works would you propose to locate them ?

3. Boys and youths of 16 years and over receive a cost of living bonus varying with age. Girls and young women also receive one from the age of 14 years. What effect does this have on costs in a piece-work shop ?

4. Prepare a labour cost sheet for a machined component, using your own figures, assuming eight operations and the following additional information :

Commenced with 150 ; 5 scrapped on operation 1 ; 5 scrapped on operation 2 ; 3 scrapped on operation 3, and 8 rejected for adjustment ; 2 scrapped on operation 4 ; and for operation 5 and 6 no spoiled ones. During operation 7 there were 5 defective forgings and two spoiled in machining. Operation 8, all correct.

5. Draw up a card to be used for recording piece-work, showing the information that you consider to be essential. State what you assume to be the methods in use of (a) recording attendance and (b) charging overheads to the products.

6. What are the general circumstances which render payment by results desirable or undesirable respectively ?

7. At a factory where a considerable number of employees are

occupied, partly indoors on bench work, and partly outdoors, changing frequently, which do you consider the most efficient method of checking their movements and accounting for their time ?

COSTING.   Part II.—Materials   Time allowed—2 hours

N.B.—*The Candidate's examination number and trade must be stated at the top of every sheet used : his name must* NOT *appear anywhere on his paper.*

Questions numbered 1, 2, 3 and 4 are compulsory.   Candidates should attempt two only out of the remaining questions numbered 5, 6 and 7.

1. What steps would you propose should be taken to avoid discrepancies between the Store-house Records and the Stores Ledgers in respect of issues of materials and stores ?

2. At a Works consisting of many and scattered departments, what arrangements would you recommend as to the physical issue of materials and stores in order to avoid waste of labour and transport ?

3. On what basis would you determine credits for scrap arisings and for materials returned to store ?

4. Describe a system that would definitely link up the Purchasing Department, Goods Receiving Department, and Cost Department; giving all information for passing invoices, checking goods received and posting to Costs.

5. Certain material in stock at the end of the financial year is found to have doubled in value, according to current market price. It is valued in stock at cost. Discuss the position created with regard to future issues, bearing in mind that estimates have been accepted for jobs which will use this material, and that these estimates were based on the market value then ruling. Assume there is a considerable quantity of the material in stock, but not sufficient to cover all orders.

6. A factory manufacturing articles in wood, in large quantities, issued timber in planks from store to the Works. Several separate designs were produced from each plank, but owing to variation in quality there were variations in the number produced per plank. How would you allocate cost of timber to each design ?

7. A contract, including a material " rise and fall " clause, has been placed. Show how this feature should be dealt with to ensure correct charges to you as purchaser.

COSTING.   Part III.—General Expenses   Time allowed—2 hours

N.B.—*The Candidate's examination number and trade must be stated at the top of every sheet used : his name must* NOT *appear anywhere on his paper.*

Questions numbered 1, 2, 3 and 4 are compulsory.   Candidates should attempt two only out of the remaining questions numbered 5, 6 and 7.

1. It is the practice in a certain factory to charge overheads to the products by means of pre-determined hourly rates. How would you propose to deal with the following under or over-absorbed overhead at the end of an accounting period :

	Overhead incurred.	Overhead absorbed.	Balance.
	£	£	£
Department A	2,000	2,200	+ 200
Department B	1,500	1,300	− 200
Department C	1,100	1,000	− 100

2. Where costs are compiled monthly (period of 4 weeks), how would you deal with the following items when charging overheads to the products :

    (a) Steam for shop heating;
    (b) Shop lighting;
    (c) Paid holidays ?

3. Explain the term " Standing Works Order," and give a representative list of such orders.

4. What items of general expense would you expect to show most change per centum as a result of a combine ? Indicate the direction of, and reasons for, these changes.

5. In using the direct-man-hour method of overhead absorption rates, prepare a statement for three departments, showing the information necessary to arrive at the rate of each.

6. In connection with a contract on an " actual cost " basis, a customer's cost auditor refuses to pass a charge upon the grounds that the rate of overhead is higher than that of competitors. Discuss the position thus created.

7. When fixing hourly rates of absorption of overheads, how would you differentiate between machines that were only occasionally used owing to

    (a) Temporary shortage of work;
    (b) Inevitable want of balance in relation to other machines that were fully employed ?

COSTING. Part IV —Methods   *Time allowed—*1½ *hours*

N.B.—The Candidate's examination number and trade must be stated at the top of every sheet used : his name must NOT *appear anywhere on his paper.*

Questions numbered 1, 2 *and* 3 *are compulsory. Candidates should attempt two only out of the remaining questions numbered* 4, 5 *and* 6.

1. What are " terminal costs " ? In what industries are they used ? Give examples.

2. What means would you adopt to ascertain the cost of defective work where job costing prevails and where defective work is not charged to overheads ?

3. A decision is required regarding a product that could be purchased outside or made in the Works. The outside quotation is somewhat in excess of the cost price. Would you consider it economical to purchase outside ? State reasons in detail.

4. How would you propose to cost the products of a brass foundry where castings are made that vary considerably as regards weight, intricacy and mixture of virgin and scrap metals ?

5. How would you lay out for costing purposes an order for a million articles where delivery extended over 18 months and there were expenses for tools, gauges, patterns, and drawings ? It should be assumed that the order was obtained in competition and that the articles differ in some respects from the normal output of the Works.

6. Devise a system to ensure recovery of all expenditure upon repair jobs where speedy results are required for charges to customer.

THE INSTITUTE OF COST AND WORKS ACCOUNTANTS
(LIMITED BY GUARANTEE)

FINAL EXAMINATION. DECEMBER, 1931

COSTING. PART I.—(General Arrangement and Assembly)

Time allowed—2½ hours

N.B.—The Candidate's examination number and trade must be stated at the top of every sheet used : his name must NOT appear anywhere on his paper.

Questions numbered 1, 2, 3 and 4 are compulsory. Candidates should attempt one only out of the remaining questions numbered 5 and 6.

1. Prepare a cost sheet for any industry with which you are familiar, showing comparative figures at the end of four separate periods.

2. In the preparation of periodical cost figures for repetition work, how would you indicate clearly the causes of fluctuations ? Illustrate your answer with two examples.

3. How would you charge out work produced by a tool room for the following purposes :

   (*a*) Use in tool room ;
   (*b*) Use in machine shop;
   (*c*) Sale?

4. At a woodworking establishment logs of various natures are bought on a cubic foot basis and converted to board or plank. There is a loss of wood during conversion, varying with the class and quality of timber.

Prepare for the use of the management a skeleton statement of the cost of conversion.

5. In the process of electro-deposition a number of jobs are treated simultaneously in the deposition baths. It is not practicable to charge the labour involved direct to the jobs. How would you propose to cost the work done ?

6. In what circumstances would you differentiate in your costs, between the time taken in (*a*) making ready or setting up for a job preparatory to the running off on a machine, and (*b*) running off the job ? What objects would you aim at securing by such differentiation ?

COSTING. Part II.—(Overhead Expenses)   *Time allowed—2½ hours*

N.B.—The Candidate's examination number and trade must be stated at the top of every sheet used : his name must NOT appear anywhere on his paper.

Questions numbered 1, 2, 3 and 4 are compulsory. Candidates should attempt one only out of the remaining questions numbered 5 and 6.

1. In setting up machine-hour rates of absorption of overheads, what provision would you make year by year for depreciation of the machines engaged in production ? How would you deal with expenses of plant of a general character ?

2. At a Works where overheads are charged to products by pre-determined hourly rates, where costs are compiled monthly and where the entire Works are closed for a week and all workers are paid, how would you treat the expense of this paid holiday in your monthly over-head statements ?

3. When considering the rate of depreciation of plant and machinery, what influence would expenditure on repairs have upon your recommendations? Give reasons for your answer.

4. During a period of industrial depression, how would you deal with the expense relating to idle plant, assuming such expense to be considerable, and that the market conditions preclude its inclusion in estimated prices? Detail the main items comprising such expense.

5. How would you charge out the expenditure incurred in the Pattern Shop?

6. Three Feeder Departments supply the manufacturing departments at pre-determined cost prices. At the end of the financial year two have made a book profit of £3,000 and £8,000 respectively, and the other has made a loss of £2,700. How would you deal with this situation?

COSTING. PART III.—(General Principles and Methods
Time allowed—3 hours

N.B.—*The Candidate's examination number and trade must be stated at the top of every sheet used : his name must* NOT *appear anywhere on his paper.*

Questions numbered 1, 2, 3 *and* 4 *are compulsory. Candidates should attempt two only out of the remaining questions numbered* 5, 6 *and* 7.

1. A firm has undertaken to reduce the time of delivery of product from 34 to 21 weeks. This will involve additional expenditure for overtime and week-end work. How would you deal with this extra expense?

2. What are the principal difficulties encountered in reconciliation of cost and financial accounts? How are they overcome?

3. The products of a manufacturing concern are wide and various. At the end of the financial year the value of Stock and Work-in-Progress is urgently required. Describe a system that would give accurate and speedy returns.

4. What methods of costing would you advocate in the case of the following manufactures? State reasons.

Ball bearings.
Beer.
Bicycles.
Biscuits.
Bricks.

5. Where it is the practice to capitalise as machinery the cost of foundations for and erection of machinery, how would you deal with expenditure of re-erection of an old machine on a new foundation? Give reasons.

6. On what broad lines would you proceed to classify between capital and revenue expenditure? How would you treat the following :

(a) Conversion of a machine from shaft to direct motor drive.
(b) Alteration of a furnace from gas to fuel-oil firing.
(c) Re-erection of a machine on a stronger foundation, the old foundation having given way.
(d) Removal and re-erection of a machine on a fresh site following a policy of rationalisation.

7. You are asked to investigate the manufacturing conditions in a factory, with a view to recommending a method of costing. What are the main considerations which would influence your decision as to the most suitable form of costing to adopt?

THE LONDON ASSOCIATION OF ACCOUNTANTS, LIMITED

FINAL EXAMINATION, JUNE, 1931.

COST ACCOUNTS AND SYSTEMS OF COSTING

Time allowed—2 hours

(Brevity and arrangement will be taken into account in marking. Please arrange your answers in their sequential order.)

1. The following is a schedule of the expenditure in three departments of a manufacturing business for 1930, viz. :

	Department		
	A.	B.	C.
	£	£	£
Direct Wages	10,116	4,690	5,928
Indirect Wages	2,725	1,106	894
Toolmakers	629	528	242
Power consumed	920	292	208
Shop Sundries	217	70	26
Repairs to Plant	548	281	75
Depreciation of Plant . . .	272	325	169
Rent and Rates	992	535	529
Stationery for Manufacturing Departments	50	32	69
Supervision Salaries . . .	1,106	427	642
Storekeeper's Wages . . .	128	156	110

Divide the oncost of each department into fixed and floating oncost and show separately the fixed and floating oncost rates, using the direct wages as the measure of the oncost in each case.

2. State briefly what is the object of distinguishing the fixed from the floating oncost in Question No. 1.

3. The following is a summary of the expenditure of a business for 1930, viz. :

	£	£
Materials consumed		24,927
Direct Wages—		
A Department	11,469	
B ,, ...	7,892	
C ,, ...	10,974	
		30,335
		55,262
Oncost—		
A Department	16,280	
B ,, ...	3,426	
C ,, ...	9,842	
		29,548
Total Manufacturing Cost		84,810
Selling, Delivery and General Administration Charges		16,962
Carriage outward		4,728
Royalties		746
Bad Debts		250
Discounts allowed to customers . . .		2,700
		£110,196

From these particulars prepare a cost of an article the direct wages costs of which are :

		s.	d.
A Department	. . . . .	10	0
B ,,	. . . . .	7	8
C ,,	. . . . .	14	2

and the material cost of which is £1 6s. 9d. Provide 2s. for Royalties and 3s. 9d. for carriage outward.

4. For 1930 the manufacturing expenditure of a business, consisting of one department only was as follows :

	£
Direct Material	14,000
Direct Wages	16,000
Departmental Oncost	10,000
Selling, Delivery and General Administration Expenses .	2,000
	£42,000

The Capital of the business was £14,000. The cost of an article made during that year is submitted in the following form for your criticism :

	£	s.	d.
Material Cost	1	1	0
Wages Cost	1	4	0
Oncost (40 per cent. of Direct Material and Labour) .	0	18	0
	£3	3	0

Do you consider that this Cost expresses the approximate cost of production and sale ? If not, state your reasons very briefly and work out if you can a more accurate cost, making provision at the same time for a profit which would yield 15 per cent. on the capital employed.

5. In a certain machine shop there were six heavy machines, the capital cost of which was as follows :

	£			£
Machine No. 1 . . .	3,000	Machine No. 4 . . .		1,500
,, No. 2 . . .	4,000	,, No. 5 . . .		5,000
,, No. 3 . . .	900	,, No. 6 . . .		600

Some of these machines were used intermittently and others were almost continually in operation. The oncost of the shop was charged to costs on the direct wages method, the shop rate being 200 per cent. Can you see any objection to this method ?

6. The following items of expenditure occur in the Accounts of a manufacturing business :

	£
Cost of removing Plant	675
Income Tax	2,684
Bonus to Employees, voted at Annual Meeting	3,000
Welfare Expenditure	682
Employers' Liability Insurance	3,759

How would you allocate each of these items of Cost ? Would you include them in cost of Manufacture or in cost of Selling, Delivery and General Administration ?

7. A cost schedule relating to a manufactured article is prepared as follows :

		s.	d.
Wages—			
Machining	. . . .	7	6
Assembling	. . . .	5	9
Oncost—			
Machining	. . . .	10	0
Assembling	. . . .	2	10
Materials	. . . .	10	0
		1 16	1
Establishment Charges	. . . . .	12	0
		£2 8	1

From these particulars calculate the Departmental oncost rates, and the rate for Establishment Charges. One place of decimals is sufficient. Why would you expect the machinery oncost to be so much higher than the assembling oncost ?

You will observe that Establishment Charges are added to Materials as well as Wages and Oncost. Why should this be so ? Be very brief in your answer.

8. Give an example of :

(1) Direct Wages.
(2) Indirect Wages.
(3) Direct Materials.
(4) Indirect Materials.

Definitions are not required.

THE LONDON ASSOCIATION OF ACCOUNTANTS, LIMITED

Final Examination, December, 1931.

Cost Accounts and Systems of Costing

Time allowed—2 hours.

(*Brevity and arrangement will be taken into account in marking. Please arrange your answers in their sequential order.*)

1. The cost of the same article produced in three different months is ascertained to be as follows :

	April.	October.	December.
	s. d.	s. d.	s. d.
Direct Wages	2 9	2 9	2 9
Oncost (based on monthly figures) .	3 10	3 5	2 6
Direct Materials	9 0	5 10	6 6
	15 7	12 0	11 9

What is the probable cause of the fluctuations in Oncost ? Can you suggest a better method of dealing with this factor of Cost ?

2. Selling, Delivery, and General Administration Expense (otherwise " Establishment Charges ") is usually added to costs as a percentage of the total manufacturing cost. Why is this ? Is it inadvisable to provide for them as a percentage on the direct wages ? Give reasons.

3. Two manufacturing departments (A and B) of a business contained 40 and 30 machines respectively, the machines in each department being substantially uniform in type, and the working conditions such as to necessitate the use of a machine hour rate for costing purposes. The number of working days in the year 1930 was 300, and the working hours per day were 8½. Allow 10 per cent. for lost time, and calculate the number of machine hours for the year in each department.

The Oncost Expense for the period was as follows, viz. :

		A. £	B. £
(a)	Building Expense (Rent, Rates, Lighting, Cleaning and Maintenance) . . .	1,500	1,000
(b)	Power Service	7,425	6,980
(c)	Tool Service	2,287	2,763
(d)	Plant Maintenance	9,471	6,490
(e)	Plant Depreciation	5,000	4,000
(f)	Stores Service	1,159	847
(g)	Management and Supervision . . .	1,725	2,275
(h)	Transporting and Labouring . . .	4,829	5,700
		£33,396	£30,055

The total Direct Wages expenditure in each
Department was £38,925   £43,718
The wage rates of the Machinists are not uniform.

Assume that all the Oncost expense falls equally on the machines, and calculate the machine hour rate of each Department.

State how you would provide for the wages of the machinists in costing the products of the machines.

4. If the machines in A Department (*see Question 3*) were not approximately uniform in type, how would you allocate to each machine :

(1) Buildings Expense (Rent, Rates, Lighting, Cleaning and Maintenance).

(2) Plant Maintenance.

(3) Management and Supervision.

5. The following is cost of a manufactured article submitted by a Cost Clerk to a Manufacturer :

	£ s. d.	£ s. d.
Direct Wages :		
A	7 6	
B	14 0	
C	11 9	
		1 13 3
Oncost :		
A	11 0	
B	1 7 0	
C	8 0	
		2 6 0
		3 19 3
Materials		2 8 4
		6 7 7
Selling, Delivery and General Administration Expense		12 9
		£7 0 4

What do you understand to be the reason for the division of direct wages into A, B and C? Why are not materials similarly dealt with?

6. What is meant by Oncost? State briefly any two methods known to you of allocating Oncost to the cost of producing manufactured goods, indicating in both cases the principle underlying the method.

7. The following schedule represents the total expenditure of a business for the year 1930 :

		£
Material consumed	. . . .	24,749
Direct Wages :		
Machine Shop	. . . . . .	5,422
Press Shop	. . . . . .	6,550
Assembling Shop	. . . . . .	8,115
Oncost Expenses :		
Machine Shop	. . . . . .	4,520
Press Shop	. . . . . .	13,755
Assembling Shop	. . . . . .	3,246
Tinning Expense	. . . . . .	4,698
Enamelling Expense	. . . . . .	3,829
		74,884
Selling, Delivery and General Administration	. . .	9,360
Debenture Interest	. . . . . .	4,000
		£88,244

The Direct Wages and other Costs of producing 500 articles of a certain type were :

Direct Wages :	£	s.	d.
Machining 506 articles (six rejected in assembling)	506	0	0
Press Shop Work (508 components, the material cost of each being 1s. (two spoilt)	44	9	0
Assembling (500 only)	68	15	0
Tinning (500 only)	37	10	0
Material (506 articles)	518	13	0

Ignoring scrap value of spoilt material, ascertain (1) the cost of producing the 500 articles, including the Selling, Delivery and General Administration cost; (2) the total cost per article; (3) the selling price necessary to show a 10 per cent. profit on the selling price.

8. The following is a schedule of the expenditure of a manufacturing business for 1930, viz. :

	Departments.		
	A.	B.	C.
	£	£	£
Direct Wages	10,116	4,690	5,928
Indirect Wages	2,725	1,106	894
Toolmakers	629	528	242
Power consumed	920	292	208
Shop Sundries	217	70	26
Repairs to Plant	548	281	75
Depreciation of Plant	272	325	169
Rent and Rates	992	535	529
Stationery for Manufacturing Departments	50	32	69
Supervision	1,106	427	642
Storekeeper's Wages	128	156	110

	£
Materials purchased	29,678
Advertising	1,259
Travellers' Salaries and Expenses	3,427
Salaries of Office Staff	3,162
Managing Director's Remuneration	1,500
Professional Charges	210
Rent and Rates of Offices and Show Rooms	2,420
Miscellaneous Expenses	192
Bank Charges other than Interest	327
Printing and Stationery	430
Sundry Trade Subscriptions	16

Calculate the oncost rate of each department, using the direct wages as the measure of the oncost. Also calculate the percentage of establishment charges to total manufacturing cost. By " Establishment Charges " is meant all charges not shown under the separate manufacturing departments.

THE LONDON CHAMBER OF COMMERCE
SENIOR COMMERCIAL EDUCATION CERTIFICATES
WEDNESDAY, MAY 16th—7 to 10 p.m.
COSTING

INSTRUCTIONS TO CANDIDATES.
Candidates must attempt all questions.

1. What advantages can be obtained from a good Costing System, in addition to that of ascertaining the cost of manufacture ?

2. A new engineering shop has been equipped at a cost of £10,000, as an addition to existing works buildings.

Write a note for the Directors' information explaining your views as to the costing of the output of this shop. Deal with the calculation of machine rates and their application, and explain what charges should be included in the costs in respect of (1) cost of operating the plant; (2) depreciation of the plant; (3) interest on the capital invested in the plant. Outline the methods by which the information needed would be obtained.

3. A colliery produced 15,000 tons of saleable coal during last month. From the following particulars prepare a Cost Sheet for the monthly meeting of the Board; you may supply any additional figures you need for comparative purposes and add any remarks or explanations which you think will be useful to the Board.

	£	s.	d.
Wages, Underground	7,500	0	0
Pitwood	1,312	10	0
Stores, Underground	750	0	0
,, Surface	937	10	0
Railway Charges	2,812	10	0
Truck Hire	562	10	0
Rates	125	0	0
Horse-keep	625	0	0
Surface Wages	3,750	0	0
Repairs and Renewals	437	10	0
Depreciation	93	15	0
Office and General Expenses	156	5	0
Insurances	281	5	0
Royalties	250	0	0

4. A multiple shop company, having 150 establishments, deals with four main commodities and "Sundries." All purchases are made by the Head Office, which charges goods out to branches at selling prices. All sales are for cash.

The management desire to keep a close supervision of :

(1) The stocks held at each of the shops;
(2) The relative selling costs of each shop.

You are required to outline your suggestions, indicating the returns which you consider each manager should make to the Head Office, and stating what use should be made by the Head Office of these returns.

5. Explain the methods adopted for the calculation and payment of wages on :

(1) Day-rates.
(2) Piece-rates.
(3) Any Premium bonus system with which you are familiar.

Describe briefly a system of wage record with which, as a cost accountant, you would be satisfied, and indicate the variations which would be necessary to adapt the system to one of the other methods of payment.

6. Describe the practice adopted in making up the Balance Sheet of any business with the operations of which you are familiar, in regard to the valuation of :

(1) Unfinished goods in course of manufacture for stock, and
(2) Contract work in progress;

and express your views upon the methods you describe.

ROYAL SOCIETY OF ARTS

STAGE III.—ADVANCED.—May, 1928

COSTING

3 *hours allowed*

(First and Second-class Certificates will be granted in this Stage.)

Candidates are required to answer ANY TEN *questions.*

1. Draw up a specimen Cost Ledger Sheet for job costing.
2. For what class of manufacture would you recommend batch costing ? Give reasons for your recommendation.
3. What information would the Cost Accountant be expected to furnish to the Chief Estimator ?
4. Criticise the statement that the percentage of Oncost to direct labour is the best test of efficiency of production.
5. What method of recording work would you recommend for a factory employing over 1000 workers, and how would you propose to deal with the information so recorded, up to the stage of posting the Cost Ledgers ? Give an idea of the numbers of transactions at each stage justifying your proposed treatment.
6. Give instances where efficiencies are indicated in costing information.
7. What advantages are to be obtained by departmentalising Oncost ?

On what basis would you allot to departments the following items of general Oncost :

(a) Expenses of Pay Office ;
(b) Expenses of Time Office ;
(c) Expenses of Cost Office ;
(d) Expenses of Wages Office ;
(e) Care and Custody of Stores ;
(f) Expenses of Ratefixers' Department ;
(g) Expenses of Examination Department ;
(h) Expenses of Welfare Department?

8. In a factory comprising a number of shops, a proposal is being considered to transfer the plant, etc., of Shop A to Shop B, after rearranging the plant, etc., already in Shop B. What information would you, as Cost Accountant, be able to furnish from your records as to contributory items of savings that should follow the proposed concentration ?

9. In establishing machine-hour rates of absorption of oncost, how would you deal with the following items :

(a) Rent of Factory ;
(b) Electricity Charges ;
(c) Charges for Maintenance of Machinery and Plant ;
(d) Depreciation of Machinery and Plant ;
(e) Charges for Shop Supervision ;
(f) Shop lighting ?

10. To what uses can a work in progress account be put ?
11. By what method would you cost an article, the manufacture of which went on uninterruptedly, and where wastage occurred at various stages of manufacture and assembly ?

ROYAL SOCIETY OF ARTS EXAMINATIONS

Stage III.—Advanced—March, 1932

COSTING

3 hours allowed

(First and Second-class Certificates will be granted in this Stage.)

1. Define the following terms :

(1) A capital service.
(2) Works cost.
(3) Control account.

2. Where standing expense orders are in use for collecting oncost expenditure, how would you arrange to ascertain the cost of specific services, *e.g.*, cost of maintenance of a particular machine or the cost of a particular experiment ?

3. Draw up a skeleton statement of a wages (pay-roll) analysis for a works which comprises several departments. At what periods would you propose that it should be rendered ? To what members of the works organisation would you suggest that it should be issued ?

4. What is meant by uniform costing ? What advantages would you consider to accrue from its adoption in an industry ?

5. In the course of compiling machine-hour rates of absorption of

II

Oncost the various expenses have been allocated to the different machines or groups of machines. In order to determine the hourly rates of a particular machine or group of machines, would you take as the divisor, into the total expenses so allocated, the maximum hours on a one-shift basis or some other figure ? Give your reasons and indicate what effect your decision may have on the amount to be included in respect of certain of the expenses.

6. Express graphically on the squared paper provided the following information. What deductions would you expect the works manager to make from it and what further information would he probably call for in this connection ?

Period.		No. Produced.	Total Cost.			Cost per Unit.		
			£	s.	d.	£	s.	d.
Jan. to March	. .	400	4200	0	0	10	10	0
April	. . . .	200	1900	0	0	9	10	0
May	. . . .	250	2062	10	0	8	5	0
June	. . . .	250	2000	0	0	8	0	0
July	. . . .	200	1700	0	0	8	10	0
August	. . . .	200	1700	0	0	8	10	0
September	. .	300	2400	0	0	8	0	0
Oct. to Dec.	. .	500	5000	0	0	10	0	0

7. A road is being constructed which involves the diversion of an hydraulic main at an estimated cost of £150. As an alternative to this diversion a new main of an improved type can be laid down at an estimated cost of £300, the old main, which stands in the books at a value of £100, being in this case abandoned. How would you deal as between capital and revenue expenditure (i) with the expenses of diversion if the former course is adopted, and (ii) with the cost of the new main and the residual value of the old main if the latter course is decided upon ?

THE CORPORATION OF ACCOUNTANTS

FINAL EXAMINATION. COSTING.

June, 1935.

2 hours allowed for this paper.

Candidates may attempt any part of a question. Reasons for an answer should be given where necessary.

1. What are the duties of a storekeeper ?

2. Draft a memorandum giving your suggestions regarding the installation of a system of recording workers' time and charging same to the Cost Accounts. State the forms you would introduce and also the entries to be recorded in the Cost Books and Financial Books. Rulings of forms are *not* required.

3. Prepare a comparative statement showing " Orders received " and " Orders executed." The figures are required for each week and comparison is to be made with the corresponding week in the previous year. Cumulative totals to date should also be shown. Insert figures for three weeks and show how the value of orders in hand but not completed can be obtained from your statement.

4. (*a*) What do you understand by " continuous stocktaking " ?

    (*b*) Suggest reasons for discrepancies discovered as a result of " continuous stocktaking " ?

5. As Accountant to a manufacturing concern, you are instructed to prepare a Statement showing Stocks of Materials and Finished Goods at the end of the years 1932, 1933 and 1934, also the Sales for the three years. It is desired to know if the stocks of Materials and Finished Goods vary in proportion to the Sales.

Draft the Statement for submission to the Directors.

The figures are as follows :

	1932.		1933.		1934.	
	Tons.	Value.	Tons.	Value.	Tons.	Value.
		£		£		£
Materials in Stock as at 31st December . .	200	200	240	280	360	450
Finished Goods in Stock as at 31st December .	50	100	60	100	80	140
Sales for year . .	1,000	2,500	960	1,920	1,080	2,430

6. From the following information write up Works Oncost Account, Office Oncost Account and Wages Control Account, as they would appear in the Cost Ledger for the month of May, 1935 :

	£	£
Wages paid		3,000
Allocated thus :		
Direct Labour	2,800	
Works Oncost, Indirect Labour	200	
Works Expenses, amount paid during month (excluding Indirect Labour)		600
Works Expenses allocated to Production as Works Oncost		750
Works Oncost Suspense, Dr. Balance as at 1st May, 1935		50
Office Expenses—amount paid during month . .		230
allocated to Production as Office Oncost		225
Office Oncost Suspense, Dr. Balance as at 1st May, 1935		25

Show the balances of Works Oncost and Office Oncost to be carried forward as at 31st May, 1935.

7. From the following information prepare a Statement for the year ended 31st March, 1935, showing :

    (a) Prime Cost ;
    (b) Works Oncost ;
    (c) Works Cost ;
    (d) Office Oncost ;
    (e) Total Cost ;
    (f) Profit or Loss.

Submit your answer in columnar form for each department separately:

	Dept. A.		Dept. B.		Dept. C.
	£	s.	£	s.	£
Materials : Stock as at 1/4/34 . .	200	0	240	0	300
Purchases for year . .	1,700	0	1,400	0	1,300
Stock as at 31/3/35 .	280	0	320	0	240
Direct Wages.	1,500	0	1,700	0	1,600
Finished Goods : Stock as at 1/4/34	300	0	167	0	560
Stock as at 31/3/35	200	0	400	0	300
Sales	5,446	0	5,200	0	5,100
Depreciation	100	0	180	0	130
Indirect Wages	352	10	479	10	220
Carriage Inwards on Materials . .	80	0	60	0	40

K K

				£
Works General Expenses.	.	.	Total for year	480
Rates, Lighting, etc. (Works) .	.	.	Do.	250
Works Office and Store Expenses	.	.	Do.	360
Upkeep and Repairs of Plant .	.	.	Do.	800

Head Office Expenses £700 and Office Salaries and Expenses £671 to be allocated as Office Oncost as follows : Dept. A, £432; Dept. B, £539 and Dept. C, £400.

Dept. A occupies half of Factory; Dept. B three-tenths; and Dept. C two-tenths.

Works General Expenses and Works Office and Store Expenses to be allocated on the basis of Direct Wages.

There are 7 machines in Dept. A; 5 in Dept. B; and 8 in Dept. C.

Using the above figures as a basis, state what price should be quoted for a contract to be undertaken by Dept. C, the prime cost elements of which are :

					£
Materials	.	.	.	.	380
Carriage Inwards		.	.	.	20
Direct Wages	.	.	.	.	440

[COPYRIGHT.] *Reproduced by Permission of the Institute.*

INSTITUTE OF MUNICIPAL TREASURERS AND ACCOUNTANTS (INCORPORATED)

INTERMEDIATE EXAMINATION.

January 16th, 1935.

COSTING.

Time allowed—1 hour.   *From 4.30 p.m. to 5.30 p.m.*

Each question carries the same number of marks.

Not more than THREE *questions should be answered. In the event of more than three questions being answered, only the first three in numerical order will be marked.*

1. Describe a scheme of costing suitable for *one* of the following activities of a local authority and submit a specimen " Cost Statement " in respect of the service chosen :

   (*a*) Electricity assisted wiring scheme;
   (*b*) Manufacture of artificial stone;
   (*c*) Disposal of refuse by incineration;
   (*d*) Centralized fleet of private cars for council purposes;
   (*e*) Municipal garage with repair shop, petrol pumps and lock-up sheds for cars.

2. How would you deal with the following items in the Cost Accounts relative to maintenance of roads :

   (*a*) Idle Time;
   (*b*) Overtime;
   (*c*) Holiday and Sick Pay; and
   (*d*) Superannuation Contributions ?

3. Describe a system of stores control which facilitates stocktaking.
4. Describe and comment on the official Costing Returns issued in connection with any *four* services administered by local authorities.

THE SOCIETY OF INCORPORATED ACCOUNTANTS AND AUDITORS

INTERMEDIATE EXAMINATION.

November, 1935.

Time allowed—1 hour.

III.—COST ACCOUNTS.

1. How would you arrive at the amount to be charged against a particular job for Depreciation of Plant and Machinery in a Factory where the rate of depreciation varied on the different items and machines ?

2. Where a business owns the Freehold of the premises, what would be a proper charge in lieu of rent, and what entries would be necessary in relation thereto in a double-entry costing system ?

3. Enumerate the books and documents which would be required for a complete costing system, adding explanatory notes where necessary.

4. The following figures show the Actual or Estimated Expenditure for one week in a Laundry. You are required to prepare a Weekly Trading Return and Statement of Costs.

	£
Working Costs :	
Productive and Stoker's Wages	375
Materials	48
Fuel	45
Lighting, Power and Water	65
Allowances	10
Upkeep Costs (including Rent, Insurance, Repairs, Depreciation and Engineers' Wages)	84
Collection and Delivery Costs (including all transport charges, motor upkeep and depreciation, baskets, etc.)	280
General Costs :	
Office Salaries	58
General Expenses	43
Management Salaries	35

Two services are maintained, viz. : (*a*) Fully Finished ; (*b*) Machine Finished. For the purpose of this question apportion all expenditure as to two-thirds to (*a*) and one-third to (*b*). The value of the work done for the week was (*a*) £758 5*s.*, (*b*) £346 10*s.*

THE SOCIETY OF INCORPORATED ACCOUNTANTS AND AUDITORS

FINAL EXAMINATION.

April and May, 1935.

Time allowed—1½ hours.

III.—COST ACCOUNTS.

FIVE *questions only to be attempted, of which question* SIX *must be one.*

1. Give an illustration of a Cost Sheet for (*a*) a Power Station, or (*b*) a Gas Undertaking, or (*c*) a Railway.

2. How far and in what particular manner has mass production affected costs of production ?

3. You are requested to draft with appropriate rulings a Time or Job Card suitable for a system where piece work is operated.

K K 2

4. From the information given below prepare a monthly Cost Sheet of Bricks made, showing cost and profit per 1,000 bricks :

Material—Coal	. . . .	1,790 tons at 30s. per ton.
Royalty	. . .	1s. 6d. per 1,000 bricks.
Stores	. . . .	£1,665
Labour—Brickmaking	. . .	£4,000
Indirect	. . .	£1,000
Oncost—Works	. . . .	25 per cent. of direct charges.
Office	. . . .	10 per cent. of works total costs.

Sales	. . . . .	7,000,000 at 55s.
Stock of finished bricks :		
1st of the month	. . .	200,000
31st ,, ,,	. . .	600,000

5. From the following figures you are requested to show the cost of each of the three processes of manufacture. The production of each process is passed on to the next process immediately on completion.

Process.	A.	B.	C.
	£	£	£
Wages and Materials . . .	640	1,200	2,925
Works Oncost	560	525	600
Production (Units)	36,000	37,500	48,000
Stock (Units from preceding process) 1st June	—	4,000	16,500
Stock (Units from preceding process) 30th June	—	1,000	5,500

COAL PRODUCTION ACCOUNT.

6. You are requested to consider the figures set out below from the point of view of standardising the costs and to make such suggestions as may appear to you advisable to that end.

	Colliery A. Cost per ton produced.		Amount.	B. Cost per ton produced.	Amount.	C. Cost per ton produced.	Amount.
	s.	d.	£		£		£
Stock . . .	—		8,750	—	10,000	—	11,500
Wages . .	23	3·64	17,478	—	18,500	—	19,000
Repairs and Re- newals . .	1	1·14	822	—	925	—	1,600
Stable Expenses	0	3·37	210	—	250	—	90
Rents, Rates and Taxes .	0	8·69	543	—	400	—	470
Royalties .	0	8·70	542	—	450	—	500
Depreciation .	0	4·41	275	—	300	—	500
Office Expenses	1	0·00	751	—	750	—	1,000
	27	5·95	29,371		31,575		34,660
Profit . .			13,379		17,425		21,340
			42,750		49,000		56,000
Sales . .			40,000		44,000		50,000
Stock . .			2,750		5,000		6,000
			42,750		49,000		56,000

	A.	B.	C.
Production	15,000 tons.	18,000 tons.	20,000 tons.
Sales	20,000 ,,	22,000 ,,	25,000 ,,
Stock at start	7,000 ,,	8,000 ,,	9,000 ,,
,, end	2,000 ,,	4,000 ,,	4,000 ,,

SECTION I.

THE LONDON ASSOCIATION OF CERTIFIED ACCOUNTANTS

FINAL EXAMINATION, DECEMBER, 1935.

COST ACCOUNTS AND SYSTEMS OF COSTING.

Time allowed—1½ hours.

Brevity and arrangement will be taken into account in marking. Please arrange your answers in their sequential order.

1. The following is a Table of Departmental Oncost rates relating to a manufacturing business :

	Fixed.	Float-ing.	Fixed.	Float-ing.	Total.	Stan-dard.
	£	£	%	%	%	%
Moulding in Iron Foundries	96	237	33	80	113	100
Finishing Shop	87	53	38	23	61	75
Dressing Shop	8	37	20	90	110	70
Smithy	33	83	17	43	60	75
Machine Shop	68	69	30	30	60	75
Fitting Shop	38	37	23	22	45	50

What is the meaning of the columns headed :
Fixed, Floating, Standard ?

In some cases the standard is exceeded and in others it falls short of the total percentages given. Can you suggest a reason for this ?

2. The following is a summary of the Manufacturing expenditure of a business, viz. :—

	£	£
Materials Purchased :		
Castings	261	
Stores	771	
Partly Manufactured Goods	701	
Factored Goods	190	
	1,923	
Less Sales of Brass and Iron Scrap	5	
		1,918
Galvanising		90
Direct Wages :		
Moulding Shops	262	
Brass Foundry	33	
Finishing Shop	229	
Dressing Shop	41	
Smithy	193	
Machine Shop	227	
Fitting Shop	166	
		1,151

		£	£
Manufacturing Overheads :			
Moulding Shop	. . . . . .	258	
Brass Foundry	. . . . . .	75	
Finishing Shop	. . . . . .	140	
Dressing Shop	. . . . . .	45	
Smithy .	. . . .	116	
Machine Shop .	. . . . . .	137	
Fitting Shop .	. . . . . .	75	
			846
Process Expenditure :			
Cupola .	. . . .	126	
Annealing	. . . . . .	104	
Total Cost of Production	. . . .		£4,235

From the details given, calculate :

(1) Departmental Oncost rates for the separate departments except the Brass Foundry and the Dressing Shop. Ignore decimal points.

(2) Describe what method you would adopt of allocating the Cupola and Annealing expenditure to individual costs of castings produced.

3. To what use can the separate departmental oncost rates asked for in question 2 be put ? Would not a general oncost rate to apply to all departments be much simpler ?

4. A manufacturer, in answer to your request for a schedule of his " Establishment Charges " provides the following, viz. :

	£
Agents' Commission	475
Carriage and Freight	747
Rent, Rates and Insurance of Warehouse	81
Warehouse Wages	170
Travelling Expenses	86
Rent of Copenhagen Store (part)	10
Rent, Rates and Insurance (Office proportion)	33
Lighting and Heating (Office proportion)	8
Repairs to Offices	12
Repairs to Warehouse	31
Office Salaries	213
Directors' Remuneration	700
Printing, Stationery, Stamps and Telephone . . .	250
Professional Charges	75
State and Employers Liability Insurances (Office) . . .	11
Depreciation of Fixtures and Fittings	27
Subscriptions and Donations	21
Bank Charges	11
Stocktaking	35
Incidentals	131
Lighting and Heating of Warehouse	17
State and Employers' Liability Insurances (Warehouse) . .	9
Bank Interest	87
Discounts Allowed	297
Bad Debts	29
Depreciation of Leasehold Premises	22

Prepare from this information a revised schedule showing in separate classifications the

(1) Selling Expense.
(2) Delivery Expense.
(3) General Administration Expense.
(4) Expense which you would disregard in estimating costs.

5. What do you understand by :

(1) Direct Wages.
(2) Indirect Wages.
(3) Direct Material.
(4) Indirect Material.

Give an example in each case.

6. The following figures relate to the costs of an Iron Foundry, viz. :

	£	£
Materials consumed—		
Pig Iron		3,620
Coke		421
Limestone and Ganister . .		68
Haulage		134
		4,243
Wages of Cupola Men . . .		360
Cupola Overheads		367
Cost of Melted Metal		4,970
Direct Wages—		
Pattern Makers	431	
Moulders	6,101	
Coremakers	918	
		7,450
Manufacturing Overheads—		
Pattern Shop	329	
Moulding Floors	5,059	
Coremaking	501	
		5,889
Other Foundry Expenditure—		
Dressing	1,921	
Sandblasting	809	
		2,730
		£21,039

Weight of good Castings moulded . . .	888 tons.
Do. Do. dressed . . .	888 tons.
Do. Do. sandblasted . .	326 tons.

A Casting weighed three cwts. The moulder's piece work rate for moulding was 19s., and the coremaker's wages in connection with the casting were 14s. The casting was dressed, and sandblasted. Calculate its cost from the above details. No Patternmaking was involved.

THE CORPORATION OF ACCOUNTANTS

FINAL EXAMINATION.   COSTING.

December, 1935.

2 hours allowed for this paper.

Candidates may attempt any part of a question.   Reasons for an answer should be given where necessary.

1. Calculate the amount of wages payable to a worker who is paid at the rate of 1s. 6d. per hour.   Time-and-a-half is paid for overtime in excess of a full day's work.   The Clock Card is as follows :

	In.	Out.	In.	Out.
Friday	8.0	12.0	1.0	5.30
Saturday	8.0	12.0		
Monday	8.30	12.0	1.0	6.0
Tuesday	8.0	12.0	1.0	5.30
Wednesday	9.0	12.0	1.0	8.0
Thursday	8.0	12.0	1.0	6.0

Normal working week is 46½ hours.

2. A manufacturer operates his own system of motor transport. How would you apportion the cost between Production Department (transporting raw materials to the works) and Sales Department (delivering finished products to customers)?

3. A Factory consists of three Production Departments (manufacturing separate products) and the usual Stores, Offices, Canteen, etc.

State how you would charge the following items of expense in preparing the Cost Accounts, and the basis on which you would allocate same to the various departments :

(a) Rates.
(b) Fire Insurance on Plant and Machinery (including Process Plant, Boilers, etc.).
(c) Workmen's Compensation Insurance.
(d) Electric Light.
(e) Electric Power.
(f) Repairs to Plant carried out by engineers on the factory staff.
(g) Packing Materials.
(h) Depreciation on Plant and Machinery.
(i) Storekeeper's Wages.
(j) Carriage Inwards on Raw Materials.

4. An amalgamation of three companies, the XL Engineering Co., Ltd., Bolts Ltd., and Nuts Ltd. has been carried through and it is arranged that the products of Bolts Ltd. and Nuts Ltd. will be assembled by the XL Co., which will take over the products at cost price plus 5%.   The methods of costing used by Bolts Ltd. and Nuts Ltd. will be continued meantime.

The following figures are representative jobs completed in the workshops of Bolts Ltd. and Nuts Ltd. :

	Bolts Ltd. Job 99.	Nuts Ltd. Job K. 27.
	£	£
Wages	400	200
Material	150	310
Oncost	55	100
	£605	£610

	Bolts Ltd. Job 197.	Nuts Ltd. Job S. 89.
	£	£
Wages	100	300
Material	310	205
Oncost	41	150
	£451	£655

	Job 282.	Job T. 19.
	£	£
Wages	300	400
Material	200	110
Oncost	50	200
	£550	£710

Prepare a statement showing the profit made by the XL Co. on Job No. 1000, the Selling Price of which is £1,300. The prime cost figures are as follows :

	Workshop.	
	Bolts Ltd.	Nuts Ltd.
	£	£
Wages	250	200
Material	150	160

The cost of assembling Job No. 1000, including selling and delivery expenses, is 25% on the prices credited to Bolts Ltd. and Nuts Ltd.

5. A manufacturer introduces new machinery in his factory with the result that production per worker is increased. The workers are paid on a piece-work basis and it is arranged that for every 2 per cent. increase in individual output over 1932 standard the rate of wages will be increased by 1 per cent. over the rate ruling in 1932. The Selling Price per article has decreased in the interval by $8\frac{1}{3}$ per cent.

Calculate the saving in material and oncost which would be required per article in 1934 as compared with 1932 to compensate the manufacturer for the losses incurred.

	1932.	1934.
	£	£
Number of Workers	175	125
Number of Articles manufactured . .	168,000	140,000
Wages Paid	33,600	
Total Sales	75,600	

6. Trial Balance of Cost Ledger as at 1st October, 1935, is as follows :

	Dr.	Cr.
	£	£
Stores Ledger Control Account (for Raw Materials)	1,000	
Work in Progress Account	880	
Finished Stock Account	1,300	
Works Oncost Suspense Account . . .	90	
Office and Administration Oncost Suspense Account	40	
Cost Ledger Control Account		3,310
	£3,310	£3,310

Write up Ledger Accounts to record the transactions for the month of October and carry down the balances as at 31st October, 1935. Profit or Loss for the month is to be shown.

	£	£
Stores Purchased		1,200
Stores issued to Production		1,100
do. Factory Repair Orders . . .		200
Carriage inwards on Stores issued to Production .		300
Wages Paid		3,200
allocated—Direct Labour	2,900	
Indirect Labour	300	
Works Expenses—payments during month . .		400
Works Oncost allocated to Production . . .		890
Goods finished during month		5,280
Sales of Finished Goods for month		6,000
Stock of Finished Goods as at 31/10/35 . . .		1,000
Value of Work in Progress as at 31/10/35 . . .		700
Office and Administration Expenses—payments during month		200
do. do. Oncost allocated to Production . . .		210

INDEX

455

distribution, 310; cost of production, 302; fixed charges, 308; fuel, 303; load factor, 309; overhead, 305; running charges, 308; services accounts, 311; tariffs to consumer, 312; transport, 310; two part costs, 308; uniform costing, 301; unit of cost, 306, 309; works cost, 302, 307

ELECTRO-PLATING, 249, 335
EMERSON WAGES SYSTEMS, 93
EMPLOYERS' LIABILITY INSURANCE, 112, 264
ENGAGEMENT OF LABOUR RECORD, 54
ENGINEERING WORKS, 22
ENGINES, 16
ENVELOPE MAKING, 249, 252
ESTABLISHMENT CHARGES, 12, 116, 404
ESTIMATES AND COSTS, CONTRASTED, 3
EXAMINATION PAPERS, 385; Institute of Chartered Accountants, 385, 386, 387; Institute of Cost and Works Accountants, 389, 390, 391, 392, 393; London Association of Accountants, 394, 395, 396, 397, 398; London Chamber of Commerce, 399, 400; Royal Society of Arts, 400, 401; Society of Incorporated Accountants and Auditors, 387, 388, 389
EXCEPTIONAL EXPENSES, 105
EXPENSE: administration, 12; analysis, plan of, 182; budgets, 6, 262, 382; chargeable, 11; departmental, 11; direct, 11; distribution, 11, 13, 110, 113, 116, 183; drawing office, 12, 109, 114; factory, 12, 108; indirect, 11; municipal, 393; production, 12; selling, 12, 109, 113, 183; summary, 136; warehouse, 110 (see also *Overhead*)
EXPERIMENT AND RESEARCH DEPT., 22, 109
EXPLOSIVES COSTS, 15, 215

FACTORY EXPENSE, 12, 108
FACTORY COST, 13
  ,, JOB COSTING, 171
  ,, LABOUR STATISTICS, 181
  ,, ORGANISATION, STANDING ORDERS, 108
FETTLING EXPENSE, 283
FINANCIAL ACCOUNTS: job costs in conjunction with, 187; reconciliation with, 162, 183, 194, 200, 311, 404, 407, 419
FINISHED MATERIALS WASTE, 116
FINISHED PARTS, 28, 40
  ,, ,, CONTROL ACCOUNT 198, 200
  ,, ,, STOCK, 29

FINISHED PARTS, STOCK, PART-, 28, 40
FIRE INSURANCE, 234, 264
"FIRST IN, FIRST OUT" PRICING, 48, 249
FIXED BONUS SCHEME, 99
FIXED CHARGES, 105, 110, 307, 308, 347
FIXED OVERHEAD, 105, 110, 308, 347
FLOURMILL, 15
FOOD PRODUCTS, 16, 207
FOREMAN, DUTIES OF, 25
FOUNDRY, 214, 267; core shop, 272, 273; cost summary, 277; cupola record, 268; fettling shop, 272, 273; indirect labour, 273; iron account, 184; job cost account, 184; machine shop, 273; materials, 279; melting dept., 272; moulding shop, 272, 273; overhead, 274, 276, 279; trading account, 347
FUEL FOR BOILER-HOUSE, 296
  ,, ELECTRICITY STATION, 302

GANTT TASK BONUS, 93
GAS MANUFACTURE, 227; supply costs, 16, 227
GENERAL EXPENSES (see *Overhead*)
GENERATING STATION, ELECTRICITY, 301
GLASS BOTTLE WORK, 207
GLEDHILL–BROOK TIME RECORDERS, 57, 71
GOLD MINE, 248
GOODS DESPATCHED NOTE, 238
GOODS RECEIVED BOOK, 35, 233
GOODS RECEIVED NOTE, 33, 233
GRAPHIC CHARTS, 372; bar, 379; circular, 379; logarithmic scale, 375; natural scale, 375; organisation, 382; pie, 379; progress, 377; ratio ruled, 375; trilinear, 380; vertical bar, 379
GUNCOTTON COSTS, 215

HALSEY PREMIUM BONUS, 95
HALSEY–WEIR PREMIUM BONUS, 95
HAULAGE EXPENSE, 165, 403, 407
HIGH WAGE PLAN OF PAYMENT, 88
HOLIDAYS, AS OVERHEAD, 109, 265
HOLLERITH, COSTING SYSTEM USING, 344; payroll, by, 82; standard costing by, 335
HOLLERITH TABULATING MACHINES, 69, 344, 417
HORSES, DEPRECIATION OF, 125
HOT ROLLING MILL, 344
HOURLY COST RATES, labour, 100, 148, 186; machine, 100, 186; printers, 262; transport, 403, 407

A STANDARD TEXT-BOOK

BOOK-KEEPING AND ACCOUNTS

By

L. CUTHBERT CROPPER, F.C.A.,
F. D. MORRIS, F.C.A., and
A. K. FISON, B.A., F.C.A.

Crown 8vo.   **994 pp.**   **Price 8s. 6d. net.**

SEVENTEENTH EDITION

THIS is the largest and the cheapest text-book ever issued on the subject. It is thoroughly exhaustive in treatment, based on the latest legislation, and, as might be expected of the authors, an *authoritative* treatise. It has long been regarded as the *standard work for students of book-keeping and accountancy*. It includes some 266 graded exercises on the subject-matter of the chapters, and a large collection of the most recent examination papers as set by the various examining bodies.

Contents : Chap. I: Elementary Theory; II: Elementary Commercial Practice; III: Books of Account—Statistical Books—The Ledger; IV: The Cash Book—The Petty Cash Book; V: The Purchases Book (Invoice Book or Bought Day Book); VI: The Sales Book (Sales Journal, Sales Day Book, or Sold Book); VII: The Journal; VIII: Bills Payable and Receivable Books—Returns Books; IX: The Trial Balance—Trading and Profit and Loss Accounts; X: The Balance Sheet; XI: A Merchant's Accounts; XII: Cheques and Bills of Exchange—Promissory Notes; XIII: Single Entry Book-keeping; XIV: Consignment Accounts—Current Accounts between Merchants; XV: Partnership Accounts; XVI: Joint Stock Companies and their Accounts; XVII: Self-Balancing Ledgers—Tabular or Columnar Book-keeping; XVIII: Departmental Accounts—Branch Accounts—Foreign Currencies; XIX: Joint Accounts—Joint Adventure Accounts—Cost Accounts— Royalties and Short Workings—The Double Account System— Goodwill—Bankruptcy and Deeds of Arrangement—Receipts and Payments Accounts—Income and Expenditure Accounts; XX: Dividend and Income Tax Accounts of Limited Companies; XXI: Investment Accounts, etc.; XXII: Bank Accounts; XXIII: Life Assurance Accounts; XXIV: The Form of Published Accounts; XXV: Hints to Examination Candidates; XXVI: How to Answer Examination Papers; XXVII: Book - keeping Examinations; XXVIII: The Book-keeper's Compendium; XXIX: Income Tax; XXX: Supplementary Exercises; XXXI: Examination Papers; Index.

From the same Publishers

FUNDAMENTALS OF INDUSTRIAL ADMINISTRATION

By

EDWARD T. ELBOURNE, M.B.E.

Industrial Consultant
Chartered Mechanical Engineer
Fellow of the Royal Statistical Society
Fellow and Hon. Director of the Institute of Industrial Administration
Author of
" Factory Administration and Cost Accounts "
" The Marketing Problem: How it is being tackled in U.S.A."
" The Management Problem," etc.

SECOND EDITION

Demy 8vo.   xx + 644 pp.   Price 15s. net

BUSINESS STATISTICS
AND
STATISTICAL METHOD

By

H. J. WHELDON, B.Com. (Lond.)

F.C.W.A., F.L.A.A., A.C.I.S.

Lecturer in Business Statistics
Author of " Cost Accounting and Costing Methods."

PRESS OPINIONS

" This book sets a new standard in the presentation of the subject."
—*The Certified Accountants Journal.*

" The success which has followed the publication of Wheldon's Cost Accounting and Costing Methods is likely to be equalled if not excelled by this book, which we have no hesitation in commending to all students."
—*The Cost Accountant.*

" A thoroughly practical application of fundamental principles to actual business needs."—*The Secretary.*

" A simple but comprehensive course in business statistics."—*The Accountant.*

Demy 8vo.   xii + 224 pp.   Price 7s. 6d. net